# Business communication
## Theory and application

# Business communication
## Theory and application

**Raymond V. Lesikar,** Ph.D.

*Professor and Chairman*
*Department of Management*
*Louisiana State University*

 *1976 Third edition*

**Richard D. Irwin, Inc.** Homewood, Illinois 60430

Irwin-Dorsey Limited Georgetown, Ontario L7G 4B3

Third Edition

6 7 8 9 0 A 5 4 3 2 1 0 9 8

ISBN 0-256-01818-9
Library of Congress Catalog Card No. 75–28943
*Printed in the United States of America*

LEARNING SYSTEMS COMPANY—
a division of Richard D. Irwin, Inc.—has developed a
PROGRAMMED LEARNING AID
to accompany texts in this subject area.
Copies can be purchased through your bookstore
or by writing PLAIDS,
1818 Ridge Road, Homewood, Illinois 60430.

# Preface

THIS third edition of *Business Communication: Theory and Application* follows the general plan of its predecessors. The wide acceptance of the previous editions suggests that the book should remain in its original mold. And so do the comments of adoptors and reviewers.

Even so, I made some changes which seem to be dictated by movements in the field. I updated the review of communication theory wherever appropriate. I worked in additional analyses of relationships between theory and applications. Because they are so important in the real world of business, I gave additional emphasis to the short forms of reports. And in response to strong suggestions from many quarters, I added a chapter on oral communication.

As in the earlier editions, the book first summarizes the appropriate areas of communication theory. Then it relates theory to applications in business. This is the approach leaders in the field have been talking about for the past two decades—perhaps longer. It is the approach which combines traditional how-to-do-it instructions with the theoretical support of why it should be done that way. Without question, this approach not only is defensible, but it has answered much of the criticism the business communication field has received in years past.

The coverage of communication theory is selective. It must be so for reasons of space economy. I have chosen those topics which seem to me most helpful to the student in developing an understanding of organizational communication. As you will see, I have relied heavily on the contributions of general semantics. Very clearly, this subject matter provides a base for understanding the problems and principles of communicating in business.

Perhaps some will feel that I have oversimplified the theory material.

Certainly it could have been covered in greater depth and with much greater sophistication. My goal, however, was to overcome the communication barriers which a discussion of "theory" typically raises in the student's mind. Such barriers can be overcome only by clear, simplified explanation. I am confident that I have succeeded in this endeavor.

My coverage of the traditional business communication areas of correspondence, report writing, and oral communication builds from the theory presented. At the appropriate places, the theory is related to application. Because the theory applies to almost every instruction given, the more obvious relations are left to the student. To do otherwise would have a cluttering effect and would be highly repetitious. It was my hope to cover the application areas with sufficient thoroughness to permit the option of building a course primarily around this material and of using the theory parts as supplementary reading.

As in all such works as this, I am indebted to many people for their assistance. Foremost, I am indebted to those scholars who have contributed over the years to the general knowledge in the fields from which I have drawn my information. Especially must I acknowledge the contributions of my dear friend and former teacher and colleague, William P. Boyd, now Professor Emeritus at The University of Texas at Austin. The effects of his teachings are literally scattered throughout this book. Those others from whom I have borrowed directly are acknowledged at specific spots of reference in the book. There are many, many others whom I cannot so recognize.

A special note of gratitude is due Berle Haggblade of California State University at Fresno and James L. Godell of Northern Michigan University who reviewed the book. Their most helpful suggestions made many contributions to the revised manuscript. In addition, I must recognize my many friends around the country who have given me their advice and suggestions from time to time. Although these helpful people must remain anonymous, I am grateful to all of them nevertheless.

Here at the scene of my work I am indebted to three truly dedicated workers. First, Karen Arnold was most thorough and punctual in her research assistance. Second, my son Ray contributed his professional advice and assistance. Third, as she has done in all of my writing efforts over the past seven years, Gloria Armistead, my loyal and efficient secretary, provided her typing expertise. To all of these most helpful people, I am truly grateful.

Finally, and most importantly, I acknowledge the assistance of my dear wife. Her patience and tolerance of what must appear to be an endless succession of writing projects deserve my most special words of gratitude.

*February 1976*                              RAYMOND V. LESIKAR

# Contents

everything: *Uniqueness illustrated. Effects on perception.* All in process: *Changes in inanimate things. Changes in the living. Error effect on perception.* Relative nature of perception. Truth and reality.

A storehouse of knowledge. The role of opinions, attitudes, and beliefs: *What the terms mean. How viewpoints are formed. How viewpoints affect communication.* The influence of emotions. The filter in summary.

Language and human progress: *The foundation of language. Classification based on similarity. Illustration: "Fido" and the "economy." Illustration: "Living" and a "home run." Illustration: Words about "mosquito." Two basic observations.* The question of meaning: *Location in the mind. Meaning and dictionaries. Living nature of language. Connotative and denotative meaning. Context as an aid to meaning. As the map fits the territory.*

Two-valued thinking: *The true dichotomy. Multivaried situations. The dangers involved. Value of specific reference.* Fact-inference confusion: *Necessity of inference. Effect on communication. Calculating the probabilities.* The blocked mind: *A result of opinions, attitudes, and beliefs. A result of allness. Extreme effects of the blocked mind. Unblocking the mind.* The static viewpoint: *The unstatic nature of things. The contributing factor of language.* Failure to discriminate: *Miscommunication from stereotypes. Judgments by category. Developing an awareness of differences.* Miscommunication summarized.

**part two**
**Applications to business**

The basic principle of adaptation: *The filter as the basis for adaptation. The technique of adapting. Cases of adaptation.* Care in word choice: *Selecting words the reader understands. Bringing the writing to life with words. Selecting words for precise communication.* Construction of sentences which communicate: *Keeping sentences short. Using words economically. Considering emphasis in sentence design. Arranging sentences for clarity.* Care in paragraph design: *Giving the paragraph unity. Keeping the paragraph short. Putting topic sentences to good use. Making the paragraph move forward.* Measuring readability: *Development of readability formulas. The Gunning Fog Index. Critical appraisal of the formulas.* A word of caution.

*sentation of reasoning. Positive coverage of refusal. Off-subject closing talk. Case refusal of a claim.* Vague and back orders: *Consideration in handling. Variations in opening possibilities. Tact in handling the delayed shipment. A pleasant ending picture. Illustrated handling of delayed order.* Credit refusals: *Strategy and the reason for refusal. The buffer beginning. Justification of the refusal. Tact in the refusal. A closing forward look. Cases in review.*

Persuasive requests: *Determination of persuasion. Attention in the opening contact. Presentation of the persuasion. Goodwill and action in the close. Approach variations illustrated.* Sales letters: *Value of sales writing. Need for preliminary knowledge. Determination of appeal. An approach to the subject. Some mechanical differences. The attention opening. Presentation of the sales material. Stress on the you-viewpoint. Completeness of the sale. Clearness and motion in the action. Urgency in the action. Recall of the appeal. A study of examples.* Collection letters: *A series of efforts. Determining the collection series. Early-stage efforts. The middle (discussion) stage. Last-resort letters.* Applications for employment: *Preliminary planning. Letters of application. The data sheet.*

An orientation to reports: *The special needs of reports. Reports defined.* Determining the report purpose: *The preliminary investigation. Needs for a clear statement of problem. Determination of factors. Use of subtopics in information reports. Hypotheses for problems of solution. Bases of comparison in evaluation studies. Need for subbreakdown.* Gathering the information needed. Organization of the report information: *Preliminary steps in determining order. Need for a written outline. Patterns of report organization. System of outline symbols. The nature and extent of outlining. Organization by division. Division by conventional relationship. Combination and multiple division possibilities. Introductory and concluding sections. Wording the outline for report use.*

Overall view of content. Greater importance of the short types. Organization and content of longer reports: *The prefatory parts. The report proper.*

Major differences in short and long reports: *Less need for introductory material. Predominance of direct order. More personal writing style. Less need for coherence plan.* Short forms of reports: *The short report. Letter reports. Memorandum reports.* Special report forms: *The staff report. The audit report. The technical report.*

*When to footnote. Mechanics of footnotes. Form of the footnote. Standard reference forms. Discussion footnotes. Placement of quoted and paraphrased information. The bibliography. Bibliography: Books. Government publications. Periodicals.*

*Standard for correctness in grammar. Standard for the use of numbers.*

# part one
## Communication theory

# 1

## The role of communication in the business organization

$O$F ALL your activities, probably communication takes up most of your time. If you are like most of us, you spend a good part of each day talking or listening to other people. And when you are not talking or listening, you are likely to be communicating in other ways—reading, writing, gesturing, drawing. Or perhaps you are just taking in information by seeing, or feeling, or smelling. All of these activities are forms of communication; and certainly you do them throughout most of your conscious moments.

Logically, something done so much must be essential to our existence. In fact, probably communication is the most essential of all our activities. It is easy to see that communication is the activity which has enabled us to develop the civilized society we know today. It is one activity which we human beings clearly do better than the other forms of life on earth; and largely it explains our dominant role. Very obviously, communication is the activity which has enabled us to organize—to work in groups. Thus, collectively we have been able to overcome barriers to our existence which individually we would not be able to overcome. But there is no need to trace further how communication contributed to the development of us human beings. The role is so very obvious to us all. We need only to conclude that communication is extremely vital to our success and well-being in civilized society.

## AN ESSENTIAL TO ORGANIZED ACTIVITY

Just as communication is vital to your existence in civilized society, it is vital to the functioning of the organizations[1] which our society has produced. In fact, we could go so far as to say that organizations exist through communication; without communication, there would be no organizations. Supporting the key role of communication in organizations are these words of two authorities on the subject:

> Communication is not a secondary or divided aspect of organization—a "helper" of the other and presumably more basic functions. Rather, it is the essence of organized activity and is the basic process out of which all other functions derive.[2]

If you need proof of the importance of communication to organized activity you need only to apply your good logic to any real-life example. Take, for example, a very simple organization. It is made up of just you and one other person. Assume that this organization has an objective—one that is unfamiliar to each of you. You may even assume that both of you know what this objective is. Now, assume that both of you no longer can communicate. You cannot read; you cannot speak; you cannot write; you cannot gesture; you cannot draw. If the two of you make any progress at all, it is likely to be individual effort. Strain your imagination as you will, there is simply no likelihood of coordinated effort resulting without communication.

Without question, communication is the ingredient which makes organization possible. It is the vehicle through which the basic management functions are carried out. Managers direct through communication; they coordinate through communication; and they staff, plan, and control through communication. Hardly an action is taken in any organization without communication leading to it.

## THE HIGH FREQUENCY OF COMMUNICATION

Just how much communicating a business organization needs depends on a number of factors. The nature of the business certainly is one. Some (such as insurance companies) have much greater need to communicate than do others (such as janitorial services). The organization plan of the company also affects the volume of communication, for much of the

---

[1] Throughout this work the term *organization* is used to refer to any goal-oriented group of people, such as businesses, churches, labor unions, and government agencies. Because business organizations are of primary concern to us, however, most of the illustrative material used pertains to them.

[2] Alex Bavelas and Dermot Barrett, "An Experimental Approach to Organizational Communication," *Personnel,* Vol. 27 (March, 1951), p. 368.

information flow is provided by the structure. Also, the people who make up the organization affect the volume of communication. As we shall point out later, every human being is different. Each has different communication needs and abilities. Thus, varying combinations of people will produce varying needs for communication.

Although the communication needs vary by company, people in organizations communicate more than most of us suspect. According to one generally accepted estimate, between 40 and 60 percent of the work time spent in a typical manufacturing plant involves some phase of communication. Of course, these percentages are only averages. Some employees spend much more of their time communicating. In fact, the higher up the organization structure the employee is, the more communicating he is likely to do. Typically, top executives spend from 75 to 95 percent of their time communicating. Unskilled laborers, on the other hand, need only the briefest of communication to do their work.

Without question, communication is important to the business organization. Because it is important, it stands to reason that business wants its communication to be well done. But all too rarely is business satisfied with what it gets. Unfortunately, to use the often quoted words of an authority in the field, "Of all the things businessmen do, they are worst at communicating."

## COMMUNICATION ILLUSTRATED: DAN'S HALF HOUR

The role of communication in organized activities is perhaps best explained by illustration of a real situation. By design, our illustration is both detailed and scant. It is detailed because it is made up of illustrations of the minute and specific communication events which occur in business. It is scant because at best it covers only a sample of the almost infinite number of events.

For this review we could select any organization, for communication is vital to every conceivable type. Our choice is the Typical Company, manufacturer of a line of quality whatsits. The Typical Company is moderately large, with scores of departments and hundreds of workers doing a thousand and one duties. It employs crews of salespeople who sell the manufactured whatsits to wholesalers over the country. Like most companies in its field, Typical works to help move its products from wholesaler to retailer and from retailer to the final consumer. And it works to keep the consumer happy with his purchase. The Typical Company is indeed typical.

Our review begins with the workday of Dan D. Worker, a clerk in Typical's order department. (We could, of course, have selected any of Typical's employees.) Dan's communication activities begin each day the moment he awakens. But for our purposes we shall pick up Dan's activities as he rides to work in a car pool with three of his fellow workers. Of course, Dan and the members of his car pool communicate as they travel. Obviously, communication has a social use, and riding to work is a form of social occasion for Dan and his friends.

Most of their talk is about trivial matters. They talk primarily to entertain and to while away the time. There is a joke or two, some comments about politics, a few words about a coming football game, and some raves about the new girl at the company switchboard. Such talk, of course, is of little direct concern to Typical except perhaps as the talk affects the general happiness and welfare of the company's workers.

In time, the conversation drifts to subjects more pertinent to Typical and its operations. Someone mentions a rumor about a proposed change in promotion policy. Then Dan and the others bring in their own collection of rumors, facts, and opinions on the subject. And in the process they form opinions and work up emotions concerning the company and its policies. This communication activity has little to do with manufacturing whatsits, nor is it related to Dan's duties at Typical. But it has affected Dan's outlook, and he just might not put out very much work for Typical today or any other day. He might not trust Typical quite so much the next time the union contract problem comes up.

When the four reach the plant, the gate guard receives the message communicated by the green sticker on the windshield and waves the car through. They drive past the most convenient parking spaces, for they receive clearly the message on signs at these sites: "Reserved for the President," "Reserved for the Sales Manager," "Reserved for the Production Superintendent," etc. As Dan enters his work area, he files past the time clock, punches his card, and thereby communicates to the payroll department a record of his attendance.

As Dan enters his work area, he engages in more social communication. He exchanges "good mornings" with each of his colleagues, and he makes small talk with two of them as they wait for the company whistle to communicate the message that it is time for work to commence. Although this small talk with his associates has little to do with manufacturing whatsits, it does help to create a happy and friendly attitude among Dan and his co-workers. And such an attitude can be conducive to productivity.

When the 9 o'clock whistle blows, Dan begins his work as order clerk. The morning mail, already delivered to his desk, produces first an order from one of Typical's salespeople in the field. Dan records the transaction on specially designed forms, indicating such information as quantities, types, salesperson credited, and sales district. And he checks the goods ordered against the inventory record which he maintains from daily communications from the warehouse.

These records Dan summarizes daily to communicate vital planning information for a number of his superiors. To the sales manager his reports supply a continuing measure of activity in the field. To the men in production they serve as a guide to output goals. And to top administration they are a part of the information needed to guide the course of the company.

After recording the vital information, Dan routes the order to the shipping department through Ms. Peevy, who serves as acknowledgment clerk as well as departmental secretary. Ms. Peevy's job is to send the buyer a specially adapted acknowledgment letter. The Typical Company uses a specially adapted letter rather than a routine form acknowledgment because the firm recognizes the goodwill-building effect of making every communication contact as favorable as possible. Obviously, individually written letters are expensive; so Ms. Peevy cheats a little by using basic form letters as an aid to quick composition. When Ms. Peevy finishes her letter, she sends the order to the shipping department, where Dan's instructions are carried out.

Contents of the next envelope Dan opens are not so positive as the first. This one is a note from a Typical's salesperson in the field who reports on a difficulty one of his customers is having with his whatsit. Dan forwards this message through interplant mail to the customer services department. Here Typical's individualized attention will be given to the problem, for Typical knows that it is good business to keep its customers satisfied. Probably someone in customer services will communicate with some of Typical's technical personnel in an effort to find the cause of the difficulty. Then they will pass on their findings to the salesperson in the field, who will personally visit his customer to report the information.

Occasionally, such problems cannot be so easily solved. When a whatsit is defective, for example, customer services will make a fair and speedy adjustment. Or if the defect occurs frequently enough, a full-scale investigation may result. Possibly one or more of the company's technical specialists will be assigned to the problem, and they will spend days or weeks or even longer periods searching for the answer to the problem. When they find the answer, they will communicate this information through some form of written report.

As Dan opens the third envelope, he recognizes the familiar off-color brown of employee relations stationery. Inside he finds a printed memorandum with an instruction sheet attached. This memorandum, signed by the president, explains the new pay plan Dan and his friends discussed on the way to work. The instructions tell Dan to post the memorandum on the department bulletin board. As Dan posts the memorandum, he reads the company's explanation. There is much there that he had not considered before, and some of the "facts" his friends used in their arguments are strongly refuted. Dan is now somewhat confused, but he begins to feel that the company may have a point or two.

On the way back to his desk, Dan passes the water cooler where James Hooker and one of the other men in the department are standing. Dan does not care much for Hooker. In fact, he has had a few run-ins with the man since Hooker joined Typical three weeks ago. Dan cannot explain exactly what went wrong. At the beginning Hooker appeared to be a pleasant enough chap. He and Dan had lunch together that first day. But soon after that time Hooker started to find fault with some of the work procedures in the department. He even pointed out some things that Dan could do "to improve operations." As Dan saw it, there was little a neophyte like Hooker could tell a man who had been on the job for almost 20 years.

As Dan passes the cooler, he grunts a barely audible and cool hello. His thoughts are even more hostile. He wonders how long it is going to take John Riley, his department head, to notice how much time Hooker spends at the water cooler, in the rest room, and at coffee. Yesterday Dan saw Hooker getting ready to go home for the day a full ten minutes before quitting time. As Dan sees it, Riley must like Hooker. The two talk together a lot, and Riley has accepted a number of Hooker's suggestions. But Riley always has had his favorites, Dan thinks.

Dan returns to his desk; but before he can resume his work, Riley walks up. "Have you given any more thought to that reporting procedure change we talked about yesterday?" Riley asks.

Riley is referring to a change he has had in mind for quite a few years. Last week he asked Hooker to do some research on the possibilities of the procedure. It was then that Hooker talked with Dan about the plan, and it was then that the two had another one of their run-ins.

Riley's words bring Dan's temper to a slow boil. "Riley certainly is sold on that asinine idea of Hooker's," he thinks to himself. "Sure, it will save time now, but it won't give us as much information. But you can't fight city hall." Dan forces a smile which belies his inward feeling as he responds: "Yes, I have, Mr. Riley. It's a great idea. We should put it into effect right away."

A few minutes later as Riley walks away, Dan glances at his watch. It is 9:30—half an hour of a typical day.

Reviewing Dan's activities, we find that most of what he does involves communication in one way or another. From the moment he left home to the moment he looked at his watch, he was giving, receiving, or handling information. Nothing that he did directly involved making whatsits, which, of course, is the Typical Company's main reason for being. Yet there is no question of the importance of his activities to Typical's operations. Obviously, Dan's work assignment more directly involves communication than do many other assignments at Typical. But there are many other communication-oriented assignments in the company; and every Typical employee's workday is spotted in varying degrees with communication in one form or another. If we were to trace the workdays of each Typical employee and combine our findings, we would come up with an infinitely complex picture of the communication that goes on at Typical. We would see that communication truly plays a major role in Typical's operations.

## MAIN FORMS OF ORGANIZATIONAL COMMUNICATION

The importance of communication in business becomes even more apparent when we consider the communication activities of an organization from an overall point of view. As we can see from a review of Dan's half hour at Typical, these activities fall into three broad categories of communication: internal-operational, external-operational, and personal.

### Internal-operational communication

Internal-operational communication consists of the structured communication within the organization directly related to achieving the organization's work goals. By "structured," we mean that such communication is built into the organization's plan of operation. By the "organization's work goals," we mean the organization's primary reasons for being—to sell insurance, to manufacture nuts and bolts, to construct buildings, and the like.

The Typical Company, to use a familiar example, has as its major work goals the making and selling of whatsits. In achieving these work goals, it has an established plan of operation, and communication plays a major role in this plan. More specifically, each of Typical's employees has an assignment in the plan. For the plan to work, some communicating must be done. In some of the assignments certain working information is needed. And so that all assignments may be performed as a harmonious and unified effort, certain coordinating information must be communicated. All this information flow is internal-operational communication.

Specifically, internal-operational communication is carried out through any number of structured activities. In the Typical Company, for example, sales reports and inventory records communicate the organization's production needs to the production planning department. And production planning communicates this need to the various production departments through production orders—forms which route each whatsit through the production departments and tell each department precisely what it must do in the manufacturing process.

Within each production unit and between production units there is, of course, additional communicating that must go on. Superiors make decisions and transmit them to subordinates. Departments exchange information, and workers communicate working information with each other. Memoranda are written, reports are prepared, conversations are held, all in the process of coordinating efforts and supplying the information needed to achieve the organization's goals. In every division of the company and in every activity, similar internal-operational communication occurs.

## External-operational communication

External-operational communication is that part of an organization's structured communication which is concerned with achieving the organization's work goals and which is conducted with people and groups outside the organization. It is the organization's communication with its publics—its suppliers, service companies, customers, and the general public.

In this category fall all of the organization's efforts at direct selling— the sales representative's sales spiel, the descriptive brochures, the telephone callbacks, the follow-up service calls, and the like. Included also are all of an organization's advertising efforts. For what is advertising but a deliberate, structured communication with an organization's publics? Radio and television messages, newspaper and magazine space advertising, and point-of-purchase display material obviously play a role in the organization's plan to achieve its work objective. Also falling in this category is all an organization does to enhance its public relations. This would include its planned publicity, the civic-mindedness of its management, the courtesy of its employees, the condition of its physical plant. All these and many more communication efforts combine to make up the organization's external-operational communication.

The extreme importance of an organization's external communications hardly requires supporting comment. Certainly, it is obvious that any business organization is dependent on people and groups outside itself for its success. It is an elementary principle of business that because a business organization's success is dependent on its ability to satisfy the needs of customers, it must communicate effectively with these customers. It is equally elementary that in today's complex business society, organizations are dependent on each other in the manufacturing and distribution of goods as well as the sale of services. And this interdependence necessarily brings about needs for communication. Just as with internal communication, these outside communications are vital to an organization's operation.

## Personal communication

Not all the communication that goes on in an organization is operational, however. In fact, much of the communication in an organization is without purpose so far as the organization is concerned. Such communication may be classified as personal.

Personal communication is all that incidental exchange of information and feeling which human beings engage in whenever they come together. Human beings are social animals. They have a need to communicate, and they will communicate even when they have little or nothing to express.

Certainly, much of the time friends spend with each other is spent in communication, for it is simply the thing to do when people get together. Even total strangers are likely to communicate when they are placed in a position together, as for instance on a plane trip, in a waiting room, or at a ball game. Such personal communication also takes place in the work situation, and it is a part of the communication activity of any business organization. Although not a part of an organization's plan of operation, personal communication can have a significant effect on the success of this plan. This effect is a result of the influence personal communication can have on the attitudes, opinions, and beliefs of the members of the organization.

Attitudes of the organization members toward the organization, their fellow employees, and their assignments directly affect the members' willingness to do their assigned tasks. And the nature of conversation in a work situation affects attitudes. In a work situation where heated words and flaming tempers often are present, the participants are not likely to make their usual productive effort. Likewise, a rollicking, jovial work situation is likely to have an equally adverse effect on productivity. No doubt somewhere between these extremes the ideal productive attitudes lie.

Also affecting the organization members' work attitudes is the extent of personal communication permitted the members. Absolute denial of the communication privilege could lead to some degree of emotional upset, for people hold dear their right to communicate. On the other hand, excessive personal communication could interfere directly with their work effort. Probably somewhere in the middle-ground area lies the optimum policy toward personal communication.

Personal communication also can help to form attitudes and beliefs, which are stronger and have more lasting effects on the mind than opinions. As was illustrated in the preceding account of Dan's workday at Typical, Dan and his car-pool friends spent some of their conversation time discussing a proposed new policy for Typical. And in talking, each helped to crystallize the opinions of the others. It is in this way that every member of an organization determines much of what he thinks about his organization, his co-workers, and his work situation in general. What he thinks can affect his relationship with the organization, and it can have a direct influence on his productivity.

## COMMUNICATION NETWORK OF THE ORGANIZATION

Looking over all of an organization's communication (internal, external, and personal), we see a most complex mass of information flow. We see an organization literally feeding on a continuous supply of information. More specifically, we see dozens, hundreds, or even thousands of individual members engaging in untold numbers of communication events throughout each working day. The picture of this network of information flow is infinitely complex.

In simplified form, this infinitely complex information flow in a modern-day organization may be likened to the network of arteries and veins in the body. Just as the body has arteries, the organization has well-established channels of information flow. These are the formal and established channels of communication—the main line of the organization's operational communication. Included here are the reports, records, and other forms which supply working information to the various parts of the organization; the orders, instructions, and messages which flow up and down the organization's authority structure; and the letters, sales presentations, advertising, and publicity which go to an organization's publics. These main channels do not just happen; they are carefully thought out, or at least they should be. They are changed as the needs of the organization change.

Our overview also shows us a secondary network of information flow corresponding to the veins of the body. This is the network made up of the thousands upon thousands of personal communications which take place in any organization. Such communications follow no set pattern but rather form an intricate and infinitely complex web of information flow linking all of the members of the organization in one way or another.

Known as the "grapevine" in management literature, this informal communication system is far more effective than a first impression might indicate. Certainly it consists of much gossip and rumor, for this is the nature of human conversation. And it is as fickle and inaccurate as the human beings who are a part of it. Even so, the grapevine carries far more information than the formal communication system; and on many matters it is more effective in determining the course of an organization. The wise manager recognizes the presence of the grapevine. He learns who the talk leaders are; and he communicates to them the information that will do the most good for the organization. That is, he keeps in touch with the grapevine, and he turns it into a constructive tool.

The foregoing review merely skims the surface; yet, hopefully, it has given you an appreciation of the importance of communication to yourself and to organizations. Hopefully, it has shown you how extensive communication is, how it permeates every segment of the organization in a most intricate and complex way. And hopefully, it has shown you that good communication is vital to the successful operation of an organization. These conclusions, combined with the convincing evidence that most organizational communication is not well done, should lead you to yet another conclusion: that communication is an area deserving increased study by those concerned with improving the operations of an organization.

## A PREVIEW TO THE PRESENTATION

In the following pages such a study is undertaken. Its approach is first to gain an understanding of what communication is—how it works and how it does not work. The material covered here borrows from many disciplines—from psychology, sociology, and linguistics, and perhaps most heavily from the new discipline of general semantics. Much of the source material used is highly sophisticated, but every effort has been made to simplify it. Perhaps some people will even look upon it as being oversimplified.

After establishing a foundation of understanding, our study shifts to applications of this theoretical material to the real-life activities of an organization. For reasons of course design, much of the emphasis concerns written communication. Specifically, we shall emphasize the areas of correspondence and report writing, for these are vital areas in today's business organization. We shall give some emphasis to other areas, especially oral communication. It should be apparent, however, that this coverage is far from complete. The almost infinite nature of the subject makes it so. Even so, the applications presented should show you the ways to handle the theoretical material in your day-to-day work in business.

## QUESTIONS AND PROBLEMS

1.  Explain the role of communication in the development of civilized society.
2.  Discuss the role of communication in organized activity.
3.  Contrast the role of communication in organizations of human beings with communication in organizations of other forms of life (for example, ants).

4. Make a list of the types of external-operational and internal-operational communication that occur at your school.

5. Review Dan's half hour and note the communications that probably were true to fact and those that were not true to fact. Are there any obvious differences in the effect of each on the organization?

6. Select an organization with which you are acquainted and construct a diagram showing its network of communications. Construct its formal communications and informal communications structure. Discuss and explain these structures.

7. At the conclusion of a long and bitter strike, the Timms Manufacturing Company found through a survey that a strong majority of the people in the community sided with the union. Give a probable explanation. What would you suggest the company do to regain the lost goodwill.

8. Mary Cabot is one of 12 workers in Department X. She has strong leadership qualities, and all of her fellow workers look up to her. She dominates conversations with them and expresses strong opinions on most matters. Although she is a good worker, her dominant character has caused problems for her superior. As the new supervisor for Department X, today you have directed the workers to change a work procedure. The change is one that has proved to be superior wherever it has been tried. Soon after giving the directive, you notice the workers talking in a group, with Mary the obvious leader. In a few minutes she appears at your office. "We've thought it over," she says. "Your production change won't work." Explain what is happening. How would you handle the situation?

9. Trace the lines of formal communication at your university. Discuss some of the more significant informal communication lines.

# 2

# A model of the process

**A** CONVENTIONAL analysis of communication begins with a definition of the term. Many such definitions exist; so we would have no difficulty finding one suitable for our use. But our approach is not conventional. We shall not use words to define words, for, as we shall see, such definitions are dangerous. Instead, we shall use an operational definition. By operational definition we mean one which demonstrates how something works. In the following pages an operational definition is presented in the form of a model.

Specifically, in our presentation of the model we shall attempt to look with scientific diligence into the phenomenon of human communication. We shall take the event of one human being communicating with another. By choice we shall use a face-to-face oral communication event, for this is the communication situation with which we are best acquainted. Later we shall adapt it to written communication. Our plan will be to take this event and place it under the microscope of our minds. We shall try to determine how the process works, and conversely, how it does not work.

In developing our model, we must lean heavily on the theoretical, for we are not dealing with a subject on which much factual support is available. The theoretical material presented, however, represents authoritative thinking[1] on the subject. Regardless of its factual bases, this

---

[1] The following discussion of the communication process is adapted from the classic description by Wendell Johnson, "The Fateful Process of Mr. A Talking to Mr. B," *Harvard Business Review*, Vol. 31, No. 1 (January–February, 1953), pp. 43–50.

presentation will give us a meaningful understanding of communication, and it will provide us with principles which can be applied successfully to real-life communication problems.

## A COMMON MISCONCEPTION

Before beginning our analysis of the model, let us dispense with a misconception which many of us have. If you are like most people, you have never really thought much about what communication really is. If you have thought about it, probably you viewed communication as a very normal human activity. This assumption is far from correct.

Human communication, at least the verbal part of it, is far from being a normal function. That is, it is not the sort of thing we would do anyway if left to nature's devices, as is the case with many of our other activities. Our hands, for example, would perform their normal functions of picking up and handling things whether we grew up with wild animals in a jungle or with civilized people. Likewise, our mouths would take in food, and our teeth and jaws would chew it in either event. And so would most of our other body parts function normally without instruction from other human beings. The same cannot be said of the major organs used in communication. Our vocal apparatus would not make words if we were not taught to make them. Neither would our brains know them nor our hands write them without instruction. Clearly, communication is a function which we must learn. It was originated by human beings, and it must be acquired from human beings.

## THE COMMUNICATION ENVIRONMENT

Study of the communication process is logically preceded by an analysis of the environment in which communication occurs. This is the environment in which each of us finds himself throughout every waking moment. It is made up of all the signs existing in the world of reality which surrounds each of us. At this moment, your sensory environment is the real world surrounding you as you read these words. It consists of all the signs your senses can detect. More specifically, it is all you can see, smell, hear, or feel in that part of the world which surrounds you.

At this point perhaps some definitions are needed, although the terms will be explained in detail in following chapters. By "world of reality" or "real world" we mean that which actually exists. It contrasts with that world which exists only in the minds of people. Thus, the real world is the world of matter and space; and it includes all the happenings in this world. As we shall see, in the minds of people there is much that does not exist in the real world.

By "signs" we mean all that from the real world which can create a stimulus in us. In other words, it is all that which our sensory receptors can detect. It is that which our eyes can see, our ears can hear, our nostrils can smell, our tongues can taste, or our flesh can touch. It may be a word spoken, the sound of objects crashing together, a printed word, the aroma of a flower, the movement of a bird, or the like. Thus, an individual sign is a portion of the real world which can create a stimulus within us.

By deduction from the preceding comment we know the meaning of "sensory receptors." The term refers to those body organs which we use to detect the signs in the real world. Specifically, we refer to our eyes, our noses, our ears, and our flesh with its ability to detect surface and temperature differences.

## Sign detection

From the infinite number of signs existing in our communication environment, our sensory receptors continuously pick up some. Or stating it another way, the signs around us continuously produce stimuli within us through our receptors. Perhaps this phenomenon can be explained best by example.

At this very moment you are looking at this printed page. On it there are words (signs) which your eyes are picking up. We hope that these are the primary signs you are receiving, but there are others. Probably you pick up some of them from time to time. Perhaps there are various noises about you—voices from another room, the ticking of a clock, a radio playing in the distance, the movements and sounds made by a roommate. From time to time you may become aware of being hot or cold, or your back may itch, or your sitting position may become uncomfortable. Thus, as you read these pages your sensory receptors continuously pick up signs from all of these parts of the reality which surrounds you.

## Sensory limitations

How many and what signs we can detect from the real world, however, are limited by our sensory abilities. In short, the human sensory receptors are limited. They are not capable of detecting all signs in the real world which we know exist. For example, our eyes can detect only a small part of the total spectrum of wave lengths, and the ability to detect within these wave lengths varies from person to person. We can see only a fraction of the distance a hawk can see. Our ears can pick up only a narrow band of the whole range of air vibrations, and the abilities of human beings to pick up sounds within these ranges vary. As we all know, dogs and birds can hear much that we cannot hear. Likewise, we can smell only the stronger odors around us. Dogs and most other animals do a much better job of smelling. And so it is for all our senses. Clearly, our senses are limited, and they detect only a small portion of the reality surrounding us.

## Selective perception

In addition to being incapable of detecting all that exists in the real world around us, our sensory receptors can pick up some signs and ignore others. Place yourself, for example, in a roomful of talking people, and notice how it is possible to tune in on one conversation and to ignore others. Or notice how you are able to focus your vision on one minute object and then to expand your view to a much broader picture. To varying extents, all of us have this ability, and we can make use of it with all our senses.

## Varying alertness and perception

Our detection or nondetection of signs depends also on our receptiveness to signs. There are times when we are keenly alert to our communication environments, and there are times when we are not so alert. Certainly, you have experienced occasions when you were sleepy, in a daze, or just daydreaming. During such times you missed many of the signs in your communication environment. When you are asleep, you detect almost none.

To this point we have shown how each of us lives in an environment of signs and how these signs are with us throughout each day. We have shown also how we vary in our abilities to detect these signs, how we can tune them in or tune them out, and how our alertness to them varies from time to time. With this knowledge of the communication environment as a foundation, we are now ready to describe the communication process.

## THE COMMUNICATION PROCESS

To illustrate our description of the communication process, we shall use two hypothetical characters. Let us call them Jones and Smith. These two people are somehow in a communication situation. Let us make it a face-to-face personal situation, for this is the most common form of human communication. Then, after we have traced the process through this basic situation, we can adapt it to other communication situations, such as that between writer and reader.

Our plan is first to describe orally the communication process as it occurs. We shall begin with Jones as he exists in his communication environment. We shall trace the development of the communication effort to the formulation of the message and the transmission of it into Smith's environment. Then we shall trace briefly the message as it communicates with Smith. Following our oral review of the process, we shall summarize with a diagram of the model (Figure 2–1) we have described. By design our description will be short, for the major phases of the process are the subjects of the following chapters.

## Reception of signals

Let us begin our illustration as Jones and Smith are talking to each other; and let us first look into the communication process as it occurs in Jones. At this moment, as in all of his conscious moments, Jones's sensory receptors are picking up signs from his communication environment. As we know, his environment is infinitely filled with signs, but Jones picks up only a few of them. Probably his eyes are picking up Smith's image as well as some of the surrounding real world. His nose may be detecting the smoke from Smith's cigar. His ears may be picking up various sounds from outside the room. But the dominant signs are likely to be the words which Smith sends into Jones's environment. Whatever they are, Jones picks up some signs, and the communication process begins.

The signs picked up now travel as stimulations through the nervous system of Jones's body and on to his brain. They go out again to the muscles and glands and feed back into the nervous system, where they bring about various reverberations of stimulations. This is the preverbal neurophysiological stage of communication. It is a stage about which we know little that is definite, yet scientists assure us that it does occur in the manner just described.

> Though our factual information is meager as yet, certainly it is sufficient to demonstrate that the nervous system is not merely a hypothetical construct. We can say with practical assurance that stimulation of our sensory end organs is normally followed by the transmission of nerve currents into the central nervous system, with a consequent reverberation effect. . . .[2]

## Flow to the brain

The reverberations Jones's nervous system develops reach Jones's brain. They enter as a continuous stream, for as we have noted, the senses continuously pick up signs from the communication environment. From time to time this stream will vary in its speed of flow and in its volume. Sometimes it will run fast and strong, as when his environment is filled with strong signs and his mind is keenly alert. At other times it will run slowly, as when Jones is in a stupor and his communication environ-

---

[2] *Ibid.*, p. 46.

ment has no signs strong enough to break the spell. Most of the time, of course, the stream runs somewhere between these extremes.

## Role of the filter

When this stream of stimuli reaches Jones's brain with all of its resulting reverberation effect, it goes through what we shall call the "filter" of the mind. In this stage Jones's brain gives meaning to the stimulations received. And the meanings given depend largely on the makeup and current condition of Jones's filter.

By "filter," we mean all that exists in Jones's mind which will influence his interpretation of any signs received. The filter is in reality all that Jones is and all that he has ever been. It is made up of all he knows and all he thinks, and it includes all he thinks he knows. It includes all of his emotional makeup; and it includes all of his opinions, attitudes, and beliefs. It is apparent that Jones's filter is unique. In fact, of the three-billion-odd filters on earth, no two are identical.

All filters differ because no two people have identical experiences, knowledge, emotional makeups, thought processes, and the like. For this not to be so, two people would have to live side by side every moment of every day. They would have to act alike and think alike. They would have to perceive identical signs from identical sensory environments, and they would have to react in exactly the same way to these perceptions. Obviously, such identical existences do not occur. In fact, the possibilities for differences in filter makeups are so great that differences outnumber similarities.

Since filters are so different, and since meaning is determined by the filter, it is apparent that meanings assigned to a given set of signs will also differ. To illustrate this major truth of the communication process, consider the different meanings Jones might give to the words "Watson is a union member." First, assume that Jones comes from an independent and individualistic rural family which has for years been critical of labor. Throughout his life Jones has heard critical comments about unions and union members. In fact, he has made some such remarks himself. Let us also assume that Jones is now a ranking officer in the company, with many years of experience in haggling with union officials. Thus, his labor experiences and his knowledge of labor unions and their membership have been quite negative. Now, as the words strain through Jones's filter, they register a somewhat unpleasant meaning.

On the other hand, had Jones been born in a family sympathetic to labor, or perhaps if he were a rabid union worker, the meaning given would be different. Instead of going through a negatively biased filter, the symbols would now go through a positively biased filter. The resulting meaning given the symbols in question would be much more favorable.

For another example, assume that Jones's receptors pick up the symbol "liberal" in a comment about some proposed legislation. If Jones's filter contains favorable references to this controversial word, a favorable reaction will come about. On the other hand, Jones's filter could contain quite negative references to the word. His experiences, for example, could have taught him that things liberal are things to be feared and despised. They could have taught him that the true connotation of the symbol lies somewhere between these extremes. Or they could have conditioned him to regard the word with suspicion and confusion. In each of these events, Jones's response to these symbols would vary.

Similar illustrations may be made with other words. In a given sentence, "house" might have one meaning to a destitute mountaineer, another to a middle-class citizen of a big city, and still another to a rich southern planter. "Capitalist" might stir up all sorts of vile responses in the mind of a dedicated communist; quite different responses could be expected from a political scientist, an economist, and a zealous American patriot. "Our forefathers" would not get identical responses from an anthropologist and from one whose experiences include hearing traditional Fourth of July orations. Our illustrations could continue through thousands of similar symbols.

The illustrations used thus far have concerned words. We have used words because they are the easiest to use and because they are the most important signs in our study of communication. Words, however, are only one of the sign forms in our communication environment.

Similar filter responses occur with other signs our receptors pick up and pass through our filters. For example, the sight of a grasshopper resting on a leaf or of ants swarming on an anthill might strike the American child as an interesting nature study. A youngster in a primitive tribe might have experiences which prompt him to see a delicious meal. The sight of a 5-foot king snake might strike terror in the mind of one conditioned to fear all snakes; yet a snake fancier would find the reptile to be a friendly and harmless pet. Cool breezes coming off the sea might mean pleasant sleeping to the vacationing tourist, good sailing for the sailboat enthusiast, and a factor to be considered by the fisherman. And so it is for all the signs our receptors pick up.

Some of the signs recorded, of course, do not bring about such clear and distinct reactions as the examples given. In fact, many bring about multiple, mixed, or confused reactions. When such an indefinite response occurs, the content of the filter is equally indefinite. It is easy to see why filters so often hold indefinite information, for little in reality is clear-cut and precise. For example, one's filter might contain hundreds of reactions concerning a certain politician. Some of them might be strongly positive, some strongly negative, and some in between. Any mention of the politician would result in a mixed reaction. So it is with much of what exists in the filter.

Obviously, the differences in filter makeups are infinite, and the foregoing discussion and illustrations barely begin to explain them. Hopefully, enough has been given to provide you with a general idea of the vital role of the filter in communication. But because this role is so vital to an understanding of communication and is in fact the heart of all communication problems, it is the subject of detailed discussion in a later chapter (Chapter 4). For the moment we have sufficient information to understand how the stimuli going through the filter are given meanings and how these meanings will differ from filter to filter.

## The symbolizing stage

The meanings Jones's filter gives the stimulations he receives react on Jones in some way. This reaction may be wholly within the mind, as when Jones is passively receiving information. In some instances his reaction may trigger strong physical movements. He may, for example, swing a clenched fist at one who, according to his filter, has insulted him. Or he may quickly jump to avoid danger when his filter gives meaning to a frantic "Watch out!" In most communication situations his response is to communicate his reaction to those with whom he is communicating.

When the reaction to symbols received is a communication response, the symbolizing stage of the communication process begins. This is the stage in which the mind searches for a means of presenting its reaction to those with whom it wishes to communicate. Since most of our communication makes use of words, which are our most common symbols, this stage is likely to consist of finding the words which will convey the meaning intended. It could, however, concern selecting facial expressions, body movements, hand signals, or any other form of symbol.

As the symbolizing stage involves the innermost workings of the mind, our knowledge of it is limited. There is evidence, however, which indicates that one's competency at this stage is related to his mental ability. Especially is one's symbolizing competency (the ability to select words) related to his knowledge of language. A knowledge of language gives one an appreciation of the strength and limitations of verbal communication. Also, such a knowledge equips one with a variety of symbol forms; and the greater the number of symbol forms in the mind, the more precise and discriminating can one be in selecting from them.

As we shall see in Chapter 5, symbolizing is a highly imperfect act. In the first place, the symbols we use do not carry perfectly clear meanings. Most have multiple meanings, and many are vague and general. Then there simply is not a sufficient supply of symbols to communicate all one thinks or sees. In addition to the inadequacy of symbols, we all have some limitation in using those which are available. It is no easy task to put in symbol form what is in our minds. Even if we have plenty of time available, as when we are writing, we are rarely satisfied with our symbolizing efforts. Our efforts are even more unsatisfactory when we symbolize our reactions in seconds or even split seconds, as when we are carrying on a conversation.

## Act of encoding

The symbolizing stage ends when Jones encodes his response. In this part of the symbolizing stage Jones sends the symbols he has selected to Smith. Since he and Smith are engaged in face-to-face communication, probably he encodes with vocal sounds (air vibrations made with his vocal cords). That is, he speaks words. But instead of words, or perhaps as a supplement to them, he might encode with body movements, gestures, or facial expressions.

As graphically summarized in Figure 2–1, the encoding of the message ends the first cycle of the communication process. This is the cycle which describes the role of the communicator (Jones, in this case) in the process. Now we begin another and identical cycle—this time to describe the role of the communicatee (Smith).

## The cycle repeated

However they are sent, the symbols encoded by Jones move into the sensory environment of Smith. Here they vie for attention with other signs Smith's receptors are capable of picking up. And just as was the case in a similar situation in the first cycle, Smith will detect only some of the many signs existing in his environment. Those he does pick up go through the nervous system and on to Smith's brain. Here they are processed through Smith's filter. It is at this point that communication is most likely to fail. As is the case with Jones's filter as well as with every other filter, Smith's filter is unique. No one else has his exact experience and knowledge. No one else has his precise emotional makeup. And no one else has his exact opinions, attitudes, and beliefs. Thus, because each of their filters is unique, the meaning Smith gives to Jones's words will differ from the meaning Jones intended. The difference, of course, may be barely discernible, in which case for all practical purposes communication will be successful. Fortunately, most human communication falls in this category. But the difference could be significant. When this is the case, miscommunication is the result.

The meaning Smith's filter gives the symbols received brings about a

**FIGURE 2–1**

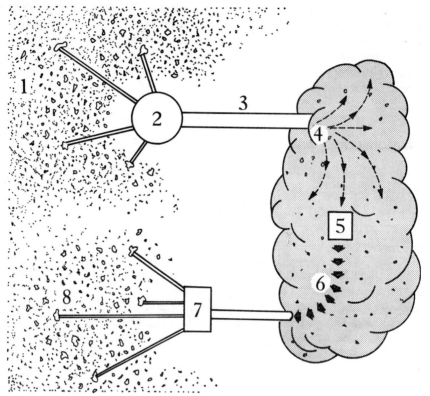

Explanation:
1. This area represents our communication environment. It is all the signs and symbols that exist in the real world that surrounds us.
2. Our sensory receptors pick up some (far from all) of the signs and symbols.
3. Those signs and symbols which are picked up go through our nervous systems and into our mental filters.
4. Our mental filters give the signs and symbols meaning. The meanings received add to the content of the filters.
5. Sometimes the meanings we form trigger communication responses.
6. We form these responses through our mental filters.
7. We send our responses as symbols through speaking, writing, etc.
8. These symbols become a part of the communication environments of others. Here they may be picked up by the sensory receptors of others, and another cycle begins.

reaction in Smith. Since he and Jones are engaged in face-to-face communication, more than likely he will communicate this reaction. Thus, the symbolizing stage begins for Smith. Now Smith's brain searches for the symbols which will convey his reaction. He encodes these symbols and sends them into the sensory environment of Jones. And then begins a third cycle, which may lead to a fourth, and a fifth, and on and on as long as both feel a need to communicate.

## THE MODEL AND WRITTEN COMMUNICATION

Although the foregoing description of the communication process applies specifically to a face-to-face situation, it generally fits written communication as well. But some significant differences exist.

### Effects of creativity

Perhaps the most significant difference between face-to-face and written communication is that written communication is more likely to be creative effort of the mind. The fact is that it is more likely to be thought out and less likely to be the spontaneous reaction to signs received by the receptors. More specifically, the message in a written communication is more likely to be a result of stimuli produced by the mind than of outside stimuli picked up by the sensory receptors.

In a report-writing situation, for example, before beginning his work, the writer has decided to communicate; or perhaps someone has decided for him. Before he begins the task of communicating, he gathers the information which will form the basis of his communication. Then, through his logical thought processes, he encodes the communication which will accomplish his communication objective. Thus, there is not likely to be an interchange of stimuli between communicants, nor is there likely to be any triggering of desires to communicate. The process is a creative and deliberative one.

On the other hand, a letter-writing situation can be an exception, at least to some extent. In a sense, a letter situation can be like a face-to-face situation in slow motion. Stimuli picked up by one person's receptors could produce a reaction which would bring about a communication response—in this case a written letter. This letter could in turn bring about a communication response in its reader's mind. Thus, a reply would be written. This reply could then bring about another reply. And the cycle could be repeated as long as each letter brings about a communication response. Even so, letters represent more deliberate and creative efforts than face-to-face communication.

## The lag of time

Most obvious of the differences in face-to-face and written communication processes is the time factor. In face-to-face communication the encoded messages move instantaneously into the sensory environments of the participants. In written communication, however, some delay takes place. Just how long the delay will be is indeterminate. Priority administrative announcements or telegrams may be read minutes after they are written. Routine letters require a day or two to communicate their contents. Research reports may take weeks in communicating their information to the intended readers. And all such written communications may be filed for possible reference in the indefinite future. They may continue to communicate for months or years.

The lag of time also makes a difference in the return information one gets from communicating. Return information, commonly called "feedback," helps greatly in determining when clear meaning is being received. In face-to-face communication, feedback is easy to get. The participants are right there together. They can ask questions. They can observe facial expressions. They can repeat and simplify whenever it appears to be necessary. In written communication, feedback is slow at best. Often it does not occur at all.

## Limited numbers of cycles

A third significant difference between face-to-face and written communication is the number of cycles typically occurring in a communication event. As previously noted, face-to-face communication normally involves multiple exchanges of symbols; thus, many cycles take place. Written communication, on the other hand, usually involves a limited number of cycles. In fact, most written communication is one-cycle communication. A message is sent and received, but none is returned. Of course, there are exceptions, such as letters and memorandums, which lead to a succession of communication exchanges. But even the most involved of these would hardly match in cycle numbers a routine, face-to-face conversation.

## THE UNIVERSAL INGREDIENTS OF HUMAN COMMUNICATION

The differences in face-to-face and written communication processes are significant, but the similarities are even more vital to our study of communication. These similarities are vital because they comprise the universal ingredients of all human communication. To know and understand them is to know and understand communication. Thus, they are the basic substance of any meaningful study of the subject.

## The communication environment

The first universal of human communication is the communication environment of those engaged in communication. All communication must enter such an environment and must compete for detection by the sensory receptors with the other stimuli which happen to be in the environment at the time.

## The filter of the mind

In all forms of human communication the stimuli picked up by the sensory receptors are passed through the filter of the mind. Because the filter is the product of all one's experiences and all his thinking, sharp differences exist in filter makeups. In fact, of all the differences between people, probably none are greater than the differences in their filters. Yet it is through these sharply different filters that people must attempt to communicate meaning.

## The encoding and decoding processes

Encoding and decoding are the third and fourth universal ingredients of the process of human communication. The universal role of these functions should be apparent. All purposeful human communication makes use of symbols (words, gestures, facial expressions, etc.), for symbols are our primary conveyors of meaning. As we human beings have thousands of symbols at our disposal, there must be the process of selecting the ones which will best carry a given message. And there must be the process of giving meaning to the message. Encoding and decoding are these processes.

## SOME FUNDAMENTAL TRUTHS OF COMMUNICATION

A review of the communication process reveals certain fundamental truths which will help us in our understanding of the subject. Three in particular stand out.

## Communication is imperfect

First is the obvious truth that communication is imperfect—that it is not the highly precise activity some people think it is. Convincing explanations support this observation. The most obvious explanation lies in the countless variations which exist in human filters. Since meanings are determined through filters, no two of which are precisely alike, there are apt to be variations in the meanings given to a set of symbols.

The imprecision of the symbols used in communication is the second explanation of communication imperfection. As will be discussed in greater depth in Chapter 5, the symbols we use (mainly words) are crude substitutes for reality. Typically, symbols have multiple and vague meanings, and they are not consistently used.

Yet another explanation of communication imprecision is that people vary in their abilities to encode meanings. Not all people know the same symbols, nor are all people equally proficient in selecting and putting together the symbols to be used in messages. For example, two people with varying encoding abilities trying to communicate the same message would select different symbols and arrangements of symbols. The result would be that the message would be changed and different meanings would be received.

## We communicate about ourselves

A second observation which we may draw from our description of the process is that when we communicate, we communicate about ourselves. In fact, in the process of symbolizing, we attempt to select symbols which tell what is going on inside us. In effect, when we communicate, we are really saying: "This is how I perceive or react to the stimuli I am receiving."

To illustrate this point, take a situation in which our two characters, Jones and Smith, are viewing a painting. Jones remarks, "This is a beautiful painting." But what Jones really is saying is, "As I view this painting as picked up by my receptors, it is pleasing to me." Viewing the same painting, Smith comments, "What a hideous painting this is!"

In reality, a painting is neither beautiful nor hideous. It is only a composition of matter. The qualities of beauty and hideousness are reactions in the minds of the viewers. Thus, what each is saying in reality is: "As I view this picture as picked up by my receptors and relayed through my nervous system and strained through my filter, the picture appears to be beautiful (or hideous) to me."

## Meaning is in the mind

A third significant observation we may draw from the process is that meaning is in the mind and not in the symbols used. In a sense, this observation is a corollary of the preceding one, but it is so fundamental to an understanding of communication that it deserves our special emphasis. It should be clear from the description of the process that symbols do not have meaning. If they did, there would be no communication problems, for communication would be precise.

Putting it another way, we can say that people have meaning in mind when they use symbols. It is their hope that the symbols they use will be given similar meaning in the minds of those with whom they communicate. The proximity of the meaning given in the minds of those involved in the communication is a measure of the success of the communication effort. As has been noted, precise agreement rarely if ever occurs.

From this observation we can gain one of the major lessons of communication—that in communication our emphasis should be on "What did he mean when he used those symbols?" rather than on "What do those symbols mean in my mind?" If all of us understood and practiced this fundamental truth, we would eliminate a major portion of the misunderstanding in the world today.

## QUESTIONS AND PROBLEMS

1. What is meant by operational definition?
2. Construct your own definition of communication. Compare it with the operational definition given in the text.
3. Although communication is not a normal function for human beings, it is for ants and bees. Discuss.
4. Explain the meaning of real world, signs, and sensory receptors.
5. Describe the sensory environment in which you are at this moment. Contrast that part with which typically you are aware with that part which you typically are unaware.
6. Without looking, describe in as much detail as possible some object you have seen many times (a watch, dollar bill, etc.). What part of the operational definition of communication does this illustrate?
7. Following an incident involving a worker and his foreman, workers who observed the incident were questioned about what had happened. Some reported that the foreman remained cool throughout the incident and attempted to calm down the worker who was yelling and shaking his fist. Some reported that both people were emotional. And some saw the worker as calm and collected and the foreman as emotional and upset. All those reporting were honorable people. Explain how this could happen.
8. Margaret Lewis, a very conscientious student, is at the last meeting of a class before a major exam. "Will we cover Chapter 7 on the examination?" she asks the professor. Laughter is heard around the room. "They are laughing because I answered your question the moment before you asked it," the professor says. Explain what happened from a communications viewpoint.
9. "Professor Oliver is really a great teacher," says Emily to her friend Bill. "He's so brilliant as a lecturer. And he's really interested in students."

Bill responded with these words: "That creep? I had him last semester. He's terrible." Explain from a communications viewpoint.

10. Explain why no two filters are quite the same.

11. From your own experience select an example of miscommunication. Use the model to explain how the miscommunication occurred.

12. The exact conversations of an organization's meeting were transcribed, typewritten, and distributed to the membership. How well does the communications model fit here? Do all the differences between face-to-face communication and written communication apply?

13. Explain each of the universal ingredients of human communication.

14. Sandra and Betty were engaged in an intellectual argument. Said Sandra after listening to Betty's argument, "You've really proved my point—not yours. You used the word 'preponderance,' which means the big majority. So what you really said was that my position has stronger support." Discuss the fundamental truth of communication illustrated here.

15. Relate the following conversation between a foreman and an employee to the fundamental truths of communication.

*Foreman:* "You stupid or something? I've told you in clear, simple English what to do. I can't tell you no plainer."
*Worker:* "I'm sorry, but I don't understand your explanation."

# 3

# Perception and reality

THE PRECEDING review of the communication process clearly shows us that when we communicate we symbolize (put in words, gestures, and so on) our reaction to the reality we perceive. But just what is reality? And how do we perceive it? The answers to these questions are basic to our understanding of communication.

## REALITY DEFINED

As we defined it in Chapter 2, "reality," or the "real world," is all that which actually exists as contrasted with that which exists only in the minds of human beings. Our definition includes all that our senses can perceive—all that we can see, smell, taste, hear, or feel. It includes also much that our senses cannot perceive.

## That which has substance

Obviously included in this definition is all that we think of as having substance—that is, all that which has physical shape and composition. Included would be most of what we can see and feel around us: the chair you sit in, the desk before you, this book, your own body. It includes all that we commonly refer to as matter—rocks, soil, water, and plants. In general, it is all that the eye can see or that the sense of touch can detect.

## Reality without substance

Reality also includes much which does not have shape or form. The invisible air you breathe is as real as the ground you walk on. Equally real is the existence of space—of nothingness. Nothingness is all about us; in fact, it is in far greater supply than the tangible parts of reality. In addition, vibrations in the air (we detect them as sounds) are certainly a part of reality. So is time. And so are the qualities of light and color. None of these parts of reality are tangible so far as our unaided senses are concerned. Yet there is no doubt about their presence.

## The reality of events

Included also in our definition of reality are all the events which take place in the real world. By events we mean any change in the relationships of the parts of reality. A car moving over a road changes its relationship with the other parts of reality which surround it. The same is true of a man slipping on a banana peel, a fist striking a table top, a wind moving the leaves in a tree. Obviously, the parts of reality are not static. They move around or in some way change their relationships with the other parts of reality.

## Position relationships

Even the static position relationships of the elements of reality are a part of reality. Illustrating this point is a tale told by a popular comedian about a man caught in the company of a married woman by the woman's husband. When asked by the husband what he was doing there, the man replied, "Everybody's got to be someplace." Aside from the humor of the anecdote, it presents a basic truth of reality: All of reality must be somewhere. Everything must have spatial relationships with other things. For example, a box may be stacked on another box. It may have objects stored inside it, and these objects are arranged in some way within the box. All such relationships of objects are a part of the reality in which we exist.

However vague our definition may be, we all know that reality does exist. We know it because we perceive some of it. Unfortunately, however, we do not perceive reality precisely. Thus, since communication is the symbolizing of our reactions to our perceptions, imprecise perceptions must result in imprecise communication. As was discussed in Chapter 2, some of the blame for our imprecise perception we may place on the limitations of our sensory organs. The remaineder of the blame we may place on our lack of understanding of reality. For this latter reason, we shall next analyze the characteristics of reality and our perceptions of them.

## THE INFINITY OF REALITY

A major reason why we human beings err in our perceptions of reality is that there is so much of it. The world of matter and events is all so tremendously involved and complex that for all practical purposes it is infinite in nature. Because of the infinite nature of reality, it is humanly impossible to know even a substantial part of all the facts involved in any one object or event; and it is likely that different people would perceive differently the parts of a given object or event. Thus, when we symbolize our reactions to reality (which is what we do when we communicate), we symbolize our reactions to a small part of the whole, and to parts which others perceive differently from us. More than likely, we are not conscious of these limitations. These concepts are perhaps best explained by illustration.

### Infinity in a sheet of paper

To illustrate the concept of the infinite nature of reality, take some familiar object around you—say a single sheet of theme paper. One common variety has a double red stripe down the left margin; and it has some 30-odd blue parallel lines running horizontally across the page. It is a rather simple thing as objects go—at least, that is how it appears to most of us at first glance. But let us take a closer look.

Close inspection with the naked eye shows us that the red lines are not so sharp and clear as they at first appeared. The lines are fuzzy, to say the least, and the intensity of color varies from place to place. The same is true of the blue lines. And the white space is not all white, for here and there are little flecks of dark matter.

These observations alone are enough to prove that countless variations exist on the paper. But our case would be even more convincing were we to give this same page a microscopic inspection. Under such an inspection we would find that each line contains many more irregularities than we are able to detect with the naked eye. We would see many more flecks in the paper; and we would see that each has a shape, color, and size unlike any of the others. We would see that the paper is made up of thousands of compressed fibers, and we would see that each of these fibers is different from any of the others. The edges of the paper would take on a different appearance. Instead of the smooth, straight line we see with the naked eye, we would see a rough and ragged edge of loose fibers.

We could take our inquiry a step further into the submicroscopic world. Here we would find that each little fiber, each fleck, each particle of dye on the lines is made up of atoms. And as we know from our study of physics, the atom is a universe in itself—a whirling mass of electrons with a nucleus composed of protons and neutrons. And there are millions upon millions of atoms in our sheet of paper. Their variations also approach infinity.

The infinite number of characteristics in our simple sheet of paper illustrates the nature of what we would find in any part of reality we would choose to examine. In fact, many parts would present even greater complexity. An automobile, an electronic computer, or a building, for example, each presents much greater complexity in overall makeup. Each consists of hundreds of distinguishable parts; and as with the sheet of paper, each of these parts has its own infinite characteristics. Without question, the world of reality is indeed infinite in its complexity.

## Limiting effects on perception

Because of the infinite nature of the real world, we have some difficulty perceiving it. Two of the major explanations of this difficulty deserve our attention. First, our sensory organs are inadequate to cope with this complexity. Second, our perceptions are not uniform.

*Inadequacy of sensory organs.* From the preceding discussions it should be apparent that our sensory organs can pick up only some of the details in a given object or event. They cannot pick up everything. Our eyes cannot detect all the minute details in reality. Our ears can detect only some of the sounds which occur around us. And so it is with our other senses. There simply are too many details in reality, and our sensory organs are too limited for our perceptions to even approach detailed completeness. Thus, we can never perceive everything about anything. In fact, at best we can perceive only a small part of the whole.

To illustrate the point, imagine that you are watching a football game. The teams line up. The ball is snapped. Then for a few seconds there is bedlam. Men block, run, and fall. The crowd roars, and the officials scurry about. Action is everywhere, and you are perceiving it. Yet how much of the reality of this event do you really perceive? How much do you miss? And when it is all over and you make some comment about it, on how much of all that took place is your comment based? Did you see the guards pull out, the linebackers close the hole, or the offensive tackle hold the opposing lineman? Did you see each muscle twitch, each facial grimace, each bead of perspiration? There is no question about it; you did not see all that happened. In fact, you missed most of it.

Because you saw so little of all that went on, can you really comment on the event accurately? "That was a well-executed play," you might say, for this may be how your senses perceived it. But is it not quite possible that had you perceived more of the situation, you might find your comment to be wrong? Could it not be that the play worked because one of the opposing players tripped on a shoestring or that an undetected clip took out a key defender? Or that some of the defenders were loafing or made key mistakes? Certainly, all these happenings are possible.

*Perception differences.* A second explanation of why the infinite nature of reality causes communication difficulty is that because of its infinite nature any object or event can be perceived in many different ways. People standing side by side looking at or listening to the same things will not receive the same perception. There are so many complexities and variations in the real world that each of us cannot perceive precisely the same ones.

Our illustration of the football play describes this phenomenon well. So many separate events occur in any one play that two people sitting side by side are likely to perceive different ones. So numerous are the possibilities, in fact, that probably no two spectators in a packed stadium will detect precisely the same ones.

Perhaps even better illustrations can be gathered from the files of almost any law enforcement agency. It is all too common for witnesses to a crime to come up with conflicting accounts of the actions witnessed. Countless cases can be found in which eyewitnesses to a given event sincerely disagree on the parts of the event. One witness may see an accused assailant angrily attacking a victim; another witness may see the accused heroically defending himself from the alleged victim. Or, for another example, a gentleman, in passing a lady on the street, may see only a well-dressed lady in a brown dress; his wife may see a clear picture of the lady and her dress down to such details as her blue eyes and her alligator shoes.

From this analysis comes a question which is basic to our understanding of communication. When people communicate their perceptions of the same objects or events, are they really communicating the same thing? When, for example, in the preceding illustration the lady discusses the dress with her husband, do they have in their minds identical concepts of the dress? Does "that dress" mean the same to the gentleman as "that dress" does to the lady? The answer is an obvious no. And so it is with all other perceptions.

## UNIQUENESS IN EVERYTHING

A second observation we may make from our inspection of reality is that everything is unique. The sheet of paper we described, for example, is so infinite in its makeup that no other sheet could duplicate it precisely. There never has been one exactly like it, and there never will be one exactly like it. So astronomical is the number of variations in each sheet that exact duplication is beyond the realm of probability.

## Uniqueness illustrated

The same observation holds true for any event or object in the world of reality. Every grain of sand on the beach is unlike every other. Every snowflake has its individual characteristics. Every human being now living or who has ever lived is different from every other one. And so it is with every puff of smoke, every hamburger, every apple, every blade of grass, every cat, and every cup of tea. Even carefully matched jewelry, standardized manufactured parts, and the like have differences at the microscopic and submicroscopic levels. Without question, uniqueness is a quality of every object in reality. No two have ever been found to be exactly the same, nor are they likely to be found.

Likewise, no two events can ever be precisely the same. For example, over the years baseball players have hit baseballs millions of times, and each hit has been unique. In the first place, the objects involved in each hit have been different. The balls have been similar, but not precisely the same. The same is true of the bats, the players, the gloves, and the like. In the second place, the continuous change occurring in all objects over time makes exact duplication impossible. A ball hit one moment is not the same ball hit a moment later. In the third place, the movements involved always will differ. Each ball hit will have its unique trajectory and speed. It will land in one unique location. In all such events there will be many very loose similarities, but never exact duplication.

## Effects on perception

Some of the differences we speak of are minute, of course. Some are so infinitesimal that we must go to the miscroscopic or submicroscopic level to find them. Because these differences are so small, it is apparent that we cannot detect them without technical aids such as the microscope. Our ears, our eyes, or any of our other sensory organs simply are not capable of detecting such differences.

Because we must go to the microscopic or submicroscopic level to find such differences, you might well ask our reason for mentioning this point. If we must go to such extremes to detect them, can these differences affect our perception of reality? The answer to this question is vital to our understanding of our perception and, conversely, our communication.

Admittedly, the foregoing analysis was presented to prove the point that everything is unique. In many respects it draws an impractical and fine line of distinction. For most practical purposes the insignificant and almost imperceptible differences in reality are of little value to us, and not being able to perceive them does not affect our communication significantly. To consider them every time we communicate would confuse us more than it would help us. But there are communication difficulties which result from the uniqueness of all parts of reality. These we should understand.

These communication difficulties stem primarily from our failure to perceive the uniqueness of the objects and events about which we communicate. More specifically, when we perceive reality, we tend to assume erroneously that similarities rather than differences exist in the real world to which our communication relates. We tend to stress similarities and to ignore differences. Because such practices are contrary to the reality about which we communicate, error in communication results. This cause of miscommunication is discussed in more detail in Chapter 6.

## ALL IN PROCESS

A third observation we can make of the real world about us is that it is a world of process. It is continually and forever changing. Nothing remains static. Nothing is now as it was before; and as things are now, they will never be again. Perhaps the foregoing discussion sounds like an overstatement; but it, too, describes reality as it really is. As in our discussion of uniqueness, in the short run the process of reality is perceptible only at the microscopic and submicroscopic levels. It is so apparent in the long run, however, that there can be no doubt about its existence. Again, illustrations best serve to prove this point.

### Changes in inanimate things

Take some object around you—say the chair in which you are sitting. As you look at it, probably you see it as being static. It looks very much the way it looked yesterday and the day before. But if you look closely, you can see evidence that it is not exactly as it once was. Here and there, you may find scratches or nicks, and maybe the color has begun to fade. In all likelihood the glue or screws that hold it together have loosened a bit. Thus, you have evidence that some change has taken place, and you know full well that similar changes will continue to take place. You know that over time the chair will receive additional scratches and its screws and glue will weaken more and more. Someday it will deteriorate to the point that it will be discarded. Perhaps it will decay on a junkpile, or it may be burned. Eventually, it will become dirt or ashes or something far different from what it is today.

Or take the illustration of a visit to a hallowed battlefield of a war fought a century or more ago. Assume that you are listening to the commentary of a guide who describes the events which took place here. "Over there on the knoll General Blain set up his command post from which he directed his battle strategy. Down there by the brook his cavalry assembled, and over there in the wooded area his infantry prepared for the charge across the meadows ahead." And on and on he talks, giving you a vivid picture of the battle fought long ago in this very place. Probably you are moved with emotion. Here you are in the very place where so much history took place.

Now let us take a look at the place as it really is. Let us look to see how much remains of the scene at the time of battle. The brook is still there, but its path has changed. And the water which flowed through it then is far, far away. How many of the trees that were there at the time of the battle are still alive, and how many of the trees now present were even seedlings then? Much of the soil on which the soldier's feet trod has long since washed away. The grass now in the meadow is a hundred generations removed from the grass the soldiers saw. What, then, remains of the place where the battle was fought? Although it may sound like a play on words, we might conclude that we are at the same place, but the place is not the same.

Such changes, of course, are obvious over long periods of time. Others are more apparent and occur more rapidly. Without refrigeration, a pail of fresh sweet milk, for example, may change to sour milk in a day or two. Sometime later, it will become clabber; and after even more time, it may become cottage cheese. A piece of ice placed on a hot stove will change to water, then to steam, and then seemingly will disappear before your eyes. White, dry flour can change in a matter of minutes to dough, then to bread. And certainly, we all marvel at the wonders of chemistry in transforming petroleum into various forms of plastics. A student of chemistry could continue this discussion through countless examples.

## Changes in the living

Just as all matter is in a constant state of change, so does all life change. So obvious a point as this hardly needs discussion, for we have only to trace our own lives back to the time of birth to prove the point. Certainly, we are not now the physical beings we once were. We are bigger and stronger than we once were; even our features are different. And we know that this physical change will continue as long as we live—that at every passing moment imperceptible changes take place and that these changes become perceptible over time.

Equally apparent but all too often overlooked are the changes which take place in our minds—in how we think and what we know. From the time of birth this process of change begins, and it continues until death. We are continually receiving new knowledge, having new thoughts, and generally taking different views of the world about us.

This point can be illustrated by a review of your own development. Go back a few years and analyze the you of that time. How different are you now from what you were then? How much more do you know today? Are there any beliefs, opinions, or attitudes which have changed? Are you the same person emotionally? Unless you are a most unusual person or one who does not comprehend this analysis, you will find vast differences. You simply are not the same person you were then. Significant changes have taken place. They are taking place now. They will continue to take place as long as you live.

## Error effect on perception

Now, no one will seriously argue that such changes do not take place, for the facts are most obvious. A problem does arise, however, from our failure to consider properly the changing nature of reality when we perceive reality. All too often we see reality as if it were static—as if it has always been the way it is and always will remain that way. And because reality simply does not remain static, such perceptions must lead to some error.

Examples of error resulting from failures to consider the process nature of reality come from all areas of human activity. A major retailer, for example, once paid a fancy fee to a consultant to get advice on how to improve his collections. The consultant suggested a procedure she had found to be highly successful in retail stores like this one. The retailer, however, brushed off the suggestion with the comment, "I tried that once. It didn't work." Further discussion revealed that the retailer had tried the plan in the 1930s, in the midst of the Great Depression. This was a time when most creditors had very little money and when no collection techniques proved to be effective. The situation had changed drastically since that time.

Even nations are guilty of this form of perception error, as is evident from a review of history. A major reason for war, for example, has been to avenge wrongs done by one nation against another generations earlier. That is, nations have often looked at past relationships with other nations as if they were in the present—as if the people responsible for these relationships still represented their nation. Thus, they have blamed inhabitants of the present for acts of their ancestors. As a result, people have hated and killed and engaged in acts which in time people not yet born may again use as justification for more war. If we look at such situations with clear, objective eyes, we see that the people involved have failed to consider the fact that reality has changed.

Among the better examples of this error are those which involve statistical comparisons. In a heated political campaign a certain candidate for mayor berated his opponent by pointing out that during his opponent's administration, expenditures exceeded those of three preceding administrations combined. It was a statement of fact. But it failed to consider the most significant fact of all—that the administration criticized covered a period of extraordinary growth which saw population more than double in size. Certainly, this great change justified at least some of the increased expenditure.

A few years ago a sportswriter noted that one of today's superstars in baseball signed a contract for more than $150,000. In the sportswriter's words, this contract was "a record in anybody's book" and that it "dwarfs the $80,000 received by Babe Ruth in his prime." Even the most elementary student of economics could point out that Ruth's $80,000 was the better salary. In the first place, Ruth's pay was not subject to today's high income tax rates. In the second place, dollars of the 1920s bought more than dollars in the 1970s. A 1925 Ford, for example, sold for $250, hardly a suitable down payment for the models 50 years later. The writer failed to take into account the very significant fact of change.

All too often each of us is guilty of this perception error in referring to our acquaintances. Our perception of a person may be based on what we knew of him at one point in time, and we tend to hold this perception. From the moment we register the perception, however, our acquaintance changes, just as everything else changes. In time, our perception may no longer fit him; yet we are not likely to alter it. As a result of this tendency, when we communicate about people, erroneous impressions may be sent or received, depending on the time of reference to the individuals concerned.

## RELATIVE NATURE OF PERCEPTION

As if the complexities resulting from its infinite, unique, and process nature were not enough, reality becomes even more complex because of variations in our perceptions of it. Some variation in perception results from shortcomings and differences in our sensory organs. As we have discussed these possibilities at some length, we may turn our attention to a second explanation of perception variation. It is that perception variation resulting from the relative positions of those perceiving an object or event. That is, we cannot all have the same point of reference in a given situation. Thus, we perceive the given situation differently.

To illustrate the point, take the words often used to berate someone's intelligence: "He doesn't know which end is up!" The chances are that this is a true statement, and it is equally true of the speaker. Actually, the direction "up" is a relative thing—in this case it is relative to the ground. But the ground is not a flat surface, for our earth is shaped like a round ball. Thus, from any point on the ball the direction up is different from the direction up at any other point. To see the point, imagine that you are looking at the earth from far out in space. Now imagine a man standing on the North Pole pointing up and another man standing on the South Pole pointing up. They are pointing in different directions. And if every person on earth were pointing up, would not each be pointing in a direction which coincided with no other?

For another example, take an automobile moving down a highway at 70 miles per hour. Inside the automobile you observe a little fly flitting from the front to the back at a speed of 20 miles per hour. Now, as you look at its movement from your point of reference inside the car, the fly clearly flew at 20 miles per hour from front to back. If, however, your reference is the side of the road, would you not see the little fly move backward at 50 miles per hour? And when its flight is done, would it not resume its sitting speed of 70 miles per hour?

These examples, of course, are the more obvious ones. But to some degree, perception of the same objects or events will vary from one person to another, depending on the points of reference. A stage play from backstage looks altogether different than it does from out front. Fight fans on one side of the ring may see hard, solid punches to the jaw; those on the opposite side may see the same blows roll harmlessly off. The crew of a bomber may see its bombs form interesting puffs of smoke as they hit their targets; people down on the ground see terrible destruction. Football spectators high up in the stands clearly see an act of pass interference committed on the field, but the official on the spot sees a skillfully executed save. Thus, we see that regardless of what reality may really be, we cannot and do not perceive it the same way. Much depends on our position of reference.

## TRUTH AND REALITY

The confusing picture of reality we have unfolded leads us to a question which man has been trying to answer throughout history. It is the question of the meaning of "truth." The question was debated by the early philosophers, and it has held the attention of scholars ever since. We are no nearer the truth today, and the foregoing discussion explains why. We have seen that the real world is so complex that it is impossible to know all about anything. And because we cannot know all about anything, is not the likelihood good that usually we do not know enough to be certain? Is there not always some risk involved with incomplete information? Then, also, because each of us sees reality in a slightly different way, there is further confusion as to just what the true reality is. Obviously, the answer to our question is as elusive now as it has ever been.

## QUESTIONS AND PROBLEMS

1. What is the relationship of reality to communication?

2. Explain the nature of reality using the reality which surrounds you at this moment to illustrate your explanation.

3. Select a simple object and explain its infinite makeup.

4. Discuss the reality around you which your senses cannot detect.

5. If uniqueness in some object cannot be detected by our sensory receptors, how can it be important to our understanding of communication?

6. Explain how an understanding of the process nature of reality helps us to understand communication.

7. Susan Hathaway has bought the same brand of automobile for 37 years. "I once owned another brand," she explained. "And I learned my lesson from that experience." Discuss the reality of this situation.

8. "Sure I know Sam Allen," an executive reported to a person considering Sam for employment. "He and I were in high school together. He's shiftless and lazy." Discuss the executive's perception.

9. A personnel executive explained that she gave importance to grades when hiring a recent college graduate. In hiring people who have been out of college for some time, however, she gave grades little importance. Discuss the reality involved in her logic.

10. "I'm sorry," a purchasing agent told the salesperson. "We buy only well-known brands. No offense, but I've never heard of your company." Discuss.

11. An ancient philosopher once noted that we cannot step into the same river twice. Discuss. *always changing*

12. A witness at court balked when taking the oath to "tell the truth, the whole truth, and nothing but the truth." He responded that he could not take the oath. Discuss.

# 4

## The filter of the mind

**W**E HAVE LEARNED from the preceding discussion that reality is infinite, unique, and forever in process. We have learned also that our ability (or perhaps *inability* would be the better word) to perceive causes difficulties in communicating. Our perception limitations, however, do not explain all of our miscommunication problems, or perhaps even a major part of them. Of major significance are our limitations in handling the perceptions we are able to register.

The handling of our perceptions, of course, involves the filter process described in Chapter 2. Specifically, it involves how we give meaning to the reality our sensory receptors pick up and pass through our minds. Thus, it is the nature of the filter to which our analysis of communication now turns.

### A STOREHOUSE OF KNOWLEDGE

Basic to our analysis of the filter is the role knowledge plays in determining meaning. As we all know, our minds serve as storehouses of knowledge. Just how knowledge is stored (learned) is a most complex subject about which psychologists long have been concerned. In general, they agree that learning involves "changes in behavior resulting from previous behavior in similar situations."[1] More specifically, it involves the basic area of classical conditioning (Pavlov and his salivating dog) and of instrumental behavior (trial-and-error, reward-and-punishment learn-

---

[1] Bernard Berelson and Gary A. Steiner, *Human Behavior,* Harcourt, Brace & World, Inc., New York, 1964, p. 135.

ing). It includes the more complex area of skills acquisition. And of greatest significance to human beings, it includes all that which we acquire through the symbolic learning process. It is the area of symbolic learning about which we are most concerned, for it is through symbols (mainly words) that the more complex forms of knowledge are acquired. Unfortunately, we know very little about symbolic learning.

Although a sophisticated analysis of how knowledge is acquired would be helpful to us in understanding communication, our present needs are served by a simplified, practical review of how knowledge affects our communication. Such a review logically begins with our first learning experiences—experiences which take place in infancy. At an early age we human beings begin to receive information picked up by our sensory receptors, and we give meanings to this information. The meanings received remain with us for varying periods. Much of the information stays with us for very brief moments—mere seconds and perhaps even fractions of seconds. Some of it remains with us for longer periods—days, weeks, months, years. Some stays with us for a lifetime.

To illustrate this point, consider your learning process at this very moment. As you read this information, you are receiving the symbols presented on this page. As you read each sentence, the exact words used are in your mind—at least for a brief moment. Very soon the exact impressions you receive will be forgotten. Later you are likely to remember only the major points presented; and as time goes on, you will forget more and more of these. Some information, of course, stays with us much longer than other information. Some never leaves us.

Thus, we can see that as our receptors bring in information to our minds, we are continuously adding to our storehouse of knowledge; and at the same time, we are continuously losing some of its content. That which is stored is forever changing. Hence, at any given moment of time our minds are equipped with a given storehouse of knowledge. At any other moment the storehouse will be somewhat different.

As our sensory organs pick up perceptions and relay them to our brains, the meanings we give these perceptions are governed by the knowledge stored at the moment. For example, assume that you live in a primitive society. Your sensory receptors have never perceived a radio, or anything resembling it. Thus, your filter contains no knowledge of this device. Now you walk into a room and hear voices and music, and there on the table before you is a little box from which the sounds appear to come. It is a most frightening phenomenon, for your mind contains no knowledge which will explain such sounds coming out of a box.

What is your reaction? Maybe you will hurl your spear through it, for surely this mysterious box is evil. All of the unknown, you have been taught to believe, is evil. And if you are a brave soul, maybe you will stand your distance and cautiously watch. Or if you are a coward, perhaps you will bolt and run away screaming, with your arms flailing about wildly.

On the other hand, assume that you are now yourself. You walk into the room and hear the music. You know that the box is a radio, for you have seen radios many times. You know that radios are sources of enjoyment—not of fear. Thus, when your perception of this radio goes to your brain, the knowledge that radios are enjoyable devices governs your interpretation. Or putting it in more technical language, the stimulus (perception of the radio) triggers a response (pleasure) which similar stimuli have triggered before and have stored in your brain.

Admittedly, this one example was selected to dramatize the role of knowledge in communication. Any bit of knowledge, regardless of its nature, could have done the job. In any event, the principle involved is the same: The knowledge stored in the mind at the time information is received influences the meaning the mind gives the information.

The knowledge stored does not have to be true knowledge, for the effects of true information and misinformation are the same. All that matters is how the mind accepts the information. If, for example, one's mind has stored the erroneous information that all snakes are dangerous, this person's reaction to a communication about snakes will be influenced by this misinformation. And the effort will be much the same until the filter receives additional information which will alter the knowledge stored. It is the same for all the knowledge stored in any mind, regardless of the degree to which the knowledge resembles reality.

## THE ROLE OF OPINIONS, ATTITUDES, AND BELIEFS

Included also in our mental filters are the viewpoints we hold about the reality in which we live. More specifically, we are referring to our attitudes, opinions, and beliefs. They differ from knowledge in that they concern matters on which there is no unanimity. Yet they are not exclusive of knowledge, for they may be well supported with factual matter. Like our storehouses of knowledge, our attitudes, opinions, and beliefs have strong influence on how we interpret the information our receptors pick up and relay through our minds.

### What the terms mean

Before we discuss the role our attitudes, opinions, and beliefs play in communication, let us define these three terms as we shall use them. In a sense, all are similar, for all refer to our viewpoints about the reality which surrounds us. They differ, however, in the degree of intensity with which we hold them.[2]

---

[2] *Ibid.*, p. 558.

Opinions are the least intense of all and refer to viewpoints concerning those areas of reality which are least critical in our lives. For example, one may have opinions on such matters as the latest fad in ladies' fashion, the merits of an advertising technique, the value of the forward pass in football, the effectiveness of closed-circuit television in teaching, or the desirability of a pending piece of legislation.

Attitudes are our viewpoints on more important matters. As we shall see, these are the intermediate matters in life. They are more vital than the everyday matters of opinions, yet they fall short of the core matters in life upon which beliefs are based. How one thinks on the question of socialized medicine, for example, might well fall in this category. Other likely examples are one's viewpoint on government regulation of business, employment of women, and labor-management relations.

Beliefs are our viewpoints on the most critical values in life. As previously implied, they concern those matters we hold most dear—matters of morality, religion, government, and the like. For example, one may believe in the immortality of the soul, in witchcraft, in academic freedom, in rugged individualism, in respect for law and order.

Obviously, our definitions are not clear-cut for the terms overlap. There are no sharp lines dividing opinions from attitudes from beliefs. What is an opinion to one person may be an attitude to another and a belief to yet another. Nevertheless, these definitions give us a general guide to understanding the makeup of this element in our filtering process.

## How viewpoints are formed

Why we think the way we think is a subject about which psychologists have long been concerned. They still have much to learn about it, but they have advanced findings which are of concern to us in our study of communication.

*Through objective reasoning.* First, we reach some of our viewpoints through rational thought processes. That is, we sometimes gather the evidence involved in a matter, weigh it, and reach a decision through objective thought processes. This is the pattern of thinking wise men have followed since the beginning of civilization. But this objective procedure is not so often practiced as we like to think. Even when it is practiced, it is likely to be influenced by the more subjective factors discussed in the following paragraphs.

Perhaps it is alarming to hear that we human beings are not the rational creatures we like to think we are, so let us illustrate the point. Take some strong belief that you have—say something concerning religion or politics. Now think of someone with a strongly different belief. Ask yourself the question, "Would I not have the same belief as he if I had lived in his environment?" Before you answer the question, assume that in early infancy you exchanged homes with this other person, and that he has lived your life and you have lived his. Instead of getting the benefits of your environment, particularly your family's teachings, you got his, and he got yours. Is it not likely that you would have his belief and he, yours? And would you not be likely to argue and defend his belief as vigorously as you now defend your own? And so it would be for many of the subjects of our attitudes, opinions, and beliefs.

*Social strata and viewpoints.* Our social strata also play a heavy role in determining our viewpoints. By "social strata" we mean the levels or segments of society into which we fall—whether we are rich, poor, or somewhere in between; Jew or Gentile; male or female; white or black; Irish, Polish, English, or Indian; Northerner, Southerner, or Westerner; and so on. To some extent, our social inheritance determines the experiences we have and the pressures society places upon us. They condition us to view reality in a way peculiar to the strata to which we belong. The result is a significant and somewhat lasting effect on our attitudes, opinions, and beliefs.

Five areas of our social structure play a significant role in determining our attitudes, opinions, and beliefs.[3] Three are major; two are relatively minor. The major ones include class, ethnic status, and residence. The minor ones are age and sex.

Although basically determined by economic status, class is also determined by factors such as education and occupation. Family status in the community may also be a determinant. Without question, one's class does determine significantly his thinking on certain matters. One born into a low-income family, for example, is subjected to hardships and deprivations which are likely to influence his viewpoints on many matters. Because he has been poor all his life, he is likely to favor legislation which will give assistance to his class; thus, in politics he is likely to be liberal. Because he has had little time for exposure to the finer things in life, he is not likely to have much appreciation for the aesthetic. And because he has lived his life in a position subordinate to others, he is likely to accept authoritarian methods with little question. His viewpoints would not likely be the same had he been born to another class.

Residence, of course, is the geographic area in which one lives. We all know that people in some areas think differently on some matters than do people in others. One born into a given area is likely to succumb to the existing thinking. Thus it is that a person from the United States South is likely to think differently on the question of states' rights than a person from the Pacific Northwest or New England. Likewise, natives of the Russian province of Georgia are destined to have viewpoints on some

---

[3] *Ibid.*, pp. 570–73.

matters different from those of people from Siberia or the Ukraine. Similar differences exist in many countries of the world.

Ethnic differences pertain to our national, racial, and religious inheritance. For example, members of minority races are likely to have strong viewpoints on matters stemming from their experiences with prejudice. On the other hand, those from nonpersecuted races enjoy a different social inheritance and may have altogether different viewpoints on such matters. For another example, the clannish living of many nationality groups in our major cities contributes to the formulation of common and different viewpoints. The Irish of New York City, the Poles in Chicago, the Chinese in San Francisco all live in a manner that sets them apart from those around them. As a result, they are likely to hold viewpoints differing from those generally held by other citizens on matters such as respect for elders, morality, recognition of authority, and importance of savings.

Religion serves as a third example of the effect of ethnic inheritance on our viewpoints. Obviously, a religion is a system of beliefs, and the systems in existence differ rather sharply. Typically, we inherit this system of beliefs from our families. We may depart somewhat from these beliefs, but most of us are likely to hold them throughout our lives.

Although minor determinants of the strata which govern at least some of our viewpoints, sex and age nevertheless play a significant role. Viewpoint differences related to sex are readily apparent. Traditionally, boys place greater importance on physical powers than do girls. In addition, boys are less emotional in their dealings with each other; they are more active in politics; they are more concerned about the technical areas. Likewise, age helps to form distinguishing viewpoints among us. In youth, we tend to be rebels in our thinking—to be different and to oppose convention and authority. As we grow older, we tend to turn toward more conservative thinking. As Samuel A. Stouffer concluded,[4] we tend to become less tolerant, to lose some of the effects of education as we grow older.

*Early influence of the family.* Just how we form our viewpoints is a most complex subject about which there is not complete agreement. There is general agreement, however, that we acquire much of our thinking from the people in our lives. That is to say, we human beings are not primarily the rational creatures we like to think we are. Rather, we are more like parrots. We tend to accept much of our thinking somewhat blindly from others.

Foremost among those who influence our thoughts are the members of our own family. At an early age we human beings begin to acquire the

---

[4] Samuel A. Stouffer, *Communism Conformity, and Civil Liberties: A Cross-section of the Nation Speaks Its Mind,* Doubleday and Co., Inc., Garden City, N.Y., 1955, p. 94.

thinking of our family. Some of this thinking we are taught deliberately, but much of it we acquire through observation. However it is done, the results are the same. Our earliest thinking on such matters as religion, politics, ethics, cultural tastes, and the like is the thinking of our family.

***Change effects of groups.*** Many of the viewpoints acquired from our social strata or our family stay with us for a lifetime. This is certainly true in such areas as religion and politics.[5] It is obvious, however, that as time goes by, we begin to question some of our attitudes, opinions, and beliefs. And occasionally we alter some of them.

As we have mentioned, some of our viewpoint changes result from logical thought processes, for we can on occasion be rational beings. More often, however, our viewpoint changes are influenced by groups to which we belong. Throughout our lives we hold membership in many groups—religious, family, social, etc. In considering our attitudes, opinions, and beliefs, we refer to these groups, and we are heavily influenced by the thinking within them. Thus, the desire to conform is a major factor in determining our attitudes, opinions, and beliefs.

A high school boy, for example, would be inclined to change a viewpoint to conform with that of his peers on matters he considers important to his membership in the group. One might discard the puritan thinking given him by a straitlaced family for the more permissive standards of his friends. Or one striving for acceptance in a street gang would be likely to adjust his viewpoints to conform with the gang's opinions on law and order and its attitudes on morality in general.

Similarly, other groups influence the thinking of all of us. If we are members of labor, we are likely to accept the prevailing viewpoint toward management held by other members of labor. If we are part of management, we are likely to assume the traditional viewpoint of management toward labor. Members of the medical profession are generally of one mind on issues such as socialized medicine. College professors are united in their beliefs in academic freedom. And so it is with all groups. Each has some effect on the thinking of its members.

It should be apparent that all people belong to many groups. One may at the same time be a member of a social set, a church, a profession, a civic organization, a hobby, a club, and a political party. As a member of these groups, he is subject to the pressures to conform to each. Obviously, he cannot always succumb to all pressures, for some must sometimes conflict. As a member of a church group, he may be under the group's pressure to accept a philosophy of charity to all the unfortunate. His professional peers, on the other hand, may favor a minimum of government help in all areas of activity. Thus, he could submit to only one of the groups' pressures. He would have to make a choice.

---

[5] Herbert H. Hyman, *Political Socialization: A Study of the Psychology of Political Behavior,* Free Press, New York, 1959, pp. 70–71.

Similar group pressures exist when one leaves one group for another. A member of labor suddenly promoted to the ranks of management finds himself facing new group pressures and leaving old ones. Likewise, a beginning teacher finds that his new group holds some different viewpoints from those he held while a member of the student group. In such cases the usual result is a change in viewpoint to conform with that of the new group.

*Self-interest as a determinant of viewpoint.* Closely related to the influence of groups[6] on our thinking are the effects of self-interest. There is no doubt about it. We hold certain viewpoints simply because it is to our best interests to do so. We human beings are basically selfish creatures, and we structure our thinking to support our selfish interests.[7]

For example, an otherwise upstanding citizen who fudges on his tax returns might build up opinions and attitudes which support his actions. "Everybody does it" might be his justification—or perhaps, "They expect you to work it close." An ambitious business person might support a policy of ruthless business dealings with the attitude that business is a dog-eat-dog activity and that ruthlessness is a necessary ingredient in successful strategy. Similarly, people of means are generally opposed to government programs which take from them and give to others. They reason that such acts discourage initiative and encourage the growth of a welfare class. The poor, on the other hand, generally support such legislation, and they support their stand with arguments such as, "It is our just share," or "Don't penalize us for the accident of birth."

## How viewpoints affect communication

Once formed, our attitudes, opinions, and beliefs tend to persist. This is not to say that they do not change, for we have shown that pressures for change are continually with us and that these pressures bring about changes in viewpoint. But the resistance to changing them is forever present; and the longer we hold a viewpoint, the greater this resistance is likely to be.

Especially is the resistance to change strong on viewpoints concerning matters in which we are emotionally involved or strongly interested. Two people of different religious convictions are not likely to convert each other, regardless of how long they argue or how logically they present their beliefs. Likewise, it is a rare case when a political conservative can change the viewpoint of a political liberal, and vice versa. In such in-

---

[6] Actually, our submission to the pressures of groups is for reasons of self-interest. We conform to the thinking of the group because we want the acceptance of the group.

[7] A. E. Mander, "Groundless Beliefs," in William G. Leary and James Steele Smith, editors, *Think before You Write,* Harcourt, Brace & World, Inc., New York, 1951, p. 8.

stances each is more interested in presenting his own case than in hearing the case of the other. And so it is with all the attitudes, opinions, and beliefs we hold. We sometimes change them, but the change comes slowly. Most of the time we resist successfully.

The facts that our mental filters contain attitudes, opinions, and beliefs and that we resist changing them play a major role in determining the meanings we give to our perceptions. When the incoming information is in accord with our viewpoints, we tend to accept it. When it runs contrary to our viewpoints, we tend to reject it. Accepted information is positively received, for it falls in place with what is already in the filter. On the other hand, information rejected produces a negative reaction. It may be upsetting and may be likely to bring about a negative communication response. Such information is not communicated easily—at least the message received is not the one intended.

## THE INFLUENCE OF EMOTIONS

Another factor in the filtering process is the emotional state of the mind at the time the mind receives the perception. Before we explain this factor, however, let us get a more precise understanding of emotions. Specifically, let us determine what they are and how they are formed. Then we shall explore the manner in which they affect communication.

Emotions may be defined as the sources of energy which make the mind work.[8] Without them, we would be in a continual stupor. Our existence would be somewhat like that of a vegetable. In addition, without emotions, we would not exist long, for the energy of emotions is a vital part of the survival effort of our species. When we perceive danger, we have the emotion of fear, which serves to protect us from that danger. When we are confronted by an antagonist, we become angry, and our anger serves in our defense against our antagonist. We love our children; thus, we protect them, thereby promoting the survival of our kind.

Our emotional energy results from an automatic response to certain of the perceptions which our sensory receptors receive and pass on to the brain. They occur much as do our reflexes. They are inevitable. Certain perceptions trigger certain emotional responses. For example, if someone bumps us, perhaps even accidentally, we tend to become angry. When someone shouts contemptuous words to us, we respond with hatred. When an attractive member of the opposite sex smiles at us, we are filled with excitement. Perhaps we are able to control our emotions in such cases, but our emotions are aroused nevertheless. We can no more stop such reactions than we can stop the eye from blinking when an object suddenly moves dangerously toward it.

[8] Edward A. Strecker, Kenneth E. Appel, and John W. Appel, *Discovering Ourselves*, Macmillan Company, New York, 1963, p. 103.

From the foregoing discussion it should be apparent that the emotions triggered play a part in determining the meanings we give to the perceptions we receive. The emotional energy brought about becomes a part of the filtering process. Thus, it plays a role in determining the meanings given to perceptions which follow. In other words, the emotional state of the mind at the moment a perception is received helps to determine the meaning the mind gives the perception.

To illustrate this point, take the case of a salesman named Smith who makes his first call on an executive named Jones. As Smith enters Jones's office, he cheerfully says "Good morning." Now, normally, such cheery words would bring about a cheerful response; but this time, let us assume that the situation is not normal. Jones has just arrived at work after an assortment of harrowing experiences. He did not sleep well last night. Breakfast was terrible. He had a fight with his wife. Traffic was unusually bad on his way to work. And now, after arriving at work, he is given a priority assignment which must be completed by noon. It is a five-hour job, so he will have to work hard to meet his deadine. Obviously, Jones is emotionally upset. Everything has gone wrong. He has more work than he has time to do, and here he is approached by a man who wants some of his valuable time. So Jones's filter gives a negative meaning to Smith's "Good morning." "What's good about it?" might well be Jones's thought, if not his response.

For another example, take an opposite situation. This time, let us assume that Jones is in excellent spirits when Smith approaches him with his cheerful "Good morning." Jones's holdings in the stock market have just advanced sharply. His business in general is unusually good. He had a good night's sleep, a most enjoyable breakfast, a pleasant conversation with his wife, and a relaxing drive to the office. His work for the day appears to be manageable. He sees Smith not as an intruder in a busy work schedule but as a friendly gentleman—one who might hold a key to more business profit. Now as the cheerful "Good morning" goes through Jones's filter, it receives the full happy connotation Smith intended.

## THE FILTER IN SUMMARY

From the foregoing discussion, we have seen that the filtering process involves principally three factors. The first is the knowledge the mind contains, for new perceptions are given meaning as they relate to what is already in the mind. Second are the viewpoints (specifically attitudes, opinions, and beliefs) which the mind holds. These viewpoints serve as determinants of acceptance for the incoming perceptions, and they play a major role in determining the emotional effect of the perceptions. Third is the emotional state of the mind, which serves as a general conditioner of the incoming perceptions.

All three of these factors are forever changing, and sometimes they behave inconsistently and illogically when we consider the influences of the emotional state of the individual. At any given moment in time the filter has a given makeup of knowledge, viewpoints, and emotional energy. Its makeup at the precise moment it receives a perception determines the meaning we give that perception.

## QUESTIONS AND PROBLEMS

1. Select an incident from your experience that illustrates how knowledge affects communication.   *religious*

2. From your viewpoints select an attitude, an opinion, and a belief. As well as you can, explain why you hold each of these viewpoints.

3. Discuss how your attitudes, opinions, and beliefs influence your communication.

4. Explain and illustrate how viewpoints can change.

5. Discuss the role of viewpoints in communicating.

6. Mary and Clara are intelligent and capable executives for the same company. Each was assigned the task of evaluating the proposed plan for promoting a new product. After long and careful thought, Mary and Clara arrived at opposite conclusions. And each was certain of being right. Each argued that information they gained through experience supported her conclusion. Explain this situation.

7. Members of Department X watched as their new supervisor entered the work area. It was the first time any of them had seen him. "Look at that square," said Mary. "That crew haircut is right out of the 50s. I'll give odds that he's a stickler for detail and a real taskmaster." Her co-workers generally agreed with her. Discuss.

8. For many months the department supervisor had been watching George. The supervisor was pleased with all that he saw and had concluded that George was the person to promote to foreman when old Mr. Koontz retired. The supervisor changed his opinion abruptly when George told him about the new motorcycle he had bought. Discuss from a communications point of view.   *image motorcycle gives*

9. Dr. Katherine Wentzel, an economic advisor to the President, was riding home in a taxi after a long day's work. She had spent the day with a committee of high-ranking legislators working on legislation designed to stimulate the economy. As she was pleased with the legislation that her work had helped to produce, she proceeded to tell the cab driver about it. To her surprise the cab driver responded with these words: "That's just more of that big brother government. Why don't they leave the economy alone and let it run without interference." Discuss.

10. Albert Dodge, a recent college graduate in engineering, is employed as a production engineer by Boone Manufacturing Company. From an article in a technical journal Albert read about a new production technique

which had proved to be highly successful when used by companies doing production work similar to that done by Boone. So he decided to try the procedure. After explaining the procedure to Wilburn Latham, the veteran foreman in charge, Albert got this response: "It won't work. I've been doing this work for 35 years. Started when I was 15. Learned it from the ground up. I know it won't work." Discuss.

11. At the age of 20 Billy Joe left his parent's farm to take a job at a factory in the city. All his life Billy Joe had been a hard worker. "A day's work for a day's pay" was a principle he believed in strongly. Billy Joe worked very hard on his new job. And for the first week he produced 150 units. The shop average was 80. After observing his production record, Billy Joe's boss remarked, "This kid is a real worker. He'll go places." The same day one of Billy Joe's fellow workers commented to another worker, "We'd better get this kid in line. He looks like a trouble maker." Discuss.

12. Professor Smiley conducted the following test among business executives. He wrote a short article advocating some fairly innovative business procedures and gave the article to two very similar groups to read. The article read by one group named a nationally known management consultant as the author. The article read by the second group identified its author as an unknown graduate student. Professor Smiley found that support for the procedure presented in the article was much stronger in the first group than in the second. Discuss.

13. For 30 years William Wills has worked as a machinist. And for most of this time he worked in an all-male environment. Recently, women workers have joined his ranks. When told that the rejection rate for work done in his shop had reached a record high, he responded: "What do you expect with women doing men's work?" When confronted with data showing that there was little difference in rejection rates of men and women workers, he replied, "That's mainly because the inspectors are women." Discuss.

# 5

# Words and meaning

O F ALL THE symbols we use in communicating, the most important by
far are words. As we have noted, we use many other symbols—facial
expressions, hand and body movements, grunts, and the like; but these
we use primarily to convey the simple message of our emotions or to
supplement our verbal communication. The bulk of our deliberate communicating we do with words. As they are the primary medium of our
communication, they deserve special study.

## LANGUAGE AND HUMAN PROGRESS

The important role of words in our communication is even more evident when we look at their influence on human progress. Our language,
which is a system of words, is credited with giving us superiority over the
other forms of life.[1] Other species, it may be pointed out, are stronger,
more efficient, and better equipped in many ways. But we human beings
alone have language,[2] and language has enabled us to combat the problems of life with unusual success.

Through our use of language, we human beings have been able to
bind time.[3] By "time binding" we mean that human beings of one genera-

[1] Irving J. Lee, *Language Habits in Human Affairs,* Harper and Row, New York,
1941, pp. 3–5.

[2] This statement is made with the knowledge that dolphins, gibbons, and other
relatively intelligent animals make some use of symbols. As interesting as the studies
of these animals may be, there has not been uncovered any evidence that these animals have a system of symbols which in any way is comparable to the language of
human beings.

[3] Alfred Korzybski, *Science and Sanity, An Introduction to Non-Aristotelian Systems and General Semantics,* 3d ed., Country Life Publishing Corp., Garden City,
N.Y., 1948, p. 376.

tion have been able to communicate with human beings of other genera-tions. From those who have lived before us, we have been able to learn from the records of their knowledge and experience. We are able to communicate our knowledge and experience to those who will live after us. And we are able to exchange knowledge with those of other times. Thus, because we have language, we human beings are the only life form which has not been limited to knowledge that can be learned from the trial-and-error experience in a single life-time. The results have been that we have built a vast storehouse of knowledge. With this knowledge we have managed to achieve our present state of superiority.

## The foundation of language

Words, like any other form of symbol, have the objective of conveying our impressions of reality. But as we have seen, reality is infinitely com-plex. It is made up of billions upon billions of objects, each different from all others and continuously changing. It is comprised of billions upon billions of events, each different from any other event that ever has taken place or will take place. The task of words to convey precisely this com-plex reality most certainly is a gigantic one.

To convey exactly the meaning of each object and event with words would require that we use new and different words for each object and event. Once used, the words would have to be discarded, for they could never again apply. They would never again apply because the precise event or object they cover would never again occur. Obviously, such a system of symbols would not work. In the first place, it would have to be as complex and involved as reality itself, and this would be an impossi-bility. In the second place, for language to be effective, some form of meaning of the symbols must be agreed upon by the participants in communication. Our mental limitations make it necessary that we achieve such agreement by repetitious use of somewhat general symbols. Thus, we human beings have been forced to form a simpler-than-reality lan-guage—a language that makes single words cover a broad area of reality. And so that some agreement on meaning can be reached, we must use these words again and again.

## Classification based on similarity

Although no one really knows how our early ancestors built our lan-guage, the finished product gives us evidence that they built it around classifications of their perceptions. Probably they began by reviewing reality, looking for similarities in what they saw. When they found simi-larities, they built classifications and devised words for them. Then, when viewing these groups, they found that broader similarities were present in some of them, and again they built classifications and selected words for them. Again and again, they combined groups into broader concepts and supplied words. They did this as long as it was practical for them to do so.

This process of classifying perceptions and combining classifications into broader concepts is not so exact as this simplified description might imply. At best, the classifications are fuzzy; they are not clearly separated. There is considerable overlap and duplication of the classification possibilities. Nevertheless, the process gives us a meaningful comprehension of the structure of language and how it relates to reality.

This general process of forming language is referred to in the writings of Alfred Korzybski[4] as the "structural differential" and more recently has been popularized by S. I. Hayakawa[5] as the "abstraction ladder." Hayakawa's words are most appropriate, for they describe the process which has occurred. In each of the steps of classification, man has abstracted from reality. From all the characteristics involved, he has selected certain ones as a basis for grouping the objects or events at each stage. That is, he has abstracted similarities and based his words on them.

## Illustration: "Fido" and the "economy"

In constructing our language, probably our ancestors began with the more obvious events and objects in life. Perhaps on one occasion members of a tribe of our ancestors perceived a certain little animal that was living around their village. Their perceptions, of course, included only some of the reality in this animal, for there was much that they could not detect. They could not perceive the bones, blood, flesh, and body organs; the cells that made up these parts; the structure of the cells; and the like. But these parts were nevertheless there.

Their perceptions were of individual animals—little four-legged, pointed-nosed, short-haired creatures. Each had its distinctive markings, its unique personality, and a body of its own. Perhaps our ancestors befriended one of these animals and induced it to live in their camp. In time, they found need to communicate about this one animal which they perceived separately from the others. So they selected a word for it. Let us say that the word was "Fido."

Our primitive ancestors had other perceptions of Fido, however. Sometimes they did not perceive him alone, but with other creatures that looked something like him. Our primitive ancestors were aware that some of these creatures were not exactly like their Fido. They had hair of different lengths, and the colors of their coats varied. Some were quite

---

[4] *Ibid.*, p. 393.

[5] S. I. Hayakawa, *Language in Thought and Action,* Harcourt, Brace & World, Inc., New York, 1949, p. 179.

small when compared with Fido, and some were much larger. Also, their noses were of different shapes, and they held their tails in different positions. In spite of these differences, our ancestors perceived some similarities. The creatures they observed all had four legs, two eyes, and a tail. Most of them barked. They wagged their tails when they were happy, and they bared their teeth and growled when they were unhappy. So our ancestors overlooked the many differences; and on the basis of the few similarities, they made a classification. They called this group "dogs."

From time to time, our tribe of ancestors had many occasions to communicate about dogs; so they constructed some higher level classifications based on some other characteristics they perceived. When they thought of the dogs that lived with them on a family basis, they linked them together with the cats, birds, and other creatures they owned. These were their "pets," and they represented a wide assortment of creatures. Their differences were infinite, but they had one thing in common. They all were owned by our ancestors, and they lived with them on a friendly basis.

Sometimes our ancestors looked upon their pets as a part of everything else they owned. They grouped them with their stone axes, their furs, their pottery, and other such items. When they had this thought, they needed another word—a shortcut to listing "pets, stone axes, furs, etc." So they formed a new word—"possessions." More than the preceding illustrations, this word grouped items that were sharply different. These items had one thing in common—they were all of the tangible things our ancestors owned.

In time, there were occasions when our ancestors viewed all of their possessions in terms of how well off they were in comparison with their neighbors. Probably they perceived that some of them had more possessions and some had less. Their references no longer were to items owned but to an idea they attached to these items collectively. They called this concept "wealth."

Still later, perhaps, there came a time when our ancestors looked at how they lived with other human beings. They perceived a system in which they and their neighbors worked to secure their wealth. They noted that they worked to make additional items of wealth and that they stored their wealth. They saw also that they bartered their wealth. All of these activities they perceived as one. They named it "the economy."

## Illustration: "Living" and a "home run"

Probably language developed in the general order just described—that is, from the specific object or event to the general reference. We can get a more meaningful and complete understanding of the classification structure of language, however, by viewing it in the opposite order—from the broad general reference to the specific. Take, for example, the events of living as they are described by our language.

In looking at these events in a broad sense, we could say that they are covered by the symbol "living." This symbol covers all that we are, or think, or do; and it includes an infinite assortment of events. If we had only to symbolize living to refer to all these events, however, we could not communicate specifically about the infinite variations covered by the word. So if we wish to make more specific references, we must divide all that part of reality covered by "living" into subdivisions and find symbols to cover each of them.

Looking at the area of reality covered by "living," we can see many possibilities for further breakdown. One possibility would be to classify all events as they affect the people involved—to classify them as "happiness" or "unhappiness." Such a classification is a two-valued one, to be sure; and we shall see in Chapter 6 the dangers of two-valued thinking. Our language is filled with such classifications.

Let us now take the subclassification of "happiness" to see what subclassifications it possesses. Of all the happiness-producing events in life, we can see that some result in a sense of security. Some result in a satisfaction of the body's needs, such as good food, sweet sounds, friends, and beauty. There are those which result in fun—those short-run pleasures which typically make us smile or laugh. Some events provide happiness through contentment, which is a problem-free state of mind. Then there is the happiness which results from the rewards one receives for his efforts. There are more, depending on how one views the subject.

Next, let us select the subclassification "fun" and review its possible components. Fun can be many things to many people, but most of us would agree on some of its subclassifications. Parties, games, television, outdoor sports, travel, and reading would pass the tests of most people.

"Games" is our next topic for breakdown. Its possibilities likewise are voluminous, for there are many types of games. There are baseball, hopscotch, football, mumblety-peg, tennis, blindman's bluff, and bridge, to name a few.

Assuming that we select "baseball" among the games for the next classification analysis, our inspection would show the game to be one of many specific types of events. In the game there are events such as pitching, hitting, running, arguing, and sliding. Within each of these categories next fall the great multitude of specific events and objects of the game. Umpires bark decisions. Players run. Pitchers throw. Balls meet leather gloves. And players hit home runs. These are the parts of reality on which all communication is based.

In the foregoing description we have reviewed the formation of words from the broadest, most general type of observation to the observation of a specific event. From this analysis we can see that our language is designed to communicate about reality at any level along the scale. We can communicate about someone hitting a home run, which is a most specific event in the broader game of baseball. We can communicate about baseball, which is one of the games which are fun for many people. We can refer to happiness, of which fun is a part. Or we can communicate about living, which is the broad umbrella under which all the others fall.

## Illustration: Words about "mosquito"

It is important to note that no one classification arrangement exists for each object or event. The possibilities are numerous and could take any number of directions, depending on the communicator's reactions to his perceptions. For example, assume that a little mosquito is now buzzing about your head. From your perception of the mosquito's buzzing, you might single it out for reference with some word. If it had a name, you might refer to it by the name. Since it does not, perhaps you will refer to it only in terms such as "that dad-burned mosquito."

You might next make some derogatory reference to all of its kind; so you would place "dad-burned mosquito" in the broader classification of "mosquito." Next, you could conceive of mosquitoes as being a part of the world of insects. At this point your reference could depart from the biological classification and shift to the effects on our lives. You could then classify insects as a nuisance, which would put them in a category with a great number of nuisance causes. Perhaps you would next consider "nuisance" as a part of the broader category of "unpleasantness," for nuisances are only one of the unpleasantries in life. Finally, "unpleasantness" would be one of the possible subclassifications of "living." Thus, the buzzing of the mosquito, and of all mosquitoes, is a nuisance; and nuisance is a form of unpleasantness, which is a part of living.

## Two basic observations

From the preceding description of the classification process, we may make two basic observations. First, it is apparent that the classifications we make in arranging word meanings are based on similarities rather than differences. Second is the obvious fact that the higher levels of classification are more difficult to comprehend than the lower forms. Both of these observations explain major problems in communication.

*Emphasis on similarities.* In his effort to devise a manageable, workable language, man has had to find some means of simplifying the reality he perceived. As we have observed, the reality to which language must refer is too complex and involved for him to have done otherwise. Thus it was that he classified the elements of the real world on the basis of similarities. In doing this, he ignored the big bulk of the differences present.

Any object in the real world will illustrate the point—a dog, a house, a chair, a radio. As was illustrated previously, in arriving at the common term *dog* for all the creatures in a class, man used a few biological similarities as a base. To be sure, the resulting classification is made up of creatures with many similar characteristics. They all have four legs, a tail, two eyes, five toes. Most, but not all, bark. Most have hair, but there are exceptions. We could name additional similarities. The point which needs to be made, however, is that all the differences in the animals have to be ignored.

Differences in dogs far outnumber similarities. In size, dogs range from the tiny Chihuahua which can stand in the palm of your hand to the 250-pound Saint Bernard. The sounds they make run the range from high-pitched yelps to deep thunderlike barks. Some dogs have floppy ears; others have erect ears; and some have ears that are between these extremes. Their hair runs the gamut from none, as with the Mexican hairless, to the long mane of a Yorkshire terrier; and it may range in coarseness from silky fine to wire-stiff. In color they are black, brown, red, white, plus a variety of combinations. We could go on and on from the more obvious differences to the differences at the microscopic level. Our eventual conclusion would be the obvious one: The differences among dogs outnumber the similarities. As we shall see in Chapter 6, this aspect of our language development is the source of some problems in communication.

*Word difficulty and the classification scale.* As we move along the classification scale from the object or event to the broadest category, the words take on a progressively increasing difficulty of comprehension. At the bottom of the scale when the reference is based on our sensory experiences, clarity is more likely to exist. If we make a reference to "that dad-burned mosquito," our words would convey a fairly accurate message to anyone around us who would also observe this one creature. As we move up the scale to a comment about the mosquito, there would still be a likelihood of clear understanding, for most of the people with whom we communicate have seen and experienced mosquitoes. When we use the word *mosquito,* they are not likely to have difficulty visualizing these creatures collectively.

When we move up the scale to the insect, we take a long step, for we cover a broad assortment of creatures. The meaning the word conveys to each person will differ somewhat, depending on his own experiences and observations of the creatures in this group. Certainly, most people will have an idea of what an insect is, but it is at best a vague one. Were we to ask them to draw a picture of the meaning they receive, we would get a confusing assortment of drawings.

Meaning becomes much more diffused when we move up the scale to "nuisance." At this point we can no longer look to reality for a picture. We cannot see a nuisance, nor can we touch it or smell it. In fact, it is not even a part of reality. Instead, it is an evaluation of some of the events in reality. It is a word about other words. Thus, if it exists at all, it exists only in the minds of people. Because minds work in so many different ways, the meaning of the word must vary somewhat from mind to mind. And because the word is not directly related to something in reality, it cannot carry anything but a vague meaning.

Similarly, the next two words in the classification scale are vague in meaning. "Unpleasantness" and "living" have no direct object or event relationship in the real world. They differ from "nuisance" not in the vagueness or their relationship; they differ primarily in the breadth of their coverage. Living encompasses unpleasantness, and unpleasantness encompasses nuisance. The indefiniteness of the meanings of all three is quite comparable.

We could make similar analyses with any classification structure, and we would have no difficulty arriving at the same conclusion. We would not fail to find that the higher in the classification structure a word is, the farther from the objects and events of the real world are its references. Thus the greater is its vagueness. Take words like *democracy, security, love, patriotism, liberal, coordination, equilibrium,* and *sin.* All of them are near the top of the scale, and all of them have nonspecific meanings. Were we to ask any group of people to define them, we would be likely to get as many definitions as there are people in the group. Because the high-level words do not have clear and precise meanings, communication which uses them cannot be clear and precise.

This is not to suggest that such words should be avoided. They definitely have a place in our communication. Generally, they refer to the more sophisticated concepts, ideas, and relationships which intelligent people have developed. The advancement of knowledge could not proceed without them. The point is, however, that we should be aware of the communication risks we run when we use them. We should be aware that not all people will agree on the meanings of the words. And we should be aware that the higher up the classification structure the word is, the greater is the likelihood of its confusion.

Although the use of higher level words is justified, the good communicator will be wary of using them. He will move down to the lower level words as often as it is necessary to achieve understanding. The reasoning for this conclusion should be apparent from the foregoing discussion. The objective of purposeful communication is to form as precise a meaning as possible in the mind of another. We can do this best by using words which make precise references in the mind. These are the words which are at the bottom of the scale—those which relate directly to the reality perceived by human beings. These are the words which bring about images of things and events man has experienced. They are far more precise than those words which have as their references relationships and intangible structures which exist only in the mind.

To illustrate the point, assume that you must communicate with one of your employees who has not been doing his job well. You could talk in words of a high level of classification to him, saying, "If you persist in your inefficiency, you will be disciplined." Probably he would get the general idea of your message. You would communicate more clearly, however, with these words: "If you make any more of these handles too small, you will be docked $3 for each one." This latter comment relates directly to the worker's experiences in the real world. As his job consists of making handles, he has lived this experience many times. He knows what size a handle should be, and he knows when one is too small. Likewise, he has seen, held, and spent dollars, and he knows what it is to lose them. The message is a clear one, for it relates directly to the employee's real world.

## THE QUESTION OF MEANING

The foregoing analysis leads to the overall conclusion that language is structured to fit in the mind. From this conclusion, one may reason further that there must be some relationship between words and meaning. To the uninformed reader, this relationship may appear to be all too obvious. Further inquiry will reveal that it is not so obvious and is in fact a most complex subject.

### Location in the mind

Perhaps the most difficult communication principle for the uninformed student to accept is that words in themselves do not have meaning. As was concluded in Chapter 2, meaning lies in the mind, not in the symbols (words are symbols) we use. Words do not naturally convey the meaning of a given object or event. A rose just as appropriately could have been called a cow, or an oak, or a dodo. All that really matters is that the symbol and the real-life object or event it represents be associated in the mind.

If words actually had meaning, our communication problems would be greatly simplified. There would be no word barriers between people. If we were to say "run" or "talk" or any other word, all people would understand us, whether they were Swedes, Germans, Chinese, or Congolese. This is the way it would have to be if meaning were in the word. But it is not. The Swedes, Germans, Chinese, and Congolese all have their own words.

## Meaning and dictionaries

That words are used to represent one and only one meaning or that they have one correct meaning is a popular misconception. As we have noted from our analysis of the communication process, meanings are determined by the filters of the mind. Thus, since all filters differ, there cannot be precise uniformity in meaning. Of course, there can be and is some general agreement as to the meanings represented by words. In no way have we intended to say that words represent completely different meanings in each mind. The differences we refer to are minute for the most part.

These general agreements on the words we use are recorded in our dictionaries. As helpful as dictionaries are, their use is distorted. In the minds of many, they are supreme authority. One would think that their makers have superhuman intelligence and are permitted to dictate correct word usage. Their role is far from this.

Actually, dictionaries are made by teams of readers (lexicographers) who cover widely the literature of the day. Primarily, they read the works of the better minds—those who have gained some measure of eminence in their respective fields. As the lexicographers read, they look to see how these people use words, and they record all manners of usage. They compile tens of thousands, perhaps millions, of usage examples. Usages they find in sufficient quantity they keep; others they throw out. The words and uses remaining make up the dictionary. Obviously, it is a dictionary of usage—not of edict.

## Living nature of language

Because minds differ, people continually use words in new ways. Sometimes they invent new words. Sometimes they borrow words from another language. Others read or hear these usages, and they follow. In time the new words and usages become accepted, and they find their way into the dictionaries. So it is that language is continually changing. Words begin, they change, they end. The result is a living language.

The living nature of language explains some of its complexity. It explains why we have so many words. To illustrate the point, take a look at the latest *Webster's New International Dictionary*. It contains some 2,600 pages, each filled with fine print. And most of the words listed have many definitions. It is estimated that the 500 most commonly used words in English have a total of 14,000 listed definitions—an average of 28 per word.

The multiplicity of word definition is so great that one can use any page in the dictionary to prove the point. The little word *cat* illustrates well the multiplicity of meaning. The most common cats are the alley types. They are different from the big jungle beasts that perform in circuses. Then there are the spiteful women known as cats. Sailors of today know a cat as the tackle used to hoist anchors, and sailors of the past knew it as a nine-cord whip used to flog them when they required discipline. To some, a cat is a type of fish; to others, it is a game. Workers on a construction job know a cat to be a heavy piece of mechanical equipment. Then there are the various slang uses of the word *cat*. Doubtless there are others.

Good illustrations are plentiful. See what you can do with *ring, head, form, spirit, fast, mark, bag,* and *stand.* Then work on some verbs such as *sweep, make, do, go, run.* The examples could go on and on. In fact, a quick look at a dictionary page will show you that multiple meanings of words are the rule, not the exception.

The fact that we have so many words and that they have so many definitions explains some of our communication problems. So many words and definitions are available that it is impossible for any two people to have precisely the same knowledge of words and definitions. If precise communication is to occur, all people involved must have a common understanding of the symbols used. Thus, with different assortments of words and definitions in their minds, is there any wonder that people often fail to communicate?

## Connotative and denotative meaning

Making the area of word meaning even more confusing is the fact that the meanings we assign to words are not determined by their real-world references alone. To be sure, some of the meanings derived from words are based on references in the real world, but many of them exist only in the mind. Those meanings which are based on references to the real world are called *denotative* meanings. Meanings which exist in the mind rather than in the real world are *connotative* meanings. Unfortunately, words have both forms of meaning.

The denotative meanings we derive from words are based on the classification process we traced earlier. These are the meanings which relate directly to the real world—the objects or events the words stand for. To illustrate, it is a denotative meaning if one can point directly to the object or event in reality and say, "This is a football," "This is a party," or "This is a dog." The meanings the words bring to mind are clearly the objects or events to which we point. Or putting it another way, these are the meanings which *inform* us of the real-life objects or events about which we communicate.

Connotative meanings, on the other hand, bring in a qualitative judgment. Thus, they add or detract from the denotative meanings. They are meanings which build inside people. They are based on experiences, biases, emotions, opinions, attitudes, beliefs, and the like rather than on references in the real world. They are the meanings which arouse some personal feeling toward the objects or events of reference.

Reviewing these definitions, we can conclude that denotative meanings are the meanings which inform; connotative meanings are the meanings which have some affective results. For example, take some object in reality—say a ragged, unshaven, dirty man walking down a road. We could use a number of words to refer to him. We could call him a tramp, a bum, a vagrant, a hobo, a vagabond, a wanderer, or a knight of the road. All of these words perform the same informative function. They point to this one man.

In the minds of most people, however, the connotations of the words differ to some degree. Not all of us will receive the same connotations from the words, but probably we shall agree on most. We see a tramp as a down-and-out and perhaps immoral fellow; a bum is even lower. "Vagrant" has less of the bad connotations of "tramp" and "bum," but the word lies in the same general category. "Hobo" has a somewhat adventurous meaning in the minds of most of us; and "vagabond" has a little bit more. "Wanderer" has none of the negative moral connotations of the preceding words—in fact, "wanderer" borders on being a favorable reference. "Knight of the road" is even more favorable; in fact, this term has elegance.

Salesmen may intend to convey the same denotative meaning with "Hello," "How are you, sir?" and "Hiya, bud." But the connotative meanings are not the same. A restaurant sign may say "crispy fried fish" or "dead fish boiled in oil" and point to the same object. But the connotations of the two expressions differ sharply. A hard worker may be referred to as aggressive, eager, or enthusiastic. Again, the denotations would be the same, but not the connotations. The same is true of the following groups of words and expressions:

> Died, deceased, croaked, kicked the bucket.
> Bout, altercation, fight, donnybrook.
> Story, fib, falsehood, lie.
> Rout, debacle, defeat, moral victory.
> Depart, go, leave, get out.
> Be silent, be quiet, shut up.
> Expectorate, eject from the mouth, spit.
> Stout, obese, fat, blubbery.

From the preceding analysis of connotative meanings, we can see that words have an emotional quality. Those that give the same information—

that is, those that point to the same objects or events—are likely to convey different messages to the mind. For this reason, any attempt to communicate a particular message involves much more than choosing words which point to the objects or events in that message. The words selected, with all their denotative and connotative effects, will determine the message a communicant receives.

The point is well illustrated by a well-known marketing research study.[6] In this study, two comparable groups were asked for the same information, but the wording in the question differed. One group was asked: "Do you think the United States should permit speeches against democracy?" The other group was asked: "Do you think the United States should forbid speeches against democracy?" As the information sought by both questions is identical, the percentages favoring government control should be about the same. They were not. To the first question, 21 percent responded "should allow" as compared to 39 percent who responded "should not forbid" to the second question. To the first question, 62 percent answered "should not allow" as compared to the 46 percent "should forbid" response to the second question. No opinions were about the same for both questions. As all other factors in the study were kept constant, the connotative meanings in the questions explain the differences.

A series of differences between a labor union and the management of a certain company serves further to illustrate connotative effects from word choice. In discussing a proposed new contract, both sides argued about every provision. Their arguments brought in some classic examples of word choice for connotative effect. Concerning a provision to change the rate of pay for certain work groups, labor charged "infringement on seniority rights." Management justified the provision with "equal pay for equal work." The matter of an employee welfare fund was referred to by labor as "an example of Christian brotherhood." By management, it was labeled "an inroad of communism." Other points of discussion brought in such emotionally charged words as "arbitrary decision," "freedom of choice," "the American way," "question of integrity," "featherbedding," "a fair deal," and "a matter of honor."

There can be no question about it: Connotative differences are real, and they have a major effect on our communication. Skillful communicators know this fact well, and they very carefully choose their words for their connotations as well as their denotations. So if you are to acquire skill in communication, you must do likewise. Specifically, you must become a student of words. Especially must you study the shades of connotative differences in the meanings of words, and you must learn how these words can enable you to achieve a desired effect.

---

[6] Donald Rugg, "Experiments in Wording Questions: II," *Public Opinion Quarterly*, Vol. 5 (March, 1941), pp. 91–92.

## Context as an aid to meaning

In spite of all the complexities of words and their meanings, we do a reasonably good job of communicating with them. A good part of the credit goes to the role context plays in determining meaning. By "context," we mean the total situation in which a word is used. Specifically, this includes, first, the physical environment in which the communication is made. Second, it includes all the information in that communication, including the words themselves. How these two factors aid in determining meaning is best shown through illustration.

*Context of the physical environment.* The word *fast* is a word of multiple meanings; thus on occasion it will give us some problem in determining which of its various meanings to use. The physical context in which the word is used, however, usually tells us the meaning. If we are at a racetrack watching the horses run and hear someone say, "She's a fast one," the odds are that the words refer to the running speed of a horse. The fact that we are at a racetrack, where horses are the center of interest, gives us this meaning. The same words heard at a party would be likely to refer to a person of questionable morals. Again, the physical context gives us the meaning. For similar reasons of context, "fast" communicated in a certain work situation at a textile mill would refer to the permanency of color of the materials. Spoken to a sailor on his job, it could refer to the permanence of a knot. If made in conversation with one who has not eaten for a few days, the word would appropriately refer to an abstinence from food. In each of these cases, physical context provides assistance in determining meaning.

Physical contexts are often so clear that they not only help to determine meaning—they also do the work of words. If at a baseball game we see the hot dog vendor come by, we do not have to say "I want to buy two hot dogs, please." We need to say only "Two," or perhaps we need only to raise two fingers. The context takes care of the rest. In World War II an American general's reply to a German ultimatum to surrender was a terse "Nuts." The context carried his full message much more accurately than a page of words would have done. Or take the case of the boss who found his workers playing cards rather than working on a high-priority job. His abbreviated comment "By tonight, or else" was crystal-clear to all concerned. Either they completed the priority job by that night, or they would be in for trouble.

*Context of the surrounding words.* Verbal contexts help to determine meaning by supplying some help in defining words. If you were to hear someone say that "George lost his 'glub' yesterday," you would not know what a "glub" is, but you know from the surrounding words that it is something that can be possessed. Next you hear that "George had gone to get some flea powder, and when he got back he found the glub's cage door open." Now the verbal context has told you much more. You know that a glub is some kind of animal, for it is kept in a cage; and if it has fleas, probably it has fur. If the conversation continued long enough, in time you would have a good idea of what a glub is like.

The significance of verbal contexts may also be shown with word omissions. As most politicians will confirm, words or expressions lifted out of the whole message may take on an entirely different meaning. For example, John Smith, a candidate for the office of governor, might quote a very prominent citizen as saying, "Smith would make a good governor." Assume that the quote is correct—that the citizen actually said the words. But what if the words were lifted from the complete statement "Smith would make a good governor if he had the intelligence to match his arrogance." In this case the lifted part is inconsistent with the whole.

## As the map fits the territory

In reviewing the preceding discussion, we can see that in a sense we live in two worlds. First, of course, is the world of reality, which we have described as an infinite and complex world. Because it is so infinite and complex, and because our sensory receptors are limited, we can perceive only parts of it.

Second is the world of words in which we live. This is the world of symbols which stand for the reality we perceive. As we have seen, this world is based on perceptions, which, as we know, are limited. It is based on inaccurate substitutes for the real thing. The conclusion from this reasoning should be apparent. The verbal world is different from the real world. To some degree it must be inaccurate. Certainly, it is incomplete, for words cannot cover all the reality in any real-world situation. The extent to which the real world and the verbal world differ is a measure of the miscommunication of a given communication effort.

In looking at the verbal world and the real world, we can see a territory-map relationship. The real world, of course, is the territory. The world of words is a representation of that territory. Just as a good map must fit the territory it represents, so must the words of our communication fit their territory. A map which has reversed the locations of Chicago and Atlanta or New York and Los Angeles or which has omitted a key highway going westward from Cleveland does not represent its territory. Some people will look at such a map, believe it, and try to use it. But they will have problems. Likewise, words which do not represent their territory are likely to cause problems. Like good maps, words must fit the reality to which they refer.

It is important also that we recognize the verbal world for what it is—a world of words and not of reality. Words are not the real world, just as a map is not the territory. As we shall see in the following chapter, we sometimes confuse this relationship. We sometimes act on words which misrepresent reality as if they were reality. We let words take the place of reality. The result is miscommunication.

## QUESTIONS AND PROBLEMS

1. Make a list of the types of symbols that we use in communicating. Give examples of each.

2. Discuss the role of language in the development of human progress.

3. Why did language develop around similarities rather than differences?

4. For each of the following objects construct an abstraction ladder of words:
   a. A bird in a tree
   b. This book
   c. Your desk
   d. A pebble on the beach

5. Are high-level abstractions ever useful and appropriate in communication? Give examples to support your discussion.

6. "It doesn't matter what the dictionary says a word means. What is important is what one means when one uses the word." Explain this statement.

7. Explain the difficulty one would have in using a 1976 dictionary to determine meaning in a book written in 1796.

8. Illustrate the multiple meanings of words with these examples:
   a. Top
   b. Fall
   c. Stick
   d. Run
   e. Show
   f. Down

9. For each of the following words make a list of words which have similar denotative meanings. Explain the connotative meanings of these words as you understand them.
   a. Carry
   b. Hamburger steak
   c. Sing
   d. Cheat
   e. Look

10. Discuss how the following statements would have different meanings in different physical environments.
    a. I'll take ten. *rest, break, money,*
    b. Save me. *life, bad news, religious*
    c. It's a hit. *baseball, record, movie*
    d. He missed a step. *sing, math, chemist*

11. Using the context implied in the following sentences, write a definition for a pfitt.

      Mary bought a pfitt last week. She used it briefly Monday before it rained. She likes the way it does the job; but she thought it was too noisy.

12. Explain the map-territory relationship to communication.

# 6

# Some malfunctions of
# communication

THAT COMMUNICATION is imperfect is clearly evident from our review in the preceding chapters. Specifically, we have seen that some of the difficulty stems from the fact that the reality about which communication is concerned is infinite and complex. Also, we have seen that our minds (filters) are conditioned to receive information in an individual manner based on each mind's accumulations. Further, we have seen that the symbols we use in our efforts to communicate are plagued with imperfections and at best only loosely fit the reality to which they refer. As if these sources of miscommunication were not enough, now we shall see that additional malfunctions are presented in our communication effort.

These malfunctions may be described as patterns of miscommunication which are common in human communication effort. Some of these patterns are products of language and result from the language imperfections discussed in the last chapter. Others involve the logical thought patterns which are a part of our cultural heritage—specifically of the system of thinking handed down to us from past generations.

Scholars led by Alfred Korzybski, the founder of the discipline of general semantics, traced these erroneous thought patterns to the teachings of Aristotle.[1] They argue that the Aristotelian system of logic has been the core of our accepted patterns of thought as well as a determinant of the structure of our language. They point out certain aspects of Aristotelian logic which are the sources of our erroneous thought pat-

---

[1] Alfred Korzybski, *Science and Sanity, An Introduction to Non-Aristotelian Systems and General Semantics*, 3d ed., Country Life Publishing Corp., Garden City, N.Y., 1948.

terns. These arguments are too involved for analysis here, but much of the following material is based on them.

## TWO-VALUED THINKING

Deeply intrenched in our culture and our language is the pattern of two-valued thinking. It is the pattern in which we recognize two and only two possibilities in a given situation. It is the "either-or" logic—the logic which concludes that something either is or is not. It accepts no middle ground.

### The true dichotomy

Now, some situations may be correctly described in two-valued terms. For example, in a lifetime you either will marry or will not marry. You either will make a million dollars or will not make a million dollars. You either will pass this course or will fail this course. Two-valued thinking is quite appropriate in these instances. It fits the realities involved.

### Multivalued situations

Not all situations involve only two values, however. In fact, most involve many values, for most concern an infinite number of gradations between extremes. For example, it is illogical to classify all people as either fat or skinny. True, some are fat, and some are skinny; but most are in between. Also, not all fat people are equally fat, and not all skinny people are equally skinny. If we were to take all the people in the world and group them from the fattest to the skinniest, we would find infinitesimal gradations along the scale. Were we to draw a line dividing the fat from the skinny, we would be separating the groups by an imperceptible weight difference.

It is the same with many other situations. Not all people are either short or tall. The weather is not always either hot or cold. One does not run at only two speeds—fast and slow. Children are not just good or bad. Students are not either intelligent or stupid. Yet in all of these situations we tend to think of just two values. Thus, when we communicate about such situations, we are neither thinking nor reporting accurately. Our words and thought do not match the reality concerned.

Much of the blame for two-valued thinking can be laid to the structure of our language. We have in English an abundance of either-or words and an extreme shortage of words in between. Take the words *sweet* and *sour*. What words do we have for in-between taste? We could say "slightly sweet," "very sweet," "slightly sour," and the like. But usually we do not. Even if we do, we have only added a few general categories. We could say the same for "stupid or intelligent," "success or failure," "rich or poor," "week or strong," "happy or sad," "love or hate." The examples are limitless.

## The dangers involved

The danger in making two-valued statements, of course, is that they do not fit reality; thus, they can lead to miscommunication. This is not to say, however, that they should be forever eliminated from our vocabularies. Two-valued statements often are convenient devices in communication. They simplify that about which we communicate; hence, they help to make the message understandable. The danger comes in when those involved in the communication think or act as if the two values exhaust the possibilities.

A written evaluation of an employee, for example, may include the words *lazy* or *industrious*. Obviously, there are degrees of laziness and industriousness, and not all people would agree on the dividing line between the two. Thus, any personnel action which fails to take these possibilities into account would be illogical and unfair.

Our thinking patterns on politics and matters of government supply us with an abundance of illustrative material on this point. On candidates for public office or matters of legislation we tend to be either for or against. And we structure our reasoning to support our stand. In structuring our reasoning, there is the tendency to think in terms of right and wrong, good or bad, conservative or liberal, and the like. As a result, we fail to recognize the reality of the situation, which in most cases involves a mixture of good and bad, right and wrong. Thus it is that a true Republican takes the stand that all which the Democrats do is wrong and all which his party does is right. A true Democrat takes the opposite position of bias.

Similarly, in viewing the role of unions, a representative of management might conclude that labor unions are bad, and in all his thinking about them he is likely to fail to see anything but the bad. A true son of labor is likely to view the same situation from a directly opposing viewpoint. Also, on matters of social concern such as civil rights, drinking, and gambling, dichotomous thinking is apt to be present. In fact, any matter on which viewpoints may be made is a probable topic for two-valued thinking.

## Value of specific reference

The only possible solution to the problem of two-valued thinking is a two-step one. First, we must continually be aware of this communication difficulty. We must keep our eyes on the reality with which we are concerned. Second, we must try as well as we can to be specific in our choice of symbols. As the first step involves an awareness of what we have been discussing, it needs no additional comment. The second, however, involves practical techniques which are best presented by illustration.

In choosing symbols that are precise, we are limited by the possibilities of our language, but most of us can do better than we do. Whenever possible, for example, we can use quantitative measures. Instead of saying "He has an excellent academic record," we can say "He has a 3.9 grade-point average." Instead of saying "He is fat," we can say "He carries 345 pounds on a 5-foot, 4-inch frame." Instead of saying "He is a safe driver," we can say "He has driven 500,000 miles without an accident."

In addition, we can use middle-ground words much better than we do. In communicating a qualitative judgment, we can use such gradations as "exceptionally good," "very good," "good," "moderately good," "moderately bad," "bad," "very bad," and "exceptionally bad." In describing taste, we can go far beyond the more general and common symbols such as "good" and "bad" or "sweet" and "sour" with words such as "sugary," "saccharine," "candied," "honeyed," "acid," "tart," "astringent," "vinegary," and "acetose." Certainly, many of these words are general, but they do convey some of the gradations of taste.

## FACT-INFERENCE CONFUSION

Sometimes we are able to communicate about actual experience—things and events we have seen or heard. For example, if we buy a new car for $5,200, we can report factually that "We bought the car for $5,200." Or if we attend a club meeting at which George is elected president, we can report factually that "George was elected president." When we can do this, it is good, for it tends to produce communication which fits reality.

Unfortunately, we cannot always be factual. Frequently, we need to communicate about something we have not personally experienced—something we do not know to be factual. That is, we frequently find it convenient to communicate about things or events we do not know—things we only infer. For example, we may see a friend with a new car. In conversation with this friend, we might say, "How much did you pay for it?" We are, of course, assuming that our friend bought this car. Could it not be that the car belongs to a friend of our friend or perhaps to his mother? He could have received it as a gift or through an inheritance. He could even have stolen it. In any event, there is at least some likelihood that our inference could be wrong. Thus, our communication would not fit reality and would in effect be a miscommunication.

## Necessity of inference

Although inferences can sometimes be wrong, we must make them if we are to engage in human communication. In the first place, we would be severely limited if we could only communicate about that which we have experienced. We could make no interpretations of the events and the reality in the world about us. We could make no predictions. We could make no evaluations. In fact, there would be very little to communicate about. To prove the point, try talking to a friend for five minutes limiting all comments to factual material. If you do it at all, you will find such communication to be dull and difficult.

In the second place, we must make inferences if we are to survive. We cannot know everything with which we must deal in life; yet living requires that we make decisions and take actions based on inferences. If in the days of the Old West two strangers met on the trail and one went for his gun, the other had no choice but to infer that his life was in danger. If the second man did not draw and attempt to shoot first, the odds were that he would not have lived long. But there was also the slim possibility that all was not as it appeared. Perhaps the first man was only attempting to shoot a rattlesnake coiled and ready to strike the other man.

When we are driving an automobile and sight an approaching car, we infer that the other driver is a normal person who will stay on his prescribed side of the road; but sometimes drivers do not. We infer that cooks and waiters in restaurants are normal, decent human beings who do not put poison in our food; there have been exceptions. If you observe a man entering your home through a window, you infer that he is up to no good; again, there are other possible explanations. Because there is much we do not know, all of life is filled with risks. If we are to live, we must take them. Thus, we must make inferences.

## Effect on communication

As necessary as inferences are to our living, they are a source of human miscommunication. The trouble is not that we make inferences; it is that all too frequently we confuse what is fact and what is inference. More specifically, we tend to make inferences from the facts we perceive, and we tend to treat these inferences as if they were facts. Thus, because we fail to see reality as it is, we cannot communicate accurately.

One of O. Henry's classic short stories illustrates this point well. It is the story of a man who owns one of the world's great jewels. At a dinner party the man shows his famous jewel to his guests, explaining that the jewel is priceless and that it was once a part of a beautifully matched pair. He passes the jewel around the table for all to inspect. The talk then turns to other things. After a time, the host asks for his jewel, but no one has it. Efforts to produce the stone fail; finally, the police are called. A personal search of all guests is called for. Everybody agrees to the search —except one man. As he steadfastly refuses to be searched, suspicion is turned on him. In the minds of all present, he is the guilty one. Why else would he refuse to be searched? As those in the room continue to talk and discuss the case, they label this one man as the guilty party. In time, someone finds the gem in a dish of food. Now the people seek some explanation for their wrong inference. The man explains that, as everyone has been told, his host's gem is one of a matched pair. It just so happens that the suspected man is the owner of the other gem. And he has the matched gem in his pocket.

O. Henry's story, of course, is an unusual one; and the odds of such a coincidence taking place are slim indeed. So let us take a more likely example. Let us assume that we are somehow involved in a sales organization and have observed that three of our top salesmen are bald-headed. From this factual information we may infer that bald-headed men make the best salesmen. Now, our communication about bald-headed salesmen or salesmen in general is clouded with this erroneous inference which our filters contain. However, the fact is only that three of our bald salesmen are good. Probably there are many other bald salesmen who are also good, but there are many more who are not as good. In all probability, the reality of this situation does not support the inference we have made.

In the first example, the inference was logical and the odds of its being wrong were long. In the second, the inference was illogical, to say the least. In either event, the result was the same. There was error. The concepts in the mind were not in accord with reality. From this observation one conclusion should be clear: there is risk in inferences. Inferences are not facts of reality. And any communication involving inferences has some probability of not being true.

## Calculating the probabilities

Although we must make many inferences in coping with the day-to-day problems of life, we can work to reduce the communication hazards they bring about. Specifically, we can be continually aware of the inferences we make. More specifically, we can attempt to calculate the probability of correctness of each of them.

Thus, when we infer that what appears to be a book on a library shelf contains pages, we should realize that the odds are perhaps a few thousand to one that our inference is correct. But we should be aware that there is always the possibility that it could be a false book—one consisting of a cover and simulated pages with the center cut out to form a secret compartment.

When we infer that because Joan Smith missed work today she is sick, the odds favor our being right. But we should be aware that there is also the possibility that our inference is wrong—that Joan Smith may be playing hooky or attending a funeral; or perhaps she is even dead. When we learn that some thieves are members of a certain organization, we are likely to infer that this organization is made up of immoral people. We should be aware that there is a very good chance that to some degree our inference is incorrect.

Actually, calculating the probability of an inference involves nothing that has not been suggested previously. First, it involves being continually aware of the nature of reality. Second, it involves using our knowledge of reality as a check on our inferences.

## THE BLOCKED MIND

A miscommunication pattern which affects us all is that of the blocked mind. As the term implies, a blocked mind is one which is closed to reality. It works on limited information, and it ignores or refuses to accept additional information. Thus, because it makes use of only a part of the information available, its communication efforts are necessarily only partially correct.

### A result of opinions, attitudes, and beliefs

One of the causes of this form of miscommunication was covered in Chapter 4 with our review of opinions, attitudes, and beliefs. There it was pointed out that our minds tend to reject or ignore information which runs contrary to our viewpoints. Our opinions, attitudes, and beliefs tend to become rigid and to resist all information which is contrary to them. As a result, they may severely impair the fidelity of our communication.

### A result of allness

A second contributor to the blocked mind is our tendency to judge the whole by a part—to assume that the part is the whole. This tendency is called "allness," and all of us are victims of it from time to time.

More specifically, allness is that attitude which implies that what one knows or says about something is all there is to know or say about it. In view of our previous discussions of reality, this is a most illogical attitude. As was explained in Chapter 3, reality is too complex, too filled with detail for any human being to know all there is to know about something. It is so detailed that in communicating about it, we must select (abstract) some of its characteristics. We ignore all the others.

For example, in talking about Wilma Cuppenheimer, we could abstract many things. We could say that she is a devoted mother, a civic worker, a Protestant, a Democrat, a college dropout, a dentist, a gardener, a friend of animals, a music lover, a heavy drinker, a tennis player, a glutton, and a spendthrift. Wilma Cuppenheimer is all of these, and hundreds of others as well. But when we communicate about Wilma, we are likely to refer to only one or two of these characteristics, at least in a single statement.

This practice of selecting one characteristic to communicate about is necessary, for communication would be meaningless if only the broadest and most general references could be made. Such narrow references, however, tend to block our minds to the reality involved. All too often, in selecting limited numbers of characteristics for communicating, we tend to think that our limited reference is the whole.

If, for example, Wilma Cuppenheimer moves into the house next door, the first information reported about her might be that she is a heavy drinker. As we have noted, this is only one of many characteristics one could communicate about the woman. Yet when we communicate about this one characteristic, we tend to consider it as being the whole and to ignore the others. As the news that Wilma is a heavy drinker is communicated through the neighborhood, opinions are likely to be formed. Thus, the whole of Wilma Cuppenheimer is considered by this one part, although the other parts would present a much more favorable impression. But unless the other characteristics are specifically brought out, there is the tendency of the mind to be blocked to their existence.

This attitude may be illustrated further by a woman who comments that a certain detergent is no good. It ruined some of her fine clothes, she may reason. Her reasoning may be entirely valid, but it may be based on incomplete evidence—on only one of the many characteristics involved. The truth may be that although it is not good for finery, the detergent may be excellent for washing greasy work clothes, for killing fleas on dogs, for removing road film from cars, for cleaning rugs, and the like. In view of these many characteristics of the detergent, the woman's comment is not in accord with reality.

## Extreme effects of the blocked mind

The problems of the blocked mind that stem from rigid viewpoints or from our tendency toward allness are with us in everyday living. And in a multitude of minor forms they tend to distort the fidelity of our communication. Some extreme forms of the pattern, however, are more likely to lead to serious communication problems.

In its most extreme form the blocked mind typifies the attitude of the dogmatist and of those among us who "know it all." All of us have had experiences with people who are adamant in their stand on certain issues. They imply that only they have the true facts—that only they are right. These attitudes are appropriately criticized by the old adage "A little learning is a dangerous thing." Until these persons realize how much there is to know about everything and how little they really know, they are not likely to unblock their minds.

Most arguments are to some extent a result of blocked minds—or more precisely, two blocked minds. The point is illustrated by almost any argument you have witnessed. For our purposes here, select any one. Unless you have selected a rare one involving people with superobjectivity, you have selected a contest of blocked minds. In all likelihood, you have selected an argument in which each participant presented his own viewpoint with more vigor than he received the views of his opponent. Probably each did more talking than listening, if he listened at all. In fact, the participants are likely to use their listening time preparing the comments they will make next. At the end of the argument neither of the participants has received much additional information; and if their viewpoints have changed at all, probably they have become more rigid than before.

## Unblocking the mind

Unblocking the mind from the effects of our viewpoints and our tendency to allness is no simple undertaking. And explaining how it can be done involves the most general of instructions. Nevertheless, it can be done, at least to some extent; and if we are to improve our communication, we must try.

In unblocking our minds for the effects of our opinions, attitudes, and beliefs, we are striving to do nothing new. Since the beginning days of civilization, intelligent human beings have sought to free their thinking from the grip of their human limitations. They have sought truth. They have striven for rational approaches to their problems. To date, however, even the best of them have failed miserably; and there is likely to be no change in the foreseeable future.

Because we cannot change the fact that we are human beings, about all we can do is to be conscious of the role our opinions, attitudes, and beliefs play in our thinking. We can be conscious of the fact that we acquire many of them through nonrational means. And most important of all, we can strive to be rational, always questioning our viewpoints and checking them with reality.

As is the case with most of the causes of miscommunication, combating the attitude of allness requires that we continually be aware of the nature of reality. More specifically, it requires that we keep in mind the fact that in communicating we must select some of the details of reality while omitting others. This is much the same advice Alfred Korzybski[2] gave in developing his discipline of general semantics when he suggested that all statements end with "etc." This symbol, he argued, keeps communicants aware of the fact that whatever is said about anything, there always is much more that could be said. Perhaps following Korzybski's suggestion would be impractical—at least until many people are aware of this device and of its meaning. But Korzybski's device is sound, and we would be wise to place a silent mental "etc." at the ends of the statements we communicate.

## THE STATIC VIEWPOINT

The failure of language and our concept of reality to account for time changes leads us to hold a static view of things. That is, we tend to ignore the fact that all things change, and our language assists us in doing this. Such a static view of the process world in which we live, of course, is not true to fact. Thus, it contributes to miscommunication.

### The unstatic nature of things

The fact that all of reality is in a state of perpetual change was explained in Chapter 3. It is a condition of fact about which we all are fully aware. Even so, we are likely to ignore it in our thinking and our communicating.

To illustrate, when we communicate about someone we knew in the past, our minds hold references formed in the past. It is these images which become a part of our communication—not the true images of the people as they are now. The truth of this communication error can be vividly described by an ex-convict who has tried to go straight. No matter how hard he may try, in the minds of many he remains the criminal they knew in the past.

Such miscommunication is not limited to references to persons. Two people talking about a place—say Chicago—may apparently agree that "It's one great town." Their filter references, however, may be from different times. One might recall her happy days living there 40 years ago; the other's references might be current. Perhaps the first person might not even like the current Chicago. And so it is with all places. The California of today is not the California of 1900, or 1875, or 1849, or of any other time. The England of today is not the England of the 1500s. Yet, in our references to these places the symbols remain the same.

Similar illustrations may be made of the changing value of currency. The United States dollar, for example, is not the dollar it was a generation ago; and that dollar is far different from its counterpart of the pre-

---

[2] *Ibid.*, p. xxxiii.

ceding generation. Yet when the old-timers talk about hard times, low pay, and the like, they are neglecting to account for these changes, even though they know better.

## The contributing factor of language

Our language contributes to our tendency to hold static viewpoints of reality, for it fails to give adequate emphasis to the timing of events. Of course, we have tense differences which give some timing to the events about which we communicate; and when there is a special need for time references, we can state specific times and dates. But these are a small part of the whole. Everything we communicate about has a place in time, and usually our language does not provide for it.

For example, when we want to communicate that "Henry Hobson is a scoundrel," there is no natural way of indicating whether we mean Henry Hobson at age 10, 21, 35, or 60. When we read that a certain eminent economist feels "that government subsidies are needed to solve the farm problem," her words do not indicate the time to which they apply. They might be quite inappropriate to the economic situation and the economist's viewpoint a few years earlier or later.

## FAILURE TO DISCRIMINATE[3]

All too often in our communication we fail to make adequate distinction between the objects and events about which we communicate. We fail to see the differences involved and instead see the similarities. As we have noted, uniqueness is common to all events and objects. Thus, seeing similarities rather than differences is contrary to the nature of things. Such failures to discriminate are common to all of us. The result is some degree of miscommunication.

Probably our language is the major cause of this error in viewing reality. As we noted in Chapter 5, words must do multiple duty if we are to keep their number manageable. Reality is too complex and involved for it to be otherwise. Thus, in forming our language, we have to categorize the events and objects in nature. As a result, we are conditioned to think in terms of similarities.

## Miscommunication from stereotypes

In thinking in terms of similarities, we frequently form stereotyped impressions. That is, we view a category of reality as having a common mold. We see a typical or common group of characteristics for the cate-

---

[3] Adapted from William V. Haney, *Communicating Patterns and Incidents,* Richard D. Irwin, Inc., Homewood, Illinois, 1960, pp. 101–9.

gory. Because everything in reality is unique, stereotypes cannot be true to fact.

To illustrate the point, the word *professor* is used to refer to tens of thousands of people. The one major thing professors have in common is that they teach at some institution of higher learning. As with all such groups, the differences among professors are infinite. Yet we are conditioned to think in terms of the similarities the word conveys. Most likely, the term *professor* conveys a generally common meaning to the minds of most of us. He is an absent-minded, long-haired, bearded gentleman, slight of build and sharp of feature. How well does this description fit your professor in this course—or any of the professors you have had?

Numerous such stereotypes are held by all of us. We are likely to picture a farmer as a tall, slender, rugged man dressed in bib overalls and with tousled hair. But how many farmers actually fit this image? We may see a business executive as a cigar-smoking, bald-headed, pot-bellied, girl-chasing man. How many actually fit this mold? We may see a show girl as a statuesque, unlettered, giddy, partying type. In reality, this type is the exception. Likewise, in our minds there are stereotypes of detectives, poets, wrestlers, students, policemen, gangsters, cowboys, and hundreds of others. Such stereotyped views of the members of any group is a gross distortion of reality, for few of the items in any classification approximate the common mold.

The effect of stereotypes on communication is that they tend to take the place of reality. Stereotype images are in our mental filters, and they have some effect on our determination of meaning. Thus, when Professor White is mentioned in a communication, our stereotype of "professor" is a part of the meaning we give to the communication. When someone says that "Henry Hatton is a poet," that stereotype plays a role in determining the meaning we give to the statement. And so it is with other stereotypes. Each plays a part in determining meaning, and usually each tends to distort reality.

## Judgments by category

An extreme form of discrimination failure is the making of common judgments to cover all things within a category. Rarely are such judgments supported by fact, for rarely are all things in a group sufficiently similar to deserve a common judgment. Most such judgments are based on very limited observation. Almost never are they based on knowledge of all members in the group. Unfortunately, we all make such judgment errors in our day-to-day communication.

The most common judgments by category spring from an incident or two—or at most, very limited observation. A professor may catch a couple of students in the act of cheating. This incident plus news of a few other incidents involving cheating might lead her to react with the judgment that "Students just don't seem to have much regard for honesty." The same professor driving home from work might be passed by a speeding carload of students. Her reaction might be that "Students drive like maniacs." And when she gets home and sees a note from her husband telling her that he is out fishing, she might respond with a judgment "Men have an easy life!"

On all three of these judgments the professor is in error, for she bases her judgments on a very small part of the whole. Certainly, there is good likelihood that at least some, if not all students, are honest. Most are safe, level-headed drivers. And there are many hardworking men who would vigorously refute her last judgment.

Such judgments are so commonplace that we make them and use them without giving them much thought. You have heard such statements as "Women are poor drivers," "Sailors are wild," "Salespeople are deceitful," and "Artists are temperamental." In varying degrees, all of these judgments are wrong, for there are exceptions to every one. In every case a failure to discriminate among the members of the category has resulted in a communication that is inconsistent with reality. Thus, some degree of miscommunication is the result.

## Developing an awareness of differences

The solution to the problem resulting from failures to discriminate is to be continuously aware of the differences that exist within all categories. By thoroughly understanding the uniqueness of reality, and by making this understanding a permanent part of our filtering process, we are not likely to make discrimination errors—at least not so many as we do now.

Again, Alfred Korzybski in his works in general semantics suggested a solution for this communication problem. His suggestion is to index our references[4]—to distinguish between the object and events about which we communicate. For example, he would distinguish between the professors communicated about, referring to them as professor$_1$, professor$_2$, professor$_3$, etc. Parties given by a certain person might be labeled party$_1$, party$_2$, etc. Unquestionably, such a system would help to avoid the confusion which develops. But like some of the other suggestions of Korzybski, they are not yet widely accepted. Until they are accepted, their meanings would not be clear to all concerned.

Even so, the suggestion is a good one, and we would be wise to follow it mentally. That is, we can each look for the differences in all things about which we communicate. So the next time you hear someone make a reference to labor leaders, students, bookies, or cabdrivers, keep in mind

---

[4] Korzybski, *op. cit.*, p. 381.

that everyone in the group is different and that stereotypes will not fit them all. And the next time you hear a general judgment of all members of a category such as "Women are fickle" or "Italian men are romantic," index the statements yourself. Ask yourself "Which women are fickle?" and "Which Italian men are romantic?" By doing so, you will be gaining a more realistic understanding of the reality about which we communicate.

## MISCOMMUNICATION SUMMARIZED

This review of patterns of miscommunication is by no means exhaustive. At best, we have pointed out the major communication violations which can be placed in categories. In forming these categories, we should take some of our own advice. We must note that wide variations occur within each category. Some violations are so mild that they hardly warrant classification as miscommunication. Others are flagrant.

In summarizing the suggestions given for correcting these miscommunication patterns, one basic bit of advice stands out. It is the advice to keep our eyes on reality. If we are to communicate better, we must become better acquainted with the real world, and we must check our communications with this real world. When our communication and the real world are not in harmony, we have miscommunication. Thus, the watchword for ridding ourselves of the miscommunication habit is "Keep in touch with reality."

## QUESTIONS AND PROBLEMS

1. Classify each of the following concepts as truly dichotomous or multivariate:
   a. Semester grades  *dic*
   b. Swimming across a river  *dic*
   c. Succeeding in one's profession  *mult.*
   d. Honesty  *mult.*
   e. Happiness  *mult.*
   f. Living  *dic*
   g. Sleeping  *mult dic*
2. What can one do to correct the error of two-valued thinking?
3. How clear is the distinction between fact and inference? Would all of us agree on what is fact and what is inference?  *no, cause we see it differently.*
4. What inferences have you made as you studied this chapter? What facts have you observed?
5. Explain how our minds can become blocked.
6. What can we do to avoid blocking the mind?
7. From your experience give an example that illustrates the effects on communication of the static viewpoint.

8.  How does language contribute to the static viewpoint?
9.  What can we do to overcome the effects of the static viewpoint?
10. Select three stereotypes that are widely held by your associates. Discuss how correct they are and how they developed.
11. For the past 20 years, the Shannon Manufacturing Company has been making a unique garden cart. At a meeting of the board of directors, the chairman of the board recommended that the company discontinue the product, backing his recommendation with the claim that the product had been a failure from the very beginning. The company's president then came to the defense of the product, claiming that it had been a success. A member of the board entered the discussion with the comment, "One thing is clear. You both cannot be right." Discuss.
12. The president of a manufacturing plant announced that rather than give across-the-board raises he would give uniform $100-a-month raises to one-half of his workers. Those that would get the raises would be those with the best records of productivity. Discuss the executive's thinking from a communication viewpoint.
13. Give examples of specific wordings which describe each of these multi-variate concepts:
    a.  Quality of work done on a job
    b.  Profitability of a sales outlet
    c.  Effectiveness of an insecticide
    d.  Odor of gases
    e.  Adhesive strength of a glue
14. Evaluate this comment: "Some of the workers are doing a good job; but the rest are not earning their pay."
15. Point out and comment on the probability of each of the inferences made in these statements:
    a.  Messenger to his boss: "Yes, I delivered the memo to the supervisor personally. I handed it to the only one who was wearing a suit."
    b.  A supervisor's memorandum to his workers: "There's been too much talking on the job. Tomorrow we are all going to work."
    c.  One customer to another: "This place is a real money maker. Did you ever see so many people buying?"
    d.  Waiter to a customer: "I'll give you this choice seat by the orchestra where you can enjoy the music."
    e.  Credit manager to assistant: "Turn down Mr. Culberson. He doesn't list one reference from a town he lived in only last year."
16. Discuss the communication malfunction illustrated by each of these statements:
    a.  Executive to a salesperson: "Sorry, but we've been buying only Drago office machines for the past 20 years. We tried the others; but none compared with Drago."
    b.  One director to another: "The person selected for this administrative job must be an engineer. Sure he has to know finance, management, marketing, and all that stuff. But we're an engineering company."

   *c.* A male interviewer to a female job applicant: "Sorry, Miss Clary. The only jobs we have are on the production line."

17. Discuss this comment. "No, I wouldn't hire Bruce for this job. He's just not the serious type. Back when we were in college together he always was the clown."

18. Evaluate this conclusion: "We have kept records of our company automobiles for over 30 years. Clearly the Curry is the most economical all-around automobile."

19. Describe the stereotype these words convey in your mind:
   *a.* Politician
   *b.* Cabdriver
   *c.* Bellhop
   *d.* Lifeguard
   *e.* Accountant
   *f.* Stockholder

# part two

## Applications to business

# 7

# General principles of
# business writing

THAT A KNOWLEDGE of communication theory can help you in your career in business should be unmistakably clear. Such knowledge gives you a better understanding of the business world of which you will be a part. It will help you to understand the people with whom you will work. And it will help you to understand and to solve the myriad of problems you will encounter in business. In addition to these broader benefits, you will also be able to apply communication theory to the more specific, practical tasks of communicating in business. Thus, it is to the practical applications of communication that our analysis now turns.

Any manageable analysis of the application of communication theory in business must be selective, for the area is very broad. For this reason, the material in this chapter and following ones is limited to those phases of applied communication in which you will need the most help. Specifically, we shall cover the area of business writing, especially the writing of correspondence and reports. Following this review of writing we shall cover briefly the more important methods of oral communication in business. Space and time limitations do not permit us to cover the important area of interpersonal communication. Fortunately, however, this area has received some review through illustrations in the preceding chapters.

## THE BASIC PRINCIPLE OF ADAPTATION

In applying communication theory to business writing, one basic principle emerges. It is the principle of adaptation—of fitting the symbols to the specific reader or readers. It is the underlying principle upon which many of the rules of good business writing are based, and it serves to temper these rules in their applications.

## The filter as the basis for adaptation

As we noted in our study of the communication process (Chapter 2), the meanings we give to the symbols and signs we receive are determined by the filters of our minds. As every filter is made up of all that the mind has retained from all the perceptions that have passed through it, no two are alike. No two can be alike, for no two can possibly have precisely the same knowledge, experience, bias, emotions, and the like. No two have the same knowledge of words, nor do any two give the same meanings to all the words held in common. The differences are so great that they present a major problem in communication.

Because filter makeups differ, especially in the knowledge of words and meanings, you must adapt your communication to fit the individual filter or filters concerned. That is, you must use symbols and concepts which will be given similar meaning in your filter and in the filters with which you communicate. Not to do so would be much like communicating in a foreign tongue.

## The technique of adapting

Adapting your words and concepts to your reader will not come naturally to you. If you are like most of us, you are not likely to adapt without conscious effort. Most of us consider writing something of a chore. We work hard to find words which express our thoughts. We work so hard that we are content to accept whatever word choice comes first to mind. Such choices of words, however, are likely to communicate only with those with filters similar to our own. They may completely miss the filter of our reader.

In adapting your writing to your reader, you should begin by visualizing your reader. You should get clearly in mind the answers to such questions as who he is, how much he knows about your subject, what his educational level is, and how he thinks. Then, when an image of your reader is in mind, you should select the symbols which will communicate to this individual.

In many business situations, adapting to the reader will mean writing down to a level lower than your own. Frequently, you will find yourself in situations in which you wish to communicate with people below your educational level, or you will be communicating with readers less knowledgeable than you are on the subject concerned. In both instances you will need to simplify your message. That is, you will need to write in the simple words and concepts your readers understand. If, for example, you must write a memorandum to a group of laborers, you would need to communicate in the everyday words of this group. Or if you must communicate on a technical subject to an educated but nontechnical reader, you would need to simplify the concepts in your message. Not to do so would be to miscommunicate, or at least to make communication difficult.

Your task in adapting is relatively simple when you are writing to a single reader or to a homogeneous group of readers. But what if you must write to a number of people with widely varying mental filters? What should you do, for example, if your readers range from college graduates to those with almost no formal education? The answer is obvious. You would have no choice but to aim at the lowest level of the group. If you write at a higher level, you will be likely to miscommunicate with those at the lower levels.

## Cases of adaptation

Illustrating this fundamental principle are the financial sections of the annual reports of some of our major corporations. In attempting to communicate the financial information, some companies see their stockholders as being uninformed on matters of finance. Perhaps they see their rank-and-file readers as widows, housewives, and others who have not had business experience. Their communication might read like this:

> Last year your company's total sales were $117,400,000, which was slightly higher than the $109,800,000 total for the year before. After deducting for all expenses, we had $4,593,000 left over for profits, compared with $2,830,000 for 1971. Because of these increased profits, we were able to increase your annual dividend payments per share from the 50 cents paid over the last ten years.

Some companies visualize their stockholders in an entirely different light and see them as being well informed in the language of finance. Perhaps they misjudge their readers, or maybe they fail to consider the readers' knowledge. In any event, these companies present their financial information in a somewhat technical and sophisticated manner, as illustrated by this example:

> The corporation's investments and advances in three unconsolidated subsidiaries (all in the development stage) and in 50 percent owned companies was $42,200,000 on December 31, 1971, and the excess of the investments in certain companies over net asset value at dates of acquisition was $1,760,000. The corporation's equity in the net assets as of December 31, 1971, was $41,800,000 and in the results of operations for the year ended December 31, 1971 and 1970, was $1,350,000 and $887,500. Dividend income was $750,000 and $388,000 for the years 1971 and 1970, respectively.

When you write to someone who is about as well-educated and informed on your subject as you are, your communication task is relatively easy. You need only to write to one like yourself, using language that is easy for you to understand. Likewise, if you are a technical person writing on a technical subject to a technical person who will understand the subject, you should write in the technical language both of you know and use. As technical language is the everyday language of the technician, this is the language which communicates quickly. Also, it is the language the technician expects. As we shall see later, however, such writing can be too technical even for the technical reader.

## CARE IN WORD CHOICE — *use short words!*

Writing in language which is adapted to your reader is not so simple as it may at first appear. To do the job well, you will need to become a student of language as well as a student of people. You can be guided in your efforts, however, by certain rules of word selection.

### Selecting words the reader understands

In general, these rules suggest that you simplify your writing. Although adaptation does not always mean simplification, in most business situations it does, and for good reason. In the first place, if you are like the typical business person, you tend to write at too difficult a level. Perhaps subconsciously you seek to impress; or maybe you just have a tendency to become stiff and formal when you write. In any event, the resulting words are not likely to make sharp, clear meanings in the reader's mind.

In the second place, usually the writer knows the subject of his message better than does the reader. Thus, the minds of the two are not equally equipped to communicate on the subject. The writer has no choice but to present the message in the more elementary words and concepts that will make meaning in the reader's mind.

A third reason for simplifying your writing is the conclusion drawn from exhaustive studies on readability—that writing which is slightly below the reader's level makes the most comfortable reading. According to the findings of such notables as Robert Gunning and Rudolph Flesch, such writing communicates best. Even if we are able to comprehend the more difficult words, we do so with effort.

**Use the familiar words.** The first rule of word selection is to use the familiar everyday words. Of course, the definition of familiar words varies by persons. What is everyday usage to some people is likely to appear to be high-level talk to others. Thus, the suggestion to use familiar language is in a sense a specific suggestion to apply the principle of adapting the writing to the reader.

Unfortunately, many business writers do not use everyday language enough. Instead, they tend to change character when they begin to put their thoughts on paper. Rather than writing naturally, they become stiff and stilted in their expression. For example, instead of using an everyday word like *try*, they use the more unfamiliar word *endeavor*. They do not "find out"; they "ascertain." They "terminate" rather than "end," and they "utilize" instead of "use."

Now, there is really nothing wrong with the hard words—if they are used intelligently. They are intelligently used when they are clearly understood by the reader, when they are best in conveying the meaning intended, and when they are used with wise moderation. Perhaps the best suggestion in this regard is to use words you would use in face-to-face communication with your reader. Another good suggestion is to use the simplest words which carry the thought without offending the reader's intelligence.

The communication advantages of familiar words over the far more complex ones is obvious from the following contrasting examples:

| *Formal and complex* | *Familiar words* |
|---|---|
| The conclusion ascertained from a perusal of the pertinent data is that a lucrative market exists for the product. | The data studied show that the product is in good demand. |
| The antiquated mechanisms were utilized for the experimentation. | The old machines were used for the test. |
| Company operations for the preceding accounting period terminated with a substantial deficit. | The company lost much money last year. |

***Prefer the short to the long word.*** Because short words tend to communicate better than long ones, you should prefer them in your writing. As has been borne out by readability studies, a heavy proportion of long words confuses the reader. Some of the explanation, of course, is that the long words tend to be the more difficult ones. In addition, however, the readability studies indicate that long words give the appearance of being hard; thus, our mental filters recieve them as hard words. The studies give evidence that even when the long words are understood, a heavy proportion of them adds to the difficulty of comprehension.

There are, of course, many exceptions to this rule. Some words like *hypnotize, hippopotamus,* and *automobile* are so well known that they communicate easily; and some short words like *verd, vie,* and *gybe* are understood by only a few. On the whole, however, word length and word difficulty are correlated. Thus, you will be wise to use long words with some caution. And you will need to be certain that the long ones you use are well known to your reader.

The following contrasting sentences clearly show the effect of long words on writing clarity. Most of the long words are likely to be understood by most educated readers, but the heavy proportion of long words makes for heavy reading and slow communication. Without question, the simple versions communicate better.

| *Heavy on long words* | *Short and simple words* |
|---|---|
| A decision was *predicated* on the *assumption* that an abundance of *monetary* funds was *forthcoming*. | The decision was *based* on the *belief* that there would be *more* money. |
| They *acceded* to the *proposition* to *terminate* business. | They *agreed* to *quit* business. |
| During the *preceding* year the company *operated* at a *financial deficit*. | Last year the company lost money. |
| *Prior to accelerating productive operation*, the foreman inspected the machinery. | *Before speeding up production*, the foreman inspected the machinery. |
| *Definitive* action was *effected subsequent* to the reporting date. | Final action was *taken after* the reporting date. |

**Use technical words with caution.**    Whatever your field will be in business, it will have its own jargon. In time, this jargon will become a part of your everyday working vocabulary. So common will this jargon appear in your mental filter that you may assume that others outside the field also know it. And in writing to those outside your field, you may use these words. The result is miscommunication.

Certainly, it is logical to use the language of a field in writing to those in the field. But even in such instances you can overdo it, for an overuse of technical words can be hard reading even for technical people. Frequently, technical words are long and hard-sounding. As we noted in the preceding rule, such words tend to dull the writing and to make the writing hard to understand. Also, the difficulty tends to increase as the proportion of technical words increases. Illustrating this point is the following sentence written by a physician:

It is a methodology error to attempt to interpret psychologically an organic symptom which is the end result of an intermediary change of organic processes instead of trying to understand those vegetative, nervous impulses in their relation to psychological factors which introduce a change of organic events resulting in an organic disturbance.

No doubt the length of this sentence contributes to its difficulty, but the heavy proportion of technical terms also makes understanding difficult. The conclusion that may be drawn here is obvious. When you write to your fellow technicians, you may use technical words, but you should use them moderately.

In writing to those outside the field, you should write in layman language. For example, a physician might well refer to a "cerebral vascular accident" in writing to a fellow physician, but he would do well to use the word *stroke* in writing to the layman. An accountant writing to a non-accountant might also need to avoid the jargon of his profession. Even though terms like *accounts receivable, liabilities,* and *surplus* are elementary to him, they may be meaningless to some people. So, in writing to such people, he would be wise to use nontechnical descriptions such as "how much is owed the company," "how much the company owes," and "how much was left over." Similar examples can be drawn from any specialized field.

## Bringing the writing to life with words

As we noted in our analysis of the communication process, our sensory receptors and our minds do not give equal attention to all our perceptions. Some they completely ignore. Others they give varying degrees of attention, ranging from almost none to the strong and vigorous. Obviously, it is the strong and vigorous perceptions which communicate best.

Applied to written communication, this observation means that symbols which are strong and vigorous are more likely to gain and hold the interest of your reader. Subject matter, of course, is a major determinant of the interest quality of communication; but even interesting topics can be presented in writing so dull that an interested reader cannot keep his mind on the subject. If you wish to avoid this possibility, you will need to bring your writing to life with words.

Bringing your writing to life with words is no simple undertaking. In fact, it involves techniques which practically defy description—techniques which even the most accomplished writers never completely master. In spite of the difficulty of this undertaking, however, you can bring your writing to life by following four simple but important suggestions: (1) You can select the strong and vigorous words, (2) you can use the concrete words, (3) you can prefer the active verbs, and (4) you can avoid overuse of the camouflaged verbs.

*Use strong, vigorous words.* Like people, words have personality. Some words are strong and vigorous, some are dull and weak, and others fall in between these extremes. In improving your writing skill, you should be aware of these differences whenever you write. You should become a student of words, and you should strive to select words which will produce just the right effect in your reader's mind. You should recognize, for example, that "tycoon" is stronger than "eminently successful business person," that "bear market" is stronger than "generally declining market," and that a "boom" is stronger than a "period of business prosperity." As a rule, you should make the strong words predominate.

In selecting the strong word, you should be aware that the verb is the strongest part of speech, and it is closely followed by the noun. The verb is the action word, and action by its very nature commands interest. Nouns, of course, are the doers of action—the characters in the story, so to speak. As doers of action, they attract the reader's attention.

Contrary to what you may think, adjectives and adverbs should be used sparingly. These words add length to the sentence, thereby distracting the reader's attention from the key nouns and verbs. As Voltaire phrased it, "The adjective is the enemy of the noun." In addition, adjectives and adverbs both involve subjective evaluation; and as previously noted, the objective approach is necessary in many forms of business communication.

**Use the concrete word.**    Interesting business writing is marked by specific words—words which form sharp and clear meaning in your reader's brain. Such words are concrete. Concrete words are the opposite of abstract words, which are words of fuzzy and vague meaning. In general, concrete words stand for things the reader perceives—things he can see, feel, hear, taste, or smell. Concrete words hold interest, for they move directly into the reader's experience. Because concrete words are best for holding interest, you should prefer them to abstract words wherever possible.

To a large extent, concrete words are the short, familiar words previously discussed. They are the words at the bottom of the abstraction ladder—the words which make sharp, clear meanings in the mind. In addition to being more meaningful to your reader, such words generally have more precise meanings than the other words. For example, this sentence is filled with long, unfamiliar words: "The magnitude of the increment of profits was the predominant motivating factor in the decision." Written in shorter and more familiar words, the idea becomes more concrete: "The size of the profit gained was the chief reason for the decision."

Concreteness involves more than simplicity, for many of the well-known words are abstract. Perhaps we can make a clear distinction between concrete and abstract wording by illustration. In the write-up of the results of an experiment a chemist might refer to the bad odor of a certain mixture as a "nauseous odor." But these words do little to communicate a clear mental picture in the reader's mind, for *nauseous* is a word with many different meanings. Were the chemist to say that the substance smelled like "decaying fish," his words would be likely to communicate a clear meaning in the reader's mind. One of the best-known examples of concreteness is in the advertising claim that Ivory soap is "99$\frac{44}{100}$ percent pure." Had the company used abstract words such as "Ivory soap is very pure," few people would have been impressed. But the firm used specific words, and millions took notice. Similar differences in abstract and concrete expressions are apparent in the following:

| *Abstract* | *Concrete* |
|---|---|
| A sizable profit | A 22-percent profit |
| Good accuracy | Pinpoint accuracy |
| The leading student | Top student in a class of 90 |
| The majority | Fifty-three percent |
| In the near future | By Thursday noon |
| A work-saving machine | Does the work of seven men |
| Easy to steer | Quick-steering |
| Light in weight | Featherlight |

**_Prefer active to passive verbs._**   Of all the parts of speech, the verbs are the strongest, and verbs are at their strongest when they are in the active voice. Thus, for the best in vigorous, lively writing, you should make good use of active-voice verbs. Certainly, this suggestion does not mean that you should eliminate passive voice, for passive voice has a definite place in good writing, especially when you wish to give emphasis to words other than the verb. But it does mean that you should use as much active voice as you logically can.

Active-voice verbs are those which show their subject doing the action. They contrast with the dull, passive forms which act upon their subjects. The following contrasting sentences illustrate the distinction:

*Active:*   The auditor inspected the books.
*Passive:*   The books were inspected by the auditor.

The first example clearly is the stronger. In this sentence the doer of the action acts, and the verb is short and clear. In the second example, the helping word *were* dulls the verb, and the doer of the action is relegated to a role in a prepositional phrase. The following sentences give additional proof of the superiority of active over passive voice:

| *Passive* | *Active* |
|---|---|
| The new process is believed to be superior by the investigators. | Investigators believe that the new process is superior. |
| The policy was enforced by the committee. | The committee enforced the policy. |
| The office will be inspected by Mr. Hall. | Mr. Hall will inspect the office. |
| A gain of 30.1 percent was recorded for Softlines sales. | Softlines sales gained 30.1 percent. |

|  |  |
|---|---|
| It is desired by this office that this problem be brought before the board. | This office desires that the secretary bring this problem before the board. |
| A complete reorganization of the administration was effected by the president. | The president completely reorganized the administration. |

*Avoid overuse of camouflaged verbs.*   Closely related to the problem of using abstract words and passive voice is the problem of camouflaged verbs. A verb is camouflaged when it appears in the sentence as an abstract noun rather than in verb form. For example, in the sentence "Elimination of the excess material was effected by the crew," the noun *elimination* is made out of the verb *eliminate*. Although there is nothing wrong with nouns made from verbs, in this case the noun form carries the strongest action idea of the sentence. A more vigorous phrasing would use the pure verb form, as in this example: "The crew eliminated the excess material." Likewise, it is stronger to "cancel" than to "effect a cancellation"; it is stronger to "consider" than to "give consideration to"; and it is stronger to "appraise" than to "make an appraisal." These sentences further illustrate the point:

| *Camouflaged verbs* | *Clear verb form* |
|---|---|
| Amortization of the account was effected by the staff. | The staff amortized the account. |
| Control of the water was not possible. | They could not control the water. |
| The new policy involved the standardization of the procedures. | The new policy involved standardizing the procedures. |
| Application of the mixture was accomplished. | They applied the mixture. |

From these illustrations and those of the preceding discussion of passive voice, two helpful writing rules may be gleaned. The first is to make the subjects of most sentences either persons or things. For example, rather than writing "Consideration was given to . . .," you should write "We consider. . . ." The second rule is to write most sentences in normal (subject, verb, object) order, with the real doer of action as the subject. It is when you attempt other orders that you are most likely to produce involved, strained, passive structures.

## Selecting words for precise communication

Good business writing requires some mastery of language—enough, at least, to enable the writer to communicate with reasonable accuracy. Unfortunately, all too often we select words as a matter of routine. We select words without carefully thinking out the meanings they will bring to the mind of our reader. Sometimes we even use words we do not understand. The result is writing which is as vague and fuzzy as our process of word selection.

Even though our words do not convey precise meanings, we can use them with much more precision than we do. We should all do a better job of learning more of the accepted uses of each word. Especially should we learn the shades of differences in the meanings of similar words and the different meanings various arrangements of words can bring about. For example, you must learn that the word *fewer* pertains to smaller numbers of units or individuals and that the word *less* relates to value, degree, or quantity. You must know the differences in connotation of similar words such as *secondhand, used,* and *antique; slender, thin,* and *skinny; suggest, tell,* and *inform; tramp, hobo,* and *vagabond.*

## CONSTRUCTION OF SENTENCES WHICH COMMUNICATE

Arranging your words into sentences which form meaning in your reader's mind is a major part of your task as a business writer. As with using words, this task is one of adaptation—of fitting the message to a particular reader or readers.

Largely, your task of adapting sentences to your reader is a mental one. On the one hand you visualize your reader; on the other you structure words into sentences which produce the intended meaning in his mind. In structuring your words, you are guided by your own best judgment, for constructing sentences clearly is a product of the thinking mind. The sentence is a form man has devised to express his thought units. Thus, clear and orderly sentences are the products of clear and orderly thinking; vague and disorderly sentences represent vague and disorderly thinking.

The technique of good thinking cannot be reduced to routine steps, procedures, formulas, or the like, for the process is too little understood. But sentences which are the products of good thinking do have clearly discernible characteristics. These characteristics suggest the general guidelines for good sentence construction which appear in the following paragraphs.

### Keeping sentences short

More than any other characteristic of a sentence, length is most clearly related to sentence difficulty. The longer a sentence is, the harder it is to understand. This relationship is convincingly borne out by the readability studies previously cited. And it is a logical conclusion which we may draw from an analysis of the operation of the mind. We all know that our minds have limitations. We know that they are limited in their abilities to handle complex information. Some minds, of course, can handle more complex information than others, but each one has its maximum limit.

Complexity in communicating with words is largely determined by the number of relationships and the volume of information expressed in the sentence. When an excess of information or relationships is presented in a single package, our minds have to work hard to grasp the message. In written communication, a repeated reading may be needed; and in the more extreme cases, even these may not produce results. Thus, like food, information is best consumed in bite sizes.

What is bite-size for the mind, however, depends on the mental capacity of the reader. Most of the readability studies conclude that writing aimed at the middle level of adult American readers should have an average sentence length of around 16 to 18 words. For more advanced readers the average can be higher. It must be lower for those of lower reading abilities. Of course, these length figures do not mean that short sentences of six or so words are taboo, nor do they mean that one should avoid long sentences of 30 or more words. Occasionally, short sentences may be used to emphasize an important fact, and long sentences may be skillfully constructed to subordinate some less important information. It is the average which should be in keeping with the readability level of the reader.

Differences brought about by sentence length are emphatically illustrated by the following contrasting sentences. Notice how much better the shorter versions communicate.

| *Long and hard to understand* | *Short and clear* |
|---|---|
| This memorandum is being distributed with the first-semester class cards, which are to serve as a final check on the correctness of the registration of students and are to be used later as the midsemester grade cards, which are to be submitted prior to November 16. | This memorandum is being distributed with the first-semester class cards. These cards will serve now as a final check on student registration. Later, they will be used for midsemester grades, which are due before November 16. |
| Some authorities in personnel administration object to expanding normal salary ranges to include a trainee rate because they fear that probationers may be kept at the minimum rate longer than is warranted through oversight or prejudice and because they fear that it | Some authorities in personnel administration object to expanding the normal salary range to include a trainee rate for two reasons. First, they fear that probationers may be kept at the minimum rate longer than is warranted, through oversight or prejudice. Second, |

would encourage the spread from the minimum to maximum rate range.

Regardless of their seniority or union affiliation, all employees who hope to be promoted are expected to continue their education either by enrolling in the special courses to be offered by the company, which are scheduled to be given after working hours beginning next Wednesday, or by taking approved correspondence courses selected from a list which may be seen in the training office.

they fear that it would, in effect, increase the spread from the minimum to the maximum rate range.

Regardless of their seniority or union affiliation, all employees who hope to be promoted are expected to continue their education in either of two ways. (1) They may enroll in special courses to be given by the company. (2) They may take approved correspondence courses selected from the list which may be seen in the training office.

## Using words economically

Of the many ways in which every thought may be expressed, the shorter ways usually are the best. In general, the shorter wordings save the reader time; they are clearer; and they make for more vigorous and interesting reading. Thus, you should strive for economy in the use of words.

Learning to use words economically is a matter of continuing effort. You should continuously be aware of the need for word economy. You should carefully explore and appraise the many ways of expressing each thought. You should know that the possibility of word economy depends on the subject matter in each case. You should know also that there are certain ways of expression which simply are not economical. These you should avoid. The more common of the uneconomical ways of expression are discussed in the following paragraphs.

*Cluttering phrases.* Our language is cluttered with numerous phrases which are best replaced by shorter expressions. Although the shorter forms may save only a word or two here and there, the little savings over a long piece of writing can be significant. As the following sentences illustrate, the shorter substitutes are better.

| *The long way* | *Short and improved* |
|---|---|
| *In the event that* payment is not made by January, operations will cease. | *If* payment is not made by January, operations will cease. |
| *In spite of the fact that* they received help, they failed to exceed the quota. | *Even though* they received help, they failed to exceed the quota. |
| The invoice was *in the amount of* $50,000. | The invoice was *for* $50,000. |

Here are other contrasting pairs of expressions:

| Long | Short |
|---|---|
| Along the lines of | Like |
| For the purpose of | For |
| For the reason that | Because, since |
| In the near future | Soon |
| In accordance with | By |
| In very few cases | Seldom |
| In view of the fact that | Since, because |
| On the occasion of | On |
| With regard to, with reference to | About |

**Surplus words.**  You should eliminate words which add nothing to the sentence meaning. In some instances, however, eliminating the words requires recasting the sentence, as some of the following examples illustrate:

| *Contains surplus words* | *Surplus words eliminated* |
|---|---|
| He ordered desks *which are of the* executive type. | He ordered executive-type desks. |
| *It will be noted that* the records for the past years show a steady increase in special appropriations. | The records for past years show a steady increase in special appropriations. |
| *There are* four rules *which* should be observed. | Four rules should be observed. |
| *In addition to these defects,* numerous other defects mar the operating procedure. | Numerous other defects mar the operating procedure. |
| His performance was good enough to *enable him* to qualify him for the promotion. | His performance was good enough to qualify him for promotion. |
| The machines *which were* damaged by the fire were repaired. | The machines damaged by the fire were repaired. |
| By *the* keeping *of* production records, they found the error. | By keeping production records, they found the error. |

**Roundabout construction.**  Of the many ways of saying anything, some are direct and to the point; others cover the same ground in a roundabout way. Without question, the direct ways are usually better, and you should use them. Although there are many forms of roundabout expressions (some of them overlap the preceding causes of excess wording), the following illustrations clearly show the general nature of this violation:

| *Roundabout* | *Direct and to the point* |
|---|---|
| The department budget *can be observed to be decreasing* each new year. | The department budget *decreases* each year. |
| The union is *involved in the task of receiving* the seniority provision of the contract. | The union is *reviewing* the seniority provision of the contract. |
| The president is *of the opinion that* the tax was paid. | The president *believes* the tax was paid. |
| *It is essential that* the income be used to retire the debt. | The income *must* be used to retire the debt. |
| *It is the committee's assumption that* the evidence has been gathered. | The committee *assumes* that the evidence has been gathered. |
| The supervisors should *take appropriate action to determine* whether the timecards are being inspected. | The supervisors *should determine* whether the timecards are being inspected. |
| The price increase will *afford* the company *an opportunity* to retire the debt. | A price increase will *enable* the company to retire the debt. |
| *During the time she was* employed by this company, Miss Carr was absent once. | *While* employed by this company, Miss Carr was absent once. |
| He criticized everyone he *came in contact with*. | He criticized everyone he *met*. |

**Unnecessary repetition.**   You should work to avoid unnecessary repetition of words or thoughts. Exception to this rule, however, is justified when you wish to repeat for special effect or for emphasis.

| *Needless repetition* | *Repetition eliminated* |
|---|---|
| *The provision of Section 5 provides* for a union shop. | Section 5 provides for a union shop. |
| *The assignment* of training the ineffective worker is *an assignment* we must carry out. | Training the ineffective worker is an assignment we must carry out. |
| *Modern, up-to-date* equipment will be used. | Modern equipment will be used. |
| *In the office* they found supplies *there* which had never been issued. | In the office they found supplies which had never been issued. |
| He reported for work Friday *morning* at 8 a.m. | He reported for work Friday at 8 a.m. |
| *In my opinion I think* the plan is sound. | I think the plan is sound. |

| The *important essentials* must not be neglected. | The essentials must not be neglected. |

## Considering emphasis in sentence design

All of the information you present in a letter, report, memorandum, or the like is not equally important to your message. Some subject matter, such as conclusions to reports or objectives of letters, plays a major role. On the other hand, some subject matter plays a supporting role—sometimes even an incidental one. A part of your task as a business writer is to determine the importance of each bit of information you present, and then to communicate this importance in your finished manuscript. By doing this you exercise some control over the information your reader's mind receives. Thus, you are more likely to communicate. As we shall see later in our study, you may give emphasis to information in a number of ways. The one way of concern to us now is by sentence design.

Short, simple sentences carry more emphasis than do long, more involved sentences. Short sentences stand out and call attention to their content. The mind gets the message without the interference of related or supporting information. Especially can you gain emphasis with short sentences when you place them in positions of emphasis such as the beginnings and endings of paragraphs. As we shall soon see, such positions call attention to the subject matter concerned.

Sentences which cover two or more items give less emphasis to the content. Within these sentences, varying emphasis may be given each item. Those items placed in independent clauses get major emphasis. Those placed in subordinate structures (dependent clauses, parenthetic structures, modifiers, and the like) are relegated to less important roles. Thus, by skillful design, or by a lack of it, you may present the same facts in distinctly different ways, as shown by the following illustrations.

In the first illustration, separate sentences are used to present each item of information. Each item gets special emphasis by this treatment; but because all are treated the same, none stand out. Also, the items obviously are not equally important and should not be given equal emphasis. In addition, the writing is elementary to the point of being ridiculous.

The main building was inspected on October 1. Mr. George Wills inspected the building. Mr. Wills is a vice president of the company. He found that the building has 6,500 square feet of floor space. He also found that it has 2,400 square feet of storage space. The new store must have a minimum of 6,000 square feet of floor space. It must have 2,000 square feet of storage space. Thus, the main building exceeds the space requirements for the new store. Therefore, Mr. Wills concluded that the main building is adequate for the company's needs.

In the next illustration, some of the information is subordinated, but not logically. The facts of real importance do not receive the emphasis they deserve. Logically, the points that should be emphasized are the conclusions that the building is large enough and the supporting evidence showing that floor and storage space exceeds minimum requirements.

Mr. George Wills, who inspected the main building on October 1, is a vice president of the company. His inspection, which supports the conclusion that the building is large enough for the proposed store, uncovered these facts. The store has 6,500 square feet of floor space and 2,400 square feet of storage space, which is more than the minimum requirement of 6,000 and 2,000 square feet, respectively, of floor and storage space.

The next illustration gives good emphasis to the pertinent points. The short, simple sentences placed for emphasis at the beginning present the conclusion. The supporting facts that the new building exceeds the minimum of floor and storage space requirements receive main-clause emphasis. Incidentals such as the identifying remarks about George Wills are relegated to subordinate roles.

The main building is large enough for the new store. This conclusion, made by Vice President George Wills following his October 1 inspection of the building, is based on these facts: The building's 6,500 square feet of floor space are 500 more than the 6,000 set as the minimum. The 2,400 square feet of storage space are 400 more than the 2,000 minimum requirement.

The following sentences illustrate more specific violations of logical emphasis. The first shows how placing an important idea in an appositional construction weakens the idea. Notice the increased emphasis given the idea (by position and by construction) in the second sentence.

*Weak emphasis:*    Hamilton's typewriter, a machine which has been used daily for almost 40 years, is in good condition.

*Strong emphasis:*    Although Hamilton's typewriter has been used daily for 40 years, it is in good condition.

The next sentence shows how an idea may be subordinated through placement in a participial construction. The idea receives more emphasis as a dependent clause in the second sentence.

*Weak emphasis:*    Having paid the highest dividend in its history, the company anticipates a rise in the value of its stock.

*Strong emphasis:*    Because it has paid the highest dividend in its history, the company anticipates a rise in the value of its stock.

## Arranging sentences for clarity

Words alone do not make a message, for their arrangement also plays a role in the meanings given by our minds. All languages have certain rules of arrangement which help to determine meaning. These rules are generally fixed in our minds, and they are a part of our filter operation. Thus, to violate them is to invite miscommunication.

As we all know, scholars of the past have thoroughly cataloged the rules of our language. And all of us have been exposed to these rules in our study of language. Contrary to what many of us may think, however, these rules of language are not merely arbitrary requirements set by detail-minded scholars. Rather, the rules are statements of logical relationships between words. Dangling participles, for example, confuse meaning by modifying the wrong words. Unparallel constructions leave erroneous impressions of the parts. Pronouns without clear antecedents have no definite meaning. The evidence is quite clear: The business writer must know and follow the conventional standards of his language.

Unfortunately, too many of us know too little about the conventional rules of English grammar. Why so many people have resisted this subject through years of drill at all levels of education is a mystery to educators. Obviously, the area is too broad for complete coverage in this book. Some of the points with which most of us have trouble, however, are presented for quick review in the Appendix of this book. You should not ignore their importance.

## CARE IN PARAGRAPH DESIGN

In writing, we do not communicate by words and sentences alone. Paragraphs also play a major role. As we shall see, how a paragraph is designed helps to organize its information as the information goes into our mental filter. In addition, the rest stop provided by paragraphing gives a psychological if not real boost to our receptiveness to messages.

How we should go about designing paragraphs is not easily put into words. Much of paragraph writing depends on the writer's mental ability to organize and to relate facts logically. Thus, it is a mental process about which we know little. There are, however, some general suggestions you would be wise to follow. They are summarized for you in the following paragraphs.

## Giving the paragraph unity

A first suggestion in paragraph design is to give the paragraph unity. Unity, of course, means oneness. When applied to paragraph construction, it means that you should build the paragraph around a single topic or idea. That is, you should include only this major topic or idea plus the supporting details which help to develop it. Exceptions to the rule of unity are the transitional paragraphs whose objectives are to relate preceding and succeeding topics.

Just what constitutes unity is not always easy to determine. All of a report, for example, may deal with a single topic and therefore have unity. The same could be said for each major division of the report as well as for the lesser subdivisions. Paragraph unity, however, concerns smaller units than these—usually the lowest level of a detailed outline. That is, in reports written with detailed outlines, each paragraph might well cover one of the lowest outline captions. In any event, one good test of a paragraph is to reduce its content to a single topic statement. If this statement does not cover the paragraph content, unity is not likely to be there.

## Keeping the paragraph short

In most forms of business writing, you would be wise to keep your paragraphs short. Short paragraphs help your reader to follow the organizational plan of the paper. Specifically, they help him to see the beginning and ending of each item covered, and they give added emphasis to the facts covered. In addition, short paragraphs are more inviting to the eye. People simply prefer to read material which gives them frequent breaks. This is true so long as the breaks are not too frequent. A series of very short paragraphs would leave an equally offensive choppy effect.

A glance at Figure 7–1 quickly shows the psychological effect of paragraph length. The full page of solid type appears to be more difficult and generally less inviting than the one marked by short paragraphs. Even if both contained exactly the same words, the difference would be present. Perhaps this difference is largely psychological. Psychological or not, it is real.

Just how long a paragraph should be is, of course, dependent upon the topic. Some topics are short; others are long; still others are in between. Even so, a general rule can be given as to paragraph length. Most well-organized and well-paragraphed business papers have paragraphs averaging around eight or nine lines. Some good paragraphs may be quite short—even a single sentence. And some may be well over the eight-to-nine-line average.

One good rule of thumb to follow is to question the unity of all long paragraphs—say those exceeding 12 lines. If inspection shows you that only one topic is present, you should make no change. But if the paragraph covers more than one topic, you should make additional paragraphs.

**FIGURE 7–1**

Contrasting pages showing psychological effects of long and short paragraphs

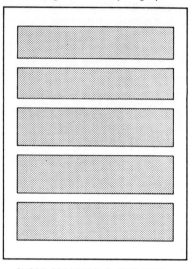

HEAVY PARAGRAPHS MAKE THE
WRITING APPEAR TO BE DULL
AND DIFFICULT.

SHORT PARAGRAPHS GIVE WELL
ORGANIZED EFFECT—INVITE THE
READER TO READ.

## Putting topic sentences to good use

In organizing your paragraphs, you will need to make effective use of the topic sentence. A topic sentence, of course, is the sentence in a paragraph which expresses the main idea of a paragraph. Around this topic sentence, the details which support or elaborate the main idea build in some logical way. Exactly how a given paragraph should build from the topic sentence largely depends on the information to be covered and on the writer's plan in covering it. Obviously, much of paragraph design must come from your mental effort. You would profit, however, by being generally acquainted with the paragraph plans most commonly used.

*Topic sentence first.*   The most widely used paragraph plan begins with the topic sentence. The supporting material then follows in some logical order. As this arrangement gives good emphasis to the major point, it will be the most useful to you as a business writer. In fact, some company manuals suggest that this arrangement be used almost altogether. As the following paragraph illustrates, this arrangement has merit.

*Illustration*

*A majority of the economists consulted think that business activity will drop during the first quarter of next year.* Of the 185 economists interviewed, 13 percent looked for continued increases in business activities; and 28 percent anticipated little or no change from the present high level. The remaining 59 percent looked for a recession. Of this group, nearly all (87 percent) believed the down curve would occur during the first quarter of the year.

***Topic sentence at end.***    Another logical paragraph arrangement places the topic sentence at the end, usually as a conclusion. The supporting details come first and in logical order build toward the topic sentence. Frequently, such paragraphs use a beginning sentence to set up or introduce the subject, as in the following illustration. Such a sentence serves as a form of topic sentence, but the real meat of the paragraph is covered in the final sentence.

### Illustration

The significant role of inventories in the economic picture should not be overlooked. At present, inventories represent 3.8 months supply. Their dollar value is the highest in history. If considered in relation to increased sales, however, they are not excessive. In fact, they are well within the range generally believed to be safe. *Thus, inventories are not likely to cause a downward swing in the economy.*

***Topic sentences within the paragraph.***    Some paragraphs are logically arranged with the topic sentence somewhere within. These paragraphs are not often used, and usually for good reason. In general, they fail to give proper emphasis to the key points in the paragraph. Even so, they may sometimes be used with good effect, as in this example:

### Illustration

Numerous materials have been used in manufacturing this part. And many have shown quite satisfactory results. *Material 329, however, is superior to them all.* Built with material 329, the part is almost twice as strong as when built with the next best material. Also, it is three ounces lighter. And most important, it is cheaper than any of the other products.

## Making the paragraph move forward

Each paragraph you write should clearly move an additional step toward your objective. Such forward movement is a good quality of paragraph design. Individual sentences have little movement, for they cover only a single thought. An orderly succession of single thoughts, however, does produce movement. In addition, good movement is helped by skillful use of transition, by smoothness in writing style, and by a general proficiency in word choice and sentence design.

Perhaps the quality of movement is easier to see than to describe. In general, it is present when the reader is made to feel at the paragraph end that he had made one sure step toward the objective. Although many arrangements can illustrate good paragraph movement, the following does the job exceptionally well:

> Three reasons justify moving from the Crowton site. First, building rock in the Crowton area is questionable. The failure of recent geological explorations in the area appears to confirm suspicions that the Crowton deposits are nearly exhausted. Second, distances from Crowton to major consumption areas make transportation costs unusually high. Obviously, any savings in transportation costs will add to company profits. Third, obsolescence of much of the equipment at the Crowton plant makes this an ideal time for relocation. New equipment could be scrapped in the Crowton area.

## MEASURING READABILITY

Much of the preceding discussion of adaptation and readable writing is supported by the findings of communication scientists over the past few decades. These studies show conclusively that different levels of readability exist. More specifically, they show that for each general level of education there is a level of writing easily read and understood. Writing that is readable to one educational level can be difficult for those below that level. To illustrate, the general level of writing that is easy reading for the college graduate is difficult for those below his educational level. A level that is easy reading for the high school senior is difficult for those below him in education. Readability levels exist for each general level of education.

### Development of readability formulas

In addition to generally supporting the basic need for adaptation, these studies have produced formulas for measuring readability. These formulas are based on the qualities of writing that show the highest correlation with levels of readability. In general, these qualities are two—sentence length and word difficulty.

Measuring sentence length is relatively easy, although a few complexities here and there do not meet the eye. Determining word difficulty, on the other hand, is somewhat complex. The studies show that word difficulty is traceable to many things—to historical origin, extent of usage, and such. But because normally the longer a word is the more difficult it is, word length is used in the formulas as a convenient gauge of word difficulty.

Of the various readability formulas used in business today, the Gunning Fog Index probably is the most popular. Other formulas are just as accurate in measuring readability, but this one is among the easiest to use.

## The Gunning Fog Index

The ease with which the Gunning Fog Index can be used is obvious from a review of the simple steps listed below. Its ease of interpretation is also obvious in that the index computed from these simple steps is in grade level of education. For example, an index of seven means that the material tested is easy reading for one at the seventh grade level. An index of 12 indicates high school graduate level of readability. And an index of 16 indicates the level of the college graduate.

The simple steps for computing the index are as follows:

1. *Select a sample.* For long pieces of writing use at least 100 words. As in all sampling procedure, the larger the sample, the more reliable the results can be. So, in measuring readability for a long manuscript one would be wise to select a number of samples at random throughout the work.

2. *Determine the average number of words per sentence.* That is, first count words and sentences in a sample selected. Then divide the total number of words by the total of sentences.

3. *Determine the percentage of hard words in the sample.* Words of three syllables or longer are considered to be hard words. But do not count as hard words (1) words that are capitalized, (2) combinations of short, easy words (*grasshopper, businessman, bookkeeper*), or (3) verb forms made into three-syllable words by adding *ed* or *es* (*repeated, caresses*).

4. *Add the two factors computed above and multiply by 0.4.* The product is the minimum grade level at which the writing is easily read.

Application of the Gunning Fog Index is illustrated with the following paragraph.

> In *general, construction* of *pictograms* follows the *general procedure* used in *constructing* bar charts. But two special rules should be followed. First, all of the picture units used must be of equal size. The *comparisons* must be made wholly on the basis of the number of *illustrations* used and never by *varying* the *areas* of the *individual* pictures used. The reason for this rule is *obvious.* The human eye is grossly *inadequate* in *comparing areas* of *geometric* designs. Second, the pictures or symbols used must *appropriately* depict the *quantity* to be *illustrated.* A *comparison* of the navies of the world, for *example,* might make use of *miniature* ship drawings. Cotton *production* might be shown by bales of cotton. *Obviously,* the drawings used must be *immediately interpreted* by the reader.

Inspection of the paragraph reveals these facts. It has 10 sentences and 129 words for an average sentence length of 13. Of the total of 129 words, 26 are considered to be hard words. Thus, the percentage of hard words is 20. From these data, the Gunning Fog Index is computed as follows.

```
Average sentence length . . . . . . . . .    13
Percentage of hard words . . . . . . . .    20
Total . . . . . . . . . . . . . . . . . . . .    33
Multiply by . . . . . . . . . . . . . . . .    .4
Grade level of readership. . . . . . . . .  13.2
```

## Critical appraisal of the formulas

Readability formulas are widely used in business today. Perhaps the reason for their popularity is the glitter of their apparent mathematical exactness. Or perhaps they are popular because they reduce to simple and workable formulas the most complex work of writing. Whatever the reason, the wise writer will look at the formulas objectively.

Unquestionably, these formulas have been a boon to improving clarity in business writing. They emphasize the main causes of failure in written communication. And they provide a convenient check and measure of the level of one's writing. But they also have some limitations.

The most serious limitation of the formulas is the primer style of writing that can result from a slavish use of them. Overly simple words and a monotonous succession of short sentences make dull reading. Dull reading doesn't hold the reader's attention. And without the reader's attention, there can be little communication.

Perhaps the formulas are most useful to the unskilled writer. By intelligent use of the formulas, he may at least be able to improve the communication quality of his work. His writing style, which was poor to begin with, does not suffer. A skilled writer, on the other hand, can violate the formulas and still communicate. Charles Dickens, for example, was a master in communicating in clear yet long sentences. So was Pope. And so are some business writers. Because most business writers fall somewhere between these extreme quality groups, the wisest course for them is to use the formulas as general guides. But never will a formula replace the clear and logical thinking that is the underpinning of all clear writing.

## A WORD OF CAUTION

Like most elements of writing, the foregoing principles must be tempered with good judgment. If followed blindly to an extreme degree, they can produce writing which takes on the appearance of being mechanical or which in some way calls attention to writing style rather than to content. For example, slavish application of the rules for short sentences could produce a primer style of writing. So could the rules stressing simple language. Such writing could be offensive to the more sophisticated reader. Your solution is to use the rules as general guides, but clear and logical thinking must guide you in your use of them.

The writing principles presented in this chapter are by no means all we may derive from communication theory. We have reviewed only the most general ones—those which may be applied in most everyday business-writing situations. The more specific applications we have reserved for coverage at the points of their best application in business-writing situations. They are liberally sprinkled throughout the application chapters which follow.

## QUESTIONS AND PROBLEMS

1. Discuss how adaptation is supported by communication theory.
2. Discuss the relationship of short and familiar words to adaptation.
3. Distinguish between active and passive voice. Discuss the advantages of emphasizing active voice.
4. Find a paragraph on some business subject that is heavy in technical words. Rewrite it for a nontechnical audience.
5. How is the suggestion to use concrete words supported by communication theory.
6. List five commonly used camouflaged verbs and rewrite them. (Do not repeat any of those given in the text.)
7. Discuss the role of sentence length in the readability of writing. Include comments on exceptions to the rule.
8. Explain the role of the topic sentence in paragraph design.
9. What is meant by paragraph unity?
10. Apply the Gunning Fog Index to the last two paragraphs of this chapter.

    *Instructions for questions 11 through 55:* Revise the following sentences to make them conform with the principles discussed in the text. They are grouped by the principles they illustrate.

## Using understandable words

(Assume that these sentences are written for high school level readers.)
11. We must terminate all deficit financing.
12. The most operative assembly-line configuration is a unidirectional flow.
13. A proportionate tax consumes a determinate apportionment of one's monetary inflow.
14. Business has an inordinate influence on governmental operations.
15. It is imperative that the consumer be unrestrained in determining his preferences.

16. Mr. Casey terminated John's employment as a consequence of his ineffectual performance.
17. Our expectations are that there will be increments in commodity value.
18. This antiquated mechanism is ineffectual for an accelerated assembly-line operation.
19. The preponderance of businessmen we consulted envision signs of improvement from the current siege of economic stagnation.
20. If liquidation becomes mandatory, we shall dispose of these assets first.

## Selecting concrete words

21. We have found that young men are best for this work.
22. He makes good grades.
23. John lost a fortune in Las Vegas.
24. If we don't receive the goods soon we will cancel.
25. Profits last year were exorbitant.

## Limiting use of passive voice

26. Our action is based on the assumption that the competition will be taken by surprise.
27. It is believed by the typical union member that his welfare is not considered to be important by management.
28. We are serviced by the Bratton Company.
29. Our safety is the responsibility of management.
30. You were directed by your supervisor to complete this assignment by noon.

## Avoiding camouflaged verbs

31. It was my duty to make a determination of the damages.
32. Harold made a recommendation that we fire Mr. Shultz.
33. We will make her give an accounting of her activities.
34. We will ask him to bring about a change in his work routine.
35. This new equipment will result in a saving in maintenance.
36. Will you please make an adjustment for this defect?

## Keeping sentences short

37. Records were set by both the New York Stock Exchange industrial index, which closed at 67.19, up 0.16 points, topping its previous high of 67.02 set Wednesday, and Standard & Poor's industrial indicator, which finished

at 123.61, up 0.20, smashing its all-time record of 123.41, also set in the prior session.

38. Dealers attributed the rate decline to several factors, including expectations that the U.S. Treasury will choose to pay off rather than refinance some $4 billion of government obligations that fall due next month, an action which would absorb even further the available supplies of short-term government securities, leaving more funds chasing skimpier stocks of the securities.

39. If you report your income on a fiscal-year basis ending in 1975, you may not take credit for any tax withheld on your calendar year 1975 earnings, inasmuch as your taxable year began in 1974, although you may include, as a part of your withholding tax credits against your fiscal 1976 tax liability, the amount of tax withheld during 1975.

40. The Consumer Education Committee is assigned the duties of keeping informed of the qualities of all consumer goods and services, especially of their strengths and shortcomings, of gathering all pertinent information on dealers' sales practices, with emphasis on practices involving honest and reasonable fairness, and of publicizing any of the information collected which may be helpful in educating the consumer.

## Using words economically

41. In view of the fact that we financed the experiment, we were entitled to some profit.

42. We will deliver the goods in the near future.

43. Mr. Watts outlined his development plans on the occasion of his acceptance of the presidency.

44. I will talk to him with regard to the new policy.

45. The candidates who had the most money won.

46. There are many obligations which we must meet.

47. We purchased coats which are lined with wolf fur.

48. Mary is of the conviction that service has improved.

49. Sales can be detected to have improved over last year.

50. It is essential that we take the actions that are necessary to correct the problem.

51. The chairman is engaged in the activities of preparing the program.

52. Martin is engaged in the process of reviving the application.

53. You should study all new innovations in your field.

54. In all probability, we are likely to suffer a loss this quarter.

55. The requirements for the job require a minimum of three years of experience.

# 8

# Correspondence: The basic elements

**A**s you move up the executive ladder in business, probably you will spend more and more of your time writing. And of all the writing you do, letters are likely to take up most of your time. In fact, if you are to be like the typical business executive, your work routine will include a period for handling the daily mail. Little that you will do the remainder of the day will be more important to your company. Yet, if you follow the practices of today's typical executives, the quality of your letter writing will rank at or near the bottom of your work activities. Hopefully, this and the following three chapters will make you an exception to this statement.

## OBJECTIVES OF THE BUSINESS LETTER

Our study of the business letter appropriately begins with an analysis of the objectives of this form of communication. That this approach is appropriate should be most obvious. As we shall see, the objectives involved in each business letter situation determine the techniques we must follow in achieving them.

### The primary goal

Primary among the letter's objectives is the immediate purpose for communicating. This goal is the one which moves us to write the letter in the first place. Perhaps we write a letter to get certain information; maybe we seek to collect money; or it could be that we are merely communicating

118

routine information to our readers. In each of these instances there is a definite need to communicate, and fulfillment of that need becomes the primary objective of the letter.

This primary objective is the obvious one, and no normal business executive would quarrel about its existence. It is not universally known, however, that it is not the only objective of a letter. There is at least one more objective in the typical business letter situation—one which may be equally important in some cases. This is the public relations objective.

## The public relations goal of the letter

In analyzing the public relations objective of the business letter, we need first to look at the overall public relations goal of the firm. It is a fundamental fact in the field of public relations that the success of a business organization is to a large extent determined by what the public thinks of the organization. In a retail operation, for example, the customer's inclination to buy again and again from the store is influenced by what he thinks of the store. Purchasers of branded products are guided in their selection among brands by the images their minds hold of the companies involved. Clients of service organizations are influenced to use organizations by the impressions they have accumulated. And so it is with all business organizations. Their customers form mental images of them. Some customers like them; some dislike them; some hold opinions somewhere between these extremes. The important point is that the more the customers like the organization, the more successful the organization is likely to be.

Whether or not a company is liked is determined by the total of the impressions its public has received of it. Throughout its existence each company makes countless impressions on the minds of its customers. Each time a customer visits a company's place of business, her mental filter records information about the organization—information about such things as the cleanliness and tidiness of the place, the friendliness of the workers, the quality of the goods and services she sees. She registers thoughts also from what she reads about the organization in the newspapers and by the advertisements the company runs. She forms a mental note each time the company's delivery truck comes by, each time she meets a company employee socially, and each time she hears a comment about the organization. She also forms notions about the company from the letters it sends her.

The total of all these impressions in the minds of the company's public determines the company's public relations. If the overall effect of these public relations is favorable, people will like the organization, and they will want to do business with it. On the other hand, if the total is heavily weighted by negative reactions, people will not be so favorably inclined to do business with the company. The obvious conclusion is that a company's public relations are important. They have a direct bearing on success and profit. Thus, organizations should work to improve their images in the minds of their public. Their effort should be a total one, covering all areas in which they make impressions.

One of the areas of impression in which a company should work for improvement is correspondence. This suggestion is valid even with companies which maintain relatively little communication with their public. As a rule, the letters that are written make strong impressions—strong for a number of reasons. In the first place, letters are highly personalized messages, for they single out a special reader. They have a more formal effect than most face-to-face situations. They receive the added impetus of the printed word, and they have the quality of permanence. Because letters make strong impressions, all organizations should work to get the maximum public relations benefit from them. Thus, we may conclude that every business letter should have the secondary objective of enhancing the company's public relations.

In determining what we should do in order to give our letters the optimum public relations effect, we need only to explore our own mental filters. Specifically, we need to ask ourselves questions such as how we like to be treated, what effects words produce on us, and what company images we like most. The answers to such questions suggest the techniques we should put to use in order to get the best public relations effort from our letters. Some of the more significant of these techniques are presented in the following pages.

## CONVERSATIONAL STYLE

Because people like people, for optimum public relations effect you should make your letters sound human. That is, you should write in words which have the effect of good conversation. This is not to say that you should write letters exactly as you would talk to the reader if you were face to face with him. Writing demands more correctness. But the words you use should be from your speaking vocabulary, and the tone of your writing should be that of good conversation. Such writing produces a warmth which all of us like. It recalls in our minds pleasant experiences with friendly people. In addition, as it uses the familiar words of our language, it is the kind of language which communicates best.

### Tendency to be formal

Contrary to what you may think, writing in a conversational manner does not come easy to all of us. In most of us there is the tendency to stiffen up, to become formal whenever we write. Instead of being the warm, friendly people we are, we become stiff and stilted. We tend to write in an unnatural manner. The results are letters which convey the impression of a cold and formal institution rather than that of a group of friendly folk doing business.

## The old "language of business"

Adding to the natural difficulty we have of writing in a conversational manner is an inherited tradition of stiff, unnatural writing. Unfortunately, the pioneer business writers using the English language developed a highly formal, unnatural style. Borrowing heavily from the legal language of the courts and the flowery expressions of the aristocracy, they developed a style of writing which became known as the "language of business." It was a highly stereotyped and cold manner of communicating and had little of the warmth that is so essential for friendly human relations. Typifying this manner of writing were such expressions as these:

| *In openings* | *In contents* | *In closings* |
|---|---|---|
| Your letter of the 7th inst. received and contents duly noted. | Please be advised | Thanking you in advance |
| We beg to advise | Said matter | Trusting this will meet with your favor |
| In compliance with yours of even date | In due course | We beg to remain |
| Your esteemed favor at hand | Inst., prox., ult. | Anticipating your favorable response |
| This is to inform you | Kind favor | Assuring you of our cooperation |
| We have before us | Kind order | Hoping to receive |
|  | Re: |  |
|  | In re |  |
|  | Said matter |  |
|  | Deem it advisable |  |
|  | Wherein you state |  |

This style of writing business letters reached its peak in the last half of the 19th century and was still very much with us in the early years of this century. In fact, the classic letter guide, *Pitman's Mercantile Correspondence,* which was a popular reference during this period, is filled with such expressions. Its introductory instructions go so far as to list this rule as the first one a correspondent should follow: "He must respect the generally recognized commercial modes of expression."[1] Illustrating this manner of word choice, the book presents this typical example:

---

[1] *Pitman's Mercantile Correspondence,* Sir Isaac Pitman & Sons, Ltd., London, n.d., p. 2.

Gentlemen,

We have to thank you for yours of 28th inst., enclosing cheque for $95.12 in payment of our invoice of 17th inst. Formal receipt enclosed herewith. Trusting to be favoured with your further orders,

> We are, Gentlemen,
>
> Yours faithfully,[2]

Fortunately, the old language of business no longer receives authoritative support. In fact, it has been under relentless attack by writing authorities for the last half century. That these efforts have been effective is unmistakably clear, for rarely do we see letters like the Pitman example in today's business. As we would expect, however, even a half century of effort is not enough to change completely the habits of business people.

In today's business letters some carry-overs from the antiquated language remain with us. As recently as the early 1960s, Richard Morris & Associates, in a study of 5,000 letters written by executives from 60 blue-chip corporations, concluded that 75 percent of the writers still overused the worn-out expressions. Thus, there are still writers among us who end their letters with "Thanking you in advance, I remain," "Trusting that you will understand my position," or the like. And there are still outcroppings of bromides such as "enclosed please find," "we wish to thank," "permit me to say," and "take the liberty."

## Use of "rubber stamps"

The language-of-business carry-overs plus some more recent additions comprise a group of words and expressions we refer to as "rubber stamps." By rubber stamps, we mean expressions we use somewhat automatically in a certain type of situation. They are expressions we use without thought. They do not fit the one case, for we would use the same expressions in any similar situations. They are used as their name implies —as rubber stamps. Because our filters have received them many times, these words produce the feeling that we are being given routine treatment. And routine treatment is far less effective than special attention in bringing about good public relations.

In addition to the language-of-business illustrations previously given, some more modern rubber stamps are commonly used. Perhaps most widely used is the "thank you for your letter" variety of opening sentence. Sincere as its intent may be, its overuse tends to place it in the routine category, and routine treatment has nowhere near the good-will-building effect that would result from specially selected words to fit the one situation involved. Also in the category is the "if I can be of any further

---

[2] *Ibid.,* p. 18.

assistance, do not hesitate to call on me" type of close. Like the preceding examples, its sincere intent may suffer from routine use. Other examples of modern-day rubber stamps are the following:

I am happy to be able to answer your letter.
I have received your letter.
This will acknowledge receipt of. . . .
According to our records. . . .
This is to inform you. . . .
In accordance with your instructions. . . .

To eliminate the timeworn expressions as well as the more modern rubber stamps, it is not necessary first to memorize long lists of the taboo words and expressions and then to avoid them. You need only to write in the language of good conversation. The worn-out words and expressions are not a part of your everyday vocabulary. If you use them at all, you have acquired them from reading the letters of others—not from your oral communicating experience. So if you will rely on your conversational vocabulary, you will be safe, and you will be writing in a style which will make a most favorable impression on your reader.

The stilted and conversational styles of writing are perhaps best described by contrasting illustrations. As you read the examples which follow, note the effects they have as they filter through your mind. Try to visualize the people who wrote each, and record your impressions of the companies they represent. You should detect marked differences.

| *Dull and stiff* | *Friendly and conversational* |
|---|---|
| This is to advise that we deem it a great pleasure to approve subject of your request as per letter of the 12th inst. | Yes, you certainly may use the equipment you asked about in your August 12th letter. |
| Pursuant to this matter, I wish to state that the aforementioned provisions are unmistakably clear. | These contract provisions are quite clear on this point. |
| This will acknowledge receipt of your May 10th order for 4 dozen Hunt slacks. Please be advised that they will be shipped in accordance with your instructions by Green Arrow Motor Freight on May 16. | Four dozen Hunt slacks should reach your store by the 18th. As you instructed, they were shipped today by Green Arrow Motor Freight. |
| Thanking you in advance. . . . | I'll sincerely appreciate |
| Herewith enclosed please find . . . | Enclosed is. . . . |
| I deem it advisable. . . . | I suggest. . . . |

I herewith hand you. . . .          Here is. . . .
Kindly advise at an early          Please let me know soon . . .
date. . . .

## YOU-VIEWPOINT

As we know from an analysis of our own mental filters, we human beings are self-centered creatures. In part, our natural tendency toward self-preservation explains this characteristic, but our self-centered nature goes beyond this. Perhaps the explanation is that basically we are selfish beings. We have structured our thinking (the whole area of our attitudes, opinions, and biases) to conform with our best interests. We want recognition; we want good things to happen to us. We like to talk about ourselves, and we like others to say good things about us. In general, we like ourselves better than we like anyone else.

Because we are self-centered, we tend to see each situation from our own point of view. In a letter-writing situation this attitude may lead us to a writer-oriented, "we-viewpoint" approach—an approach which places emphasis on us and our interests rather than on our reader and his interests. Such approaches obviously do not bring about the most positive responses in our reader, for he also is self-centered. The resulting effect is not conducive to building goodwill, nor does it help in getting him to do things you want him to do. You can achieve more positive results by writing in your reader's point of view.

### What it is

Called the "you-viewpoint" or the "you-attitude," this approach involves seeing the situation from your reader's standpoint and choosing words and strategy which will bring about a favorable response in his mind. To some extent it involves using second-person pronouns, for the words *you* and *your* clearly call attention to the reader and his interests. But the you-viewpoint goes much deeper. It is an attitude of mind. As an attitude of mind, the you-viewpoint can take many forms. It involves seeing a situation from the reader's point of view rather than from your own. It involves placing your reader in the center of things—talking to him and about him. Sometimes it may involve just being friendly and treating the other person the way he likes to be treated. And at times it may involve skillfully handling people with carefully chosen words in order to get a desired reaction from them. It involves all these things and more.

### The you-viewpoint illustrated

Like most techniques of writing, the you-viewpoint may be understood best through illustration. First, take the case of a writer whose letter objective is to present a favorable message. If he writes from his self-centered point of view, he could herald his message with words such as "I am happy to report. . . ." A you-oriented writer, on the other hand, would write something like "You will be happy to know. . . ." The messages are much the same, but the effects are different.

In a letter reporting to a new customer that his charge account has been approved, the we-viewpoint approach might take this form: "We are pleased to have your new account." The words might be favorably received by some readers, but some may see a self-centered retailer gleefully clapping his hands at the prospect of more business. The you-viewpoint approach would use words like this: "Your new charge account is now open for your convenience."

Perhaps no group is more aware of the technique of you-viewpoint presentation than the advertising copywriters. Although no one from this group would do so, a writer-oriented presentation of the message of a razor manufacturer might go like this: "We make Willett razors in three weights—light, medium, heavy." Instead, the professional copywriter would bring the reader into the center of things and talk about the product in terms of the reader's satisfaction. Probably he would come up with something like this: "So that you may choose the one razor that is just right for your beard, Willett makes razors for you in three weights—light, medium, and heavy."

Even in fairly negative messages, the you-viewpoint may be effectively used to help the reader see the most positive aspect of the situation. For example, take the case of the executive who must write a letter denying a professor's request for assistance on a research project. The answer, of course, is bad news; but it is even worse when presented in these we-viewpoint words: "We cannot comply with your request to use our office personnel on your project, for it would cost us more than we can afford." A writer skilled in word selection and the advantages of you-adaptation could cover the same ground but with much more positive results. His strategy might be to view the situation from his readers's point of view, find the one explanation which would be most convincing to this one reader, and then present this explanation in you-viewpoint language. His response might take this form: "As a business professor well acquainted with the need for close economy in all phases of office operation, you will understand why we must limit our personnel to work in our office."

The following contrasting examples provide additional proof of the different effects changes in viewpoint produce. Although they are given without explanation, with a bit of imagination you should be able to supply information on the situations they cover.

| *We-viewpoint* | *You-viewpoint* |
| --- | --- |
| I have seven years' experience as a direct-mail copywriter. | Seven years of practical experience as a direct-mail copy- |

We are happy to have your order for Kopper products, which we are sending today by Railway Express.

We sell the Forever cutlery set for the low price of $4 each, and suggest a retail price of $6.50.

Our policy prohibits us from permitting outside groups to use our equipment except on a cash rental basis.

We have been quite tolerant of your past-due account, and must now demand payment.

writer will equip me to cultivate your mail solicitations.

Your selection of Kopper products should reach you by Saturday, as they were shipped by Railway Express today.

You can reap a nice $2.50 profit on each Forever set you sell at $6.50, for your cost is only $4.

As our office is financed by your tax dollar, you will appreciate our policy of cutting operating costs by renting our equipment.

If you are to continue to enjoy the benefits of credit buying, you have no choice but to clear your account now.

## A point of controversy

Use of the you-viewpoint is a matter of some controversy. Its critics point out two major shortcomings. They say that it is insincere; and they say that it is a manipulative technique. In either event, they argue the technique is dishonest. It is better, they say, to just "tell it as it is."

These arguments have some merit. Without question the you-viewpoint can be used to the point of being obviously insincere. It can be and usually is a prime ingredient of obvious flattery. Proponents of the technique counter with the argument that insincerity and flattery need not, in fact should not, be the result of you-viewpoint effort. The objective is to treat people courteously—the way they like to be treated. People like to be singled out for attention. They naturally are more interested in themselves than in the writer. Overuse of the technique, they argue, does not justify disuse. Their argument is supported by recent research on the subject. The findings of one major study[3] show that a majority of personality types, especially the friendlier and more sensitive, react favorably to you-viewpoint treatment. A minority, mainly the less sensitive and harsh personalities, are less susceptible.

On the matter of the use of the you-viewpoint to manipulate, we must again concede a point. It is a technique of persuasion. And persuasion

---

[3] Sam J. Bruno, *The Effects of Personality Traits on the Perception of Written Mass Communication,* doctoral dissertation, Louisiana State University, Baton Rouge, 1971.

may have illegitimate goals. Proponents of the you-viewpoint counter this argument by saying that it is the goal and not the technique that should be condemned. Goals can be quite legitimate, and persuasion techniques used to reach legitimate goals are most legitimate.

The answer to the question appears to be somewhere between the extremes. As is the case in most controversies, this question is not a two-valued one. One does not have to use the you-viewpoint exclusively; neither does he have to eliminate it. He can take a middle ground. He can use the you-viewpoint when it is the friendly, sincere thing to do. And he can use it in persuasion when his goals are legitimate. In such cases, using the you-viewpoint is not deceptive. It is "telling it as it is"—or at least, as it should be. It is with this attitude in mind that we apply the technique in the following chapters.

## ACCENT ON POSITIVE LANGUAGE

Whether your letter achieves its goal will depend to a large extent on the words you use to carry your message. As you know, there are many ways of saying anything, and each way conveys a meaning different from all others. Much of the difference, of course, lies in the connotations of the words.

### Effects of words

Words which stir up positive meanings in the reader's mind usually are best for achieving your letter objectives. This is not to say that negative words have no place in business writing. They do. They are strong, and they give emphasis. There are times when you will want to use them. But most of the time your need will be for positive words, for such words are more likely to produce the effects you seek. If you are seeking some action, for example, they are the words most likely to persuade. They tend to put the reader in the right frame of mind; and they place emphasis on the more pleasant aspects of the objectives. In addition, positive words create the goodwill atmosphere we seek in most letters.

On the other hand, negative words produce the opposite effect. The negative meanings they produce in the mind may stir up your reader's resistance to your objective. Also, they are likely to be highly destructive of goodwill. Thus, in reaching your letter-writing goals, you will need to study carefully the degree of negativeness and positiveness your words convey. You will need to select those words which do the most for you in each case.

In selecting your words, generally you should be wary of those with strongly negative connotations. These are the words which convey meanings of unhappy and unpleasant events; and usually such thoughts detract from your goal. Included in this group would be words such as *mistake, problem, error, damage, loss,* and *failure.* There are also words which deny—words such as *no, do not, refuse,* and *stop.* Included also are all those words which by their sounds or connotations have unpleasant effects. Although not all of us hold similar connotations of such words, probably we would agree on these: *itch, guts, scratch, grime, sloppy, sticky, bloody, nauseous.* Or how about *gummy, slimy, bilious,* and *soggy?* Run all of these negative words through your mind. Study the meanings they produce. You should have no difficulty seeing how they tend to work against most objectives you may have in your letters.

## Examples of word choice

To illustrate the positive-to-negative word choices you have in handling letters, take the case of a corporation executive who must write a local civic group denying its request to use the company's meeting facilities. To soften the refusal, however, the executive can let the group use a conference room, which may be somewhat small for its purpose. Of the many ways of wording his response, the executive could come up with this totally negative one:

> We *regret* to inform you that we *cannot* permit you to use our clubhouse for your meeting, as the Ladies Book Club asked for it first. We can, however, let you use our conference room; but it seats *only* 60.

Review of the word connotations clearly brings out the negative words (in italics); first, the positively intended message "We *regret* to inform you" is an unmistakable harbinger of coming bad news. "Cannot permit" contains an unnecessarily harsh meaning. And notice how the one goodnews part of the message is handicapped by the limiting word "only."

Had the writer searched for more positive ways of covering the same situation, he might have written this tactful response:

> As the Ladies Book Club has reserved the clubhouse for Saturday, the best we can do is to offer you our conference room, which seats 60

Not a single negative word appears in this version. Both approaches achieve the letter's primary objective of denying a request, but the effects on the reader differ sharply. There is no question as to which technique does the better job of building and holding goodwill for the company.

For a second illustration, take the case of a correspondent who must write a letter granting the claim of a customer for some cosmetics damaged in transit. Granting a claim, of course, is the most positive ending such a situation can have. Even though he has had a somewhat unhappy experience, the customer is receiving what he wants. An unskilled writer, however, can so thoroughly recall the unhappy aspects of the problem with negative language that the happy solution is moved to the background. As this negative-filled version illustrates, the effect on the reader is destructive of his goodwill:

> We received your claim in which you *contend* that we were responsible for *damage* to three cases of Madame Dupree's lotion. We assure you that we sincerely *regret* the *problems* this has caused you. Even though we feel in all sincerity that your receiving clerks may have been *negligent,* we shall assume the *blame* and replace the *damaged* merchandise.

Obviously, this version grants the claim grudgingly, and only if there were extenuating circumstances would the company profit by such an approach. The words "in which you contend" clearly imply some doubt of the legitimacy of the claim. Even the sincerely intended expression of regret serves only to recall to the reader's mind the ugly picture of the event that has caused all the trouble. And negatives like "blame" and "damage" serve only to strengthen this recollection. Certainly, such an approach is not conducive to goodwill.

In the following version of the message the writer uses only positive aspects of the situation—what he can do to settle the problem. He does it without a single negative word. He makes no reference to the situation being corrected or to his suspicions concerning the legitimacy of the claim. The goodwill effect of his approach is more conducive to continued business relations with the reader.

> Three cases of Madame Dupree's lotion are on their way to you by Railway Express and should be on your sales floor by Saturday.

For additional illustration, compare the differing results obtained from the following contrasting positive-negative versions of letter messages. Italics mark the negative words.

| *Negative* | *Positive* |
|---|---|
| You *failed* to give us the fabric specifications of the chair you ordered. | So that you may have the one chair you want, will you please check your choice of fabric on the enclosed card? |
| Smoking is *not* permitted anywhere except in the lobby. | Smoking is permitted in the lobby only. |
| We *cannot* deliver until Friday. | We can deliver the goods on Friday. |

Chock-O-Nuts don't have that *gummy, runny* coating that makes some candies *stick* together when it gets hot.

The rich chocolate coating of Chock-O-Nuts stays crispy good throughout the summer months.

You were *wrong* in your conclusion, for paragraph 3 of our agreement clearly states. . . .

You will agree after reading paragraph 3 of our agreement that. . . .

We *regret* that we *overlooked* your coverage on this equipment and apologize for the *trouble* and *concern* it must have caused you.

You were quite right in believing that you have coverage on the equipment. We appreciate your calling the matter to our attention.

## OVERALL TONE OF COURTESY

If you can develop a courteous relationship with your reader, you will have the ideal atmosphere for success in most letter situations. Friendly people working together are likely to solve the problems they may have and to want to do business with each other. In developing a courteous tone in your letter, the techniques previously discussed will help. Certainly, writing in conversational tone, strategically emphasizing the reader's viewpoint, and carefully selecting positive wordings all generate courtesy. They all do much toward putting the reader in a favorable frame of mind. But your efforts should go beyond this.

### Singling out your reader

Courteous treatment in a letter involves many things. For one, it involves singling out your reader and writing directly to him. Letters that appear routine, that sound like form letters which could be used for any number of similar readers in a similar situation, simply do not affect us positively. They produce cold and impersonal effects as they filter through the mind. They leave us with the negative impression of routine treatment.

In individually tailoring your letter to your reader, you can make reference to him by name within the letter. Our names are dear to us, and a strategic sprinkling of references such as "as you will agree, Ms. Smith," adds to the effectiveness of the letter. A basic technique is to make your letter fit the facts of the one case rather than to use broad statements that cover a variety of similar situations. For example, a writer of a letter granting a professor permission to quote company material in the professor's book could close with this catchall comment: "If we can be of any further assistance, please call on us." Or he could make a specific reference to a fact from the one case: "We wish you the best of success on the book." Without question, the latter approach does the better job.

## Refraining from preaching

Unless you are careful, sometimes your words will take on a lecturing tone—much like that of the traditional Sunday sermon. Except in rare cases in which the reader looks up to the writer, such a preaching tone is offensive. We tend to be somewhat independent creatures. We want to be treated as equals. We do not want to be bossed. Any implication that our relationship with our reader is otherwise would be likely to stir up negative impressions in his mind. With the reader antagonized, the chances for our letter's success are dimmed.

Preaching usually comes about unintentionally, frequently when the writer is attempting to explain or justify something. A writer of a sales letter may insult his reader with these preachy words:

> You must take advantage of savings like this if you are to be success-ful. The pennies you save pile up, and in time you will have dollars.

Perhaps the point made is quite appropriate, but telling the reader something he knows very well as if he does not know it is insulting. If the words "As you know" had prefaced this message, the offense would be lessened. Merely letting the reader know that you know he knows reduces the effect of the preachiness.

Likewise, flat obvious statements fall in the preachy category. Statements like "Rapid turnover means greater profits" are very obvious to the experienced retailer and would be likely to produce negative reactions. So would most statements including words such as "you need," "you want," "you must," for they tend to talk down to the reader. Another form of the preaching tone takes this obvious question-answer pattern: "Would you like to make a deal that would make you a 38-percent profit? Of course you would!" What intelligent, self-respecting reader would not be offended by such an obvious question?

## Doing more than is expected

One sure way for you to gain goodwill is to do a little bit more than you have to for your reader. We are all aware of what the little extra acts can do in other areas of our personal relationships. Too many of us, however, do not use them in our letters. Perhaps in the mistaken belief that we are gaining conciseness, we include only the barest of essentials in our letters; the result is letters which give the effect of brusque, hurried treatments. Such treatments are inconsistent with our effort to build goodwill and frequently with our primary objectives.

The writer of a letter refusing a request for use of some of the company's equipment, for example, needs only to say no to accomplish his primary objective. This curt answer, of course, would be blunt and totally devoid of courtesy. A goodwill-conscious writer would take the time to explain and justify his answer, and he might even make suggestions for alternative steps the reader might take. The wholesaler who uses a brief extra sentence to wish one of his retailers good luck on a coming promotion has productively used his time. So has the insurance agent who includes a few words of congratulations in his letter to a policyholder who has earned some distinction. Likewise, a salesman uses good judgment when he includes in his acknowledgment letter some helpful suggestions about using the goods ordered. And the writer for a retail operation, or any other form of selling organization, could justifiably include in his letters to customers a few words about new merchandise received, new services provided, price reductions, and such.

To those who will say that these suggestions are inconsistent with the need for conciseness, we must answer that the information we speak of is needed to achieve the second objective of every business letter—the building of good public relations. Conciseness concerns the number of words needed to say what you must say. Never does it involve leaving out information that is vital to any of your objectives. On the other hand, nothing we have said should be interpreted to mean that anything or any amount of extra information is justified. You must take care that you use no more or less than you need to achieve your objectives.

## Avoiding anger

Perhaps it is unnecessary to say that you should hold your temper in your letters. There may be times when anger is justified, and letting off steam may be beneficial to us emotionally. But anger helps us to achieve the objective of a letter only when the objective is to antagonize the reader. There is no question about the effect of angry words. They destroy goodwill. Also, they bring about anger in the reader's mind. And with both writer and reader angry, there is little likelihood that the two can get together on whatever it is the letter is about.

To illustrate the effect, take the case of an insurance company correspondent who must write a letter to a policyholder. She must tell the policyholder that he (the policyholder) has made a mistake in interpreting the policy and is not covered on a case in question. Now, the correspondent may feel that any fool should be able to read his policy, so she might respond with words such as these:

> If you had read Section IV of your policy, you would know that you are not covered on accidents which occur on water.

In a sense, we might say that this statement "tells it as it is." The information is true. But it shows anger and therefore lacks tact. A more tactful writer would refer to the point of misunderstanding in a more positive and impersonal manner:

As a review of Section IV of your policy indicates, you are covered on accidents which occur on the grounds of your residence only.

Most statements made in anger do not even concern information needed in the letter. They are superfluous comments added to permit the writer to give vent to his emotions. They may take many forms—sarcasm, insults, or exclamations. You can see from the following examples that it is better to omit them from your letters:

No doubt you expect us to hold your hand.

I cannot understand your negligence.

This is the third time you have permitted your account to be delinquent.

We will not tolerate this condition.

Your careless attitude has caused us a loss in sales.

We have had it!

We have no intention of permitting this condition to continue.

## Showing sincerity

If your letters are to be effective, people must believe you. You must convince them that you mean what you say and that your efforts to be courteous and friendly are well intended. That is, your letters must have the quality of sincerity.

The best way of getting sincerity into your letters is to believe in the techniques you use. If you honestly want to be courteous, if you honestly feel that you-viewpoint treatments lead to harmonious relations, and if you honestly feel that tactful treatment spares your reader's sensitive feelings, you are likely to apply these techniques sincerely, and your sincerity will show in your writing.

*Overdoing the goodwill technique.* There are, however, two major check areas to which you might be alert. First, you will need to avoid overdoing any of your goodwill techniques. Perhaps through insincerity in what you are doing, and perhaps as a result of an overzealous effort, the techniques previously discussed can be overdone. It is easy, for example, to make too many references to your reader by name in your efforts to write the letter directly to him. And as shown in the following example, the you-viewpoint effort can go beyond the bounds of reason:

So that you may be able to buy Kantrell equipment at an extremely low price and sell at a tremendous profit, we now offer you the complete line at a 50-percent price reduction.

Likewise, this one, included in a form letter from the company president to a new charge customer, has a touch of unbelievability:

> I was delighted today to see your name listed among Morgan's new charge customers.

Or how about this one, taken from an adjustment letter of a large department store?

> We are extremely pleased to be able to help you and want you to know that your satisfaction means more than anything to us.

*Avoiding exaggeration.*  As a second check area for sincerity, you will need to watch out for exaggerated statements. Most exaggerated statements are easy to see through; thus, they can give a mark of insincerity to your letter. Exaggerations, of course, are overstatements of facts. Although a form of exaggeration is conventional in sales writing, even here there are bounds of propriety. The following examples clearly overstep these bounds:

> Already thousands of new customers are beating paths to the doors of Martin dealers.
>
> Never has there been, nor will there ever be, a fan as smooth-running and whispering-quiet as the North Wind.
>
> Everywhere women meet, they are talking about the amazing whiteness Supreme gives their clothes.

Probably most exaggerated comments involve the use of superlatives. All of us use them, and only rarely do they fit the reality about which we communicate. Words like *greatest, most amazing, finest, healthiest,* and *strongest* are seldom appropriate and not often believed. Other strong words may have similar effects—for example, *extraordinary, stupendous, delicious, more than happy, sensational, terrific, revolutionary, colossal,* and *perfection.* Such words cause us to question; rarely do we really believe them.

## TECHNIQUES OF EMPHASIS

The letters you write will contain a number of points of information, and all of them may be vital to the message. They do not all play equally important roles in achieving the letter's objectives. Some points, such as the statement of the letter's primary objective, are more important than others, such as the supporting information. Likewise, for goodwill effect the pleasanter information requires more emphasis than do the more negative aspects of your message.

As we know from our study of the communication process, the alert mind continuously receives information, but some of the information it records with greater emphasis than others. The process is the same when the mind receives the information in a letter. That is, the mind will give different degrees of stress to the points in a letter. Because it is vital to the success of a letter that the reader give each point its due stress, we need to use certain techniques to assist him in determining the importance of points. Specifically, we need to use certain emphasis techniques. There are four major ones: position, space, structure, and mechanical devices.

## Emphasis by position

The beginnings and ends of a unit of written communication carry more emphasis than do the center parts. This is true whether the unit is the letter, a paragraph of the letter, or a sentence within the paragraph. Perhaps the fresh mental energy of the reader as she begins reading each unit explains the beginning emphasis, and the recency of impression of the ending points may explain ending emphasis. Whatever the explanation, exhaustive research on advertising copy has borne out this conclusion.

Viewing the letter as a whole, the beginning sentence and the closing sentence are the major emphasis positions. Thus, you must be especially mindful of what you put in these places. The beginning and ending of the internal paragraphs are secondary emphasis positions. Your design of each paragraph should take this matter into account. To a lesser extent, the first and last words of each sentence carry more emphasis than the middle ones. So even in the design of your sentences, you can help determine the emphasis your reader will give the points in your message. In summary, your organization plan should place the points you want to stand out in these beginning and ending positions. Those points you do not want to emphasize you should bury within these emphasis positions.

## Space and emphasis

How much you say about something determines how much emphasis you give it. The more you say about something, the more emphasis you give it; and the less you say about it, the less emphasis you give it. If your letter devotes a full paragraph to one point and a scant sentence to another, the former receives more emphasis. Thus, in giving the desired effect in your letter, you will need to take care to say just enough about each bit of information you have to present.

## Sentence structure and emphasis

As we noted in Chapter 7, short simple sentences call attention to their content. Conversely, long involved ones do not. In applying this emphasis technique to your writing, you should consider carefully the possible sentence arrangements for your information. The more important information you should place in short simple sentences so that it will not have to compete with other information for the reader's attention. The less important information you should combine, taking care that the relationships are logical. In your combination sentences the more important material should be cast in independent clauses. The less important information should be relegated to subordinate structures.

## Mechanical means of emphasis

Perhaps the most obvious of the emphasis techniques are those using various mechanical devices. By "mechanical devices," we mean any of those things we can do physically to give the printed word emphasis. Most common of these devices are the underscore, quotation marks, italics, and solid capitals. Lines, arrows, and diagrams drawn on the page can also call attention to certain parts. So can the use of color, special type, and drawings. For obvious reasons of propriety, these techniques are rarely used in letters, with the possible exception of sales letters.

## COHERENCE IN THE LETTER

Your letters are made up of independent bits of information. But these bits of information do not communicate the whole message in your reader's mental filter. A part of the message is told in the relationships of the facts presented. Thus, if your message is to be communicated successfully, you must do more than communicate information. You must also make these relationships clear. Making these relationships clear is the task of giving coherence to your letter.

The one best thing you can do to give your letter coherence is to arrange the information in an order of logic—an order appropriate for the strategy of the one case. So important is this matter of letter organization that it is the primary topic of discussion in the three following chapters. Thus, we shall postpone discussion of this vital part of coherence. But logical organization usually is not enough. Various aids are needed to bridge across or tie together the information presented in the plan. These aids are known as transitional devices. We shall discuss four of the major ones: tie-in sentences, repetition of key words, use of pronouns, and link words and phrases.

## Tie-in sentences

By structuring your strategy so that one idea sets up the next, you can skillfully relate the ideas. That is, the sentences are designed to tie in two successive ideas. Notice in the following example how a job applicant tied together the first two sentences of his letter:

> As a result of increasing demand for precision instruments in the Billsburg boom area, won't you soon need another experienced and trained salesman to call on your technical accounts there?
> With seven successful years of selling Morris instruments and a degree in civil engineering, I believe I have the qualifications to do this job.

Contrast the smooth connecting sentence above with the abrupt shift this second sentence would make:

> I am 32 years of age, married, and am interested in exploring the possibilities of employment with you.

For another case, compare the following contrasting examples of sentences following the first sentence of a letter refusing an adjustment on a trenching machine. As you can see, the strategy of the initial sentence is to set up the introduction of additional information which will clear the company of responsibility:

*The initial sentence*

> Your objective review of the facts concerning the operation of your Atkins model L trencher is evidence that you are one who wants to consider all the facts in a case.

| *Good tie-in* | *Abrupt shift* |
|---|---|
| In this same spirit of friendly objectivity, we are confident that you will want to consider some additional information we have assembled. | We have found some additional information you will want to consider. |

## Repetition of key words

By repeating key words from one sentence to the next, you can make smooth connections of successive ideas. The following successive sentences illustrate this transitional technique. The sentences come from a letter refusing a request to present a lecture series for an advertising clinic.

> Because your advertising clinic is so well planned, I am confident that it can provide a really *valuable* service to practitioners in the community. To be truly *valuable*, I know you will agree, the program must be given the *time* a thorough preparation requires. As my *time* for the coming weeks is heavily committed, you will need to find someone who is in a better position to do justice to your program.

## Use of pronouns

Because they refer to words previously used, pronouns make good transitions between ideas. Thus, you should use them from time to time in forming idea connections. Especially should you use the demonstrative pronouns (*this, that, these, those*) and their adjective forms, for these words can be used clearly to relate ideas. The following examples illustrate this technique:

> Ever since the introduction of our model V ten years ago, consumers have suggested only one possible improvement—automatic controls. During all this time, *this* improvement has been the objective of Atkins research personnel. Now we proudly report that *these* efforts have been successful.

## Transitional words

Most of your thought connections you make with transitional words. These are words we all know, and we make good use of them in most of our communications. You should also make good use of them in bridging the ideas in your letters. Included in this group are words such as *in addition, besides, in spite of, in contrast, however, likewise, thus, therefore, for example,* and *also.* A more complete list appears in Chapter 14 where we review transition in report writing. That these words bridge across ideas is easy to see. Each gives a clue to the nature of the connection between what has been talked about and what comes up next. "In addition," for example, lets the reader know that what is to be discussed next is an enumeration which builds on what has been discussed. "However" clearly indicates a contrast in ideas. "Likewise" shows that what has been said and what is coming next are similar.

## A word of caution

Nothing that has been said should imply that these transition devices should be used automatically or arbitrarily in your writing. Much of your subject matter will flow smoothly without them. When they are used, however, they should be used naturally. They should blend in with the writing inconspicuously. They are devices all of us use. The trouble is that we do not always use them enough.

Perhaps the best advice concerning how to use transition is to review your writing, looking for abrupt shifts of subject matter. At these points you should consider the use of one of these devices. You should make the device blend into your writing so that it does not appear to be stuck in.

## AN APPROACH TO LETTER PROBLEMS

Your approach to planning each letter should also make good use of your knowledge of communication theory. Your efforts should be largely mental. You should analyze the communication process in the one situation, looking at the one message and its effect on the one reader. On the basis of your analysis, you should build the one letter which will do the best possible job in the one case.

### Determination of primary objective

You should begin your mental effort by getting clearly in mind your primary objective—that is, your main reason for writing the letter. It may be that you need information, that you seek to collect money, that you wish to acknowledge an order, or the like. You may even have more than one objective, as when you wish both to give information and to ask for information in the same letter, or when you must both acknowledge an order and clear a vague order in the same message. Then, of course, there is always the secondary public relations objective which all good business letters have.

### Selection of direct or indirect plan

After determining what your letter must do, your next logical step is to visualize the communication process as your objectives are conveyed to your reader. You must look into your reader's mental filter to see what his reaction to your message is likely to be. If your analysis reveals that your message will be well received, you have no major obstacle to successful communication. You can move directly to your objective without slow explanation or other introductory remarks. This plan of presentation we shall call the "direct" plan, and it will be our choice for most of the letters we write in business.

On the other extreme, if your analysis reveals that your reader is not likely to receive your objective favorably, you have obstacles to overcome before your communication can be successful. That is, in some way you will need to prepare your reader to receive your message. Perhaps you will try to overcome his resistance to your objective through persuasion. Or maybe you will seek to soften the effect of your message on him with explanation. In any event, you will have to precede talk about your objective with some form of conditioning matter. Such a plan we shall refer to as "indirect."

## Choice in the middle ground

Obviously, some letter situations are neither bad news nor good news. They lie somewhere between these extremes. They could even vary in their effects on individual readers, for as we have seen, mental filters and their reactions to reality vary sharply. In this broad middle ground you will have to use your best judgment as to whether the direct or the indirect approach will be best for the individual case.

Your decision should be based primarily on how it appears that the reader's mind will receive the message. If the decision is a close one, however, you will have to base your choice on what you think will be the response in the one case. Frequently, the information in your message will be routine business matter and will have neither very positive nor very negative effects on your reader. In such cases, you will be wise to use directness, for directness is the timesaving approach. If, however, it appears that a direct presentation of the information is startling to the reader or that his filter would expect some kind of explanation or introductory comment, some manner of indirectness is advisable. More specific analyses of the approach choices are discussed in the chapters which follow.

## The plans illustrated

To illustrate these two basic plans, we may use the case of a letter written by an oil company president to a customer, informing the customer that he has won $50,000 in a contest sponsored by the company. Certainly, the news is good. There is no question about how it will be received in the reader's filter. The writer of the letter should not dally one moment with explanation or other comment. He should move directly into his primary message with words like "The enclosed $50,000 check is your first-prize money for our contest." Any introductory comment such as "We received your contest entry" or "It has been a great pleasure for us to conduct a contest" merely slows down the message and wastes the time of all concerned. Even a positive "It gives me great pleasure to be able to give you good news" is slow and time-wasting.

When the news is bad, as in the case of a correspondent who must refuse a claim for adjustment, a direct approach would be hard on goodwill. Such beginning words as "I must refuse your claim" certainly make a negative impression in the reader's mind. They are exactly opposite to what he had hoped to hear. If the writer hopes to convince her reader that the decision is a just one, these harsh words do not put the reader in a frame of mind to listen. In many negative-news letters, only if the reader's mind can be conditioned with justifying information will the reader be able to accept the basic objective.

*Contrasting examples in two good-news letters.* Perhaps the advantages of these approaches can be seen better by contrasting applications to good-news and bad-news situations. For a good-news situation, we shall use the case of a company which is writing a college professor telling him that the company is granting her request for certain production records for use in a research project. Even though the company asks that its name not be used in any publication, the news is basically good. Now let us see what the slow and indirect approach would do to the message.

Dear Professor White:

We have received your May 2nd inquiry in which you ask for our January–March production records for use in your study. As this request has been referred to me for attention, we are pleased to report that we are very much impressed with the work you are doing. We want to help, so we are sending you all of the record sheets you asked for.

We regret to say, however, that we cannot permit you to use our name in your printed results or to identify the statistics as ours in any way. Our industry is a very competitive one, and we work hard to keep our production secret. We must insist that you comply with this restriction.

We are happy to assist you in this instance and regret again that we must ask you to guard our identity.

Sincerely yours,

The letter, of course, illustrates more than indirectness. It makes overuse of negatives which stir up antagonisms in the reader's mind. Its slow approach to the good news, however, is painfully obvious. Almost a full paragraph of introductory trivia precedes the favorable answer. The result is wasted words and wasted time. Compare this slow approach to the timesaving directness of the following version:

Dear Professor White:

Enclosed with our compliments is a copy of the production records you asked for in your May 2nd letter. We hope you will find it useful in your project. As you will understand, much of the information concerns company secrets which our competitors should not know. So we must request that our identity be kept anonymous in any published use of the data.

The work you are doing will be valuable to all of us in the industry. We wish you the best of luck in your work and look forward to reading your results.

Sincerely yours,

There should be no question about it. This is the superior plan. In addition to using more positive language, it gets directly to the point.

Thus, it wastes no words. Its directness and tact produce a goodwill effect.

*Contrasting examples of bad-news letters.* A contrasting pair of letters presents equally convincing proof of the value of the indirect approach in handling bad-news problems. The case concerns a department store correspondent who must write a charitable organization denying a request for a contribution. The following is the direct approach an unschooled letter writer might use:

> Dear Ms. Smith:
>
> We regret to inform you that we cannot grant your request for a donation to the Association's scholarship fund.
>
> There are so many requests for contributions made of us each year that we have found it necessary to budget a definite amount each year for this purpose. Our budgeted funds for this year are exhausted, so we simply cannot consider additional requests. However, we shall be able to consider your request next year.
>
> We deeply regret our inability to help you and trust that you understand our position.
>
> Sincerely yours,

Part of the bad effect produced by this letter is traceable to the overuse of negative wording. But the direct opening statement of the refusal certainly does not put the reader in the right frame of mind to hear the explanation the writer makes. Her mind receives the bad news, and the resulting negative reaction serves as a barrier to all else that may follow. In fact, she may not even read beyond the first sentence.

The more deliberate indirect approach used in the following version certainly does a better job:

> Dear Ms. Smith:
>
> Your efforts to build the scholarship fund for the Association's needy children are most commendable. We wish you good successs in your efforts for this worthy cause.
>
> We here at Aaron's are always willing to assist worthy causes whenever we can. That is why each January we budget for the year the maximum amount we feel we are able to contribute to worthy causes. Then we distribute this among the various deserving groups as far as it will go. As our budgeted contributions for this year have been made, the best we can do is to place your organization on our list for consideration next year.
>
> We wish you the best of luck in your efforts to help educate the deserving children of the Association members.
>
> Sincerely yours,

The superiority of this letter is also determined in part by its use of more positive wording. In fact, it makes the refusal without so much as using a single negative word. But its major advantage lies in its indirect approach. Its friendly opening contact sets the explanation which follows. Then the reader hears the explanation before the refusal—while he is in a mood to listen. Thus, when he receives the refusal, he knows why it must be so. If it is possible to get him to understand the writer's position, this approach is likely to succeed.

## The structure of the letter

With the general approach of your letter determined, your next step is to build the specific structure of your letter. This is largely a creative effort. It is an effort in which you construct your letter in your mind. You analyze the facts involved in your one case. You explore the strategy possibilities, keeping in mind your one reader and how his mental filter will react to the alternative strategy possibilities. In the end you should develop a specific plan—a strategy which will get done the problem at hand.

The general strategy plans discussed in the following chapters illustrate this mental effort in some detail. As you will see, these discussions are arranged by letter situations which are grouped in three broad categories. First are those situations which can best be handled by directness. Primarily, these are the good-news situations. Second come the indirect letter situations involving bad-news messages. And third are those letter situations requring more persuasive efforts. Although the second two groups have much in common, they have sufficient differences to justify separate analysis.

## Selection of the words

After you have built the plan of your letter in your mind, your final step is to select the words which will produce your message. It is at this stage that you make use of the writing principles previously described. Especially will you be concerned with those principles which will produce the goodwill tone, for building goodwill is a vital part of the plan you have created. This final step should produce for you the letters which will accomplish the objective which prompted you to begin the letter-writing effort.

## A CONCLUDING AND FORWARD LOOK

From the preceding review you should have a general idea of how business letters should be written. But to this point you have reviewed only the general tools with which to work. Now your task is to apply them—to fit them to particular letter situations. As you will see, each letter situation is an individual case to be solved, requiring a particular strategy and application of the basic elements discussed.

## QUESTIONS AND PROBLEMS

1. If it were not for the need to maintain goodwill, business letters would be much easier to write. Discuss.
2. What is conversational style, and how do we acquire it?
3. "The you-viewpoint is dishonest. It's not sincere." Discuss.
4. Distinguish between positive and negative words. When would you use each?
5. Discuss the various ways we can achieve courtesy in a letter.
6. Explain how the goodwill techniques discussed in this chapter are supported by communication theory.
7. Is anger ever justified in a business letter? Discuss.
8. Can the goodwill technique be overdone? Explain.
9. Look through letter examples in the following three chapters and find three examples of good transition.
10. Explain and illustrate the primary emphasis technique available to the business writer.
11. Write three pairs of contrasting sentences illustrating (*a*) positive and negative wording, (*b*) we- and you- viewpoint. (Avoid using examples similar to those in the text.)

# 9

# Correspondence: Situations requiring directness

**F**ORTUNATELY, you will be able to write most of your business letters in the direct order. This is good because it will save time for both you and your reader. It will save you time because it is a relatively simple letter arrangement. It will save your reader time because it presents the message concisely and quickly. Without question, this order has advantages. You will want to use it whenever your letter objective permits.

As we noted in the preceding chapter, the direct order clearly is best for good-news messages. Such messages find no resistance in the reader's mental filter; thus, there is no reason for delay. The plan is also best for most neutral messages—that is, messages that basically are neither good nor bad news. Usually such messages concern the routine exchanges of information businesses need. Businesses recognize such needs, and they participate in the exchanges willingly and routinely. Thus, such letters need little or no explanation or persuasion to get action. A simple and direct-to-the-point presentation is sufficient.

In covering the direct order of letter arrangement, we shall review the basic situations which normally require this treatment. Our coverage will not be complete, but it will include most of the types of direct letter problems you will encounter in business. In covering these situations, we shall point out suggested plans for treating them. Hopefully, you will see these plans as flexible guides to problem solving and not as rigid patterns to follow. As we shall stress again and again, each problem must be thought out and solved on its own unique facts. Even so, a similarity exists within problem types; and you will find that these plans work with most similar problems.

Although each letter situation presents its own problem facts and solution possibilities, the following discussion of common types of situations usually requiring directness should be helpful. The letter types presented are not intended to be complete. They do, however, cover most of the direct-order letter situations you will encounter in business. As we have noted, the procedures suggested are meant to serve primarily as general guides. They should not become fixed in your mind as rigid patterns of solutions to be followed blindly. Nevertheless, you should find these guides helpful in most comparable situations.

## THE ROUTINE INQUIRY

Letters which seek information are among the most common written in business. Because the exchange of information is common, the people involved are likely to conclude that such requests are reasonable, and they probably will grant them. Thus, when you are involved in such a situation, your analysis of the effects your objective will have on the reader is likely to lead to the conclusion that a direct plan is in order. Exceptions, of course, should be made when your request is a negative one, or when it is requiring explanation or conditioning. As we shall see later, such problems are handled better with an indirect plan.

After you have made the general conclusion that your request can be handled better through a direct approach, your thoughts should shift to developing the specific plan. In your mind you should organize your letter from beginning to end. And as you did in reaching your decision to use the direct approach, you should base your organization of the letter on your analysis of your reader's reactions to your message. Your analysis generally will lead you to proceed as follows.

### A question beginning

Because you have decided to use the direct approach, you will begin the routine inquiry with words that get right down to the main objective. Or, more specifically, since your objective is to ask for information, you will start out asking for information. Such directness is commendable, for it moves fast—just as most people in business want their routine to move. Also, it has the provocative form of a question. Because questions stand out from other sentences, they command extra attention in the mind. Thus, they are likely to communicate better than other sentence forms.

The nature of the question you use depends upon the nature of the problem involved, but two basic approaches are available to you. First, you could begin with a question that is a part or all of the letter's objective. If the objective involves just one question, it could be that question. If it involves a number of questions, it could be one of that number—preferably a major one. For example, in a problem in which the objective is to get answers to five questions about a company's product, the opening question could be one of the five: "Does Duro-Press withstand high temperatures and long exposure to sunrays?"

Second, should you feel that such a beginning sentence produces a startling effect, you may use a general question covering the more specific one—for example: "Will you give me, please, the answers to the following questions about your new Duro-Press products?" This general-question approach is not so direct and timesaving as the other, for all the specific questions still must be asked. But because it uses the question form of sentence, it has a mind-arresting effect. Also, it appears to be more logical to some people.

Probably the direct approach appears somewhat illogical to some because our minds have been conditioned to the indirect approach traditional writers use for such cases. The traditional inquiry begins with an explanation of the situation, and it follows the explanation with the questions to be asked. Obviously, the approach is slower than the direct one. Its effect in the mind is likely to be somewhat passive, and passive impressions frequently communicate weakly or not at all.

## Adequate explanation

Because your reader is likely to need information to assist him in answering your questions, you may need to include some explanation. As you attempt to visualize how your question will be received in your reader's mind, you should be aware of just how much or how little knowledge he already has and how much he needs to have about your situation in order to answer. If you misjudge his knowledge, he might not be able to answer, or at best he would have some difficulty answering. An inquiry about a certain product, for example, might go to a person who knows all the answers to your questions. The answers which apply in your case, however, may be determined by the specific use you plan to give the product. Unless you explain this specific use, the person cannot tell you what you want to know.

Where and how you include the necessary explanation information depend on the nature of your letter. Usually, general explanatory material that fits the entire letter is best placed following the direct opening sentence. Here it helps to reduce any startling effect a direct opening question might have. Frequently, it fits logically into this spot, serving as a qualifying or justifying sentence for the entire letter. Sometimes, in letters which ask more than one question, you will need to include explanatory material with some of the questions. If this is the case, the explanation fits best with the questions to which it pertains. Such letters may take on an organization pattern of alternating questions and exposition.

### Structured questions

If your inquiry involves just one question, you have achieved your primary objective with the initial sentence. After any necessary explanation, and after a few words of friendly closing comment, your letter is done. If multiple questions are involved, however, you will need to give some thought to their organization.

Because the mind has difficulty grasping all parts of a complex message, you will need to make certain that your questions stand out. You may make them stand out in a number of different ways. First, you may make certain that each question is in a sentence to itself. Combining two or more questions in a single sentence de-emphasizes each and invites the reader's mind to overlook some.

Second, you can structure your questions in separate paragraphs wherever this practice is logical. It is logical only when you have enough explanation and other comment about each question to justify a paragraph.

Third, you can number your questions, either in words (first, second, etc.) or with arabic numerals (1, 2, 3, etc.). Either form of number calls special attention to the words which follow them. Also, numbers serve as a convenient check and reference guide to answering the inquiry.

Fourth, you can structure your questions in question form. True questions stand out, but the sentences that merely hint at a need for information are not likely to cause much attention. The "It would be nice if you would tell me . . ." or "I should like to know . . ." variety really are not questions. They do not ask—they merely suggest. Questions that stand out are those written in question form—those using direct requests such as "Will you please tell me . . . ?" "How much would one be able to save . . . ?" "How many contract problems have you had . . . ?" and the like.

### Goodwill in the ending

Because it is the natural thing for friendly people to do, you should end routine inquiry letters with some appropriate, friendly comment. This is how you would end a face-to-face communication with the reader, and there is no reason to do otherwise in writing. To just end your letter after asking the questions would be like turning your back on someone after a conversation without saying goodbye. Any such abrupt ending would register negative meanings in your reader's mind and would defeat your goodwill efforts.

Just what you should say in the close to make a goodwill impression is a matter to be determined by the facts of the case. Your letter will receive a more positive reaction in your reader's mind if you use words selected specifically for the one case. The general "A prompt reply will be appreciated" or "Thank you in advance for your answer" varieties do little to create a sense of personal attention in the reader's mind. A much more positive reaction results from something like "If you will get this refrigeration data to me by Friday, I shall be most grateful."

## Direct inquiries illustrated

The direct inquiry is illustrated by the following examples. Even though they follow the same general plan, you will note that they differ in their internal structure. That they differ internally is evidence that the specific facts of each situation are the major determinants of the structure of the letter.

*An inquiry about advertised land.* The first illustration concerns a routine request for information from a realtor. Obviously, the reader will welcome the inquiry, for he wants to sell the property. Thus, the writer can afford to get right down to his objective. He wants the answers to four specific questions, so he begins the letter with one of them. Because such opening directness can produce a startling effect, he quickly brings in the explanatory information which justifies the inquiry. Next in the letter he brings in the remaining questions he wants answered. Wherever explanation is needed to help the reader in making his answer, it is worked in. The close of the letter is a courteous request for quick handling combined with a reference to possible quick action on the property, which is a most encouraging bit of information to the reader.

Dear Mr. Phillips:

Does the 1,200-acre tract you advertise in the July 1st issue of the *Daily Sentinel* have deep frontage on the river? A client of mine is seeking such a tract for an industrial site, and it appears that your listing could meet his needs. My client's manufacturing plant will require reasonably level, well-drained ground; so would you please give me a description of the terrain of the tract, including minimum and maximum elevation readings?

Also, will you give me a description of all public roads leading to the property? As the site must also be accessible to highway transportation, the presence of all-weather roads in the area is most important.

Should your answers meet my client's requirements, I shall want to inspect the property. As we wish to move fast on this project, may I have your answer right away? *A specific date would be more effective.*

Sincerely yours,

*A request for convention information.* The second illustration follows a somewhat different plan from the first. Rather than beginning with one of the specific questions to be asked, it starts with a general question—one that serves as a topic statement for the letter. Although not so direct as the preceding letter beginning, this one appears to be more logical in the minds of many people. Thus, it may produce more favorable results.

As you will note, following the initial general question and, in fact, worked in with it is some of the explanatory information the reader needs in answering the letter. Next comes the specific question, with additional explanation material where needed. An individually tailored and friendly compliment marks the letter's close.

Dear Ms. Briggs:

Will you please help the National Management Forum to decide whether it can meet at the Lakefront? The Forum has selected your city for its 1977 meeting, which will be held August 16, 17, and 18. In addition to the Lakefront, we of the convention committee are considering the De Lane and the White House. In making our decision, we shall need the information requested in the following questions.

Can you accommodate a group such as ours on these dates? Probably about 600 delegates will attend, and they will need about 400 rooms.

What are your convention rates? We need assurance of having available a minimum of 450 rooms, and we would be willing to guarantee 400. Would you be willing to reserve for us the rooms we shall require?

What are your charges for conference rooms? We shall need eight for each of the three days, and each should have a minimum capacity of 60. On the 18th, for the one-half-hour business meeting, we shall need a large assembly room with a capacity of 500. Can you meet these requirements?

Also, will you please send me your menu selections and prices for group dinners? On the 17th we plan our presidential dinner. About 500 can be expected for this event.

As convention plans must be announced in the next issue of our bulletin, may we have your response right away? We look forward to the possibility of being with you in 1977.

Sincerely yours,

## INQUIRIES ABOUT PEOPLE

Letters asking for information about job applicants fall in the routine inquiry group, but they involve a special problem. Because they are about people, these letters involve certain elements of privileged communication not present in other letters. For obvious reasons of courtesy, we human beings just do not exchange personal information about ourselves indiscriminately. We have moral as well as legal rights which must be protected. Inquiries about us must protect these rights.

## Privileged communication

Probably the best guide for you to follow in inquiring and reporting about people is to pursue truth and to act in good faith. In pursuing truth, you will make careful distinction between fact and opinion. For the most part, you will seek and give facts. Opinion, when it must be used, should be clearly labeled as opinion and should be supported by fact. In acting in good faith, you should seek and give only that information which is needed for business purposes. You should give and receive such information only when the person concerned has authorized it. And you should hold all such information in confidence. Because these points are so vital to fair treatment in inquiries about people, you will want to cover them in your letters.

## Question content

Letters inquiring about job applicants vary even more in their content. What you will need to know in any given case depends on the job to be done. For a sales job, for example, you would need to know about the applicant's personality—how she meets and gets along with people, how she talks, how aggressive she is, and the like. Such information might be only incidental in considering one for work as an accountant. Thus, the coverage of your content for such letters should fit the one case at hand.

Aside from the need to cover the privileged aspects of communication and the basic content differences, letters about people are much like those previously described and illustrated. As the following examples show, they begin directly, they bring in exposition whenever necessary, and they close in friendly fashion.

## An inquiry about a job applicant

The writer of the following letter did an excellent job of analyzing the work her applicant was seeking to do. Then she asked the specific questions which would help her to determine whether this one applicant could do the job. The letter begins directly, with a topic sentence form of question which serves to justify the inquiry as well as to give some needed introductory information. Next, it presents additional introductory information which serves also to cover the privileged aspects of the case. Then in following paragraphs the mixed pattern of question and exposition covers and explains the information needed. The questions are all stated in clear question form. Thus, they stand out and are easy to answer. The close is a courteous, individually tailored one which brings in another of the privileged aspects of the communication.

Dear Ms. Borders:

Will you help me to evaluate Mr. Rowe W. Hart, who is applying for work as office manager in my insurance firm? Mr. Hart has given your name as reference, indicating that he worked for you from 1972 to 1975.

In the job of office manager, Mr. Hart would be in charge of an office force of 11. The position demands leadership ability and a working knowledge of human relations. Frankly, does he have these qualifications?

Work on the job requires a thorough understanding of good office procedures. Ours is an expanding operation, and the office manager would need to adapt office procedures to meet company growth. Did Mr. Hart show this level of understanding of office administration in his work with you?

Work in our office is not steady and frequently reaches heavy peaks. To meet these peaks, our office manager must be a hard and durable worker. Does Mr. Hart have the stamina and drive to handle such an assignment?

The man for the job will have responsibility for a major part of our company's equipment. Also, he will be responsible for some of the company's expenditures. Thus, it is highly important that he be morally reliable. Do you have knowledge of anything in Mr. Hart's background which might make him a questionable risk for this assignment?

We shall, of course, hold your answers in strict confidence. And we shall appreciate whatever help you are able to give Mr. Hart and us.

Sincerely yours,

## FAVORABLE RESPONSES

When you answer an inquiry and can comply with your reader's wishes, you are telling your reader what he wants to know. The news is good, and you need not delay it. In such cases you would be wise to choose the direct pattern.

### Situation identification

In analyzing your reader's response to a favorable reply, you should note first that there is some need for identification of the situation. Yours is an answer to a letter from him. It may be that recently he has written many letters, as is the case with many business executives. His mind may be so crammed with details that the specific inquiry you are answering may not immediately be clear to him. So for reasons of quick, clear communication, you will want to identify his inquiry somewhere early in your letter.

One good way of identifying his inquiry is through use of a subject line—a mechanical device usually appearing near the salutation of the letter (see Appendix B). You may place it in any of a number of specific places—on a line between the salutation and the first sentence of the letter, to the right and on the same line as the salutation, between the salutation and the inside address, or in the upper right corner of the letter layout. Usually, the subject line contains some identifying term such as "Subject," "About," or "Reference," followed by appropriate descriptive words. The words take no one correct form, but as a minimum should include the nature of the letter and a by-date reference to the inquiry being answered. Applied to some typical response situations, something like these examples might be used:

*Subject:* Reply to your January 13th inquiry about the Little Mole trencher
About your April 27th inquiry concerning Ms. Lois Ray

You may also place the necessary identification material in the body of the letter. Because your reader should know this information early if it is to help in the communication of the basic message, it should come in the first sentence or two. Preferably, you should place it in incidental form, for it does not deserve the importance of a separate sentence. Thus, you should place it as an incidental comment somewhere in the opening. Words like "As requested in your July 7th inquiry" typify this technique.

## Good-news beginnings

Because nothing you have to say will make a better impression on your reader, you should begin with the favorable response. If your letter is an answer to a single question asked, your opening words should give this one answer. For example, a letter granting the reader's request to use certain equipment might begin like this: "Yes, you may use our duplicating equipment on the weekend of the 13th."

Your response to an inquiry involving a number of questions can use either of two approaches. One is to begin with an answer to one of the questions asked—preferably the most important one. Certainly, the approach should create a favorable effect in your reader's mind. It tells him something he wants to know. These specific answers to major questions illustrate this type of opening statement:

We have been using the Atlas lifts in our Wellsburg warehouse since early January with good results.
The Craft-O-Matic can be adapted to handle the small jobs you mentioned in your April 16th inquiry.

Your second possibility is to begin with a general statement heralding a favorable answer. This approach is not so direct as the first, for it really does not answer the question asked. It does, however, tell your reader that he will get what he wants. And it has the effect of direct treatment without the risk of startling the reader. These examples illustrate the technique:

> You certainly may have the answers to the questions you ask in your May 3rd letter.
>
> As you requested in your December 1st inquiry, here are the answers to your questions about Tiger-Craft products.

*slow beginning →*

Either of these beginnings is a great improvement over the indirect approach used by altogether too many business people. The almost conventional "Your April 1st letter has been received" or "Thank you for your April 3rd inquiry" beginnings certainly do not tell the reader what he wants to hear. They delay the main message of the letter. And as in the case of the first example, sometimes they are obvious.

## Construction of answers

If your problem concerns just one question, you have little to do after handling it in the opening. You answer it as completely as the situation requires, and you bring in whatever explanation or other information you need to achieve your objective. Then you are ready to close the letter.

If, on the other hand, your problem concerns two or more questions to be answered, you proceed to answer them. Thus, the body of your letter becomes a series of answers—answers to the specific questions your reader asks. As in all clear writing, you should work to place your answers in some logical order, perhaps in the order your reader used in his letter to you. You may even wish to number your answers, especially if your reader numbered his questions. Or you may elect to arrange your answers by paragraphs, so that each will stand out clearly in your reader's mind, thereby aiding the communication process.

## Handling negatives

When your response concerns some bad news along with the good news, you will need to handle the bad news with care. Bad news stands out. Unless you are careful, it is likely to receive more emphasis than it deserves. So, in order to give the bad news its appropriate emphasis, usually you will need to subordinate it. Conversely, you will need to emphasize the good-news part.

In giving proper emphasis to your information, you will of course make full use of the techniques of emphasis. Especially will you use position. That is, you will place good news in positions of high emphasis—at the beginnings and endings of the paragraphs as well as of the letter. The bad news you will place in secondary positions. In addition, you will want to consider the effects of space emphasis by covering the negative news quickly. Also, you will take care in selecting your words and arranging your sentences. That is, you will make judicious use of the pleasant, happy words that create good feeling. In general, your goal should be to present all of your information so that your reader gets the effect you intend for him to have.

## Consideration of "extras"

For the optimum in goodwill effect you should consider including with your answers some of the extra comments, suggestions, and so forth, which serve to build goodwill. These are the things you say and do which are not really required of you. Included would be an additional comment or question which shows an interest in the reader's problem, some extra information which may prove to be valuable, or a suggestion for use of the information supplied. In fact, it could be anything which does more than skim the surface with hurried, routine answers. Such "extras" frequently spell the difference between success and failure in the goodwill effort.

Illustrations of how such "extras" can enhance the goodwill effects of a letter are as broad as the imagination. A business executive answering a college professor's request for information on company operations could supplement the specific information requested with suggestions of other sources of information on the subject. An executive answering questions on his experiences with a computer could bring in helpful data not covered in the inquiry. Or a technical writer could take time to supplement some highly technical answers with helpful explanations. Obviously, such "extras" as these are of genuine service to the reader. Their goodwill effects are equally obvious.

## Cordiality in the close

As in most routine business letter situations, you should end the letter with friendly, cordial words which make clear your willing attitude. As much as possible, your words should be adapted to the one case. For example, a writer ending a letter answering questions about his company's experience with duplicating equipment might close with these words:

> If I can help you further in deciding whether to purchase the Multi-Cater, please write me again.

Or an executive writing to a graduate student giving him answers to certain questions for a thesis project could use this paragraph:

If I can give you any more of the information you need for your study of executive behavior, please write me. I wish you the best of luck on the project.

## Favorable replies illustrated

Illustrating the direct approach for good news is a letter written by an executive of a major shirt manufacturer. The executive's letter objective is to grant the request of a graduate student who has asked the company's cooperation in his thesis project. Specifically, the student has asked for sample shirts, which he plans to use in a study of consumer knowledge of price-quality relationships.

The letter begins with the good news, bringing in the identifying material incidentally. But it does much more than just to give an affirmative answer. Notice how it emphasizes the more positive aspects of the message. It does not just say that the company will help or that it will send the shirts. It practically gets the shirts to the reader, and it clearly says that the company is glad to cooperate. The remainder of the letter consists of friendly goodwill talk, although it does handle the question of disposing of the shirts after the research has been done. The letter's major strength in goodwill building lies in the sincere interest the writer shows in the reader's project. Its attitude of interest is further displayed in the friendly, personalized, and individually tailored close.

Dear Mr. Massey:

The Arrow shirts you requested in your June 10th letter are being rushed to you by air express as our way of helping you in the very worthwhile study you propose for your thesis.

Your study, using six of our model A-22 shirts, should offer some real insights into the price-quality relationship question for consumers. These shirts are, as you requested, free from identifying marks and labels. assorted colors, standard-point collar, barrel cuff. After you have used the shirts, you may dispose of them as you wish.

Good luck, Mr. Massey, on your project; we'll be eagerly looking forward to receiving the promised copy of your study.

Sincerely yours,

The second illustration of a favorable response is a letter from the manufacturer of a mildew-free paint to an inquiring customer. This manufacturer's product is Chem-Treat paint. In response to its advertising, the manufacturer has received an inquiry from a prospective user. The prospective customer asks many questions: Is the paint really mildew-free? Is there proof? Does the company guarantee results? Is it safe? How much does a gallon cover? Will one coat do the job on new wood? The company can answer all of the questions positively, except the last one. Two coats are required for all unpainted surfaces.

Analysis of the letter shows a direct beginning with a good-news answer. It includes no identification reference, probably on the assumption that this writer has little correspondence and would have no problem recalling the inquiry she wrote earlier. The letter presents the favorable answers in logical order, giving each the positive wording and emphasis it deserves. Notice though, how the one negative answer (about new surfaces) is subordinated by position, volume of treatment, and structure. A more positive aspect of the answer immediately follows the negative part. The close is goodwill talk, with some subtle selling strategy thrown in. "We know that you'll enjoy the long-lasting beauty of this mildew-free paint" points positively to purchase and successful use of the product.

Dear Ms. Mullins:

Yes, Chem-Treat paint will prevent mildew or we will give you back every penny of your purchase price. We know it works, for we have subjected it to exhaustive tests under all common conditions. It proved to be successful in every case.

If you will carefully follow the directions on each can, Chem-Treat paint is guaranteed safe. As the directions state, you should use Chem-Treat only in a well-ventilated room—never in a closed, tight area.

One gallon of Chem-Treat usually is enough for one-coat coverage of 500 square feet of previously painted surface. For the best results on new surfaces, you will want to apply two coats. For such surfaces you should figure about 200 square feet per gallon for a good heavy coating that will give you five years or more of beautiful protection.

We sincerely appreciate your interest in Chem-Treat paint, Ms. Mullins. We know that you'll enjoy the long-lasting beauty of this mildew-free paint.

Sincerely yours,

## ROUTINE ACKNOWLEDGMENTS

Another good-news letter is the routine acknowledgment. An acknowledgment letter is one sent to those who place an order to let them know the status of that order. An acknowledgment is routine when the order can be handled without problem—that is, when the goods can be delivered. Many routine acknowledgments are routine to the point of being form letters. In fact, some companies use printed, standard notes, sometimes with checkoff or write-in blanks to be filled in with information on the specific order. Some individually written letters are used, however, especially with new accounts and with large orders.

When properly written, the individually written acknowledgment letter can do much more than acknowledge an order, although this task remains its primary goal. The letter can serve as a goodwill-building device. By taking on a warm, personal, human tone, it can reach out and give the reader a hearty handshake. It can make her feel good about doing business with a company that cares about her, and it can make her continue to want to do business with the company.

## Acknowledgment in the beginning

As with other good-news letters, you should begin a routine acknowledgment directly—getting to the point of your objective right away. Because this letter has a more than usual goodwill need, you will want to work especially hard to make the most positive impression with your opening words. You could, for example, report the news directly with words such as these:

> Your July 7th order for assorted Mandy Candies will be shipped Monday by Green Arrow Motor Freight.

They do not produce the positive effect, however, of words which play up the receiving rather than the sending of the goods:

> Your assorted Mandy Candies which you ordered July 7 should be on your sales floor by Wednesday. They will leave our warehouse Monday by Green Arrow Motor Freight.

## Goodwill talk and resale

The typical acknowledgment letter concentrates on the goodwill function and sometimes even does some selling and reselling. It may tell of new products or new services, and it may tell about the goods being ordered. Your goodwill talk could be built from any of these topics which appear to be appropriate in the individual case.

Somewhere in the letter, as a matter of courtesy, you will need to express your appreciation for the order. After all, you are making a sale, and some form of thank-you is appropriate. If you are acknowledging a first order, your new customer deserves a warm welcome.

## A friendly, forward look

Your ending of an acknowledgment letter appropriately is a friendly, forward look. What you use here as subject matter depends on what you used in your goodwill and selling efforts earlier in the letter. If you elected to stress resale of the merchandise ordered, your close might well comment about enjoyable and profitable use of the product. If one of your objectives in the letter happens to be sales promotion, you could urge your reader to give an additional order; or if you choose a goodwill, customer-welcome theme, you could look ahead to additional opportunities to serve. In any event, you would do well to make your close tie in with the material which preceded it. And you would do well to make it fit the one case.

## Routine acknowledgments illustrated

The following two letters illustrate individually written acknowledgment letters. The first is almost in the form-letter category. It adapts to the specific situation by bringing in the facts of this one order. But obviously, its goals are limited to covering acknowledgment details and saying thank you for the order.

Dear Ms. Hammond:

You should have your Art-Grain paneling early next week, for it was shipped from our Kalamazoo warehouse this morning. Northern States Transport is the carrier. As you requested, you will be billed for the $368.50 cost on the first with the usual 2/10, n/30 terms.

We sincerely appreciate your continued business. We look forward to serving you again with quality Art-Grain products.

Sincerely yours,

In addition to acknowledging the order and expressing gratefulness, the writer of the second letter extends a warm welcome to a new customer, and it includes some resale talk about the product. The writer's apparent objective is to build a friendly relationship with this new customer and to give the information which may help in selling the products concerned. Letters such as this take time. Thus, they are not justified in all acknowledgment situations. Selectively used, however, they can be powerful tools in building profitable accounts.

Dear Mr. Gilmer:

Subject:    Shipment of goods on your
order No. 3172B

Your selection of Wonder Lures should reach you by Wednesday, for they were sent by Railway Express this morning. As you instructed, we are sending them c.o.d. Total payment will amount to $42.44, which includes our state sales tax.

As this is your first order from us, I welcome you to the Sports Distributors, Inc., circle of fine dealers. Our representative, Mr. Carl Forman, has told us of the growth your new company has had in the area. We shall be happy to do whatever we can to help you further your success.

Probably we can help you most by continuing to supply you with the best in sports equipment. We work hard to make each Wonder Lure to perfection, and I think we have succeeded. Under Uncle Billy Wonder's careful supervision, each lure is handcrafted, as have been all Wonder Lures for the past 53 years. As you may know, Uncle

Billy limits our line to only six lures—every one tested by him personally and guaranteed to be the best. It has to be a mighty good lure to replace one of the six. There is no question about it—Wonder Lures will complement the good reputation you are building.

We genuinely appreciate your order, Mr. Gilmer. And we look forward to a mutually rewarding relationship in the years ahead.

Sincerely yours,

## PERSONNEL EVALUATION REPORTS

Replies to inquiries about job applicants usually are received favorably. You can expect a favorable reaction regardless of how positive or negative the information in the letter may be. The reader is getting what she asked for. Since her reaction will be positive, you should begin these reports in the direct order.

### Directness in the opening

As you would do with the favorable-reply letter, you begin an evaluation report by telling the reader something she wants to hear. Preferably, you should answer one of the more significant questions asked you. It should be one which deserves this position of emphasis—one which serves as introductory material for the remainder of the report. For example, a report might begin with a statement of how long the person has worked for you. Such a statement serves to qualify all else which follows. Or for another example, if you are writing a report which contains nine favorable points and one unfavorable one, you would be overemphasizing the negative one by beginning with it. You would do better to select one of the nine—one which is consistent with the overall evaluation of your subject.

Should a direct move to one of the answers appear to produce a startling effect, you may use the less direct approach, which begins by telling the reader that you are complying with his request. Such a beginning might use these words:

As you requested in your May 8th letter, following is my evaluation of Mr. Garton L. Ford.

Like similar beginnings cited in preceding direct letters, this one tends to explain while retaining the effects of directness.

Employee evaluation reports are written in response to inquiries; so they have some need for early identification in order to tie in quickly with the correspondence being answered. You may wish to use the subject block for this purpose. Or you may wish to acknowledge the preceding letter incidentally, as is done in the illustration sentence above. Also, since they concern confidential information, these reports require the same privileged communication treatment given to the inquiry letters they answer. Thus, somewhere in the letter you will need to consider labeling the information as confidential; and you will want to make it clear by word or implication that the report has been authorized, that it was requested, and that the information is to be used for business purposes only.

## Systematic presentation of facts

Most of the remainder of your report should concern the information the reader wants. If your reader's inquiry includes specific questions, your response should include the answers to these questions. On the other hand, if his inquiry is a general one, you must decide what he needs. Your content decision should be guided by your analysis of the work for which the applicant is being considered. You should select for presentation those points which are important in doing the work.

You should present your information in as orderly and systematic a manner as you can devise. If you are only answering a reader's questions, you would do well to organize your information around his questions. If his inquiry is a general one, leaving the content up to you, you will need to find some logical order of organization. Especially should you seek to organize so that you eliminate overlap and repetition. In general, you should work to keep related information together, and you should find a sequence which will permit the information to flow naturally and smoothly.

## The problem of fair reporting

As a fair-minded writer, you will want to be careful that your employee evaluation reports convey a correct picture. To present a job applicant in too positive a light would be unfair to your reader, and to present your subject too negatively would be unfair to him. Your task will be to find just the right picture and to try hard to convey this picture with your words.

Conveying a true picture, as we have noted in our study of words, is no simple undertaking. Words have imprecise and inconsistent meanings in our minds. But words do not present the only difficulties in our efforts to make a truthful report. Perhaps even more important is the material you select for presentation and the emphasis you give this information.

In selecting the information for presentation, you should make a careful distinction between fact and opinion. For the most part, your report should contain fact. But sometimes opinions are sought. If you choose an opinion, it should be clearly labeled as opinion; and it should be supported by fact.

Even if every item in your report is verifiable fact, the report could be unfair. The reason is that negative points tend to stand out. They overshadow the positive ones. For example, you could write all day about the merits of a certain person; but if you ended with the comment that he was arrested for theft, this one negative point would be likely to stand out above everything else. Perhaps in some minds it would erase all else.

The fact that negatives stand out means that in your letter report you will need to be very careful in handling negative points. You will want to give them only the emphasis they deserve—just enough to convey the true picture in your one case. Frequently, this need for fair treatment requires that you subordinate the negative point of your report. Not to do so would be to give these points more emphasis than they deserve.

To illustrate, take a report on a person who, in spite of a physical disability, has a good record. If you place this one negative point in the first or last sentence, you make it stand out. It may stand out too much even if you place it within the letter at a paragraph beginning or ending, or if you spend a full paragraph on the details of this one point. If the disability is to receive its due emphasis, you must treat it in more subordinate fashion.

Nothing that has been said should be interpreted to mean that shortcomings of the subject of your report should be hidden, or that any form of wrong information should be communicated. Quite the contrary is intended. If your subject is a scoundrel, your words should show that he is a scoundrel. If he is a model human being, your words should reflect this status. Purely and simply, your task is to communicate a true picture, whatever that picture may be. You can communicate a true picture only by using emphasis devices to place every fact in the perspective due it.

## Natural friendliness in the close

As you should do in all friendly business letters, you should close employee evaluation reports with some appropriate goodwill comment. A sentence or two usually will do the job. As in other similar situations, you should strive to make it fit the one case. Above all, you should avoid the "rubber stamps" that so often find their way into this type of letter.

## A case example

Illustrating good technique in a personnel evaluation report is the following letter. The writer of this letter has a well-qualified person to write about—a new holder of a doctoral degree who is looking for work as a university instructor. Although the man is well-qualified, he has a number of minor weaknesses which in all honesty must be covered. He is a good but not brilliant scholar; he has a slight speech problem; and he sometimes irritates others with his extreme preoccupation with his work. The writer covers all three of these negative points in subordinate fashion, giving each the emphasis he feels it deserves. The result is a fair appraisal of a generally good applicant.

Especially commendable in the letter is the writer's logical organization of the subject matter. Notice how the direct opening gives a summary evaluation of the applicant. And notice how this evaluation sets up the three areas of discussion which form the organization plan of the letter. The plan is a most orderly one.

Dear Dean Koogan:

Dr. Harlan A. McQueen, about whom you inquired in your January 31st letter, is a competent scholar, a diligent worker, and a capable teacher in the classroom.

His scholarship is evidenced by his 3.7 grade-point record (4.0 basis) with us as well as his good undergraduate record at Southern Illinois University. In the two classes he had with me, he did good work, making A's in each. Although I did not find him to be a brilliant student of management, he did demonstrate a marked degree of scholarly inquisitiveness. With this inquisitiveness I fully expect him to make some normal contribution to his field of research. At times I have felt that he tends to get lost in the minutiae of detail and to overlook the obvious.

Perhaps Dr. McQueen's outstanding quality is his extreme dedication to work. Of all the graduate students I have known, I have observed none who works more diligently than he. What he lacks in native intelligence, he overcomes with tireless dedication. So dedicated and interested in his work is he that he sometimes forgets that all those around him do not share his enthusiasm for his topic of interest.

During the three years I have known him, he served as a graduate assistant under my direction. He does a commendable job in the classroom in spite of a slight hesitancy in speech. He prepares his classwork diligently, and he extracts good work from his students. He is sincerely interested in his students, and he spends much time counseling them.

In summary, Dean Koogan, I recommend Dr. McQueen to you as a teacher of industrial management. If I can help you further in your evaluation of him, please write me again.

Sincerely yours,

## CLAIM LETTERS

When things go wrong between a business and its customers, someone usually makes an effort to right the wrong. Usually, the person is the one offended. The offended person begins by calling the trouble to the attention of those responsible. Sometimes she takes this step through a letter. When she does, the letter she writes is a claim letter.

## Directness in spite of negativeness

As you analyze a claim situation, you will see clearly that it is a situation steeped in negativeness. Goods have been damaged or lost, a product has failed to perform, service has proved to be ineffective, or the like. It is truly an unhappy situation for the writer. Usually, when the news you have to present is bad, you will elect to use an indirect approach. In this case, however, you will use a direct one—and for good reason.

In the first place, most business executives want to please their customers. When they do not please, they want to know about it. They want to make the adjustment necessary to make the customer happy. There is no need to persuade the customer to do the right thing. Neither is there need to break the news gently.

In the second place, directness lends strength to your claim. To begin directly with the trouble emphasizes it and shows your confidence in reporting it. In fact, some readers would interpret indirectness as weakness. Since your chances of getting a favorable adjustment depend in large part on the strength of your claim, you will want to use the arrangement which will contribute to strength.

## Need for identifying facts

Because the claim letter is about a particular transaction, item of merchandise, service call, or the like, you will need to bring in the necessary identification material early in the letter. What you bring in depends on what is needed in each case—invoice number, order date or number, serial number of product, etc. You should include enough to permit your reader to determine quickly just what your claim is about. Without this information, your reader's mental filter would be thoroughly confused.

As in the letter situation previously discussed, such identification can be handled incidentally or by subject line. Should you elect to use the subject line, you may be hesitant to identify the situation, since it is negative. Your directness logically can start right here, however, through the use of words which lend strength to your claim. The following examples illustrate this manner of identification:

> *Subject:*  Breakage of Tira cologne
> shipped on invoice No. 317A
> dated July 4, 1976
>
> *Subject:*  Failure of model N pump,
> serial No. 31510,
> purchased May 15, 1976

## Forthright statement of what is wrong

In writing the claim that will communicate with the courteous firmness and strength that you want, you should tell the trouble right away. Preferably you should do it in the first main clause, for any other arrangement would weaken your case. Your initial statement should move as far as is possible into the facts of the situation. If there are details of identification not covered in the subject line, you might need to work these into your letter, perhaps somewhere near the beginning. But this you should do incidentally.

In some instances, you may wish to do more than just name the problem. You may wish to explain also any special effects the problem may have caused. A broken machine, for example, may have stopped an entire assembly line. Or damaged merchandise ordered for resale may have cost the buyer a loss in sales, or perhaps even a loss of customers. By interpreting the breakage, loss, or the like in terms of its effect, you strengthen your claim. And sometimes you may need a stronger approach to enable you to get the relief you seek. The following two first sentences of claim letters illustrate this technique:

> The total content of 8 of the 11 cartons of Sea Mist cologne was broken on arrival and could not be used for our advertising promotion.

> The model H freezer (serial No. 71312) we purchased from you last September has suddenly quit working, destroying $312 of frozen foods in the process.

## Explanation of facts

After indicating what is wrong, your next logical step is to present the supporting facts. This you should do in a straightforward manner, being as factual and objective about it as you can. You will need to take care to tell your reader just what went wrong, what evidence you have, the extent of the damage—in fact, everything you know which could affect the decision.

In presenting the facts of the case, you will have to watch your words carefully. Any words which tend to accuse the reader of wrongdoing or which imply a distrust of his sincerity will work against your claim. So will words which give an impression of anger. Although anger may work effectively in some cases, it is not likely to be effective in cases which require persuasion to convince the reader. As we have noted, angry and accusing words tend to put the reader on the defensive and to arouse resistance. With resistance aroused, your chances of receiving a successful settlement are diminished.

## Choice in handling the error

The facts you present should build convincing proof of your claim. So after you have presented them, you may logically move to the handling of your claim. How you handle your claim is to some extent a matter for you to decide, although the facts of the case may clearly point to one of the possibilities as being the superior one.

One possibility is to state specifically what you want the reader to do to correct the wrong. Perhaps you will want your money returned, or new merchandise, or free repairs. Clearly stating what you want strengthens your case, for giving you something short of what you seek gives the adjuster an added negative hurdle to clear.

When you know that your reader and her company have a most favorable adjustment reputation, you may wish to let them determine what is to be done. Such companies will try hard to make an equitable adjustment. In fact, they often do more than is necessary and more than you would dare ask them to do.

## Doubt-removing friendliness in the close

Your final friendly words should remove all doubt about your cordial attitude. For added strength, when strength is needed to support a claim, you could express grateful appreciation for what you seek. This suggestion does not support use of the timeworn "Thanking you in advance" wording. Instead, something like "I shall be grateful if you can get the new merchandise to me in time for my Friday sale" would be better.

## Two claim situations

Illustrating the direct approach to establishing a claim, the following letter begins with a clear statement of what went wrong and the effects of the error. Then, in a tone that shows firmness without sign of anger or accusation of wrongdoing, it relates precisely what went wrong. It asks for a specific remedy, and it covers disposition of the damaged merchandise. Its ending uses some subtle persuasion by implying confidence in the reader, yet it leaves no doubt as to the continued friendship of the writer.

Dear Ms. Golby:

> *Subject:*    Damage to Fireboy extinguishers,
> your invoice 341A

The corroded condition of all of the Fireboy extinguishers received today makes them unfit for sale.

At the time of delivery the condition of your shipment was called to our attention by the Red Arrow Freight Company driver. Upon inspection, we found all boxes thoroughly soaked with fluid. Further inspection revealed that at least six of the extinguishers had leaked acid from the cap screws. As a result, the chrome finish of all units has been badly damaged.

As the Fireboy has been our best seller, will you rush 24 replacements for the defective units right away? Also, will you please instruct me as to what I should do with the defective units?

I am aware, of course, that errors like this will happen in spite of all precautions, and I am confident that you will take care of this problem with your usual courtesy.

Sincerely yours,

A second illustration follows the same general plan, but it differs in one application. Its opening does not clearly name the trouble. Instead, it merely reports that the product is defective. Obviously, it is not so direct as the preceding opening. It has some added strength, however, in the moral trap of the words indicating that the reader "will want to know" about the trouble.

Dear Mr. Samuels:

*Subject:* Malfunction of Stay-Cool
model M, serial No. 37471

You will want to know, I feel sure, that the Stay-Cool window air conditioner I ordered from you on May 7 is not performing well.

Apparently, the difficulty is in the thermostat, for the unit will not maintain a consistent temperature. Although the compressor does cut on and off automatically from time to time, the room temperature fluctuates widely between changes.

In addition, the unit arrived with a defective temperature control knob. It was severely cracked, and after short use it broke completely. I had not intended to do anything about so small a matter, but I feel certain that you will want to take care of this matter, also.

As you have no repair representative convenient to me, I should be happy to install these two parts myself. So will you please send them to me? Should you wish, I shall gladly send you the defective ones.

As the weather is becoming unbearable, I shall appreciate your promptness in mailing the parts to me.

Sincerely yours,

## ADJUSTMENT GRANT

When you can grant a claim, the situation is a happy one for your reader. So, when you transmit the decision by letter, there is no reason to justify or explain. Instead, you should present your message in the direct order that is appropriate for other presentations of favorable news.

## Need to overcome negative impressions

Even though your basic objective is a good-news one, your situation is not all positive. If you will place yourself in your reader's situation to see things through his mental filter, you will understand why. As the reader sees it, something bad has happened—goods have been damaged, equipment has failed to work, sales have been lost, and the like. He has suffered some unpleasant experiences, and the ugly pictures of them remain in his mind. His ill feelings are likely to be focused in two directions—on your company and on your product or service.

Granting the claim is likely to take care of any ill feelings your reader may have toward you or your company. Certainly, by doing what the reader wants you to do you have helped to improve your relations with him. But just correcting the error is not likely to regain any of the confidence he may have lost in your product or your service. At this stage, he could conclude that you are a nice group of people but your products or services are bad.

## Direct presentation of decision

Because the basic news is good, you should begin your adjustment-grant letters with a direct statement of your answer. You need spend no words in introductory explanation or conditioning talk. Since your letter is a response to one the reader wrote, however, you will need to identify the preceding correspondence. This you can do by incidental reference within the first sentence, or by use of a subject line.

The news you have to present is certain to create a favorable response, and you should take full advantage of it. For the best effect, you should select words that go as far as words can go to enhance the positiveness of your answer. You may even be able to present your decision in terms of customer satisfaction, as is done in this example:

> The enclosed check for $82.50 is our way of proving to you that we at Strickland's value your satisfaction highly.

## Avoidance of negatives

In the opening as well as throughout the letter, you will want to avoid using words which tend to recall unnecessarily in your reader's mental filter the bad situation you are correcting. Your goal is to change your reader's mental picture of your company and your product from negative to positive, and you do not help your case by recalling memories of what went wrong. Your emphasis should be on what you are doing to correct the wrong—not on the wrong itself.

Illustrating the point are the truly negative words which describe the situation—words like *mistake, trouble, damage, broken,* and *loss.* Also negative are the apologies which begin some letters of this type. Even though well intended, the somewhat conventional "We sincerely regret the inconvenience caused you" type of comment does not produce optimum results. Equally negative are such general references as "problem," "difficulty," and "misunderstanding." Even though you may need to talk about the problem somewhere in the letter, you should try to do so using a minimum of negative words.

### Regaining lost confidence

After your good news has put your reader in a happy frame of mind, he is likely to be receptive to whatever else you will say. He now knows that you are on his side—that he has won his case. The situation is now ideal to work on your secondary objective of regaining confidence lost.

Except in those cases in which the cause of the difficulty is routine or incidental, you will need to try to regain lost confidence. Just what you must do and how you must do it depend on the facts of the case. You will need to survey the one situation to see what the facts are. If something can be done to correct a bad procedure or a product defect, you should do it. Then you should present this information to your reader as convincingly and positively as you can. If what went wrong was a rare, unavoidable event, you should explain this situation to your reader. Sometimes you will need to explain how a product should be used or cared for, and sometimes you will need to resell the product. Whatever it is that you can do and say that will regain lost confidence, you should do and say.

In attempting to regain lost confidence, you must be especially mindful of your choice of words. Since you will be talking about what went wrong, it will be easy to slip into negative references. As you can see from the example letters, it is possible to write about negative things without using negative words.

### Happiness in the close

Regardless of how positively you handle the preceding parts of the letter, the problem is still filled with negative elements. So, for the best in goodwill effect, you will need to end the letter on a happy note. Your final words should do as much as you can to move your reader's mind away from the unpleasant situation which caused the adjustment problem.

Your choice of subject matter for the close again depends on what is appropriate for the one case. It could be a forward look to happy future relations, a comment about a product improvement, talk about announcements of a coming promotion, and the like. You should include not a word which recalls to his mind the negative situation. Even an apology would be negative, for it would bring back to mind that for which the apology is being made.

## Two case illustrations

The logic of this direct approach to granting adjustments is applied in the following illustrations. The first concerns acceptance of a legitimate claim for fire extinguishers damaged in transit. After making proper identification of the transaction involved and of preceding correspondence, it states the good news in words which add to the happiness of the message. With a reader-viewpoint explanation, it leads into a review of what happened. Without as much as a single negative word, it makes clear the cause of the problem and what has been done to prevent its recurrence. After handling the essential matter of disposing of the damaged merchandise, it closes with positive talk which is far removed from the problem of the claim.

> Dear Ms. Watson:
>
> *Subject:*   Your December 3rd report
>    on invoice 1348
>
> Two dozen new and thoroughly tested Fireboy extinguishers should reach your sales floor in time for your Saturday promotion. They were shipped early today by Red Line Motor Freight.
>
> As your satisfaction with our service is important to us, we have thoroughly checked all the Fireboys in stock. In the past, we have assumed that all of them were checked for tight seals at the factory. We learned, thanks to you, that now we must systematically check each one. Already we have set up a system of checks as part of our normal handling procedure.
>
> When you receive the new Fireboys, will you please return the original group by motor freight? Of course, we shall bear all transportation charges.
>
> As you may know, the new Fireboys have practically revolutionized the extinguisher field. Their compact size and efficiency have made them the top seller in the field in a matter of only three months. We hope that they will play their part in the success of your coming sale.
>
> Sincerely yours,

The second illustration follows much the same plan. It differs primarily in the nature of its explanation. It can make no face-saving explanation of what happened or what it will do to prevent recurrence of the happening. It can only make a plea of the human error with which all businesses are plagued from time to time. It makes the plea most positively and convincingly.

Dear Ms. Brown:

*Subject:*    Your October 3d inquiry
concerning order No. A4170

Your Mecca sterling cutlery properly monogrammed with an Old English B should reach you in a day or two. It is our evidence to you that Mecca's century-old record for satisfaction is as genuine as the sterling itself.

Because we value your satisfaction so much, we have carefully looked into the handling of your order. As you probably guessed, we found it was just one of those rare situations which even the most careful human beings occasionally get into. Two people read and checked the order, and two people overlooked the "Old English monogram" specification. You will agree, I feel sure, that even in the best-run businesses such things happen. Even so, we are redoubling our efforts to continue to give the fast, dependable service Mecca customers have come to expect over the years.

We know that your Mecca sterling will enhance many a dinner party through the years ahead. And we wish you the best in enjoyment from your set.

Sincerely yours,

## ORDER LETTERS

Letters which order goods are not so often written nowadays as they once were. Most orders today either are placed orally with salespeople or are made on standard order forms. Nevertheless, some orders must be made by letter. And when they are written, they carry more importance than most other business letters.

### Clear and forthright authorization

Order letters mean business and profits for the reader; so you will want to use the direct approach which is appropriate for the good-news letter. Since your basic objective is to order goods, your first main words should authorize shipment—in clear, specific language. Your words should say, in effect, "Please send me. . . ." Any wording which merely hints or suggests ("I am in need of . . ." or "I should like . . .") falls short of the ideal.

### Specific coverage of the sale

The remainder of your letter is an exercise in clear and orderly coverage of the details your reader needs to know. Your letter is likely to contain many facts, and unless these facts are arranged in good order, they are likely to overwhelm or confuse your reader's mind. As we have noted, the mind can receive only a limited number of facts in one message, so we must work to keep the facts in the best possible order for quick comprehension.

There is no one best sequence to use for the descriptive information needed in an order. You would, however, be wise to begin with the quantity and units you need. Then, in the sequence illustrated, you may list these descriptive parts:

Catalog number
Basic name (including trade names and brands when helpful)
Points of description (color, size, weight, etc.)
Unit price
Total price

In finished form, a description might read like this:

3 dozen   No. 712AC, Woolsey claw hammer,
          drop-forged head, hickory
          handle, 13 inches overall length,
          16 ounces, at $12.74 per dozen........$37.22

For quick and easy communication you will need to arrange this descriptive information in orderly and neat fashion. There is no one best form, although the illustration letter below gives one good arrangement. Most acceptable arrangements keep the quantities and units in a clear column to the left. The remaining description is set off to the right with carry-over lines dropping under the preceding beginnings of the description (see example letter on page 173). Price extensions appear to the right of the listing and are also set off in a clear column.

In addition to describing the items ordered, you will need to include other vital information. You will need to give whatever shipping instructions are necessary and any information regarding payment (charge, cash, c.o.d.). Some of this information you may work into the beginning of the letter, following the beginning authorization statement. The remainder you may include with your closing remarks. The essential point is that you include all the reader needs to know to fill your order.

## A cordial close

You should end the order letter with a short and friendly comment relating to the order. As was mentioned earlier, it could even include some of the shipping instructions not covered previously. It should not demand, command, or talk down. But it would be quite appropriate to request early action, as in this example:

As we have promised to make our first delivery on the 17th, will you please get the supplies to us by the 13th at the latest? We shall sincerely appreciate it.

## An order illustrated

The specimen order letter which follows shows good form in arranging the detailed facts in an order. It authorizes the shipment right away, as it should; it covers the necessary shipping details clearly and quickly; and it ends with appropriate cordiality. It meets the requirements of a good order letter in every respect.

Dear Ms. Green:

Please send me the office supplies listed below by prepaid parcel post at the address above. I am ordering from your September 7th price list.

| | | |
|---|---|---|
| 10 reams | No. 321A, Scroll bond paper, white, 257-rag, 8½ by 11 inches, 20-pound, @ 3.25 . . . . . . . . | $ 32.50 |
| 4 boxes | No. 106B, carbon paper, 8½ by 11 inches, medium weight, @ $4.40 . . . . . . . . | 17.60 |
| 5 dozen | No. 1171A, typewriter ribbons, Royal, black record, medium-inked, @ $10.50 . . . . . . . . . . . . . | 52.50 |
| 5 each | No. 215H, typewriter stands, Luddell model K, 26 inches high, 161 by 24-inch top, black enamel, @ $9.60 . . . . . . . . | 48.00 |
| | | $150.60 |

Please charge the amount to me on the usual 2/10, n/60 terms. As our supplies of these items are nearly depleted, I shall appreciate any rush service you can give this order.

Sincerely yours,

# Letter problems—1

1. As director of training for the Permian Oil Company (headquarters Houston, Texas), you have received a brochure describing Clarion University's Executive Development School. The practical educational program described in the brochure appears to be just what Permian needs to sharpen the administrative skills of a select group of its promising executives. So you decide to write for some details not covered in the brochure.

Because Permian would send six people to the program each year for at least three years, you'd like to know whether quantity discounts can be given from the $1,460 package cost of the six-weeks session. Before you send anyone to such a program, you will certainly need to check out the program. So you will ask for names of companies that have sent people in the past. Then there is another question that bothers you. Some of the executives you want to send are technical people (engineers, scientists, etc.) who have had no business course work. You wonder whether they will be at a disadvantage competing with people trained in the business disciplines. Also, some of your people are likely to want college credit for the work. So you'll need to check into this matter.

Write the letter to Dr. David. A. Wattle, director of the program.

2. Assume that you have just been promoted to the position of director of South American activities for the Remingway Manufacturing Company, builders of heavy-duty construction equipment. You have all the qualifications for the job except one—your Spanish is lousy. You will have to learn the language—and fast.

In discussing the matter with a good friend, you learn about a Professor Roberto Rodriguez at Carter University who conducts a high-intensity Spanish language course. As your friend tells it, Professor Rodriguez can work with individuals on an all-day basis for two seven-day weeks. And he guarantees fluent Spanish at the end of the course. This course sounds just like what you need.

So you decide to write Professor Rodriguez asking him for details of his course. You'll need to know information about cost, verification of success of the program, dates, and the nature of the program. Then there may be other information you will need to know. Think through the situation and write a letter to the professor seeking the information you need.

3. You are director of training for the Campbell Chemical Company. At last month's meeting of the Training Directors Association, one of the directors present told you about an excellent training film titled "General Semantics and Decision Making." The film is sold by the National Management Institute, a new company in the training aids area. You would like to know more about the film; so you decide to write the company.

Although you would appreciate any information the National Management Institute can give you about the film, you will certainly want to know its cost, both rental and outright purchase. Also, you'd like to know its length, in minutes, as well as the general nature of its contents. Then there is the matter of audience level (top executive, supervisors, workers) at which the film aims. Write the letter. Since you don't know the name of the appropriate person at the National Management Institute, address the letter to the sales department.

4. In today's *Wall Street Journal* you saw the following advertisement:

> Commercial building on 14.2 acres, outskirts of Denver, 14,500 sq. ft. Suitable for small manufacturing operation or storage. $250,000. Write Box 1731, Denver, CO 80209.

This property may be just what one of the clients of your commercial real estate firm is looking for. The place and the price is right. But the right place will need to be on a railroad. Your client will have little need for the extra acreage. Thus, you'll need to know whether the building could be bought separately. Also, because of current borrowing conditions, your client would like to receive owner financing for about 65 percent of the total—for ten years, if possible.

Write the letter that will get you the information you and your client need.

5. In the role of president of a professional society (your choice) you are considering holding the organization's next annual convention at sea.

The idea came to you last week when you saw in *Business Week* an advertisement of Caribbean Conventions, Inc., a New Orleans based convention booking agency.

The advertisement described exotic Caribbean cruises which can be used to combine business with pleasure. The cruises take a number of routes in the Caribbean (Virgin Islands, Jamaica, Martinique, Trinidad), ranging from seven to fifteen days. The advertisement promised reduced rates for all conventions. It specified that all replies should indicate desired dates, number in group (including members of families), and time of trip.

Write the letter that will get you the information you and your organization will need to decide whether it will have its next convention at sea. Supply whatever specific facts you may need in your inquiry (numbers to attend, dates, etc.)

**6.** In your search for a business in which to invest your time and money, you find this advertisement in today's *Wall Street Journal:*

> FRANCHISE AVAILABLE: Fastest growing car rental business in the country. Franchises available in many choice cities. National advertising. Dynamic promotion. Nationwide reservation system. Highly competent professional advisory service. Training program. A sure money maker. Write Scotsman Car Rental, P.O. Box 1792, Chicago, IL 60611.

You are interested if you could get a franchise in —— (your choice of city) and if you could swing the finances. Write the letter that will get you the information you will need in making your decision.

**7.** Select an advertisement of a product a business might purchase. Then write a letter to the company asking for the information the business would need before buying. So that your instructor may better evaluate your inquiry, clip the advertisement and attach it to your letter.

**8.** In your search for a place to invest the $10,000 you have saved, you observed a coin-operated duplicating machine at a local hotel. The idea appeared to be a good one. In fact, you can think of a number of other locations where these machines could be placed profitably.

On the machine you found the manufacturer's name and address. The machine is called the Kopy Kaatz, and it is manufactured by the Kaatz Manufacturing Company, 3417 Parkway, Cleveland, OH 44118. Now you will write an inquiry for information on the availability of the machines, terms of sale, and the other details you will need in order to wisely invest your money. Address the letter to the sales manager.

**9.** As the sales manager for National Chemical Products, Inc., write a letter to Ms. Martha Goodman, Marketing Manager, Wayside Inns, Inc. From a business acquaintance you have learned that the Wayside Inns hotel and motel system is promoting a special discount plan for businesses that will sign a quantity contract with them. Because National's salesmen have been running very high expenses lately, you think the idea worth looking into.

You are generally acquainted with the Wayside Inns organization. Its hotels and motels blanket the nation. They are moderately priced, comfortable, and clean. Most have restaurant and lounge facilities. But you don't know the details of the discount plan. Certainly, you will need to know the extent of the discount, the commitments necessary to get it, and the priorities contract companies have. Write the letter that will get you this and any other information you feel you need.

## FAVORABLE REPLIES

**10.** Today's mail brings to you, director, Executive Development School, Clarion University, an inquiry from the Permian Oil Company (see Problem 1). The training director of that company wants the answers to some questions about your school. You can answer all of them positively, but one must be answered somewhat negatively.

The negative answer is to the question about quantity discounts. You just do not make them. Your program is planned to break even, and any cut in cost would result in losses that the program cannot afford.

On the positive side, the course can carry five semester hours of elective credit in business administration. But one must be admitted as a student to the university prior to beginning the program. You are sending a brochure describing the university's admission policies and procedures.

There should be absolutely no problem for technically trained executives. In fact, the course is designed for them. You are delighted to send the names of companies that have sent executives to the program. So you include the names and addresses of those training directors of companies in Houston (make up this information). Of course, you will want to work a bit to keep the reader interested in your school.

**11.** Professor Roberto Rodriguez can indeed teach one to be fluent in Spanish (Problem 2) in two weeks. But it takes hard work and personal instruction every working hour of the day for the period. And the cost is high ($2,500 for the period, including room, board, and instructional materials). The professor's technique is to take the students into his home and let him live with the Rodriguez family for the two weeks. The student hears and speaks only Spanish. Almost every minute of every day he is either studying, talking, or reading Spanish. There is little rest—for the student or the professor. But the system works; and the professor can prove it by a long list of successful users of the instruction. The next open two-week period begins on the 16th of next month.

Make up any of the specific details needed and write the letter for the professor.

**12.** Move into the office of the sales manager of the National Educational Institute and answer the letter of the director of training of Campbell Chemical Company (Problem 3).

To answer the questions about the nature of the film, you are sending your specially prepared brochure. Although the brochure does a good job of explaining how the film teaches general semantics and shows how general semantics can help one become a better decision maker, you can point out in your letter how three of the leading university-sponsored executive development programs (Harvard, Stanford, Chicago) are using the film. The film runs for 36 minutes. Although originally aimed at middle and upper management levels, the film is easily understood by any reasonably intelligent adult. You have evidence that it has been successfully used in at least six foreman training schools. The film rents for $50 for a three-day period, and it sells for $360. The charge for a rental could be applied to the sale price if they would want to try the film first.

As your company is just getting started in the business, you'll work especially hard to cultivate this sale.

**13.** As the owner of the building advertised in the *Wall Street Journal,* answer the letter inquiring about the property (Problem 4).

Fortunately, you can answer all but one of the questions positively. A railroad spur runs through the back part of the property. You would be willing to sell only the building; but to have access to the railroad, one would need to buy about five acres of the land. You are asking $190,000 for the building and these five acres. A mortgage at the current bank rate of interest would be quite acceptable to you—after a down payment of a third of the cost. You will send photos of the building to this out-of-town purchaser. But you will invite him to inspect it personally at a time of his choosing.

Write the letter that will get the information to this potential purchaser.

**14.** In answering the inquiry about your Caribbean convention cruises (Problem 5), you will send a beautifully illustrated brochure. Most of the required information is there—cost, dates, accommodations, etc. But there is some additional information which you must send in a letter.

As the brochure gives only standard prices, you'll need to explain that groups exceeding 50 delegates (not counting family members) get a 10 percent discount on all costs, including costs of family members. Groups exceeding 100 get 15 percent. The maximum number of delegates you can take care of on one trip is 150. Any group exceeding 50 gets free use of meeting rooms up to a maximum of three rooms. All dates given in the brochure are open except May 7–21 and August 3–17, which are filled. Other dates are likely to fill soon; so you suggest a quick decision.

Write the letter that will give the reader the information needed to make this decision.

**15.** As sales manager for Scotsman Car Rental, answer the letter you received from Michael P. Patterson, a potential purchaser of a franchise (Problem 6). Your printed brochure will answer most of the questions he asked. But there are a few that you will have to handle in a letter.

Mr. Patterson wants a franchise for his home town of Stockton, California. One is available there; and so is one for near-by Sacramento, which you feel offers more potential. Patterson can get either for a Class B investment, which as described in the brochure requires approximately $65,000 cash. Whether the office location Patterson suggested in his letter would be suitable for a Scotsman operation you cannot say. But you would send your location expert to make a site evaluation before reaching a final franchise agreement.

Write the letter to Mr. Patterson transmitting the brochure and giving him the additional information.

**16.** Select an advertisement, brochure, or other material describing a product that a business executive might want to get more information about before buying. The product can be one for resale; or it can be one to be consumed or used by the business. Next, assume that you are a sales correspondent for the manufacturer of this product. Make a list of the questions the business executives would be likely to ask. Then write a letter answering these questions. To assist your instructor in evaluating your work, attach your list of questions and the advertisement, brochure, etc., to the letter.

**17.** As sales manager for the Kaatz Manufacturing Company (Problem 8) answer the inquiry from a prospect for your Kopy Kaatz duplicating machine.

The Kaatz people have a heavy-duty model specially built for coin operation. And they would be quite willing to sell direct to anyone interested. The company sells only on a cash basis. But local banks usually are eager to lend money on purchases of copying machines.

A brochure which you will enclose with your letter answers most of the questions the prospect asks about the machines—their construction, operating information, prices, and such. You can point out in your letter, however, that you would give a 6-percent discount for purchase of 10 machines and 8 percent for 20 or more. Also, in response to a question about repairs and maintenance, you will report that you have a repair contract with the Ellis Business Machines Company, which is in the prospect's hometown. Thus, you can promise quick and reliable service when needed. Also, you'll gladly supply the list of profitable owners of the machine. In fact, you're including such a list. Report all this information and anything else you think appropriate in your letter.

**18.** Take over for Ms. Martha Goodson (Problem 9) and answer the inquiry about Wayside Inns' discount plan.

The plan is simple and works this way. Wayside Inns will grant quantity discounts to any business willing to join its plan. Joining requires that the business guarantee using a specified number of rooms per year.

For a guaranteed use of 500 rooms, a 10-percent discount is given. For 1,000 rooms the discount is 15 percent; and for 2,000 and more it is 20 percent. These savings are even more meaningful when Wayside's already moderate prices are considered (typically $16–$26 per single). In addition to the discount, contracting companies will receive Wayside's very best service, which includes coast-to-coast toll-free reservation service and assistance in finding a suitable room when Wayside's rooms are all booked. The discounts do not apply to restaurant and lounge charges. But you may want to note that charges here are already moderate.

## INQUIRIES, PROSPECTIVE EMPLOYEES

**19.** Assume the position of office manager of a major manufacturing company. You desperately need someone to take charge of the customer correspondence work of the office. Mainly, this job involves handling customer inquiries and complaints. It is this person's task to see to it that the customer is fairly treated and that the public relations of the company is enhanced. Clearly, the person for this job must be a first-rate letter writer. And he must be a skilled diplomat as well. Of course, this person must also live and work with others; so you're concerned about his personal qualities as well. And there are also matters of character (reliability, honesty, loyalty, etc.).

One of the applicants for this job is Ms. Shelly Levy, an attractive young woman who appears to have all the necessary qualities. As she formerly did similar work for Batt and Company, Cleveland, Ohio, you'll need to write her immediate superior there. Her name is Ms. Carolyn Hrushka. Write her a letter asking her the pertinent questions.

**20.** As personnel manager for Sunset Appliance Company you need more information about Loraine Walpole before adding her to your sales staff. The job for which you are considering her involves selling a wide assortment of home appliances to homeowners as well as to building contractors. The ideal person for the job is one who is aggressive and self motivated—one who will go out and get the business rather than wait for the business to come in.

In reviewing Ms. Walpole's work record, you note that she sold real estate for the Vance Realty Company for four years. She listed Mr. Kenneth W. Vance, president of that organization, as one of her references. Write Mr. Vance and ask him the pertinent questions about this prospective employee.

**21.** Assume that you have your degree and are seeking the job of your choice. You have just concluded an interview with a firm of your choice. As is customary, you gave the interviewer a list of your references, including the name of the professor who knows your work best.

Now switch roles with the person who interviewed you. Write a letter to the professor. Make certain to ask for the really meaningful information the professor can report.

**22.** In the position of president of Tull-LaCase, Inc., manufacturers and distributors of precision instruments, you are looking for a qualified person for the position of controller in your firm. One outstanding applicant is Robert E. Valdez, a young man of 34. Mr. Valdez is a CPA and has 12 years of experience with the rival firm of Higgins and Booker Instruments, Inc. As Mr. Valdez explained his situation to you, his chances for advancement in his present job are blocked by people with more seniority. He explained further that his boss, Thomas E. Schwartz, knows that he is seeking other employment. In fact, he listed Schwartz as one of his references.

Write Mr. Schwartz for the information you will need before hiring a controller for your firm.

**23.** Play the role of your professor in this course. You have been appointed chairman of the search committee to find someone to fill a vacant administrative position at your school (dean, department head, or such—as determined by your professor).

Advertisement of the position has brought in a wide assortment of applicants, which your committee now must evaluate. In order to get the proper information for evaluation, now you must write the references furnished by each applicant. So you decide to work up a standard letter which will get the information you need.

Write the letter, addressing it to Dean Mary E. Pharr, and ask her about Dr. Michael E. Sellers, who is one of the applicants.

**24.** Imagine that you are the owner of Night Owl, Inc., a small chain of neighborhood convenience stores. You need information on Ms. Patricia Comisky, who is seeking work as an assistant store manager. She appears to be an attractive, aggressive, and personable woman—the type you want for this job. On the other hand, there are a number of question marks in her background which make you want to know more about her.

You are concerned about the fact that she has not stayed very long on any one job. In fact, she has had five different jobs over the past seven years. Perhaps her last boss, Mr. Herman A. Schmaltz, owner-manager, Schmaltz Groceries, Inc., can fill you in on this information. Perhaps, also, he can evaluate Ms. Comisky's suitability for the job.

Using your imagination logically to supply you with the supplementary information you may need, write the letter to Mr. Schmaltz.

## PERSONNEL EVALUATIONS

**25.** Take over for Ms. Carolyn Hrushka at Batt and Company (Problem 19) and write an evaluation of Shelly Levy.

You know Shelly Levy very well. She worked under your direction for four years, and she worked hard. There is no question about Shelly's letter writing ability. She's good at it. And she knows how to build good public relations with words. She's fast and she's efficient. Also, she is a loyal hard worker. Rarely did she leave the office until all incoming work for the day had been done.

Although she is good at handling difficult situations in writing, she doesn't do quite as well in her personal relations. While with you, she was involved in a number of office conflicts. Apparently she has some problem getting along with her co-workers. She gave other reasons for leaving, of course, but you suspect that unhappiness with her co-workers was involved in her decision. In spite of her personal shortcomings, you'd hire her back in a minute if you had the chance.

Using your logical imagination, you may generate any other facts you feel you will need. Write the letter.

**26.** As Kenneth W. Vance (Problem 20) write a letter evaluating Ms. Loraine Walpole. As you view Loraine's record, you recall that she has more than the usual ability for selling. She is a highly personable and articulate young woman. As far as you know, her character is excellent. She was highly aggressive—in fact, too much for selling real estate, you feel. But she was effective. In fact, she was your top salesperson her last year with you.

You were sorry to see her leave after four years with you. You are not certain just why she left. She said merely that she wanted to move to another town. Her reasons were personal, she said, and had nothing to do with the work or the company. Assuming any other factual information which may need to be reported, write this letter.

**27.** It's not easy to write an accurate and fair letter about yourself, but that is your assignment. Specifically, your task is to assume the role of the professor whom you have listed as a reference in your application for a job of your choice. In this role, you will carefully evaluate your scholastic record, your relation with the professor, your activities—in fact, everything which the professor should report. Then write the letter.

**28.** Assume the role of controller of Higgins and Booker (Problem 22) and evaluate Roberto E. Valdez. Mr. Valdez is indeed one of your better accountants. In fact, you'd like to keep him. You see a good future for Roberto at Higgins and Booker, but apparently he is impatient and wants to move up now. He is a deserving young man. You will certainly help him to leave, if this is his preference.

In general, you can give Roberto a very high rating on his knowledge and ability as an accountant. He knows the field and has the mental ability to handle the job he seeks. As he has not yet had experience in administration, however, you can only speculate as to his potential for such work. You see him as somewhat detail-minded—perhaps not so much management-oriented as he should be. He is an exceptionally fine human being—courteous, sensitive, logical, honest.

With this general picture of the man in mind, make up any specific facts you may need to write a fair evaluation of Mr. Valdez.

**29.** Fill in for Dean Mary E. Pharr (Problem 23) and answer a letter inquiring about Dr. Michael E. Sellers. Dean Pharr has known Dr. Sellers for the 11 years he has been at her university. She has been his immediate superior for the past five years. She knows the man to be a very personable and capable individual. As chairman of his department for the past three years, he has done an outstanding job. His department has run smoothly, and he is well liked by his subordinates. He does press hard for funds at budget time—perhaps too hard. But certainly he has the best interest of his people in mind when he does it.

In addition to being a capable administrator, Dr. Sellers has a good record for scholarship. He has published widely and has served in a number of offices in his professional associations. In addition, he has presented a number of scholarly papers at professional meetings.

You may use your imagination to supply any details you may need. But keep them consistent with the general description of the man given above.

**30.** Evaluate Ms. Patricia Comisky for Night Owl, Inc. (Problem 24).

You remember the woman well. She worked for you as an assistant manager for a little over a year. She did a reasonably good job for you. In fact, you were considering promoting her to a manager's position. That is, you were until she phoned in one day after pay day to tell you that she was quitting. She gave little reason except that she wanted a change. As you recall, her leaving left you shorthanded for a few days.

In spite of this incident, you want to be fair to Ms. Comisky and to the

Night Owl. The woman has ability. She is attractive, personable, and intelligent. Unquestionably, she is a hard worker.

Using your imagination to supply any additional information you need, write the letter.

## CLAIMS

**31.** You are the manager of the Closet, a men's clothing store catering to the college and young executive set. Your order No. 3147 from Shamrock, Inc., came in today—in a mess. Of the ten dozen assorted shirts in the order, 37 have clearly visible faded or stained spots on them. There is no way you would dare sell them to your discriminating customers.

Certainly you are not going to keep the shirts—much less pay for them. You will have to write the Shamrock people telling them what happened. Because you have your store's tenth anniversary sale next week, you will want replacements for the shirts right away. Write the letter that will get the action desired from Shamrock. Assume any additional information you may need.

**32.** As owner of Building Supplies, Inc., you saw an advertisement for Uncle John's smoked turkeys. At $25 for a ten-pound bird, you thought they would make excellent Christmas gifts for your better customers. So you ordered two dozen of them.

Today the birds arrive. But most of them are in no shape to be given as Christmas presents. The decorative metal cans in which they were packed are badly scarred. They simply are not the "beautifully decorated holiday tins" the advertisement described. In fact, they are quite plain and appear to have been used previously for some other purpose.

If you are to give the turkeys as Christmas presents, you'll have to have the replacement containers within a week. And if Uncle John's can't do it, you want your money back. Write Uncle John's and take care of this problem.

**33.** With your college work behind you, you are a management trainee with International Stores, Inc. Currently, you are working in the shipping and receiving department of one of the major outlets in this major chain of department stores. After working some 30 minutes on a claim letter, your boss, Alonzo Walker, tosses his rough draft of a letter on your desk. "I'm no college graduate," he says. "You're the one who should be writing this. How about reworking it for me?"

The letter, addressed to the shipping manager of Lancelot Toiletries, Inc., goes like this:

Gentlemen:

Received goods your invoice No. 1473A. Wish to advise that 14 cases of Lancelot men's cologne damaged and unfit for sale. Contents were poorly packed. Result was breakage which spilled over remainder of contents. Request replacement shipment immediately, as items are advertised for annual sale beginning one week from Saturday. Instructions needed on disposition of damaged merchandise.

Thanking you for all courtesies, I remain,

Yours sincerely,

Judged by standards you learned in college, the letter is bad. You will revise it thoroughly.

**34.** Because you thought it would wear as well as its manufacturer claimed in advertisements, you selected Toughie vinyl tile for the floors of your office building. "One floor for a lifetime," the advertisement stressed.

Now you have reason to doubt these words. After only two years of use, the entrance areas and all heavily traveled areas in your office complex clearly show the effects of wear. At these places the top layer of tile has clearly worn away. As the pattern has been destroyed in these places, the floor looks bad. You'll have to replace all the floors in the building—a total of 6,250 square feet. Of course, you think the manufacturer should stand behind the product—and pay for it all. That is, you think they should pay for the tile plus replacement labor.

Write the letter.

**35.** As vice president in charge of advertising for Albeef, a 100-percent meat dog food, you have a beef to make to the producers of *An Hour with Minnie Morrison*. For the past two weeks spot ads on this show have told of your high-quality, all-meat dog food.

Things were running well until yesterday's show. That was when outspoken Minnie followed your commercial with the comment, "Why all this emphasis on all meat? What's wrong with cereals? If humans can eat cereals, why can't dogs?"

Clearly, this comment did Albeef no good. You'll want to put a stop to that kind of talk and to get some compensation for the bad publicity. Frankly, you think the producer should give you back the $32,000 you paid for the advertising. So you'll write a letter designed to get the charges cancelled. You'll try, also, to get Minnie to say something special about Albeef on the next show. If these things aren't done, you'll cancel all remaining advertisements.

**36.** As owner of the Wig Shop, you have a claim to make against Carr-Biglowe Wig Manufacturing Company. A few months ago you began stocking this company's line of quality human hair wigs. Retailing for $400 and up, these quality wigs should give your shop a touch of class—you thought.

Within the past two weeks two of your good customers have returned

Carr-Biglowe Model 12 wigs and demanded their $424 back. Of course, you gave it to them. Now you will write the company to get them to give you your money back.

Inspection of the two returned wigs and the seven other Model 12s you have in stock shows that the hairs are not securely fastened. They pull out easily. The other Carr-Biglowe models don't appear to have this defect—just the Model 12s. You don't dare sell any of the seven you have on hand, and you're anticipating hearing from the owners of the other five you have sold.

Obviously, you have a problem. Write the letter that will solve this problem for you. (Make appropriate assumptions for sales prices, shipping costs, invoice numbers, and any other specific facts you may need.)

37. As owner-manager of your own furniture store, you have been working hard getting ready for your big promotion commemorating your tenth anniversary. One of the items you plan to offer at a special discount is the Sandman mattress. In fact, you have prepared your full-page advertisement, and the Sandman occupies a prominent position in it. The advertisement will run this weekend and the big sale will begin Monday.

Things were running smoothly until today's delivery by Arrow Transit. They delivered the four dozen Sandman mattresses you had ordered; but 27 of them are badly soiled and faded. It appears like water damage. It's obvious the mattresses weren't injured in transit, for the heavy brown paper in which they were wrapped shows no sign of damage.

You have enough mattresses for the first day or two of the sale, but you'll want replacements by Wednesday. Write the letter that will get them to you by that date.

## ADJUSTMENT GRANTS

38. As shipping manager for Shamrock, Inc. (Problem 31), you are somewhat embarrassed about the Closet's claim concerning 37 damaged shirts. Of course, you'll make the claim good. You're sending personally inspected replacements by Wing Motor Freight today. And the Wing people guarantee delivery within two days.

Your check on your shipping operations reveals what happened. A fire in the warehouse last month brought fire extinguishers into use. The result was a number of damaged shirts. You thought all of the damaged merchandise had been destroyed; but apparently someone overlooked these.

Write the letter that will tell the Closet people what they want to hear. And try to regain any confidence that may have been lost.

39. Play the role of the adjustment manager of Daakin Instrument Company, manufacturers of a popular line of electronic calculators. Today's mail brings in one of your models with this terse letter attached:

Gentlemen:

I am returning the accompanying D610 calculator which I bought through your advertisement in last month's *Accountant's Journal*. It has not worked properly from the day I got it. Please send me my money back.

Sincerely,
Mable Carson

Your money-back guarantee means exactly what it says. So you'll send a check for the $189.50 instrument. But you'd like the lady to know the facts of the case. Inspection shows the calculator had one minor defect— a defect that occurs no more than once in every 2,500 calculators. She still has her need for a calculator, and you'd like her to give the D610 another chance. You would send her one you inspected personally.

**40.** Play the role of Uncle John (Problem 32) and handle the claim of the owner of Building Supplies, Inc. Apparently, one of the temporary packing clerks you added for the Christmas season made a bad mistake. He packed the turkeys in the plain tins you use for discount sales to those who buy direct from the smokehouse outlet rather than the special holiday gift tins.

Of course, you will do what you can to correct the matter. So you will send 24 holiday containers for the turkeys by Roadrunner Motor Freight. They guarantee delivery in two days. Then the Building Supplies owner can put each turkey in the gift container and send it to the lucky customer. They can just throw away the old containers.

In your letter you'll want to explain things so that you can regain any confidence lost. And to make them think more kindly toward you, you're sending them a 15-pound turkey—compliments of Uncle John.

**41.** Take over for the shipping manager of Lancelot Toiletries and answer the claim letter of Alonzo Walker (Problem 33). A quick check through your shipping department reveals no clear information. The young lady who packed the merchandise insists that the fault is not hers. In fact, she shows proof that everything was in good order when the carrier picked up the shipment. As things appear to you, the carrier is at fault.

You will look into this question later, but right now you need to get good merchandise into the hands of Mr. Walker's store. You'll send the merchandise by White Wing Transport, Inc., today. The shipment will arrive within 40 hours, the White Wing people assure you—in plenty of time for the promotion mentioned in Walker's letter. As for the damaged merchandise, you'll ask Walker to dispose of it in any way he sees fit. He may want to destroy it. You'll want to work to regain any confidence lost.

**42.** Play the role of the adjustment correspondent for Carr-Biglowe Wig Manufacturing Company (Problem 36) and handle the claim from the Wig Shop. It's embarrassing, but the company did turn out a bad run of Model 12 wigs. In fact, you were in the process of calling in all that had been sold.

Unfortunately, your production foreman changed manufacturing techniques—without authorization. He had a novel idea which he thought would work. It didn't.

Now you have to work to correct the damage that has been done. You have taken measures to make certain such errors won't happen again. You are calling in all Model 12s from the stores. And you will ask the stores to call in all they have sold and replace them with good wigs which you are sending to them immediately.

Write the letter which will handle the Wig Shop's claim and regain any lost confidence.

**43.** In the role of sales manager of the Hawkins-Continental Hotel, you must answer the letter of Philip Bordeaux, who was convention chairman of the Ancient Order of Vipers. This fraternal organization held its annual national convention at your hotel last week. It was a most profitable meeting for the hotel, as the group used 450 rooms, held two dinners, and used the hotel restaurants and shops heavily.

In his letter, Mr. Bordeaux vigorously calls your attention to the bill he received from you. He was charged $280 for the complimentary suite he used; $1,200 for the ballroom, which you had told him was free with hotel-catered banquet; and $12 for automobile storage, which he paid in cash as he left the hotel.

The man is right on the first two items; and you'll take his word on the auto storage matter. The errors were human ones, and you'll accept the blame for not communicating instructions properly to the billing people. You hope the man will remember the good services you and your staff tried so hard to give him. You'd like more of his organization's future business. Write the letter that will help you to get it.

**44.** Send Maxine Strelsky a new Coffee Master 2000. In her letter to you, she explained how she had taken her coffee maker to a local repair man seven times in the past year and that she was fed up with the appliance. You can't understand what happened because the product has been most reliable. Complaints have been extremely low. Perhaps she would have had better results if she had taken it to the authorized factory service agent in her town (AAA Appliance Company). The machine is delicate and requires trained people to repair it.

Write the letter that will get the new product to Maxine. And try to regain her lost confidence.

## ORDERS

**45.** Select at least three items from advertisements in a newspaper, trade publication, or the like. Write a letter ordering these items. Make certain that you give all the information needed to complete the sale (size, color, weight, material, etc.). Take care to cover the cost portion, including shipping costs and manner of payment. And don't forget to give proper shipping instructions. For the benefit of your instructor, clip the advertisements to your letter.

**46.** Today you returned to your small clothing store from your annual trip to the regional trade fair. You are looking through some of the literature you picked up. This one especially attracts your interest:

"Alpine Jeans—the best in sports shorts. Functional European design. Added American comfort and easy care. Tailored with double-stitched seams for durability—kept the slim look and four practical pockets in front (two pockets in rear, also). Cut for action. Comfortable. Also available in slack length, shipped unhemmed. Made from cool, lightweight Tundra cloth, 50 percent cotton, 50 percent dacron. Easy care—just wash and wear 'em. Colors: tan, brown, jungle green. Men's even waist sizes: 28–44. Women's even sizes: 8–20. Slacks: $16.50 postpaid. Shorts: $14.00 postpaid."

You will order an assortment of styles, sizes, and colors. You make the selection based on what you think you can sell. Send cash with the order.

**47.** Play the role of president of the Thrifty Building Supply Company. In your efforts to select a truly distinctive Christmas gift to give to your loyal contractor customers, you recall a visit you made to the shop of a western jeweler on your last trip through New Mexico. After some searching, you find the little brochure you picked up describing his work. One item you liked especially is described as follows:

"Bucking Bronc cuff links, 14-carat gold, set with chip rubies. Two sizes: massive, $33.50; and regular, $24.75."

The second item is described in these words:

"Longhorn tie clasp. 14-carat gold longhorn head, chip rubies for eyes. Massive, $35.50; regular, $27.50."

You will order 16 of the cuff links, regular, and 12 of the tie clasps, regular. Be sure to handle shipping instructions and payment. As the items are to be Christmas gifts, you'll need them no later than December 10.

**48.** The Fireguard steel file cabinets you saw adveritsed in today's *Wall Street Journal* are just what you need for your office. You'll order six of them direct from the manufacturer. The ad described the product as capable of withstanding 1,800 degree heat for an hour. A plunger system locks all doors. The 4-drawer model is 25x18x52 and the 2-drawer model is 25x18x29. Colors are sand, tan, or green. Shipping weights are 140 and 190 pounds for the 2-drawer and 4-drawer models, respectively. They sell for $235 and $275 plus transportation. C.o.d. orders are invited.

You want four of the 4-drawer and three of the 2-drawer models. Your color preference is sand. As you need the cabinets right away, ask for rush shipment.

# 10

## Correspondence: Indirect letters

I N SOME letter situations your reader will not be likely to react favorably to a direct presentation. When you judge that this is the case, you should organize your letter in an indirect order. Certainly, you will want to use the indirect order when your basic message contains bad news, for a direct presentation of bad news would produce a harshly negative effect. And you will want to use it in some of the neutral situations when directness would bring about an awkward or startling effect. In fact, you will want to use the indirect order whenever your logical judgment tells you that your goals will be served best by this slower and more involved approach. Your decision on directness or indirectness for any given letter should be determined by what you think the reader's reaction will be to your objectives. Sometimes your decision will be clear-cut, as is the case with most of the situations analyzed in this chapter and the preceding ones. Sometimes the decision will be a close one.

In the pages which follow appear analyses of some of the more common types of indirect letters. All represent letter situations which are in the bad-news category, and rarely would anything other than the indirect approach achieve their goals. As in the preceding chapter, the letter types presented here do not exhaust the possibilities for this order of treatment. By carefully following these analyses, however, you should gain an insight for developing strategies that will help you solve all similar problems.

## REFUSED REQUEST

Refusal of a request is definitely a bad-news message. Your reader has asked you for something, and you are denying her what she seeks. The degree of negativeness involved in each refusal varies, of course, but one has to strain the imagination to find a refusal that clearly is positive. So, as the general rule, you should handle refused requests in the indirect order.

As is true with most general rules, however, sometimes you can justify making exception. If, for example, you feel that the negative answer will be treated strictly as routine and will not need care in presenting, you may elect to use directness. Likewise, you may choose directness when you and your reader clearly have a relationship which requires frank exchanges. And, of course, you may choose to use directness any time you are not concerned about goodwill effect. But such exceptions are rare, and you would be wise to use indirectness in most refusals.

The reason you should use the indirect order in refusing most requests is obvious. Your objectives are to say no and, usually, to maintain goodwill. You can do the first simply enough, for little skill is required to say no. Maintaining goodwill, however, requires much more of your writing skill. It requires that you explain your decision—that you convince your reader that it is fair and reasonable. Were you to begin with the negative answer, you would put your reader in a negative frame of mind. She would not be in the best mood to receive whatever you have to say that will explain your decision. Thus, your best strategy is to explain first—to take your reader through your reasoning and to lead her logically to your decision.

### Strategy development

Developing the strategy which will maintain goodwill and justify your decision is largely a mental process. You will need to search through the facts of the one case for the best possible explanation to use. You will need to place yourself in your reader's position and attempt to view the situation as she perceives it through her mental filter. Then you will have to work out something to say that will lead her to accept your decision as a fair and logical one.

It may be that your decision must be made because of a policy of your company. In such a case you will be wise to think through the justification of your policy. If the policy is a fair one, as all policies should be, you should see reasons why it benefits your reader as well as your company. For example, a policy of refusing to accept returns on goods bought on sale obviously benefits the house; but it also benefits the customer. Only by cutting the costs of returns can the house give the customer the low sale price. A policy of selling only through retail outlets can be justified on the basis of providing better service to the customer. Such reasoning makes convincing explanation.

In some instances you may need to refuse simply because the facts of the case justify a refusal. When this is the case, your task of building goodwill is more difficult, for you can use little reader-viewpoint reasoning. You can only review the facts of the case which justify your decision, taking care not to accuse or insult. Probably your best strategy would be to appeal to the reader's sense of fair play.

Each letter situation, of course, will have its own set of facts for you to evaluate. In the end, you should develop a reasoning which should work on your one reader in the one case.

## Opening contact and setup of the plan

With your strategy in mind, you should next turn to the task of putting it into letter form. Usually, you cannot just blurt out your explanation or justification, for such directness would be just as awkward as beginning with the refusal. Instead, your best course is to begin with some comment which meets the reader on neutral ground. It should imply neither a yes nor a no answer. It should be on the subject enough to clearly inform the reader that you are writing about her request. In this regard, you may also include an incidental reference to her letter somewhere in the opening. Most important of all, the opening should set up the presentation of your strategy which will justify your decision.

Exactly what is appropriate for the beginning words of your letter must be evaluated in light of the facts of the individual case. As the technique is best described through illustration, let us take a typical case. It is the case of an executive who must write the president of a professional group that the executive's company cannot cooperate in a study to determine background characteristics of the company's successful executives. The reason for the refusal is simply that more high-ranking employees' time would be required to do the work than the company can spare at the moment. In the beginning paragraph illustrated below, the writer starts with a neutral comment which is on the subject of the request. She makes a by-date reference to previous correspondence, leaving no question about the specific situation involved. Then, by labeling the project as one deserving "the help of business leaders whenever they are able to give it,"she sets up her explanation that her company is not able to give the assistance requested at this time.

Your study of executive characteristics described in your July 3rd letter should be of general interest to us all, and it should be of genuine practical use in the search for executive talent. Certainly, it is a worth-while project—one that deserves the help of business leaders whenever they are able to give it.

## Presentation of the reasoning

As we have implied, the reasoning which justifies your decision should flow logically from your opening. Your opening sets it up; so now you present whatever facts and reasoning you have selected to justify your decision. You present it as convincingly as you can.

In presenting your strategy convincingly, you will need to make good use of the rules of emphasis. You may need to highlight the happier aspects of your problem and to subordinate the gloomier ones. You will need to watch your words carefully, working to avoid the negatives which may offend a sensitive reader. Also, you will need to make good use of the you-viewpoint in your presentation. Since your effort will be designed to change your reader's thinking (more specifically, to convince him of your way of thinking), you will need to consider carefully the effects of every word and thought which go into this part of your letter.

## Positive handling of the refusal

Your handling of the refusal logically follows your reasoning. If you have built the groundwork of explanation and fact convincingly, the refusal comes as a logical conclusion. And it comes as no surprise. If you have done your job well, it may even be supported by your reader. Even so, because it is the most negative part of your message, you will need to avoid overemphasizing it. You will want to say it quickly, clearly, and positively; and you will want to keep it away from positions of emphasis.

In stating your refusal quickly, you should cover the ground in a minimum of words. To labor the point for three or four sentences when a single clause would do the job gives heavy emphasis to the refusal. You should give it not one word more than is necessary to do the job.

In stating the refusal clearly, you will need to make certain that there is no doubt about your decision. Sometimes, in the effort to be positive, we become evasive and unclear. For example, the writer who uses the words "it would be better if . . ." to carry the refusal would not communicate the decision to all people. Equally vague would be refusals conveyed in words like "these facts clearly support the policy of . . .".

In making your refusal positive, you need to study carefully the effects of your words. Harsh negatives such as "I refuse," "will not," and "cannot" clearly stand out. So do the timeworn apologies like "I deeply regret to inform you . . ." and "I am sorry to say . . . ." Usually, you can make your stand clear by a positive statement of policy. For example, instead of writing that your "policy does not cover damage to buildings not connected to the house," you could say that your "policy covers damage to the house only." Or instead of using words like "We must refuse," a wholesaler could deny a discount with something like "We can grant discounts only when . . .".

If you can make a compromise of any kind, you may use it to cover your refusal. That is, by saying what you can do, you can clearly imply what you cannot do. For example, if you write "The best we can do is . . . ," you make it clear that you cannot do what the reader has requested. Yet you do it in the most positive way the situation will permit.

## Off-subject goodwill close

Even though you have handled the refusal skillfully, it is the most negative part of your message. The news is disappointing, and it is likely to put your reader in an unhappy state of mind. If you are to achieve your goodwill objective, you must move the reader from this unhappy state. So, in the close of your letter you should shift to thoughts that are more pleasant—to off-subject material about happier things.

What you may include as subject matter for a particular letter depends again on the facts of the situation. It should be positive talk appropriate to the one case. If you have made a counterproposal, for example, you could discuss some aspect of it. If the reader's request concerns a project, you could make some suggestion concerning it, or perhaps express a wish for its success. In fact, you may use anything which makes appropriate subject matter for the situation, as long as it serves your goal of goodwill building.

Ruled out, of course, are the well-intended but negative final apologies or requests for understanding. To end with "Again, may I say that I regret that we must refuse . . ." or "I sincerely hope that you understand why we make the decision" clearly parades the negative views through the reader's mind.

## A case in refusal strategy

Good tact and strategy in a refusal are illustrated by the case of an office manager who refuses the request of a trade-book author. The author has asked the office manager for some of the best letters in the company's files. She wants to use them as examples in a correspondence guidebook she is writing. The request is an unreasonable one, for it would require going through many file drawers—perhaps all 40,000 of the company's letters on file. So the office manager must refuse.

In building the strategy for her refusal, the office manager concludes that the author will certainly want quality letters in the book, for the book will be no better than the letters. But not just any clerk can recognize quality letters. The work will require someone with ability. And because of the volume of work needed, it will require time. So the office manager selects a compromise. She will invite the author to use the files personally.

Her letter follows the general plan suggested in preceding pages. It begins away from the request—on neutral ground as far as the answer is concerned. But it is on the subject of the inquiry, and it sets up the explanation which follows. The explanation proceeds quickly, using a positive you-viewpoint approach. It presents the refusal without using a single negative word. It tells what the comapny can do and clearly implies what it cannot do. The close moves away from the refusal to more positive talk about the book.

Dear Ms. Howard:

Your *Correspondence Guidebook* should be a worthy contribution to business literature as well as a really practical aid to the business executive.

The practical value of the book, as I see it, depends largely on the quality of its illustrations. Your book demands illustrations that meet all the criteria of good correspondence. But getting the quality of illustration you need will require careful checking by someone who knows good writing, and going through the 40,000 letters in our files will take considerable time. For these reasons, I am sure you will understand why the best we can do is to make our files open to you or your staff. We would, of course, be happy to provide working space for you, and we assure you our very best cooperation. If you wish to use our files in this way, please let us know.

Please let us know, also, if we can help you further. We look forward to seeing the book. It is likely to get good use in the offices here at Merrit & Company.

Sincerely yours,

## ADJUSTMENT REFUSALS

Claims which you must refuse make another bad-news situation. Fortunately, most claims are legitimate, and most companies try hard to do what they can to correct any damage or mistakes they may have caused. But sometimes claims are not well founded. They may be based on wrong information. They may even approach fraudulence. On such occasions the company is likely to say no.

Saying no clearly and diplomatically in such cases requires your utmost effort in strategy and writing skill. You may be dealing with someone who is worked up emotionally about the situation giving rise to the claim—someone whose mental filter contains incomplete knowledge and biased judgments on the case. He may honestly feel that he has been wronged and that the only right action is for you to come through with an adjustment. Of course, some will know that their claims are weak, perhaps even fraudulent. Even these people have biased opinions on the matter. All are likely to resist any effort to justify a claim refusal.

## Determination of basic strategy

Your strategy in refusing a claim involves finding some way of overcoming your reader's negative mental reaction to your message. Your refusal, of course, is based on legitimate reasons. The facts support you, but your reader is not aware of them. To win your case, you must present these facts to him, and you must make him believe them. In your presentation you must appeal to his basic human honesty. Because you are dealing with a matter on which there is initial disagreement, you will need to select your words with great care, giving thought to the connotations they are likely to form in your reader's mind. Unquestionably, the problem requires the indirect approach and the utmost in strategy.

You should begin planning your strategy in adjustment refusal situations by reviewing all the facts involved. Your review should bring out the facts of the case as completely and clearly as you can identify them. Of course, they should support a refusal; otherwise, your action is not justified. Then, with the facts in mind, you should search for possibilities of presenting them so that they will be accepted. This effort is a mental one. You should place yourself in the reader's position, limit yourself to his knowledge of the situation, and search for means of presenting your case to him. You should look for reader-viewpoint reasoning wherever it logically can be supported. Then, with your strategy in mind, you should fit it into the general plan presented in following paragraphs.

## Opening setup of the reasoning

Your objective in the opening is to set up the review of facts which will justify your decision. Because you are answering a letter the reader has written to you, you will need to make this matter clear. Probably the best way of doing this is through an incidental reference to his letter early in your letter. A subject line would also do the job; but because the letter has a bad-news message, it would have to be neutral as to the decision. Nothing like "Refusal of your July 19th claim" would be appropriate.

In setting up a review of the facts involved, you will need to exercise your logical imagination. You will need to find some point on which you can begin communicating. It should be a point which in no way implies a yes or a no answer. It should be pertinent to the situation, for something far afield would create a startling effect. And perhaps most important of all, it should lead to the review of facts which will follow.

The subject matter for your opening contact could be almost anything which fits the situation. It could be some point on which you and the reader can agree—perhaps some point in his claim letter. For example, in a claim letter about an air-conditioning unit that was not cooling a house satisfactorily, the adjustment correspondent used this opening sentence:

> You are correct in believing that a two-ton Deep Kold window unit should take care of the ordinary five-room house.

The sentence makes contact on a point of common agreement. At the same time, it sets up the reasoning which will justify the refusal: that the house in question has many features which make it far from the ordinary five-room house. A statement showing concern for the reader's well-being might be effective in some cases. An interior decorator might begin a refusal with these contact words:

> Assisting young couples to enjoy beautifully decorated homes at budget prices is one of our most satisfying goals. We do all that we reasonably can to reach it.

From this goodwill contact, the writer could shift smoothly to reasoning that shows that the company does all one can reasonably expect of it, and that making the adjustment is beyond that reasonable limit.

In some cases a statement showing mutual respect for honest intentions could form the basis for opening contact:

> Your straightforward report of the 13th shows that you are one who wants to get all the facts and to base a fair decision on them. That is why I am confident that you will want to consider the following information.

Clearly, the statement sets up a review of the new information which follows. The new information, of course, will justify the refusal.

## Presentation of reasoning

The reasoning which supports your decision should follow your opening as a logical outgrowth of it. Your objective in this part of your message is to convince. To convince, you should first have sound logical reasoning. Farfetched facts and unsupported claims just will not do the job. Your information should be believable.

In addition to using information that convinces, you should use your best skill in writing to make your facts sound convincing. Especially should you make good use of positive language, for negatives have an irritating effect in the mind and thereby work against conviction. For similar reasons, you should avoid any inclination to question the reader's sincerity or honesty or to talk down to or insult him. Statements such as "If you had read the contract, you would have known . . ." or "Surely you knew that . . ." do little to convince. Instead, they do much to antagonize.

## Positive coverage of refusal

Your reasoning, of course, should build up your case. It should take your reader logically and systematically to the refusal. Then you should refuse. If you have done your job well, your refusal should appear to be the logical outcome of what you have given beforehand. It should leave no startling effect. In fact, if you have done your job well enough, your decision should be the only one that the facts of the case support.

As with all similar refusal problems, you should word your refusal clearly and positively. To be clear, your refusal should leave no doubt in anyone's mind. There should be no need to question. To be positive, you again will need to study the effect of your words. You may find it possible to refuse without using a single negative word. Perhaps you can imply what you can do. Also, you will need to keep your refusal words away from emphasis positions.

## Off-subject closing talk

Because your refusal is negative, you should follow it with some appropriate comment which is away from the subject of the refusal. No negative apologies are in order. Neither are any words which recall the problem giving rise to the claim. Probably a good general topic would be some more agreeable aspect of customer relations—new products, services, uses of products, industry news, or the like. Any friendly comment that appears logical in the one case will suffice.

## Case refusal of a claim

In the following example of a refused adjustment, a small manufacturer of furniture has made a claim to the Do-Craft Company, manufacturer of heavy fabrics. The claim contens that a certain Do-Craft fabric bought numerous times over the past year has badly faded and discolored. The furniture manufacturer includes with the claim three faded samples of the fabric, and they prove the point. Already the manufacturer had a number of complaints from buyers, and the claims total $545. The furniture manufacturer wants cash payment on these claims.

Inspection by the fabric manufacturer reveals that the fabrics were exposed to strong sunlight for long periods of time. The fabrics in question are strictly for inside use, and all of Do-Craft's advertising and catalog descriptions clearly emphasize the point. Do-Craft is not responsible and does not intend to pay the claim. Because the furniture manufacturer is a good customer, however, Do-Craft hopes to make him see the justice of the decision and to remain friends.

The Do-Craft letter begins in a friendly tone and on a point of agreement. In addition, the beginning sets up the review of facts. Without accusations, anger, or negative words of any kind, it relates the facts of the case—facts which clearly free the Do-Craft people from any blame. The refusal is clear, although more by implication than by direct wording. It is skillfully handled, without resort to negative words or undue emphasis. The close shifts to helpful suggestions which apply to the one case. Friendliness permeates the entire letter.

Dear Ms. Sanderson:

Certainly, you have a right to expect the best possible service from Do-Craft fabrics. Every Do-Craft product is the result of years of experimentation, and we manufacture each yard under the most careful controls we know how to impose. We are determined that our products will do for you what we say they will do.

Because we do want our fabrics to please, we carefully ran the samples of Do-Craft fabric 103 you sent us through our laboratory. Exhaustive tests show that each has been subjected to long periods in extreme sunlight. As we have known this limitation quality of Do-Craft from the beginning, we have clearly noted it in all our advertising in the catalogs from which you ordered, and with a stamped reminder on the back of every yard of the fabric. Under the circumstances, all we can do concerning your request is to suggest that you change to one of our outdoor fabrics. As you can see from our catalog, all in the 200 series are recommended for outdoor use.

Probably you will be interested also in the new Duck Back cotton fabrics listed in our 500 series. These plastic-coated cotton fabrics are most economical, and they will resist sun and rain remarkably well. If we can help you further in your selection, please call on us.

Sincerely yours,

## VAGUE AND BACK ORDERS

Not all orders can be acknowledged as positively as we illustrated in Chapter 9. Sometimes the persons ordering do not specify all of the information needed to complete the transactions; so you have to write them letters to clear up their vague orders. Then, sometimes you are out of the goods wanted, and you have to write those who order, telling them when they will receive the goods. Both situations are in the bad-news category. Those placing the order are not getting what they want right away. They must wait.

## Consideration in handling

In some areas of business, back orders and vague orders are somewhat routine. They are accepted as normal, and no one gets excited about them. In such situations the news is reported routinely, perhaps on printed forms or as notations on a copy of the order form. When the customer clearly will be disappointed in the news, however, a more tactful means of presentation is needed. In such cases you will want to write a letter, and you will be wise to write it in the indirect order used for most bad-news messages.

In planning your strategy for this form of acknowledgment letter, you should first review the facts of the case. If your reader's order is vague, the fault is hers. In such cases you are free of blame, but the situation is still negative. She is not getting what she wants now. Also, any tactless reference to her error could bring about resentment. If some of your reader's goods must be placed on back order, the fault may be yours; at least, it is not hers. In either event, you will need to give careful thought to the handling of the negative points.

## Variations in opening possibilities

Your opening for the letter will depend on how much your letter must do. If a number of items were ordered, you could have to acknowledge any combination of goods that you are shipping, goods that you must place on back order, and goods that were vaguely described. When you are sending some of the goods (the usual case), you may begin with this good-news part of your message, as illustrated in this beginning sentence:

> Your durable Rockwood roofing, which you ordered October 1, should be in Oxford well before your Wednesday deadline, as the shipment left our Cleveland warehouse this morning.

When you have only vague orders or back orders to handle, your opening should make a positive, friendly contact and serve as a buffer for the following bad news. Probably the most appropriate possibility is to begin with a grateful acknowledgment of the order. Or if the order is the first one, a new-customer welcome would be appropriate. Whatever you say, however, should be sincerely and individually written for the one case. The rubber-stamp "Thank you for your order" long ago lost its personalized effect. So has the "We are happy to have your order" variety. A more effective approach is one like this:

> Your January 31st order of Williams janitorial supplies is receiving our best attention, and we are sincerely grateful to you for it.

Other opening possibilities include a wide range of friendly, pertinent conversation topics that might go on between reader and writer. It could be some comment on the significance of the order:

> Your large April 9th order appears to indicate continued good business in the Burtville area.

It could also be some friendly remark reflecting business relationships:

> It's always good to receive an order from our friends at Morrison's Supply.

## Tact in handling the delayed shipment

After the friendly opening comment, you will need to move into the bad-news part. Your work here is largely an exercise in positive writing and writing in the you-viewpoint. In handling the vague order, for example, you should ask for the information you need without pointing an accusing finger at the reader for leaving out necessary information. Certainly, she made a mistake, but nothing is gained by saying "You failed to specify the color of umbrella you want." You gain much more in goodwill by something like this:

> So that you may have just the right color of umbrella to complement your wardrobe, will you please check your choice of the colors listed on the enclosed card?

The sentence not only handles the matter diplomatically; it makes the action easy to take. She has only to check and mail a card. In cases in which additional information would be helpful to the decision, you would be wise to supply it. In the illustration above, for example, a color chart or fabric samples could be sent.

Your handling of any back-order information should place primary emphasis on the most positive part of this bad news. That is, rather than tell your reader that you "can't ship the goods until the 9th," you can get the goods moving toward her with words like "We shall be able to rush the Old New Orleans pralines to you by the 9th." Of course, since the back order is your fault, it may deserve some explanation. If there is a logical one, present it—especially if the explanation shows good demand for the product or in some other way enhances the demand for it. Words like "As our supply of this very popular product should be replenished by rush shipment due Friday" do the job well. Should your back order be for a long period of time, you may choose to give your reader a way out if she wishes. Something like "Unless we hear from you by the 10th" following the back-order handling should take care of this matter.

## A pleasant ending picture

Like all good acknowledgment letters, you should end this one on some positive topic. If you are handling a vague order, you might choose to end with a request for the information you seek. If skillfully handled, this question can make a positive ending. In other situations you will need to find some specifically adapted goodwill talk. It could be talk about enjoyable use of the product. If you have not already done it earlier in the letter, it could be an expression of your gratefulness for the order. It could even be some resale talk about the products ordered—something which will enhance your reader's interest in the product. In some cases such resale talk may be sprinkled appropriately throughout the letter, especially if there is some likelihood that the reader will not wish to wait for the goods.

## Illustrated handling of delayed order

Good technique in handling order delays is illustrated in the following letter. The case concerns an order for a number of items of individual equipment. Some can be sent right away. One item must be placed on back order. Another requires additional information before it can be sent.

Generally, the letter follows the plan just described. Since some goods are being sent, it uses this information to form the good-news opening contact. It handles the vague order without mentioning the reader's negligence. Instead, it presents the choice from the reader's point of view, and it gives the reader information which should help him to make a choice. The back-order news is presented in its most positive light, with emphasis on receipt of the goods rather than on the delay, and with reselling words which tend to make the product more desirable. The close is a sincere expression of gratefulness, with a forward look to continued friendly relationships.

Dear Mr. Fletcher:

By noon tomorrow, your three new Baskin motors and one Dawson 110 compressor should reach your Meadowbrook shops ready to use on the production line. As you requested, we marked them for your West Side loading dock and sent them by Warren Motor Express.

So that we can be certain of sending you the one handcart for your special uses, will you please review the enclosed description of the two models available? As you will see, the model M is our heavy-duty design, but its extra weight is not justified for all jobs. When you have made your choice, please mark it on the accompanying card and mail the card to us. We'll send your choice to you as soon as we know it.

Your 3 dozen 317 T-clamps should reach you by the 13th. As you may know, these very popular clamps have been in short supply for some time now, but we have been promised a limited order by the 11th. We are marking 3 dozen for rush shipment to you.

It is always a pleasure to do business with your fine organization. We look forward to serving you again with quality industrial equipment.

Sincerely yours,

## CREDIT REFUSALS

Letters which refuse an application for credit carry an unusually negative message. Their major objective of denying credit to someone who wants it obviously is negative, for it goes against the reader's wishes. The situation is made more negative, however, by the very nature of the subject. Credit is tied to personal things a person holds dear—morals, acceptance in society, character, and integrity. Unless skillfully handled, a refusal of credit is likely to be interpreted in the mind as a reflection on the person personally. A situation as negative as this clearly requires that you use the indirect order of organization in handling it.

Perhaps some people will argue that there is no need for you to be concerned about the sensitive feelings of your reader. You are declining his business, they may say, so why spend time trying to avoid offending him? Why not just give him a quick, curt no and let it go at that? If you will carefully study the situation, the answer should be clear to you.

In the first place, being nice to people is personally gratifying to us all—at least, it should be. All the rewards in business are not measured in cold dollars and cents. There are emotional satisfactions to be gained, and kind treatment—by us and to us—produces one of them.

In the second place, being nice to people is profitable in the long run, and perhaps even in the short run. All prospective credit customers who are turned down have needs, and they are going to satisfy them somewhere. The chances are that they will have to buy for cash, for if you turn them down, others are likely to turn them down also. So someone is going to get their cash business, and if you handle them positively, it might be you. In addition, the fact that you must turn them down now does not mean that they never will be good credit customers. Many good credit accounts today were bad risks sometime in the past. By not offending credit applicants now, you may keep them as friends of your company until they improve their ability to handle credit.

## Strategy and the reason for refusal

In studying your case to find the best strategy for breaking the bad news to your reader, you should first consider the reason for your refusal. If your applicant is a bad moral risk, you have a most negative situation. You cannot tell him bluntly that you are refusing because his character is not up to par. The mental filters of even the lowest characters would be likely to react negatively to such moral accusations. Instead, your plan will need to be more roundabout. Probably you will be wise only to imply the reason, and you will not want to promise any future credit extension. As your only interest in him would be as a cash customer, you might want to work for whatever cash business he might be able to give.

If you are refusing because your applicant has a weak capital position, your task is an easier one. Short capital is not a reflection on one personally. In fact, one's ability to pay hardly is related to his personal qualities. Thus, you can broach the subject more directly. And you can talk more optimistically about future credit possibilities should his financial situation change.

## The buffer beginning

As in all letter situations requiring indirect treatment, you should begin the credit refusal letter with some comment that will set up the strategy you have selected. In addition, it should be friendly, neutral talk that will imply neither a yes nor a no answer. And it should be sufficiently close to the specific situation so that your reader recognizes the letter as a reply to his request for credit.

Your specific choice of subject is again a matter for your logical imagination. Almost anything will do which sounds natural and sincere in the one situation and which meets the requirements listed above. If an order accompanies the credit request, you could use some form of reference to it. Perhaps it could be a compliment, a statement of the order's significance, a few words about the merchandise ordered, or the like. The following opening illustrates such possibilities:

> Your January 22nd order for Rock-Wire roofing shows good planning for the rush months ahead. As you will agree, it is good planning which marks the path of the progressive business.

Clearly, the opening ties in with the inquiry being answered. Also, it sets up the strategy with the reference to planning. In following sentences the writer points out his observations over the years that the best-planned businesses hold to a 2-to-1 ratio of current assets to liabilities. Thus, he justifies the refusal on this basis.

If no order accompanies the request, any pleasant talk that fits the situation will do. Probably an expression of appreciation for the request for credit is the most often used subject matter. Because this approach is so often used, it has lost some of its effectiveness; but it is always appropriate and requires less imaginative effort on your part. If you do use it, try for some variation in wording from the timeworn "Thank you for your application" variety as the following opening illustrates:

> We are sincerely grateful for your credit application, Ms. Spangler, and will do all that we reasonably can to help you in getting your business started.

The writer follows this sentence with an explanation showing that granting the application is beyond what could be expected under the circumstances.

### Justification of the refusal

As was mentioned earlier in the discussion of basic strategy for the letter, how you explain your refusal depends on your reason for refusing. If you are refusing on moral grounds, you need to say little. Readers with bad credit records know their credit status, and it takes only an implication or two to let them know that you also know. There is no need at all to say bluntly anything like "Your credit record is bad." The illustration sentence given for handling the refusal part of the letter (see next section) implies much without actually saying it.

For refusing the applicant with good character but weak finances, you should discuss the reasons for refusing with whatever frankness you feel your relationship with the applicant permits. You will want to justify your credit policy as well as you can in terms of the applicant's benefits as well as yours. Perhaps you can show her how experience has proved that cash buying is the wiser policy for a business executive in her financial position. Or you may seek her agreement as a reasonable person on the matter of reasonable credit precautions being good business. Whatever your explanation, it should be sound, believable, and convincing; and it should flow logically to the refusal which follows.

### Tact in the refusal

Your wording in the refusal also depends on the strategy you have selected. If your refusal is for moral reasons, after a brief incidental reference or two to the reasons for the refusal, you can refuse, probably through implication rather than direct words. Words like these do the job clearly yet positively:

As our credit check gives us insufficient evidence to grant you credit at this time, we invite you to join the tens of thousands who save on Deal's discount prices.

Applicants being turned down because of weak finances likewise should be refused positively. In such cases, however, you can look hopefully to the future. For a study in contrasting effects, read carefully the following sentences. The first one is blunt and tactless:

For these reasons, we must refuse all applicants whose current assets-to-liabilities ratio falls below 2 to 1.

This one does the job well:

Thus, for the best interests of both of us, we must postpone credit buying until your current assets-to-liabilities ratio reaches 2 to 1.

## A closing forward look

Because the refusal is bad news, you should follow it with some more pleasant talk. It could be on a variety of topics, as long as they fit the one case and accomplish the goodwill objective. Perhaps the best choice is something that will suggest cash buying. In fact, you might invite the applicant to buy for cash with you, perhaps supporting your invitation with talk about low prices, merchandise, service, and the like. How much you say and how far you go toward driving for a cash sale should depend on your judgment of the reader. This goodwill talk might well mark the end of your letter, with your last words taking a forward look to whatever future relations appear to be appropriate. Two such closes are these:

As one of Myers' cash customers, you will continue to receive the same courtesy, quality merchandise, and low prices we give to all our customers. We look forward to serving you soon.

For your buying convenience, we are sending you our new spring catalog. We look forward to serving you through your orders.

## Cases in review

Illustrating variation in credit refusal are the two following letters. The first is a routine refusal used by a department store. Because the store must handle its credit applications on a mass basis, it does not choose to write individual letters in each case. Thus, the letter is general, and it is short. Yet it covers all that needs to be covered. It explains the reasons for the refusal in positive language, and it ends with a pleasant forward look.

Dear Mr. Sands:

We sincerely appreciate your interest in an account with White-Horton & Company. Whenever we can, we are always willing to serve you.

In determining what we can do for you regarding your December 9th request for credit, we made the routine checks you authorized. The information we have received permits us to serve you only as a cash customer. But as you know, cash buying here at White-Horton's discount prices can make a very real saving for your budget.

We hope to see you in the store again very soon, and we look forward to the opportunity of serving you.

Sincerely yours,

The second letter refuses credit to a mercantile customer who is short of finances. Under the "sound business practice" theme, the letter explains the refusal in a you-viewpoint manner that is meaningful to this one reader, the owner of a laboratory supply business. The letter covers the refusal without harsh, negative words, but through telling what can be done rather than what cannot be done. It does more than is usually expected in such a case: It suggests an alternative. In addition, it works for cash buying in the off-subject close.

Dear Ms. Haines:

Your June 3rd order for Bell precision instruments suggests that Technicians Supplies is continuing to make progress. We sincerely hope that this is the case and that the good growth of the past year will continue.

To assure yourself of that continued growth, we feel certain you will want to follow the soundest business procedures wherever possible. As you may know, most financial experts say that maintaining a reasonable indebtedness is a must for sound growth. About a 2-to-1 ratio of current assets to liabilities is a good minmum, they say. In the belief that the minimum is best for all concerned, we extend credit only when this ratio is met. In your case, perhaps we shall be able to review the application soon. At the rate your organization is growing, your current assets-to-liabilities ratio should reach this sound status soon.

Some companies we know have achieved sound status in record time by taking advantage of every possible saving. One in particular is the very significant 5 percent discount we and most firms like us give for timely cash payments. Your saving on your current order, for example, would amount to $87.30. This percentage added to your cash holdings would help a lot to improve the ratio. Even if you would need to borrow locally, the cash saving on the volume of your purchases would be significant.

We hope that you will soon find it possible to reap these savings with us. We hope also that Bell Instruments will be your partner in progress through the years ahead.

Sincerely yours,

# Letter problems—2

## REFUSED REQUESTS

1. You are sales manager for Sampson Sporting Goods, Inc., manufacturers of a complete line of tennis and golf equipment. Sam Gray, owner of the Sports Shop in Monterey, California, has written you a persuasive letter asking for exclusive rights to Sampson products in his area. As Sampson policy is to sell to any retailer willing to stock Sampson products, you will have to say no. You don't want to offend the man; so you'll try to justify your policy to him. The Sampson people feel they can best satisfy the growing demand for their low-cost, quality products by offering them widely. Sampson's plan appears to be working for hundreds of retailers as well as for Sampson. Explain your position to Sam Gray so convincingly that he will want to handle Sampson products anyway.

2. Addressed to you, president of Continental Industries, Inc., is a letter from the president of your former university. On the 12th of next month he wants you to address his senior students at their annual Career Day convocation. "Just give them some tips on how to go about landing a job," he said in his letter.

You'd like to go, and you are honored by the request. But you can't. You are scheduled to attend the annual stockholders meeting in New York on the 11th and to address the Atlanta Sales Executive Club on the night of the 12th. You can suggest a substitute—Betty Styles, your vice president in charge of sales. Ms. Styles is a most capable person, who is rapidly gaining a reputation as a speaker and leader in business. Write the letter that will convey this information to the president.

**3.** As sales manager of Madeline Mallory Fashions, Inc., manufacturers of a middle-priced line of ladies clothing, you receive a letter from Nancy Canady, owner of Nancy's Dress Shop. Apparently Nancy doesn't know much about her business. In fact, her letter states that she has been in the business only three months.

It seems that Nancy bought more clothing than she can sell. She wants to return $1,640 of the purchases she made ten weeks ago. You can't accept. It's just not done this way in business. There is an element of risk in retailing styled merchandise, which is why there is a premium on wise buying. No manufacturer would be in business long if he had to take care of every retailer's errors. Typically, retailers take care of their errors by discounting the clothes at the end of the season. In fact, the price structure is designed to permit such sales.

Apparently the lady needs a lesson in retailing practices. Your explanation of your refusal will give it to her. And you will do it in such a way as to keep her business.

**4.** Today's mail brings two letters to your sales executive desk. One is an invitation from Becker Industries, Inc., inviting you to work up cost estimates for installing your NoFire fire control system in their mammoth office building. This is the biggest sales possibility you have had in your three years with NoFire. The commission here would more than double your last year's income.

The second letter is a persuasive request from the board of a national philanthropic association (you name it). The association asks you to serve as chairman for the local fund drive. You'd like to do the work, for the cause is a worthy one. But you can't this year. Write the letter that will refuse and make the board understand.

**5.** In your new position as a vice president for National Chemical Company you have just selected Dorothy Cooper as your administrative assistant. Without question, she is the best of the six applicants for the job. Her aptitude test placed her at the top, her scholastic record was the best, and she impressed you most in the interviews.

Now that you have made the selection, you have the task of informing the other applicants that they were not selected. One of them is Robert E. Wise, Jr. Unfortunately, Robert E. Wise, Sr., is an old friend, and he has actively worked to get his son this job. You know you have made the right decision, but now you'll have to explain it to Robert (and his dad) in a letter.

**6.** Place yourself in the position of public relations director of the Olympic National Life Insurance Company and refuse a request from Nathaniel Bush, managing director of the American Collegiate Internship Program, to become a sponsoring company of this organization. This nonprofit organization is made up of a number of sponsoring businesses which give working internships to business administration students during summer vacations. The program is most worthwhile, and it has a proven record of success. Even so, the Olympic administration has elected not to join. And it is your job to give the verdict to Mr. Bush. Although the Olympic administration views this program as a deserving one, it feels that the company simply cannot join. It costs money to hire the students, pay their expenses, train them, etc. Rarely could Olympic expect to get profitable work out of a new employee in a short summer period. So participation in the program would have to be viewed strictly as philanthrophic. And it is not that Olympic doesn't want to do its share. Actually its contributions in the form of scholarships to deserving students is sizeable—as much as it can stand at the moment.

Your job is to think through the situation and write a letter that will handle the refusal so that Mr. Bush will understand.

**7.** As manager of the Stark Hotel, you have received a persuasive letter from Ms. Clara Pettigrew, president of the City Garden Club. It seems that the club will hold its annual garden show on the 19th and 20th of next month. They would like to use your grand ballroom for the affair—free of charge. As Ms. Pettigrew puts it, "the publicity the Stark would get from having the show would be worth much more than the cost of the room."

You will have to refuse the request. To give in to it would likely open the door to a flood of similar requests from other organizations. Like any business organization, your hotel has to operate at a profit. It can't go around giving away a $500-a-night facility any easier than a merchant can give away $500 in merchandise.

You'll have to think through the situation a bit further to build a convincing explanation. But do your best, for the club members represent an influential group in the local population.

**8.** Assume that you are a student representative and chairman of your school's campus traffic committee. The committee has concluded a meeting at which it considered a request for open parking on campus from the local chapter of Student's for Action. By open parking is meant no parking privileges for anyone. Students, faculty, staff—all would be equal on a first-come, first-serve basis.

After considering the pros and cons of the question in a four-hour session, the committee voted unanimously to retain the present system, which gives faculty, staff, and handicapped students priorities. The arrangement makes sense, the committee believes. And they ask you to convey their reasoning in a letter which gives the answer to the request.

**9.** For the past six months, Ms. Malvina Thorn of the White Sands Hotel, Tampa, Florida, has been working on you to schedule your annual sales convention at her place. You were impressed with the facilities of the White Sands, and the price offer was most reasonable. But your sales managers voted to go to the mountains instead. So you selected the Red Hill Lodge in southwestern Colorado.

Probably the group will want to go to a beach resort next year, although you can't be certain. Anyway, Ms. Thorn worked very hard and gave you some very valuable information. So now you will write her a letter telling her your decision and making certain that she is handled in a friendly fashion. Make up any facts you may need as long as they don't change the nature of the assignment.

**10.** A professor in the management department of a major university, you have been active in writing cases for use in your policy course. One of these cases, the Gassie Manufacturing Company, received considerable attention at the last regional meeting of the International Case Writers Association last month. As a result of this favorable discussion, Professor Althea Crittendon of Midway University has written you asking to use the case in a textbook she is writing.

You are flattered at the request, but you have other places for the case. You hope someday to use it in a textbook of your own. Thus, you will have to deny Professor Crittendon's request. As the professor is an old friend, you'll work especially hard to handle the matter carefully.

**11.** In the role of public relations director for the Balboa Manufacturing Company, answer a letter written by Ms. Mary Keene, a third-grade teacher from a nearby city. Ms. Keene has asked to bring her class of 24 students on a visit through your factory next Friday. She is certain the Balboa people won't mind; and she'll have a couple of mothers along to keep the kids in line.

Because of potential dangers throughout the plant, Balboa management doesn't even permit adult groups to visit the production areas. There is just too much that could go wrong. You know it will be a disappointment to the kids, for Ms. Keene's letter tells how excited they are about it. As a compromise, you would be willing to visit her class and show film on your operations. You also would bring along some sample products as gifts for the kids.

Write the lady and handle this difficult assignment.

**12.** As sales manager for Talbot-Shannon Laboratories, Inc., you must write Alton E. Buffington telling him that you didn't select him as manager of the southern region. Alton was a finalist in the selection process, but the nod went to Charlie Cooper. These two candidates were neck and neck in the final selection, but Cooper had a little edge in experience and sales record.

Without question Buffington is an excellent performer. He has potential, and you feel that sooner or later he will move up in the organization. So you will write him a letter that will give him the answer and will have him looking forward to productive work in the future.

## REFUSED CLAIM

13. Assume the position of adjustment manager of the National Electronics Manufacturing Company and deny the claim of Oscar R. Tweedy. Mr. Tweedy mailed you an irate claim for full money back for the NE150 printing calculator he bought through your mail order sales for $247, including tax. Along with the letter he returned the calculator with instructions to "junk it."

Inspection of the instrument reveals that it isn't working because it apparently received a heavy jolt. The broken parts can be repaired easily. You can't give the man his money back, but you will repair the instrument for him at a $9.85 cost. Your one-year guarantee doesn't cover damage from unusual or harsh treatment, which is evident in this case.

14. "Your Ironware luggage is more ware than iron," writes Mrs. Beatrice Wascom. "It already has a bad scratch on it. I want my $185 back for the two pieces I ordered last month. I am returning them to you today."

When the luggage arrives, your inspection does indeed find an ugly scratch on one bag. Apparently the bag received a severe blow. The blow probably would have destroyed any competing luggage, for Ironware is made of a truly durable patented material. But even the most durable material can be damaged in extreme cases.

As you see it, Mrs. Waskom's bags have passed one severe test, probably protecting her clothing while doing it. The product has performed well. You see no reason for refunding her money. But you will repair the damaged bag so that it will look like new. And you'll do it at no cost. Sign the letter as the sales manager for Ironware, Inc.

15. You are in charge of all mail-order adjustments for Casey-Stamps, Inc., one of your area's quality department stores. Today's mail brings you the following letter from one of your out-of-town customers.

Dear Sir:

I am returning the dress I bought from you last Thursday when I was in your city. Please send me the full amount I paid, which was $159.95 plus tax of $9.60. When I got home I realized the dress just doesn't fit right. I am enclosing the sales slip. Thank you for your kind attention to this matter.

Sincerely,
Mrs. Clara Salach

Upon checking out the transaction you find that the dress was bought on sale. And all merchandise bought on sale cannot be returned. If you had to allow for the cost of returns, you could not offer the goods at the low sale price. Anyway, the lady got a real bargain. The dress originally sold for $239.95.

Although Casey-Stamps doesn't return merchandise bought on sale, it does free alterations. So you can promise her a good fit if she will bring the dress into the store the next time she is in town. Write the letter handling this situation skillfully.

**16.** As sales manager of the Highlander Hotel, today you receive a claim letter from Ruth Hooper, convention chairman for the National Association of Office Managers. Ten days ago NAOM held its annual convention at your hotel. It was a good meeting for all concerned. But Ms. Hooper doesn't like the bill for 300 dinners at $10.50 that you sent her. "We sold only 216 tickets," she writes, "and didn't consume 200 meals."

Checking through your correspondence with the lady you find that she estimated that 300 would attend. You had asked her to give you a final count by noon of the day of the dinner. She didn't. So you prepared 300 meals and watched much of the food go to waste.

Clearly the fault is not yours. You cannot grant her claim. But you want to make her understand why you must refuse, and you want to keep her happy. You'd like to get the group back for another convention.

**17.** As owner-manager of Green Thumb Nurseries, Inc., you must refuse a claim made by Peter C. Cappell, an out-of-town contractor. Late last spring Mr. Cappell worked out a deal with you to sell him plants for landscaping a subdivision he was building. The total sale amounted to $23,714, about a 25-percent discount from your usual retail price.

Now Mr. Cappell claims that approximately $6,200 of the plants failed to survive. He wants replacement plants or his money back. You cannot give him either. The survival of plants depends as much on their planting and the care they are given throughout the first month as on their condition at the time of sale. You know the plants were in good condition when they were shipped. Mr. Cappell's employees did the planting and the caretaking; so the blame must fall on him.

Try to make the man accept your decision as a just one. As a goodwill gesture, you can offer to replace the dead plants at your cost—which you estimate to be $5,600.

**18.** Ms. Marilyn Chapman wants her $90 back for the course in business communication she took from the National Business Institute. In Ms. Chapman's words, "I didn't get nothing from the course." As registrar for the Institute, you must refuse her claim.

After reviewing Ms. Chapman's record, you understand her attitude. She barely passed the course, with a D grade. From Thelma Brindley, the course instructor, you learn that the lady put out little effort. Her lessons appeared to have been handled hurriedly and with little reading of the assigned text material.

But it takes just as much time to handle a bad student as it does a good student. So you must refuse. Of course, you'll do it so the lady will accept your decision as a fair one.

**19.** Stecher Learning Aids, Inc., rents and sells educational film to business and educational institutions. Its standard rental charge is $75 (maximum three days), and its sales prices range from $350 to $550 per film. Rental charges may be applied to the purchase price of the film if purchase is made within 30 days of rental.

Twelve months ago, Mary Cole, claim director for the Schroeder Manufacturing Company, rented seven films for an in-house executive training program; and two months ago she rented the same seven films again. Then a week later she wrote Stecher that she had decided to buy the films. Stecher then billed the Schroeder Company for $2,650 (cost of the films) less $525 (rental)—total of $2,125. In today's mail, you (the Stecher sales manager) receive a letter from Ms. Cole presenting a claim for an additional deduction of $525 for the first rental twelve months ago. Stecher doesn't allow such deductions for good business reasons. Think through the situation and write a letter that refuses this claim and justifies the decision.

**20.** It's election time in your state, and your printing company has enjoyed receiving some profitable jobs from the candidates. One in particular was a $16,000 order for posters for the Sally Sands for Governor organization.

Today you receive a letter from Samuel Gotleib, the Sally Sands campaign manager. He presents the claim that the posters were inferior in quality. "The colors are not as sharp and clear as the sample you showed us," he writes. "As we don't have time to wait, we must use them. Yet we feel a 25-percent adjustment is in order."

You don't intend to give the adjustment. It's not just because you're against Sally Sands, but you feel justice is on your side. Mr. Gotleib selected an inferior cardboard for the job—against your advice. The sample posters he looked at were made on better quality cardboard. He could have had the quality he wants had he been willing to pay the additional 15 percent for the better cardboard. He elected the cheaper route.

Now you must write Mr. Gotleib and refuse his claim. But you'll want to handle the matter diplomatically. Sally just could win the election.

## CREDIT REFUSALS

**21.** As proprietor of the Fashion Plate, a dress shop for the fashionable ladies of your town, you have the task of refusing the credit application of Ms. Nancy Malek. Nancy is a records clerk in the tax assessor's office. She makes only a modest salary. But apparently she spends her money faster than she makes it. Her record for payment around town is slow at best. Because Nancy is a personable lady and because she will spend money somewhere in the years ahead, you'll work hard to reduce the negative effect of the refusal.

**22.** Your credit check of the Walshak Mercantile Company told you something that you didn't detect when you talked personally with Dennis Walshak about his credit application. In fact, when you talked with him, you felt that the check would be routine and that the $8,950 order accompanying his request was certain to go through. But the credit check shows different information. Without question, Mr. Walshak has extended his credit too far. For the past year he has been slow to pay. And his credit obligations are much too high.

So even though you would like to have the sale, you must refuse the credit. If you handle the situation well, you may be able to get the man's cash business.

**23.** For 55 years Planters Mercantile Company has been serving the members of the community. Through most of this time, credit was liberally given; and the company prospered.

In recent years, however, the situation has begun to change. The liberal credit policy appears to be backfiring. Instead of making money, the company is losing money. So the company has decided to strengthen its policy.

As a trainee in the credit department, you have been assigned the task of writing a form letter refusing credit. Most of the customers in the area are farmers and wage earners; so you will want to adapt your letter to them. As all of these people will spend some money in the community in the years ahead, you'll try to refuse as positively and with as much convincing explanation as you can.

**24.** Write a personal letter for Lloyd's Department Store refusing credit to Dr. Viola Fahrendorf. Your credit check showed that this young physician owes just about everybody in town.

Probably two reasons explain Dr. Fahrendorf's situation. First, she apparently is a spendthrift of the first order. Second, her income has been severely hampered by some legal problems she has encountered recently.

Whatever the reason, you must refuse. But because the lady is a prominent physician and because she does have good money to spend, you'll work hard to keep her goodwill.

**25.** Bradshaw Brothers Grocery has applied to W and J Wholesale Grocers for credit with a limit of $5,000. As the W and J credit manager, you will have to turn them down.

In a nutshell, Bill and Joe Bradshaw are long on character but short on capital. They have worked hard to build their grocery store. They have a good business—good sales and loyal customers, but currently their assets-to-liabilities ratio is dangerously low. Simply put, they are just too far in debt. As you see it, giving them more credit would hurt them more than it would help them.

But you feel that Bill and Joe will make it in the long run. So you'll handle the matter carefully. You'd like to get their cash sales until they are strong enough to afford credit.

**26.** It won't be easy to refuse credit to Wade Walden, but that's what you must do. This old friend of yours has applied to you for credit to help finance the inventory he needs to open Sports Unlimited, a retail sporting goods store. He wants $12,000 worth of merchandise now on 90-day terms.

The financial information which Wade furnished you with his request for credit presents a weak picture. Apparently, Wade is entering business primarily on character and courage. He has little capital. Your employer, the Cavanaugh Company, just does not extend credit in cases like this.

There are good business reasons for Cavanaugh's policy. Think them out and use them as a basis for your refusal of credit to Wade Walden.

## VAGUE AND BACK-ORDER ACKNOWLEDGMENTS

**27.** Your small importing firm has had good success with its newly acquired line of Iberian Crafts leather goods. So good has been sales, in fact, that shipments from Madrid haven't kept up with sales. So you must handle a number of back orders.

One is from the Crescent Gift Shop of New Orleans, which you feel deserves special attention. This is their first order, and it's a nice one. They want two dozen Iberian Holiday handbags at $324 a dozen, an assortment of tooled leather men's belts for $362, and a dozen Iberian Ambassador men's billfolds at $132. You have the belts and the billfolds in stock; but the handbags will have to wait. The Iberian people promise you delivery within six weeks.

Handle the situation with your best writing effort. And include a new customer welcome.

**28.** As sales manager for the Colonial Clock Works you have a rush order for six of your Timemaster grandfather models. The order is from DeWare's Clock House, one of your newer customers.

Unfortunately, you will need more information before you can fill the order. You make the clock in walnut, pecan, and oak; and no material was specified. Also, the DeWare buyer made no mention of his choice of dial faces. Both arabic and roman numeral dials are available. To make matters even worse, the price quoted in DeWare's order is from an old price list table. Timemasters now sell for $479 at your factory (they quoted $447).

Write the letter that will straighten out this situation.

**29.** In your role as owner, the Book House, you are in the process of filling a mail order for seven books. The order is from old Professor Michael Chutz, who is now retired and living in his Colorado resort home.

Five of the books you have; and you're sending them out today. One (*Outline of Southern History* by Hal Calvin) is out of print. You have located a copy in an out-of-town bookstore and will get it to him within a week. The other book poses a problem. You can find no book by Ethan A. Chaffee titled *Generals of the South*. The man has written two books that might fit this description: *Generals in Grey* and *Generals of the American Revolution*. So you'll need to find out which book the professor wants.

Write the letter that will handle this problem. As Professor Chutz specified, you are billing him for the books. But because you are not shipping all of the books now, you will bill him as you send them.

**30.** Play the role of sales manager for Digi-lator, Inc., manufacturers of a combination digital watch and minicalculator. You are faced with the problem of telling eager retailers they will have to wait about two months on their orders. The extreme popularity of your product has placed your company well behind in production.

One of the orders is from Rose Marie Grimes, owner of Grimes Jewelers in Augusta, Maine. She wants one dozen, and she marks the order *rush*.

Write the letter to Ms. Grimes that will handle the case. Probably this letter will serve as a model for the others you must write.

**31.** Assume the position of manager of mail-order sales for Denson-Cappozola Department Store and write a letter to Ross Comeaux. Apparently Mr. Comeaux saw your advertisement in the local paper ten days ago. Today you receive his order, written in his almost illegible handwriting. The man wants one of your Town House smoking jackets at $57.50, burgundy and black and two pairs of your McGruder slacks, midnight blue and tan at $42.00 each. He specifies that you send the goods c.o.d.

Unfortunately, you can't send either item right away. Your smoking jacket sold out the third day. You have more on order. They should be in within a month. You have a good supply of the slacks, but you can't send them until you know the man's size.

**32.** Mrs. Damon Klug wants her order for the seven dozen Politz shoes she selected in time for the opening of her Happy Feet Shoe Store in two weeks. You can send her most of them—all except the two Politz Duchess pumps in camel tan and white. These stylish, pigskin shoes are extremely popular this year—so popular, in fact, that production is well behind orders. You can get them for the lady within a month.

As sales manager for the Politz Shoe Company, you must write Mrs. Klug telling her the status of her order. Perhaps you'll want to make some suggestions about other shoes that you could get for her in time for the opening date. But you want to keep the Duchess shoes on back order, also.

**33.** You are in charge of mail-order sales for Durham's, one of the nation's largest department stores. As you read the order from Mr. Albert Overdyke, you become exasperated. The man has an almost illegible handwriting.

In response to your advertisement in the state edition of the local newspaper, Mr. Overdyke asks for "one of those number 12-A crepe sport shirts. . . ." The next few words are hard to read. Is it "light grey" or "lime green"? And is the size 15½–34 or 16½–34? You can't be sure. He has the price right—$21.37, including tax.

The second item he ordered is easier to describe. He wants two pairs of your Vega brand slacks in dark green and brown. Unfortunately, you have sold out of these popular slacks. You have reordered and expect delivery in 10 days.

Using your imagination to supply any additional information you feel is necessary, write the letter that handles this situation.

**34.** Place yourself in the position of the owner of the Classic Uniform Company and handle a difficult letter problem. Your advertisement in *Harmony Magazine* appears to be paying off. Already you have received seven orders for uniforms from men's glee clubs. The latest one, from the Boones Valley Harmoneers, is for 28 blue blazers with white slacks. Appropriate sizes and other specifications are in order. All is well except for the fact that you can't meet their requirements of delivery within 30 days. The problem is your backlog of work from prior orders, all of them requiring rush treatment. The best you can promise is delivery in 60 days.

Using your imagination to supply any facts you may need, write the letter that will convey the bad news to the Harmoneers. Convince them that your slacks and blazers are worth waiting for. Address the letter to C. Calvin Combs, manager.

# 11

# Correspondence:
# Persuasive letters

SOME OF YOUR business letter objectives are likely to incur the resistance of your reader. It may be that she will view your goal as contrary to her best interests. She may feel that your objective is contrary to her wishes. Or perhaps she just may have little or no interest in your message. In any event, if you are to succeed with your letter, you must overcome this resistance. Specifically, you must alter the filter makeup of her mind so that she will accept your objective as fair and reasonable. The techniques you use in this effort are those of persuasion.

In analyzing a persuasion situation from a communications point of view, we may begin by looking at your main objective. In general, it is to communicate a message which will make your reader come around to your way of thinking. At the outset, however, your reader does not accept your objective. If she were likely to do so, you would use the simpler direct approach. As things stand, her mental filter contains facts, impressions, or viewpoints which in some way make her oppose your objective. If you are to succeed in turning her thinking around, you will need to overcome the barriers which exist in her mental filter.

In overcoming these barriers, you will need to analyze the resistance in the mind of your reader. You will need to try to see the problem through your reader's mind. You will need to consider all that makes up her thinking on this point—her experience, biases, attitudes, and the like. You will have to anticipate the objections she might have. Then, with her viewpoint analyzed, you should do some good hard thinking to find explanations and arguments for overcoming her objections. That is, you will need to work out in your mind just what you can say that will convince her to come over to your side. To do the job well will require all your best in human evaluation, in logical reasoning, and in convincing writing.

The specific organization plan you should use in persuasion problems will vary depending on the facts of the case. In general, however, you should follow the indirect order. The indirect order is justified because in persuasive situations you anticipate that your reader's first reaction to your objective will be to oppose it. Thus, the message your letter brings is unfavorable; and as we know, unfavorable messages are best handled indirectly. In fact, we may view persuasion letters as just a special type of unfavorable letters. We discuss them in a separate chapter because they have some unique problems.

Our plan for study of this form of letter is again to take up some of its representative types. First, we shall analyze a routine persuasive request letter. This is the basic type of persuasion letter, and our approach to it sets the pattern for most of the other persuasion letters. Next, we shall move into more specialized areas of persuasion: sales, collections, and applications. As in preceding chapters, our review is selective, but it is representative of the major types you will find in business. If you study the analyses used in each of the following situations, you should have little difficulty adapting to any of the problems in persuasion.

## PERSUASIVE REQUESTS

Requests which are likely to encounter resistance require a slow, deliberate approach. As we noted in Chapter 9, the fast-moving direct order is preferable in most inquiries; but to begin with a request the reader is likely to oppose would be to invite failure. Very obviously, you must change this negative mental attitude if you are to achieve your objective. Thus, in such cases you should sacrifice the speed and simplicity of directness. In its stead, you should elect the slower approach of persuasion.

### Determination of persuasion

Your planning of the persuasive request letter is a matter for your logical imagination. You will need to place yourself in your reader's position, and you will need to think through his mind as well as your own. Specifically, you will need to determine any objections he might have. Then you will have to build arguments or explanations which will overcome them.

In some cases your thinking will be comparable to that used by the orderly and logical debater. You will think through the problem noting the points of opposition; and you will develop the counterpoints and arguments to these points. In other cases, you may need to see your reader on your objective through the use of basic appeals. For example, you may be able to build an argument showing how your reader stands to gain directly from your objective in time, money, and such. Or perhaps you can show how he stands to gain in goodwill or prestige. Sometimes you may be able to persuade by appealing to his aesthetic side—to his love of beauty, excitement, serenity, and the like. When such appeals as these will not do the job, you may be able to use the altruistic appeal— the pleasant feeling one gets from doing a good turn. In any event, your task is to build the most convincing strategy you can devise for your specific situation.

### Attention in the opening contact

Armed with the strategy which will convince your reader that he should grant your request, you are ready to fit it into a plan for presentation. As we have noted, the best plan for such letters is an indirect one. Thus, your opening will not give away your goal. Instead, it will serve as a form of buffer for your main objective.

As in other indirect letters, your opening has the basic objective of setting up the strategy of your presentation. In persuasion situations, however, it has a second objective. Because you usually are writing to someone who has not invited your correspondence and who may not even care to see it, your opening must also gain your reader's interest. A flat, dull statement would do little to begin the change which must be made in your reader's mind. You can get better results from some interest-arresting question or statement which will start his mental activity. Because of its natural interest value, a question form of beginning is especially good, if, of course, it is appropriate to your strategy. The following beginning sentences illustrate some of the possible variations.

From a covering letter of a questionnaire seeking medical doctors' opinions:

> What, in your opinion as a medical doctor, is the future of the private practice of medicine?

From a letter requesting contributions for handicapped children:

> While you and I dined heartily last night, 31 orphans at San Pablo Mission had only dried beans to eat.

From a letter seeking cooperation of business leaders in promoting a fair:

> What would it mean to your profits if 300,000 free-spending visitors were to come to our town during a single week?

## Presentation of the persuasion

Following your interest-arresting opening, you should proceed with your objective of persuading your reader. Your task here involves a logical and orderly presentation of the reasoning you have selected to convince your reader.

As in all convincing arguments, you should do more than merely list the points which support your stand. You should help to put over your points with words and structures which add to their persuasiveness. Since you are trying to penetrate a resisting mind, you will need to make good use of you-viewpoint adaptation in your discussion. You will need to pay careful attention to the connotations of your words and the clarity of your expression. And because your reader may tend to become impatient if you delay your objective for long, you will need to make your words travel fast.

## Goodwill and action in the close

After you have done the selling job, you logically move to the action you seek. You have prepared the reader for what you want; and if you have done a good job, she is ready to accept your proposal.

As with all negative parts, your request requires care in word choice. You will want to avoid all words which tend to detract from it. You will want to avoid words which bring to mind ugly pictures and things which might work against you. Words which bring to mind reasons for refusing are especially harmful, as in this example:

> I am aware that business people in your position have little free time to give, but will you please consider accepting an assignment to the board of directors of the Children's Fund?

The following positive tie-in with a major point in the persuasion strategy does a much better job of asking:

> Because your organizing skills are so desperately needed, will you please serve on the board of directors of the Children's Fund?

Whether your request should end your letter will depend on the needs of the case. In some cases you will need to follow your request with additional words of explanation and conviction. Especially is this procedure effective when your persuasion effort must be long and you simply cannot keep your objective from your reader through the presentation of all your reasoning. On the other hand, less involved presentations might well end with the request. Even in this latter case, however, you may want to follow the request with words which leave the reader thinking about the theme of your persuasion plan. As illustrated at the end of the following letter, this procedure associates the request with the advantage the reader will enjoy if she agrees to the request.

## Approach variations illustrated

That persuasive requests make good use of the imagination is illustrated by the following examples. All generally follow the plan just described, yet each adapts to the specific situation and readers involved. The first is a request sent to noncontributors by the solicitation committee of a city's Junior Achievement program. The letter's opening has good interest appeal, and it sets up the overall plan. Perhaps its special need for explanation slows the movement to the persuasion effort somewhat. But the explanation helps in the persuasion effort. Its strength comes from a strong you-viewpoint slant, and it leads directly to the action close.

Dear Mr. Williams:

Right now—right here in our city—620 teen-age youngsters are running 37 corporations. With their only adult help being advice from some of your business associates who work with them, the kids run the whole show. Last September they applied for a charter and elected officers. They selected products for manufacture—antifreeze, candles, and chairs, to name a few. They issued stock—and they sold it, too. With the proceeds from stock sales, they set up a production operation. Now they are producing and marketing their products. This May they will liquidate their companies and account to their stockholders for their profits or losses.

You, as a public-spirited citizen, will quickly see the merits of the Junior Achievement program. You know the value of such realistic experience to the kids—how it teaches them the operations of business and how it sells them on the merits of our American system of free enterprise. You can see, also, that it's an exciting and wholesome program—the kind we need more of to combat delinquency. After you have considered these points and others you will find in the enclosed brochure, I know you will see that Junior Achievement is a good thing.

Like all good things, Junior Achievement needs all of us behind it. During the three years the program has been in our city, it has had enthusiastic support from local business leaders. But with the over 900 students on the waiting list this year, our plans for next year call for expansion. That's why I ask that you help make the program available to more youngsters with a $25 contribution (it's deductible). Please make your check payable to Junior Achievement, and sent it right away. You will be doing a fine thing for the kids in our town.

Sincerely yours,

The next letter uses the interest-gaining narrative approach to gain the attention of prospective contributors for Father Flanagan's Boys Town. Its appeal is subtle, coming mainly through the sympathy aroused from the story told. It is powerful persuasion. It illustrates how far the imagination may range in finding an effective approach.

My dear Friend:

A knock at the door—a swirl of snow over the threshold and standing in the warm glow of the hall light was little Joe. His thin jacket was drawn tightly around his small body. "I'm here, Father, I'm here for an education," he blurted out.

Like other homeless boys, Joe dropped out of school at an early age. He had made his lonely way over hundreds of miles to Boys Town, determined to better himself by continuing his education. Now he stood there, cold, hungry, and forlorn, his big eyes pleading. A hot meal and a warm clean bed for the night—again I had found a room for one more boy. Joe proved to be an adept student and now, a leading citizen in his community, he follows his profession like other Boys Town graduates as shown on the back of this letter.

During the past 47 years about 11,000 homeless boys have come to Boys Town. They were sad of heart, sensitive, and with many hidden heartaches because some tragedy had robbed them of their home and parents. Here they begin life all over again, in clean, healthy surroundings. Through understanding and individual counseling we give them a feeling of contentment and a sense of dignity. They receive an excellent education in our well equipped and fully accredited schools.

As Christmas approaches our hearts go out to these unfortunate boys and for the other homeless ones who will be coming to Boys Town. Will you help me provide for them? Here are your Boys Town Christmas seals. Please keep them and use them and send me in the enclosed envelope $1, $2, $5, or more as your heart dictates.

In appreciation of your kind generosity our boys will elect you an Honorary Citizen of Boys Town and I will send your certificate with my acknowledgment. May your Christmas be especially happy since you have extended a helping hand to our unfortunate and helpless boys. Thank you and God bless you!

Sincerely,

Somewhat different from the preceding example is the letter sent to a famous scientist by a college group seeking the scientist's participation in a campus program. Certainly, its opening is in the interest-gaining category, and it does a good job of setting the stage for explanation. Because of the nature of this problem, more than the usual explanation is needed; but much of the dulling effect of explanation is counteracted with fast, lively writing. It uses less persuasion than the first letter, but in this case the facts included also tend to persuade, especially the reference in the end to preservation of the conference proceedings in a time capsule.

Dear Dr. von Braun:

The "World of 2076"—what is it?

It's a program—an exciting, stimulating program designed to challenge the mind, shake the webs of youth, and awaken a keen sense of responsibility for the challenges of life in the future. Yes, the "World of 2076" is a program for projecting 18,000 University students into the possible, predictable coming century. From this "trip" the young leaders of tomorrow should return better prepared for the mushrooming complexities of tomorrow.

You, Dr. Von Braun, living today with these complexities of the future, can well appreciate the need for instilling the challenges of tomorrow in the youth of today. To accomplish such a task is no simple matter, but it is a task to which we have committed ourselves for the Spring of 1976.

For 14 weeks the full facilities of the Union will concentrate on making our student body time-travelers into the future. To aid us, we are enlisting the materials and talents of some of America's most dynamic companies (I.B.M., General Electric, Boeing, the Rand Corporation) and some of the greatest minds in each area which the program will cover.

You will be particularly interested in one major segment of the program: "Outer Space: On to the Stars." Because of your unique experience and position, you can provide insights into the frontier of space as no other speaker can. So we want you to deliver the key lecture on this topic. Will you accept this challenge of helping us prepare for the future? Our flexible schedule will allow us to fit this entire segment of the program around your presentation—any time from February to March that will be convenient for you. Of course, an honorarium and complete expenses will be provided.

Dr. Von Braun, your part of this challenging program will be an invaluable part of the total effort in this "projection." We know that when our time capsule of the complete record of the project is opened in 2076 your words will again point up the importance of thinking ahead. Your answer to this challenge will help bring the future a step closer. As we must complete plans by the semester's end, may we have your answer soon?

Sincerely yours,

## SALES LETTERS

Probably you will never write a sales letter—a real one, that is. With small exceptions, sales letters are written by professional writers who specialize in selling by the written word. They get to be professionals, first, by having a talent for writing and, second, by long, hard practice. Why then, you might ask, should you know how to write sales letters?

## Value of sales writing

Even though you are not likely to be called on to write sales letters, you benefit much from the experience of writing them, although your efforts may appear amateurish. Especially do you benefit from experience in using the techniques of selling which all sales letters employ. The experience you gain will help you in writing other letters, for in a sense every letter you write is a sales letter. In every letter case you are selling something—an idea, a line of reasoning, your company, yourself. And to do this selling in each of these letter situations, you use the general techniques of selling.

Even in your daily life you will find good use for the selling technique. From time to time, all of us are called on to sell something. If we are engaged in selling goods and services, our sales efforts will, of course, be frequent. In other areas of business our selling effort may consist only of selling such intangibles as an idea, our own competency, and the good-will of the firm. In all such cases you can make good use of the selling techniques. Thus, sales writing and the techniques used in it actually are more valuable to you than you might at first think. After you have studied the section, you should see why.

## Need for preliminary knowledge

Before you can begin writing, you must know something about your product and your readers. Knowing your product is an obvious require-ment. You simply cannot sell most goods and services unless you know something about them. To sell, you have to tell your prospect what he needs to know about the product—how it is made, how it works, what it will do, what it will not do, and the like. Thus, as an initial step in sales writing, you will need to study very carefully that which you propose to sell.

Next, you will need to know something about the people who will read your message, especially their needs for your product. In the progressive business organization a marketing research department or agency will gather this information. If you do not have such an agency to supply you with the necessary information, you will need to use your best logic to help you. The nature of the product should give you some of the guidance you need. For example, industrial equipment would be likely to be bought by men with technical backgrounds. Expensive French perfumes and cosmetics would be most attractive to ladies in high income brackets. And burial insurance would appeal to the older members of the lower economic strata.

## Determination of appeal

With your product and prospect in mind, you are ready to begin the imaginative work which will create your letter. Although this is the area about which we know so little, it does involve selecting the appeals you will use in the letter. By appeals, we mean those strategies which we may use to present a product to make it desirable to the reader. We could, for example, introduce our product in terms of its beauty. We could present its taste qualities. We could stress the fun the product will give, or how it will make one more attractive to members of the opposite sex. Or we could attempt to sell our audience through an appeal to profits, savings, durability, and the like.

For convenience in studying them, we may divide appeals into two broad groups. In one group are the emotional approaches to persuasion— those which affect how we feel. Included here are all the appeals to our senses—tasting, smelling, feeling, hearing, and seeing. They include also all strategies designed to arouse us through love, anger, pride, fear, and enjoyment. Rational appeals are the appeals to reason—to the thinking mind. Included in this group are persuasion efforts based on saving or making money; doing a job better, more quickly, or more efficiently; and getting better use of a product.

In any given case the possible appeals available to you are many, and you need to consider all that fit your product. Which ones you select should be based on an analysis of product and prospect as well as a consideration of the prospect's need for the product. Some products, for example, are well suited to emotional selling. Products and services like perfume, travel, style merchandise, candy, and exotic cuisine clearly lend themselves to emotional reasons for buying. On the other hand, products like automobile tires, tools, or industrial equipment are best sold through appeals in the rational area. Automobile tires, for example, are not bought because they are beautiful, because they move us aesthetically, or the like. People buy them for very rational reasons—because they are durable, because they grip the road, because they are safe.

How the product will be used by the buyer may be a major determinant of the best sales strategy to use. Cosmetics sold to the ultimate user might well be sold through emotional appeals. The same product sold to a retailer, who is interested only in reselling the product, would require rational appeals. Such a reader would have interests in the emotional qualities of the product only to the extent that they would influence his customers to buy from him. His main concern about the product involves questions such as the following: Will it sell? What is the likely turnover? How much money will it make?

## An approach to the subject

When you have selected the basic appeals to use, you should next turn to the task of putting your presentation in writing. It is at this point that your imagination comes into full play. Writing sales letters is as creative an activity as writing short stories, plays, and novels. It is an exercise in applied psychology and the artful manipulation of language. The variations in techniques and approaches it uses are infinite, and the only means of judging them is by the sales success of the letter.

Because sales writing involves so much about which we know so little, it cannot be reduced to a formula. Even so, in the following paragraphs we shall study what might be regarded as a classic pattern—the pattern into which most sales letters fit. And we shall describe certain considerations and techniques which are generally used. As you study this material, you should keep in mind that only your imagination limits what you may do in sales writing. In the final analysis, what is good is determined by what will achieve your goals.

## Some mechanical differences

A part of your effort in putting your thoughts on paper concerns the mechanical arrangements you will give the letter. Sales letters may differ in many ways from ordinary business letters in their physical arrangements. With small exception, they are mass-produced rather than individually typed. They may use inside addresses that are individually typed; but this costly but effective technique all too often is substituted by impersonal salutations, such as "Dear Student," "Dear Mr. Homeowner," or "Dear Sir." One widely used technique is to eliminate the salutation and inside address and to place the beginning words of the letter in the form of these parts. As shown in the following illustration, this arrangement gives the letter what appears at first glance to be a normal layout. The letters can be mass-produced without the cost of individually typed inside addresses.

IT'S GREAT FOR PENICILLIN
BUT YOU CAN DO WITHOUT IT
ON YOUR ROOF. . . .

We're referring to roof fungus, which, like penicillin, is a moldlike growth. However, the similarity ends there. Unlike penicillin, roof fungus serves. . . .

Sales letters may use a variety of mechanical techniques to gain attention. Pictures, lines, diagrams, and cartoons are common; so is the use of varying colors of type. Devices such as coins, stamps, sandpaper, rubber bands, pencils, and paper clips may be affixed to the letter to gain interest and help put over the appeal. One letter, for example, was mailed on scorched pages to emphasize the theme of "some hot news about fire insurance." A letter with a small pencil glued to the page used the theme that "the point of the pencil is to make it easy to order" a certain magazine. As you can see, the imagination possibilities in sales writing are boundless.

## The attention opening

Although how you begin the sales letter can vary to the extent of your imagination, your words must meet one fundamental requirement. They must gain attention. Not to do so would insure the failure of your letter. The reason for the attention need of the opening should be apparent from your own experience. Sales letters are sent without invitation. They are not likely to be received favorably and, in fact, may even be unwanted. So, unless the opening words do something to overcome the barriers and gain the reader's attention, the letter travels to the wastebasket unread.

Your plan for gaining attention is a part of your creative effort. But whatever you do, it should assist in presenting the sales message. That is, it must help to set up your strategy. It should not be just attention for attention's sake. Attention is really easy to get if nothing else is needed. For example, a small explosion set off when the reader opens the envelope would gain attention, as would an apparatus which would give him an electric shock, or a miniature stink bomb. But these devices would not be likely to assist in the selling. Unless the attention is favorably directed, animosities or irritations are likely to build up, and the letter is doomed.

One of the most effective attention-gaining techniques is to use a statement or question which introduces a need the product will satisfy. For example, a rational-appeal letter to a retailer would clearly tap his strong needs with these words:

Here is a proven best seller—and with a 12-percent greater markup!

Another rational-appeal beginning is this first sentence of a letter seeking to place metered typewriters in hotel lobbies:

Can you use an employee who not only works free of charge but who also pays you for the privilege of serving your clientele 24 hours a day?

Yet another rational-appeal beginning is this opening device from a letter selling a trade publication to business executives:

How to move more products,
Win more customers,

And make more money
. . . for less than $1 a week

For an illustration of a need-fulfilling beginning of an emotional-appeal approach, study these words which begin a letter selling a fishing vacation at a lake resort:

> Your line hums as it whirs through the air. Your lure splashes and dances across the smooth surface of the clear water as you reel. From the depths you see the silver streak of a striking bass. You feel a sharp tug. And the battle is on!

As you can see, the preceding paragraph begins to cast an emotional spell around the reader, which is what emotional selling should do. It puts a rod in the reader's hand, and it takes him through the thrills of the sport. To an addicted fisherman, the need is clearly established. Now he will be willing to listen to see how the need can be fulfilled.

As was mentioned previously, gimmicks are sometimes used to gain interest, but a gimmick is effective only if it supports the theme of the letter. One company made effective use of a penny affixed to the page top with these words:

> Most pennies won't buy much today, but this penny can save you untold worry and money—and bring you new *peace of mind*.

A paper manufacturer used a letter with small samples of sandpaper, corrugated aluminum, and smooth glossy paper fastened to the top of the page with these first words:

> You've seen the ads—
> you've heard the talk—
> now feel for yourself what we mean by *level-smooth*.

Another opening approach is the story technique. Most people like to read stories, and if you can start one interestingly, your reader should want to hear the rest of it. Following is the interest-catching beginning of a four-page masterpiece used by *Time* magazine:

> The girl in my office doorway was blond . . . real blond.
> Her dress was as short as a cop's temper and tighter than a landlord's pocketbook. Her coat had orphaned a lot of little minks . . . and the ice on her wrists was the non-melting kind.

## Presentation of the sales material

After you have gained your reader's attention and have set up the strategy of your selling effort, you develop this strategy. What you do in this part of the letter is, of course, a product of the thinking and planning you did at the beginning of your preparation. In general, however, you will try to develop a need for your product, and you will present your product as a fulfillment of that need.

The plan of your selling effort may vary with your imagination, but it will follow certain general patterns determined by your choice of appeals. If you select a predominantly emotional approach, for example, your opening probably has established an emotional atmosphere which you will continue to develop throughout the letter. Thus, you will sell your product in terms of its effects on your reader's senses. You will describe your product's appearance, texture, aroma, and taste so vividly and clearly that your reader will mentally see it, feel it—and want it. In general, you will seek to create an emotional need for your product.

If your basic strategy happens to be appeal strictly to your reader's rational thought processes, your sales description is likely to be based on factual material. In such a case, you will describe your product more in terms of what it can do for your reader than how it appeals to his senses. You will write matter-of-factly about such qualities as durability, savings, profits, and ease of operation. Differences in these two sharply contrasting appeals are shown in the illustrations beginning on page 235.

## Stress on the you-viewpoint

In no area of business communication is you-viewpoint writing more important than in sales writing. As we noted in our discussion of the makeup of our mental filters, we human beings are selfish creatures. We are persuaded best through our own self-interest. Thus, in our sales writing we would do well to present our points in terms of our reader's interests. More specifically, we should make good use of the pronoun *you* and the implied *you* throughout our presentation.

The techniques of you-viewpoint writing are best described through illustration. For example, in a letter seeking to sell to a retailer, the writer may wish to stress what the manufacturer will do through advertising to help the retailer sell the product. He could present this information in matter-of-fact fashion: "Star mixers will be advertised in *Time* for the next four issues." Or he could present the information in terms of what it means to the reader: "Your customers will read about the new Star mixers in all January issues of *Time*." For another example, instead of merely quoting price in impersonal language like "a 4-ounce bottle costs $2.25 and you can sell it for $3.50," the reader's interests are better served with something like "You can sell the 4-ounce size for $3.50 and make almost a 55-percent profit on your $2.25 cost." The following contrasting examples further illustrate the value of the technique:

| *Matter-of-fact statements* | *You-viewpoint statements* |
|---|---|
| We make Aristocrat hosiery in three colors. | You may choose from three lovely shades . . . |
| The Regal has a touch as light as a feather. | You'll like its feather-light touch. |
| Lime-Fizz tastes fresh and exciting. | You'll like the fresh, exciting taste of Lime-Fizz. |
| Baker's Dozen is packaged in a rectangular box which has a bright bull's eye design. | Baker's Dozen's new rectangular package fits compactly on your shelf, and its bright bull's eye design is sure to catch the eyes of your customers. |

### Completeness of the sale

Although what information you present and how you present it is a matter of your best judgment, you must present sufficient information to complete the sale. You should leave none of your reader's questions unanswered; nor should you fail to overcome any of his likely objections. You must work to include all such basic information in your letter. And you should make it clear and convincing.

In your effort to include all necessary information, you may choose to use any of a variety of supplementary sales material—booklets, leaflets, brochures, and the like. When you use such supplements, you should take care to coordinate all the parts of your mailing so that you have a unified sales presentation. As a general rule, you should use the letter to carry your basic sales message. More specifically, in your letter you should not shift a major part of your sales effort to an enclosure. Instead, you should use the enclosures primarily to supplement the sales letter—to supply the descriptive, pictorial, and other information that is too detailed for including in the letter. So that all the parts of your mailing fit together into a unified sales effort, you might well direct the reader's attention to each of them. You can do this best through incidental references in the text of the letter.

### Clearness and motion in the action

After you have sold your reader on your product or service, the next logical step is to ask for the sale you seek. After all, this is what you have been working for all along; and it is a very natural conclusion to the sales effort you have made.

Just how you will word your drive for action will depend somewhat on your strategy in the letter. If your selling effort is strong, your action may also be strong, even approaching a command. If you use a milder approach, you could make it a direct question. In any event, the drive for action should be crystal-clear—in no way resembling a hint. For best effect, it should take the reader through the motions of whatever will be necessary to complete the transaction, as is typified by these examples:

> Just check your preferences on the enclosed stamped and addressed order form. Then drop it in the mail today!
>
> Won't you please permit us to deliver your Tabor recorder on approval? The number is 348-8821. Dial it now, while it's on your mind.
>
> Mail the enclosed card today—and see how right the *Atlantic* is for you!

### Urgency in the action

Because action is sometimes delayed and forgotten, you would do well to include in your request some urge for immediate action. "Do it now," "While it's on your mind," or "Act today" illustrate some of the possible versions of this technique. Especially can you use this technique effectively when you tie it in with a practical reason for taking the action, such as "to take advantage of this three-day offer," "so that you can be ready for the Christmas rush," or "so that you will be the first in your community."

### Recall of the appeal

Yet another effective technique for the close of a sales letter is to insert a few words which bring back to the reader's mind the basic appeal you have used. The strategy here should be clear. By associating the action with the benefits your reader will gain by taking the action, you can add strength to your bid for a sale. Illustrating this technique is a letter selling Ever-Flame cigarette lighters to retailers. After building its sales effort around a high-turnover, high-profit theme, the letter makes a drive for action and follows it with these words:

> . . . and start taking your profits from the fast-selling Ever-Flame lighter.

Or, for another example, a letter selling a fishing resort vacation could follow its action words with these words recalling the joys described earlier in the letter:

> It's your reservation for a week of battle with the fightingest bass in the Southland.

## A study of examples

Evidence of the creative nature of sales letter writing is shown best by example. A thorough review of possibilities, however, would be voluminous and could not possibly fit into the space requirements of this book. Our course, therefore, is to select a limited number of diverse types of letters to illustrate some of the variations possible.

First is a letter selling the services of a restaurant consultant. Because of the very nature of the service, a strongly rational appeal is justified. Notice especially how the description of the service is presented in you-viewpoint language.

Dear Ms. Collins:

"Killshaw is adding $15,000 a year to my restaurant's profits!"

With these words, Bill Summers, owner of Boston's famed Pirate's Cove, joined the hundreds of restaurant owners who will point to proof in dollars in assuring you that I have a plan that can add to your profits.

My time-proved plan to help you add to your profits is a product of 28 years of intensive research, study, and consulting work with restaurants all over the nation. I found that where food costs exceed 40 percent, staggering amounts slip through restaurant managers' fingers. Then I traced down the causes of these losses. I can find these trouble spots in your business—and I'll prove this to you in extra income dollars!

To make these extra profits, all you do is send to me, for a 30-day period, your guest checks, bills, and a few other things I'll tell you about later. After these items have undergone my proved method of analysis, I will write you an eye-opening report that will tell you how much money your restaurant should make and how to make it.

From the report, you will learn in detail just what items are causing your higher food costs. And you will learn how to correct them. Even your menu will receive thorough treatment. You will know what "best sellers" are paying their way—what "poor movers" are eating into your profits. All in all, you'll get practical suggestions that will show you how to cut costs, build volume, and pocket a net 10 to 20 percent of sales.

For a more detailed explanation of this service, you'll want to read the enclosed information sheet. Then won't you let me prove to you, as I have to so many others, that I can add money to your income this year? This added profit can be yours for the modest investment of $500 ($200 now and the other $300 when our profit plan report is submitted). Just fill out the enclosed form and place it along with your check in the addressed and stamped envelope that is provided for your convenience.

That extra $15,000 or more will make you glad you did!

Sincerely yours,

Written on clear plastic in red, black, and blue type, the following letter seeks to sell *Popular Science* subscribers on renewing their subscriptions. Although the words may appear to place undue emphasis on the writer, the slant deftly brings out the reader's point of view. The personal tone of the writing adds to its effectiveness.

Dear Friend:

Here's an honest-to-goodness attempt to make everything between us as CLEAR as CRYSTAL—

Frankly, I'm thoroughly confused because out of the thousands of readers whose subscription expired with yours several months ago, you're one of the very small handful who have not renewed yet. Whatever it is that's holding up your renewal, I wish you'd let me know about it because you're a good customer and we miss you.

I'm sure you haven't lost your hearty interest in the latest news on cars and car repairs, inventions, home workshop projects and ideas, aviation, mechanics, and the hundreds of other exciting things POPULAR SCIENCE brings to your doorstep every month. I'm sure you'll find the lively new features and money-saving home repair articles lined up for coming issues of POPULAR SCIENCE even *more* inviting than ever!

Chances are you've been intending to renew all along, but just keep putting it off. To make certain you don't delay another minute, I'm going ALL OUT with a special bargain offer that can't be *repeated!*

I'm going to SLASH the regular rate of $8.40 a year DOWN TO ONLY $6—SAVING YOU A FULL 28%! That means you'll get 12 crisp, new issues of POPULAR SCIENCE for only 50¢ a copy. You save even more by renewing for 2 or 3 years!

So get on the band wagon. Join the vast majority who have already renewed their subscriptions. All you have to do is fill in and return the enclosed postage-free order card TODAY. If it isn't convenient to send your remittance now, don't worry about it because your credit is TOPS with me.

This is CLEARLY a bargain you shouldn't miss!

Sincerely yours,

Letters to dealers typically are all rational appeal, as is the next example. Because dealers are always interested in profit makers, this one starts out with a direct statement of a claim. The remainder of the letter is devoted to proving the claim. It does it with good you-viewpoint description which interprets the product features in terms of customer satisfaction, sales, turnover, profits, and the like.

Dear Ms. Sullivan:

Here's a new, fast-selling profit maker that's a "must" for the progressive automobile accessory store. It's Drive-Rest—a long-needed support for the driver's right arm that will sell to your comfort-seeking truck- and car-owner customers.

Your customers will like the fast, easy adjustment that moves Drive-Rest up or down, right or left, and into the desired position (a Drive-Rest solution to a problem that has long kept major automobile manufacturers from placing permanent drivers' right arm rests in their cars). Best of all, they'll be sold on the relaxed, "easy-chair" ride the Drive-Rest will give them.

Your salespeople will have smooth sailing in selling customers on Drive-Rest's overall construction. Its sturdy support bar of special alloy aluminum is insulated for fullest protection to clothing and upholstery. The rest itself is cushioned with foam rubber and upholstered with a durable material in several colors.

Drive-Rest will be a "natural" to feature to the throngs of vacationers who will soon be shopping for items that will add comfort and pleasure to summer driving. There will be additional sales to the front- and backseat riders, too. We'll furnish the mats that will bring them in for the sale.

Profitable sales will continue beyond the vacation period. Weekend drivers, salespeople, truck drivers—in fact, all who want driving comfort on those long straightaway drives—will keep your profits coming in the year around. And profits are good, too. You get the Drive-Rest for 50 percent and 10 percent off the suggested selling price of $12.95 (no excise tax added) on terms of 2/10, n/30, f.o.b. Houston, Texas. All armrests are packed in individual boxes. Shipping weight is 36 per 100 pounds, and they take third-class freight rate. Look over the enclosed catalog sheet—then mail your order for Drive-Rest.

The profits will make you glad you did.

Sincerely yours,

Some products, such as travel, jewelry, and perfume, lend themselves to purely emotional appeals. Because the reader must be approached in terms of his own enjoyment of the product, as many senses as possible are brought into play in the writing. Such a situation is shown in the next example, which seeks to stimulate reservations for an airline's special weekend package tours. Throughout the letter, as many descriptive words as possible are used to paint vivid mental pictures of desirable aspects of the tours. The rather negative aspect of cost is subordinated in the middle of a paragraph, surrounded by pleasantly positive material. Finally, the action-drive close pushes the reader to act *now* for his own enjoyment, and the final words bring back to his mind the appeals developed in the sales pitch.

Dear Mr. Petti:

You slide back in the deep plush chair, champagne tickles your nose, the hills of Georgia float swiftly away 30,000 feet below—and cares of the week are left far behind in the steady whine of the jets.

Three more glasses, a mouth-watering selection of hors d'oeuvres, and suddenly you're deplaning and swept up in the never-ending excitement of America's fun capital—New Orleans. As the uniformed door-man of the world famous Royal Orleans welcomes you to the understated elegance of the hotel's crystal chandeliered and marbled lobby, you understand why this "city that time forgot" is the perfect place for a completely carefree adventure—and that's what you're on—a fabulous Delta Jet-Set Weekend. Every detail is considered to give you the ultimate in enjoyment. You'll savor New Orleans as it's meant to be experienced—gracious living, unsurpassed cuisine, jazz-tempo excitement.

After settling in your magnificent Royal Orleans "home," you're off to dinner at Antoine's—spicy, bubbling Oysters Bienville, an exotic salad, trout almondine, selected fromages, all mellowed with a wine from one of the world's most famous cellars, and topped off with spectac-ular cherries flambé. A memorable meal sets you up for the night spot tour of many splendored delights—the spots where jazz was born, the undulating strippers, Pete Fountain's chic club, and the rollicking sing-a-long of Pat O'Brien's where a tall, frosty Hurricane signals the close of a perfect evening. Then, just before returning to the hotel, time for a steaming cup of dark, rich French Market café au lait and some extra special doughnuts.

Saturday morning dawns bright and crisp—perfect for casual brows-ing through the "treasure" shops of the Quarter—the world of artists, antiques, and astonishing sights awaits you. From noon, you are escorted through some of the famous areas of the city—the Garden District (where the elegance of the past lives on), the lake area, and the most famous historical sights of the Quarter. Late afternoon finds you ap-proaching famed Elmwood Plantation for an exclusive cocktail party and dinner—you'll practically hear the moan of ol' river steamers on the mighty Mississippi before you.

Night ends back in the Quarter—with the particular pleasure of your choice. But don't sleep too late Sunday! Unforgettable "breakfast at Brennan's" begins at 11:00 and two hours later you'll know why it is the most famous breakfast in the world! Wrap up your relaxed visit shopping in the afternoon, then the mighty Delta jet whisks you back to Atlanta by 7:00. This perfect weekend can be yours for the very special price of only $175, which includes transportation, lodging, and noted meals. Such a special vacation will be more fun with friends, so get them in on this bargain—you owe yourself the pleasures of a Jet-Set Weekend in America's fun capital.

This Jet-Set Weekend to dream about becomes a reality starting right now—a quick call to the Delta Hostess at Peachtree 4-0663 confirms your reservation to escape to the fun, the food, and the fantasy of New Orleans, land of excitement. The city is swinging—waiting for you!

Sincerely yours,

To sell an unusual new fabricated product, here's a rather unusual letter—with touch as light and fast as that of the product it describes. It also illustrates a common industrial use of direct mail—to get inquiries or leads for the personal salesperson. For that reason it does not mention the price at all.

Dear Mr. Buchstein:

Before you read the rest of this letter, won't you pick up that sample strip of Burlon and give it the works? It's *two* strips—see? Stuck together like two cockleburs. But pick up the tabs at the bottom and pull them apart. Press them back together. Test for the *side* pull, to see how firmly they hold together. Now the tabs again—how easily they slip apart.

Now you know—it's a pushbutton zipper—a closer with no gadgets.

Already you see what to do with it—what it can mean for your line of children's jackets . . . raincoats . . . shirts . . . any garment that has to be fastened somewhere.

Picture your sales copy to mothers of children who have trouble starting the fastener, to the man in a hurry to button up that raincoat, "Fingertouch fastening—no buttons, no slides, no metal, no plastic teeth. Press the edges together—they are fastened to hold. Pull up gently from the bottom—they come apart so quickly and quietly."

Your engineering curiosity will be shooting questions at us like "How does it work, anyway? How *good* is it?"

Well, it works like a cocklebur—like ten thousand of them, in fact. That gray top strip is packed with microscopic nylon hairs with infinitesimal fish-hook tips—so small that you can rub them on soft skin without feeling the points. The blue strip's surface is merely soft nylon yarn. Press the two together and your nylon-cockleburs, or Burlon, grasp the yarn firmly. That's all there is to it. They pull apart so easily from the botom up.

How *good?* Well, you'll find you can wash or dry-clean Burlon. It won't corrode. It won't jam. It holds its grip indefinitely. And try it now to see how light and flexible it feels and works. In strips ranging from a half inch to 2 inches wide, it is adaptable to any garment-closure problem you might have.

In order to work this startling new fastener into your fall-production specifications, wouldn't you like to have one of our men come and show you the whole range of demonstrations and tests and help figure your needs for different garments and fabrics? Just use the handy air-mail-paid card to describe your needs and tell us that you'd like to see the Burlon man.

Mail it this morning to get in an early itinerary.

Sincerely yours,

## COLLECTION LETTERS

When your customers do not pay their bills on time, you will be forced to make some effort to collect. More than likely, in your efforts you will use letters, for letters are conventional devices for collecting money. Because your collection efforts will involve getting your readers to do something they are reluctant to do, probably you will need to use persuasion in your approach. As we shall see, however, in some instances you will use approaches that do not fall in the conventional persuasion pattern. In spite of these exceptions, the overall collection effort may be regarded as persuasive.

## A series of efforts

If you follow the conventional business patterns, your efforts to collect will consist of a series of steps which build up progressively. At first, you will send your debtor only routine notices of payment due. If these notices do not bring in the money, you will send additional notices, and then you add strength to the notices with a few words reminding the reader of the past-due obligation. Your reminder could be in the form of a sticker or a stamped message on the bill, or it could be a short printed note or a letter.

If your reminder fails to work, you will then move to stronger efforts. You will write letters urging payment. Depending on your policy, you may write any number of letters, each building up its persuasive appeal to pay. Then, should your persuasive letters fail to convince your reader that she should pay, you will write one last one. At this stage you will be ready to sever business relations with your debtor by taking some step to force her to pay.

This progression from sending bills to last-resort action may be graphically viewed as a stairway (see Figure 11–1), with each step representing a collection effort. Early in the collection effort, we need only to send reminders. Fortunately, they work with most customers. During this stage we assume that our customer *will pay*—she needs only to be reminded. Later, we move into the middle stage of collection, where we shift to an attitude that we must convince our customer that she *should pay.* This is the truly persuasive stage, and it makes up the bulk of the collection series. Finally, we move to the last-resort action. Usually, it is a single step in the series—a final letter seeking to convince the debtor that she *must pay.*

## Determining the collection series

How many steps you may choose to use in a collection effort or how much time should elapse between steps should be based primarily on the class of credit risk with whom you are dealing and on the conventions of your business. For example, if you are collecting for an exclusive dress shop catering to good credit risks, probably you would move slowly in your efforts. You would send a number of reminders before resorting to persuasive effort. Then you would move slowly through a series of per-

**FIGURE 11–1**

Diagram of the collection procedure

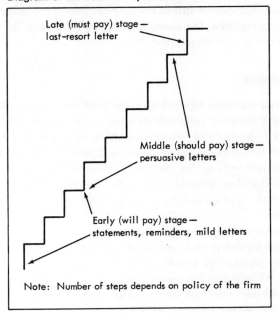

Late (must pay) stage —
last-resort letter

Middle (should pay) stage —
persuasive letters

Early (will pay) stage —
statements, reminders, mild letters

Note: Number of steps depends on policy of the firm

suasive letters, reaching last-resort action only after giving the reader every opportunity to respond. Your collection efforts might extend over a long period—perhaps even a year or more.

On the other hand, if you are collecting from a bad credit risk, you would move faster through your collection efforts; and you would not take many steps. In extreme cases you might jump quickly from routine statements to strong persuasion. Then, should the persuasion not work, you might move just as quickly to last-resort action. Such a series could reach its end in a matter of a few weeks.

Convention requires that your collection efforts with mercantile accounts move at a faster rate than those for the individual consumer. You will find that businesses expect and receive payments on a timely basis from other businesses; and when payments lag, collection efforts move fast. Because business dealings are more impersonal, your collection efforts with business accounts can be more matter-of-fact and more calm and rational in their approach.

Individual consumer accounts vary greatly in the treatment you should give them. Probably you would be wise to classify them on some basis. Some classification by type of risk would fit most collection operations. Also, some classification by type of account may be helpful. Open accounts represent the most selective type of credit risk; thus, they are handled slowly and tactfully. Budget accounts, cycle accounts, and other credit plans used for more questionable risks require a more aggressive collection effort. Installment accounts traditionally permit little laxness in payment, and move to strong action quickly.

## Early-stage efforts

As long as it appears that your customers have good intentions of paying but have forgotten or have just put it off, you should use tact in dealing with them. At first, you will be wise to follow the lead of most companies by sending a duplicate of the original bill. For added strength, you might elect to add a few reminder words to the bill, perhaps as a sticker, a rubber-stamp message, or a printed insert. Such reminders can take many forms. Typically, they carry messages such as "Please," "May we remind you," "Probably you have forgotten," and "Just a friendly reminder."

If your reminders fail to bring in the money, you will need to begin your collection letter efforts. Except in cases in which your series must move quickly, your first letter should be in the reminder stage. Actually, such letters are not truly persuasive. At least, they do not follow the conventional persuasion pattern covered in this chapter. But because they are a part of the overall persuasive buildup of the series, we shall discuss them here.

If you follow the lead of most companies, your first collection letter will use a direct pattern of organization. At the beginning you will courteously come to the point and remind your reader of his past-due account. Because your assumption at this stage is that the reader *will pay,* your goal is to remind her more pointedly than you have done in the past. But because the account is not long past due, you have no cause to use strong appeals for payment. Your message may contain some appropriate goodwill talk—as much as is necessary to convince your reader of your friendly intent. Obviously, such messages need not be long. Usually, two or three short paragraphs are adequate.

Although such letters follow no definite pattern, the following two are typical. The first one is quite direct in its beginning, getting right down to the basic question. But its tactful words clear it of any overly negative effect. Its goodwill content and closing invitation to trade clearly mark it as a friendly reminder.

Dear Ms. Adams:
Won't you take a brief moment to write a check for the $148.50 now four months past due on your account? We know how easy it is to let such matters slip by, and we are confident that you will appreciate this friendly reminder.

If you choose to bring your check into the store personally, you'll enjoy seeing the new fall suits which are beginning to arrive. Perhaps you will want to take advantage of the preseason discounts Loren's charge customers can get on purchases made before the 15th.

We look forward to seeing you in the store again soon.

Sincerely yours,

The second letter, which is from a major publisher to a subscriber, reminds the reader while helping her to save face by offering a possible explanation. Its positive words clearly mark it as a friendly reminder.

Dear Subscriber:

Like many other subscribers, you probably have the systematic habit of settling your accounts at a regular time every month.

For this reason, we almost wish the enclosed bill were larger—then you wouldn't have overlooked it. The amount is so small, you must have lost sight of it the last time you cleaned up your monthly bills.

If so, won't you send us your check today?

This will clear your books . . . ours, too . . . and will be much appreciated.

Many thanks!

Cordially,

A milder type of reminder letter is one which appears to have some purpose for being sent other than to collect money. Usually, such letters are basically goodwill letters. They may tell of new merchandise, promotions, services, and such. But in telling of these goodwill topics, they slip in the reminder of the past-due account. Such letters truly follow a sandwich pattern, with the payment reminder placed between two sections of noncollection material.

Obviously, this type of letter is best used when the accounts can be handled on an individual, personal basis. Because not many companies feel that they can afford to give their accounts such treatment, this approach is not widely used. Nevertheless, it has merit, and it is worthy of your consideration whenever the situation will permit.

The following illustration shows how this form of letter begins away from the subject of collection and on a topic which justifies the letter's being sent. After some discussion of this topic, it slips into a reminder of the past-due account, and then it moves back to the other friendly talk.

Dear Ms. Vinton:

As one of Brock's discriminating charge customers, you will be well pleased when you see the new fashions we have selected for the fall. They're coming in fast now and will be ready for our annual preseason preferred-customer sale next week. As you would expect, our buyers have made their usual careful selections from the creations of both Arno and d'Antoni, as well as the leading American fashion houses.

You may inspect these exciting fashions on the 15th or 16th from

7–9:30 p.m. As a preferred customer, you will be entitled to the usual 10-percent preseason discount; and of course, you may add it to your account. While you are doing it, perhaps you will wish to pay the $178.40 now four months past due, which no doubt you have just overlooked. We know you will enjoy this annual event and that you will find something made especially for you.

We look forward to having you with us.

Sincerely yours,

## The middle (discussion) stage

If your customer fails to respond to your reminders, you will need to write her letters which use more pressure. That is, you will have to convince her that she *should pay*. Specifically, you will have to select some basic appeal and present it convincingly so that it moves her to pay. Obviously, your technique is that of persuasion, and you will follow the general plan for persuasive letters previously described.

*Analysis of the strategy.*   As in other situations involving persuasion, at the outset your reader's wishes run contrary to your own. You want her to pay; she has shown by ignoring your reminders that, at best, she is not strongly motivated to pay. Thus, she is not likely to receive your message favorably. In fact, she probably does not want to read your letter. Very obviously, you will have to gain her attention from the beginning if you are to get her to read what you have to say.

In persuading your debtor that she should pay, you will need to build some convincing strategy. As in other persuasion cases, you will need to view the situation as it appears in your reader's mental filter. You will need to select some basic appeal and to fit it into your reader's mind as convincingly as you can. You may, for example, select a "fair-play" appeal, and build a case for fairness showing that for her promise to pay you have given her something she wanted and now it is only fair that she come through with payment. Similarly, you could build your persuasion around appeals to pride, the value of a good credit record, and the protection of social standing. Numerous other appeals are possible.

After you select your appeal, you develop it through your imagination. More specifically, you think out the reasoning which will convince your reader that she should pay her bill. How strong you choose to be in your appeal should depend on how far along the collection effort you are. In most cases your first motivation letter should be relatively mild and should have some goodwill content. If these letters fail to bring in money, however, the following letters should get stronger in their persuasion and should decrease in goodwill content.

*Attention in the opening.*   As we have noted, your collection letter is uninvited, perhaps even unwanted. Thus, your opening words have a special need to gain attention. Your reader has received reminders from you. She knows that she owes you. More than likely, she intends to pay you—in time—when it is convenient for her. She may quickly label your letter as just another dun and put it aside. So if this letter is to have a chance of succeeding, it must gain attention right away.

In gaining your reader's attention, you will need to use your imagination to find some interesting opening words. Whatever words you select, they should also help to set up your basic appeal in the letter. The possibilities for opening, of course, are unlimited and are best explained by illustration.

One successful letter begins with this question:

When they ask about you, what shall we tell them?

Written late in the collection series, the letter used the appeal of the danger of losing a good credit reputation. The opening truly is a persuasive question. It makes one want to read further to learn just what is to be told about her. Clearly, it sets up discussion of the appeal.

Another interest-gaining question is this one:

How would you write to a good friend on an embarrassing subject?

The question is personal, it is interesting, and it sets up the persuasion of the letter. This persuasion, of course, builds around the human situation of friends communicating on a subject that is not conducive to friendship. The appeal it sets up is that of the reader's moral obligation to a friend.

Another successful beginning asks a question about the product for which the debtor owes:

How are you and your Arctic air-conditioning system making it through these hot summer months?

This opening has the subtle advantage of working on the reader's conscience through a friendly human question. The appeal it sets up is that of fair play—of persuading the reader to carry out her end of a bargain from which she is receiving enjoyment.

***Persuasive presentation of the appeal.*** Following the opening contact, you should present the appeal you have selected. Your beginning sentence has set it up; so it is the logical thing to do. And because your opening has set it up, the transition to it should be smooth.

Presenting the appeal is mainly a matter of adapting to your reader's point of view. You study the appeal for its you-viewpoint possibilities; then you present it in these terms. The technique is much like that of selling. You've searched through your imagination for reasoning that will move your reader to take the action you want her to take. You try to show the advantages she will receive from taking it. And you present it all in the carefully selected language that will convince her.

In writing this part, you should be careful that your words carry just the right degree of force appropriate for the one case. Early in the collection series, the facts of the case may call for mild persuasion. The farther along the collection series you progress, however, the more forceful you can afford to be. In addition, you will need to take care that you do not insult, talk down, lecture, or show exasperation to your reader. As we have noted in other related situations, an angry reader tends to resist, and resistance leads to failure. Instead, your tone should be wholesome and friendly. You will need to keep in mind that throughout this stage of collection you hope to collect, to maintain cordial relations, and perhaps even to continue business with the debtor. Were you not to feel this way about the account, you would move to the more forceful and effective last-resort letter.

**The closing drive for payment.**    After you have made your persuasive appeal, the logical end result is to ask for the payment. In doing this, you should bring in a reference to the reader's past-due account (how much, how long past due, perhaps even what for), and you should ask that she pay it. You should ask directly, in words that form a clear question—not in words which merely hint at payment. "Won't you please write a check for $37.50 today and mail it to us right away?" is stronger and more effective than "We shall appreciate your writing and sending your check for $37.50."

In collection letters, as in sales letters, a closing reference to a benefit to be gained by taking the action adds strength to the appeal. For example, a letter which stresses an appeal to the advantages of a prompt-pay record for a business could effectively end with these words:

> Won't you please write out and mail a check for the $274.80 right now while you're thinking about it? It's your best insurance of keeping your invaluable prompt-pay record.

**Illustrations of approach variations.**    Because collection letters are so much a product of the creative mind, the variations possible are best shown by illustration. As you would expect, the examples selected do not cover all the variations which might be used. They represent only a small selection from a whole that is limited only by the imagination.

The first example comes early in the collection series of a distributor to a retail customer. It builds around an appeal to the reader's pride in his credit record. By beginning with an excerpt from the debtor's credit report, it ranks high in interest value.

> Dear Mr. Black:
> He is of Scotch-Irish descent, a native of Springfield, Illinois. Twenty-seven years of experience in retail hardware operations. Hard working, reliable, and competent manager. Pays promptly, usually discounts. . . .

This is a part of the report we received on you when you applied for credit with us. It's an excellent report, and you have every right to be proud of it. It shows that you are a man of your word—that when you promise to pay, you come through with the payment. And you have proved it over a period of 27 years.

In view of your good record, we are concerned that your account has slipped into the delinquent group. Certainly, a man of your reputation will want to take care of this matter right away. So won't you please write and mail a check for the $488.50 now 60 days past due on invoice 704A? Your good record tells us that you will.

Sincerely yours,

Using an appeal to the advantages to be derived from prompt payment, the following letter proved to be very effective with a retail account. Part of its effectiveness may be explained by its interest-gaining question opening as well as the straightforward, logical approach it takes.

Dear Ms. Carr:

Have you wondered how we are able to sell quality hand tools at 10 percent under our competitors? As you know, the low price permits you to take an additional markup and still beat competition.

A part of the explanation lies in our selective credit policy. We grant credit only to the most reliable firms—those that have earned their good credit reputation. As they pay us promptly, we can keep down collection costs. And we can pass these savings on to you.

As you were reported to us as an excellent credit risk, we know that you will want to join our other prompt-pay customers. So will you please send us a check today for the $845.53 now 30 days past due on your order for assorted hand tools? You will be helping all of us to profit.

Sincerely yours,

The next letter builds around an appeal to pride supported by the advantages of a prompt-pay record. Although much of the persuasion is presented without actual you-references, its you-viewpoint adaptation is clearly implied.

Dear Mr. Stevenson:

You don't belong in that group!

Every day Massey's deals with hundreds of charge customers. More than 99 percent of them come through with their obligations to pay. We mark them as "prompt pay," and the doors to credit buying are opened to them all over town. Less than 1 percent don't pay right away. Of course, sometimes they have good reasons, and most of them tell us about it. And we work something out. But a few allow their good credit records to tarnish.

Somehow, you have permitted your account to place your name in this last group. We don't think it belongs there. Won't you please remove it by writing us a check for the $137.75 now over four months past due? It would place you in the group in which you belong.

Sincerely yours,

Written near the end of the collection series, the next letter uses an appeal to the value of a good credit reputation. Its short and direct question opening quickly gains attention. It talks directly to the reader, interpreting the effects of her credit record on her personally.

Dear Ms. Matson:

How much is it worth to you? It's your credit record I am referring to, and it's a most important question to you now that it hangs in the balance.

The good reports we got on you when you opened your account told us that you have handled your promises to pay promptly for a long time. We know that you must want to maintain this good rating, for it means so much to you. Aside from the obvious advantages of credit buying, it is important to you personally. The community and your friends judge you by how you fulfill your promises. It is vital to your own peace of mind to know that you have fulfilled your promises to pay.

Because your credit record means so much to you, it is hard to understand how you have permitted your account of $371.43 to run six months past due. Won't you please save your good credit record by sending us payment today?

Sincerely yours,

A next-to-last letter to a retail customer is the following illustration. Obviously, it is stronger than the preceding one, for it talks more of the effects of nonpayment than of the advantages of paying. It presents a rather doleful picture of the consequences of not paying.

Dear Ms. Carmichel:

What shall we report about you?

As you may know, all members of the Capital Credit Bureau must report their long-past-due accounts for distribution to the members. At the moment your own account is in the balance, and we are wondering whether we shall be forced to report it. We are concerned because what we must say will mean so much to you personally.

A slow-pay record would just about ruin the good credit reputation you have built up over the years. You wouldn't find it easy to buy on credit from Capital Bureau members (and this includes just about every credit-granting business in town). Probably your credit privileges would be cut off completely. It would take you long years to regain the good reputation you now enjoy.

So won't you please avoid all this by mailing a check for the $474.80 now nine months past due? It would stop the report and would save your credit record.

Sincerely yours,

## Last-resort letters

Hard as you may try, not all of your collection letters will bring in the money. Some of your debtors will ignore your most persuasive efforts. Because you cannot continue your collection efforts indefinitely, you will need to take some last-resort action with these debtors. And you will use your final letter in the collection series to inform them of this impending effort.

A number of last-resort actions are available to you at this stage. One of the most common ones is to report the account to some credit interchange group, such as the credit bureau in the community to which most retailers belong. Another is to sell the account to a collection agency, with full authority to take legal steps if necessary. Yet another is to take the delinquent to court. You will need to decide on the action appropriate to your case. In making your decision, you will be guided by such considerations as the customs in the field, the nature of the account, and the image of your organization.

*Justification of directness.* In selecting the letter plan for the last-resort letter, you should think in terms of what must be done to collect the money. Up to this point, you have tried the milder persuasive methods. They have not worked. Something stronger is needed.

As we learned from our earlier discussion of letter psychology, there is strength in directness. We have not used it through the middle stage of the series because directness in such cases can destroy goodwill. Until now, we have been concerned about maintaining goodwill. We have wanted to salvage the account, but now we have reached the point where we are more interested in collecting the money. So we can justify using our strongest plan—the plan of directness.

*Direct presentation of last-resort action.* For the strongest effect as well as for interest-gaining purposes, you should begin the last-resort letter with a clear statement of your action. That is, you should tell the reader right away just what you are going to do. Although your reader probably knows very well why you are taking the action, it is likely to help your case if you can bring in some justification of your decision. It could be that she has delayed later than she thinks. Something like this would do the job well:

> Your failure to pay the $378.40 now seven months past due on your account leaves us no choice but to report you to the Omaha Credit Bureau.

*Interpretation of the action.* Following your direct opening should come your persuasion. Again, in selecting it, you need to place yourself in your reader's position. You need to think through your last-resort action to see just how it will affect her. It may mean that she will lose her credit-buying privileges. Or it may mean court costs, loss of prestige, personal embarrassment, and the like. Whatever the effects, you should reason them out, and you should think about how you can best present them to make your reader understand them. Then you should describe these effects in clear, convincing language.

In describing the doleful effects of the last-resort action, you will need to watch the tone of your words. Certainly, you are no longer handling the reader with the tact you used in earlier efforts. But you still wish to avoid inviting her anger, for even at this stage anger invites resistance. So, instead of a tone of exasperation, your words should show a genuine concern for the predicament the reader is in. You wish it had not turned out this way, but her actions leave you no other course.

*The action close.*    After you have painted a vivid picture of what will happen to her if the last-resort action is taken, you should give your reader a chance to avoid these consequences. Thus, in your close you should set a deadline for payment, or perhaps for other arrangements; and you should urge her to meet this deadline. As in other persuasive efforts your final words should recall to her mind what she will gain (or avoid) by taking the action. The following close meets these requirements well:

> We won't report you to Capital Credit Bureau until the 15th; so won't you please help yourself by sending us your check by that date? It's the one way you can save your credit reputation.

The effectiveness of the direct approach to collection is well illustrated by the following letter. Its opening strength is high in interest value, and its interpretation of the effects of the action is vividly described in terms of the reader's viewpoint. In spite of its sternness, it reflects a spirit of helpfulness and concern for the reader's welfare.

> Dear Mr. Perry:
>
> Your failure to answer all of our seven requests for payment of the $317.10 now 12 months past due leaves us no choice but to take you to court for collection. We sincerely want to avoid this action, for it would be unpleasant for both of us. Especially would it be unpleasant for you.
>
> For you, it would mean that you would be forced to pay. You would pay not just the $317.10 you owe, but court costs also. In addition, you would pay attorneys' fees.
>
> Also, legal action would be embarrassing to you. As you know, it's the kind of information people talk about. Your friends would pick it up. So would other businessmen. Results might well be an end to your credit buying. And your credit reputation would be injured permanently.
>
> You can avoid the effects of court action only by paying before the 17th—the day we shall turn your account over to our attorney. Won't

you please help yourself by mailing your check by that date? It's the only way you can avoid the cost and embarrassment of going to court.

Sincerely yours,

## APPLICATIONS FOR EMPLOYMENT

Of all the letters you will write, the one that will mean the most to you personally is likely to be the application letter. Even though recruiters now come to your campus to hire prospective graduates, application letters frequently are written. The campus recruiters may ask you for follow-up information, or even for a formal written application. You may want work with a company that does not visit your campus, or you may wish to answer advertisements you see. In both cases you are likely to write letters. Then, after your first job, you are likely to change employment a time or two. On such occasions you will find that application letters are especially useful.

In a very real sense, the application letters you write are sales letters. They sell your ability to do work. And because they are sales letters of a sort, they make good use of the planning that goes into sales letters. Also, they make good use of the strategy employed in the traditional sales letter.

### Preliminary planning

As with the sales letter, your planning should begin with a study of the product to be sold (you) and of the work you seek to do. Studying the product means taking personal inventory. It means listing all the pertinent facts you can present about yourself—everything that might have a bearing on your ability to do the work. Studying the job means learning as much as you can about the company concerned—about its policies, its plans, and its operations in general. It also means learning the requirements of the work the firm wants done. Sometimes you can get this information through personal investigation. Often, however, you will have to develop it through your own good judgment.

After you have assembled the preliminary information, you are ready to plan your application. First, you will need to decide whether a data sheet (a summary sheet of your background facts) will accompany the letter. Because the data sheet and letter combined give more thorough coverage, this arrangement is likely to do the better job for you. If for some reason, however, more streamlined presentation appears to you to be desirable, the letter alone is quite acceptable. Letters sent without accompanying data sheets normally contain more detail, for they have the whole selling job to do.

## Letters of application

When you have decided what your mailing will consist of, you next turn to the construction of your letter. With the job requirement in mind, you begin the task of constructing the letter by relating the facts from your background which will qualify you to do the job. You arrange the facts for logical and orderly presentation. Then you present them much as a sales writer would present his sales points, adapting them to the reader's needs whenever it is practical to do so. Although, as in the sales letter, your specific plan of presentation can vary somewhat with your imagination, a general review of a conventional pattern appears in following paragraphs.

*Attention need in the opening.* As in the sales letter, you should open the application letter with some statement or question which gains interest and which sets up the review of information which follows. The attention need is especially important in letters prospecting for a job—that is, letters sent without invitation. Such letters are likely to reach the desk of a busy executive who has many things to do other than reading application letters he has not asked for. Unless his favorable interest is gained right off, the letter's chances for success are lessened. Even invited letters have an attention need. They probably will compete with many others, and those that stand out favorably are most likely to succeed.

In choosing an appropriate opening, you should, of course, make good use of your imagination, for the letter plan is to some extent a creative one. But your imagination should be guided by the nature of the work you seek. If, for example, the work you seek requires imagination and extrovert qualities, your opening might show imaginative thinking and vivid writing. At the opposite extreme, an application for a more conservative position, say as an accountant or a bank employee, would require a more restrained opening.

In choosing the best opening for your one case, you will need to consider whether your letter is invited or prospecting. If it has been invited, your best beginning is to make some reference to the work to be done. It should begin qualifying you for it and should make some reference to the source of your invitation. This one meets the requirements:

> Does your interest in finding an accountant, as indicated in your ad in today's *Career,* center upon finding a young man well grounded in theory and experienced in petroleum accounting?

In addition to fitting the work sought, the opening clearly sets up the review of qualifications which follows. This review is structured around the three areas mentioned in the sentence.

Because it has more interest need, and because one can do more research on it, a prospecting application letter can make more use of imagination in the opening. As we have mentioned, this letter should be consistent with the nature of the job sought. One good interest-gaining possibility is to begin on a topic which shows good understanding of the reader's operation or of the work he wants done, as in this example:

> Now that Taggart, Inc., has expanded operations to Central America, can you use a broadly trained business administration graduate who knows the language and culture of the region?

Another possibility is some statement or question which focuses attention on a need of the reader—a need the writer seeks to fill. The following penetrating question illustrates this approach:

> When was the last time you interviewed a young college graduate who wanted to sell and who had successful sales experience?

Applications for the more conservative types of work may justify a more conventional beginning, even though they may fall short of the interest requirement. How far you should go depends on the field concerned and the people to whom you write. But never should you use dull and unimaginative forms such as "This is to apply for . . ." or "Please consider this my application for. . . ." Something like the following would please the conservative accountant or banker and would at the same time set your application apart from its competition:

> On the suggestion of Mr. William M. Hawkes of your staff, I submit the following summary of my qualifications for work as your loan supervisor.

***Selection of content.***   Following the opening contact, of course, you will present the information which qualifies you for the work you seek. This task involves more than assembling a mass of detail and parading it before your reader. As you would do in a sales letter, you should carefully review the job requirements, and you should select the data which qualify you for the work.

If your letter is an invited one, you may gain some information about the job requirements from the source of your invitation. If you are answering an advertisement, for example, you may find in it some of the requirements the employer specifies. Or if you are writing following an interview, comments made in the interview will give you some idea of the job requirements. If you are prospecting for a job, your own research, coupled with your best logical analysis, should help you to determine what qualifications your reader will be most impressed by, and you should use these as the basis for your presentation.

In any event, you will be concerned generally with three broad areas of background information: education, experience, and personal details.

Perhaps a fourth—references—could be added, although it is not precisely an area of your background information. References are a standard part of the data sheet; if you choose not to have a data sheet, your letter might well include them.

How much you include of each and how much emphasis you give each should depend on the job requirements. Most jobs you will be seeking as a new college graduate will have strong educational requirements, so you will be wise to stress these requirements. When you apply for a job in later years, after you have gained working experience, it will be your experience that will be most likely to qualify you for the work you seek. Then you will stress experience, and you will place education in a secondary position. Your personal details are generally important for most jobs, although they are especially important for work involving contacts with people, such as sales, personnel, and management training.

If a data sheet accompanies your letter, you may be inclined to rely too much on the data sheet. You should remember that the letter is the persuasive part of your mailing. It is the part which does the selling. The data sheet merely lists details. Thus, your letter should contain all of the major points around which you build your case. The data sheet will include these parts, plus the supporting details. As the two are really parts of a team effort, your letter would profit from an appropriate reference to or comment about the data sheet.

*An order for conviction.*   Your order for presentation of the facts about you is a part of the strategy your creative mind will work out. But it is likely to follow one of three general arrangements. First and most likely to fit your needs is an arrangement around some logical grouping of your information, such as education, personal details, and experience. A second possibility is to present the information chronologically, showing consistent progress throughout your lifetime in preparation for the work you seek. Third is any of a number of possible arrangements by requirements for the job. Whatever plan you select, it should be the one which permits a logical and convincing presentation of fact.

Merely presenting facts does not assure conviction. You will need also to present the facts in words which make the most of what you have to say. You could say, for example, that you "held a position" as a sales manager; but it is much more concrete and convincing to say that you "supervised a sales force of 14." Likewise, you do more for yourself by writing that you "earned a degree in business administration" than by saying that you "spent four years in college." And it is more effective to say that you "learned cost accounting" than to say that you "took a course in cost accounting."

You can help your case, also, by presenting your information in reader-viewpoint language whenever it is practical to do so. More specifically, you should work to interpret the facts in terms of what they mean to your reader and to the work he wants done. For example, an applicant could present a cold recital of facts like this:

> I am 21 years old and have an interest in mechanical operations and processes. Last summer I worked in the production department of a container plant.

Or he could interpret the facts, fitting them to the one job:

> My creative ability has been whetted all of my 21 years by the desire to build, repair, or work with many objects and ideas. This interest in mechanical operations and processes would make me at home whether in Craft-Technicians' precision machine shop, manufacturing units, or offices. The summer experience in the production department of a container plant, as listed on the enclosed data sheet, stands as proof of my capability for doing hard work.

Since you will be writing about yourself, you may find it difficult to avoid overusing I-references, but you should try. An overuse of I's sounds egotistical, and it focuses too much of the attention on the often-repeated word. Some I's, however, should be used, for the letter is a personal one. To strip it of all I-references would be to rob it of some of its personal warmth. Thus, you should be concerned with the degree of I-references. You want not too many, not too few.

*Action drive in the close.* Your strategic presentation of background facts logically leads to the action which forms the close of your letter. The action you use may be whatever is appropriate in your case. It could be a request for an interview, if distance permits; it could be an invitation for additional correspondence, perhaps to answer questions the reader may have; or it could be a suggestion that the reader write to your references. Rarely would you wish to ask for the job, at least not in a first letter. You are concerned mainly with getting negotiations under way.

Your action words should be clear and direct, preferably in question form. And as in the sales letter, they may be made more effective by following them with words which recall to the reader's mind a benefit he will receive by taking the action. The technique is illustrated in this action request:

> If I have described a promising personnel man, Mr. Sellers, may I have the privilege of an interview? A collect wire or a letter will bring me in at your convenience to talk about how I can help in your personnel work.

*Review of examples.* The following application letters generally illustrate the techniques we have described. First is a prospecting letter of a new college graduate. Perhaps it leaves too much to the accompanying data sheet, but it does a good job of interpreting the data and adapting to the work.

Dear Mr. Stark:

How often do you find an employee who understands the basic problems of management and yet can talk with workers on their own level? My background, education, and experience have given me this ability, Mr. Stark, and I want to use it to help your department grow, just as Ford is growing.

Having been born and reared by working parents in a poor, highly organized section of New York City, I am aware of the worker's attitude toward his employer and his union. More insight was gained when I worked for a year in New York's garment district as a shipping and receiving clerk. In four years of Navy life, "John Doe" was my constant associate; and once again, as a graveyard-shift riveter in the Boeing airplane factory, I was part of labor. I speak the workers' language, Mr. Stark; and what is more important, they will talk to me! You know how important such a factor can be in labor relations.

A college education, including specialized studies in labor relations, economics, psychology, and all of the other learning which led to my Bachelor of Business Administration degree, has helped to give me a well-balanced view of labor-management problems. In addition, I am up on all of the important new issues you are now facing. Added to my background and education is a deep fascination for the field of labor relations. Here is a dynamic area, constantly challenging even the most imaginative and resourceful mind. It is the type of work to which I could devote all of my energy for a lifetime.

My business education has been well rounded to prepare me to handle all the technical details relating to labor relations work. From by knowledge of statistics, I could make meaningful correlation studies and other comparisons for you. My study of report writing would assure you of getting clear and informative reports. And my knowledge of labor law would help me to cope with the day-to-day problems you face. As you will see from the enclosed data sheet, I have planned my curriculum for this one area of work.

If this brief description meets the requirements for work in your office, may I hear from you soon? I could visit you any time at your convenience to talk about how I could help in your labor relations work.

Sincerely yours,

Also a prospecting letter, the next one does a good job of selecting and talking about the facts which qualify the writer for the work. It is somewhat heavy in the use of I-references. But by his interpretations, the writer makes it clear that he knows the work to be done.

Dear Mr. Wilson:

Now that work is starting on the West Channel Canal and the docks at Bell City, won't the Port Commission need an additional employee who has learned and studied cargo and ship operation?

With my unlimited chief mate's license in the merchant marine, five years of experience as a naval officer in shipboard and dockside cargo operations, and a college degree in foreign trade, I believe I have the qualifications for this work.

As you know, the dock's acquisition will mean a greater influx of ships into the port, and my five years of experience in the U.S. merchant marine taught me how to solve and cope with various types of cargo-loading and -unloading operations, cargo plans, manifests, and other documents. I have been in the major ports of Europe, South America, Africa, and the Pacific islands, where I studied at first hand port and harbor facilities, and I could apply this knowledge to your operation.

I served as hull officer for a reserve fleet group while on duty with the Navy and was responsible for the work performance of three junior officers and 120 enlisted men. This tour of duty taught me how to get along with people and yet to be able to direct their work activities. For two years I served as first lieutenant on a refrigeration ship, where I was directly responsible for loading, maintaining, and unloading quick-frozen and perishable cargoes. As you can see, Mr. Wilson, experience has given me a thorough grounding in the activities that are conducted in your port.

Currently, I am supplementing my experience with a study of foreign trade here at the university. In January I shall earn my Bachelor of Science degree, which will supplement the Bachelor of Science degree I received from the United States Merchant Marine Academy, Kings Point, New York, in 1967. Through courses in foreign trade, international business, import and export practices, and water transportation, I have gained a thorough understanding of port operations.

After you have verified the above facts with the references I have listed on the attached data sheet, won't you write or call me, naming a time when we can talk further concerning my employment with the Port Commission?

> Sincerely yours,

The next letter is in response to an advertisement. It wisely selects the three main points stressed in the advertisement and builds the applicant's case around them. It does a good job of adapting to the work involved.

Dear Ms. Alderson:

Sound background in advertising . . . well trained . . . work well with others. . . .

These key words in your July 7th advertisement in the *Times* describe the person you want, and I believe I am that person.

For the past four years I have gained experience in every phase of retail advertising working for the *Lancer*, our college newspaper. I sold advertising, planned layouts, and wrote copy. During the last two summers I got more firsthand experience working in the advertising department of Wunder & Son. I wrote a lot of copy for Wunder, some of which I am enclosing for your inspection; but I also did just about everything else there is to do in advertising work. I enjoyed it, and I learned from it. I am confident that this experience would help me to fit in and contribute to the work in your office.

In my concentrated curriculum at the university I studied marketing, with a specialization in advertising. As you will see from the attached data sheet, I studied every course offered in advertising and related fields, and I believe that my honor grades give some evidenc that I worked hard and with sincerity. I am confident that upon my graduation in June I can bring to your organization the firm foundation of knowledge and imagination your work demands.

Understanding the importance of being able to get along well with people, I actively participated in Sigma Chi (social fraternity), the First Methodist Church, and Pi Tau Pi (honorary business fraternity). From the experience gained in these associations, I am confident that I can fit in harmoniously with your close-knit advertising department.

If I have convinced you of my sincerity and capability, may I meet with you and talk with you? I could visit your office at any time convenient to you to talk about doing your advertising work.

Sincerely yours,

## The data sheet

Although it is not persuasive in the usual sense and not really a letter, the data sheet now deserves our attention. As we have mentioned, it may be a vital part of the application plan; and even though its plan may not be persuasive, it does contribute to the overall persuasion effort.

The data sheet, sometimes called "vita" an "resume," is an orderly summary of the background data on an applicant. In general, it contains all of the information presented in the letter, plus supporting and incidental details. It is designed for quick reading, and usually is an orderly listing of facts grouped by subtopics of the application information. Rarely does it use sentences—just facts, tabulated and arranged for the best possible physical appearance.

As you would expect, variations in plan and content of data sheets exist, but for all purposes we may consider two basic types. One is the general data sheet. It is designed to cover all possible employment opportunities in which an applicant might be interested (see Figure 11–4 on page 265). Thus, its contents are not selected with one specific job in mind. It is the kind an applicant would send to a hundred different companies, and it would be appropriate for each. The second is a personalized data sheet. It is specifically written for one company and for one job. Most of its contents are the same as in the general type, but there is some selectivity in the information presented. And it adapts some of the wording to the one case. Because it is individually tailored for the one job and company, it is most effective.

*Selection of background facts.*  In writing your data sheet, you should begin with the information you assembled when you took inventory of your background facts prior to writing the letter. From this collection of data, you should select all that you feel your employer will need to properly evaluate you. You will list the points covered in your letter, for these are the most important; but you will include much more. Much of what you will include will be details which would clutter up the letter; yet they are details which tell your prospective employer something he needs to know about you.

*Arrangement by groups.*  After you have selected the facts that you will include, you next arrange them into groups on some basis of likeness. Most probably you will arrange them by the conventional categories of "Experience," "Education," "Personal Qualities," and "References." In some cases the information might be organized by job requirements or on some chronological basis. Then there are other possibilities which your imagination might work out.

*Wording of the headings.*  Your next task is to devise headings (captions) for each of your subclassifications of data as well as for the data sheet itself. If you are writing the general, conventional type of data sheet, you may use plain topic captions such as "Experience," "Education," and "Personal Details," and your title for the entire data sheet might read something like "Personal Data Sheet of John Pettit."

A more interesting, effective, and therefore the recommended plan is to make the caption do more for you by using words which enhance the information they cover. This technique is best described by illustration. As shown in the following main captions for data sheets, the words can be adapted as well as possible to the one job and the one case.

PREPARATION OF DAVID S. HANDY
TO SELL ILCO PRODUCTS

WHY WILMA WYNN IS QUALIFIED AS A FASHION BUYER

WILLIAM O. HOBSON'S QUALIFICATIONS
FOR GENERAL ACCOUNTING WORK
WITH HUGGINS, INC.

Likewise, with some effort you can make the wording of the subcaptions do more for you. Instead of the topic caption "Education," you may choose a stronger and more concrete wording such as "Specialized Study in Accounting." Instead of "Employment," you may use "Experience in Petroleum Accounting." And rather than the routine "References," you may use the more informative "Men Who Can Vouch For Him." These are but a few of the possibilities available to you. Your imagination can supply more appropriate ones for your background facts.

*Presentation of the data.*    The content of the listed parts in each data sheet will vary, but you will want to make certain that the facts you present contain the essential details. In covering your working experience, you will need to identify your jobs completely, including dates, places, firms, and duties. You will need to indicate whether it is full- or part-time employment. And you will want to make certain that you present the information so that it does the most for you. For example, in describing a job, you might write "1974–76: Office manager for Conway, Inc."; but it would be more accurate and more helpful to give this fuller description: "1974–76: Office manager for Conway, Inc., supervising a staff of 14."

Because your education is likely to be your strongest selling point for your first job after graduation, probably you will need to present it in some detail (as the years go by and your experience grows, you will give more emphasis to experience and less to education). You will need to cover institutions, dates, degrees, and areas of study as a minimum. For some jobs you will need to bring out specific courses.

How much detailed coverage you give to your personal qualifications depends somewhat on the work you seek. For work which involves dealing with people, you should give strong emphasis to the personal details. For a more technical position, such as that of research specialist, accountant, or program analyst, you should list only a minimum of information. In any event, you will need to list sufficient data to give your reader a general idea of what you are like. As a minimum, you should include age, marital status, health, participation in social and civic organizations, and honors and awards. In addition, you might consider physical description, hobbies, athletic interests and participation, race, and religion.

For most jobs, application references are necessary, so you will need to include some. How many you include will depend on how much experience you have had. You should list at least one reference for every major job you have had in recent years. Should you base your claim heavily on your education or your personal characteristics, you should include references who can vouch for these areas. As a minimum, you should include three. Six would be a fair maximum. Of course, your list should include accurate mailing addresses, with appropriate titles.

*Some points on wording.*    As the data sheet is merely a listing of information, you should write it impersonally. That is, you should write it without using personal (I, you) references. Also, as in all good writing, the points you list should be grammatically consistent. You should give the same grammatical form to all points in a single group. If, for example, one caption is a noun phrase, all others on a par with it should be noun phrases. In the following four captions all but the third one (which is an adjective form) are noun phrases. The inconsistency is corrected by adding a noun to the third one, as is shown in the right column, making it a noun phrase.

| | |
|---|---|
| Specialized study | Specialized study |
| Experience in promotion work | Experience in promotion work |
| Personal and physical | Personal and physical qualities |
| Qualified references | Qualified references |

Likewise, the parts listed in a subgroup should be consistent in form. Notice how the understood words of the following items shift:

Born in 1952
Single
Have good health
Active in sports
Ambitious

To complete these abbreviated statements, you would have to add "she was" to the first, "she is" to the second, "I" to the third, "I am" or "she is" to the fourth, and "she is" to the fifth. Any changes which would make all of them fit the same understood words would be appropriate.

*Attractive physical makeup.*   It goes without saying that the physical makeup of your data sheet will tell as much about you as most of your factual information. Certainly, an arrangement of type and space that is pleasing to the eye is a requisite for the best possible results. Thus, you will want to take care to insure the good physical appearance of your work.

As you would expect, there is no one best set of mechanical rules for constructing data sheets. Your best procedure is to approach the task much as a printer would, with the objective of working out an arrangement of type and space that meets the eye's requirement for spacing. Even so, there are some fairly specific suggestions you might keep in mind as you set up the information.

Your overall margins on top, left, and right sides of the page look better if they are no smaller than an inch. A minimum margin of about 1½ inches is good for the bottom. Your listing of the items looks best by rows (columns) if the items are short and can be set up with two uncrowded rows, one on the left and one on the right side of the page. Longer items of information are more appropriately set up in lines extending across the page. In any event, you will do well to avoid long and narrow columns of data with large sections of wasted space showing on either side. Likewise, any arrangement which gives a heavy, crowded effect offends the eye. Extra spacing between subdivisions and indented patterns for subparts and carry-over lines are especially effective in pleasing the eye.

*Some examples of data sheets.*   The three examples of data sheets shown in Figures 11–2, 11–3, and 11–4 generally adhere to the content and form instructions given. The first (Figure 11–2) presents its information in a manner bordering on the narrative. It is especially commendable

**FIGURE 11–2**

A personalized narrative data sheet

THE SCHEME BY WHICH DAVID R. ANDERSON PREPARED HIMSELF FOR LEGAL OFFICE

WORK WITH BORRON, OWEN, BORRON, AND DELAHAYE

Permanent address:
1366 Hyacinth Street
Baton Rouge, Louisiana 70803
Telephone 433-6605

Experience That Produced Versatility

1964-1974   Active duty with United States Navy, six years of which was in rating of yeoman, first class. Navy work was primarily clerical and administrative in nature, involving shorthand (100 w.p.m.) and typing (70 w.p.m.). One of rating requirements was understanding of court-martial procedure. As senior petty officer, assumed responsibility for offices assigned to, both ashore and afloat.

1958-1964   Printer's devil with The Columbia County Journal, Waldo, Arkansas, from 1958 to 1960. In 1960 became apprentice printer in composing room of The Houston Post, Houston, Texas. Left the Post with fourth-year apprentice standing in 1964 to enter United States Navy.

1971-1974   Achieved some success in free-lance fiction and article writing. Articles appeared in U. S. Naval Institute Proceedings, Our Navy, and Three Quarters. Fiction appeared in Stars and Stripes.

1974-1976   Served as Business Manager and Assistant Editor of Delta, student literary magazine of Louisiana State University.

Education That Accentuated Positive Effort

1960-1964   Attended Reagan High School, Houston, Texas, graduating in upper twenty-five percent of class.

1972-1974   While on active duty with navy, commenced part-time prelaw study at Iowa State College, Ames, Iowa. During this time also studied correspondence courses through General Extension Division, Louisiana State University.

1974-1976   Completed prelaw curriculum in General Business at Louisiana State University with a scholastic standing of 3.53 out of a possible 4.00. Courses studied included Business Statistics, Business Management, Elementary French, General and Labor Economics, Business Law, and many other courses designed for a broad business background for the legal profession.

**FIGURE 11–2** *(continued)*

2

<u>Personal</u> <u>Traits</u> <u>That</u> <u>Make</u> <u>for</u> <u>Reliability</u>

Facts and Figures:    Born in Texarkana, Arkansas, on August 20, 1942;
                              have Irish-English ancestry; weigh 175 pounds;
                              72 inches tall.

Physical Condition:    No known physical defects other than slight vision
                              impairment which is easily corrected by glasses.

Marital Status:    Married, with one eight-year-old daughter.

Outdoor recreation:    Golf, hunting, fishing.

<u>References</u> <u>That</u> <u>Will</u> <u>Speak</u> <u>Objectively</u>

From last job:                               From childhood background:
Rear Admiral E. T. Seaward, USN (Ret.)      Mr. M. H. Doerge
126 North Riverside Drive              608 Peddie Street
Ames, Iowa 50010                     Houston, Texas  77019

College Professor:                       Personal:
Dr. P. F. Boyer                         Mr. C. G. Neal
Professor of Finance                  7343 Thurow Street
College of Business Administration      Houston, Texas  77017
Louisiana State University
Baton Rouge, Louisiana 70803

**FIGURE 11–3**

A typical personalized data sheet

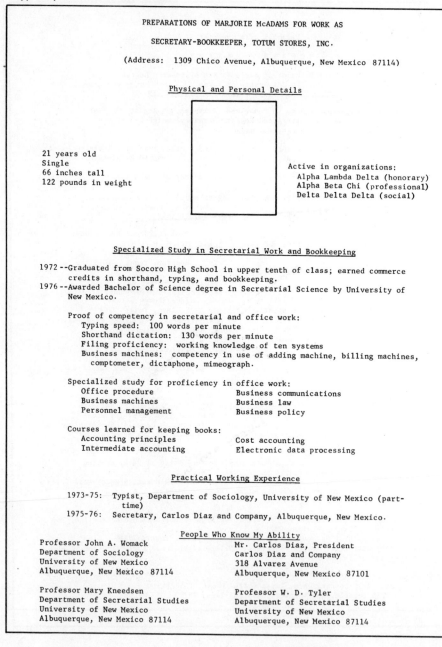

PREPARATIONS OF MARJORIE McADAMS FOR WORK AS

SECRETARY-BOOKKEEPER, TOTUM STORES, INC.

(Address:  1309 Chico Avenue, Albuquerque, New Mexico 87114)

<u>Physical and Personal Details</u>

21 years old
Single
66 inches tall                          Active in organizations:
122 pounds in weight                       Alpha Lambda Delta (honorary)
                                           Alpha Beta Chi (professional)
                                           Delta Delta Delta (social)

<u>Specialized Study in Secretarial Work and Bookkeeping</u>

1972 --Graduated from Socoro High School in upper tenth of class; earned commerce
       credits in shorthand, typing, and bookkeeping.
1976 --Awarded Bachelor of Science degree in Secretarial Science by University of
       New Mexico.

       Proof of competency in secretarial and office work:
           Typing speed:  100 words per minute
           Shorthand dictation:  130 words per minute
           Filing proficiency:  working knowledge of ten systems
           Business machines:  competency in use of adding machine, billing machines,
           comptometer, dictaphone, mimeograph.

       Specialized study for proficiency in office work:
           Office procedure              Business communications
           Business machines            Business law
           Personnel management         Business policy

       Courses learned for keeping books:
           Accounting principles
           Intermediate accounting      Cost accounting
                                        Electronic data processing

<u>Practical Working Experience</u>

   1973-75:  Typist, Department of Sociology, University of New Mexico (part-
             time)
   1975-76:  Secretary, Carlos Diaz and Company, Albuquerque, New Mexico.

<u>People Who Know My Ability</u>
Professor John A. Womack              Mr. Carlos Diaz, President
Department of Sociology              Carlos Diaz and Company
University of New Mexico             318 Alvarez Avenue
Albuquerque, New Mexico 87114        Albuquerque, New Mexico 87101

Professor Mary Kneedsen              Professor W. D. Tyler
Department of Secretarial Studies    Department of Secretarial Studies
University of New Mexico             University of New Mexico
Albuquerque, New Mexico 87114        Albuquerque, New Mexico 87114

**FIGURE 11–4**

A general-purpose data sheet

Personal Data Sheet of

M O R R I S  E · M A S S E Y

Candidate for Bachelor of Business Administration Degree
The University of Texas
June 1976

OCCUPATIONAL PREFERENCES
    Type of Work:  Retail Advertising,
    Manufacturer's Advertising Depart-
    ments, Manufacturer's Salesman.
    Location:  No preferences.
    Travel:  Willing to travel.

PERSONAL AND FAMILY DATA
    Date and Place of Birth:  June 13, 1954, Waco, Texas.
    Height: 5'8".  Weight:  150 lbs.  Health:  Excellent.
    Marital Status:  Single.  Hobbies and Sports:  Swimming, reading, tennis.

SCHOOLS ATTENDED
    1969-1972, Waco High School, Waco, Texas.
    1972-1976, The University of Texas, Austin, Texas.

ACADEMIC PREPARATION
    Major:  Advertising.        24 semester hours.
      Fundamentals of advertising, retail advertising (writing and production),
      selling, advanced advertising, marketing research, sales management, principles
      of retailing, psychology in advertising.
    Other Business Administration Courses Included:
      Accounting-9 hours, business law-6 hours, business writing-5 hours, management-
      3 hours, finance-6 hours, statistics-7 hours, basic marketing-3 hours.
    Outside the College of Business Administration:
      Economics-6 hours, mathematics-8 hours, engineering drawing-3 hours, psychology-
      6 hours, chemistry-8 hours.
    Grade Point Averages:  Major - 3.3 out of 4.    In all courses - 3.2 out of 4.
    Proportion of College Expenses Earned: 25%.

COLLEGE HONORS AND ACTIVITIES
    The University of Texas:  Member, Alpha Delta Sigma; Co-Chairman of Round-Up
    Committee; President, Royal Co-Operative House; Delta Sigma Pi-Senior Vice-
    President, Historian, Outstanding Member Award; Inter-Coop Council; Senior Class
    Secretary; CBA; College of Business Council, American Marketing Association.

BUSINESS EXPERIENCE
    June-Sept. 1973, Bellman, Mammoth Hotel, Yellowstone National Park, Wyoming.
    June-Sept. 1974, Bellman, Raleigh Hotel, Waco, Texas.
    June-Aug. 1975, Assistant Co-ordinator for Summer Entertainment, Student Activities
    Office, The University of Texas, Austin, Texas.

REFERENCES
    Dr. William Brown, Professor of Marketing, College of Business Administration, The
    University of Texas, Austin  78712
    Ed B. Price, Dean of Students, The University of Texas, Austin  78712
    Dr. Stanley Arbingast, Graduate Advisor, College of Business Administration, The
    University of Texas, Austin  78712

ADDRESSES
    Permanent:  2010 Conner, Waco, Texas 76711.  Phone: 755-2113
    Austin: 2210 Enfield, Apartment #5, Austin, Texas 78703

for its completeness in conveying the applicant's achievements. The second example (Figure 11–3) is typical of the data sheet that should be sent by the college graduate with limited experience. It gives good emphasis to education, selecting those education points which help qualify the applicant for the specific job. The third example (Figure 11–4) is typical of the printed type that many college graduates have processed for mass distribution to prospective employers. Because they must fit so many companies and no one job, they are usually general in their content.

# Letter problems—3

## PERSUASIVE REQUESTS

1. Although not a union in the usual sense, the Fraternal Order of Policemen of Mudville voices its members' interests on matters such as pay, working conditions, and community relations. With one or two exceptions, its membership consists of the Mudville Police Department.

Last night at the organization's monthly meeting, the discussion centered on the need for an across-the-board pay increase for Mudville policemen. There was emotional talk about how Mudville salaries had dropped well behind national and regional levels, how financial hardships were forcing some to take on second jobs, how some were leaving the force, and such. At the end of the discussion, the group voted unanimously to request a pay increase of a 10-percent minimum. They elected you (their executive secretary) to present their case in writing.

So now you must write a persuasive letter to the mayor and the city council members which will persuade them to do what they can to grant the officers a pay increase. (You may make up facts to support your case; but be realistic about it.) At this stage you are persuading—not threatening. You are representing a group of loyal, dedicated servants who feel they have a very legitimate case for better pay.

2. Now that you are a successful business executive, you find yourself more and more involved in civic work. Your current involvement is with United Cancer Society. You are chairman of this year's money-raising drive for your state.

On the 20th of next month, the organization will hold its kick-off rally—an inspirational meeting of all district campaign workers. For it you want a keynote speaker who can build enthusiasm as well as one whose name will add prestige to the affair. The first name that comes to mind is the governor (or another personality your instructor may designate) of your state.

It is your job to write this celebrity a letter that will persuade him (or her) to participate. There is no pay, of course—only the rewarding feeling he will get from doing something good. (You may fill in any details you may need—dates, times, places, etc.)

**3.** In addition to your normal administrative duties at the Tri-D Manufacturing Company, you have been assigned the task of coordinating the car pool program. Specifically, your assignment is to encourage the plant's 2,400 workers to form car pools and to help them in doing so.

The reasons for car pooling should be obvious to all. First, of course, there is the need to save precious energy. There is also the benefit of reducing the heavy congestion on roads leading into the plant. Then there is the acute shortage of parking space at the plant. And there are personal benefits—money savings, friendly associations, etc.

As a first step in your plan to sell the idea to the employees, you will write a form letter to all plant personnel. In it you will do your best to convince the workers of the benefits of car pooling. And you will offer to help them in any practical way. (You can supply them with names of employees who live in their area.) Address the letter to Hilda Aaron, who is first on your list of employees.

**4.** Last year Patrolman Henry A. Washington lost his life attempting to apprehend a suspected narcotics peddler. It was a tragic loss, for Henry was an outstanding police officer as well as an excellent human being. He left behind a young wife, three young children, and very little wealth. In recent weeks, the family has begun to suffer.

As a civic-minded citizen of your community, you have joined with others in an effort to raise a Henry A. Washington Fund to help the Washington family. In fact, you are president of the organization. As president it is your job to plan and carry out the first collection campaign.

Your plan is to write letters to a select list of citizens of your town. In your letter you will attempt to persuade the readers to contribute generously to the fund. Although you haven't yet decided on the persuasive strategy you will use, it will be the most convincing and practical plan you can devise. (You may make up any facts you feel are needed. But don't do anything to change the nature of the problem.)

**5.** As executive director of the Small Business Advisory Service it is your task to build membership in your organization. The assignment is no routine one, for membership means work. The only benefit a member gets is a good feeling from doing a good deed.

In a nutshell, the SBAS is an organization of retired executives who give their time freely in advising and generally assisting small businesses. The work is sometimes long and hard; but most members enthusiastically report that it is rewarding.

Your plan for building membership is to write a letter to a select list of retirees in your community. You will make your letter so persuasive they will want to join right away. (You may make up any specific facts you feel you need.)

**6.** You have joined some civic-minded citizens in protesting the proposed destruction of one of the historical landmarks in your city (your instructor will specify the landmark). It so happens that this landmark has been bought by a giant out-of-town investment group. They plan to tear down the building and to build an apartment complex on the site.

Your group has had productive conversations with the investment group. In fact, you have gotten them to agree to abandon their building plans if they can get their purchase price back. (You may determine the price by estimating the value of the building you have selected.)

Now your group faces the task of raising the money to buy back the building. It will start with a mail campaign to leading area citizens. The letter will be a persuasive one—one that will make a public-spirited citizen want to contribute to this cause. As president of this organization, you have the assignment of writing this persuasive letter. Address it to any one of the prominent citizens in your town. (You may use your imagination to supply any specific information you may need.)

**7.** In your job as a writer of direct-mail copy, you have been given the task of writing a letter for the local chapter of HEXCON (Hire an Ex-Convict) Association. The goal of this organization is to help ex-convicts find employment upon their release from prison.

The assignment interests you, for you strongly believe in HEXCON's goal. You know that a job is the first requirement for successful rehabilitation. You know, also, how difficult it is for these unfortunate people to find jobs. So you will do your very best on this assignment.

You will write the letter to leading employers in the area. You will use your best persuasion to get them to hire some ex-convicts. Write the letter for the signature of Matilda Strelsky, president. Enclose an addressed card on which the reader can indicate his willingness to cooperate in the program. An association member will call on him later to work out hiring details.

**8.** In your position as president of your city's Chamber of Commerce, you are spearheading a campaign to win the state's cleanest city title this year. This award given annually by the state association of chambers of commerce has eluded your town in the past, although your town came in second last year.

Cleaning up the town is no simple task, but one part of it involves cleaning up the business establishments. So as a first step you will write a form letter to be sent to every business owner in town. It will appeal to the owners' civic pride and ask them to do what they can to spruce up their businesses. You want each to do what needs to be done—things like keeping rear alleys clean of trash, repairing visible damage to buildings, painting, etc.

Address the letter to William Adcock of Adcock Furniture, whose name is first on your alphabetized list.

**9.** For years the National Management Association has held its annual meeting in late December (between Christmas and New Year's Day). The period was selected initially because this is a slack period for most business executives. In recent years, however, you have noticed considerable grumbling about the date, particularly from family people. For many, it ruins the holiday season. For some, it means leaving the family on Christmas Day in order to make the convention.

As a member of the association's board of directors, you feel that a change of date is in order—at least on an experimental basis. So you decide to present your viewpoint to the other members of the board. You will do it in a letter which you will address to each board member. Your letter will be sufficiently persuasive, you hope, to move the members to vote your way when you propose the change at the board meeting in Chicago next month.

Before writing the letter, you will need to think through the situation carefully and determine the advantages of the change. (Make up any factual information you may need as long as it is realistic and in line with the problem.)

**10.** As convention chairman of your local chamber of commerce, write a letter that will persuade the American Association of Technical Writers to hold their annual convention in your city. You have learned from a member of the association that this group is considering your city along with several other cities. So it is not as if they had never thought of the idea.

Your plan is to present the highlights of your persuasion in a letter. The incidental material you will furnish in some brochures which you will enclose. As you see it, the directors should be interested in two things: (1) a city that will be interesting to visit and (2) a city with hotels that can take care of the Association's needs.

Information you have gathered tells you that the Association's meetings typically attract about 125 members. About half bring their families and make the meeting a vacation. The group meets for two and a half days, with meetings running through the working hours of the day. Their evenings are free.

Address the letter to Cleo Sklar, the Association's president. You will send similar letters to each member of the board.

## SALES

11. Take over as sales manager of the Flat-Rate Rent-a-Car Company and write a letter to business executives. The goal of your letter will be to sell the executives on renting your cars when they travel.

Your company is one of the new ones trying to compete with the old, established companies. You have facilities in all the major U.S. cities and many of the smaller ones. But you do not yet blanket the nation as your competitors do.

Your main appeal is price. You don't have expensive airport booths, computers, and executive offices. Thus, you can pass on the savings to your customers. The saving is sizeable—about 55 percent under the major competition. For example, your compact rents for a flat $12 a day and standard models for $16. There is no charge for mileage, although the customer does pay for gas used.

Although the competition justifies their higher prices by claiming better service, Flat-Rate emphasizes service, also. A phone call on arrival at an airport usually leads to delivery of a car before the traveler's luggage. Your check-out procedure requires only a minute. Your return procedure is equally fast, and it ends with the customer being delivered to the airport.

Include with your letter a special introductory offer card which will entitle the reader to a 20-percent discount the first time he uses your service. It is good for 30 days. Address your letter to any of the executives on your mailing list.

12. Write a letter designed to bring in new members for the Travelers Association. This new organization is designed to meet the needs of those women and men who must travel for a living. In a nutshell, it provides these benefits:
1. *The Traveler*—a monthly magazine with tips and items of interest for the traveler.
2. Discounts at 4,500 hotels and motels.
3. Discounts on car rentals—from 10 to 20 percent, including some of the budget companies that normally do not discount.
4. An extensive vacation plan, including a variety of group trips to the finest resorts here and abroad.
5. A voice in Washington through the organization's lobbyist.

6.  Term life insurance coverage, the amount determined by the following annual membership fee schedule:

| Insurance coverage | Annual membership fee |
|---|---|
| $ 50,000. . . . . . . . . . | $ 30.00 |
| 100,000. . . . . . . . . . | 55.00 |
| 150,000. . . . . . . . . . | 75.00 |
| 250,000. . . . . . . . . . | 112.50 |
| 500,000. . . . . . . . . . | 200.00 |

Include with your letter a return card. The card provides space for checking the membership fee desired. It also permits payment by credit card with spaces for recording card account numbers. Address the letter to any name on your prospect list.

13. As an account executive with the Dearborne Advertising Agency, you must write a sales letter for the Mirror Bay Hotel. Located on the Mississippi Gulf coast, this is truly one of the nation's better resort hotels. It provides just about everything a vacationer would want—golfing on the beautiful 18-hole course, tennis on ten Rubico courts, a marina with a wide assortment of rental boats, deep-sea fishing on the hotel's own *Southern Belle,* and fishing off the hotel's pier. Bicycles can be rented. And there are miles of hiking trails in the area. Then, of course, for those who like swimming, there is the broad, sandy beach as well as the hotel's beautiful pool. To top it off, there is the excellent food that has earned the dining room a four-star rating from the International Gourmet Association. Truly, Mirror Bay is a wonderful spot.

The full facilities of the club are available at a reasonable $75-a-day rate per couple ($45 for singles). This price includes room, breakfast and dinner, and use of most of the hotel's facilities. Golfing, tennis, bicycles, boating, and deep-sea fishing cost extra.

The letter will go to a select group of professional people in surrounding states. If you need additional information, supply it as long as it doesn't change the nature of the assignment.

14. Select from a current magazine an advertisement on a product that could be sold profitably to business executives. Preferably select an advertisement that presents a thorough description of the product. Then write a sales letter for this product. Be careful that your writing does not borrow the wording in the advertisement. In other words, make your letter original in its wording from start to finish. Include a descriptive brochure and an order card with your letter. Address it to the first business executive on your list (for class purposes clip the advertisement to your letter.)

**15.** To your direct-mail office today comes Molly Lee Azar, owner of Business Scanners, Inc. Realizing that business executives have a very difficult time keeping up with the voluminous literature in the field, Ms. Azar thought of the idea of starting a business reading service.

Her service is a simple one. In a nutshell, she and her staff summarize 45 of the leading business publications. She sells these summaries to business executives. The summaries come out monthly and cover all major articles (exclusive of current events). From this publication, an average reader can cover in one hour of reading what would take 30 to 40 hours of reading time. Cost of the service is $120 a year. A subscribing company may obtain extra copies at $1 per copy.

Ms. Azar wants you to work up for her signature a sales letter that will induce business executives to subscribe to her service. You will include a stamped and addressed order card with the letter.

**16.** As the direct-mail manager for Business Gifts, Inc., write a sales letter for your newest product—polished marble paper weights.

Your company specializes in selling items that businesses can give to their customers—calendars, ash trays, ball-point pens, etc. Mainly the items are a form of advertising and have the giving company's name prominently displayed on them. Sales are usually in large quantities.

The paper weights you have added to your line appear to be ideal for your business. They are beautiful rectangles of highly polished Italian marble (measuring in inches 2½x2½x1). The giving company's name is affixed to the marble in the form of a bronze seal designed to the specifications of the company. The idea, of course, is to get these paper weights on customers desks where they will continually advertise the giver's name.

You can sell these ideal gifts only in lots of 100 at $260 per 100, including shipping costs. You can give a 5-percent discount on orders of 500 or more and 10 percent on orders of 1,000 or more. Included in the cost is the design of the company's seal.

You will include with your letter a brochure which displays the choices available. You will also include a stamped and addressed order card. Address the letter to any of the business executives on your mailing list.

**17.** Write a letter selling a package tennis vacation to Tennis Unlimited. Located in a resort area near you (your instructor may select the place), Tennis Unlimited features 48 individual cottages, all comfortably furnished, a club house with restaurant and lounge, a swimming pool, ten Har-Tru outdoor courts and four Dynaturf indoor courts. Its resident pro is Hal Gunn, a former world class professional player. Hal has four competent associates. Without question, Tennis Unlimited is a quality tennis resort.

Package rate per person is $55 per day with double occupancy and $70 per day with single occupancy. Included in the price is breakfast and dinner, a guarantee of three hours minimum court time each day, and one hour per day of group instruction. Private instruction is available at $10 per half hour.

Using your imagination to supply the additional details you may need, write the letter. It will be mailed to a list of affluent tennis enthusiasts. Include an illustrated brochure and an addressed reservations request card.

**18.** As a writer of direct mail, you have been hired by your favorite bank to write a sales letter. This letter will be sent to new citizens of the town in the effort to sell them on depositing their money in this bank.

Because you need to know your product before you can sell it, you will first learn things about your bank—things like the advantages the bank can offer, the services it provides, etc. Then, with this information gathered, you'll arrange it strategically and present it so convincingly that a new citizen will want to use the bank's services.

You will enclose a special introduction card with your letter which will entitle the bearer to a valuable gift (leather-bound check book with a supply of 200 personalized checks). Address the letter to Anthony R. Capri.

**19.** The dean of your college has a list of local National Merit Scholars who have indicated an interest in a major in your discipline. Take over for him and write a letter to these students selling them on your college for their education.

As you will be selling a product that you know well, probably you will not need to spend time investigating your product before writing. But you will need to take mental inventory of the selling points you can stress in your letter—things like physical facilities, library, faculty, and curricula.

Enclose a current brochure on your college, a catalog, and an application form. Your drive for action will seek to get the reader to submit the application form.

**20.** Select your favorite brand of quality chocolate-covered candy and write a sales letter for it. You will send the letter to a list of local business executives. Your objective is to get them to buy a five- or ten-pound gift box for their spouses for Valentine's Day. Price for the candy is high—about 50 percent above retail. But the service more than makes up for the difference. Specially selected singing messengers will deliver the candy—on Valentine's Day.

You haven't yet decided what appeal to use in your letter. But you know that it will be whatever appeal is likely to induce executives to give their spouses candy on a special occasion. You will include a descriptive brochure and an order form designed for easy use. Payment can be made on credit card. Sign the letter as the sales manager for the Candy Corner.

## COLLECTIONS

(These problems are arranged by series. The stage in the series is identified at the beginning of each problem.)

### City Office Supply series

**21.** (Early Stage) The local office of Minuteman Insurance Company, Carolyn Lowe, manager, owes your City Office Supply store $1,240.55 for an assortment of office supplies. You sent this firm the original invoice 75 days ago with terms of 2/10, n/30. Thirty days later (on the due date) you sent the first formal notice, and thirty days later you sent the second formal notice.

Today you're ready to try your first letter. You suspect Ms. Lowe needs to be reminded, but you will try to make it a gentle one. This account has been a good one over the years.

**22.** (Middle Stage) It is now 21 days after your first letter to Carolyn Lowe and her Minuteman Insurance Company. You have not received payment. So it is time to try again to collect the $1,240.55 now over two months past due.

You will write the company a somewhat stronger letter this time. For a basic appeal you'll stress the value of a prompt-pay record. As the customer is a valued one with a long history of profitable relations with you, you'll be careful not to insult or offend. But you will be strong enough to convince the lady that she should pay.

**23.** (Middle Stage) Your last letter to Minuteman Insurance Company didn't work. Now, another 15 days later, you will write again.

This time, you will try a stronger appeal. You will stress the fair-play theme—that is, you will emphasize how you did something for them when they needed it. Now it's only fair that they take care of their end of the obligation. Use your best persuasion to drive home the point; but remember, you are not yet ready for threatening talk.

**24.** (Middle Stage) Carolyn Lowe and her Minuteman Insurance Company still haven't paid. Fifteen days after you wrote them stressing the fair-play appeal, you wrote them again. Now, another 15 days later, you'll have to write yet another letter.

In this letter you will use some negative appeal for the first time. You will talk about the danger of losing a good credit reputation. Even so, it won't be threatening; nor will it show anger. If this one does not bring in the money, the next letter will be the last one.

**25.** (Last Resort) After five futile attempts you will try one more letter to collect from Minuteman. If they do not pay, you will turn over the case to your attorney for collection. Your letter will show Ms. Lowe how essential it is that she come through with payment. Not to do so would cost her heavily in court fees as well as damage to reputation. You will give Ms. Lowe and Minuteman 15 days from today before you will take final action.

## The Parisian Shop series

**26.** (Early Stage) The Parisian Shop, your exclusive ladies clothing store, has served the high-income buyers of your community for seven months. So far, business has been good. Especially have credit sales been good. But recently you have been faced with a problem that was certain to occur sooner or later—the problem of collection. To your disappointment, you find that some of your elegant ladies are slow to pay.

Now, you are in the process of working out a collection procedure for these customers. You have decided on the following plan. First, you will send your monthly statement. You will send a second statement the next month. The following month (when the bill is two months past due) you will send a statement with a printed reminder. If this reminder does not bring in the money, you will send a first reminder form letter the next month.

This reminder letter will follow a "may we tie a string around your finger" theme. Its reasoning will be that you know the reader must have forgotten and will appreciate a reminder. Write the letter.

**27.** (Middle Stage) If the first letter doesn't do the job, 30 days later the Parisian Shop will send a second form letter. This one will get down to collection talk, but it will take a positive approach. Its appeal will be to the social rewards of keeping an impeccable credit record.

Write this letter. Make some provisions for mentioning the amount owed and time past due.

**28.** (Middle Stage) Your collection plan for the Parisian Shop is to write a third letter 30 days later and a fourth after another 30 days. By this time the account is six months past due. A stronger appeal is in order.

In this fourth letter you will stress the fair-play appeal. As in the other letters, make some provision for mentioning the amount owed and the time past due. Write this fourth letter.

**29.** (Last Resort) Fifteen days after the fourth letter in the Parisian Shop's form collection comes another persuasive letter. This one talks rather directly about the advantages of maintaining a good credit record and asks for the money with some force. If it doesn't work in 15 days, a last-resort letter is sent.

As Parisian doesn't want the negative publicity associated with forced collection, it sells its long overdue accounts to the City Collection Agency with full authorization to take legal action. Thus, the last letter Parisian writes warns of this impending action. It talks with friendly directness of what this action will mean to the reader. And it urges the reader to pay within 15 days so as to avoid these consequences. Write this last letter.

## Bargain Cellar series

**30.** (Middle Stage) The Bargain Cellar is a bargain basement clothing operation that caters primarily to low-income families. It grants credit on a selective basis. But because of the income level of its customers, it maintains a vigorous collection procedure.

If payment is not made within 15 days of the initial statement, the store sends a second statement with a printed reminder. If this does not do the job in 15 days, they send a persuasive form letter. By most standards, this letter would be classified as middle stage. It talks rather directly about the value of maintaining a good credit reputation. Write this letter.

**31.** (Middle Stage) If the Bargain Cellar's first letter doesn't collect in 15 days, they move to a second persuasive form letter. This one talks rather directly and negatively about the consequences of losing a good credit reputation. And it makes it clear that this is what is likely to happen to the reader if he doesn't pay up. Write this letter.

**32.** (Last Resort) The Bargain Cellar doesn't believe in waiting long. If they don't collect in another 15 days, they are ready for last-resort action. So they write a third form letter. This one points out clearly that unless payment is made within 15 days they are turning the account over to their attorney with full authorization to go to court. And it talks convincingly and with concern about the consequences of this action. Write this letter.

## Wicker Wholesale Grocers series

**33.** (Early Stage) As collection manager for Wicker Wholesale Grocers handle the account of Dykus Super Mart. This small-town grocery store made a $1,766 initial purchase from you 60 days ago on terms of 2/10, n/30. On the due date you sent a statement, and 15 days later another statement with a printed reminder. Now an additional 15 days later, you still have not received their money. So you will write them a first letter.

This first letter will be a friendly reminder, for you're not yet ready to do anything to hamper relations with this new customer. Your letter will stress the theme that probably they have overlooked this matter. Much of the letter will concern goodwill material. Address the letter to Mark Dykus, owner.

**34.** (Middle Stage) The friendly reminder to Mark Dykus didn't work. Now, 20 days later, you'll have to write him again.

This time your letter will have to be persuasive. You'll appeal to the man's pride, showing how a good credit record is a part of one's character.

**35.** (Middle Stage) Try again to collect from Mark Dykus and his Dykus Super Mart. It's another 20 days later. In this letter you'll talk about the value of a good credit rating to one's success in business. You'll try to present the case so convincingly that he'll want to pay. But take care not to threaten. You'll do that next time—if he doesn't pay.

**36.** (Last Resort) Unfortunately, Mark Dykus didn't respond to your persuasive request. So you'll have to take drastic action. This $1,766 account now is 90 days past due. If payment is not received within 15 days of the date of your letter, you will turn the matter over to your lawyers. They will then force collection through the courts.

Write a letter to Dykus telling him of this action, describing its consequences and giving him a chance to pay up and avoid the consequences.

## Roberto Lopez Associates series

**37.** (Early Stage) Roberto Lopez Associates, a management consulting firm, has had some difficulty collecting from the Horton Machine Works. About four months ago the Horton firm came to Roberto Lopez with serious operational problems. Mr. Lopez worked with the Horton people personally for nine successive ten-hour days. He worked out Horton's problems; and the Horton people said they were well satisfied.

After completing the job, Roberto Lopez Associates billed Horton $4,760 for services rendered ($50 per hour plus expenses). Thirty days later Horton had not paid; so Lopez sent a duplicate bill. Now an additional 30 days later Horton still hasn't paid.

Roberto Lopez feels it's time to send a gentle reminder. As he had very friendly relationships with John Horton, owner-manager, the letter will take the approach that payment has been overlooked and that a friendly reminder will be appreciated. Write the letter.

**38.** (Middle Stage) Roberto Lopez is terribly disappointed that his reminder letter didn't bring in Horton's money. Now, 30 days later, he will write a second letter. This one will stress the fair-play appeal (We've given you something you needed; now how about doing something for us). Write the letter for Mr. Lopez.

**39.** (Middle Stage) Thirty days after sending the second letter to Horton's Machine Works, Roberto Lopez had to write another letter. It didn't work. Now, 15 days later, he's ready to try his hand at letter writing again. If this letter doesn't work, the next letter will threaten last-resort action.

This fourth letter will stress the advantages of keeping a good credit record. And it will give convincing argument to support the appeal. Write the letter.

**40.** (Last Resort) Roberto Lopez doesn't like to do it, but he feels that he must take last-resort action to collect the $4,760 Horton Machine Works owes him. If Horton doesn't pay within 15 days, Roberto Lopez Associates will take the matter to court. The letter will explain vividly the effects of this action. It makes the Horton people see that they have no choice but pay. Write the letter for Lopez.

## Applications

**41.** Assume that you are completing your degree requirements this semester and are looking for a job. Find an advertisement for a job for which you would be qualified. Then write a letter of application for the job. For class purposes, clip the advertisement to your letter. Assume that a data sheet accompanies the letter.

**42.** Write the data sheet to accompany the letter in problem 41, above.

**43.** Move yourself ten years into the future. Your career development has been fairly successful, though not sensational. To this point you have been employed by one major firm (you name it) and have gained excellent experience. But the road to advancement with this firm appears to have only limited possibilities. So you have decided to look elsewhere for a suitable position.

Your search for a new position turns up one good possibility. The job is with a major competitor of your present employer; and the position would represent a logical move up from your present status.

Making only logical assumptions about your development and experience over the ten-year period, write the letter. Assume that a data sheet accompanies the letter.

**44.** Write the data sheet that accompanies problem 43, above.

**45.** Assume that you are in your last term of school and that graduation is just around the corner. Your greatest interest is in finding work which you like and in which you could support yourself now and a family later as you win promotions.

No job of your choice is revealed in the want ads of newspapers and trade magazines. No placement bureau has provided anything to your liking. So you decide to do as any good salesman does: survey the product (yourself), then the market (companies which in the scope of their operations could use a person who can do what you are prepared to do), then advertise (send the company a data sheet with a covering application letter). Such a procedure sometimes creates a job where none existed before; sometimes it establishes a basis for negotiations for the "big job" two, three, or five years after graduation. And very frequently, it puts you on the list for the good job which is not filled through advertising or from the company staff. Assume that a data sheet accompanies the letter.

**46.** Write the data sheet to accompany problem 45, above.

**47.** Move the calendar to your graduation date so that you're now ready to sell your working ability in the job market for as much as you can get and still hold your own. Besides your wide canvass of likely firms with the aid of prospecting letters and your diligent followups of family "contacts," you've decided that you won't overlook anything especially good in the ad columns of newspapers and magazines. A look through the library copies of the latest issues available of big town publications turns up the following prospects worth looking over that you think you could handle. (You may change publication and place names to fit your section of the country.)

a. ACCOUNTING TRAINEE. Small CPA firm needs recent college graduate with accounting major. Excellent opportunity to grow with company. Must be hard worker, intelligent, and personable. Excellent starting salary and fringe benefits. Write P.O. Box 2174, City.

b. MANAGEMENT TRAINEE. Business administration or engineering graduate preferred. Must be intelligent, hard-working, and personable. Apply by letter only to Personnel Department, Moran Chemical Company, Box 1001.

c. BANKING TRAINEE. Large bank has opening for college graduates with good foundation in finance. Training programs designed to give thorough foundation in all areas of bank operation. Applicants must be mature, intelligent, and personable. Good salary and fringe benefits. Excellent opportunity for advancement. P.O. Box 171, City.

*d.* SALES.   Major publisher of college textbooks wants representative to call on college profesors in region. Must be college graduate, self-motivated, stable, and personable. Above average starting pay and good advancement. Write Sales Manager, Holly Publishing Company, P.O. Box 3699, City.

*e.* ADMINISTRATIVE ASSISTANT.   High-ranking executive in large corporation needs assistant to relieve him of detail work. College degree in business administration preferred. Must be hard worker, have good communications skills (written and oral), and willing to do detail work. Send letter and resume to Box 2037, City.

*f.* HOTEL MANAGEMENT TRAINEE.   Young college graduate for career in hotel administration. Training covers all phases of hotel operations. Applicants must be personable, hard-working, mature, and intelligent. Write Placement Officer, DeVoe Hotels, Inc., 3175 Burgess Avenue, City.

*g.* ASSISTANT CONTROLLER.   Recent college graduate in accounting preferred. Excellent opportunity to get broad experience quickly. Must be able to assume responsibility and advance with fast growing small manufacturing company. Must be personable, hard-working, and mature. Box 217, City.

*h.* MERCHANDISING TRAINEE.   Large department store chain seeks college graduates in business administration for trainee program. Must be willing to relocate throughout career. Must have potential for top management—willing to work, personable, intelligent. Write Personnel Manager, P.O. Box 909, City.

*i.* OFFICE MANAGER.   Local insurance agency needs bright young college graduate. Will train for position. Must know office administration and have good letter writing ability. Excellent salary and fringe benefits. Box 3007, City.

*j.* MARKETING RESEARCH.   College degree with specialized training in marketing research and procedure required, including computer use and statistics. Company is national leader in field. Excellent opportunity to get broad experience in field. Box 2901, City.

*k.* EXECUTIVE SECRETARY.   President of successful small business needs college-trained secretary. Must be qualified in typing, dictation, and office procedures. Pleasing personality essential. Top salary and benefits. Write Box 409, City.

*l.* INDUSTRIAL SALES.   National manufacturer of chemicals wants aggressive salesmen to call on industrial buyers. College degree with major in engineering, chemistry, or business administration preferred. Guaranteed income during six months training period; unlimited income from commission plan thereafter. Must be personable, aggressive, and self-motivated. Write Sales Manager, Box 47, City.

*m.* DEPARTMENT STORE BUYER.   Major department store seeks recent college graduate for training as buyer of ladies fashion goods.

Must be personable, willing to travel, and have interest in fashion. Excellent pay and benefits. Write Personnel Director, P.O. Box 1714, City.

Assume that you *do* want a job, and concentrate on the ad describing the work you would like most or could do best—then write a letter which will get that job. Your letter will first have to survive the siftings which winnow out the dozens (sometimes hundreds) of applicants who lack the expected qualifications. Toward the end you'll be getting into strong competition in which small details may make the little extra margin of superiority that will get you an interview and a chance to campaign further.

Study your ad for what it says and even more for what it implies between the lines. Weigh your own preparation even more thoroughly than you weigh the chosen ad. You may imagine far enough ahead to assume completion of all the courses which are blocked out for your degree. You may build up your case a bit on what you actually have. Sort out the things that line up for the *one* job, organize them strategically, and then present them. Assume that you've attached a complete data sheet (possibly with picture).

**48.** Write the data sheet to accompany Problem 47, above.

# 12

# Reports: The problem and its organization

## AN ORIENTATION TO REPORTS

**H**ow MUCH you will communicate through reports in business will depend on the nature of your organization. But the odds are that you will use reports and that you will use them a lot. Reports are vital to the communication needs of all large organizations; and the larger the organization, the greater the need for reports is likely to be. Also, the more technical and complex the work within the organization is, the more likely it is that reports will be needed. As today's movement is toward progressively larger and more technical business operations, your likelihood of communicating extensively through reports is good.

### The special needs of reports

Communicating through reports involves applying many of the principles of clear writing used in letters, especially those discussed in Chapter 7. Certainly, there is much in common in all forms of writing. Reports, however, have some special needs which make it desirable that you study them separately. The most important of these needs are those related to the special communication problems caused by the extent of information some reports must present. Although many reports are no longer than a long business letter, many others contain great masses of information. Presenting vast quantities of data for the best possible communication results involves many problems worthy of study.

From a review of the communication process, we can see easily the difficulty of communicating voluminous material. The sensory receptors are selective, and the mental filters are deficient in giving meaning to what the receptors pick up. As a result, much of any involved message will be missed. Thus, you, as a report writer, must do whatever you can to help in the communication of the mass of information which makes up your report.

As you will learn from the following pages, you can help to communicate voluminous material in a number of ways. You can present the information in an order carefully worked out to give maximum understanding to the information. You can work hard to show the relationships of various parts of the report, making them fit logically together in the reader's mind. You can make good use of visual helps when words alone would not do the best job. You can summarize from time to time, and you can mark the reader's path through the information with forward-guiding references and concluding remarks. These and other things you can do to overcome the major communication barrier of a report, make up the bulk of the discussion which appears in the following pages.

## Reports defined

Most of us know, or think we know, what business reports are, for they are commonplace in 20th-century life. But probably we would be hard pressed to find words to define them. In fact, definitions in current use range from one extreme to the other. Some are so broad as to include almost any presentation of information. Others limit reports to only the most formal types. For our purposes, this middle-ground definition is adequate: A business report is an orderly and objective communication of factual information which serves some business purpose.

Careful inspection of this definition reveals the identifying characteristics of the business report. As an *orderly* communication, a report is given some care in preparation. And care in preparation distinguishes a report from the casual, routine exchanges of information which continually occur in business. The *objective* quality of a report is its unbiased approach to the facts presented. The report seeks truth, regardless of its consequences. The word *communication* is broad by definition, covering all ways of transmitting meaning (speaking, writing, drawing, gesturing, and so on). The basic ingredient of the report is factual information—events, records, and the various forms of data that are communicated in the conduct of business. Not all reports are business reports. Research scientists, medical doctors, ministers, students, and many others write reports. To be classified as a "business report," a report must *serve some business purpose.*

Even though this definition of a business report is specific enough to be meaningful, it is broad enough to take into account the variations to be found in reports. For example, some reports do nothing more than present facts. Others go a step further by including interpretations. Still others proceed to conclusions and recommendations. There are reports that are formally dressed both in writing style and in physical appearance. And there are reports that evidence a high degree of informality. The definition given permits all of these variations.

## DETERMINING THE REPORT PURPOSE

Your work on a report logically begins with your efforts to get the problem (purpose) clearly in mind. As elementary and basic as this step may appear to be, all too often it is haphazardly done. And all too often it is the cause of the failure of a report to achieve its mission.

### The preliminary investigation

Getting a problem in mind largely is a matter of gathering all the information needed to understand it and then applying your best logic to the problem. Gathering the pertinent information involves a variety of activity, depending on your problem. It may mean gathering material from company files, talking over the problem with experts, searching through bibliographical references, and/or discussing the problem with those authorizing it. In general, this preliminary investigation should be pursued until you have whatever information is necessary for you to understand clearly the purpose of your report.

### Needs for a clear statement of problem

After you have sufficient information to understand your problem, your next logical step is to state it clearly. Preferably you should state it in writing. Stating the problem in writing is good for many reasons. A written statement is preserved permanently; thus, you may refer to it time and again without danger of changes occurring in it. In addition, other people can review, approve, and evaluate a written statement; and their assistance sometimes may be valuable. Most important of all, putting the problem in writing forces you to do, and to do well, the basic initial task of getting the problem in mind. In this way, this practice serves as a valuable form of self-discipline.

The problem statement normally takes one of three forms. One is the infinitive phrase: To determine the cause of decreasing sales at Store X. Another and equally good form is the question: What are the causes of decreasing sales at Store Y? A third and less popular form is the declarative statement. Although somewhat dull and not so solution-oriented as the other two, this form nevertheless gives a good indication of the problem. An example of it is the following: Company X sales are decreasing, and it wants to know the cause for this decline.

## Determination of factors

From the problem statement you should next turn to the mental path of determining its needs. Within the framework of your logical imagination you should look for the factors of the problem. That is, you should look for the subject areas that must be investigated in order to satisfy the overall objectives. Specifically, these factors may be of three types. First, they may be merely subtopics of the broader topics about which the report is concerned. Second, they may be hypotheses that must be subjected to the test of investigation and objective review. Third, in problems that involve comparisons they may be the bases on which the comparisons are made. Obviously, the process is a mental one, involving the intricate workings of the mind. Thus, we can describe it only in a most general way. You begin the process by applying your best logic and comprehensive abilities to the problem. The same mental process that helped you to comprehend your problem now should assist you in determining the structure of the solution.

## Use of subtopics in information reports

If the problem concerns primarily a need for information your mental effort should produce the main areas about which information is needed. Illustrating this type of situation is the problem of presenting for Company X a report that reviews the company's activities during the past quarter. Clearly, this is a routine and informational type of problem— that is, it requires no analysis, no conclusion, no recommendation. It requires only that information be presented. The mental process in this case is concerned simply with the determining of which subdivision of the overall subject should be covered. After thoroughly evaluating the possibilities, the investigator may come up with the following factor analysis.

*Problem statement:* To review operations of Company X from January 1 through March 31.

*Factors:*
1. Production
2. Sales and promotion
3. Financial status
4. Plant and equipment
5. Product development
6. Personnel

## Hypotheses for problems of solution

Some problems by their nature seek a solution. Typically, such problems seek an explanation of a phenomenon or the correction of a condition. In analyzing such problems, the researcher must seek possible explanations or solutions. Such explanations or solutions are termed *hypotheses*. Once they are determined, hypotheses are tested and their applicability to the problem is either proved or disproved.

Illustrating problem analysis for this type of situation is the problem of a department store chain that seeks to learn why sales at one of its stores are dropping. In preparing this problem for investigation, the researcher logically would think of the possible explanations (hypotheses) of the decline in sales. He would be likely to think of more explanations than would be workable, so his task would be one of studying, weighing, and selecting. After such a study session, he may come up with explanations such as these.

> *Problem statement:* Why have sales declined at the Milltown Store?
> *Factors:*
> 1. Change in competition in the area
> 2. Exceptional changes in area economy
> 3. Merchandising deficiency

Logically, in the investigation that follows the researcher would test each of the above hypotheses. Perhaps he would find that one, two, or all apply. Or perhaps he would find that none is logical. Then he would have to advance additional hypotheses for further evaluation.

## Bases of comparison in evaluation studies

When the problem concerns evaluating something, either singularly or in comparison with others, the researcher seeks to determine the bases for the evaluation. That is, he seeks to determine what characteristics he will evaluate. In some cases, the procedure may concern more than naming the characteristics. It may include also the criteria to be used in evaluating each characteristic.

The problem of a company that seeks to determine which of three cities would be best for opening a new factory illustrates this technique. Such a problem obviously involves a comparison study of the cities, and the bases for the comparison are the factors that determine success for the type of factory involved. After careful mental search for these factors, the investigator will be likely to come up with a plan such as the following.

*Problem statement:* To determine whether Y Company's new factory should be built in City A, City B, or City C.

*Factors:*
1. Availability of labor
2. Abundance of raw material
3. Tax structure
4. Transportation facilities
5. Nearness to markets
6. Power supply
7. Community attitude

## Need for subbreakdown

Each of the factors selected for investigation may have factors of its own. In the last illustration, for example, the comparison of transportation in the three cities may well be covered by subdivisions such as water, rail, truck, and air. Labor may be compared by categories such as skilled and unskilled. These breakdowns may go still further. Skilled labor may be broken down by specific skills: machinists, plumbers, pipefitters, welders, and such. The subdivisions could go on and on, and they should be made so far as it is helpful to the investigator.

The value of this step of finding the factors of the problem is obvious: it serves as a guide to the investigation that follows. In addition, it gives the problem the first semblance of order, and the value of order in any complex process cannot be questioned.

## GATHERING THE INFORMATION NEEDED

With the problem clearly in mind, your next step in your work on the report is to gather the information you need. How you collect your information is determined by the unique nature of your problem. It may, for example, require some form of primary research, such as a survey or an experiment. Or it may require research of a secondary nature—library research, research through company records, and the like. Whatever method is required, it is likely to be one for which your work has prepared you. For this reason, and because the subject of research methodology is so complex and involved, we shall move past this major step in report preparation. Thus, we shall assume that the research has been done—that you now have collected all of the essential data your problem requires.

## ORGANIZATION OF THE REPORT INFORMATION

With your research completed, you next find yourself with a mass of information on your subject. This is the material with which you will build your report. Your next logical step is to give this material the order in which it will appear in your report.

## Preliminary steps in determining order

In all likelihood, your research findings will be in some form of disorder. They may be in the form of stacks of note cards, reams of questionnaires, sheets of recordings, and such. In this condition they are almost useless. You must do something to them before they can be made meaningful in your report.

What you do to give your findings their first semblance of order depends on the nature of the information you have assembled. If you have conducted library research, for example, you will need to assort your findings by some means of grouping or classifying. If you have conducted a survey or an experiment, it may mean tallying results into categories of likeness, constructing tables, computing central-tendency measurements, and the like. Or if your research is from your memory, this step of putting the information in orderly form would mean only logically arranging the thoughts in your mind.

With your information organized for better understanding, you may now begin to apply it to your problem. This, of course, is a mental task, and we can give no formula for doing it. Generally, it involves fitting your findings to your problem—that is, analyzing them and applying them to your objectives in the one case. Your task is one of good, hard thinking—of using good logic and good knowledge in giving meaning to your research. The end result will be that from this thinking the report story will begin to emerge. You will decide what you are going to say and how you will say it.

## Need for a written outline

After you have given your findings meaning and know generally what your report will say, you are ready to begin arranging your material in the order it will take in your report. Your work here will involve constructing an outline. As you know, an outline is simply a plan for the writing task which follows. It is to you, the writer, what the blueprint is to the construction engineer or what the pattern is to the dressmaker. In addition to guiding your efforts, the outline compels you to think before you write. And when you think, your writing is likely to be clearer.

Although your plan may be written or mental, you will be wise to use a written plan for all but the shortest problems. In longer reports, where tables of contents are needed, the outline forms the basis of this table. Also, in most long reports, and even in some short ones, the outline topics may serve as guides to the reader when placed within the report text as captions (or heads) to the paragraphs of writing they cover.

## Patterns of report organization

After you have made your information ready for outlining, and before you begin the task, you should decide on the writing sequence, or pattern, you will use in your report. The possible sequences are many, but they fall into these definite patterns: logical, direct, and chronological. Although the emphasis at this stage of report preparation is on the selection of a sequence for the whole of the report, these patterns may be followed in any writing unit, be it sentence, paragraph, major section, or the whole.

In the *logical* arrangement you present the findings in inductive order —moving from the known to the unknown. You precede the report findings with whatever introductory material is necessary to orient the reader to your problem. Then you present the facts, possibly with their analyses. And from these facts and analyses, you derive concluding or summary statements. In some problems you may include a recommendation section. Thus, in report form this arrangement is typified by an introductory section, the report body (usually made up of a number of sections), and a summary, conclusion, or recommendation section.

Illustrating this plan is the following report of a short and rather simple problem concerning a personnel action on a subordinate. For reasons of space economy, only the key parts of the report are presented.

> Numerous incidents during the past two months appear to justify an investigation of the work record of Clifford A. Knudson, draftsman, tool design department. . . .
>
> The investigation of his work record for the past two months reveals these points:
>
> 1.   He has been late to work seven times.
> 2.   He has been absent without acceptable excuse for seven days.
> 3.   On two occasions he reported to work in a drunken and disorderly condition.
> 4.   Etc.
>
> The foregoing evidence leads to one conclusion: Clifford A. Knudson should be fired.

Contrasting with the logical sequence is the *direct* arrangement. In this sequence you present the subject matter in deductive fashion. First, you present conclusions, summaries, or recommendations; and you follow them with the facts and analyses from which they are drawn. A typical report following such an order would begin with a presentation of summary, conclusion, and recommendation material. The report findings and the analyses from which the beginning section is derived comprise the following sections. Written in direct order, the same report recommending that Knudson be fired would look like this:

Clifford A. Knudson, draftsman, tool design department, should be fired. This conclusion is reached after a thorough investigation brought about by numerous incidents during the past two months. . . .

The recommended action is supported by this information from his work record for the past two months:

1. He has been late to work seven times.
2. He has been absent without acceptable excuse for seven days.
3. On two occasions he reported to work in a drunken and disorderly condition.
4. Etc.

In the *chronological* arrangment you present the findings in the order in which they happened. Obviously, such an arrangement is limited to problems of an historical nature or problems which in some other way have a relation to time. The time pattern followed may be from past to present, from present to past, from present to future, or from future to present. A report following an order of time might begin directly with the chronological review of facts (see examples below), with an introductory section, or with a conclusion, summary, or recommendation. In other words, the chronological order may be combined with either of the two preceding orders. In such cases it is the arrangement of the findings (the report body) to which the chronological sequence applies. Again, the report on Knudson illustrates this arrangement.

Clifford A. Knudson was hired in 1974 as a junior draftsman in the tool design department. For the first 18 months his work was exemplary, and he was given two pay increases and a promotion to senior draftsman. In January of 1976, he missed four days of work, reporting illness, which was later found to be untrue. Again, in February. . . .

All of these facts lead to the obvious conclusion: Clifford A. Knudson should be fired.

## System of outline symbols

In constructing your outline, you will use some system of symbols to designate the levels of importance of your parts. Thus, a word about systems of symbols is necessary at this point. The most common system of outline symbols is the conventional form with which you are familiar:

I.  First degree of division
    A.  Second degre of division
        1.  Third degree of division
            *a*)  Fourth degree of division
                (1)  Fifth degree of division
                    (*a*)  Sixth degree of division

A second system of symbols is the numerical (sometimes called *decimal*) form. This system makes use of whole numbers to designate the major sections of a paper. Whole numbers followed by decimals and additional digits indicate subsections of the major sections. That is, an additional digit to the right of the decimal designates each successive step in the subdivision. Illustration best explains this procedure:

1.   First degree of division
   1.1   Second degree of division
      1.11   Third degree of division
         1.111   Fourth degree of division
2.   First degree of division
   2.1   Second degree of division
      2.11   Third degree of division (first item)
      2.12   Third degree of division (second item)
         2.121   Fourth degree of division (first item)
         2.122   Fourth degree of division (second item)

You should take care with numbers over ten. For example, 1.19 shows that this is item 9 of the third degree of division—not the 19th item of the second degree. The latter division would be written 1.(19).

## The nature and extent of outlining

In general, you should build the outline around the objective of the investigation and the findings. With the objective and findings in mind, you build the structure of the report in imagination. In this process you hold large areas of facts and ideas in your mind, shifting them about until the most workable arrangement becomes clear. A workable arrangement is that order which will enable you to present the findings in their clearest and most meaningful form.

The extent of the task of outlining will differ from problem to problem. In fact, in many instances much of the work may be done long before you consciously begin the task of constructing an outline. The early steps of defining the problem and determining its subproblems may lay the groundwork for final organization. If you use a questionnaire or other form in gathering information, possibly its structure has given the problem some order. The preliminary analysis of the problem, the task of classifying and tabulating the findings, and possibly preliminary interpretations of the findings may have given you the general idea of the report's story. Thus, when you begin to construct the outline, the work before you may be in varying degrees of progress. Obviously, the task of outlining will never be the same for any two problems. Even so, the following general and systematic procedure for outlining may prove helpful.

## Organization by division

This procedure is based on the concept that outlining is a process of dividing. The subject of division is the whole of the information you have gathered. Thus, you begin the task of organizing by surveying the whole for some appropriate and logical means of dividing the information.

After you have divided the whole of the information into comparable parts, you may further divide each of the parts. Then you may further divide each of these subparts, and you may continue dividing as far as it is practical to do so. Hence, in the end, you may have an outline of two, three, or more levels (or stages) of division. You designate these levels of division in the finished outline by some system of letters or numbers such as the two systems we have discussed.

## Division by conventional relationship

In dividing the information into subparts, you have the objective of finding a means of division that will produce equal and comparable parts. Time, place, quantity, and factor are the general bases for these divisions.

Whenever the information you have to present has some chronological aspect, organization by *time* is possible. In such an organization the divisions of the whole are periods of time. Usually, the periods follow a time sequence. Although a past-to-present or present-to-past sequence is the rule, variations are possible. The time periods you select need not be equal in length, but they should be comparable in importance. Determining comparability is, of course, a subjective process and is best based on the facts of the one situation.

A report on the progress of a research committee serves to illustrate this possibility. The time period covered by such a report might be broken down into the following comparable subperiods:

The period of orientation, May–July
Planning the project, August
Implementation of the research plan, September–November

The happenings within each period might next be arranged in the order of their occurrence. Close inspection might reveal additional division possibilities.

If the information you have collected has some relation to geographic location, you may use a *place* division. Ideally, the division would be such that like characteristics concerning the problem exist within each geographic area. Unfortunately, place divisions are hampered by the fact that political boundary lines and geographic differences in characteristics do not always coincide.

A report on the sales program of a national manufacturer illustrates a division by place. The information in this problem might be broken down by these major geographic areas:

New England
Atlantic Seaboard
South
Southwest
Midwest
Rocky Mountain
Pacific Coast

Another illustration of organization by place is a report on the productivity of a company with a number of manufacturing plants. A major division of the report might be devoted to each of the company's plants. The information for each of the plants might be further broken down by place, this time by sections, departments, divisions, or the like.

*Quantity* divisions are possible whenever your information has quantitative values. To illustrate, an analysis of the buying habits of a segment of the labor force could very well be broken down by income groups. Such a division might produce the following sections:

Under $2,000
$2,000 to under $4,000
$4,000 to under $7,000
$7,000 to under $10,000
$10,000 to under $15,000
Over $15,000

Another example of division on a quantitative basis is a report of a survey of men's preferences for shoes. Because of variations in preferences by ages, an organization by age groups might be used. Perhaps a division such as the following would be appropriate:

Youths, under 18
Young adult, 18–30
Adult, 31–50
Senior adult, 51–70
Elderly adult, over 70

*Factor* breakdowns are not so easily seen as the preceding three possibilities. Frequently, problems have little or no time, place, or quantity aspects. Instead, they require that certain information areas be investigated in order to meet the objectives. Such information areas may consist of a number of questions which must be answered in solving a problem.

Or they may consist of subjects which must be investigated and applied to the problem.

An example of a division by factors is a report which seeks to determine the best of three cities for the location of a new manufacturing plant. In arriving at this decision, one would need to compare the three cities on the basis of the factors which affect the plant location. Thus, the following organization of this problem would be a logical possibility:

Worker availability
Transportation facilities
Public support and cooperation
Availability of raw materials
Taxation
Sources of power

Another illustration of organization by factors is a report advising a manufacturer whether to begin production of a new product. This problem has few time, place, or quantity considerations. The decision on the basic question will be reached by careful consideration of the factors involved. Among the more likely factors are these:

Production feasibility
Financial considerations
Strength of competition
Consumer demand
Marketing considerations

## Combination and multiple division possibilities

Not all division possibilities are clearly time, place, quantity, or factor. In some instances, combinations of these bases of division are possible. In the case of a report on the progress of a sales organization, for example, the information collected could be arranged by a combination of quantity and place:

Areas of high sales activity
Areas of moderate sales activity
Areas of low sales activity

Although not so logical, the following combination of time and quantity is also a possibility:

Periods of low sales
Periods of moderate sales
Periods of high sales

The previously drawn illustration about determining the best of three towns for locating a new manufacturing plant shows that a problem may sometimes be divided by more than one characteristic. In this example the information also could have been organized by towns—that is, each town could have been discussed as a separate division of the report. This plan, however, is definitely inferior, for it separates physically the information which must be compared. Even so, it serves to illustrate a problem with multiple organization possibilities. The presence of two characteristics is common. The possibility of finding three or even four characteristics by which the information may be grouped is not remote. As a rule, when multiple division possibilities exist, those not used as a basis for the major division might serve to form the second and third levels of division. In other words, the outline to this problem might look like this:

    II.  Town A
         A.  Worker availability
         B.  Transportation facilities
         C.  Public support and cooperation
         D.  Availability of raw materials
         E.  Taxation
         F.  Sources of power
   III.  Town B
         A.  Worker availability
         B.  Transportation facilities
         C.  Public support and cooperation
         D.  Availability of raw materials
         E.  Taxation
         F.  Sources of power
    IV.  Town C
         A.  Worker availability
         B.  Etc.

Or it might look like this:

    II.  Worker availability
         A.  Town A
         B.  Town B
         C.  Town C
   III.  Transportation facilities
         A.  Town A
         B.  Town B
         C.  Town C
    IV.  Public support and cooperation
         A.  Town A
         B.  Town B
         C.  Town C

The plan of organization selected should be the one which best presents the information gathered. Unfortunately, the superiority of one plan over the others will not always be so clear as in the illustration above. Only a careful analysis of the information and possibly trial and error will lead to the plan most desirable for any one problem.

## Introductory and concluding sections

To this point, the organization procedure discussed has been concerned primarily with arrangement of the information gathered and analyzed. It is this portion of the report which comprises what is commonly referred to as the report "body." To this report body may be appended two additional major sections.

At the beginning of a major report may be an introduction to the presentation (the reason why the examples above begin with II rather than I), although some forms of today's reports eliminate this conventional section. Appended to each major report may be a final major section in which the objective is brought to head. Such a section may be little more than a summary in a report when the objective is simply to present information. In other instances it may be the section in which the major findings or analyses are drawn together to form a final conclusion. Or possibly it might lead to a recommended line of action based on the foregoing analysis of information.

## Wording the outline for report use

As the outline in its finished form is your table of contents and may also serve as caption guides to the paragraphs throughout the written text, you should take care in constructing its final wording. In this regard you should consider a number of conventional principles of construction. Adherence to these principles will produce a logical and meaningful outline to your report.

*Topic or talking caption?*  In selecting the wording for the outline captions, you have a choice of two general forms—the topic and the talking captions. Topic captions are short constructions, frequently one or two words in length, which do nothing more than identify the topic of discussion. The following segment of a topic-caption outline is typical of its type:

II. Present armor unit
    A.  Description and output
    B.  Cost
    C.  Deficiencies
III. Replacement effects
    A.  Space
    B.  Boiler setting
    C.  Additional accessories
    D.  Fuel

Like the topic caption, the talking caption (or "popular" caption, as it is sometimes called) also identifies the subject matter covered. But it goes a step further. It also indicates what is said about the subject. In other words, the talking caption summarizes, or tells the story of, the material it covers, as in the following illustration of a segment of a talking outline:

II. Operation analyses of armor unit
   A. Recent lag in overall output
   B. Increase in cost of operation
   C. Inability to deliver necessary steam
III. Consideration of replacement effects
   A. Greater space requirements
   B. Need for higher boiler setting
   C. Efficiency possibilities of accessories
   D. Practicability of firing two fuels

Following is a report outline made up of captions that talk:

I. Orientation to the problem
   A. Authorization by board action
   B. Problem of locating a woolen mill
   C. Use of miscellaneous government data
   D. Logical plan of solution
II. Community attitudes toward the woolen industry
   A. Favorable reaction of all cities to new mill
   B. Mixed attitudes of all toward labor policy
III. Labor supply and prevailing wage rates
   A. Lead of San Marcos in unskilled labor
   B. Concentration of skilled workers in San Marcos
   C. Generally confused pattern of wage rates
IV. Nearness to the raw wool supply
   A. Location of Ballinger, Coleman, and San Marcos in the wool area
   B. Relatively low production near Big Spring and Littlefield
V. Availability of utilities
   A. Inadequate water supply for all but San Marcos
   B. Unlimited supply of natural gas for all towns
   C. Electric rate advantage of San Marcos and Coleman
   D. General adequacy of all for waste disposal
VI. Adequacy of existing transportation systems
   A. Surface transportation advantages of San Marcos and Ballinger
   B. General equality of airway connections
VII. A final weighting of the factors
   A. Selection of San Marcos as first choice
   B. Recommendation of Ballinger as second choice
   C. Lack of advantages in Big Spring, Coleman, and Littlefield

The report outline below is made up of topic captions:

I.   Introduction
    A.   Authorization
    B.   Purpose
    C.   Sources
    D.   Preview
II.  Community attitudes
    A.   Plant location
    B.   Labor policy
III. Factors of labor
    A.   Unskilled workers
    B.   Skilled workers
    C.   Wage rates
IV.  Raw wool supply
    A.   Adequate areas
    B.   Inadequate areas
V.   Utilities
    A.   Water
    B.   Natural gas
    C.   Electricity
    D.   Waste disposal
VI.  Transportation
    A.   Surface
    B.   Air
VII. Conclusions
    A.   First choice
    B.   Alternate choice
    C.   Other possibilities

*Parallelism of construction.*    Because of the many choices available, you are likely to construct an outline which has a mixture of grammatical forms. Some report writers believe that such a mixture of forms is acceptable and that each caption should be judged primarily by how well it describes the material it covers. The more precise and scholarly writers disagree, saying that mixing caption types is a violation of a fundamental concept of balance.

This concept of balance they express in a simple rule—the rule of parallel construction: All coordinate captions should be of the same grammatical construction. That is, if the caption for one of the major report parts (say part II) is a noun phrase, all equal-level captions (parts III, IV, V, etc.) would also have to be noun phrases. And if the first subdivision under a major section (say part A of II) is constructed as a sentence, the captions coordinate with it (B, C, D, etc.) would have to be sentences.

The following segment of an outline illustrates violations of the principle of parallel construction:

A. Machine output is lagging (sentence)
B. Increase in cost of operation (noun phrase)
C. Unable to deliver necessary steam (decapitated sentence)

You may achieve parallelism in any one of three ways—by making the captions all sentences, all noun phrases, or all decapitated sentences. If you desire all noun phrases, you could construct such captions as these:

A. Lag in machine output
B. Increase in cost of operations
C. Inability to deliver necessary steam

Or, as all sentences, you could make them like this:

A. Machine output is lagging
B. Cost of operations increases
C. Boiler cannot deliver necessary steam

*Variety in expression.* In the report outline, as in all forms of writing, you should use a variety of expressions. You should not overwork words and expressions, for too frequent repetition tends to be monotonous, and monotonous writing is not pleasing to the discriminating reader. The following outline excerpt illustrates this point well:

A. Chemical production in Texas
B. Chemical production in California
C. Chemical production in Louisiana

As a rule, if you make the captions talk well, there is little chance of such monotonous repetition occurring, for it is unlikely that your successive sections would be presenting similar or identical information. That is, captions which are really descriptive of the material they cover are not likely to use the same words. As an illustration of this point, the outline topics in the foregoing example can be improved simply through making the captions talk:

A. Texas leads in chemical production
B. California holds runner-up position
C. Rapidly gaining Louisiana ranks third

## QUESTIONS AND PROBLEMS

1. For each of the following problem situations, write a clear statement of the problem and list the factors involved. When necessary, you may use your imagination logically to supply any additional information needed.
   a. A manufacturer of breakfast cereals wants to determine the characteristics of its consumers.

    *b.*   The manufacturer of a toothpaste wants to learn what the buying public thinks of its product in relation to competing products.

    *c.*   Southwestern Oil Company wants to give its stockholders a summary of its operations for the past calendar year.

    *d.*   A building contractor engaged to build a new factory for Company X submits a monthly report summarizing its progress for the period.

    *e.*   The Able Wholesale Company must prepare a report on its credit relations with the Crystal City Hardware Company.

    *f.*   The supervisor of Department X must prepare a report evaluating the performance of his secretary.

    *g.*   Baker, Inc., wants a study made to determine why turnover of its employees is high.

    *h.*   An executive must rank three of his subordinates on the basis of their suitability for promotion to a particular job.

    *i.*   The supervisor of production must compare three competing machines for a particular production job.

    *j.*   An investment consultant must advise a client on whether to invest in the development of a lake resort.

    *k.*   A consultant seeks to learn how a restaurant can improve its profits.

2. Explain the concept of outlining as a division process.

3. Select a hypothetical problem with a time division possibility. What other division possibilities does it have? Compare the two possibilities as the main bases for organizing the report.

4. Assume that you are writing the results of a survey conducted to determine what styles of shoes are worn over the country for various occasions by women of all ages. What division possibilities are possible here? Which would you recommend?

5. For the problem described above, use your imagination to construct topic captions for the outline.

6. Select one of the divisions formed in Question 4 and construct the subcaptions. Use talking caption form.

7. Point out any violations of grammatical parallelism in these captions:
    *a.*   Region I sales lagging
    *b.*   Moderate increase seen for Region II
    *c.*   Region III sales remain strong

8. Point out any error in grammatical parallelism in these captions:
    *a.*   High cost of operation
    *b.*   Slight improvement in production efficiency
    *c.*   Maintenance cost is low

9. Which of the following captions is logically inconsistent with the others?
    *a.*   Agricultural production continues to increase.
    *b.*   Slight increase is made by manufacturing
    *c.*   Salaries remain high
    *d.*   Service industries show no change

10. Select an editorial, feature article, book chapter, or the like that has no captions. Write talking captions for it.

# 13

# Reports: Determination of makeup

**A**FTER YOUR OUTLINE is in finished form, you next turn to the task of planning the makeup of your report. This task is complicated by the fact that reports are far from standardized in regard to their physical arrangement. The variations existing among reports are countless. In fact, report types in use are so numerous as to almost defy meaningful classification. Even so, if you are to determine the makeup of a specific report, you must know the possibilities of choice available. Thus, you should be acquainted with some workable approach to a summary of all reports.

## OVERALL VIEW OF CONTENT

Such an approach is presented in the following paragraphs. It should be pointed out, though, that the concept of this approach is quite general. It does not account for all possible reports nor the countless variations in the report makeup. But it does serve to help you grasp the relationship of all reports.

To understand this relationship, you might view the whole of reports as resembling a stairway, as illustrated in Figure 13–1. At the top of this stairway is the formal, full-dress report. This is the form used when the problem is long and the problem situation is formal. In addition to the report text (usually introduction through conclusion), this formal report has these prefatory parts: title fly, title page, letters of transmittal and authorization, table of contents, and synopsis.

As the need for formality decreases and the problem becomes smaller, the makeup of the report also changes. Although these changes are far

302

from standardized, they follow a general order. First, the somewhat use-less title fly drops out. This page contains nothing other than the title, and the title information appears on the next page. Obviously, the title fly is used strictly for reasons of formality. Next in the progression, the synopsis (summary) and the transmittal letters are combined. When this stage is reached, the report problem usually is short enough to permit its summary in a relatively short space. A third step down, the table of contents drops out. The table of contents is a guide to the report text, and such a guide serves little value in a short report. Certainly, a guide to a 100-page report is necessary, but a guide to a one-page report is illogical. Somewhere between these extremes a dividing point exists. You should follow the general guide of including a table of contents whenever it appears to be of some value to the reader.

Another step down, as formality and length requirements continue to decrease, the combined letter of transmittal and synopsis drops out. Thus, the report now has only a title page and report text. The title page remains to the last because it serves as a very useful cover page. In

**FIGURE 13–1**

Progression of change in report makeup as formality requirements and length of the problem decrease

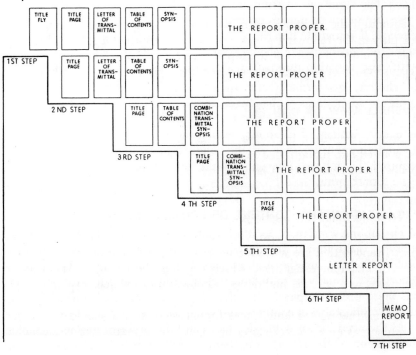

addition, it contains the most important of the identifying information. Below this short-report form is a report which reinstates the letter of transmittal and summary and presents the entire report in the form of a letter—thus, the letter report. And finally, for short problems of even more informality, the memorandum (informal letter) form may be used. Two of these steps, the first and fifth, are illustrated at the chapter end. The seventh is illustrated in Appendix A.

As previously mentioned, at best this analysis of report change is general, and perhaps it oversimplifies changes in report structure. Few of the reports actually written coincide exactly with its steps. Most of them, however, fit generally within the framework of the diagram. Knowledge of this relationship of length and formality should be helpful to you as you begin planning the report for your problem.

## GREATER IMPORTANCE OF THE SHORT TYPES

Of all the reports described in the foregoing review, by far the most important are those at the bottom of the stairway (see Figure 13–1). Specifically, these are the short, letter, and memorandum reports. These are the reports organizations use most of all to communicate the internal operational information they need in order to function. And in all likelihood, they are the type of reports you will write most often in the years ahead.

Although the shorter reports are the most numerous and important, our plan in the following pages is to first review the long, formal report. This is the one depicted at the top of the stairway. We take this approach because much of the subject matter of this review applies equally well to the shorter, less formal plans. In a sense, the shorter, informal report forms are adaptations of the longer, formal forms. Much of what we must know about overall organization, introduction contents, concluding-summary sections, and about writing in general is most thoroughly covered through a review of the long, formal report. When you have acquired this information, you should be able to adapt it easily to the lesser report forms.

## ORGANIZATION AND CONTENT OF LONGER REPORTS

Although not so numerous as the shorter forms, the longer, more formal reports that are written tend to be highly important. Usually they concern major investigations, which explains their length. And usually they are written for high-level administration—which explains their formality.

In constructing the long, more formal reports, you should view your task much as an architect views his. You have a number of components with which to work. Your task is to select and arrange components to meet the requirements of the given situation.

The components in your case are the report's prefatory parts. As we noted in our review of the structure of reports (Figure 13–1), the longest, most formal report contains all of these parts. As length and formality requirements decrease, some of the parts drop out. Thus, it is your decision as the architect of the report to determine which of these parts are needed to meet the length and formality requirements of your situation.

In order to make this decision and in fact to carry it out, you need first to be acquainted with the parts. Thus, in the following paragraphs we shall review them. In addition, we shall review the remaining parts of the longest, most formal report. For convenience in discussion, the following review arranges the parts by groups. First are the prefatory parts—those which are most related to the formality and length of the report. Then comes the report proper, which, of course, is the meat of all reports. It is the report story. The parts before and after it are to some extent mainly trappings. The final group consists of appended parts. These contain supplementary materials. As a rule, these materials are not essential to the report presentation. They are included largely to serve any special interests the reader may have in the problem or to help the reader in his use of the report.

*Prefatory parts:*
    Title fly
    Title page
    Letter of authorization
    Letter of transmittal, preface, or foreword
    Table of contents and table of illustrations
    Synopsis
*The report proper:*
    Introduction
    The report findings (usually presented in two or more major divisions)
    Conclusions, recommendations, or summaries
*Appended parts:*
    Bibliography
    Appendix
    Index

## The prefatory parts

*Title fly.* First among the possible prefatory report pages is the title fly (see page 322). As a rule, it contains only the report title. The wording of the title should be so carefully selected that it tells at a glance what is covered in the report. That is, it should fit the report like a glove, covering all of the report information snugly—no more, no less.

For completeness of coverage, you may build your title around the five *W*'s of the journalist: *who, what, where, when, why.* Sometimes, *how* may be added to this list. In some problems, however, not all of the *W*'s are essential to complete identification; nevertheless, they serve as a good checklist for completeness. For example, a title of a report analyzing the Lane Company's 197*x* advertising campaigns might be constructed as follows:

| | |
|---|---|
| *Who:* | Lane Company |
| *What:* | Analysis of advertising campaigns |
| *Where:* | Not essential |
| *When:* | 197*x* |
| *Why:* | Implied |

Thus the title emerges: "Analysis of the Lane Company's 197*x* Advertising Campaigns."

Obviously, you cannot write a completely descriptive title in a few words—certainly not in a word or two. Extremely short titles are as a rule vague. They cover everything; they touch nothing. Yet it is your objective to achieve conciseness in addition to completeness; so you must also seek the most economical word pattern consistent with completeness. Occasionally, in the attempt to achieve conciseness and completeness at once, it is advisable to use subtitles.

*Title page.* Like the title fly, the title page presents the report title. But in addition, it displays other information essential to the identification of the report. In constructing your title page, you should include the complete identification of yourself and the authorizer or recipient of the report. You may include also the date of writing, particularly if the time identification is not made clear in the title. The page is mechanically constructed and is precisely illustrated in Appendix A and in the report illustration on page 323.

*Letter of authorization.* A report may be authorized orally or in writing. If yours is authorized in writing, you should insert a copy of this document (usually a letter or memorandum) after the title page. If your report is authorized orally, you may review the authorization information in the letter of transmittal and/or the introductory section of the report.

The primary objective of the letter of authorization is that of authorizing the investigator to begin the investigation. In addition, the letter contains a brief statement of the problem, with some indication of the limiting factors, together with the scope of the investigation and the limitations (if there are any). Perhaps the use of the report might also be mentioned, as well as when the report is needed and how much the cost of preparation is to be. The letter may follow any of a number of acceptable organization patterns. The outline below describes one acceptable arrangement and content:

1. Direct, clear authorization of the investigation.
2. Explanation of the objective in clear, unmistakable words.
3. Description of areas of the problem requiring investigation. This description may be an explanation of the subdivisions of the problem.
4. Limitations (such as time and cost) and special instructions.

*Letter of transmittal, foreword, preface.* Most formal reports contain some form of personal communication from writer to reader (see page 324). In most business cases the letter of transmittal makes this contact. In some formal cases, particularly where the report is written for a group of readers, a foreword or preface performs this function.

The letter of transmittal, as its name implies, is a letter which transmits the report to the intended reader. Since this major message is essentially positive, you should write the letter in direct style. That is, in the beginning you should transmit the report directly, without explanation or other delaying information. Thus, your opening words should say, in effect, "Here is the report." Tied to or following this statement of transmittal usually comes a brief identification of the subject matter of the study and possibly an incidental summary reference to the authorization information (who assigned the report, when, etc.).

If you choose to combine the letter with the synopsis, as may be done in some forms of reports, the opening transmittal and identification may be followed by a quick review of the report highlights, much in the manner described in the following discussion of the synopsis. But whether the letter of transmittal does or does not contain a synopsis of the report text, you should generally use the letter to make helpful and informative comments about the report. You may, for example, make suggestions about how the report information may be used. You may suggest follow-up studies, point out special limitations, or mention side issues of the problem. In fact, you may include anything which helps your reader to understand or appreciate the report.

Except in very formal instances, the letter allows you to more or less chat with your reader. Such letters may well reflect the warmth and vigor of your personality. Generally, you should make good use of personal pronouns (*you, I, we,* etc.). A warm note of appreciation for the assignment or a willingness and desire to further pursue the project may mark your close.

Minor distinctions sometimes are drawn between forewords and prefaces, but for all practical purposes they are the same. Both are preliminary messages from writer to reader. Although usually they do not formally transmit the report, forewords and prefaces do many of the other things done by letters of transmittal. Like the letters of transmittal, they seek to help the reader appreciate and understand the report. They may, for example, include helpful comments about the report—its use,

interpretation, follow-up, and the like. In addition, prefaces and forewords frequently contain expressions of indebtedness to those helpful in
the research. Like the letters of transmittal, they usually are written in the
first person, but seldom are they as informal as some letters. Arrangement
of the contents of prefaces and forewords follows no established pattern.

*Table of contents and list of illustrations.*    If your report is long
enough for a guide to its contents to be helpful, you should give it a table
of contents. This table is the report outline in its finished form with page
numbers. If the report has a number of tables, charts, illustrations, and
the like, a separate table of contents may be set up for them. The
mechanics of construction of both of these contents units are fully described in Appendix A.

*Synopsis.*    The synopsis (also called the epitome and précis) is the
report in miniature. It concisely summarizes all the essential ingredients
of the report. It includes all of the major facts as well as major analyses
and conclusions derived from these facts. Primarily, it is designed for the
busy executive who may not have time to read the whole report, but it
may also serve as a preview or review for those who very carefully read
the report text.

In constructing the synopsis, you simply reduce the parts of the report
in order and in proportion. As your objective is to cut the report to a
fraction of its length (usually less than one eighth), much of your success
will be determined by your skill in directness and word economy. With
space at a premium, loose writing is obviously costly. But in your efforts
to achieve conciseness, you are likely to find your writing style dull. Thus,
you must work hard to give this concise bit of writing a touch of color
and style interest to reflect the tone of the main report.

Although most synopses simply present the report in normal order
(normally from introduction to conclusion), there is some usage nowadays of a more direct opening (see Figure 13–2). Such a plan shifts the
major findings, conclusions, or recommendations (as the case may be) to
the major problem of emphasis at the beginning. From this direct beginning the summary moves to the introductory parts and thence through
the report in normal order.

## The report proper

Your presentation of the report contents may follow any of a number
of general arrangements. Most companies prefer the more conventional
arrangements (direct, logical, chronological) discussed earlier. Some
companies prefer to prescribe a definite arrangement for all reports, particularly for the technical ones. Description of two such reports, the technical research paper and the staff study, appears at the chapter end
(pages 319–20). Most of the variations, however, are only rearrange-

**FIGURE 13–2**

Diagram of the synopsis in normal order and in direct order

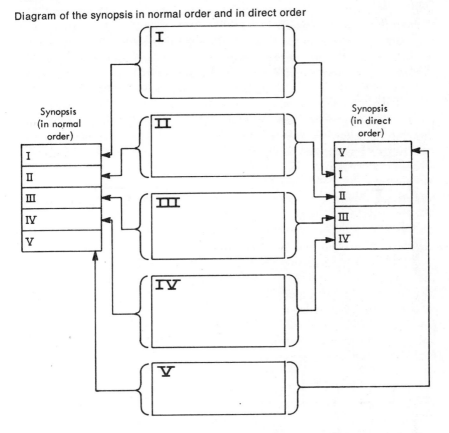

ments of the same general information. Thus, you should be able to adapt to other arrangements the following review of the makeup of the body of a conventional logical-order report.

*Introduction.* The purpose of the introduction of the report is to orient the reader to the problem at hand. In this undertaking you may include scores of possible topics, for you may include anything which will help your reader to understand and appreciate the problem. Although the possible contents are varied, there are certain general topics of coverage you should consider.

1. *Origin of the report.* The first part of your introduction might well include a review of the facts of authorization. Some writers, however, leave this part out entirely. If you decide to use this section, you will present facts such as when, how, and by whom the report was authorized, who wrote the report, and when the report was submitted.

This section is particularly useful in reports which have no letter of transmittal.

2. *Purpose.* A vital part of almost every report you will write is a description of the purpose of your investigation. Called by other names (objective, problem, object, aim, goal, mission, assignment, proposal, project, etc.), the purpose of the report is the value to be attained by the solving of the problem. It may be a long- or short-term value, or a combination of both.

You may state the purpose of your report in an infinitive phrase (". . . to propose standards of corporate annual reports"), or in the form of a well-phrased question ("What retail advertising practices do Centerville consumers disapprove of?"). Usually, you will need no more than a single sentence for this major purpose.

You will also need to state collateral, or secondary, purposes in this section. If a major problem is solved, collateral values are achieved. By stating these values, you help to convince the reader of the worthwhileness of your report. In other words, you should use a positive approach by telling what the solved problem can do for your reader.

3. *Scope.* If the scope of the problem is not clearly covered in any of the other introductory sections, you may need to include it in a separate section. By "scope," we mean the boundaries of the problem. In this section, in good, clear language you should describe the exact coverage of the problem. Thus, you tell your reader exactly what is and what is not a part of the problem.

4. *Limitations.* With some problems, you will find limitations which are of sufficient importance to warrant presenting them as a separate section of the introduction. By limitations, we mean anything which in some way has worked to impede the investigation or in some way has a deterring effect on the report. The illustrative list of limitations to a report investigation problem might include an inadequate supply of money for conducting the investigation, insufficient time for doing the work, unavoidable conditions which hampered objective investigation, or limitations existing within the problem under investigation.

5. *Historical background.* Sometimes a knowledge of the history of the problem is essential to a thorough understanding of the report. Thus, you may need to include in your introduction a section on the history of the problem. Your general aim in this part should be to acquaint your reader with some of the issues involved, some of the principles raised, and some of the values which might be received if more research were done. Also, in this section you may orient the readers and help to give them a better understanding of the report situation. This better understanding will theoretically help the readers and you, the writer, to solve some of the problems which may arise in the future.

6. *Sources and methods of collecting data.* It is usually advisable to tell the readers how you have collected the report information, whether through bibliographical research, through interviewing, and the like. If bibliographical research has been used, for example, you may give the library sources consulted and the major publications. If this latter list is long, you would be wise to append to the report a bibliography. Or, as another example, if your report has used interviewing, your description would cover such areas of the survey as sample determination, construction of the questionnaire, procedures followed in interviewing, facilities for checking returns, etc. Whatever the technique used, you should describe it in sufficient detail to allow the reader to evaluate the quality of the work done.

7. *Definitions.* If your report is to make use of words likely to be unfamiliar to the reader, you should define these words somewhere in the report. One practice is to define each such word at the time of its first use in the report text. A more common practice, however, is to set aside a special section in the introduction for definitions.

8. *Report preview.* In long reports you should use a final section of the introduction to preview the report layout. In this section you should tell the reader how the report will be presented—what topics will be taken up first, second, third, etc. And of even greater importance, you should give the reasons why you follow this plan. Thus, you give your reader a clear picture of the road ahead, so that he may logically relate the topics of the report as he comes to them.

As previously noted, the sections discussed are listed only for the purpose of suggesting possible introduction content. In few reports will you need all of the topics mentioned. And in some instances you will be able to combine some of the topics; in other instances you may further split them into additional sections. In summary, you should tailor your introduction to fit the one report.

***The report body.*** That part of the report which presents the information collected and relates it to the problem is the report body. Normally, it comprises the bulk of the content of a report. In fact, in a sense this part is the report. With the exception of the conclusion or recommendation section which follows, the other parts of the report are merely trappings. It is the report body to which most of our comments in this chapter and the following ones pertain.

***The ending of the report.*** You may end your report in any of a number of ways: with a summary, a conclusion, a recommendation, or a combination of the three.

1. *Summary.* For some reports, particularly those which do little more than present fact, the end may consist of a summary of the major findings. Frequently, these reports follow the practice of having minor

summaries at the end of each major division of the report. When you follow this practice, your final summary should simply recap these summaries. This form of summary, however, should not be confused with the synopsis. Like the summary, the synopsis presents a review of major findings; but unlike the summary, it contains the gist of the major supporting facts.

2. *Conclusions.* You draw your conclusions by inference (induction or deduction) from the facts and discussion in the body. Conclusions follow facts, even though in some reports they are placed at the beginning (the psychological arrangement).

Your conclusion should flow logically from the facts; but since this is a human process of interpretation, faulty conclusions may result. Consequently, conclusions are subject to opinions, be it rightly so or not.

For easy reference, you may tabulate your conclusions. But the arrangement of them is open to question. Sometimes you will feel that the most important ones should be placed first; sometimes you will want to list them according to the arrangements discussed in the findings. Also, you may combine them with recommendations. In some cases, where the conclusion is obvious, you may omit it and present only a recommendation.

3. *Recommendations.* The recommendations are the writer's section. Here you state your opinion based on the conclusions. Of course, you may not state your recommendations if you are not asked to; but if you are asked, you state them completely, including who should do what, when, where, why, and sometimes how.

You may include alternative courses of action. But you should state your preferences. Since you are familiar with the findings, you should not leave your reader on the horns of a dilemma. You should state his desired action and then leave him to choose his own course. Since you are likely to be in a staff position, you should give your advice for a line person to accept.

**Appended parts.** Sometimes it is desirable that you append special sections to the report. The presence of these parts is normally determined by the specific needs of the problem concerned.

1. *Appendix.* The appendix, as its name implies, is a section tacked on. You use it for supplementary information which supports the body of the report but which has no logical place within the body of the report. Possible contents might include questionnaires, working papers, summary tables, additional references, other reports, etc.

As a rule, you should not include in the appendix the charts, graphs, sketches, and tables which directly support the report. Instead, you should place them in the body of the report where they support the findings. Reports are best designed for the convenience of the reader.

Obviously, it is not convenient for the reader to thumb through many pages in order to find an appendix illustration to the facts he reads in the report body.

2. *Bibliography.* When your investigation makes heavy use of bibliographical research, you should normally include a bibliography (an identifying list of the publications consulted). The construction of this formal list is described in the appendix of this book.

3. *Index.* An index is an alphabetical guide to the subject matter of a piece of writing. It is used primarily with long manuscripts in which it would be difficult to find a specific topic were a subject guide not available. But few of the reports you will write will be of a length sufficient to justify the use of an index.

## MAJOR DIFFERENCES IN SHORT AND LONG REPORTS

The foregoing discussion of report parts obviously concerns the longer and more formal types. Certainly these types are significant in business, and we cannot know report writing without knowing how to construct them. Even so, we should keep in mind that most reports written in industry are shorter and more informal. As you can see by inspecting the examples at the chapter end, these shorter forms of reports appear to be quite different.

Even though much of what we learned concerning the long, formal report applies equally well to the other forms, certain differences exist. By concentrating on these differences, we can adapt quickly our knowledge of report writing to the wide variety of short, informal reports. Four areas of such differences stand out as most significant: (1) less need for introductory material, (2) predominance of direct (psychological) order, (3) more personal writing style, and (4) less need for a coherence plan.

### Less need for introductory material

One major content difference in the shorter report forms is their minor need for introductory material. Most reports at this level concern day-to-day problems. Thus, these reports have a short life. They are not likely to be kept on file for posterity to read. They are intended for only a few readers, and these few know the problem and its background. The reader's interests are in the findings of the report and any action they will lead to.

This is not to say that all shorter forms have no need for introductory material. In fact, some have very specific needs. In general, however, the introductory need in the shorter and more informal reports is less than that for the more formal and longer types. But no rule can be applied across the board. Each case should be analyzed individually. In each case, you must cover whatever introductory material is needed to prepare your reader to receive the report. In some shorter reports, an incidental reference to the problem, authorization of the investigation, or such will do the job. In some extreme cases, you may need a detailed introduction comparable to that of the more formal report. There are reports, also, that need no introduction whatever. In such cases, the nature of the report serves as sufficient introductory information. A personnel action, for example, by its very nature explains its purpose. So do weekly sales reports, inventory reports, and some progress reports.

## Predominance of direct order

Because usually they are more goal-oriented, the shorter more informal reports are likely to use the direct order of presentation. That is, typically such reports are written to handle a problem—to make a specific conclusion or recommendation of action. This conclusion or recommendation is of such relative significance that it by far overshadows the analysis and information that support it. Thus, it deserves a lead-off position.

As noted earlier, the longer forms of reports may also use a direct order. In fact, many of them do. The point is, however, that most do not. Most follow the traditional logical (introduction, body, conclusion) order. As one moves down the structural ladder toward the more informal and shorter reports, however, the need for direct order increases. At the bottom of the ladder, direct order is more the rule than the exception.

Your decision of whether or not to use the direct order is best based on a consideration of your readers' likely use of the report. If the readers need the report conclusion or recommendation as a basis for an action they must take, directness will speed their effort. A direct presentation will permit them to quickly receive the most important information. If they have confidence in your work, they may not choose to read beyond this point, and they can quickly take the action the report supports. Should they desire to question any part of the report, however, it is there for their inspection. The obvious result would be to save the valuable time of busy executives.

On the other hand, if there is reason to believe that your readers will want to arrive at the conclusion or recommendation only after a logical review of the analysis, you should organize your report in the indirect (logical) order. Especially would this arrangement be preferred when your readers do not have reason to place their full confidence in your work. If you are a novice working in a new assignment, for example, you would be wise to lead your readers to your recommendations or conclusion by using the logical order.

## More personal writing style

Although the writing that goes into all reports has much in common, that in the shorter reports tends to be more personal. That is, the shorter reports are likely to use the personal pronouns *I, we, you,* and such rather than a strict third-person approach.

The explanation of this tendency toward personal writing in short reports should be obvious. In the first place, the situation that gives rise to a short report usually involves more personal relationships. Such reports tend to be from and to people who know each other—people who normally address each other informally when they meet and talk. In addition, the shorter reports by their nature are apt to involve a personal investigation. The finished work represents the personal observations, evaluations, and analyses of their writers. They are expected to report them as their own. A third explanation is that the shorter problems tend to be the day-to-day routine ones. They are by their very nature informal. It is logical to report them informally, and personal writing tends to produce this informal effect.

As is explained in Chapter 14, your decision on whether to write a report in personal or impersonal style should be based on the circumstances of the situation. You should consider the expectations of those who will receive the report. If they expect formality, you should write impersonally. If they expect informality, you should write personally. Second, if you do not know the readers' preferences, you should consider the formality of the situation. Convention favors impersonal writing for the most formal situation.

From this analysis, it should be apparent that either style can be appropriate for reports ranging from the shortest to the longest type. The point is, however, that short-report situations are most likely to justify personal writing.

## Less need for coherence plan

As is pointed out in Chapter 14, the longer forms of report need some form of coherence plan to make the parts stick together. That is, because of the complexities brought about by length, the writer must make an effort to relate the parts. Otherwise, the paper would read like a series of disjointed minor reports. What the writer does is to use summaries and introductory forward-looking sentences and paragraphs at key places. Thus, the reader is able to see how each part of the report fits into the whole scheme of things.

The shorter the report becomes, the less is its need for such a coherence plan. In fact, in the extremely short forms (such as memorandum and letter reports), little in the way of wording is needed to relate the parts. In such cases, the information is so brief and simple that a logical and orderly presentation clearly shows the plan of presentation.

Although coherence plans are less frequently used in the short forms of reports, the question of whether to include them should not be arbitrarily determined by length alone. Instead, the matter of need should guide you in your choice. Whenever your presentation contains organization complexities that can be made clear by summaries, introductions, and relating parts, these coherence elements should be included. Thus, need rather than length is the major determinant. But it is clearly evident that need for coherence decreases as the report length decreases.

## SHORT FORMS OF REPORTS

As was noted earlier, the short forms of reports are by far the most numerous and important in business. In fact, the three types represented by the bottom three steps of the stairway (Figure 13–1) make up the bulk of the reports written in business. Thus, a review of each of these types is necessary for a coverage of the subject.

### The short report

One of the more popular of the less imposing reports is the conventional short report. Representing the fourth step in the diagram of report progression, this report consists of only a title page and the report text. Its popularity may be explained by the middle-ground impression of formality it gives. Inclusion of the one most essential of the prefatory parts gives the report at least a minimum appearance of formality. And it does this without the tedious work of preparing the other prefatory pages. It is ideally suited for the short but somewhat formal problem.

Like most of the less imposing forms of reports, the short report may be organized in either the direct or indirect order, although direct order is by far the most common plan. As illustrated by the report at the chapter end, this most common plan begins with a quick summary of the report, including and emphasizing conclusions and recommendations. Such a beginning serves much the same function as the synopsis of a long, formal report.

Following the summary are whatever introductory remarks are needed. As noted previously, sometimes this part is not needed at all. Usually, however, there follows a single paragraph covering the facts of authorization and a brief statement of the problem and its scope. After the introductory words come the findings of the investigation. Just as in the longer report forms, the findings are presented, analyzed, and applied to the problem. From all this comes a final conclusion and, if needed, a recommendation. These last two elements—conclusions and recommendations—may come at the end, even though they also may appear in the beginning summary. Sometimes, not to include a summary or a conclusion would end the report abruptly. It would stop the flow of reasoning before reaching its logical goal.

The mechanics of constructing the short report are much the same as those for the more formal, longer types. As illustrated at the chapter end, this report uses the same form of title page and the same layout requirement. Like the longer reports, it uses captions. But because of the report's brevity, the captions rarely go beyond the two-division level. In fact, one level of division is most common. Like any other report, its use of graphic aids, appendix, and bibliography is dependent on its need for them.

## Letter reports

As the wording implies, a letter report is a report written in letter form. Primarily, it is used to present information to someone outside the company, especially when the report information is to be sent by mail. For example, a company's written evaluation of one of its credit customers may well be presented in letter form and mailed to the one who requests it. An outside consultant may write a report of analyses and recommendations in letter form. Or an organization officer may elect to report certain information to the membership in letter form.

Normally, letter reports present the shorter problems—typically, those that can be presented in three or four pages or less. But no hard and fast rule exists on this point. Long letter reports (10 pages and more) have been used successfully many times.

As a general rule, letter reports are written personally (using *I, you, we* references). Exceptions exist, of course, as when one is preparing such a report for an august group, such as a committee of the United States Senate or a company's board of directors. Other than this point, the writing style recommended for letter reports is much the same as that for any other report. Certainly, clear and meaningful expression is a requirement for all reports (see page 347).

Letter reports may be arranged either in the direct or indirect order. If the report is to be mailed, there is some justification for using an indirect approach. As such reports arrive unannounced, an initial reminder of what they are, how they originated, and such is in order. A letter report written to the membership of an organization, for example, may appropriately begin with these words.

As authorized by your board of directors last January 6th, the following review of member company expenditures for direct-mail selling is presented.

If one elects to begin a letter report in the direct order, he would be wise to use a subject line. The subject line consists of some identifying words, which appear at the top of the letter, usually immediately after or before the salutation. Although they are formed in many ways, one acceptable version begins with the word "Subject" and follows it with descriptive words that identify the problem. As the following example illustrates, this identifying device helps to overcome any effect of confusion or bewilderment the direct beginning may otherwise have on the reader.

Subject:   Report on direct-mail expenditures of
           association members, authorized by board of
           directors, January, 1976.

Association members are spending 8 percent more on direct-mail advertising this year than they did the year before. Current plans call for a 10-percent increase for next year.

Regardless of which beginning is used, the organization plan for letter reports corresponds to those of the longer, more formal types. Thus, the indirect order letter report follows its introductory buildup with a logical presentation and analysis of the information gathered. From this presentation, it works logically to a conclusion and/or recommendation in the end. The direct order letter report follows the initial summary-conclusion-recommendation section with whatever introductory words are appropriate. For example, the direct beginning illustrated above could be followed with these introductory words.

These are the primary findings of a study authorized by your board of directors last January. As they concern information vital to all of us in the association, they are presented here for your confidential use.

Following such an introductory comment, the report would present the supporting facts and their analyses. The writer would systematically build up the case that supported the opening comment. With either order, when the report is sent as a letter it may close with whatever friendly goodwill comment is appropriate for the one occasion.

## Memorandum reports

Memorandum reports are merely informal letter reports. They are used primarily for routine reporting within an organization, although some organizations use them for external communicating. Because they are internal communications, often they are informally written. In fact, they frequently are hurried, handwritten messages from one department or worker to another department or worker. The more formal memo-

randum reports, however, are well-written and carefully typed composi-
tions (see page 345) that rival some more imposing types in appearance.

As far as the writing of the memorandum is concerned, all the instructions for writing letter reports apply. But memorandum reports tend to
be more informal. And because they usually concern day-to-day problems, they have very little need for introductory information. In fact, they
frequently may begin reporting without any introductory comment.

The memorandum report is presented on somewhat standardized
interoffice memorandum stationery. The words *To, From,* and *Subject*
appear at the page top (see page 349), usually following the company
identification. Sometimes, the word *Date* also is included as a part of the
heading. Like letters, the memorandum may carry a signature. In many
offices, however, no typed signature is included, and the writer merely
initials after the typed name in the heading.

## SPECIAL REPORT FORMS

As noted previously, this review describes only generally the forms of
the reports used in business. Countless variations exist. Of these variations, a few deserve special emphasis.

### The staff report

One of the most widely used reports in business is the staff report.
Patterned after a form traditional to the technical fields, the staff report is
well adapted to business problem solving. Its arrangement follows the
logical thought processes used in solving the conventional business problems. Although the makeup of this report varies by company, the following arrangement recommended by a major metals manufacturer is
typical:

> *Identifying information:* As the company's staff reports are written
> on intercompany communication stationery, the conventional identifica-
> tion information (*To, From, Subject, Date*) appears at the beginning.
> *Summary:* For the busy executive who wants his facts fast, a sum-
> mary begins the report. Some executives will read no further. Others
> will want to trace the report content in detail.
> *The problem (or objective):* As in all good problem-solving proce-
> dures, the report text logically begins with a clear description of the prob-
> lem—what it is, what it is not, what its limitations are, and the like.
> *Facts:* Next comes the information gathered in the attempt to solve
> the problem:
> *Discussion:* Analyses of the facts and applications of the facts and
> analyses to the problem follow. (Frequently, the statement of facts and
> the discussion of them can be combined.)

*Conclusions:*   From the preceding discussion of facts come the final meanings as they apply to the problem.

*Recommendation:*   If the problem's objective allows for it, a course of action may be recommended on the basis of the conclusions.

## The audit report

The short-form and long-form audit reports are well known to accountants. The short-form report is perhaps the most standardized of all reports—if, indeed, it can be classified as a report. Actually, it is a stereotyped statement verifying an accountant's inspection of a firm's financial records. Its wording seldom varies. Illustrations of this standard form can be found in almost any corporate annual report.

Composition of the long-form audit report is as varied as the short form is rigid. In fact, a national accounting association, which made an exhaustive study on the subject, found practices to be so varied that it concluded that no typical form exists. Although the audit report illustrated at the chapter end (page 349) covers a somewhat simple and limited audit, it shows one acceptable form.

## The technical report

Although it generally follows the plan of the conventional formal report, the technical research report has some identifying characteristics. Exact makeup of the research report differs from company to company, but the following description is typical of this form.

The beginning pages of the research report are much like those of the traditional formal report. First come the title pages, although frequently a routing or distribution form for intercompany use may be worked into them, or perhaps added to them. A letter of transmittal is likely to come next, followed by a table of contents and illustrations. From this point on, however, the technical report is likely to differ from the traditional one. These differences are mainly in the treatment of the information usually presented in the synopsis and the introduction of the conventional formal report.

Instead of the conventional synopsis, the technical report may present the summary information in various parts, such as "findings," "conclusions," and "recommendations." Parts of the conventional introductory material also may be presented in prefatory sections. The "objective" is the most likely part in this area, although "method" is also a widely used section.

The text of the technical report usually begins with introductory information. The remaining information may be organized much like any conventional report, or it may follow a predetermined and somewhat mechanical arrangement. One such arrangement is "facts," "discussion," "conclusions," and "recommendations."

## QUESTIONS AND PROBLEMS

1. Discuss the effects of formality and problem length on the model of report makeup described in the chapter (Figure 13–1).

2. A good report title should be complete and concise. Are not these requirements contradictory? Explain.

3. Discuss the relative importance of the title fly and the title page in a report.

4. Distinguish among letter of transmittal, foreword, and preface.

5. Describe the role and content of a letter of transmittal.

6. Why is personal style typically used in the letter of transmittal?

7. What is the basis for determining whether a report should have a table of contents?

8. Discuss the construction of the synopsis.

9. Why do you think the synopsis includes the facts and figures in addition to the analyses and conclusions drawn from them?

10. Some reports need little or no introduction; others need very long ones. Why is this so?

11. Give examples of report problems that would require introductory coverage of methods of collecting data, historical background, and limitations.

12. Give examples of report problems that require an ending summary. An ending conclusion. An ending recommendation.

13. Why is direct order usually used in the shorter types of reports? When is indirect order desirable for such reports?

14. Give examples of short forms of reports that are appropriately written in personal style. Do the same for impersonal style.

15. Is it correct to say that the shorter forms of reports have little need for coherence? Discuss.

16. What determines the need for coherence aids in the short forms of reports?

17. Describe the organization of the conventional short report.

18. What types of problems are written up as letter reports? As memorandum reports? Explain the differences.

19. What is meant by saying that the order of the staff study report is a problem-solving order?

20. Discuss the differences between the technical reports and the other business reports.

**FIGURE 13–3**

Illustration of a long, formal report

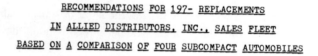

RECOMMENDATIONS FOR 197- REPLACEMENTS

IN ALLIED DISTRIBUTORS, INC., SALES FLEET

BASED ON A COMPARISON OF FOUR SUBCOMPACT AUTOMOBILES

The illustration which appears in the following pages typifies the long, formal report. Although this report is competently constructed and well illustrates this traditional form, it is not submitted as a model in all respects. Because of the need to disguise the names of the branded products involved, perhaps the report has lost some of its realism. Nevertheless, it represents an orderly, thorough, and objective solution to a somewhat complex problem.

**FIGURE 13–3**    *(continued)*

RECOMMENDATIONS FOR 197- REPLACEMENTS

IN ALLIED DISTRIBUTORS, INC., SALES FLEET

BASED ON A COMPARISON OF FOUR SUBCOMPACT AUTOMOBILES

Prepared for

Mr. Norman W. Bigbee, Vice-President
Allied Distributors, Inc.
3131 Speedall Street, Akron, Ohio 44302

Prepared by

George W. Franklin, Associate Director
Midwestern Research, Inc.
1732 Midday Avenue, Chicago, Illinois 60607

April 13, 197-

**FIGURE 13–3** *(continued)*

---

**MIDWESTERN RESEARCH, INC.**
1732 Midday Avenue
Chicago, Illinois
60607


April 13, 197-

Mr. Norman W. Bigbee
Vice-President in Charge of Sales
Allied Distributors, Inc.
3131 Speedall Street
Akron, Ohio 44302

Dear Mr. Bigbee:

In your hands is the report on the four makes of
subcompact automobiles you asked me to compare last
January 3.

To aid you in deciding which of the four makes you
should buy as replacements for your fleet, I gathered what I believe to be the most complete information available. Much of the operating information
comes from your own records. The remaining data are
the findings of both consumer research engineers and
professional automotive analysts. Only my analyses
of these data are subjective.

I sincerely hope, Mr. Bigbee, that my analyses will
aid you in making the correct decision. I truly
appreciate this assignment. And should you need any
assistance in interpreting my analyses, please call
on me.

Sincerely yours,

*George W. Franklin*

George W. Franklin
Associate Director

**FIGURE 13–3**   *(continued)*

**FIGURE 13–3**    *(continued)*

**FIGURE 13-3**    (*continued*)

Epitome

That SC-C is the best buy for Allied Distributors, Inc.,
in replacing its present sales fleet is the recommendation of this study. Authorized by Mr. Norman W. Bigbee,
Vice-President, on January 3, 197-, this recommendation
is submitted on April 13, 197-, to give the company an
insight into the problem of replacing the approximately
50 two-year-old subcompact cars in its present sales
fleet. The basis for this recommendation is an analysis
of cost, safety, and construction factors of four makes
of subcompact cars (SC-A, SC-B, SC-C, and SC-D).

The four cars do not show a great deal of difference in
ownership cost (initial cost less trade-in allowance after two years). On a per-car basis, SC-B costs $919 for
two years, which is $106 under SC-C, $168 under SC-A,
and $181 below SC-D. These differences become more mean-
ingful, however, when interpreted in terms of a 50-car
fleet purchase. A purchase of 50 SC-B's would save $5,300
over SC-C, $8,400 over SC-A, and $9,050 over SC-D. Operating costs, however, favor SC-C. Its cost-per-mile
estimate is $0.04001 as compared with $0.04158 for SC-A,
$0.04224 for SC-D, and $0.04338 for SC-B. A composite
of all costs for 50 cars over the two years the cars
would be used shows SC-C to be least costly at $110,027.
SC-A is second with a cost total of $114,345; SC-D is
third with $116,160; and SC-B is the most expensive with
a cost figure of $119,295.

On the qualities that pertain to driving safety, SC-C is
again superior to the other cars. It has the best brakes
of the group and is tied with SC-A for the best weight
distribution. It is second in acceleration and is again
tied with SC-A for the number of standard safety devices.
SC-A is second over-all in this category, having the second best brakes of the group. SC-B is last here because
of its poor acceleration and poor brakes.

Construction features and handling abilities place SC-C
all by itself. It scores higher than any of the other
cars in every category. SC-A and SC-D are tied for second place here, and again SC-B is last, having poor steering and handling qualities.

vi

**FIGURE 13–3**   *(continued)*

RECOMMENDATIONS FOR 197- REPLACEMENTS

IN ALLIED DISTRIBUTORS, INC., SALES FLEET

BASED ON A COMPARISON OF FOUR SUBCOMPACT AUTOMOBILES

I.   ORIENTATION TO THE PROBLEM

A.   The Authorization Facts

This comparison of the qualities cf four brands of subcompact automobiles is submitted April 13, 197-, to Mr.
Norman W. Bigbee, Vice-President, Allied Distributors,
Inc. Authorized by Mr. Bigbee at a meeting in his office
January 3, 197-, this investigation has been made under
the direction of George W. Franklin, Associate Director
of Midwestern Research, Inc.

B.   Problem of Selecting Fleet Replacements

The objective of this study is to determine which model
of subcompact automobile Allied Distributors, Inc.,
should select for replacements in its sales fleet.  The
Company's policy is to replace all two-year-old models
in its sales fleet annually, and approximately fifty automobiles will be replaced this year.

As the replacements involve a major capital outlay, and
as the sales fleet expenses constitute a major sales cost,
the proper selection of a new model presents an important problem. The model selection must be economical, dependable, and safe.  Allied is considering four subcompact automobiles as replacement possibilities.  As instructed by Mr. Bigbee, for reasons of information security, they are identified in this report only as SC-A
(Subcompact A), SC-B, SC-C, and SC-D.

1

**FIGURE 13–3**   *(continued)*

2

C.  Reports and Records as Sources of Data

The selection of the replacement brand is based on a
comparative analysis of the merits of the four makes.
Data for the comparisons were obtained from both company records and statistical reports.  Operating records
of ten representative cars of each make provide information on operating costs.  These reports are summaries
compiled by salesmen-drivers and represent actual performance of company cars under daily selling conditions.
Additional material enumerating safety features, overall driving quality, and dependability was acquired from
the reports of the Consumers Union of United States, Inc.,
Automotive Industries, and Bond Publishing Company's periodical, Road and Track.  Mr. Bigbee furnished the trade-
in allowances granted on the old models.  From this material extensive comparisons of the four makes are presented.

D.  A Preview to the Presentation

The findings of this report are presented in logical order.  Comparative analyses treat three major fields:
operating costs, safety features, and total performance.
Operating costs constitute the major consideration in
comparison and therefore command primary attention.
This category is broken down into single cost areas with
comparisons of the four makes in each area.  The most
efficient and economical make in each area is specified.

Safety features constitute the second field of comparison.  Again the field is subdivided into single areas,
and the outstanding automobile in each area is noted.
Finally, the total performance and durability of the four
makes is considered.  Throughout the report graphic displays emphasize particular comparisons and analyses.

In reaching a final recommendation, the outstanding qualities of each make are summarized, and the four makes are
objectively compared.  This comparison serves as the basis for the final conclusion and recommendation.

II.  THE MAJOR FACTOR OF COST

Conceivably, an adequate and logical breakdown of the
problem should be followed; and it is, therefore, natural
to begin with cost.  First interest is in original cost,

**FIGURE 13–3** (*continued*)

3

"What is the fleet discount price?" Of second interest in a natural thinking process are the cash differences after trade-in allowances for the old cars. These figures clearly indicate the cash outlay for the new fleet.

### A.  Initial Costs Favor SC-B

From Table I it is evident that SC-B has the lowest window sticker price before and after trade-in allowances. It has a $181 margin which must be considered in the light of what features are standard on SC-B in comparison with those standard on the other cars. That is, the SC-B may have fewer standard features included in its original cost and, therefore, not be worth as much as the SC-A, SC-C, or SC-D.

TABLE I
ORIGINAL COST OF FOUR BRANDS
OF SUBCOMPACT CARS IN 197-

| Make | Window sticker prices | Trade-in value for two-year-old makes* | Cash costs after trade-in allowance |
|------|------|------|------|
| SC-A | $2,091 | $1,004 | $1,087 |
| SC-B | 1,919 | 1,000 | 919 |
| SC-C | 2,040 | 1,015 | 1,025 |
| SC-D | 2,200 | 1,100 | 1,100 |

*Trade-in value for SC-A and SC-B are estimates
Sources:  Primary and Road and Track

It is clear that where features are listed as standard they do not add to original cost, but where listed as options they do. As will be shown in a later table, the SC-D has many more standard features than do the other makes. In addition to a study of standard features, a close look at trade-in values and operating costs will also be necessary to properly evaluate original cost.

**FIGURE 13–3**   *(continued)*

<br>

4

Further discussion of these facets will be postponed until they are fitted into our comprehensive study of safety
features and operation cost-per-mile estimate.

### B.   Trade-in Values Show Uniformity

As a logical follow-up of original cost, trade-in values
usually offer some conclusive data for consideration.
Trade-in values are the variable in determining original
cost when stripped prices are fairly uniform.  In this
study the trade-in values are fairly uniform, varying
only by $100 from highest of $1,100 for the SC-D to lowest of $1,000 for the SC-B (Table I).

Although fairly uniform, these figures appear to be more
significant when converted to total amounts involved in
the fleet purchases.  A fleet of 50 SC-B's would cost
$45,950.  The same fleet of SC-C's, SC-A's, and SC-D's
would cost $51,250, $54,350, and $55,000 respectively.
Thus, $5,300 could be saved by purchasing SC-B's over
SC-C's; $8,400 could be saved in relation to SC-A's; and
$9,050 could be saved when compared to SC-D's.

### C.   Operating Costs Are Lowest for SC-C

SC-C has the lowest maintenance cost of the four, .00563
cents per mile; but SC-D is close behind with .00590 cents.
Both of these are well below the SC-B and SC-A figures of
.00781 and .00789 respectively.  The components of these
values, as shown in Table II, are estimates of repairs and
resulting loss of working time, miscellaneous, and tire
replacements.

It should be stressed here how greatly repair expense
influences the estimates.  Actually, two expenses are involved, for to the cost of repairs must be added the expense of lost time by the salesmen.  Obviously, a salesman without a car is unproductive.  Each hour lost by car
repairs adds to the cost of the car's operation.

As shown in Table II, the hours lost per repair for each
make are the same (five hours).  Thus, the important consideration is the number of repairs and the costs of these
repairs.  On this basis, the SC-C has the lowest total
cost burden at $310.  SC-D ranks second with $325.  SC-B
is third with $430, and SC-A is last with $434.

**FIGURE 13–3**　(*continued*)

5

TABLE II
COMPARISON OF REPAIRS AND RELATED
LOST WORKING TIME FOR FOUR MAKES
OF CARS FOR TWO YEARS

| Make | Number of Repairs | Repair Expense | Working Hours Lost* | Total Burden |
|------|-------------------|----------------|---------------------|--------------|
| SC-A | 8 | $234 | 40 | $434 |
| SC-B | 8 | 230 | 40 | 430 |
| SC-C | 6 | 160 | 30 | 310 |
| SC-D | 6 | 175 | 30 | 325 |

*Based on hourly wage of $5
Source:  Allied Distributors, Inc., Operating Records

As shown in Table III, SC-A has the best record for oil
and gas economy with a per-mile cost of .01719 cents.
SC-C with a cost of .01901 cents, is second; SC-B is
third with .01964 cents; and SC-D is last with .02096
cents.  Computed on the basis of 55,000 miles (the two-
year mileage average for company cars), these costs mean
a $174.35 margin per car for SC-A over SC-D, or $8,717.50

TABLE III
COST-PER-MILE ESTIMATE OF OPERATION

| | SC-A | SC-B | SC-C | SC-D |
|---|------|------|------|------|
| Depreciation | $0.01590 | $0.01583 | $0.01527 | $0.01538 |
| Gas | 0.01657 | 0.01852 | 0.01657 | 0.01852 |
| Oil | 0.00122 | 0.00122 | 0.00244 | 0.00244 |
| Tires | 0.00129 | 0.00093 | 0.00048 | 0.00035 |
| Repairs | 0.00414 | 0.00413 | 0.00301 | 0.00365 |
| Miscellaneous | 0.00246 | 0.00275 | 0.00214 | 0.00190 |
| Total | $0.04158 | $0.04338 | $0.04001 | $0.04224 |

Source:  Allied Distributors, Inc., Operating Records

**FIGURE 13–3**   *(continued)*

6

for the fleet of 50 cars. Compared with SC-C, there is
a margin per car of $67.10, or a fleet total of $3,355.
SC-B comparisons show a per car margin of $101.75, or a
fleet total of $5,087.50.

### D.  Cost Composite Favors SC-C

Consolidation of all the cost figures (see Table III)
shows SC-C to be the most economical make. Total cost
per mile for SC-C is .04001 cents, as compared with .04158
cents for SC-A, .04224 for SC-D, and .04338 for SC-B.
These figures take on more meaningful form when converted
to total fleet costs over the two-year period the cars will
be owned. As shown in Chart 1, a fleet of 50 SC-C's would
cost Allied a total of $110,027, which is $4,317 under the

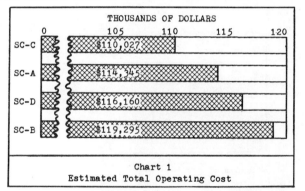

Chart 1
Estimated Total Operating Cost

$114,345 total cost of SC-A. SC-D, with a total cost of
$116,160, would cost $6,132 more than SC-C. SC-B, with
the highest total cost of $119,295, would cost $9,267
more than SC-C.

### III.  EVALUATION OF SAFETY FEATURES

Although costs receive major consideration in the selection of replacements, the safety features of each make
must also be analyzed. In fact, as salesmen spend a large

**FIGURE 13–3** *(continued)*

part of their time traveling and thus need maximum protection from hazards encountered in driving, the lowest
operating expense may be sacrificed in order to obtain
added safety features.

A.  <u>SC-D</u> <u>Is</u> <u>Best</u> <u>Equipped</u> <u>With</u> <u>Safety</u> <u>Devices</u>

Only SC-D has as standard equipment all five of the extra
safety devices considered desirable by The Consumers
Safety Council.  The SC-D is fully equipped with front
disc brakes, vacuum brake assist, adjustable seatbacks,
flow-through ventilation, and anti-glare mirror, as shown
in Table IV.  The SC-D's braking system differs from that

TABLE IV
LIST OF STANDARD
SAFETY FEATURES

| FEATURE | SC-A | SC-B | SC-C | SC-D |
|---------|------|------|------|------|
| Front Disc Brakes | Yes | No | Yes | Yes |
| Vacuum Brake Assist | No | No | No | Yes |
| Adjustable Seatback | No | No | No | Yes |
| Flow-through Ventilation | Yes | No | Yes | Yes |
| Anti-glare Mirror | No | No | No | Yes |

Source:  <u>Road</u> <u>and</u> <u>Track</u>

of the SC-A's and SC-C's in that it provides vacuum assistance.  The SC-B does not equip its cars with either
disc brakes or vacuum assistance.

SC-A and SC-C are tied in the field of safety features
with two out of the possible five shown in Table IV.  The
SC-B, although offering three of these features as options,
does not provide any of the possible five.

Now that the Federal Government has legislated the basic
safety requirements, such as, seat belts, padded dash-
boards, collapsible steering column, and shatter-proof
windshields, the extra safety features of the SC-D are
even more welcome.

**FIGURE 13–3**   *(continued)*

8

B.  <u>Acceleration</u> <u>Adds</u> <u>Extra</u> <u>Safety</u> <u>to</u> SC-D

A life-saving factor that differs greatly among the four
makes is acceleration.  It is important as a safety "on-
the-spot" need--something to have when in a pinch.  Especially is it important in low-powered subcompact automobiles.  When needed, acceleration should be available
in the safest car.  It should never be depended on by a
driver to the extent of his taking chances because he
knows that it is available, but it must be included in
any brand comparison.

While SC-C's acceleration time from 0 to 30 miles per
hour is the fastest in the group, the SC-D leads in both
0 to 60 mph times and in the ¼ mile acceleration runs.
As shown in Chart 2, SC-C reached 30 mph .3 seconds sooner

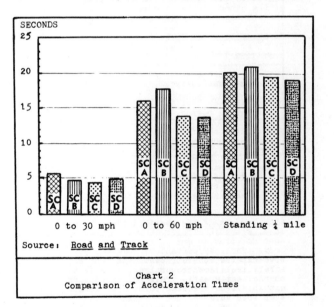

Source:  <u>Road</u> <u>and</u> <u>Track</u>

Chart 2
Comparison of Acceleration Times

**FIGURE 13–3**   *(continued)*

than SC-B, and .5 and 1.5 seconds sooner than SC-D and SC-A, respectively. SC-D reached 60 mph .4 seconds sooner than SC-C, which is not a very significant length of time. The SC-D, however, achieved this same speed a full 3 seconds faster than SC-A, and 4.5 seconds sooner than SC-B.

### C.  Weight Distribution Is Best in SC-A and SC-C

Weight distribution affects not only the acceleration of an automobile, but also the effectiveness of its brakes and its handling abilities. The correct proportion of weight on the rear wheels balances the car and in doing so controls body movements in cornering and braking. The problem is generally caused by the placement of the engine in the front of the automobile. The arrangement of the other essential heavy items at various spots on the chassis results in the best distribution.

As shown in Table V, SC-A and SC-C are tied in this cate-

TABLE V
COMPARATIVE WEIGHT DISTRIBUTIONS,
BRAKING DISTANCES, AND CORNERING ABILITIES

|  | SC-A | SC-B | SC-C | SC-D |
|---|---|---|---|---|
| Distribution, rear, % | 47 | 45 | 47 | 43 |
| Braking, 80-0 mph, ft. | 330 | 331 | 321 | 390 |
| Brake fade, % increase in pedal effort | 30 | 33 | 14 | 43 |
| Control, panic stop | good | fair | excel | fair |
| Lateral acceleration, in g units | 0.680 | 0.685 | 0.611 | 0.614 |
| speed achieved, mph | 32.0 | 32.1 | 30.2 | 30.3 |

Source:  Road and Track

gory. Their 47 percent is near the 50 percent automotive experts consider best. In contrast, SC-D carries a relatively low proportion (43 percent) of its weight on the rear wheels. This low proportion of weight is not good from the standpoint of traction on slippery roads that seem to be common throughout the Allied sales territory. The SC-B is between the two extremes with 45 percent of its weight on its rear wheels.

**FIGURE 13-3**   *(continued)*

10

### D.  SC-C Has Best Braking Quality

At speeds of 80 miles per hour, SC-C stops in the shortest distance (321 feet); but SC-A (330 feet) and SC-B
(331 feet) are not far behind.  SC-D is well back (390
feet).  In tests simulating panic-stop situations, SC-C's
brakes also prove superior to the others, rank "excellent" by test standards.  On the same test scale, SC-A's
brakes rank "good" and SC-B's and SC-D's brakes rank
"fair."  SC-C brakes also are more resistant to fade than
are the other three.  In stops from 80 miles per hour,
all makes exhibit good braking control except SC-B.  Its
stops are far less consistent than the others.

An over-all review of safety features shows SC-C to have
a very slight advantage over the other cars.  Its brakes,
weight distribution, and stopping distance lead to this
conclusion.  SC-A is second, scoring high in all categories except acceleration and standard safety features.
SC-D is third with the best acceleration but poor braking action.  SC-B is last, having only scored highly in
cornering ability.

### IV.   RIDING COMFORT AND OVER-ALL CONSTRUCTION

Few things affect the day's work of a traveling salesman
more than the ride he gets in his car.  Thus, the factors
of handling ease and general riding quality should be
considered in selecting his car.  Somewhat related to
these factors are the over-all qualities of construction
of the cars in question.

### A.  SC-C Ranks First in Handling

The SC-C, with near perfect steering, is over-all best
handling car of the group.  As shown in Table VI, SC-C
exceeds all of the other makes when values are assigned
to each category.  SC-A, which is second in this area,
is quick and predictable in handling.  During emergency
situation tests, however, it jarred and rocked severely
around bumpy corners.  SC-D, while exhibiting normal
handling characteristics during routine driving, performed miserably when subjected to emergency handling
tests.  SC-B suffered from being knocked off course by
almost any small bump.  When smoother roads were encountered, SC-B's handling was judged somewhat below average.

**FIGURE 13–3**   *(continued)*

11

```
                        TABLE VI
                COMPARATIVE COMFORT AND RIDE

            Front   Rear   Ride  Ride Handl- Steering
          seating seating light full   ing   effort
                          load load
```

| | Front seating | Rear seating | Ride light load | Ride full load | Handling | Steering effort |
|---|---|---|---|---|---|---|
| Excellent | | | | | | |
| Good | | | | | SC-C | |
| Fair-to-good | SC-C<br>SC-A<br>SC-D | SC-C | SC-A | | SC-D<br>SC-A | |
| Fair | SC-B | | SC-C | | SC-B | |
| Fair-to-poor | | SC-D | SC-D | SC-C<br>SC-D | | |
| Poor | | SC-A<br>SC-B | SC-B | SC-B<br>SC-A | | |
| Low | | | | | | |
| Low-to-moderate | | | | | | SC-B<br>SC-A<br>SC-C |
| Moderate | | | | | | SC-D |

Source:  Consumers Union of United States, Inc.

### B.   SC-C Gives Best Ride

While it is true that SC-A's ride has been judged superior to SC-C's when loaded lightly, SC-C comes out first
over-all because of the quickly deteriorating ride SC-A
exhibits when its load is increased.  SC-C's superior
ride and directional stability are the best in the group
primarily because of its fully independent suspension.
A rarity in any front engined car, much less a car in
this price field, SC-C's front bucket seats are judged
fair-to-good in comfort--relatively high rating in economy car circles.  As shown in Table VI SC-C's rear seat-
ing comfort is the best in the group.

### C.   SC-C Is Judged Most Durable

The SC-C is assembled with better-than-average care.
In fact, Consumer Research engineers have found only 16
minor defects in the car.  In addition, the SC-C has a
better-than-average record for frequency of repairs.

**FIGURE 13–3**   *(concluded)*

12

SC-D, second in this category, has only 20 problems.
Some of these problems are judged to be serious, however.
For instance, in the tests run the starter refused to
disengage after a few hundred miles had accumulated on
the car. The car's ignition timing, idle mixture, and
idle speed were incorrectly set. An optically distorted
windshield and inside mirror were discovered. In spite
of all these defects, the SC-D ranks above SC-A and SC-B
on durability.

Clearly, SC-C leads in all categories of riding comfort
and over-all construction. It handles best. It gives
the best ride. And it has some definite construction
advantages over the other three.

### V. RECOMMENDATION OF SC-C

Normally, this simulation cannot be merely a count of
rankings on the evaluations made, for the qualities carry
different weights. Cost, for example, is the major factor
in most such decisions. In this instance, however, weighting is not necessary for one automobile is the clear leader on all three of the bases used for evaluation. Thus,
it would lead in any arrangement of weights.

From the data presented, SC-C is the best buy when all
costs are considered. The total difference on a purchase
of 50 automobiles is a significant $5,300 over the second-
place brand. SC-C has a slight edge when safety features
are considered. And it is the superior car in handling
ease, ride quality, and construction. These facts point
clearly to the recommendation that Allied buy SC-C's this
year.

**FIGURE 13–4**

Illustration of a short report

RECOMMENDATIONS FOR DEPRECIATING DELIVERY TRUCKS

BASED ON AN ANALYSIS OF THREE PLANS

PROPOSED FOR THE BAGGET LAUNDRY COMPANY

Submitted to

Mr. Ralph P. Bagget, President
Bagget Laundry Company
312 Dauphine Street
New Orleans, Louisiana 70102

Prepared by

Charles W. Brewington, C.P.A.
Brewington and Karnes, Certified Public Accountants
743 Beaux Avenue, New Orleans, Louisiana 70118

April 16, 197X

In the following pages appears a short report written in the direct order (recommendation and summary first). As its introduction reviews the background facts of the problem, most of which are known to the immediate reader, the report apparently is designed for future reference. For reasons of convention in the accounting field, the writing style of the report is somewhat reserved and formal.

**FIGURE 13–4**   *(continued)*

RECOMMENDATIONS FOR DEPRECIATING DELIVERY TRUCKS

BASED ON AN ANALYSIS OF THREE PLANS

PROPOSED FOR THE BAGGET LAUNDRY COMPANY

I. Recommendations and Summary of Analysis

The Reducing Charge method appears to be the best method to depreciate Bagget Laundry Company delivery trucks. The relative equality of cost allocation for depreciation and maintenance over the useful life of the trucks is the prime advantage under this method. Computation of depreciation charges is relatively simple by the Reducing Charge plan but not quite so simple as computation under the second best method considered.

The second best method considered is the Straight-Line depreciation plan. It is the simplest to compute of the plans considered, and it results in yearly charges equal to those under the Reducing Charge method. The unequal cost allocation resulting from increasing maintenance costs in successive years, however, is a disadvantage that far outweighs the method's ease of computation.

Third among the plans considered is the Service Hours method. This plan is not satisfactory for depreciating delivery trucks primarily because it combines a number of undesirable features. Prime among these is the complexity and cost of computing yearly charges under the plan. Also significant is the likelihood of poor cost allocation under this plan. An additional drawback is the possibility of variations in the estimates of the service life of company trucks.

II. Background of the Problem

Authorization of the Study. This report on depreciation methods for delivery trucks of the Bagget Laundry Company is submitted on April 16, 19X2, to Mr. Ralph P. Bagget, President of the Company. Authorization for this report was given orally by Mr. Bagget to Mr. Charles W. Brewington, Brewington and Karnes, Certified Public Accountants, on March 15, 19X2.

Statement of the Problem. Having decided to establish branch agencies, the Bagget Laundry Company has purchased delivery trucks to transport laundry back and forth from the central cleaning plant in downtown New Orleans. The problem is to select the most advantageous method to depreciate the trucks. The trucks have an original cost of $3750, a five-year life, and a trade-in value of $750

Method of Solving the Problem. Study of Company records and a review of the authoritative writings on the subject have been used in seeking a reliable solution to the Bagget Laundry Company's problem. Alternative methods of depreciating delivery trucks have been selected through the experience and study of the writer. Conclusions are based on generally accepted business principles as set forth by experts in the field of depreciation.

1

**FIGURE 13–4**   *(continued)*

Steps in Analyzing the Problem   The depreciation methods evaluated in this report are discussed in order of their rank as a solution to the problem.  No attempt has been made to isolate the factors discussed under each method.  Since each method contains fixed factors, a comparison of them directly would be meaningless, because they cannot be manipulated.  The method of computation, amount of depreciation each year, and effect of maintenance costs are the factors to be considered.  The Reducing Charge method will be discussed first.

III.   Marked Advantages of the Reducing Charge Method

The Reducing Charge method, sometimes called the Sum–of–the–Digits method, is an application of a series of diminishing fractions to be applied over the life of the trucks. The fractions to be applied to the five–year life of the delivery trucks are computed by adding the sum of the years (the denominator) and relating this to the number of position of the year (the numerator).  Each fraction is applied against the depreciable value of the trucks.  Computation of the depreciable value is made by subtracting the trade-in value from the original cost.  The depreciable value for the delivery trucks is $3000 ($3750 – $750).

This method results in larger depreciation costs for the early years, with subsequent decreases in the latter years.  Since maintenance and repair costs can be expected to be higher in later years, however, this method provides a relatively stable charge for each year as shown in Table I.

Table I

DEPRECIATION AND MAINTENANCE COSTS FOR
DELIVERY TRUCKS OF BAGGET LAUNDRY FOR 19X0-19X4
USING REDUCING CHARGE DEPRECIATION

| End of Year | Depreciation | | Maintenance | Sum |
|---|---|---|---|---|
| 1 | 5/15 ($3000) = | $1000 | $  50 | $1050 |
| 2 | 4/15 ($3000) = | 800 | 250 | 1050 |
| 3 | 3/15 ($3000) = | 600 | 450 | 1050 |
| 4 | 2/15 ($3000) = | 400 | 650 | 1050 |
| 5 | 1/15 ($3000) = | 200 | 850 | 1050 |
| | Totals | $3000 | $2250 | $5250 |

However, since in actual practice the maintenance charges will not be exactly proportionate, the periodic charges shown will not be exactly the same.

The Reducing Charge method combines the most desirable combination of factors to depreciate the delivery trucks.  The equalization of periodic charges is considered to be the prime factor.  Although computation of this method is relatively easy, it is slightly more complicated than Straight–Line depreciation, which is the next method discussed.

**FIGURE 13–4** *(continued)*

3

IV . Runner-up Position of Straight-Line Method

Compared to the Reducing Charge method, Straight-Line depreciation is easy to compute .
The depreciable value of each truck (S3000) is divided by the five-year life of the truck to
arrive at an equal depreciation charge each year of S600.

Since the maintenance cost of operating the truck will increase in later years, however,
this method will result in much greater periodic charges in the last years . As illustrated in
Table II, the inequality of the periodic charges is the major disadvantage of this method.
This method is very popular in the business world today, but where it is shown that maintenance costs will grow in later years, it is not usually recommended . The stand taken by
many authorities is similar to the following:

> Straight-Line depreciation is the method most widely used in busi-
> ness today . It has the advantage of simplicity and under normal
> plant conditions offers a satisfactory method of cost allocation . For
> a plant to have normal conditions two factors must exist:  (1) accum-
> ulation of properties over a period of years so that the total of depreci-
> ation and maintenance costs will be comparatively even, and (2) a
> relatively stable amount of earnings each year so that depreciation
> as a percentage of net income does not fluctuate widely .[1]

| Table II |
| --- |
| DEPRECIATION AND MAINTENANCE COSTS FOR DELIVERY TRUCKS OF BAGGET LAUNDRY FOR 19X0–19X4 USING STRAIGHT-LINE DEPRECIATION |

| End of Year | Depreciation | Maintenance | Sum |
| --- | --- | --- | --- |
| 1 | 1/15 (S3000) = S 600 | S  50 | S 650 |
| 2 | 1/15 (S3000) =   600 | 250 | 850 |
| 3 | 1/15 (S3000) =   600 | 450 | 1050 |
| 4 | 1/15 (S3000) =   600 | 650 | 1250 |
| 5 | 1/15 (S3000) =   600 | 850 | 1450 |
| | Totals      S3000 | S2250 | S5250 |

However, the trucks considered in this report have not been purchased over a period of
years . Consequently, the Straight-Line method of depreciation will not result in equal
periodic charges for maintenance and depreciation over a period of years . Although this
method is used by many companies in preference to more complex means, it is selected as
second choice for depreciating delivery trucks . The prime disadvantage cited is the unsatisfactory cost allocation it provides . The Service-Hours method which will be discussed
next has this same disadvantage .

[1] Wilbur E. Karrenbrock and Harry Simons, Intermediate Accounting, South-Western Publishing Company, Cincinnati, Ohio, 1968, p.44.

**FIGURE 13–4**    *(concluded)*

4

## V. Poor Rank of Service-Hours Depreciation

The Service-Hours method of depreciation combines the major disadvantages of the other ways discussed. It is based on the principle that a truck is bought for the direct hours of service that it will give. The estimated number of hours that a delivery truck can be used efficiently according to automotive engineers is one-hundred thousand miles. The depreciable cost ($3000) for each truck is allocated pro rata according to the number of service hours used.

The difficulty and expense of maintaining additional records of service hours is a major disadvantage of this method. The depreciation cost for the delivery trucks under this method will fluctuate widely between first and last years. It is reasonable to assume that as the trucks get older more time will be spent on maintenance. Consequently, the larger depreciation costs will occur in the initial years. As can be seen by Table III, the periodic charges for depreciation and maintenance hover between the two previously discussed methods.

The periodic charge for depreciation and maintenance increases in the later years of ownership. Another difficulty encountered is the possibility of a variance between estimated service hours and the actual service hours. The wide fluctuations possible make it impractical to use this method for depreciating the delivery trucks.

The difficulty of maintaining adequate records and increasing costs in the later years are the major disadvantages of this method. Since it combines the major disadvantages of both the Reducing Charge and Straight-Line methods it is not satisfactory for depreciating the delivery trucks.

| Table III |
| :-: |

| DEPRECIATION AND MAINTENANCE COSTS FOR<br>DELIVERY TRUCKS OF BAGGET LAUNDRY FOR 19X0-19X4<br>USING SERVICE-HOURS DEPRECIATION |
| :-: |

| End of<br>Year | Estimated<br>Service-Hours | Depreciation | Maintenance | Sum |
| :-: | :-: | :-: | :-: | :-: |
| 1 | 30,000 | $ 900 | $ 50 | $ 950 |
| 2 | 25,000 | 750 | 250 | 1000 |
| 3 | 20,000 | 600 | 450 | 1050 |
| 4 | 15,000 | 450 | 650 | 1100 |
| 5 | 10,000 | 300 | 850 | 1150 |
|  | 100,000 | $3000 | $2250 | $5250 |

**FIGURE 13–5**

Illustration of a memorandum report

MEMORANDUM                                    THE **M**URCHISON **C**O. **I**NC.


July 21, 197–


TO:         William T. Chrysler
            Director of Sales

FROM:       James C. Colvin, Manager
            Millville Sales District

SUBJECT:  Quarterly Report for Millville Sales District

### SUMMARY HIGHLIGHTS

After three months of operation I have secured office facilities, hired and developed
three salesmen, and cultivated about half the customers available in the Millville Sales
District. Although the district is not yet showing a profit, at the current rate of development it will do so this month. Prospects for the district are unusually bright.

### OFFICE OPERATION

In April I opened the Millville Sales District as authorized by action of the Board of
Directors last February 7th. Initially I set up office in the Three Coins Inn, a motel
on the outskirts of town, and remained there three weeks while looking for permanent
quarters. These I found in the Wingate Building, a downtown office structure. The office
suite selected rents for $340 per month. It has four executive offices, each opening into
a single secretarial office, which is large enough for two secretaries. Although this
arrangement is adequate for the staff now anticipated, additional space is available in
the building if needed.

### PERSONNEL

In the first week of operations, I hired an office secretary, Miss Catherine Kruch.
Miss Kruch has good experience and has excellent credentials. She has proved to
be very effective. In early April I hired two salesmen--Mr. Charles E. Clark and
Mr. Adam E. Knapper. Both were experienced in sales, although neither had worked in apparel sales. Three weeks later I hired Mr. Otto Strelski, a proven salesman
who I managed to attract from the Hammond Company. I still am searching for someone for the fourth subdistrict. Currently I am investigating two good prospects and
hope to hire one of them within the next week.

### PERFORMANCE

After brief training sessions, which I conducted personally, the salesmen were assigned the territories previously marked. And they were instructed to call on the accounts
listed on the sheets supplied by Mr. Henderson's office. During the first month

**FIGURE 13–5**   (continued)

Memorandum                                    -2-                                    July 21, 197–

Knapper's sales totaled $17,431 and Clark's reached $13,490, for a total of $30,921.
With three salesmen working the next month, total sales reached $121,605. Of the
total, Knapper accounted for $37,345, Clark $31,690, and Strelski $52,570. Although
these monthly totals are below the $145,000 break-even point for the three subdistricts,
current progress indicates that we will exceed this volume this month. As we have
made contact with only about one half of the prospects in the area, the potential for
the district appears to be unusually good.

**FIGURE 13–6**

Illustration of a letter report

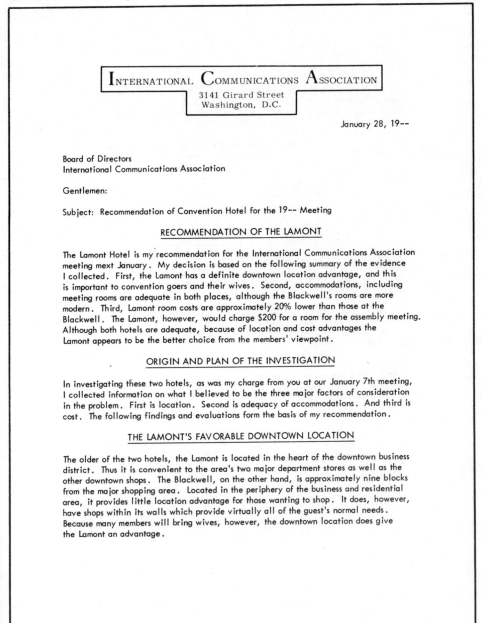

INTERNATIONAL COMMUNICATIONS ASSOCIATION
3141 Girard Street
Washington, D.C.

January 28, 19--

Board of Directors
International Communications Association

Gentlemen:

Subject: Recommendation of Convention Hotel for the 19-- Meeting

### RECOMMENDATION OF THE LAMONT

The Lamont Hotel is my recommendation for the International Communications Association meeting mext January. My decision is based on the following summary of the evidence I collected. First, the Lamont has a definite downtown location advantage, and this is important to convention goers and their wives. Second, accommodations, including meeting rooms are adequate in both places, although the Blackwell's rooms are more modern. Third, Lamont room costs are approximately 20% lower than those at the Blackwell. The Lamont, however, would charge $200 for a room for the assembly meeting. Although both hotels are adequate, because of location and cost advantages the Lamont appears to be the better choice from the members' viewpoint.

### ORIGIN AND PLAN OF THE INVESTIGATION

In investigating these two hotels, as was my charge from you at our January 7th meeting, I collected information on what I believed to be the three major factors of consideration in the problem. First is location. Second is adequacy of accommodations. And third is cost. The following findings and evaluations form the basis of my recommendation.

### THE LAMONT'S FAVORABLE DOWNTOWN LOCATION

The older of the two hotels, the Lamont is located in the heart of the downtown business district. Thus it is convenient to the area's two major department stores as well as the other downtown shops. The Blackwell, on the other hand, is approximately nine blocks from the major shopping area. Located in the periphery of the business and residential area, it provides little location advantage for those wanting to shop. It does, however, have shops within its walls which provide virtually all of the guest's normal needs. Because many members will bring wives, however, the downtown location does give the Lamont an advantage.

**FIGURE  13–6**   *(continued)*

Board of Directors                    -2-                    January 28, 197-

## ADEQUATE ACCOMMODATIONS AT BOTH HOTELS

Both hotels can guarantee the 600 rooms we will require. As the Blackwell is new
(since 1969), however, its rooms are more modern and therefore more appealing.
The 69-year-old Lamont, however, is well preserved and comfortable. Its rooms
are all in good repair, and the equipment is modern.

The Blackwell has 11 small meeting rooms and the Lamont has 13. All are adequate
for our purposes. Both hotels can provide the 10 we need. For our general assembly
meeting, the Lamont would make available its Capri Ballroom, which can easily
seat our membership. It would also serve as the site of our inaugural dinner. The
assembly facilities at the Blackwell appear to be somewhat crowded, although the
management assures me that it can hold 600. Pillars in the room, however, would
make some seats undesirable. In spite of the limitations mentioned, both hotels
appear to have adequate facilities for our meeting.

## LOWER COSTS AT THE LAMONT

Both the Lamont and the Blackwell would provide nine rooms for meetings on a
complimentary basis. Both would provide complimentary suites for our president and
our secretary. The Lamont, however, would charge $200 for use of the room for the
assembly meeting. The Blackwell would provide this room without charge.

Convention rates at the Lamont are $13-$15 for singles, $15-$19 for double-bedded
rooms, and $16-$20 for twin-bedded rooms. Comparable rates at the Blackwell are
$15-$18, $18-$23, and $19-$25. Thus the savings at the Lamont would be approximately 20% per member.

Cost of the dinner selected would be $9.00 per person, including gratuities, at the
Lamont. The Blackwell would meet this price if we would guarantee 600 plates.
Otherwise, they would charge $10. Considering all of these figures, the total cost
picture at the Lamont is the more favorable one.

Respectfully yours,

*Willard K. Mitchell*

Willard K. Mitchell
Executive Secretary

**FIGURE 13–7**

Illustration of a long-form audit report

---

To: William A. Karnes                                          Date: May 3, 19--

From: Auditing Department

Subject: Annual Audit, Spring Street Branch


### Introduction

Following is the report on the annual audit of the Spring Street branch. Reflecting conditions existing at the close of business May 1, 19--, this review covers all accounts
other than Loans and Discounts. Specifically, these accounts were proofed:

|  |  |
|---|---|
| Accounts Receivable | Savings |
| Cash Collateral | Suspense |
| Cash in Office | Series "E" Bonds |
| Collections | Tax Withheld |
| Christmas Club | Travelers Checks |
| Deferred Charges | |


### Condition of Accounts

All listing totals agreed with General Ledger and/or Branch Controls except for these:

Cash in Office . . . . . . . . . $1.17 short
Tax Withheld . . . . . . . . . .     .21 short
Travelers Checks . . . . . . . .     .97 short


### Exceptions Noted

During the course of the examination the following exceptions were found:

Analysis. The branch had 163 unprofitable accounts at the time of the audit. Losses on
these accounts, as revealed by inspection of the Depositors Analysis Cards, ranged from
$7.31 to $176.36 for the year. The average loss per account was $17.21.

Proper deductions of service charges were not made in 73 instances in which the accounts
dropped below the minimum.

Bookkeeping. From a review of the regular checking accounts names were recorded of
customers who habitually write checks without sufficient covering funds. A list of 39 of
the worst offenders was submitted to Mr. Clement Ferguson.

---

**FIGURE 13–7**   *(continued)*

A check of deposit tickets to the third and fourth regular checking ledgers revealed six accounts on which transit delays recorded on the deposit tickets were not correctly transferred to the ledger sheets.

During the preceding month on 17 different accounts the bookkeepers paid items against uncollected funds without getting proper approval.

Statements.   Five statements were held by the branch in excess of three months:

| Account | Statement Dates |
|---|---|
| Curtis A. Hogan | Sept. through April |
| Carlton I. Breeding | Dec. through April |
| Alice Crezan | Nov. through April |
| Jarvis H. Hudson | Jan. through April |
| W. T. Petersen | Dec. through April |

Paying and Receiving.   During the week of April 21-27, tellers failed to itemize currency denominations on large (over $100) cash deposits 23 times.  Deposits were figured in error 32 times.

Savings.   Contrary to instructions given after the last audit, the control clerk has not maintained a record of errors made in savings passbooks.

The savings tellers have easy access to the inactive ledger cards and may record transactions on the cards while alone.  When this condition was noted in the last report, the recommendation was made to set up a system of dual controls.  This recommendation has not been followed.

Safe Deposit Rentals.   Rentals on 164 safe deposit boxes were in arrears.  Although it was pointed out in the last report, this condition has grown worse during the past year.  Numbers of boxes by years in arrears are as follows:

| | |
|---|---|
| 2 to 3 years | 87 |
| 3 to 4 years | 32 |
| 4 to 5 years | 29 |
| over 5 years | 17 |
| Total | 165 |

Stop Payments.   Signed stop payment orders were not received on three checks on which payment was stopped:

| Account | Amount | Date of Stop Payment |
|---|---|---|
| Whelon Electric Company | $317.45 | Feb. 7, 197– |
| George A. Bullock | 37.50 | April 1, 197– |
| Amos H. Kritzel | 737.60 | Dec. 3, 197– |

**FIGURE 13–7**     *(concluded)*

Over and Short Account. A $23.72 difference between Tellers and Rack Department was recorded for April 22. On May 1 this difference remained uncorrected.

William P. Bunting
Head, Auditing Department

Copies to:

W. F. Robertson
Cecil Ruston
W. W. Merrett

# Reports: Techniques
# of writing

**W**HEN YOU HAVE collected and organized your information and have determined the arrangement your report will have, you next turn to the task of writing. This task, of course, is the primary one in your effort to communicate the report contents, although the others certainly have their effects. As you know, communication is not easy. In a report it is unusually difficult because of the complex mass of information that must be communicated in most cases. Unless you make a very special effort to communicate the mass of information in your report, you are likely to fall short of your communication objective.

Much of what you can do in communicating the information in your report we discussed in our analysis of clear writing (Chapter 7). All of these principles of clear writing apply to report writing, and you would do well to keep them in mind as you write your report. In addition, however, there are some general characteristics of good report writing with which you should be acquainted. These are adaptation, objectivity, time viewpoint, transition, and interest. We shall discuss them in the pages which follow.

## NEED FOR ADAPTATION

From our analysis of the communication process, we can conclude that the communication abilities of people differ. Thus, you and your reader will not have precisely the same communicating ability. In fact, you are likely to differ sharply. The fact that you and your reader differ in communication ability is perhaps the major barrier to successful report communication—or to any other form of communication, for that matter. Obviously, if you use words which are not in the mental filter of your reader, communication does not occur. For written communication to be successful, the words used must mean the same to both you and your reader.

From this analysis, one fundamental requirement for report writing is clear. This is the need for adapting the writing to the specific reader or readers. Unfortunately, the novice is not likely to adapt his writing to the reader without conscious effort. More than likely, he finds writing such a chore that he is content to accept whatever wording comes first to mind. Such wording may communicate well with someone like the writer, but not so well with the specific reader intended.

In order to adapt your writing, you should begin by visualizing your reader. You should determine such things as who your reader is, how much he knows about the subject, what his educational level is, and how he thinks. Then, keeping this image of your reader in mind, you tailor your writing to fit this one person.

Your task is relatively simple when you write to a single reader or homogeneous group of readers. But what if you write to a group with varying characteristics? What if, say, your audience comprises people ranging from college graduates to grade school graduates? The answer should be obvious. In such cases you have no choice but to aim at the lowest level of the group. To aim higher would be to exclude the lower levels from your message.

In cases in which you are better educated or better informed on the subject area than your reader, adaptation means simplification. A company executive writing to the rank-and-file employee, for example, would need to write in the simple words the reader understands. Likewise, a technical person writing to a nontechnical reader would need to simplify the writing. But when this technical person writes to a fellow technician, he would do well to use the technical vernacular which is easily understood and expected by such people. As the following examples show, few technical writers were better aware of this fundamental rule than the late Albert Einstein. In writing on a technical subject to a nontechnical audience, he skillfully wrote down to their level:

> What takes place can be illustrated with the help of our rich man. The atom M is a rich miser who, during his life, gives away no money (energy). But in his will he bequeaths his fortune to his sons M′ and M″, on condition that they give to the community a small amount, less than one thousandth of the whole estate (energy or mass). The sons together have somewhat less than the father had (the mass sum M′ and M″ is somewhat smaller than the mass M of the radioactive atom). But the part given to the community, though relatively small, is still so enormously large (considered as kinetic energy) that it brings with it a

great threat of evil. Averting that threat has become the most urgent problem of our time.[1]

But when writing to fellow scientists, he wrote in words which they understood and expected:

> The general theory of relativity owes its existence in the first place to the empirical fact of the numerical equality of the inertial and gravitational mass of bodies, for which fundamental fact classical mechanics provided no interpretation. Such an interpretation is arrived at by an extension of the principle of relativity to co-ordinate systems accelerated relatively to one another. The introduction of co-ordinate systems accelerated relatively to inertial systems involves the appearance of gravitational fields relative to the latter. As a result of this, the general theory of relativity, which is based on the equality of inertia and weight, provides a theory of the gravitational field.[2]

## REQUIREMENT OF OBJECTIVITY

The communication objective in a report is difficult enough without your own opinions, biases, and attitudes becoming a part of it. Your reader's mental filter will have your reader's biases, and her biases will become a part of her interpretation of meaning. Over this you have little control. But you do have control over your own writing effort. Thus, you should do whatever you can to present truth as well as it is humanly possible to do so. More specifically, you should strive to maintain an attitude of objectivity in your writing.

Maintaining an attitude of objectivity concerns both your attitude and your writing style. You can have an objective attitude by divorcing your own prejudices and emotions from your work and by fairly reviewing and interpreting the information you have uncovered. Thus, you should approach your problem with an open mind and look at all sides of each question. Your role is much like that of a judge presiding over a court of law. You are not moved by personal feelings. You seek truth, and you leave no stone unturned in quest of it. You make your decision only after carefully weighing all of the evidence uncovered.

### Objectivity as a basis for believability

A report built on the quality of objectivity has another ingredient that is essential to good report writing: believability. Perhaps biased writing can be in language that is artfully deceptive and may at first glance be

---

[1] Albert Einstein, *Out of My Later Years,* Philosophical Library, Inc., New York, 1950, p. 53.

[2] Albert Einstein, *Essays in Science,* Philosophical Library, Inc., New York, 1934. p. 50.

believable. But such writing is risky. If at any spot in the report the reader detects bias, she will be suspicious of the whole work. Painstaking objectivity, therefore, is the only sure way to believable report writing.

## Objectivity and the question of impersonal versus personal writing

Recognizing the need for objectivity in their work, the early report writers strove to develop a writing style which would convey this attitude. They reasoned that the source of the subjective quality in a report is the human being. And they reasoned that objectivity is best attained by emphasizing the factual material of a report rather than the personalities involved. So they worked to remove the human being from their writing. Impersonal writing style was the result. By impersonal writing is meant writing in the third person—without *I*'s, *we*'s, or *you*'s.

In recent years, impersonal writing has been strenuously questioned by many writers. These writers point out that personal writing is more forceful and direct than is impersonal writing. They contend that writing which brings both reader and writer into the picture is more like conversation and therefore more interesting. And they answer to the point on objectivity with a reply that objectivity is an attitude of mind and not a matter of person. A report, they say, can be just as objective when written in personal style as when written in impersonal style. Frequently, these critics counter with the argument that impersonal writing leads to an overuse of passive voice and a generally dull writing style. This last argument, however, lacks substance. Impersonal writing can and should be interesting. Any dullness it may have is wholly the fault of the writer. As proof, one has only to look at the lively style used by writers for newspapers, newsmagazines, and journals. Most of this writing is impersonal—and usually it is not dull.

As in most cases of controversy, there is some merit to the arguments on both sides. There are situations in which personal writing is best. There are situations in which impersonal writing is best. And there are situations in which either style is appropriate. You must decide at the outset of your work which style is best for your one situation.

Your decision should be based on the circumstances of each report situation. First, you should consider the expectations or desires of those for whom you are preparing the report. More than likely, you will find a preference for the impersonal style, for, like most human beings, business people have been slow to break tradition. Next, you should consider the formality of the report situation. If the situation is informal, as when the report is really a personal communication of information between business associates, you should use personal writing. But if the situation is formal, as is the case with most major reports, you should use the conventional impersonal style.

Perhaps the distinction between impersonal and personal writing is best made by illustration.

| Personal | Impersonal |
|---|---|
| Having studied the various advantages and disadvantages of using trading stamps, I conclude that your company should not adopt this practice. If you use the stamps, you would have to pay out money for them. Also, you would have to hire additional employees to take care of the increase in sales volume. | A study of the advantages and disadvantages of using trading stamps supports the conclusion that the Mills Company should not adopt this practice. The stamps themselves would cost extra money. Also, use of stamps would require additional personnel to take care of the increase in sales volume. |

## LOGIC OF PRESENT-TIME VIEWPOINT

A major problem in keeping order in a report is that of fitting all of the details in their proper place in time. Not to do so would be to confuse the reader and to bring up unnecessary barriers in the communication effort. Thus, it is important that in your report you maintain a proper time viewpoint.

Maintaining a proper time viewpoint in the report is a problem for even the seasoned writer. Illogical shifts from one tense to another detract generally from the writing and mar the accuracy of the presentation. Consistency in time viewpoint is the one logical solution to the problem. But whether the consistent time viewpoint should be past or present is a matter on which opinions differ.

Some authorities favor a consistent past viewpoint. They assume that all the data collected, as well as the research and the writing of the report, are past events by the time the report is read. Thus, they conclude that it is logical to report a result from the current survey in words such as "22 percent of the managers *favored* a change." And they would write a reference to another part of the report in words like these: "In Chapter 2, this conclusion *was* reached."

A more logical approach is to write in the present-time viewpoint. In following this viewpoint, you would present as current all information which is current at the time of writing. For example, a presentation of the results of a recent survey might be made in words like these: "Twenty-two percent of the managers *favor* a change." Or a reference in the report to another part of the report might be in words like "In Chapter 2, this conclusion *is* reached." Information which is clearly in the past or in the future at the time of writing, however, you should present in a past or future tense. For example, survey findings likely to be obsolete at the time of writing might be worded thus: "In 1939, 44.2 percent of the managers *favored* this plan." Or a predicted figure for the future might be reported in these words: "According to this projection, the value of these assets will exceed $32 million by 1980." A present-time viewpoint should in no way be interpreted to mean that every verb must be in the present tense. Nor should it ever result in placing a single event awkwardly in time. Adherence to this viewpoint simply involves placing all facts in their logical place in time at the time of writing.

## STRUCTURAL AIDS TO REPORT COHERENCE

Smooth flow of thought and clear relationships between the facts presented are essential to successful communication of the report information. Unless the relationships of the details are made clear, unless the readers are made to see the logic of your presentation, they are not likely to receive the full communication effect of your report message. The writing technique which gives your report this desired effect is coherence.

Perhaps the one best contributor to coherence is good organization—a topic discussed in detail in Chapter 12. By relating facts in a logical, natural sequence, you can give some degree of coherence to the writing. But logical arrangement of facts alone is not always enough. Particularly is this true in the long and involved report in which the relationships of the parts are complex and are not so easily grasped by the reader. In such a report you need to make a special effort to structure the report so that the relationships are clear. Specifically, you can structure the report story by using concluding and summary paragraphs to mark the report's progress. You can use introductory and preview paragraphs to show major relationships. And you can use transitional sentences and words to show relationships between the lesser parts.

### The use of introductory, concluding, and summarizing sections

The extent of use of introductory, concluding, and summarizing sections depends on the report. Perhaps the best rule for you to follow is to use them whenever they are needed to relate the parts of the report or to move the report message along. In general, these sections are more likely to be needed in the longer and more involved reports. In such a report you are likely to follow a traditional plan of connecting structure.

This plan, as described in Figure 14–1, uses these special sections to tie together all the parts of the report. Because it serves to keep the readers aware of where they have been, where they are, and where they are going, the plan helps them to find their way through complex problems. Also, placement of forward-looking and backward-glancing sections permits the casual readers to dip into the report at any place and quickly get their bearing.

As noted in Figure 14–1, you may use three types of sections (usually a paragraph or more) to structure the report. One is the introductory preview. Another is the section introduction. And still another is the conclusion or summary sections, either for the major report parts or for the whole report.

For a longer report you may use a section of the report introduction (see Chapter 13) to tell the reader of the report's organization plan. Generally, this preview covers three things: topics to be discussed, their order of presentation, and the logic for this order. Having been informed of the basic plan, the readers are then able to understand quickly how each new subject they encounter in the following pages fits into the whole. Thus, a connection between the major report parts is made. The following paragraphs do a good job of previewing a report comparing four brands of automobiles for use by a sales organization:

> The decision as to which light car Allied Distributors should buy is reached through a comparison on the basis of three factors: cost, safety, and dependability. Each of these major factors is broken down into its component parts, which are applied to each make being considered.
>
> Because it is the most tangible factor, cost is examined first. In this section the four makes are compared for initial and trade-in values. Then

**FIGURE 14–1**

Diagram of the structural coherence plan of a long, formal report

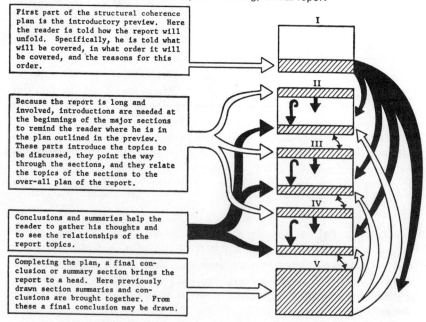

they are compared for operating costs as determined by gasoline mileage, oil usage, repair expense, and the like. In a second major section the same comparison is used to determine car safety. Driver visibility, special safety features, brakes, steering quality, acceleration rate, and traction are the main considerations here. In a third section, dependability of the cars is measured on the basis of repair records and salesmen's time lost because of automobile failure. In a final section, weights are assigned to the foregoing comparisons, and the brand of automobile best suited for the company's needs is recommended.

In addition to the introductory preview, you may help show relationships between the major report topics by introductory and summary sections placed at convenient spots throughout the report. You may use sections occasionally to remind the readers of where they are in the progress of the report. Also, you may use these sections to elaborate on the relationships between the report parts and, in general, to give detailed connecting and introductory information. The following paragraph, for example, serves as an introduction to the final section of a report of an industrial survey. Note how the paragraph ties in with the preceding section, which covered industrial activity in three major geographic areas, and justifies covering secondary areas.

> Although the great bulk of industry is concentrated in three areas (Grand City, Milltown, and Port Starr), a thorough industrial survey needs to consider the secondary, but nevertheless important, areas of the state. In the rank of their current industrial potential, these areas are the Southeast, with Hartsburg as its center; the Central West, dominated by Parrington; and the North Central, where Pineview is the center of activities.

The following summary-conclusion paragraph gives an appropriate ending to a major section. The paragraph brings to a head the findings presented in the section and points the way to the subject of the next section.

> These findings and those pointed out in preceding paragraphs all lead to one obvious conclusion. The small-business executive is concerned primarily with subject matter which will aid him directly in his work. That is, he favors a curriculum slanted in favor of the practical subjects. He does, however, insist on some coverage of the liberal areas. Too, he is convinced of the value of studying business administration. On all of these points he is clearly out of tune with the bulk of big-business leaders who have voiced their positions in this matter. Even the most dedicated business administration professors would find it difficult to support such an extremely practical concept. Nevertheless, these are the small-business executive's opinions on the subject; and as he is the consumer of the business education product, his opinion should at least be

considered. Likewise, his specific recommendation on courses (subject of the following chapter) deserves careful review.

Proper use of paragraphs such as these forms a network of connection throughout the work. The longer the report, the more effective they are likely to be.

## Communication value of transition

Transition, which literally means "a bridging-across," may be formed in many ways. In general, transitions are made by words, or sentences, placed in the writing to show the relationships of the information presented. They may appear at the beginning of discussion on a new topic and may relate this topic to what has been discussed. They may appear at the end as a forward look. Or they may appear internally as words or phrases which in various ways tend to facilitate the flow of subject matter.

Whether you should use a transition word or sentence in a particular place depends on the need for relating the parts concerned. Because the relationship of its parts may be seen merely from a logical sequence of presentation, a short report might require only a few transitional parts here and there. A long and involved report, on the other hand, might require much more transitional help.

*A word of caution.* Before more specific comments on transition are given, one fundamental point must be made clear. You should not make transitions mechanically. You should use them only when there is need for them, or when leaving them out would produce abruptness in the flow of report findings. You should not make them appear to be stuck in; instead, you should make them blend in naturally with the surrounding writing. For example, you should avoid transitional forms of this mechanical type: "The last section has discussed topic X. In the next section topic Y will be analyzed."

*Transitional sentences.* Throughout the report, you can improve the connecting network by the judicious use of sentences. You can use them especially to form the connecting link between secondary sections of the report, as illustrated in the following example of transition between sections B and C of a report. The first few lines of this illustration draw a conclusion for section B. Then, with smooth tie-in, the next words introduce section C and relate this topic to the report plan.

[Section B, concluded]

. . . Thus the data show only negligible difference in the cost for oil consumption [subject of section B] for the three brands of cars. [Section C] Even though costs of gasoline [subject of section A] and oil [subject of section B] are the more consistent factors of operation expense, the picture is not complete until the cost of repairs and maintenance [subject of section C] is considered.

Additional examples of sentences designed to connect succeeding parts are the following. By making a forward-looking reference, these sentences set up the following subject matter. Thus, the resulting shifts of subject matter are both smooth and logical.

These data show clearly that Edmond's machines are the most economical. Unquestionably, their operation by low-cost gas and their record for low-cost maintenance give them a decided edge over competing brands. *Before a definite conclusion as to their merit is reached, however, one more vital comparison should be made.*

(The final sentence clearly introduces the following discussion of an additional comparison.)

. . . *At first glance the data appear to be convincing, but a closer observation reveals a number of discrepancies.*

(Discussion of the discrepancies is logically set up by this final sentence.)

Placement of topic sentences at key points of emphasis is still another way of using a sentence to improve the connecting network of the report. Usually, the topic sentence is best placed at the paragraph beginning where the subject matter can very quickly be related to its spot in the organization plan described in the introductory preview or the introduction to the section. Note, in the following example, how the topic sentences emphasize the key information. Note also how the topic sentences tie the paragraphs with the preview (not illustrated), which no doubt related this organization plan

*Brand C accelerates faster than the other two brands, both on level road and on a 9-percent grade.* According to a test conducted by Consumption Research, brand C attains a speed of 60 miles per hour in 13.2 seconds. To reach this same speed, brand A requires 13.6 seconds, and brand B requires 14.4 seconds. On a 9-percent grade, brand C reaches the 60-mile-per-hour speed in 29.4 seconds and brand A in 43.3 seconds. Brand B is unable to reach this speed.

*Because it carries more weight on its rear wheels than the others, brand C has the best traction of the three.* Traction, which means a minimum of sliding on wet or icy roads, is most important to safe driving, particularly during the cold, wet winter months. As traction is directly related to the weight carried by the rear wheels, a comparison of these weights should give some measure of the safety of the three cars. According to data released by the Automobile Bureau of Standards, brand C carries 47 percent of its weight on its rear wheels. Brands B and A carry 44 and 42 percent, respectively.

*Transitional words.* Although the major transition problems concern connection between sections of the report, there is need also for transition between lesser parts. If the writing is to flow smoothly, you will need to relate clause to clause and sentence to sentence and paragraph to paragraph. Transitional words and phrases generally serve to make these connections.

The transitional words you may use are too numerous to relate, but the following review is a clear picture of what these words are and how they can be used. With a little imagination to supply the context, you can easily see how such words relate succeeding ideas. For better understanding, the words are grouped by the relationships they show between subjects previously discussed and those to be discussed.

| *Relationship* | *Word examples* |
|---|---|
| Listing or enumeration of subjects | In addition |
|  | First, second, etc. |
|  | Besides |
|  | Moreover |
| Contrast | On the contrary |
|  | In spite of |
|  | On the other hand |
|  | In contrast |
|  | However |
| Likeness | In a like manner |
|  | Likewise |
|  | Similarly |
| Cause-result | Thus |
|  | Because of |
|  | Therefore |
|  | Consequently |
|  | For this reason |
| Explanation or elaboration | For example |
|  | To illustrate |
|  | For instance |
|  | Also |
|  | Too |

## The role of interest in report communication

Like all forms of good writing, report writing should be interesting. Actually, the quality of interest is as important as the facts of the report, for without interest, communication is not likely to occur. If their interest is not held—if their minds are allowed to stray—the readers cannot help missing parts of the message. And it does not matter how much the readers want to read the report message; nor is their interest in the subject enough to assure communication. The writing must maintain this interest. The truth of this reasoning is evident to you if you have ever tried to read dull writing in studying for an examination. How desperately you wanted to learn the subject, but how often your mind strayed away!

Perhaps writing interestingly is an art. But if it is, it is an art in which you can gain some proficiency if you work at it. If you are to develop this proficiency, you need to work watchfully to make your words build concrete pictures, and you need to avoid the "rubber-stamp" jargon or technical talk so often used in business. You must cultivate a feeling for the rhythmic flow of words and sentences. You must remember that back of every fact and figure there is some form of life—people doing things, machines operating, a commodity being marketed. The secret of quality writing is to bring the real life to the surface by concrete diction and vigorous active-voice verbs in so far as possible. But at the same time, you should work to achieve interest without using more words than are necessary.

Here a word of caution may be injected. Attempts to make writing style interesting can be overdone. Such is the case whenever the reader's attention is focused on how something is said rather than on what is said. Good style, to be effective, simply presents information in a clear, concise, and interesting manner. Possibly the purpose and definition of style can best be summarized by this objective of the report writer: Writing style is at its best when the readers are prompted to say "Here are some interesting facts" rather than "Here is some beautiful writing." Specific suggestions for writing interestingly are presented in the following chapter.

## QUESTIONS AND PROBLEMS

1. Are adaptation and simplification the same? Explain.
2. Find a paragraph written for a high level of readership. Rewrite it for a lower level. Point out the differences.
3. Certainly not all reports written in business are written objectively. In fact, many have deliberate bias. In the light of this information, why should we stress objectivity in a college course in report writing?
4. Explain how the question of personal and impersonal writing is related to objectivity.
5. Explain the differences between present- and past-time viewpoints.
6. Is it incorrect to have present, past, and future tense in the same report? In the same paragraph? In the same sentence?
7. Using your imagination to supply the information needed, write an introductory paragraph for a section of a long, formal report.

8.  For the same report, write a typical summary paragraph bringing to a close one of the major sections.

9.  For the same report, show your knowledge of transition by writing three pairs of connecting sentences. In each pair, one sentence will end a paragraph and the other will begin the next paragraph.

# 15

# Reports: Visual
# communication aspects

PERHAPS CONFUCIUS was not precisely correct when he said "a picture is worth a thousand words." But we can quarrel only with the number in the statement. As we know from our study of communication theory, words are imprecise conveyors of meaning. We know that this is so, for we must make a limited number of words cover an infinite number of variations in reality. At best, they fit reality loosely. Thus, there is little wonder that we frequently have difficulty communicating through words.

Because your reports frequently must communicate complex and voluminous information, you are likely to have difficulty making words do the job. In a statistical analysis, for example, you are likely to get your reader lost in a maze of data as you tell the report's story in words. Or in a technical report you are likely to have difficulty attempting to use words to describe a process or a procedure. Frequently, in such cases you will need to use pictures of one kind or other to help communicate your information.

Pictures, or "graphic aids," as we call them in report writing, are an essential part of many reports. Rarely do they take the place of words, for words are essential for communicating the information in most reports. Their role is more a supplementary one—one of assisting the words to communicate the report content. In addition to this communication role, graphic aids also serve to present minor supporting details not covered in words. They help to give emphasis to the key points of coverage. Also, they serve to improve the physical appearance of the report, thereby making it more inviting and readable.

### Foresight in planning

If you are to use graphic aids effectively, you must plan them with foresight and care. Such planning is a part of the task of organizing the report.

As you approach the task of planning your graphic aids, you should keep in mind your fundamental purpose of communicating. Thus, you should never arbitrarily select some random number of illustrations to include. Nor should you judge the completeness of graphic presentation in a report by the number of illustrations used. Instead, you should plan each graphic aid for a specific communication reason. Each one should help to present your report information. Each one should be included because it is needed.

### Relationship of need to the plan

Just what graphic aids you will need to communicate a report's story, however, is not easy to determine. Much depends on your overall plan. If you plan to cover the subject in detail, the role of the graphic aids is to emphasize and to supplement. Specifically, they point up the major facts discussed and present the detailed data not covered in the writing. On the other hand, if you plan to present the facts in summary form, you may use the graphic aids to work more closely with your text.

The first of these arrangements (complete text supplemented by graphic aids) is conventional and is best for all studies when completeness is a main requirement. The second plan (summary text closely helped by graphic aids) is gaining in importance. It is especially used in popular types of reports, such as those addressed to the general public. As illustrated in Figure 15–1, this plan produces fast-moving, light reading—the kind the public likes. In addition to the public, many top executives prefer this plan. With the increasing demands on their time, these executives prefer that the reports they read give them the facts quickly and easily. Short, summary reports, helped by an abundance of clear graphic aids, do this job best. Frequently, because of the need for a complete report for future reference and the need for presentation of summary information to the top executives, both kinds of reports are written for the same problem.

### Preferred placement within the report

For the maximum communication effect, you should place the graphic aids which help tell the report story within the report and near the text

**FIGURE 15–1**

Page from a popular report illustrating use of a summary text closely helped by graphic aids

# Lifetime Careers in the Steel Industry

The record shows clearly that steelworkers spend many of their working years with one company. A recent survey revealed that those holding jobs with the same steel company for 10 or more years constituted 71 percent of the wage employees in the industry. Over one-fifth of steel industry employees had been in the employ of the same steel company 25 years or longer.

An age analysis showed a mature work force engaged in steelmaking. The average age of steel's wage employees was 43.

## YEARS OF SERVICE IN THE SAME COMPANY

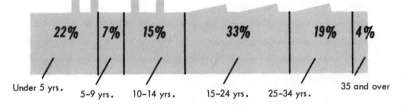

| 22% | 7% | 15% | 33% | 19% | 4% |

Under 5 yrs.    5–9 yrs.    10–14 yrs.    15–24 yrs.    25–34 yrs.    35 and over

*Steelworkers average 16.5 years*
*of service in the same company*

## AGE

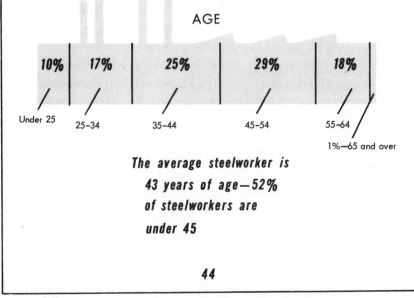

| 10% | 17% | 25% | 29% | 18% |

Under 25    25–34    35–44    45–54    55–64

1%—65 and over

*The average steelworker is*
*43 years of age—52%*
*of steelworkers are*
*under 45*

Source: American Iron and Steel Institute, *Charting Steel's Progress,* 1967.

they will illustrate. In such positions, they are likely to be seen at the time they need to be seen.

Exactly where you should place each illustration is determined by its size. If the graphic aid is small, taking up only a portion of the page, you should place it so that it is surrounded by the writing covering it. If the graphic aid requires a full page for display, you should place it immediately following the page on which it is discussed. When the discussion covers several pages, however, the full-page illustration is best placed on the page following the first reference to its content.

There is some acceptance of the report arrangement in which all of the illustrations are placed in the appendix. Aside from the time saved by the typist, there is little that can be said for this practice. Certainly, it does not work for the convenience of our readers who must flip through pages each time they wish to see the graphic presentation of a part of the text.

The graphic aids which you wish to include but which do not tell a specific part of the report's story you should place in the appendix. Included in this group are all graphic aids which belong within the report for completeness, yet have no specific spot of coverage within the study. As a rule, this group is comprised of long and complex tables which may cover large areas of information. These tables may even cover the data displayed in a number of charts and other more graphic devices which generally are constructed to illustrate very specific spots within the report.

Whether you place the illustrations within or at the end of the text, you should key them to the text portions they cover by means of references. That is, you might well call the reader's attention to illustrations which cover the topic under discussion. Such references you can make best as incidental remarks in sentences containing significant comments about the data shown in the illustration. You may use numerous incidental wordings, such as these:

. . . , as shown in Chart 4. . . .
. . . , indicated in Chart 4. . . .
. . . , as a glance at Chart 4 reveals. . . .
. . .    (see Chart 4). . . .

## General mechanics of construction

In planning the illustrations, and later in the actual work of constructing them, you will be confronted with numerous questions of mechanics. Many of these questions you must solve through intelligent appraisal of the conditions concerned in each instance. But the mechanics fall into general groups, the most conventional of which are summarized in the following paragraphs.

*Size determination.* One of the first decisions involved in constructing a graphic aid is that of determining how large it should be. The answer to this question should not be arbitrary, nor should it be based solely on your convenience. Instead, you should seek to give the illustration the size that its contents justify. If, for example, an illustration is relatively simple, comprising only two or three quantities, a quarter page might be adequate. Certainly, a full page would not be needed to illustrate the data. But if a graphic aid is made up of a dozen or so quantities, more space would be justified—possibly even a full page.

With extremely complex and involved data, it may be necessary to make the graphic aid larger than the report page. Such long presentations must be carefully inserted and folded within the report so that they open easily. The fold selected will, of course, vary with the size of the page, so there is no best fold that can be recommended. You would do well to survey whatever possibilities are available to you.

*Layout arrangement.* The layout of any graphic aid is influenced by the amount of information being illustrated. But whenever it is practical, it is best to keep the layout of the illustration within the normal page layout.

*Rules and borders.* You should arrange rules and borders of any form of graphic presentation to help display and to make clear the data presented. Thus, you should determine their use chiefly through careful planning. As a general practice, however, you should set off graphic aids of less than a page from the text by a lined border which completely encloses the illustration and its caption. You may use this arrangement for full-page illustrations as well, although with such pages the border does not serve so practical a purpose. You should not extend the borders beyond the normal page margins. An exception to this rule is, of course, the unusual instance in which the volume of data to be illustrated simply will not fit into an area less than the normal page layout.

*Color and crosshatching.* Color and/or cross-hatching appropriately used helps the reader to see the comparisons and distinctions. In addition, they give the report a boost in physical attractiveness. Color is especially valuable for this purpose, and you should use it whenever practical.

*Numbering.* Except for minor tabular displays which are actually a part of the text, you should number all illustrations in the report. Many schemes of numbering are available to you, depending on the makeup of the graphic aids.

If you have many graphic aids which fall into two or more categories, each category you may number consecutively. For example, if your report is illustrated by six tables, five charts, and six maps, you may number these graphic aids Table 1, Table 2, . . . Table 6; Chart 1, Chart 2, . . . Chart 5; and Map 1, Map 2, . . . Map 6.

But if the illustrations used are a wide mixture of types, you may number them in two groups: tables and figures. To illustrate, consider a report containing three tables, two maps, three charts, one diagram, and one photograph. You could group these graphic aids and number them Table I, Table II, and Table III, and Figure 1, Figure 2, . . . Figure 7. By convention, tables are never grouped with other forms of presentation. *Figures* represent a sort of miscellaneous grouping which may include all illustration types other than tables. It would not be wrong to group and number as figures all graphic aids other than tables even if the group contained sufficient subgroups (charts, maps, etc.) to warrant separate numbering of each of these subgroups.

As the preceding examples illustrate, tables are conventionally numbered with capital roman numerals (I, II, III, etc.). All other forms of illustration use the arabic numerals (1, 2, 3, etc.). There is some tendency nowadays, however, to use arabic numerals for all forms. Obviously, the most important rule to follow in regard to numbering is that of consistency.

*Construction of title captions.* Every graphic aid should have a title caption which adequately describes the contents. Like the captions used in other parts of the report, the title to the graphic aid has the objective of concisely covering the illustration contents. As a check of content coverage, you might well use the journalist's five *W's—who, what, where, when, why.* Sometimes you might include *how* (the classification principle). But as conciseness of expression is also desired, it is not always necessary to include all of the *W's* in the caption constructed. A title of a chart comparing annual sales volume of Texas and Louisiana stores of the Brill Company for the 1974–19– period might be constructed as follows:

| | |
|---|---|
| *Who:* | Brill Company |
| *What:* | Annual sales |
| *Where:* | Texas and Louisiana |
| *When:* | 1974–19– |
| *Why:* | For comparison |

The caption might read, "Comparative annual sales of Texas and Louisiana branches of the Brill Company, 1974–19–."

*Placement of titles.* Titles of tables conventionally appear above the tabular display. Titles to all other graphic presentations usually are below the illustration. There is convention, too, for placing table titles in a higher type (usually solid capitals without the underscore in typewritten reports) than titles of all other illustrations. But nowadays these conventional forms are not universally followed. There is a growing tendency to use lowercase type for all illustration titles and to place titles of both tables and charts at the top. These more recent practices are simple and logical; yet for formal reports you should follow the conventional arrangement.

*Footnotes and acknowledgments.* Occasionally, parts of a graphic aid require special explanation or elaboration. When these conditions come up, just as when similar explanations are made within the text of the report, you should use footnotes. Such footnotes are nothing more than concise explanations placed below the illustration and keyed to the part explained by means of a superscript (raised number) or asterisk, as shown in Figure 15–2. Footnotes for tables are best placed immediately below the graphic presentation. Footnotes for other graphic forms follow the illustration when the title is placed at the bottom of the page.

Usually, a source acknowledgment is the bottom entry made on the page. By source acknowledgment is meant a reference to the body or authority which deserves the credit for gathering the data used in the illustration. The entry consists simply of the word *source* followed by a colon and the source name. A source note for data based on information gathered by the United States Department of Agriculture might read like this:

Source: United States Department of Agriculture.

If the data were collected by you or your staff, two procedures may be followed. You may give the source as "primary," in which case the source note would read:

Source: Primary.

Or you may omit the source note.

## Construction of tables

A table is any systematic arrangement of quantitative information in rows and columns. Although tables are not truly graphic in the literal meaning of the word, they are instrumental in communicating information. Therefore, you may appropriately consider them a part of the graphic-aids planning of your report. The purpose of a table is to present a broad area of information in convenient and orderly fashion. By such an arrangement, the information is simplified, and comparisons and analyses are made easy.

Two basic types of tables are available to you—the general-purpose table and the special-purpose table. General-purpose tables are arrangements of a broad area of data collected. They are repositories of detailed statistical data and have no special analytical purpose. As a rule, general-purpose tables belong in the report appendix.

Special-purpose tables, as their name implies, are prepared for a special purpose—to help to illustrate a particular phase of the text. Usually, they consist of data carefully drawn from the general-purpose tables. Only those data are selected which are pertinent to the analysis, and sometimes these data are rearranged or regrouped to better illustrate their special purpose. Such tables belong within the text near the spot they illustrate.

Aside from the title, footnotes, and source designation previously discussed, the table consists of stubs, captions, and columns and rows of data, as shown in Figure 15–2. Stubs are the titles to the rows of data, and captions are the titles to the columns. The captions, however, may be divided into subcaptions—or column heads, as they are sometimes called.

**FIGURE 15–2**

Good arrangement of the parts of a typical table

| TABLE NO. TITLE OF TABLE | | | | |
|---|---|---|---|---|
| Stub Head | CAPTION HEAD | | | |
|  | Subcaption | Subcaption | Subcaption | Subcaption |
| Stub | X X X | X X X | X X X | X X X |
| Stub | X X X | X X X | X X X | X X X |
| Stub | X X X | X X X | X X X | X X X |
| Stub | X X X | X X X | X X X | X X X |
| " | " | " | " | " |
| " | " | " | " | " |
| " | " | " | " | " |
| " | " | " | " | " |
| " | " | " | " | " |
| " | " | " | " | " |
| TOTAL | X X X | X X X | X X X | X X X |

Footnotes

Source Note:

As you should plan the text tables specifically, their construction is largely influenced by their illustration purpose. Nevertheless, a few general rules may be listed:

1. If rows tend to be long, repeat the stubs at the right.
2. Use the dash or the abbreviation *n.a.*, but not the zero, to indicate that data are not available.
3. Key the footnote references to numbers in the table with asterisks, daggers, double daggers, etc. Numbers followed by footnote reference numbers might cause confusion.
4. Make totals and subtotals whenever they help the purpose of the table. You may include totals for each column and sometimes for each row. Usually, you will make row totals, but when you desire to give emphasis to the totals, you may place them at the left. Likewise, you should include column totals at the bottom, but you may place them at the top of the column when you want to emphasize these totals. You should separate the totals from their data by a ruled line, usually a double one.
5. Make clear the units in which you record the data. Unit descriptions (bushels, acres, pounds, and the like) are appropriately placed above the columns as part of the captions or subcaptions. If the data are in dollars, however, you should place the dollar mark ($) before the first entry in each column.

## The simple bar chart

Simple bar charts are graphic means of comparing simple magnitudes by the lengths of equal-width bars. You should use such charts to show quantity changes over time, quantity changes over geographic distance, or quantitative distances.

The principal parts of the bar chart are the bars and the grid. The bars may be arranged horizontally or vertically, and each has in its beginning a title identifying the quantity being illustrated. The grid upon which the bars are placed is simply a field carefully ruled by line marks arithmetically scaled to the magnitudes illustrated. Usually, a finely marked grid is made as a preliminary step in constructing a bar chart, and the bars are then placed on the grid. But the final drawing of the chart is best made to show only sufficient grid lines to help the reader's eye measure the magnitudes of the bars. These scaled grid lines are carefully labeled with numerals, and the unit in which the values are measured is indicated by a scale caption appearing below the values in a vertical bar chart and above the values in a horizontal bar arrangement.

Although there are numerous acceptable variations in bar-chart con-

**FIGURE 15–3**

Illustration of good arrangement of the parts of a simple bar chart

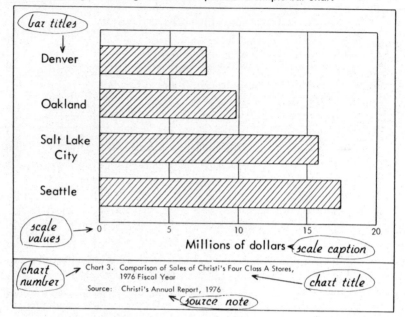

struction, a basic pattern should be helpful to you. Such a pattern, as illustrated in Figure 15–3, is generally adequate.

## Variations of the bar chart

In addition to the simple bar chart just described, you may use a number of other types of bar charts in presenting a report. The more commonly used of these variants are the multiple bar chart, the bilateral bar chart, and the subdivided or component-part bar chart.

*Multiple bar charts.* Comparisons of two or three variables within a single bar chart are made possible by the use of multiple bars distinguished by cross-hatching, shading, or color. That is, the bar representing each of the variables being compared are distinguished by these mechanical means, as illustrated in Figure 15–4. The key to the variables is given in a legend, which may be placed within the illustration or below it, depending on where space is available. Generally, it is confusing and therefore inadvisable to make multiple comparisons of this type when more than three variables are involved.

*Bilateral bar charts.* When it is necessary to show plus or minus

**FIGURE 15–4**

Multiple bar chart

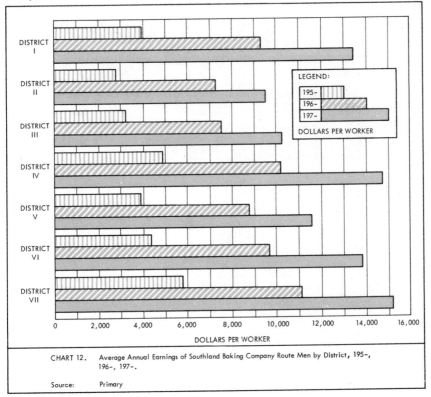

CHART 12.    Average Annual Earnings of Southland Baking Company Route Men by District, 195–, 196–, 197–.

Source:    Primary

deviations, you may use bilateral bar charts. The bars of these charts begin at a central point of reference and may go either up or down, as illustrated in Figure 15–5. Bar titles may be written either within, above, or below the bars, depending on which placement best fits the illustration. Bilateral bar charts are especially good for showing percentage change, but you may use them for any series in which minus quantities are present.

*Subdivided bar charts.* If it is desirable for you to show the composition of magnitudes being compared, you may use subdivided bar charts. In this form of chart, cross-hatchings, shadings, or colors are first assigned to each of the parts to be shown; then the bars are marked off into their component parts, as Figure 15–6 illustrates. As in all cases where cross-hatching or color is used, a legend is employed to guide the reader.

A form of the subdivided bar chart frequently is used to compare the composition of variables by percentages. This chart differs from the typi-

**FIGURE 15–5**

Bilateral bar chart

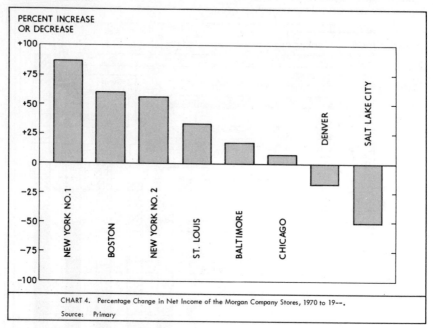

CHART 4.    Percentage Change in Net Income of the Morgan Company Stores, 1970 to 19--.

Source:    Primary

cal bar chart principally in that the bar lengths are meaningless in the comparisons. All the bars are of equal length, and only the component parts of the bars vary. As depicted in Figure 15–7, the component parts may be labeled, but they may also be explained in a legend.

## Pie-chart construction

Also of primary importance in comparing the percentage composition of variables is the pie chart (Figure 15–8). As the name implies, the pie chart illustrates the magnitude being studied as a pie, and the component parts of this whole appear as slices of this pie. The slices may be individually labeled, or cross-hatching or coloring with an explanatory legend may be used. As it is difficult to judge the value of each slice with the naked eye, it is advisable to include the units of value within each slice. A good rule to follow is to begin slicing the pie at the 12 o'clock position and to move around clockwise. It is usually best to show the slices in descending order of magnitude.

**FIGURE 15–6**

Illustration of a subdivided bar chart

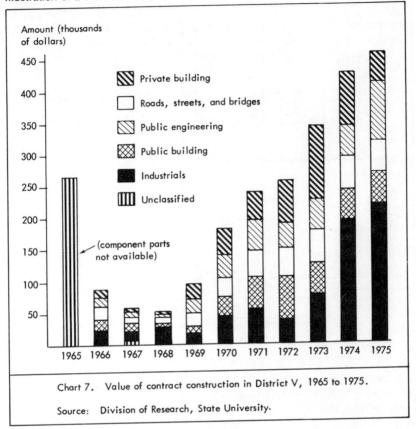

Chart 7.   Value of contract construction in District V, 1965 to 1975.

Source:   Division of Research, State University.

You should never use pie diagrams to show comparisons of two or more wholes by means of varying the areas of wholes. Such comparisons are almost meaningless. The human eye is totally inadequate to judge the relative areas of most geometric shapes.

## Arrangement of the line chart

Line charts are best used to show the movements or changes of a continuous series of data over time, such as changes in prices, weekly sales totals, and periodic employment data. You may plot them on an

**FIGURE 15–7**

Illustration of a subdivided bar chart

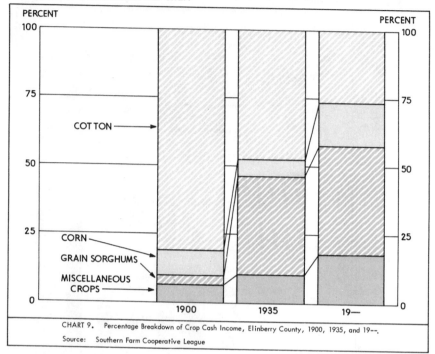

CHART 9.   Percentage Breakdown of Crop Cash Income, Elinberry County, 1900, 1935, and 19--.

Source:   Southern Farm Cooperative League

arithmetic, semilogarithmic, or logarithmic grid; but since the arithmetic plot is most common to business reports, it is described here.

In constructing a line chart, you should plot the item to be illustrated as a continuous line on a grid. On the grid, you should plot time on the horizontal axis ($X$-axis). You should plot the values of the series on the vertical axis ($Y$-axis). You should mark clearly the scale values and time periods on the axis lines, as shown in Figure 15–9.

You may also compare two or more series on the same grid on a line chart (Figure 15–10). In such a comparison, you should clearly distinguish the lines by color or form (dots, dashes, dots and dashes, and the like). You should clearly label them by a legend somewhere in the chart. But the number of series that you may compare on a single grid is limited. As a practical rule, four or five series on a single grid should be a maximum.

It is possible, also, to show component parts of a series by use of a line chart—sometimes called a belt chart. Such an illustration, however, is limited to one series to a chart. You should construct this type of chart, as shown in Figure 15–11, with a top line representing the total of the series.

**FIGURE 15–8**

Illustration of a pie chart

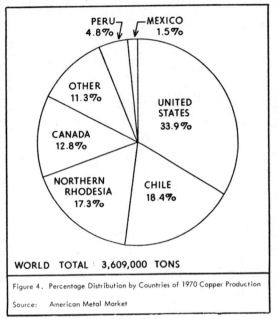

PERU
4.8%

MEXICO
1.5%

OTHER
11.3%

UNITED
STATES
33.9%

CANADA
12.8%

NORTHERN
RHODESIA
17.3%

CHILE
18.4%

WORLD TOTAL : 3,609,000 TONS

Figure 4. Percentage Distribution by Countries of 1970 Copper Production

Source:     American Metal Market

**FIGURE 15–9**

Example of a line chart with one series

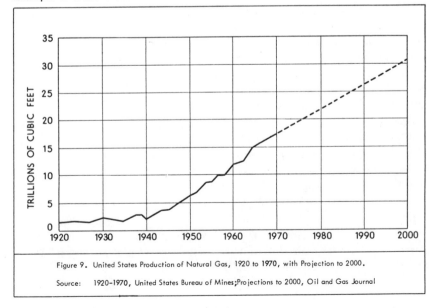

Figure 9. United States Production of Natural Gas, 1920 to 1970, with Projection to 2000.

Source:     1920-1970, United States Bureau of Mines;Projections to 2000, Oil and Gas Journal

**FIGURE 15–10**

Illustration of a line chart comparing more than one series

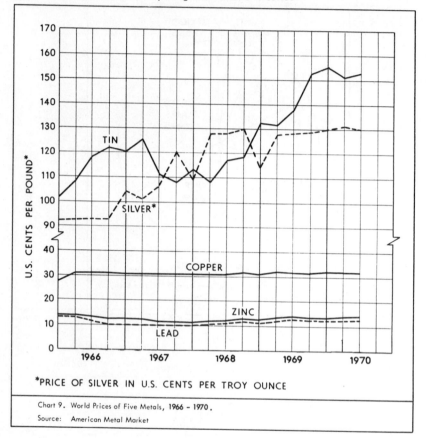

*PRICE OF SILVER IN U.S. CENTS PER TROY OUNCE

Chart 9. World Prices of Five Metals, 1966 – 1970.

Source:   American Metal Market

Then, starting from the base, you should cumulate the component parts, beginning with the largest and ending with the smallest. You may use cross-hatching or coloring to distinguish the parts. The differences between the cumulative totals show the values of the last component parts brought into the cumulation.

Even though the line graph is one of the simplest charts to construct, you should be aware of three common pitfalls. First of these is the common violation of the rule of the zero origin. The Y-scale (vertical axis) must begin at zero, even though the points to be plotted are relatively high in value. If most of the points to be plotted are relatively high in value, the comparison may be facilitated by breaking the scale some-

**FIGURE 15–11**

Illustration of a component-part line chart

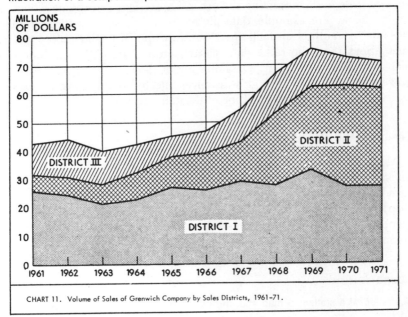

CHART 11. Volume of Sales of Grenwich Company by Sales Districts, 1961–71.

where between zero and the level of the lowest plotted value. Of the numerous means of showing scale breaks, these two techniques are recommended:

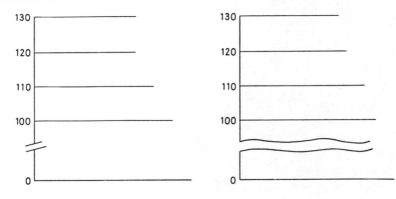

Second, equal magnitudes on both X- and Y-scales should be represented on the grid by equal distances. Any deviation from this rule would distort the illustration, thereby deceiving the reader.

A third common violation of good line-chart construction concerns the determination of proportions on the grid. It is easy to see that by expanding one scale and contracting the other, impressions of extreme deviation can be made. For example, data plotted on a line chart with time intervals one sixteenth of an inch apart certainly appear to show more violent fluctuations than the same data plotted on a chart with time intervals plotted a half inch apart. Only the application of common sense can prevent this violation. The grid distances selected simply must be such as will tend to make the presentation of the data realistic.

## Design of the statistical map

Maps may also be used to help communicate quantitative information. They are primarily useful when quantitative information is to be compared by geographic areas. On such maps the geographic areas are clearly outlined, and the differences between areas are shown by some graphic technique. Of the numerous techniques that may be used, four are most common.

**FIGURE 15–12**

Illustration of a statistical map showing quantitative differences of areas by cross-hatching

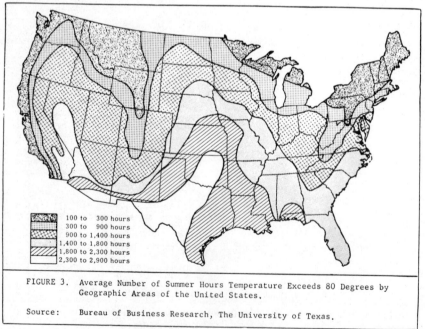

100 to    300 hours
300 to    900 hours
900 to 1,400 hours
1,400 to 1,800 hours
1,800 to 2,300 hours
2,300 to 2,900 hours

FIGURE 3.    Average Number of Summer Hours Temperature Exceeds 80 Degrees by Geographic Areas of the United States.

Source:    Bureau of Business Research, The University of Texas.

1. Possibly the most popular technique is that showing quantitative differences of areas by color, shading, or cross-hatching (Figure 15–12). Such maps, of course, must have a legend to explain the quantitative meanings of the various colors, cross-hatchings, and so forth.
2. Some form of chart may be placed within each geographic area to depict the quantities representative of that area, as illustrated in Figure 15–13. Bar charts and pie charts are commonly used in such illustrations.
3. Placing the quantities in numerical form within each geographic area, as shown in Figure 15–14, is another widely used technique.
4. Dots, each representing a definite quantity (Figure 15–15), may be placed within the geographic areas in proportion to the quantities to be illustrated for each area.

## Construction of the pictogram

A pictogram is a bar chart which uses pertinent pictures rather than bars to put over the information. For example, a company seeking to show graphically its profits from sales could use a simple bar chart for the purpose. Or the firm could use instead of bars a line of coins equal in length to the bars. Coins might be selected because they depict the

**FIGURE 15–13**

Statistical map showing comparisons by charts within geographic areas

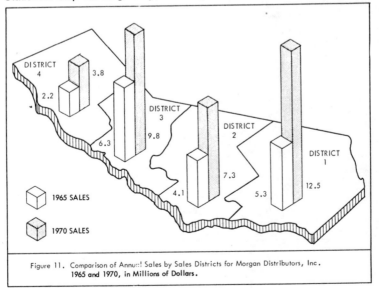

Figure 11. Comparison of Annual Sales by Sales Districts for Morgan Distributors, Inc.
1965 and 1970, in Millions of Dollars.

## FIGURE 15-14

Statistical map showing quantitative differences by means of numbers placed within geographic areas

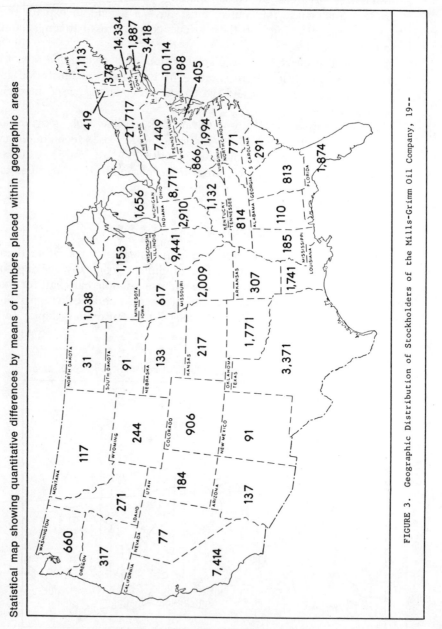

FIGURE 3. Geographic Distribution of Stockholders of the Mills-Grimm Oil Company, 19--

**FIGURE 15–15**

Illustrations of a statistical map using dots to show quantitative differences by geographic areas

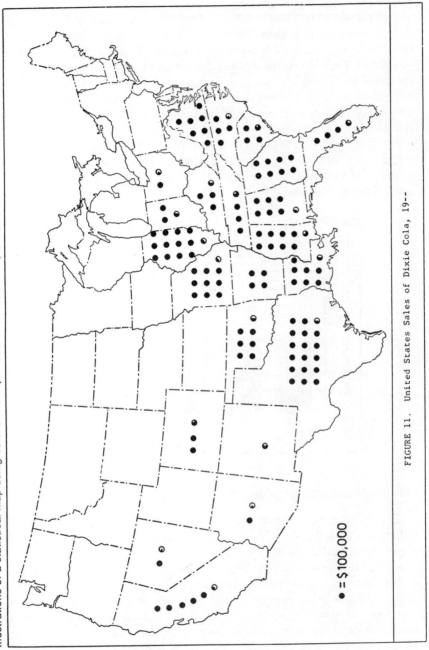

● = $100,000

FIGURE 11.  United States Sales of Dixie Cola, 19––

information to be illustrated. This resulting graphic form, as illustrated in Figure 15–16 is the pictogram.

In general, when constructing a pictogram, you should follow the procedure you used in constructing bar charts. In addition, you should follow two special rules. First you must make all of the picture units of equal size. That is, you must make the comparisons wholly on the basis of the number of illustrations used and never by varying the areas of the individual pictures. The reason for this rule is obvious. The human eye is grossly inadequate in comparing areas of geometric designs. Second, you should select pictures or symbols which appropriately depict the quantity to be illustrated. A comparison of the navies of the world, for example, might use miniature ship drawings. Cotton production might be shown by bales of cotton. Obviously, the drawings used must be immediately interpreted by the reader.

**FIGURE  15–16**

Illustration of the pictogram

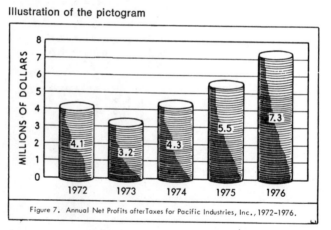

Figure 7.   Annual Net Profits afterTaxes for Pacific Industries, Inc., 1972–1976.

## Miscellaneous graphic aids

The graphic aids discussed thus far are those most commonly used. Others are sometimes helpful in assisting in the task of communicating. Photographs and drawings may sometimes serve a useful communication purpose. Diagrams, too (see Figure 15–17), may help to make simple a complicated explanation or description, particularly when technological procedures are being communicated. Then there are many almost nameless types of graphic presentation—most of which are combinations of two or more of the more common techniques. Since anything in the way of graphic design is acceptable as long as it helps to communicate the true story, the possibilities of graphic-aid design are almost unlimited.

**FIGURE 15–17**

Example of the use of a diagram

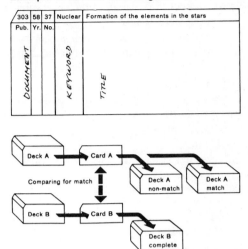

**Lookup with the IBM Collator**

In this system, reference cards are automatically segregated during a lookup operation. Then a bibliography may be listed directly from the cards selected.

For each keyword, there is a deck of IBM cards—one card per document indexed under that word.

When the collator finds a "match," only the card from Deck A is segregated. After the first two decks are compared, the segregated "match" cards go back into the Deck A feed and are compared with Deck C. This process continues until all decks are compared.

Source: International Business Machine Corporation, *Information Retrieval,* 1961.

## QUESTIONS AND PROBLEMS

1.  For the past 20 years, Professor Kupenheimer has required that his students include five graphic aids in the long, formal report he requires them to prepare. Evaluate this requirement.

2.  Because it is easier to do, a report writer prepared all of his graphic aids on separate pages. Each one took up the full page. Some of these graphic aids were extremely complex; some were very simple. Comment on this policy.

3.  "I have placed every chart near the place I write about it. The reader can see it without any *additional* help from me. It just doesn't make sense to direct his attention to them with words." Evaluate this comment.

4. A report has five maps, four tables, one chart, one diagram, and one photograph. How would you number these graphic aids?

5. How would you number this composition of graphic aids in a report: seven tables, six charts, nine maps?

6. Construct a complete, concise title for a bar chart which shows annual attendance at home football games at your school from 1960 to the present.

7. The table prepared in Question 6 requires an explanation for the years 1970 to the present. In these years one extra home game was played. Explain how you would do this.

8. For each of the areas of information described below, which form of graphic aid would you use? Explain your decision.

   *a.* Record of annual sales for the Kenyon Company for the past 20 years.

   *b.* Comparison of Kenyon Company sales, by product, for this year and last year.

   *c.* Monthly production in units for the automobile industry.

   *d.* Breakdown of how the average middle-income family in your state disposes of its income dollar.

   *e.* Comparison of how middle-income families spend their income dollar with similar expenditures of low-income families.

   *f.* A comparison of sales for the past two years for each of the B&B Company's 14 sales districts. The districts cover all 50 states and Puerto Rico.

   *g.* National production of automobiles from 1930 to the present, broken down by the manufacturer.

9. Discuss the logic of showing scale breaks in a chart.

10. Discuss the dangers of using illogical proportions in constructing a grid for a chart.

11. Discuss the techniques that may be used to show quantitative differences by area on a statistical map.

12. Select some data that are ideally suited for presentation in a pictogram. Explain why a pictogram is good for this case.

13. Discuss the dangers of using a pictogram.

14. For each of the following sets of facts (*a*) determine the graphic aid (or aids) that would be best, (*b*) defend your choice, and (*c*) construct the graphic aid.

   (1) Average (mean) amount of life insurance owned by Fidelity Life Insurance Company policyholders. Classification is by annual income.

| Income | Average life insurance |
|--------|------------------------|
| Under $5,000 . . . . . . . . . . . | $ 5,245 |
| $ 5,000–9,999 . . . . . . . . . . | 14,460 |
| 10,000–14,999. . . . . . . . . . | 26,680 |
| 15,000–19,999. . . . . . . . . . | 39,875 |
| 20,000–24,999. . . . . . . . . . | 51,440 |
| 25,000 and over . . . . . . . . . | 76,390 |

(2) Profits and losses for D and H Food Stores, by store, 1971–75, in dollars.

| | Store | | | |
|------|-----------|-------|------------|-------|
| Year | Able City | Baker | Charleston | Total |
| 1971 . . . . . . . . | 13,421 | 3,241 | 9,766 | 26,428 |
| 1972 . . . . . . . . | 12,911 | −1,173 | 11,847 | 23,585 |
| 1973 . . . . . . . . | 13,843 | −2,241 | 11,606 | 23,208 |
| 1974 . . . . . . . . | 12,673 | 2,865 | 13,551 | 29,089 |
| 1975 . . . . . . . . | 13,008 | 7,145 | 15,482 | 35,635 |

(3) Share of real estate tax payments by ward for Bigg City, 1965 and 1975, in thousands of dollars.

| | 1965 | 1975 |
|--------|------|------|
| Ward 1 . . . . . . . . . . . . . . . | 17.1 | 21.3 |
| Ward 2 . . . . . . . . . . . . . . . | 10.2 | 31.8 |
| Ward 3 . . . . . . . . . . . . . . . | 19.5 | 21.1 |
| Ward 4 . . . . . . . . . . . . . . . | 7.8 | 18.2 |
| City total . . . . . . . . . . | 54.6 | 92.4 |

(4) Percentage change in sales by salesman, 1972–73, District IV, Abbott, Inc.

| Salesman | Percentage change | Salesman | Percentage change |
|----------|-------------------|----------|-------------------|
| John Abraham | + 7.3 | Wilson Platt | + 7.4 |
| Wilson Calmes | + 2.1 | Carry Ruiz | +11.5 |
| Todd Musso | − 7.5 | David Schlimmer | − 4.8 |
| Clifton Nevers | +41.6 | Phil Dirks | − 3.6 |

(5)    Net income from operations of seven largest U.S. banks, with percentage of profit derived from foreign operations, 1974–1975.

| Bank | 1975 Operations net (millions) | Foreign (percent) | 1974 Operations net (millions) | Foreign (percent) |
|------|------|------|------|------|
| Bank America . . . . . . . . . . . . | $178.4 | 25 | $166.5 | 20 |
| 1st Nat'l City . . . . . . . . . . . . | 168.2 | 42 | 145.1 | 38 |
| Chase Manhattan . . . . . . . . . . | 147.7 | 20 | 139.3 | 15 |
| J. P. Morgan . . . . . . . . . . . . . | 109.1 | 30 | 102.0 | 25 |
| Mfgrs. Hanover . . . . . . . . . . . | 77.9 | 28 | 85.2 | 24 |
| Chemical . . . . . . . . . . . . . . | 72.5 | 15 | 77.4 | 10 |

# Report problems

## SHORT PROBLEMS (MEMORANDUM AND LETTER REPORTS)

1. *Should the Baker Manufacturing Company begin the practice of gift-giving?* The management of the Baker Manufacturing Company is considering giving presents to its industrial customers, just as many of its competitors do. In fact, corporate gift-giving has become so commonplace in the industry that Baker officials have begun to question the wisdom of continuing to avoid this practice. They have asked you, an administrative assistant to the president, to do some research on the matter. As you know, the practice of corporate gift-giving consists of giving presents to certain officials of the organizations with which a firm does business. Usually, the gifts have nominal value, consisting of such goods as wines, liquors, golf balls, cheeses, fruits, and leather goods. They are intended as goodwill gestures—as expressions of appreciation for business. Although some officials (including some at Baker) look on the practice as a mild form of bribery, most consider it to be ethical as long as the gift values are kept low and the gifts are uniformly given.

In getting information to guide you in making your recommendation, you used the facilities of your research staff to conduct a small survey of other companies in the field. Using your industry's trade directory, you mailed questionnaires to 484 companies. You received an even 100 returns. Your tabulations to the various questions on the questionnaire appear at the end of the assignment.

Your report will present your survey findings with whatever analyses and applications to your problem you feel are appropriate. Even though you have all these survey results, you will arrive at your recommendation somewhat subjectively. The facts are not all that clear. Regardless of how you recommend, your report will present all the survey statistics for whatever possible future use they may have.

Because the problem is not an involved one, you will use your company's short-form report (including only title page and text). You will write the text in direct order, beginning with your recommendation and immediately supporting it with the major evidence.

*Answers to survey questions in percentages*

1.  Has your company ever given business gifts?
    yes  72%      no  38%
2.  Does business gift-giving help build your business?
    yes  53%      no  47%
3.  Did you send more gifts this year than last year?
    more  52%      fewer  48%
4.  How much did they cost?
    a.  under $5          38%
    b.  $5–$9.99          33%
    c.  $10–$14.99        17%
    d.  $15–$19.99        5%
    e.  $20–$25           6%
    f.  more              1%
5.  Did everyone receive the same gift or a different gift?
    same  58%      different  42%
6.  Who received the business gifts?
    a.  customers/clients    58%
    b.  suppliers            22%
    c.  other               20%
7.  Why do you give business gifts?
    a.  goodwill             46%
    b.  appreciation         54%
8.  Do you give business gifts on the same occasions every year?
    yes  78%      no  22%
9.  If yes, on what occasions?
    a.  Christmas            84%
    b.  birthday            15%
    c.  wedding            0
    d.  other              11%
10. How does your company distribute business gifts?
    a.  mail                49%
    b.  in person           45%
    c.  messenger           6%
11. What location are they sent to?
    home  45%      office  55%
12. Have you ever received a business gift?
    yes  88%      no  12%

**2.** *Pointing out customer irritation to Consolidated Restaurants.* Assume the role of restaurant consultant and take on the problems of your newest client, Consolidated Restaurants, Inc. This major restaurant organization owns and operates two nationwide chains. One, the Big Dollar chain, caters to low-income and middle-income families with economy-priced meals. The other, The Steak House, aims at a slightly higher clientele, mainly middle-income and upper-middle-income families. At the moment, Consolidated's directors are unhappy about both of their organizations. Sales have been dropping and are well below national averages. That is why you have been called in.

With your usual thoroughness, you have made a careful study of kitchen operations, menu designs, purchasing, and such. These areas are a major part of your investigation and will comprise the bulk of the final report you will write for Consolidated Restaurants.

In addition, however, you have been working on the matter of customer satisfaction. In fact, you and your research staff have conducted a

Question: Which three of the things on this list irritate you most when eating out in a restaurant?

| | | Income | | | | |
|---|---|---|---|---|---|---|
| | Entire sample | $10,000 and over | $7,000– $9,999 | $5,000– $6,999 | $3,000– $4,999 | $3,000– and under |
| *Customer's complaints* | % | % | % | % | % | % |
| Can't get attention of waiter or waitress. . . . . . . . . . . | 46 | 55 | 50 | 52 | 36 | 36 |
| Paying extra for second cup of coffee. . . . . . . . . . . . | 42 | 46 | 47 | 43 | 40 | 30 |
| Menu run outs early in meal period . . . . . . . . . . | 21 | 26 | 24 | 23 | 21 | 12 |
| Paying extra for substitutions . . . . . . . . . . . . . | 20 | 20 | 21 | 22 | 19 | 18 |
| Menu hard to read . . . . . . . . | 19 | 14 | 17 | 20 | 25 | 20 |
| Paying extra for toasted bread in a sandwich. . . . . . | 18 | 18 | 17 | 16 | 18 | 20 |
| Having separate tabs put on one check . . . . . . . . . . . | 11 | 13 | 11 | 13 | 10 | 9 |
| Paying extra for Roquefort cheese salad dressing . . . . . | 9 | 13 | 10 | 8 | 9 | 4 |
| Being given a small plate to use at a buffet table . . . . . . | 8 | 8 | 7 | 7 | 10 | 7 |
| Being given a small salad bowl . . . . . . . . . . . . . . | 5 | 8 | 5 | 5 | 4 | 4 |
| Not especially irritated by any of them . . . . . . . . . . | 20 | 18 | 21 | 22 | 16 | 20 |
| Don't know . . . . . . . . . . . | 13 | 7 | 8 | 10 | 20 | 26 |
| Totals* . . . . . . . . . . . | 232 | 246 | 238 | 241 | 228 | 206 |
| Number of interviews. . . . . . | 1681 | 363 | 399 | 345 | 291 | 251 |

(Income Undesignated—32)

*Totals exceed 100% because of multiple responses.

survey of 1,681 people who eat in restaurants at least once a month in an effort to learn what, if anything, they do not like about the service they get. Your findings here will also be a part of your final report. But because this information can be helpful to Consolidated's management right away, you decide to present it now in short-report form. Your report will cover the survey findings, of course, but also it will point out any recommendations for change that may be apparent. The data for your presentation are summarized in the table on page 393.

**3.** *Recommending job termination for Mr. Kennedy.* You are the office manager for the Houghton and Smith Wholesale Grocery Company, and today you must write a personnel action report on one of your subordinates. It is a chore you had hoped not to do, but the actions of Christopher A. Kennedy leave no other choice.

Six months ago, Mr. Kennedy began work as an order clerk, a position for which he was qualified by seven years of experience with the Midville Wholesale Grocery Company. Although he was given a good recommendation from a Midville executive, rumors you have heard recently indicate that it was a courtesy recommendation. The rumors indicate that during the last two years at Midville Kennedy developed an alcoholism problem and had to be dismissed. Apparently, the Midville executive who wrote the recommendation felt that the man deserved another chance—but with another company.

Anyway, you now have the problem. For the first two months, Kennedy appeared to be trying hard to do a good job. He did not miss a single day of work. Although he made a few errors, some of them costly for the company, you attributed them to his newness on the job. In the third month, however, he made a sharp turn for the worse. In this month, he missed work four days, each one explained by a claim of illness. He was late for work six times, once by over two hours. His errors increased, too, although you failed to keep a record of them.

In the third month, you sensed a problem, so you began to keep a log on his attendance and work record. Absences for these three months were three, three, and five. His times tardy were six, two, and five. Errors in his work have been numerous and have affected over 6 percent of the orders he has handled. (You expect something near zero.) You can attribute at least three lost accounts to his errors.

He is a friendly fellow who tries hard to do his job. But it is apparent that he is drinking heavily. In the three conferences you have had with him, he admitted he had a drinking problem, and each time he promised to quit. But you have not noticed any change, except for the worse. In fact, after your last conference with him he reported for work the following morning in a drunken condition and had to be sent home.

As today ends the six-month probationary period all company employees go through before being given a permanent appointment, you must make your recommendation on Mr. Kennedy. You must recommend that he be dismissed, and you will support the recommendation with adequate facts. (You may use your imagination to supply additional details so long as they do not change the general image set in the problem description.) Write your report in memorandum form. Use the direct order.

**4. *Reporting an errant subordinate for good reason.*** As much as you dislike doing such things, today you must report Roger A. Tucker for improper conduct and neglect of duty.

Mr. Tucker joined your sales force about eight months ago after over 18 years of sales experience with your rival company, Temple Brothers, Inc. At first, Tucker did a reasonably good job for you, making his quotas each of the first five months. Since that time, however, sales have dropped. In fact, last month he sold only 44 percent of quota, as compared with 68 percent the month earlier and 76 percent the preceding month.

About six weeks ago, you learned from an old customer in Tucker's territory that this customer had apparently been dropped from Tucker's route without explanation. Further investigation revealed that at least five other customers were also dropped, apparently without cause.

You called in Tucker, talked with him, and learned that marital trouble was to blame. Tucker admitted not making many of his regular calls, and promised to do better, saying his troubles were behind him.

In following weeks, he showed no improvement. In fact, his work deteriorated more. Three additional talks with the man produced only promises for improvement, but improvement never occurred. His sales continued to drop, and you continued to hear about lost and dissatisfied customers.

You really do not know just how many customers have been lost or the exact extent of the damage done. But you know that something has to be done soon. So you will recommend that Tucker be relieved of his sales duties. As basically he is a capable man with problems, you will recommend that the company keep him in some other capacity—if he is willing.

Using standard memorandum form, write a report, stating your recommendation and backing it up with supportable reasoning. Use your imagination to supply details not given.

**5. *Choosing a retail outlet for Tachert suits.*** Assume the position of administrative assistant to Gregory A. Huddleston, sales manager for A. R. Tachert, Inc., manufacturers of men's quality suits. You have been sent to Hill City to investigate two retail outlets as possible dealerships for Tachert suits. Each of the two stores has indicated an interest in handling your line, but one to a town the size of Hill City is Tachert's policy.

For the past three days, you have been in Hill City, getting all the pertinent information on the two stores. As you analyzed your findings, you kept in mind Tachert's reputation as a prestige product. As Tachert suits are somewhat conservatively styled and in the higher price range, they appeal primarily to the successful professional man.

Quality customers, however, are not your only consideration in selecting an outlet. You want one that can bring about quantity sales. And you want one that gives the kind of service that is consistent with Tachert quality. Also, you will need to consider such factors as store location, growth potential, and the physical facilities.

Now you are ready to begin your analysis of the facts you have assembled (see summary below). You will present your report to Mr. Huddleston in the company's standard memorandum report form.

### Compton Clothiers

Located on Main Street in the heart of the business district. New men's store (one year old) in modern, spacious (80 × 120 feet sales area) building. Bright, well-lighted interior, neatly arranged stock. Owned by Henry T. Compton, a dynamic and young businessman who makes use of aggressive marketing technique. Store has 4 salesmen, 3 under 30 and 1 about 40. All use aggressive sales approaches. Store carries wide range of clothing from medium to high priced and for young and old. Handles four brands of men's suits: R. E. Allen (middle priced), Wall Street (middle priced), J. H. Conrad (upper middle priced), and I. A. Chapman (high priced). Advertises heavily—about one and one-half pages per week. Annual sales about $650,000.

### Hill City Men's Store

Oldest store in town (1887) and in original building located one block off main business street. Building is in excellent repair and store is attractive and elegant, although obviously old. Store area is small (35 × 60 feet). Owner is Theodore E. Krutcher, about 60 and a grandson of the founder. Mr. Krutcher is an easy-going, gregarious type who greets many of his customers by name. Two salesmen employed, ages over 50. Use soft-sell approach. Stresses service. Carries conservative upper middle (J. H. Conrad, Baxter Brothers) and high priced (Ross and Baker, C. Kaperton) brands. Light advertiser (total of about one-half page a week). Annual sales of $300,000.

Analyze these facts and make your recommendation to Mr. Huddleston. Present your report to him in a direct-order memorandum report.

**6.** *Selecting a site for a National service station.* As a junior executive in charge of site selection for the National Oil Company, you must select one of three sites that have been recommended for a new service station in Springville. You have collected the following data on these prospective locations.

### Hill Avenue and 37th Street

Commercial area. Lot 150 × 100 feet. Corner location. Cost of $25,000. Traffic count per day (7 A.M. to 9 P.M.), 4,200 cars. Distance from nearest company station, 3.1 miles.

### 311 Delmont Street

Commercial area. Lot 200 × 100 feet. Noncorner location. Cost of $24,000. Traffic count per day, 9,000 cars. Distance from nearest company station, 3.9 miles.

### Avenue G at Independence Street

Commercial area. Lot 150 × 150. Corner location. Cost of $30,000. Traffic count per day, 6,500 cars. Distance from nearest company station, 2.1 miles.

All the sites have relatively the same amount of competition in the immediate area. Each has one competing station within a distance of five blocks. Your task is to evaluate these alternative sites and to recommend one. Present your recommendation and analysis in a memorandum report. Write it in the direct order.

7. *Selecting the best laundry service for Maxwell Cafeterias.* Assume the position of a management consultant hired by the Maxwell Cafeterias of St. Louis. One of the many problems you have been asked to solve for this company is how it should handle its linen and laundry. Specifically, should they own their own cloth equipment and have it laundered? Or should they rent this equipment?

According to information you have gathered, the Maxwell people will need about $2,500 worth of such equipment from the beginning, and its life expectancy is about 2 years. You can get a monthly laundry rate of $60, including pickup and delivery. Weekly costs of renting the comparable equipment needed are as follows.

| | | |
|---|---|---|
| 540 . . . . . . . . | 54" tablecloths | @ $ .12 each |
| 2,100 . . . . . . . | napkins | @ $1.75 per 100 |
| 175 . . . . . . . . | aprons | @ $ .15 each |
| 84 . . . . . . . . | dresses | @ $ .50 each |
| 35 . . . . . . . . | coats (waiters) | @ $ .45 each |
| 140 . . . . . . . . | dish towels | @ $ .03 each |

Your task is to prepare the alternative possibility and to write a recommendation for the Maxwell people. Do it in standard memorandum form, using direct style order of presentation.

8. *Recommending a store manager for Econo-Mart's new store.* Next month in Camp City, Econo-Mart, a regional chain of food stores, will open its newest outlet. It is now looking for someone to manage that store, and you, an interviewer in the organization's personnel department,

have completed screening applicants in the Camp City area. From the nine who applied, you have narrowed the field down to three. Now you must evaluate them and rank them for the job. You will write your recommendations in a conclusion-first order memorandum addressed to Conrad Carlisle, personnel manager.

A summary of the basic biographical data on the three is as follows.

|  | Philip S. Towne | Bill A. Sweet | Ralph T. Story |
|---|---|---|---|
| Personal details | Age 45, married, 6 children, good health. | Age 36, married, no children, service-connected disability but otherwise good health. | Age 28, single, good health. |
| Experience | 21 years with Ero Grocery Co., duties as stock clerk, cashier, assistant manager (2 years). 3 years as manager White's Drive-In Grocery. | 12 years U.S. Army, rank master sergeant, duties in food services and supply. 5 years with Dugan Grocery Co., duties as cashier, manager of produce department (3 years). | 3 years as route salesman for Matron Baking Co. 3 years with H & H Super Market, duties as stock clerk, cashier, and assistant manager (1 year). |
| Education | High school, 3 years State University, major in education. | High school, Teague Business College 6 months. | High school, 2 years State University (mainly night school), major in business administration. |
| Score on management potential test* | 78 | 81 | 89 |
| Major comments made by references | Hard-working, steady, and loyal. Honest beyond question. Well-liked by all who know him. Easygoing. | A hard worker. Friendly but has quick temper, honest. Drives subordinates hard. | Hard-working. Extremely ambitious. Occasionally has run-ins with other workers. Honest. Works subordinates hard. |

*Scores: grade of 60, passing; 75, average; 85 and above, outstanding.

**9.** *Recommending an office manager for Econo-Mart.* Using the same general instructions given in the problem above, evaluate and rank the following three applicants for the position of office manager for the home office of Econo-Mart Stores, Inc. For varying reasons, the organization has decided to hire from the outside rather than to promote from within.

|  | *Warren T. Childs* | *Tim T. Terrell* | *Adolph A. Raska* |
|---|---|---|---|
| Personal details | Age 42, single, good health. | Age 35, married, three children. | Age 32, divorced, one child. |
| Experience | 4 years with Case Brick Co. as office clerk. 9 years with Ross Wholesale Co. as order clerk (6 years), chief of shipping and orders department (3 years). 9 years as office manager, Hess Wholesale Grocery Co. | 3 years U.S. Army, rank sergeant, duties primarily in office administration. 11 years with Butler Bros. Food Stores as records Clerk (3 years), chief records section (5 years) and assistant office manager (3 years). | 4 years U.S. Army, rank first lieutenant, Adjutant General Corps, duties in office administration. 7 years with Crow Mfg. Co., duties of management trainee (1 year), personnel assistant (3 years), chief of records section (3 years). |
| Education | High school, 1 year Moss Business College. | High school, 3 years Eastern University, major in accounting. | High school, B.S. from Eastern University, major in marketing. |
| Scores on aptitude tests Office procedures | 76 | 81 | 89 |
| Management potential | 87 | 82 | 76 |
| Comments by references | A hard-working, self-made man. Handles subordinates well. Strong character. | Well-liked and easygoing. Dependable but not highly ambitious. | Not a strong personality, but intelligent. Works hard. Well-liked by those who know him but is not gregarious. |

**10.** *A progress report on Global's new sales district.* One month ago, you were transferred by Global Insurance, Hartford, Connecticut, to Boon City to expand Global's sales coverage to this area. It is time now to make a progress report to the home office. Frankly, you do not have much to show in the way of real sales results, but you have put in a lot of work, and you think you have made good progress. As you recall, Geoffrey Curtis, district manager and recipient of your report, assured you that Global did not expect profits right off—that moving into a new territory requires time and patience.

In preparing your report, you first make random notes of the various things you have done during the month. Garbled as they are, your notes look like this.

Rented three-office suite, Hall Building, $210 per month.

Hired secretary (Miss Cleo Struble) at $450 per month. Picked from 11 applicants. Appears to be highly efficient—good work so far.

Visited two local newspapers. Bought space to announce Global's entry to area—cost $212 and $180 for 4-column, 8-inch ads in *Daily Herald* and *Evening Star*, respectively. Got free publicity in business news sections of both papers. (You will attach clippings of ads and articles.)

Bought office furniture: 3 executive desks at $205 each; 3 swivel chairs at $45 each; 7 straight chairs at $26 each; 1 stenographic desk at $145; 1 typist's chair at $28; 1 manual typewriter at $178; office supplies (stationery, stamps, paper clips, etc.), $67; 5 metal 3-drawer file cabinets at $117 each; 2 coat-trees at $13 each; 3 bookshelves at $54 each.

Visited Chamber of Commerce. Got names of 17 business leaders likely to help in finding agents. Visited all 17. Got names of seven prospects. Interviewed all seven. Four not interested. One ruled out—short on personality. Two were interested.

*George Smathers:*  Took Global's aptitude test—made 97 (exceptional). Has 13 years' sales experience, but not in insurance. Sold business machines, securities, and industrial chemicals. Hired him. Have spent much time training him both in office and on sales calls. Man is eager—a born salesman. Good personality, high morals, intelligent. No sales yet, but several good prospects lined up. This man will go places.

*William A. Tucker:*  A proved insurance salesman, with nine years of experience. Now with Central Life, but is considering a change. Hasn't yet taken Global's aptitude test. Have discussed employment possibilities with him three times. Is definitely interested. Will continue discussion. Good chance of hiring him.

These are the major facts you have to report, although you may think of additional minor details as you write the report. You will use Global's conventional memorandum report form.

11. *Investigating a personnel problem in department 3–N.*  Today's assignment in your role as special assistant to George B. Dymkus, director of employment relations of Southwestern Aircraft, Inc., takes you to department 3–N. Your objective is to investigate charges brought to you by Karl Connerly, the union steward who represents the workers of this department. According to Connerly, union members in department 3–N have been discriminated against in the awarding of overtime work. Nonunion workers have been getting the lion's share of overtime.

On arriving at the department, you discuss the matter with Wilfred Knudson. Knudson's version of the story goes like this: Of the eight workers in the department, five are members of the union and three are not. The three nonunion workers have had more overtime than the others, but they deserve it. Knudson claims that he gives overtime on the basis of seniority and productivity—nothing else. This policy, he points out, is permitted in the contract with the union. If the nonunion workers got most of the overtime, Knudson says, it is because they have seniority and are better workers.

After talking to Knudson, you go to the files that contain the department's records. Here you find data that should prove or disprove Knudson's claim and, in fact, should point to the solution of the whole problem. After an hour or more of poring over these records of the past six months, your summary notes look like this.

| Employee and union status* | Hours of overtime work | Years employed | Productivity (average daily units performed) | Percent rejection (not meeting inspection) |
|---|---|---|---|---|
| George Graves (U) . . . . . . . . . | 0 | 14 | 30 | 0.08 |
| W. Wilson Davis (U). . . . . . . . . | 0 | 1 | 21 | 0.09 |
| Kermit Crowley (U) . . . . . . . . | 10 | 3 | 32 | 0.07 |
| Walter H. Quals (U). . . . . . . . . | 60 | 8 | 26 | 0.01 |
| Hugo Detresanti (U) . . . . . . . . | 60 | 7 | 30 | 0.03 |
| Ralph A. Andrews (NU) . . . . . . | 40 | 35 | 26 | 0.02 |
| Will O. Rundell (NU) . . . . . . . . | 70 | 17 | 35 | 0.03 |
| Thomas A. Baines (NU) . . . . . . | 90 | 12 | 43 | 0.03 |

* U, union; NU, nonunion.

Now your task is to analyze these data and to present your finding to Dymkus in the form of the standard memorandum report used by the company. In addition to analyzing the data, you will recommend a course of action on the problem.

**12. *Will contests bring profits to Food King?*** John H. Gromman, newly appointed advertising and promotion manager for Food King, Inc., has an idea to increase sales, and thereby increase profits, for the chain of 142 stores. He thinks that contests at each store, with an abundance of prizes, would more than pay off. Such contests, he concludes, have been tried by other stores, and they appeared to work.

George Clemmons, however, does not think very much of the plan; and George Clemmons happens to be Food King's president. So to prove or disprove the value of contests, Clemmons suggests that the company conduct an experiment. You, as director of research, get the assignment.

The first step is to devise a contest for the experiment. With Gromman's assistance, you settle on a contest involving a simple drawing for prizes. With each purchase of $10 or more, the customers receive entry blanks, which they endorse and deposit in a large box. Drawings are made weekly to determine the winners of such prizes as washing machines, radios, electric mixers, and toasters.

For your experiment, you select two comparable and homogeneous groups of five stores—one as the experimental group and the other as a control group. In one group of stores (group A) contests are held; none are held in the other stores (group B). After one month of contests, with weekly drawings and prizes galore, the contests are stopped. Because you believe the contests may have some long-run effect on sales, you decide to analyze operations for the following months. You later find three months to be adequate. Now you assemble the data in preparation for your analysis.

Although you considered using a variety of data (traffic flow, size and number of purchases, cost of the contests), you conclude that net profits tell the whole story in summary fashion. Here are the profit figures you assembled.

| Group | Store | Month before contests | Month of contests | Month after | Second month after | Third month after |
|-------|-------|-----------------------|-------------------|-------------|--------------------|-------------------|
| A | 1 | 32 | 29 | 39 | 34 | 32 |
|   | 2 | 31 | 27 | 38 | 33 | 30 |
|   | 3 | 30 | 27 | 33 | 31 | 31 |
|   | 4 | 33 | 25 | 37 | 34 | 33 |
|   | 5 | 30 | 28 | 38 | 31 | 29 |
| B | 6 | 29 | 30 | 31 | 30 | 32 |
|   | 7 | 30 | 32 | 31 | 30 | 30 |
|   | 8 | 31 | 31 | 30 | 30 | 32 |
|   | 9 | 33 | 34 | 33 | 32 | 32 |
|   | 10 | 30 | 31 | 31 | 30 | 30 |

Write up your analysis of these data, and then draw conclusions from your analysis. Write up your work in a form that is appropriate for this situation.

**13.** *A memorandum report on changing coffee consumption.* As director of marketing research, Morning Cheer Coffee Company, you have just returned from a national meeting of marketing research directors. At the meeting you picked up the results of a survey conducted by one of your counterparts for a soft-drink company. The information pertains to changing patterns of coffee consumption; and it is most significant, you think, to the top brass of Morning Cheer. It is information that could change the future of the organization. So important is it that you decide to send the information to your superiors.

All you have is a table (see Table 1) of figures. You will need to analyze, interpret, and arrange it for meaningful presentation. You decide to write it up in a memorandum report. Send it to Mrs. Clara Bacha, vice president in charge of marketing, with copies to other top officers.

**TABLE 1**

Coffee drinking by age group (cups per day)

| Group | 1962 | 1965 | 1966 | 1967 | 1968 | 1969 | Change 1962–69 |
|-------|------|------|------|------|------|------|----------------|
| 10–14. . . . . . | 0.18 | 0.12 | 0.13 | 0.19 | 0.15 | 0.09 | −50.0% |
| 15–19. . . . . . | 1.09 | 0.77 | 0.97 | 0.82 | 0.67 | 0.81 | −25.7 |
| 20–24. . . . . . | 2.99 | 2.42 | 2.25 | 2.22 | 2.24 | 2.04 | −31.8 |
| 25–29. . . . . . | 3.88 | 3.25 | 3.45 | 3.21 | 3.06 | 3.03 | −21.9 |
| 30–39. . . . . . | 4.50 | 4.01 | 4.21 | 3.99 | 4.06 | 3.89 | −13.6 |
| 40–49. . . . . . | 4.44 | 4.16 | 4.05 | 4.48 | 3.99 | 4.10 | − 7.7 |
| 50–59. . . . . . | 3.83 | 3.54 | 3.81 | 3.20 | 3.69 | 3.73 | − 2.6 |
| 60–69. . . . . . | 3.01 | 2.96 | 3.09 | 3.16 | 3.07 | 2.92 | − 3.0 |
| 70 plus . . . . . | 2.39 | 2.47 | 2.66 | 2.50 | 2.39 | 2.36 | − 1.3 |
| *All ages.* . . . . | *3.12* | *2.79* | *2.86* | *2.84* | *2.72* | *2.68* | *−14.1* |

\*Source: Pan American Coffee Bureau.

**14.** *Reporting on the outlook for energy for the National Oil Company.* As administrative assistant to Chris Kuzel, vice president in charge of production for the National Oil Company, you have just returned from a seminar on the outlook for energy in the United States. Held on the campus of Central University, this one-day seminar was attended by members of all major oil companies. You were the representative of National.

Now that you are back, you must prepare a report on the information you picked up for the benefit of those who did not attend. They are eager to know what you found out, for the subject is of major interest to people in the oil industry. For some time the industry has been concerned about the dwindling reserves and the ever-increasing consumer demands. In order to plan properly for the years ahead, industry leaders need to keep abreast of the best available information on this situation.

Looking over the notes you took, you find four tables (see Tables 1, 2, 3, and 4). These contain the highlights of what you heard; and your rough notes scribbled after each table help explain some of the table contents and add other bits of pertinent information. The tables were prepared by statisticians at Central's Bureau of Business Research. Data for 1960 to 1970 are actual. For the years 1975 to 1985, the information consists of projections. In general, the information presents a rather dismal outlook.

Because the report will be read by National's administrative hierarchy, you will construct it to fit this audience. Certainly you will want to include some graphic aids. And probably you will arrange the report in direct order, for the readers will want to get to the basic message right away.

**TABLE 1**

Demand for energy by consumer sector (1960–70 actual; 1975–85, estimated), millions of barrels per day (oil equivalent)

| Year | Industrial and other | Residential- commercial | Transportation | Total |
|------|------|------|------|------|
| 1960 . . . . . . . . | 9.2 | 7.6 | 4.3 | 21.1 |
| 1965 . . . . . . . . | 11.4 | 8.4 | 6.0 | 25.8 |
| 1970 . . . . . . . . | 14.4 | 10.7 | 7.5 | 32.6 |
| 1975 . . . . . . . . | 18.4 | 13.6 | 10.3 | 42.3 |
| 1980 . . . . . . . . | 23.6 | 16.6 | 12.4 | 52.6 |
| 1985 . . . . . . . . | 29.3 | 19.6 | 14.6 | 63.5 |

**TABLE 2.** Energy demand by fuel sources, millions of barrels per day (oil equivalent)

| Total | Oil | Synthetic oil & gas* | Gas | Coal | Hydro- power* | Nuclear power | Total |
|------|------|------|------|------|------|------|------|
| 1960 . . . | 9.2 | — | 5.9 | 4.7 | 1.3 | — | 21.1 |
| 1965 . . . | 10.6 | — | 8.1 | 5.3 | 1.8 | — | 25.8 |
| 1970 . . . | 13.8 | — | 10.9 | 5.7 | 2.2 | — | 32.6 |
| 1975 . . . | 19.2 | — | 12.3 | 7.1 | 2.4 | 1.3 | 42.3 |
| 1980 . . . | 24.4 | — | 11.9 | 8.8 | 2.4 | 5.1 | 52.6 |
| 1985 . . . | 26.7 | 2.1 | 11.6 | 12.5 | 2.4 | 8.2 | 63.5 |

*Predicted future development

## Notes scribbled for Table 1:

1. Energy demand to grow at annual rate of 4.3 percent over next 15 years.
2. Demand will nearly double between 1970 and 1985.
3. Transportation should maintain its share—23–24 percent.
4. Fastest-growing sector is industrial—will be 47 percent of total by 1985.

## Notes scribbled for Table 2:

1. Full development of all sources required if 1985 demands are to be met.
2. Nuclear energy to grow most—11 percent by 1985.
3. Hydropower growth is limited by availability of dam sites.
4. Coal's share will grow to 20 percent by 1985. Growth contingent on finding way to remove sulfur from flue gas and mining more low-sulfur western coal reserves.
5. Natural gas limited in supply—can't exceed 21 percent of total for this reason. A drop from 33 percent in 1970.
6. Great increase in demand for oil from 1970 to 1985, but percentage of whole actually will drop.
7. Synthetic oil and gas manufactured from coal and oil shale will begin to come into the picture around 1980—assumes solving of certain technical and economic problems by then.

**TABLE 3.** U.S. gas supply, in trillions of cubic feet per year, 1960–85

| | Year | | | | | |
|---|---|---|---|---|---|---|
| | *1960* | *1965* | *1970* | *1975* | *1980* | *1985* |
| Domestic production (known reserve) . . . . | 13.2 | 16.0 | 21.8 | 16.7 | 10.2 | 7.8 |
| Domestic production (future reserve) . . . . . | — | — | — | 4.7 | 9.1 | 12.4 |
| Canadian imports . . . . . | 0.9 | 1.2 | 1.6 | 1.8 | 2.1 | 3.0 |
| Liquified natural gas imports . . . . . . . . | — | — | — | 0.4 | 1.0 | 2.0 |
| Synthetics . . . . . . . . . | — | — | — | 0.4 | 1.1 | 2.0 |
| Demand . . . . . . . | 14.1 | 17.2 | 23.4 | 27.6 | 34.0 | 40.0 |

**TABLE 4.** U.S. petroleum supply and demand, millions of barrels per day, 1960–85

| | Year | | | | | |
|---|---|---|---|---|---|---|
| | *1960* | *1965* | *1970* | *1975* | *1980* | *1985* |
| Domestic production (known reserves) . . . . . . | 8.0 | 8.9 | 11.6 | 9.1 | 6.3 | 5.5 |
| Domestic production (future reserves) . . . . . . | — | — | — | 2.5 | 4.5 | 5.0 |
| Imports (Western Hemisphere) . . . | 1.3 | 2.3 | 2.4 | 4.0 | 4.5 | 4.5 |
| Imports (Eastern Hemisphere) . . . | 0.7 | 1.1 | 1.3 | 4.5 | 10.0 | 13.0 |
| Demand . . . . . . . . . . | 10.0 | 12.3 | 15.8 | 20.1 | 25.6 | 28.0 |

Notes scribbled for Table 3:

1. Demand for natural gas has increased about 6 percent per year in past.
2. Future demand to exceed supply greatly.
3. Decline in domestic production includes production from Prudhoe Bay field on North Slope of Alaska.
4. Imports of liquefied natural gas and manufacture of synthetic gas just beginning—will grow.
5. Total will not meet demand (see Table 3).

Notes scribbled for Table 4:

1. Domestic production peak in early 1970s—then gradual decline.
2. Production from currently known reserves to decline from 78 percent of total in 1970 to 21 percent in 1985.
3. Production from Prudhoe Bay field in Alaska included in figures from 1975 on.
4. Domestic production to satisfy about 38 percent of demand in 1985.
5. Offshore production could increase as a result of presidential directive accelerating lease sales.

6. Western Hemisphere sources could improve through better economic incentives and by resolving problems holding up exploration in frontier areas such as Santa Barbara Channel and Alaska.

**15.** *An inspection report on cleanliness of a service station.*  Assume that you are a management trainee for —————— Oil Company. You are assigned to work with Edmund E. Clore, director of customer services.

Clore's job is mainly that of trying to get the managers of the company's service stations to be more customer-minded. Especially has he been working to get them to keep up the appearance of their stations. In fact, for the last month he has been conducting a "clean station" campaign.

So far, the campaign has had good results. Customer opinion reports (forms placed in rest rooms to be filled out and mailed in by customers) have been most complimentary on this point. But as might be expected, a few negative reports have come in. Mr. Clore assigns you the task of checking them out.

Specifically, your task is to go to each station, posing as a customer. While there you will inspect the whole operation for its neatness and cleanliness. Then you will write a memorandum report on each station summarizing your findings. (For class purposes, select one station in your area and make the inspection. Prepare the report that summarizes your observations.)

**16.** *Reporting on a conference to Durkee-Schwest administration.*  As a junior executive on the staff of the Durkee-Schwest Advertising Agency, you were sent as the firm's representative to a special conference sponsored by the National Association of Advertising Agencies. Theme of the conference was "Should advertising agencies advertise themselves?" Now that you are back, you must inform your superiors about the conference highlights.

The conference discussions were highlighted by the presentation of a survey of advertising agencies conducted by the association. In fact, the survey was the central theme of the conference, for most of the discussions centered around its findings. Thus, you conclude that your report also can build around the survey.

Because Durkee-Schwest administrators typically communicate somewhat informally and directly, you decide that a memorandum report is in order. And you plan to write it in personal style. You will address it to Collis Y. Durkee, president, with copies to all top administrators of the agency. (For class purposes, assume whatever facts you may need about the conference, the agency, etc.) The survey findings which will form the heart of the report are as follows:

Percent of agencies that advertise . . . . . . . . . . . .    42
Percent of agencies that do not advertise. . . . . . . .    58

## Annual expenditures on advertising:

| Dollar investment in advertising | Percent of agencies |
|---|---|
| Under $5,000 . . . . . . . . . . . . . . . . . . . | 47% |
| $   5,000–$  9,999 . . . . . . . . . . . . . . . | 24 |
| $ 10,000–$ 24,999 . . . . . . . . . . . . . . . | 13 |
| $ 25,000–$ 49,999 . . . . . . . . . . . . . . . | 5 |
| $ 50,000–$ 74,999 . . . . . . . . . . . . . . . | 1 |
| $ 75,000–$ 99,999 . . . . . . . . . . . . . . . | 1 |
| $100,000–$199,999 . . . . . . . . . . . . . . . | 2 |
| More than $200,000 . . . . . . . . . . . . . . . | 0 |
| No answer . . . . . . . . . . . . . . . . . . . . | 7 |

## How they advertise:

| Media | Percent using each |
|---|---|
| Direct mail, letters, brochures. . . . . . . . . . . | 84% |
| Business publications. . . . . . . . . . . . . . . . | 38 |
| Newsletters, external house organs . . . . . . . . | 27 |
| Newspapers . . . . . . . . . . . . . . . . . . . . . | 20 |
| Consumer magazines . . . . . . . . . . . . . . . . | 9 |
| Outdoor boards . . . . . . . . . . . . . . . . . . . | 5 |
| AM radio. . . . . . . . . . . . . . . . . . . . . . . | 3 |
| Network television . . . . . . . . . . . . . . . . . | 1 |
| FM radio. . . . . . . . . . . . . . . . . . . . . . . | 0 |
| Spot television. . . . . . . . . . . . . . . . . . . . | 0 |
| Other. . . . . . . . . . . . . . . . . . . . . . . . . | 5 |

## Why they advertise:

| | Percent of respondents |
|---|---|
| Secure new business interviews . . . . . . . . . . Interest clients in our agency when they are ready to make a change; condition potential clients to our personal calls; pave way for new business calls. | 29% |
| Establish name . . . . . . . . . . . . . . . . . . . Recognition of agency; distinguish us from other agencies; visibility; pleasant familiarity. | 20 |
| Establish reputation as well-balanced. . . . . . . Tell we are a full-service agency; of the scope or range of our agency's services; of close personal service; of our service for all types of clients. | 16 |

|                                                                                                                                                                                                                                    | *Percent of respondents* |
| --- | --- |
| Establish and keep reputation. . . . . . . . . . . <br> General comments: favorable image; good image; good agency personality; show our experience and stature in the industry; quality image; institutional. | 12 |
| Establish reputation as creative agency. . . . . . <br> (Comments were not more specific than to use the word "creativity.") | 12 |
| Keep name known . . . . . . . . . . . . . . . . <br> Keep name before influentials; remembrance; reminder advertising. | 9 |
| Don't know . . . . . . . . . . . . . . . . . . <br> No attempt made to measure results; difficult to measure; just started the program; too early to evaluate; can't answer. | 9 |
| Difficult to trace, but we feel it is generally beneficial . . . . . . . . . . . . . . . . | 3 |
| Not effective at all . . . . . . . . . . . . . . . | 1 |
| Establish reputation as businesslike. . . . . . . <br> We are profit-oriented; our advertising is realistic; our advertising reflects realities of the marketplace; we do effective advertising; not a "far-out agency"; we are professionals. | 9 |
| Establish reputation as marketing agency . . . . <br> Show that we are marketing-oriented; good at marketing strategy. | 7 |
| Identify agency with its accounts . . . . . . . . | 6 |
| Inform prospects about agency activities. . . . . <br> Disseminate the agency's news; inform of new developments in our agency. | 3 |
| Public service . . . . . . . . . . . . . . . . . . <br> Promote and clarify the effectiveness of advertising; show how advertising is good for the community and nation; social action messages, e.g., advertising and free speech. | 3 |
| Establish reputation as capable of providing international service. . . . . . . . . . | 2 |
| Gain and keep respect and confidence . . . . . . <br> Keep clients' confidence and trust; make clients proud to be served by us. | 2 |
| Inform prospects about agency's size. . . . . . . | 1 |
| General, nonspecific answers . . . . . . . . . . . <br> Make clients aware of the type of advertising we do; show our capabilities and philosophy; show that we believe in advertising (because we do it ourselves); agency growth; youthfulness of agency; hardworking employees; show agency leadership; tell our policies and goals. | 45 |

Effectiveness of advertising:

| *Effectiveness* | *Percent* |
|---|---|
| Very or quite effective; good; excellent . . . . . | 37% |
| Satisfactory; reasonably effective . . . . . . . . . Has helped some; OK; we consider it a sound investment; long-range effectiveness is good; it appears to be accomplishing its objectives; worth what we invest; prospects are impressed with it; contributes to our general reputation; results in some contacts from potential customers. | 32 |
| Not much effect. . . . . . . . . . . . . . . . . . Marginal; not good; we are dubious; only moderately effective; limited; not as good as it should be; not completely satisfied; only fair. | 18 |

## PROBLEMS OF INTERMEDIATE LENGTH

1. *Should Thrift Way Food Stores use trading stamps?* Thrift Way Food Stores, a large chain operating in your area, has for years resisted the use of trading stamps. More recently, however, the firm's management has wavered somewhat in its stand. Perhaps recent losses in its share of the market to trading-stamp-using competitors is responsible for this change in viewpoint. Whatever the reason, the company is now considering trading stamps; and you as an administrative assistant to president Cyrus H. Knudson have been asked to assist.

By next Monday morning, when the board of directors meets, Mr. Knudson has requested that you have in readiness a report on the effects which adoption of a trading stamp plan would be likely to have on Thrift Way operations. Of course, the report will have to be written in a form appropriate for presentation to the board. According to Mr. Knudson's specifications, your report should be based primarily on whatever operating statistics you can uncover from bibliographical sources.

After exhaustive research you have collected a mountain of information. In examining your data you find that one item, a report of a study conducted by Dr. Carlos A. Haire of the Retailing Science Institute which was published in the June, 1975, issue of *Retailing Science,* a trade publication, apparently holds the key to the whole problem. In fact, after careful scrutiny, you conclude that your entire study will be built around information contained in the following four tables which you extracted from the report. These compare the index of retail prices in stamp and nonstamp stores; the index of sales volume in stamp and nonstamp food chains; the percentage distribution of retail sales by stamp and nonstamp food chains; and net profits as a percentage of total sales for stamp and nonstamp food chains.

Index of retail prices in stamp and nonstamp stores for 21 cities in period after stamps were added, August 1974–March 1975 (index before stamps, November 1971–August 1973 = 100)

| Commodity group | Price index after stamps were added | | Price change in stamp stores in relation to nonstamp stores percent |
| --- | --- | --- | --- |
| | Nonstamp stores index | Stamp stores index | |
| Cereal and bakery products . . . . . . . | 103.3 | 104.4 | +1.1 |
| Dairy products . . . . . . . . . . . . . . | 103.7 | 104.5 | +0.8 |
| Fruits and vegetables . . . . . . . . . . . | 106.9 | 104.9 | −2.1 |
| Meats, poultry, and fish . . . . . . . . . | 94.2 | 95.3 | +1.3 |
| Other foods . . . . . . . . . . . . . . . . | 98.2 | 99.7 | +1.6 |
| Average, all foods. . . . . . . . . . . . . | 100.1 | 100.7 | +0.6 |

Index of sales volume for 5 stamp and 5 nonstamp food chains, 1969–75 (index of sales for 1969–72 = 100)

| Group | Before stamps | | | | | After stamps | |
| --- | --- | --- | --- | --- | --- | --- | --- |
| | 1969 | 1970 | 1971 | 1972 | 1973 | 1974 | 1975 |
| 5 stamp chains. . . . . . | 93 | 95 | 102 | 110 | 120 | 137 | 148 |
| 5 nonstamp chains . . . | 90 | 98 | 104 | 109 | 114 | 118 | 126 |
| Chain average . . . . . . | 91 | 97 | 103 | 109 | 116 | 125 | 134 |

Percentage distribution of retail sales by 5 stamp and 5 nonstamp food chains, 1969–75

| Group | Share before stamps | | | | | Share after stamps | |
| --- | --- | --- | --- | --- | --- | --- | --- |
| | 1969 | 1970 | 1971 | 1972 | 1973 | 1974 | 1975 |
| 5 stamp chains. . . . . | 37.2 | 36.6 | 36.9 | 37.6 | 38.8 | 40.7 | 41.2 |
| 5 nonstamp chains . . | 62.8 | 63.4 | 63.1 | 62.4 | 61.2 | 59.3 | 58.8 |
| Total. . . . . . . . | 100.0 | 100.0 | 100.0 | 100.0 | 100.0 | 100.0 | 100.0 |

Net profits as a percentage of total sales for 5 stamp food chains and 5 nonstamp food chains, 1969–75

| Group | Before stamps | | | | | After stamps | |
| --- | --- | --- | --- | --- | --- | --- | --- |
| | 1969 | 1970 | 1971 | 1972 | 1973 | 1974 | 1975 |
| 5 stamp food chains . . . . | 1.03 | 1.12 | 1.24 | 1.34 | 1.33 | 1.24 | 1.30 |
| 5 nonstamp food chains . . | .91 | .90 | .89 | .92 | .96 | 1.06 | 1.17 |

2. *Interpreting survey findings for State Mutual Insurance.* For the past month Business Research, Inc., has been actively working on a survey for the State Mutual Insurance Company. In a nutshell, the objective of the survey was to find out why people buy automobile insurance and how they buy it. In all, they conducted 1,600 interviews from a scientifically designed sample of policyholders over the geographic area served by the company.

The research has been completed, and the findings have been tabulated. Now, as an analyst for Business Research, you have the assignment of interpreting, organizing, and presenting the findings in report form. In interpreting the findings you will keep in mind that State Mutual intends to use them to good advantage in forming its marketing strategy. Especially does it hope to find information useful in improving sales techniques. The organization plan you plan to use will be one that will give appropriate emphasis to the highlights of your presentation. And the report format you choose will be one befitting the formality of this one situation. (For class purposes, you will need to use your logic and imagination to supply the facts you would know if you really were in this situation—research methodology, current company practices, etc.) You will address the report to Mr. Conrad A. Dunbar, vice president in charge of marketing.

Tabulations of the findings by question are as follows:

*Question:* How did you first get in touch with your present company— that is, how did you hear about it?

46%—Through a friend, neighbor or relative.
23%—Know the agent (good friend, neighbor, relative).
8%—Don't remember.
4%—Through car dealer or person who sold respondent the car.
4%—Saw or heard company's advertising and called company.
3%—Agent called on respondent.
3%—Other agent recommended it.
2%—Friend or relative worked for the company.
2%—Carried other kinds of insurance with company.
1%—Through bank or loan company where car was financed.
7%—Other sources.

*Question:* The last time you bought auto insurance did you "shop around"—that is, did you get prices from different companies? (Yes or no)

18%—Did shop.
82%—Did not shop.

*Question:*    (If "yes" to previous question) How did you go about finding the names of companies to contact?

8%—Friends, relative, neighbors.
2%—Phone book.
2%—Advertising.
3%—Went to different insurance offices.
2%—Other.
3%—Don't remember.

*Question:*    What reasons were most important to you in choosing the company you did: . . . Any others? (Probe)

24%—Save money, cheaper.
18%—Good company, reputable, reliable, good service.
17%—Agent is a friend, relative, neighbor, etc.
17%—Heard about company through friends, relatives.
12%—Better coverage, different types.
12%—No reason given.
9%—Settle claims promptly, fairly.
2%—Insured through finance company—no choice.
2%—Conveniently located.
2%—Heard about agent through friends.
1%—Insurance in connection with job.
1%—Offered payment plan
1%—Wanted all insurance with one company.
6%—Other reasons.

*Question:*    Do you think there is a big difference in what different companies would charge for the same kind and amount of auto insurance, or a small difference, or do you think that they all charge about the same?

38%—Insurance charges are about the same.
24%—There is a big difference in insurance charges.
21%—There is a small difference in insurance charge.
17%—Don't know.

*Question:*    (If difference between companies indicated) Do you think that the cost of your present car insurance is higher than most companies, lower than most other companies, or about the same?

73%—Lower than most companies.
21%—Don't know.
5%—Higher than most companies.
1%—About the same as most companies.

*Question:* When you bought your present policy, did you contact the agent, or did he contact you?

> 25%—He contacted me.
> 72%—I contacted him.
> 3%—Don't remember or question not appropriate.

*Question:* (If respondent contacted agent, ask:) How did you first get his name?

> 31%—Through friends, relatives, neighbors.
> 19%—Knew agent.
> 6%—Saw advertising.
> 6%—Don't remember.
> All other reasons accounted for 3% or less each.

*Question:* What were the main sales points the agent made about your present insurance?

> 39%—Don't remember.
> 18%—Trusted agent, didn't have to give sales talk.
> 14%—Costs less.
> 12%—Trusted person who recommended agent.
> 10%—Better coverage, more protection.
> 6%—Company has good reputation.
> 4%—Fair handling of claims.
> 1%—Insured through finance company or bank.
> 5%—Other reasons.

*Question:* People give different reasons for taking out auto insurance. Which one of these do you think is *most* important to most people?

> 89%—Cover responsibility for damage to other fellow.
> 5%—Required by law.
> 3%—Cover against damage to own car.
> 3%—Other and none.

*Question:* Here are some of the things about auto insurance companies that some people feel are important. (Show set of 7 yellow cards.) Now can you tell me which one of these is most important to you personally? (Record "1" below and ask.) And of these left, which one is the most important? (Record "2" and proceed until all cards have been ranked.)
Percent ranking feature as number 1:

> 23%—Quick settlement of claims.
> 18%—Fair treatment by company.
> 17%—Well-known company.
> 15%—Low cost of insurance.

13%–Good service from local agent.

7%–Claim adjusters in all parts of the United States.

2%–Installment plan for payments.

*Question:*  (For each company bought from previously, but not now carried)

Why do you no longer carry (each company) insurance on your car?

Of those switching from State Mutual, the following reasons were given:

50%–No reason given.

18%–State Mutual rates too high; present company cheaper.

16%–Agent is personal friend. (State Mutual agent died, got sick, left the town, switched companies, etc.)

10%–Poor claims handling.

9%–Poor service—did not bill promptly.

9%–Other company had better coverage.

6%–Let insurance expire.

5%–Insured through finance company, loan company, insurance payments made with car payments.

24%–Other reasons.

Of those switching to State Mutual, the following reasons were given:

47%–No reason given.

21%–Rates too high. State Mutual cheaper.

7%–State Mutual has better coverage.

6%–State Mutual agent is personal friend.

3%–Let insurance expire.

3%–Insured through finance company, loan company, bank company selected, included with car payments, etc.

3%–Poor claims handling by other company.

2%–Poor service from other company.

11%–Other reasons.

**3.** *Studying the substitute milk market for Better Foods.*  For the past few years, Better Foods, Inc., has been keeping an eye on the progress made by milk substitutes manufactured by its competitors. Better Foods has been reluctant to enter the market, for it judged the chances for success of the new product to be risky. But now that the product has been on the market for a few years, the company is beginning to suspect that it just might be enjoying some success.

As a research specialist in the product development department of Better Foods, you have been given the assignment of looking into the situation. Specifically, they want you to determine whether the product is here to stay. And if it is, they want you to tell them things they need to know in introducing a new product—who uses it, what they do and don't like about it, and so on. You will not be given the funds to conduct primary research of your own. Instead, your superiors refer you to a three-market comparison study supported by the Milk Industry Foundation and conducted by two distinguished university researchers (David L. Call, Massachusetts Institute of Technology; and L. John Wilkerson, Cornell). The three areas covered in the study were the Buffalo and Niagara frontier area, central Arizona, and southern California. As the New York part of the study was conducted earlier, it did not cover all points, so it is not included in Tables 7 and 8. In each area, milk substitutes had been available for different time periods. The findings of this study (see Tables 1 through 9) should give Better Foods much of what they want. They give a good measure of consumer awareness and attitudes pertaining to the product; they show the extent of usage; and they give some pertinent information on the types of people who use the product. In general, the data answers most of the questions a company needs answered as it makes the decision and plans to bring out a new product.

You will write the report for Mr. Carry E. Schlimmer, vice president of product development. Give it the makeup appropriate for this one situation.

**TABLE 1**

Status of milk substitute in three markets

|  | New York (Niagara frontier) | Arizona (central) | California (state) |
|---|---|---|---|
| Length of time substitutes have been available . . . . . | 6 months | Several years | 12–21 months |
| Substitutes as percent of relevant Class I . . . . . . . | 1.02% (June) | 10.80% (July) | 1.25% (July) |
| Recent trend in sales (May to August) . . . . . . | Down (1.1%–0.86%) | Up (9.1%–11.7%) | Steady (1.27%–1.34%) |
| Type of label . . . . . . . . | Melloream or vegetable oil product | Trade name | Imitation milk |
| Typical price differential (per half gallon) . . . . . . . | 13¢ (Average) | 8–10¢ | 8–9¢ |

**TABLE 2**

Product mixes purchased by families using fluid milk substitutes

| Product mix | New York | | Arizona | | California | |
|---|---|---|---|---|---|---|
| | Percent of families | Percent of purchases | Percent of families | Percent of purchases | Percent of families | Percent of purchases |
| Milk, skim, imitation... | 22.7% | 23.1% | 13.4% | 17.1% | 8.9% | 9.1% |
| Milk, imitation... | 45.5 | 54.2 | 31.5 | 35.9 | 53.6 | 52.8 |
| Skim, imitation... | 11.4 | 8.6 | 16.5 | 14.2 | 10.7 | 11.5 |
| Imitation.... | 20.4 | 14.1 | 38.6 | 32.8 | 26.8 | 26.6 |

**TABLE 3**

Consumer purchasers of fluid milk substitutes

| | New York (Niagara frontier) | Arizona (central) | California (southern) |
|---|---|---|---|
| Number of households surveyed ....... | 1,400 | 1,300 | 1,500 |
| Percentage of households: | | | |
| Regular weekly purchasers.......... | 3.2% | 9.8% | 3.7% |
| Occasional purchasers ............ | 5.7 | 18.3 | 6.7 |
| Purchased at least once............ | 8.9 | 28.1 | 10.4 |
| Purchase plans of those purchasing at least once: | | | |
| Plan repeat purchases............. | 59.2 | 61.4 | 51.9 |
| Undecided.................... | 9.6 | 12.6 | 14.8 |
| Do not plan repeat purchases ........ | 31.2 | 26.0 | 33.3 |
| Regular purchasers .............. | 36.0 | 34.5 | 35.2 |

**TABLE 4**

Family income and purchase of milk substitutes

| Total annual family income | Proportion of users in sample | | |
|---|---|---|---|
| | New York | Arizona | California |
| Less than $7,500 ............. | 7.9% | 24.9% | 8.2% |
| $7,500–$15,000. ............. | 11.4 | 33.0 | 13.1 |
| More than $15,000 ............ | 17.6 | 26.5 | 10.0 |
| Refuse and do not know ........ | 3.8 | 22.2 | 9.2 |
| All income groups............ | 8.9 | 28.1 | 10.4 |

**TABLE 5**

Children in the household and purchase of milk substitutes

| Number of persons under 16 years | Proportion of users in sample | | |
| --- | --- | --- | --- |
| | New York | Arizona | California |
| 0 . . . . . . . . . . . . . . . . . | 5.9% | 22.3% | 8.1% |
| 1–2 . . . . . . . . . . . . . . . | 10.0 | 30.3 | 11.1 |
| 3–4 . . . . . . . . . . . . . . . | 11.1 | 38.1 | 14.5 |
| 5 or more . . . . . . . . . . . . | 25.4 | 46.3 | 21.6 |
| All groups . . . . . . . . . . . . | 8.9 | 28.1 | 10.4 |

**TABLE 6**

Reasons for not purchasing fluid milk substitutes by those who correctly defined the product

| Reason | New York (142 families) | Arizona (67 families) | California (116 families) |
| --- | --- | --- | --- |
| Satisfied with milk . . . . . . . . . . . . . . . | 39% | 19% | 31% |
| No stated reason . . . . . . . . . . . . . . . . | 32 | 25 | 28 |
| Unsure of quality or nutritional value . . . . . . . . . . . . . . . | 5 | 25 | 20 |
| Dislike substitute or new products . . . . . . . | 18 | 24 | 10 |
| Not available in market. . . . . . . . . . . . . . | 4 | 5 | 5 |
| Miscellaneous . . . . . . . . . . . . . . . . . . . | 2 | 2 | 6 |

**TABLE 7**

Consumers opinions on calorie content of milk substitutes

| Opinion of users of substitute | Arizona | California |
| --- | --- | --- |
| More calories than whole milk. . . . . . . . . . . . . . . . | 3% | 3% |
| Same number of calories as whole milk . . . . . . . . . . | 10 | 13 |
| Fewer calories than whole milk . . . . . . . . . . . . . . . | 67 | 63 |
| Do not know . . . . . . . . . . . . . . . . . . . . . . . . . | 20 | 21 |
| Total. . . . . . . . . . . . . . . . . . . . . . . . . . . . . . | 100 | 100 |

**TABLE 8**

Consumers opinions on cholesterol and milk substitutes

| Opinion of users of substitute | Arizona | California |
| --- | --- | --- |
| Produces more than whole milk. . . . . . . . . . . . . . | 4% | 3% |
| Produces the same amount as whole milk . . . . . . . . | 7 | 10 |
| Produces less than whole milk. . . . . . . . . . . . . . . | 53 | 54 |
| Do not know . . . . . . . . . . . . . . . . . . . . . . . . . | 36 | 33 |
| Total. . . . . . . . . . . . . . . . . . . . . . . . . . . . . . | 100 | 100 |

**TABLE 9**

Consumers opinion on the taste of fluid milk substitutes

| Opinion on taste of substitute | New York | Arizona | California |
|---|---|---|---|
| Better than milk. . . . . . . . . . . | 12% | 9% | 11% |
| Same as milk. . . . . . . . . . . . . | 62 | 50 | 44 |
| Worse than milk. . . . . . . . . . . | 24 | 33 | 36 |
| Do not know . . . . . . . . . . . . | 2 | 8 | 9 |
| | | *Regular users only* | |
| Better than milk. . . . . . . . . . . | — | 21 | 19 |
| Same as milk. . . . . . . . . . . . . | — | 57 | 61 |
| Worse than milk. . . . . . . . . . . | — | 17 | 16 |
| Do not know . . . . . . . . . . . . | — | 5 | 4 |

**4.** *Interpreting market price data for Dr. Shane's Liniment.* For some time the Dr. Shane Drug Company has been concerned about the price structure of its principal product, Dr. Shane's Liniment. Unfortunately, in recent years the company has not enjoyed the best relations with its wholesalers; nor the situation in retail sales been any more encouraging.

In the mind of Calvin E. Hicks, vice president in charge of distribution, much of the blame lies in the company's antiquated price structure. It has made little effort to maintain retail prices of its products; nor has it attempted to maintain firm policies on terms of sale, discounts, and such. As Mr. Hicks sees it, a firm policy with wholesalers and a maximum retail price maintained by printing prices on the package would improve the situation.

Before he can recommend such changes, however, he needs some information. From you, his administrative assistant, he wants an analysis of the retail price structure of Dr. Shane's Liniment. Specifically, he wants to know how wide a distribution exists in retail prices, and whether these differences exist by type of retail outlet. This information, he feels, will help him in making his appraisal of the situation.

Through the assistance of marketing research professors at six strategically selected universities, you have gathered prices paid on 44,521 transactions for the 4-ounce size of Dr. Shane's Liniment. And you have arranged them by type of retail outlet (see Table 1). Now, with the preliminary work done, you are ready to begin your analysis. You plan to organize the findings so that they will best serve the needs of Mr. Hicks. And you will present them in a report form that is appropriate for the occasion. Use your logic and imagination to supply any other information you feel that you need.

**TABLE 1**

Analysis of 44,521 separate retail sales of Dr. Shane's Liniment (unit sales by type of outlet at each price reported)

| Retail price | Neighborhood independent | Centrally located independent | Chains | Cut-rate | Dept. stores | Total |
|---|---|---|---|---|---|---|
| 59¢ | 1 | — | — | — | — | 1 |
| 69 | — | — | 144 | — | — | 144 |
| 71 | — | — | 204 | — | — | 204 |
| 72 | — | — | — | — | 36 | 36 |
| 73 | — | — | — | 50 | — | 50 |
| 74 | — | — | 80 | — | — | 80 |
| 76 | — | — | 112 | — | — | 112 |
| 77 | — | 6 | 240 | — | 36 | 282 |
| 79 | — | — | 641 | 174 | 24 | 839 |
| 80 | 1 | — | — | — | — | 1 |
| 81 | — | 36 | 62 | 492 | 400 | 990 |
| 83 | — | 290 | 1,480 | 273 | 24 | 2,067 |
| 84 | — | 2 | 1,000 | 152 | 504 | 1,658 |
| 85 | — | 16 | — | 6 | — | 22 |
| 86 | — | 12 | 156 | 313 | — | 481 |
| 87 | — | 1 | 992 | 269 | 415 | 1,677 |
| 88 | — | — | 168 | 36 | — | 204 |
| 89 | 130 | 572 | 3,889 | 1,780 | 28 | 6,499 |
| 90 | 53 | 47 | 96 | 48 | — | 244 |
| 91 | — | 39 | 434 | 192 | — | 665 |
| 92 | — | 198 | — | — | — | 198 |
| 93 | — | 3 | 562 | 24 | 12 | 601 |
| 94 | 4 | — | 672 | 46 | 8 | 730 |
| 95 | 10 | 91 | 384 | 42 | 30 | 557 |
| 96 | 20 | 24 | — | 24 | — | 68 |
| 97 | 18 | 251 | 1,101 | 255 | 371 | 1,995 |
| 98 | 1,422 | 998 | 4,482 | 2,213 | 590 | 9,705 |
| 99 | 143 | 168 | 1,279 | 94 | 40 | 1,723 |
| 100 | 860 | 776 | 1,347 | 724 | 154 | 3,861 |
| 101 | — | — | — | 2 | — | 2 |
| 102 | 24 | — | 69 | 6 | — | 99 |
| 103 | 26 | — | 1 | — | — | 27 |
| 104 | — | — | — | — | 36 | 36 |
| 105 | 30 | — | 158 | 36 | — | 224 |
| 106 | 5 | — | — | — | — | 5 |
| 107 | — | — | 746 | 45 | 18 | 809 |
| 108 | 67 | 39 | 26 | 38 | 45 | 215 |
| 109 | 765 | 431 | 544 | 438 | 31 | 2,209 |
| 110 | 206 | 25 | 345 | 318 | 18 | 912 |
| 112 | 9 | 4 | — | — | — | 13 |
| 113 | 18 | 2 | — | — | — | 20 |
| 114 | 6 | — | 144 | — | — | 150 |
| 115 | 192 | 67 | — | 21 | — | 280 |
| 118 | 3 | — | — | — | — | 3 |
| 119 | 573 | 594 | 398 | 339 | — | 1,904 |
| 120 | 48 | 52 | — | 6 | — | 106 |
| 122 | 1 | — | — | — | — | 1 |
| 123 | 10 | — | — | — | — | 10 |
| 124 | — | — | 12 | — | — | 12 |
| 125 | 522 | 181 | 89 | 25 | — | 817 |
| 128 | — | 5 | — | — | — | 5 |
| 129 | 160 | 157 | 81 | 59 | — | 457 |
| 130 | — | 4 | — | — | — | 4 |
| 134 | 3 | 6 | — | — | — | 9 |
| 135 | 52 | 80 | — | 24 | — | 156 |
| 139 | 93 | 168 | 8 | 12 | — | 281 |
| 140 | 4 | 3 | — | — | — | 7 |
| 145 | 1 | — | — | — | — | 1 |
| 150 | 16 | 36 | — | — | — | 52 |
| Total | 5,496 | 5,384 | 22,145 | 8,576 | 2,920 | 44,521 |

**5.** *Determining store location factors for a grocery chain.* Save-a-Lot Food Stores, Inc., plans to expand its chain of 127 stores, all located in the United States Northeast, to 157 over the next three years. Quite naturally, they want to make the best possible selections of store sites. To guide them in their selections, they have commissioned your research firm, Northeast Research Associates, to gather some pertinent information on grocery shopping patterns.

The information they seek is what Quinn O. Phlug, president of Save-a-Lot, believes is a key to location success. Mr. Phlug has followed the practice of locating all his stores in high-density population sections of the larger metropolitan areas. His strategy has paid off. He attributes his success to his belief that convenience is of major importance in selecting a grocery store and that people travel only limited distances in buying their groceries. He wants you to test this hypothesis for him. He wants you to do a thorough job of research—so thorough that it covers all information pertinent to the basic question. After several conferences with president Phlug, you designed your research. Then you conducted your research. In the process, you conducted 5,735 usable interviews of Save-a-Lot customers at store locations chosen at random. Now the research is behind you. The questionnaires have been tabulated. The findings are before you in the form of summary Tables 1 through 5. All that remains for you to do is to analyze the data and to present them in report form.

In presenting the report, you will select a form that is appropriate for this somewhat formal situation. Also,you will make good use of graphic aids to assist your words in telling the report story. (For class purposes, you may fill in any additional facts you may need about the research or the problem.) Address the report to Mr. Phlug.

**TABLE 1**

Sales to customers according to method of travel

|  | Walk | Automobile | Public conveyance |
|---|---|---|---|
| Percent of customers . . . . . . . | 57.5% | 40.6% | 1.9% |
| Percent of sales . . . . . . . . . | 38.2% | 60.6% | 1.2% |
| Average purchase . . . . . . . . | $7.40 | $16.60 | $8.30 |

**TABLE 2**

Frequency of visit to store

|  | Once or twice a week | Three or more times a week |
|---|---|---|
| Walk . . . . . . . . . . . . . . . . . . . . | 34.3% | 65.7% |
| Automobile . . . . . . . . . . . . . . . . | 60.8 | 39.2 |
| Public conveyance . . . . . . . . . . . | 65.2 | 34.8 |

**TABLE 3**

Customer sales according to distance from store

|  | Percent of customers | Percent of sales | Average purchase |
|---|---|---|---|
| Less than ¼ mile . . . . . . . | 38.2% | 29.2% | $ 7.80 |
| ¼-½ mile. . . . . . . . . . . | 29.9 | 29.1 | 10.31 |
| ½-¾ mile. . . . . . . . . . . | 9.7 | 11.1 | 12.74 |
| ¾-1 mile . . . . . . . . . . . | 6.6 | 8.3 | 14.16 |
| Beyond 1 mile. . . . . . . . | 15.6 | 22.3 | 15.90 |

**TABLE 4**

Percentage of sales in typical Save-a-Lot store classified by location and distance traveled

| Distance traveled to store | Typical major shopping center | Typical neighborhood location |
|---|---|---|
| Less than ¼ mile . . . . . . . . . . . . | 18.6% | 53.5 |
| ¼-½ mile. . . . . . . . . . . . . . . | 26.2 | 20.4 |
| ½-¾ mile. . . . . . . . . . . . . . . | 14.5 | 5.8 |
| ¾-1 mile . . . . . . . . . . . . . . . | 4.1 | 3.5 |
| Beyond 1 mile. . . . . . . . . . . . . | 36.6 | 16.8 |

**TABLE 5**

Reason for buying at store patronized

| Reason | Percentage giving* |
|---|---|
| Convenience . . . . . . . . . . . . . . . . . | 47.6% |
| Price . . . . . . . . . . . . . . . . . . . . . | 40.2 |
| Quality . . . . . . . . . . . . . . . . . . . . | 36.2 |
| Personnel and service . . . . . . . . . . . . | 29.0 |
| Friends . . . . . . . . . . . . . . . . . . . . | 10.4 |
| Miscellaneous . . . . . . . . . . . . . . . . | 23.7 |
| No reason . . . . . . . . . . . . . . . . . . | 6.7 |

*Some gave more than one reason.

**6.** *Analyzing survey results on compensation plan for Continental Business Machines.* Place yourself in the position of administrative assistant to Mr. Eugene C. Forsyth, vice president in charge of sales, Continental Business Machines. Today he hands you a table he received in the mail compiled by the National Industrial Conference Board (see Table 1). The table summarizes findings of the board's survey of a cross section of

**TABLE 1**

Characteristics of basic types of compensation plans*

| Relationship of type of compensation plan to phases of company policy and operation | Salary | | Salary and incentive | | Commission | |
|---|---|---|---|---|---|---|
| | No. of Cos. | Percent | No. of Cos. | Percent | No. of Cos. | Percent |
| 1. Simplicity and low cost of operation | | | | | | |
| Fully meets requirements . . . | 116 | 81.1 | 158 | 86.3 | 50 | 82.0 |
| Only moderately effective . . . | 19 | 13.3 | 20 | 10.9 | 6 | 9.8 |
| Leaves a lot to be desired . . . | 8 | 5.6 | 5 | 2.7 | 5 | 8.2 |
| 2. Fairness to both company and salesmen | | | | | | |
| Fully meets requirements . . . | 90 | 63.4 | 140 | 76.9 | 47 | 75.8 |
| only moderately effective . . . | 32 | 22.5 | 35 | 19.2 | 10 | 16.1 |
| Leaves a lot to be desired . . . | 20 | 14.1 | 7 | 3.8 | 5 | 8.1 |
| 3. Attracting desirable salesmen | | | | | | |
| Fully meets requirements . . . | 96 | 67.6 | 148 | 80.9 | 54 | 87.1 |
| Only moderately effective . . . | 36 | 25.4 | 28 | 15.3 | 7 | 11.3 |
| Leaves a lot to be desired . . . | 10 | 7.0 | 7 | 3.8 | 1 | 1.6 |
| 4. Retaining desirable salesmen | | | | | | |
| Fully meets requirements . . . | 102 | 71.3 | 162 | 88.5 | 58 | 93.5 |
| Only moderately effective . . . | 37 | 25.9 | 19 | 10.4 | 4 | 6.5 |
| Leaves a lot to be desired . . . | 4 | 2.8 | 2 | 1.1 | — | — |
| 5. Rewarding salesmen for special effort | | | | | | |
| Fully meets requirements . . . | 54 | 40.3 | 110 | 62.5 | 47 | 78.3 |
| Only moderately effective . . . | 47 | 35.1 | 49 | 27.8 | 9 | 15.0 |
| Leaves a lot to be desired . . . | 33 | 24.6 | 17 | 9.7 | 4 | 6.7 |
| 6. Maintaining adequate sales control | | | | | | |
| Fully meets requirements . . . | 104 | 74.3 | 136 | 76.4 | 44 | 72.1 |
| Only moderately effective . . . | 24 | 17.1 | 33 | 18.5 | 14 | 23.0 |
| Leaves a lot to be desired . . . | 12 | 8.6 | 9 | 5.1 | 3 | 4.9 |
| 7. Safeguarding company-customer relations | | | | | | |
| Fully meets requirements . . . | 129 | 90.8 | 161 | 89.9 | 46 | 75.4 |
| Only moderately effective . . . | 13 | 9.2 | 14 | 7.8 | 14 | 23.0 |
| Leaves a lot to be desired . . . | — | — | 4 | 2.2 | 1 | 1.6 |
| 8. Stability of salesmen's incomes in good and bad periods | | | | | | |
| Fully meets requirements . . . | 124 | 86.7 | 136 | 75.6 | 28 | 46.7 |
| Only moderately effective . . . | 18 | 12.6 | 29 | 16.1 | 19 | 31.7 |
| Leaves a lot to be desired . . . | 1 | 0.7 | 15 | 8.3 | 13 | 21.7 |
| 9. Keeping sales-cost ratio at a minimum | | | | | | |
| Fully meets requirements. . . | 91 | 64.5 | 130 | 73.4 | 46 | 76.7 |
| Only moderately effective . . | 37 | 26.2 | 38 | 21.5 | 10 | 16.7 |
| Leaves a lot to be desired. . . | 13 | 9.2 | 9 | 5.1 | 4 | 6.7 |
| 10. Compensating for nondirect-selling | | | | | | |
| Fully meets requirements. . . | 106 | 84.8 | 113 | 69.8 | 31 | 55.4 |
| Only moderately effective . . | 17 | 13.6 | 30 | 18.5 | 14 | 25.0 |
| Leaves a lot to be desired. . . | 2 | 1.6 | 19 | 11.7 | 11 | 19.6 |

TABLE 1 (*continued*)

| Relationship of type of compensation plan to phases of company policy and operation | Salary | | Salary and incentive | | Commission | |
|---|---|---|---|---|---|---|
| | No. of Cos. | Percent | No. of Cos. | Percent | No. of Cos. | Percent |
| 11. Developing new business | | | | | | |
| Fully meets requirements. . . | 84 | 58.3 | 131 | 74.4 | 48 | 77.4 |
| Only moderately effective . . | 44 | **30.6** | 36 | 20.5 | 9 | 14.5 |
| Leaves a lot to be desired. . . | 16 | 11.1 | 9 | 5.1 | 5 | 8.1 |
| 12. Providing satisfactory subsistence income to salesmen | | | | | | |
| Fully meets requirements. . . | 114 | 81.4 | 158 | 88.3 | 58 | 85.5 |
| Only moderately effective . . | 25 | **17.9** | 19 | 10.6 | 8 | 12.9 |
| Leaves a lot to be desired. . . | 1 | 0.7 | 2 | 1.1 | 1 | 1.6 |
| 13. Adjusting compensation to territory differentials | | | | | | |
| Fully meets requirements. . . | 79 | 64.2 | 115 | **69.3** | 34 | 59.6 |
| Only moderately effective . . | 32 | **26.0** | 32 | 19.3 | 10 | 17.5 |
| Leaves a lot to be desired. . . | 12 | 9.8 | 19 | 11.4 | 13 | **22.8** |
| 14. Prompt payment after performance | | | | | | |
| Fully meets requirements. . . | 99 | 84.6 | 138 | 82.1 | 56 | **94.9** |
| Only moderately effective . . | 12 | 10.3 | 23 | 13.7 | 2 | 3.4 |
| Leaves a lot to be desired. . . | 6 | 5.1 | 7 | 4.2 | 1 | 1.7 |
| 15. Producing largest profitable volume | | | | | | |
| Fully meets requirements. . . | 69 | 53.5 | 103 | 60.2 | 44 | **72.1** |
| Only moderately effective . . | 39 | 30.2 | 54 | 31.6 | 14 | 23.0 |
| Leaves a lot to be desired. . . | 21 | **16.3** | 14 | 8.2 | 3 | 4.9 |
| 16. General acceptance by salesforce | | | | | | |
| Fully meets requirements. . . | 87 | 61.3 | 138 | 75.8 | 56 | **90.3** |
| Only moderately effective . . | 49 | **34.5** | 38 | 20.9 | 6 | 9.7 |
| Leaves a lot to be desired. . . | 6 | 4.2 | 6 | 3.3 | — | — |
| 17. Meeting special requirements of our business | | | | | | |
| Fully meets requirements. . . | 92 | 68.1 | 137 | 77.8 | 42 | 73.7 |
| Only moderately effective . . | 32 | 23.7 | 34 | 19.3 | 13 | 22.8 |
| Leaves a lot to be desired. . . | 11 | 8.1 | 5 | 2.8 | 2 | 3.5 |
| 18. Promoting profitable lines | | | | | | |
| Fully meets requirements. . . | 68 | 54.8 | 101 | 58.7 | 38 | **64.4** |
| Only moderately effective . . | 35 | 28.2 | 50 | 29.1 | 14 | 23.7 |
| Leaves a lot to be desired. . . | 21 | 16.9 | 21 | 12.2 | 7 | 11.9 |
| 19. Providing maximum incentive to salesmen | | | | | | |
| Fully meets requirements. . . | 46 | 34.3 | 102 | 59.6 | 48 | **81.4** |
| Only moderately effective . . | 48 | **35.8** | 49 | 28.7 | 8 | 13.6 |
| Leaves a lot to be desired. . . | 40 | **29.9** | 20 | 11.7 | 3 | 5.1 |

Source: National Industrial Conference Board.

\* As indicated by managements' appraisal of their respective compensation plans in terms of 19 specific factors affected by type of plan.

Note: Boldface figures indicate predominating characteristic of compensation plan (exceeding other types by 5% or more).

American management on salespersons' compensation plans. As you glance over the table's contents, you see that it contains answers to 19 pertinent questions related to the three basic means of compensation: salary, salary and commission, and commission. And although it includes only the tabulated findings (no analyses, no conclusions), you can see that it just might hold the answers to some questions Continental has been concerned about.

After giving you the table, Mr. Forsyth explains what he wants you to do with it in these words:

> As you know, for the past few years the directors have been questioning our straight-salary method of paying our salespersons. Some favor salary plus commission; some favor straight commission. I've heard so many arguments on the matter that I am confused, to say the least. This study made by the National Industrial Conference Board just might help us to clear up this question. I want you to analyze it and tell me what it shows that will help us to make the right decision. No, I don't think you can recommend an action for Continental on the basis of these findings; but I think you can come up with some conclusions on good and bad points of the basic plans.

With these words in mind, you begin your work on the data. Certainly in organizing the data you'll have to find some broad bases for combining questions. You just can't organize such a report into 19 separate sections. And you'll have to present the finished report in a form that Mr. Forsyth would be willing to take to the directors' meeting, if he elects to do so. And, of course, you'll consider using some graphic aids to help put over the material. (For class purposes, you may make any logical assumptions of facts that you would have at your disposal if you actually were in this situation.)

7. *Advising the board on the question of using deal campaigns to help sell food products.* At last week's meeting of the board of directors, Warner Foods, Inc., the major topic of concern was Warner's sagging sales of margarine, shortening, and oils. During the past six months the firm's two major competitors made substantial gains at Warner's expense. So far as Warner can determine, the gains were made through aggressive selling and promotion—factors which the Warner's sales staff feels that it can adjust to. But such adjustments take time. What the Warner directors want now is something that will pick up the lost ground in a hurry.

One possible approach, as some of the directors view the situation, is to begin a series of deal campaigns with each product. "Deals" are any form of coupon, gift, or gimmick arrangement designed to stimulate sales. For example, coupons giving a discount on the purchase price of a product may be mass mailed to consumers; or gift certificates may be packed within a product's container. The possible variations are infinite.

They all have one thing in common, however. They are costly, frequently to the point of causing temporary losses. They are effective only if they can cultivate repeat customers.

Although Warner has never used deal campaigns, their competitors have used them extensively. And so have many other manufacturers of foods and other household products. Over the years, however, Warner management has viewed deal campaigns with a high degree of skepticism, especially since Warner products are high in quality and price and appeal to the higher income and social groups.

Margarine, shortening, and oils: Percentage of families reporting specified number of deals and percent of total deals accounted for in each category, during July 197X, St. Louis, Missouri.

| Number of deals per family | Margarine | | Shortening | | Oils | |
| --- | --- | --- | --- | --- | --- | --- |
| | Dealing families | Portion of total deals | Dealing families | Portion of total deals | Dealing families | Portion of total deals |
| 1. . . . . . . . . | 29.6% | 6.6% | 34.5% | 11.3% | 60.2% | 35.7% |
| 2. . . . . . . . . | 23.5 | 10.4 | 19.5 | 12.8 | 24.5 | 29.1 |
| 3. . . . . . . . . | 10.7 | 7.1 | 17.2 | 17.0 | 7.7 | 13.6 |
| 4. . . . . . . . . | 8.6 | 7.7 | 6.9 | 9.0 | 3.4 | 8.0 |
| 5. . . . . . . . . | 4.5 | 5.0 | 6.9 | 11.3 | 3.4 | 10.1 |
| 6. . . . . . . . . | 4.1 | 5.5 | 6.1 | 12.1 | — | — |
| 7. . . . . . . . . | 4.1 | 6.4 | 1.1 | 2.6 | .8 | 3.5 |
| 8. . . . . . . . . | 1.7 | 2.9 | 2.7 | 7.1 | — | — |
| 9. . . . . . . . . | 1.7 | 3.3 | 2.7 | 7.9 | — | — |
| 10. . . . . . . . . | 1.2 | 2.8 | .4 | 1.2 | — | — |
| 11. . . . . . . . . | .4 | 1.0 | .4 | 1.4 | — | — |
| 12 or more. . . . | 9.9 | 41.3 | 1.6 | 6.3 | — | — |
| Total . . . . . . | 100.0% | 100.0% | 100.0% | 100.0% | 100.0% | 100.0% |

Because the directors are skeptical about deal campaigns, they are reluctant to begin them without knowing more about them. So, in an effort to become better informed, they have called on the research department for help. You, the senior research specialist, have been given the assignment.

As board chairman Peter Darwin explained it to you, your assignment is to gather the best available information on effectiveness of deals. The board will expect your recommendation, too; but you may wish to qualify it since you are not going into the financial aspects of the problem in detail. Also, any consideration of the financial aspects would depend on the nature of the specific campaign selected.

The board meets again in about two weeks; so there isn't time for primary research. Secondary research will have to be used. After a few

Dealing and nondealing households by characteristics

| Household characteristics | Buying households | | Purchases by dealing households | | Purchases by all households | |
|---|---|---|---|---|---|---|
| | Dealing households | Nondealing households | Deal (pounds) | Nondeal (pounds) | Deal (pounds) | Nondeal (pounds) |
| Race and nationality: | | | | | | |
| Native white | 54% | 46% | 10.0 | 90.0 | 6.4% | 93.6% |
| Foreign-born white | 51 | 49 | 10.1 | 89.9 | 6.0 | 94.0 |
| Nonwhite | 22 | 78 | 5.7 | 94.3 | 1.6 | 98.4 |
| Income: | | | | | | |
| Low (under $4,000) | 39 | 61 | 10.0 | 90.0 | 4.8 | 95.2 |
| Medium ($4,000–$7,999) | 55 | 45 | 9.4 | 90.6 | 6.0 | 94.0 |
| High ($8,000 and over) | 53 | 47 | 9.9 | 90.1 | 6.1 | 93.9 |
| Size of household: | | | | | | |
| Small (1 or 2 persons) | 39 | 61 | 14.1 | 85.9 | 7.0 | 93.0 |
| Medium (3 or 4 persons) | 53 | 47 | 8.9 | 91.1 | 5.4 | 94.6 |
| Large (5 or more persons) | 55 | 45 | 8.5 | 91.5 | 5.1 | 94.9 |
| Education: | | | | | | |
| 8 years or less | 43 | 57 | 11.0 | 89.0 | 5.3 | 94.7 |
| 9–12 years | 47 | 53 | 7.9 | 92.1 | 4.4 | 95.6 |
| 13 years or more | 59 | 41 | 11.6 | 88.4 | 8.5 | 91.5 |
| Age of housewife: | | | | | | |
| Under 45 years | 54 | 46 | 9.2 | 90.8 | 5.8 | 94.2 |
| 45–64 years | 44 | 56 | 11.0 | 89.0 | 5.9 | 94.1 |
| 65 years or older | 38 | 62 | 10.8 | 89.2 | 4.4 | 95.6 |

hours of fruitless work you give up on your company library; but you find exactly what you want at a nearby university library. It is a report conducted just last year by the marketing research division of the United States Department of Agriculture and appears in Bulletin 943, dated August 31, and titled "Effectiveness of Coupon and Special Offers." In the somewhat brief but information-packed tables below you see the basis of your analysis.

Sales increases attributed to deal campaigns and effect of campaigns on profits; average (mean) of six companies, one campaign each

| *Sales* | *Percent higher than before campaign* |
|---|---|
| During campaigns. . . . . . . . . . . . . . . . . . . . . . . . . . . . . . . | 16.3 |
| One month after campaign. . . . . . . . . . . . . . . . . . . . . . . | 9.1 |
| Three months after campaign . . . . . . . . . . . . . . . . . . . . | 5.9 |
| Six months after campaign. . . . . . . . . . . . . . . . . . . . . | 3.6 |
| Twelve months after campaign . . . . . . . . . . . . . . . . . . | 1.8 |

Net profit before and after campaign, 5.1% of gross sales; net profit during campaign, 2.1% of gross sales.

After you have studied the data and made your analysis, prepare the report for the board. Give the report whatever formality the board is likely to expect; and since the information is largely quantitative, you will support your presentation with appropriate graphic aids.

8. *Reporting the stability and growth of the food brokerage business.* At the last meeting of the National Food Brokers Association, the membership voted to conduct a survey of its members to determine its stability as well as its past and present growth. As a staff research analyst for the group, the work fell on your shoulders.

First, you designed a somewhat simple questionnaire. Then, you mailed it to all of the Association's 2,115 members. Of this number, 1,073 returned the questionnaire—a response of better than 50 percent. Next, you tabulated your responses and compiled them in a form suitable for your analysis (see tables below). It is now time to begin analyzing the data and to construct a report that will convey your findings.

As the project is neither major nor highly formal, you have been instructed to write it up in the form of a memorandum report. The report will be duplicated by mimeograph and mailed to all the cooperating members. You will write the report in the direct order, beginning with a quick review of major findings. Even though the report is somewhat short and informal, you may find need for some graphic aids.

Questionnaires received, 1,100 (52 percent of the membership).
Age of the brokerage firm (1,073 firms reporting):
 Total number of years in business, 32,481.
 Average age, 30.27 years.
 Oldest company reporting, 120 years old.

Number of years in business by age groups (1,073 firms reported):

| Age group | Number of firms | Percent |
|---|---|---|
| 1 to 10 years . . . . . . . . . . | 159 | 15 |
| 11 to 20 years . . . . . . . . . . | 317 | 29 |
| 21 to 30 years . . . . . . . . . . | 169 | 16 |
| 31 to 40 years . . . . . . . . . . | 154 | 14 |
| 41 to 50 years . . . . . . . . . . | 95 | 8.8 |
| 51 to 60 years . . . . . . . . . . | 73 | 7 |
| 61 to 75 years . . . . . . . . . . | 60 | 6 |
| 76 to 100 years . . . . . . . . . | 33 | 3 |
| 100 years or more. . . . . . . . . | 13 | 1.2 |

Length of service of accounts (1,073 firms reported):

| Age group | Number of accounts | Percent |
|---|---|---|
| 5 years or less . . . . . . . . . | 7,886 | 35 |
| 6 to 10 years . . . . . . . . . . | 5,069 | 23 |
| 11 to 15 years . . . . . . . . . . | 3,617 | 16 |
| 16 to 20 years . . . . . . . . . . | 2,366 | 10 |
| 21 to 30 years . . . . . . . . . . | 1,839 | 8.2 |
| 31 years or more . . . . . . . . | 1,647 | 7.8 |

Accounts served for 21 years or more, total 3,486:

| Length of service | Number of accounts |
|---|---|
| 21 to 30 years . . . . . . . . . . . . . . . . . . . | 1,839 |
| 31 to 40 years . . . . . . . . . . . . . . . . . . . | 1,114 |
| 41 to 50 years . . . . . . . . . . . . . . . . . . . | 344 |
| 51 to 60 years . . . . . . . . . . . . . . . . . . . | 135 |
| 61 to 75 years . . . . . . . . . . . . . . . . . . . | 41 |
| 76 to 100 years. . . . . . . . . . . . . . . . . . . | 11 |
| Over 100 years . . . . . . . . . . . . . . . . . . . | 2 |

**9.** *Determining the need for a restaurant in your university community*
(requires research). Warren's, Inc., a national food service chain, is

considering placement of one of its eating facilities in your university community. It has hired you to analyze the need for such a facility and to recommend the appropriate action.

The Warren organization actually consists of two food service systems. One is made up of 327 short-order stands, bearing the name The Dog House. As the name implies, The Dog House specializes in a variety of hot dogs, although it handles a well-rounded assortment of sandwiches, ice creams, and soft drinks. The other chain consists of 132 small-scale cafeterias, bearing the name Serve'nSave. These restaurants offer a streamlined menu of typical, tasty American food at low prices. They operate on a self-service plan.

From you, the Warren people want recommended answers to two basic questions: First, is there need for additional eating facilities in the university community? Second, if there is a need, which of the two types of Warren's operations would be best?

In answering these questions, you will survey the eating facilities in the area, evaluating each as to its menu offering, prices, service, and convenience of location. From your analysis, you will base your recommendation.

You will write the report in typical short-report form, consisting of title page and text. The text you will begin in direct order, leading off with your recommendations and following them with a quick summary of supporting information. The more detailed presentation of the report material will follow. Address the report to Mr. Kenneth A. Warren, president.

**10.** *Analyzing performance of the Bay City Store.* As an administrative assistant to president Frederick B. Green, American Stores, Inc., you have been assigned the task of reviewing the year's operating record of each of the food chain's 36 stores. Your objective is to compare each store's performance, by individual department, with the all-store averages. Then, you will inform each store manager of his store's performance.

The report that you will write to each store manager will be in memorandum form, with a copy for president Green and two other top executives. You will organize each report in the direct style of presentation, with the major observations at the beginning. As you will try hard to be objective in your work, you will take care to point out good as well as bad performances.

First of the 36 stores you will work on is the Bay City Store. Its performance summary by departments and the all-chain average are as follows:

## Profit and loss, Bay City Stores by departments

| | Total store | Gro- ceries | Meats | Pro- duce | Dairy | Baked goods | Frozen foods | H & BA | Other non- foods |
|---|---|---|---|---|---|---|---|---|---|
| Sales | 100% | 100% | 100% | 100% | 100% | 100% | 100% | 100% | 100% |
| Margin on sales | 18.1 | 16.7 | 18.8 | 23.2 | 14.4 | 16.4 | 27.1 | 31.3 | 25.8 |
| Expenses: | | | | | | | | | |
| Personnel | 7.2 | 5.9 | 11.8 | 14.1 | 3.2 | 4.5 | 6.6 | 7.2 | 4.0 |
| Wrapping supplies | .7 | .4 | 1.4 | .7 | .5 | .5 | .3 | .3 | .2 |
| Utilities | .4 | .2 | .4 | .8 | .7 | .1 | 2.4 | .2 | .3 |
| Laundry | .1 | — | .1 | — | — | — | — | — | — |
| Insurance, outside service, telephone, bad checks, over-short, miscella- neous | .2 | .2 | .2 | .2 | .2 | .1 | .2 | .2 | .2 |
| Repairs, maintenance | .2 | .1 | .2 | .3 | .4 | .1 | 2.5 | .1 | .1 |
| Rent, depreciation of leasehold improvements | 1.8 | 1.6 | 1.2 | 2.8 | 1.4 | 1.2 | 2.1 | 1.2 | 1.5 |
| Licenses, taxes | .2 | .2 | .2 | .2 | .2 | .2 | .2 | .2 | .3 |
| Depreciation equipment | .5 | .4 | .6 | 1.3 | .9 | .3 | 3.3 | .3 | .2 |
| Advertising, promotion | .4 | .8 | .5 | .5 | .4 | .5 | .3 | .5 | .7 |
| Stamps | 2.1 | 2.0 | 2.0 | 2.0 | 2.0 | 2.0 | 2.0 | 2.0 | 2.0 |
| All other overhead | 1.1 | 1.3 | 1.2 | 1.2 | 1.2 | 1.2 | 1.2 | 1.2 | 1.2 |
| Total expenses | 14.9 | 13.1 | 19.8 | 24.1 | 11.1 | 10.7 | 21.1 | 13.4 | 10.7 |
| NOP (before taxes) | 3.2 | 3.6 | (−1.0) | (−.9) | 4.3 | 5.7 | 6.0 | 17.9 | 15.1 |

## Average for all American Stores profit and loss statement by departments

| | Total store | Gro- ceries | Meats | Pro- duce | Dairy | Baked goods | Frozen foods | H & BA | Other non- foods |
|---|---|---|---|---|---|---|---|---|---|
| Sales | 100% | 100% | 100% | 100% | 100% | 100% | 100% | 100% | 100% |
| Margin on sales | 18.8 | 16.7 | 18.3 | 28.9 | 15.2 | 16.1 | 25.7 | 32.1 | 26.0 |
| Expenses: | | | | | | | | | |
| Personnel | 6.0 | 4.9 | 8.3 | 12.8 | 3.8 | 4.9 | 5.7 | 3.8 | 3.1 |
| Wrapping, supplies | .7 | .4 | 1.5 | .8 | .5 | .5 | .3 | .2 | .2 |
| Utilities | .5 | .2 | .5 | .9 | .7 | .1 | 2.4 | .2 | .3 |
| Laundry | .1 | — | .1 | — | — | — | — | — | — |
| Insurance, outside service, telephone, bad checks, over-short, miscella- neous | .2 | .2 | .2 | .2 | .2 | .1 | .2 | .2 | .2 |
| Repairs, maintenance | .2 | .1 | .2 | .3 | .4 | .1 | 1.6 | .1 | .1 |
| Rent, depreciation of leasehold improvements | 1.4 | 1.4 | 1.0 | 2.7 | .9 | 1.0 | 1.8 | 1.2 | 1.6 |
| Licenses, taxes | .2 | .2 | .2 | .2 | .2 | .2 | .2 | .2 | .3 |
| Depreciation equipment | .7 | .4 | .7 | 1.4 | 1.0 | .3 | 3.2 | .3 | .2 |
| Advertising, promotion | .8 | .6 | .9 | 1.0 | .9 | .8 | .5 | 1.0 | 1.3 |
| Stamps | 2.0 | 2.0 | 2.0 | 2.0 | 2.0 | 2.0 | 2.0 | 2.0 | 2.0 |
| All other overhead | 1.2 | 1.2 | 1.2 | 1.2 | 1.2 | 1.2 | 1.2 | 1.2 | 1.2 |
| Total expenses | 14.0 | 11.6 | 16.8 | 23.5 | 11.9 | 11.2 | 19.0 | 10.4 | 10.5 |
| NOP (before taxes) | 4.8 | 5.1 | 1.5 | 5.4 | 3.3 | 4.9 | 6.6 | 22.0 | 15.5 |

**11.** *Solving a problem on your campus* (requires additional research). On all college campuses, some common problems exist. At least, they exist in the minds of many of the faculty, students, and staff. From the list of problem areas that follows, select one you regard as a problem at your institution.

For the problem that you select, you will first gather all the significant information that concerns it. When you are thoroughly acquainted with the facts of your problem, you will gather whatever authoritative information you can concerning how it may be solved. Perhaps your research will involve looking through bibliographical sources to find out what has been done on other campuses. It may involve getting information or opinions from the various people on campus who are involved in the problem. When you have all this information, you will carefully analyze your problem in the light of all available knowledge. Then you will arrive at a recommended solution.

So that the situation will appear to be realistic, you may assume the appropriate role or position at your college. Present your work in suitable report form.

Your problem area possibilities are as follows (some are broad and will need to be made specific).

Library operation
Campus security
Athletic ticket sales policies
Administration regulation of social
 activities
Dress regulations
Student government
Registration procedure
Faculty-student relations

Orientation program for freshmen
Curriculum improvement
Increasing enrollments
Cheating
Improving cultural atmosphere on
 campus
Class attendance policies
Scholastic probation policies
Parking

## LONG PROBLEMS

1. *Determining the outlook for investments in the* —— *industry* (requires additional research). Assume that you are employed in the investments research department of the Whitmore Foundation, a philanthropic trust with over 300 million dollars of invested funds. You have been assigned the task of determining the general outlook for investments in the —— industry (choose one from list below).

Specifically, you will review past and present status of the industry's profits, sales, production, and the like. From these reviews you may be able to detect trends which may continue into the immediate future. Too, you will gather all facts and authoritative opinion relating to future growth. From all of this you hope to be able to make a somewhat specific recommendation about investments in the industry in general.

Although your report will concern the industry rather than a specific company (or companies), you are likely to refer frequently to the major firms in the industry. And your recommendation might point out the industry leaders. Write your report in a form appropriate for the formality of this situation. Submit it to the Investment Board, Whitmore Building, 317 Parkhurst Avenue, New York City 10018. Industries to choose from:

| A. | Aircraft | I. | Tobacco |
|----|----------|----|---------|
| B. | Electronics | J. | Paper |
| C. | Chemicals | K. | Food Processing |
| D. | Aluminum | L. | Automotive |
| E. | Steel | M. | Petroleum |
| F. | Textile | N. | Publishing |
| G. | Shoes | O. | Clothing (men's, women's |
| H. | Pharmaceuticals |  | or children's) |

2. *Interpreting a survey to help in planning Cotton Teens advertising.*
As a research assistant for Durway-Barlow Advertising Agency you
have been called into the office of your boss, Reginald W. Conway, the
agency's director of research. From Mr. Conway you learn that the
agency has landed the lucrative account of Cotton Teens, Inc., manufacturers of a line of cotton ready-to-wear clothing for teenage girls. As
usual, planning for the first advertising campaign will utilize pertinent
research information.

Fortunately, Mr. Conway feels that he already has the information he
needs for his purpose in some survey information given him by the Cotton Teens people. This survey, a reliable one conducted by Cotton Teens
own research staff less than a year ago, contains the answers to the
primary question facing the account executive. It helps to answer the
question of to whom the advertising should be directed; and it sheds
some light on the question of what appeals should be stressed.

The survey information still is in raw form—tabulated only by questions
asked. It now must be analyzed and adapted to Cotton Teens advertising. And this is where you come in. Mr. Conway asks you to study the
tables below and to "see what's in them that will help us plan a campaign." You will, of course, write up your analysis and adaptation of the
statistics in good report form. Since the material is statistical, no doubt
you will make good use of graphic aids.

*Question:* "Which *one* of these six materials would you say: You have had
most experience with? Is best to wear in hot weather? Is best to wear in cold
weather? Lasts longest? Keeps its shape best? Is easiest to care for? Is least
likely to wrinkle? Is the best value for its money?" (1,751 girls and 368 mothers
were asked each of these questions.)

|  |  |  |  | Fibers |  |  |  |
|---|---|---|---|---|---|---|---|
| Question answered | Cotton | Rayon | Nylon | Orlon | Dacron | Wool | Not ascertained |
| Most experience with? |  |  |  |  |  |  |  |
| Girls . . . . . . . . . . . . . . | 95% | * | 1% | * |  | 4% | 1% |
| Mothers . . . . . . . . . . . | 98 | * | 2 | * |  | 2 | * |

| Question answered | Fibers | | | | | | |
|---|---|---|---|---|---|---|---|
| | Cotton | Rayon | Nylon | Orlon | Dacron | Wool | Not ascertained |
| **Best to wear in hot weather?** | | | | | | | |
| Girls . . . . . . . . . . . . . . | 87 | 2% | 9 | * | 1% | * | 1 |
| Mothers . . . . . . . . . . . . | 93 | 1 | 4 | * | 1 | | 1 |
| **Easiest to care for?** | | | | | | | |
| Girls . . . . . . . . . . . . . . | 54 | 1 | 28 | 6% | 4 | 6 | 1 |
| Mothers . . . . . . . . . . . . | 47 | * | 34 | 9 | 6 | 4 | 2 |
| **Keeps its shape best?** | | | | | | | |
| Girls . . . . . . . . . . . . . . | 51 | 1 | 10 | 12 | 2 | 20 | 6 |
| Mothers . . . . . . . . . . . . | 40 | 1 | 13 | 11 | 5 | 26 | 8 |
| **Best value for the money?** | | | | | | | |
| Girls . . . . . . . . . . . . . . | 49 | 1 | 6 | 6 | 2 | 22 | 14 |
| Mothers . . . . . . . . . . . . | 60 | | 11 | 3 | 3 | 14 | 9 |
| **Lasts longest?** | | | | | | | |
| Girls . . . . . . . . . . . . . . | 36 | 1 | 11 | 5 | 1 | 39 | 8 |
| Mothers . . . . . . . . . . . . | 32 | 1 | 19 | 2 | 2 | 36 | 9 |
| **Least likely to wrinkle?** | | | | | | | |
| Girls . . . . . . . . . . . . . . | 7 | 2 | 31 | 11 | 6 | 35 | 8 |
| Mothers . . . . . . . . . . . . | 5 | 1 | 42 | 10 | 11 | 24 | 8 |
| **Best to wear in cold weather?** | | | | | | | |
| Girls . . . . . . . . . . . . . . | 6 | * | 1 | 5 | 1 | 86 | 2 |
| Mothers . . . . . . . . . . . . | 13 | 1 | 4 | 5 | 2 | 74 | 3 |

Percentages may add to more than 100 because some respondents gave more than one answer.
Asterisk indicates less than 1 percent.

*Question:* "Would you tell me everything you dislike about cotton?"

| Unfavorable characteristics | Girls | | | | | | | | | | Mothers | |
|---|---|---|---|---|---|---|---|---|---|---|---|---|
| | U.S. total | | 14 Years | | 15 Years | | 16 Years | | 17 Years | | | |
| | % | Total | % | Total | % | Total | % | Total | % | Total | % | Total |
| **Appearance and styling** . . . . . . . . | | 24 | | 17 | | 25 | | 23 | | 34 | | 15 |
| Wrinkles easily . . . | 23 | | 17 | | 24 | | 22 | | 30 | | 15 | |
| Not good for dressup wear . . . | 1 | | * | | 1 | | * | | 1 | | * | |
| Catches lint . . . . . | 1 | | 1 | | 1 | | 2 | | 3 | | * | |
| **Care and laundering.** . . | | 9 | | 6 | | 11 | | 12 | | 8 | | 14 |
| Requires washing (often) . . . . . . . | 3 | | 2 | | 2 | | 5 | | 4 | | 1 | |
| Requires ironing (often) . . . . . . . . | 3 | | 2 | | 4 | | 4 | | 3 | | 6 | |
| Difficult to iron. . . . | 2 | | 2 | | 2 | | 2 | | 1 | | 3 | |
| Difficult to wash . . . | 1 | | 1 | | 1 | | * | | * | | 3 | |
| Requires starching (often) . . . . . . . | 1 | | 1 | | 1 | | 2 | | 1 | | 2 | |

|  | | Girls | | | | |
| Unfavorable characteristics | U.S. total | 14 Years | 15 Years | 16 Years | 17 Years | Mothers |
|  | % Total | % Total | % Total | % Total | % Total | % Total |
| Poor appearance after starching. . . . | 1 | * | 1 | * | * | * |
| Doesn't dry quickly . | * | * | 1 | | | * |
| All other care and laundering. . . . . . | * | | | | * | * |
| Durability . . . . . . . . | 8 | 7 | 8 | 8 | 10 | 8 |
| Doesn't hold colors; fades, runs. . . . . . | 5 | 5 | 5 | 6 | 5 | 6 |
| Not durable; frays, ravels, splits, tears . . . . . . . . | 1 | 1 | 1 | 1 | 2 | 2 |
| Doesn't hold shape; shrinks, stretches. . . . . . | 1 | 2 | 2 | 1 | 1 | 1 |
| Flimsy, limp. . . . . . | 1 | * | * | 1 | 2 | |
| Weight and comfort. . . | 1 | 2 | 1 | * | 1 | |
| Too hot, heavy . . . . | 1 | 1 | * | | 1 | |
| Too sheer, thin . . . . | * | 1 | * | * | | |
| Scratches, itches, sticks, clings. . . . . | * | 1 | * | | * | |
| All other . . . . . . . . | 1 | 1 | * | 1 | 1 | * |
| Dislikes nothing about cotton . . . . . | 60 | 64 | 59 | 64 | 53 | 66 |
| Not ascertained . . . . . | 4 | 6 | 4 | 3 | 4 | 4 |
| Number of Cases . . . | 1,751 | 468 | 450 | 445 | 382 | 368 |

Percentages (left column) add to more than their group totals (right column) and these add to more than 100 because some respondents gave more than one answer.
Asterisk indicates less than 1 percent.

*Questions:* "Which of these items do you and your mother *usually* shop for together?" "Who *usually* makes the final decision about what to buy—you or your mother?" (1,751 girls)

| | Shopping done by | | | | Final decision made by | | | |
| Items of clothing | Daughter | Mother | Both | Not ascertained | Daughter | Mother | Both | Not ascertained |
|---|---|---|---|---|---|---|---|---|
| Dresses . . . . . . . . . | 20% | 4% | 72% | 4% | 42% | 15% | 39% | 4% |
| Skirts. . . . . . . . . . . | 36 | 3 | 57 | 4 | 54 | 10 | 32 | 4 |
| Sweaters . . . . . . . . | 43 | 7 | 46 | 4 | 58 | 10 | 26 | 6 |
| Blouses . . . . . . . . . | 50 | 6 | 40 | 4 | 61 | 9 | 25 | 5 |
| Rainwear. . . . . . . . | 16 | 6 | 41 | 37 | 28 | 13 | 24 | 35 |
| Slips and petticoats . . . . . . | 48 | 13 | 35 | 4 | 57 | 14 | 24 | 5 |
| Anklets. . . . . . . . . | 66 | 11 | 17 | 6 | 71 | 9 | 14 | 6 |

*Question:* "Generally speaking, at what age do you think a girl is old enough to do her own shopping and pick out her own clothes?"

| Suggested age at which girl is old enough to shop | Girls | | | | | |
|---|---|---|---|---|---|---|
| | U.S. total | 14 Years | 15 Years | 16 Years | 17 Years | Mothers |
| Under 14 years . . . . . . . . . . | 7% | 11% | 6% | 5% | 8% | 5% |
| 14 years . . . . . . . . . . . . . . | 18 | 26 | 17 | 16 | 13 | 14 |
| 15 years . . . . . . . . . . . . . . | 21 | 15 | 27 | 23 | 18 | 11 |
| 16 years . . . . . . . . . . . . . . | 21 | 18 | 17 | 24 | 25 | 21 |
| 17 years . . . . . . . . . . . . . . | 9 | 8 | 11 | 8 | 11 | 13 |
| 18 years . . . . . . . . . . . . . . | 6 | 4 | 6 | 10 | 7 | 12 |
| 19 years . . . . . . . . . . . . . . | 2 | 1 | 2 | 1 | 2 | 1 |
| 20 years or over . . . . . . . . . . | 1 | 1 | 2 | * | * | 1 |
| Qualified answers . . . . . . . . . | 7 | 5 | 7 | 7 | 7 | 17 |
| Not ascertained . . . . . . . . . . | 8 | 11 | 5 | 6 | 9 | 5 |
| Number of cases . . . . . . . . | 1,751 | 468 | 450 | 445 | 382 | 368 |
| Median age named (years) . . . | 15.8 | 15.4 | 15.7 | 16.0 | 16.1 | 16.4 |

Asterisk indicates less than 1 percent.

*Questions:* "Have you shopped for and bought a dress within the past 12 months?" If bought dress: "Did you plan to use the dress as an everyday or a dressup dress?" If did not buy dress: "Have you shopped for and bought a skirt within the past 12 months?"

| Purchase of dress or skirt | U.S. total | | Age of girls | | | | | | | |
|---|---|---|---|---|---|---|---|---|---|---|
| | | | 14 Years | | 15 Years | | 16 Years | | 17 Years | |
| | % | Total | % | Total | % | Total | % | Total | % | Total |
| Bought dress. . . . . . . | | 76 | | 68 | | 76 | | 79 | | 83 |
| Everyday dress . . . . | 13 | | 11 | | 14 | | 12 | | 16 | |
| Dressup dress . . . . . | 51 | | 47 | | 51 | | 54 | | 52 | |
| For both purposes . . | 12 | | 10 | | 11 | | 13 | | 15 | |
| Bought skirt . . . . . . . | | 15 | | 17 | | 16 | | 14 | | 11 |
| Bought neither . . . . . | | 9 | | 15 | | 8 | | 7 | | 6 |
| Number of cases . . | | 1,751 | | 468 | | 450 | | 445 | | 382 |

*Question:* "Now, let's tie together all of your ideas about materials. What I'd like is your *general, overall* opinion. Would you tell me everything you like about cotton?"

| Favorable characteristics | Girls U.S. total % | Total | 14 Years % | Total | 15 Years % | Total | 16 Years % | Total | 17 Years % | Total | Mothers % | Total |
|---|---|---|---|---|---|---|---|---|---|---|---|---|---|
| Care and laundering. . . . . | | 79 | | 77 | | 75 | | 80 | | 83 | | 83 |
| Easy to wash and care for . . . . . . . . | 59 | | 59 | | 53 | | 65 | | 57 | | 65 | |
| Easy to iron . . . . . . . . | 36 | | 39 | | 33 | | 34 | | 37 | | 25 | |
| Starches well . . . . . . . | 14 | | 10 | | 15 | | 15 | | 15 | | 13 | |
| Washable; no dry cleaning required . . . . | 9 | | 10 | | 8 | | 9 | | 10 | | 12 | |
| Good appearance after laundering. . . . . | 8 | | 5 | | 11 | | 7 | | 10 | | 11 | |
| Doesn't require frequent washing . . . . | 2 | | 2 | | 3 | | 1 | | 2 | | * | |
| Less expensive to keep clean. . . . . . . . | 1 | | 1 | | 1 | | 2 | | 2 | | 3 | |
| Easy to bleach. . . . . . . | 1 | | | | 1 | | 1 | | 1 | | 3 | |
| Requires little or no ironing . . . . . . . | * | | * | | 1 | | * | | 1 | | * | |
| Dries quickly . . . . . . . | * | | * | | 1 | | * | | | | | |
| All other care and laundering. . . . . . . | * | | * | | * | | * | | | | 1 | |
| Weight and comfort. . . . . | | 31 | | 33 | | 29 | | 33 | | 27 | | 20 |
| Light weight, cool . . . . | 22 | | 23 | | 22 | | 25 | | 19 | | 18 | |
| Doesn't scratch, itch, stick, cling. . . . . . . | 4 | | 3 | | 4 | | 4 | | 4 | | 2 | |
| Warm, heavy. . . . . . . | 3 | | 4 | | 2 | | 4 | | 2 | | 1 | |
| Comfortable. . . . . . . | 2 | | 4 | | 2 | | 2 | | 1 | | 1 | |
| Manageable; stays tucked in place . . . . . | 1 | | * | | 1 | | 1 | | 1 | | | |
| Absorbs perspiration . . . | * | | | | * | | * | | * | | 1 | |
| Appearance and styling. . . | | 31 | | 26 | | 34 | | 32 | | 34 | | 29 |
| Looks neat, fresh, crisp, doesn't wrinkle . . . . . . . | 20 | | 14 | | 23 | | 19 | | 24 | | 19 | |
| Looks nice, good, pretty . . . . . . . . . | 11 | | 13 | | 11 | | 11 | | 10 | | 12 | |
| Good for everyday wear; simple, informal. . . . . . . | 3 | | 1 | | 3 | | 3 | | 2 | | 2 | |
| Durability . . . . . . . . . | | 28 | | 26 | | 27 | | 26 | | 33 | | 51 |
| Durable; doesn't fray, ravel, split, tear . . . . . | 19 | | 18 | | 18 | | 17 | | 23 | | 42 | |
| Holds colors; doesn't fade, run. . . . . . . | 9 | | 8 | | 11 | | 9 | | 9 | | 17 | |
| Holds shape; doesn't shrink, stretch. . . . . . | 6 | | 6 | | 5 | | 4 | | 8 | | 7 | |
| Variety and selection. . . . | | 22 | | 21 | | 23 | | 21 | | 23 | | 24 |
| Variety of colors, prints, patterns . . . . . | 15 | | 14 | | 15 | | 15 | | 14 | | 14 | |
| Variety of styles, large selection. . . . . . | 6 | | 7 | | 5 | | 4 | | 8 | | 4 | |
| Variety of fabrics, weaves, materials . . . . | 3 | | 2 | | 3 | | 3 | | 4 | | 7 | |
| Comes in variety of garments . . . . . . . | 3 | | 2 | | 4 | | 3 | | 4 | | 7 | |
| Suitable for more occasions, seasons. . . . . | 17 | | 15 | | 17 | | 20 | | 15 | | 12 | |
| Less expensive. . . . . . . | 11 | | 9 | | 11 | | 15 | | 10 | | 23 | |
| Popular; in style. . . . . . | 3 | | 4 | | 3 | | 3 | | 1 | | * | |
| Easy to sew, mend . . . . . | 3 | | 3 | | 2 | | 4 | | 3 | | 2 | |
| Suitable for teenager's type, personality . . . . . | 1 | | 1 | | 1 | | 2 | | 1 | | 1 | |
| Practical . . . . . . . . . . | 1 | | 1 | | * | | 1 | | 1 | | 3 | |
| All other. . . . . . . . . . | 2 | | 2 | | 2 | | 2 | | 2 | | * | |
| Likes nothing about cotton . . . . . . . . . | 1 | | 1 | | 1 | | 1 | | * | | * | |
| Not ascertained . . . . . . | 3 | | 4 | | 5 | | 1 | | 3 | | 2 | |
| Number of cases . . . | 1,751 | | 468 | | 450 | | 445 | | 382 | | 368 | |

Percentages (left column) add to more than their group totals (right column) and these add to more than 100 because some respondents gave more than 1 answer.

Asterisk indicates less than 1 percent.

**3.** *A report on loans of the World Bank* (requires additional research). Mr. Eugene Black, president of the International Bank for Reconstruction and Development (The World Bank) has asked you, as general projects director, to study various projects that have begun or have been completed with the aid of loans from the bank. Some of the points that you will research and report on are:

1. To what companies or industries were loans made.
2. When and for how much were the loans made.
3. What were the amounts of the loans and at what interest rates.
4. How were the loans secured (or guaranteed).
5. For what purposes were the loans made.
6. Degree of progress of the projects.
7. Future outlook for the role of the World Bank.

Of course, you will want to present the latest data available. You know that many countries have received money from the bank, but as an organized and efficient researcher you will approach the research one step at a time. Choose from the following list one (1) country to investigate.

| | | | | | |
|---|---|---|---|---|---|
| A. | Colombia | H. | Tanganyika | O. | Spain |
| B. | Mexico | I. | Jamaica | P. | Syria |
| C. | Cuba | J. | Jordan | Q. | Uganda |
| D. | British Guiana | K. | Libya | R. | Venezuela |
| E. | Ceylon | L. | Malaya | S. | Thailand |
| F. | Iraq | M. | Nicaragua | T. | Surinam |
| G. | Guatemala | N. | Nigeria | | |

Your report will be fairly general; however, it should be specific enough to determine if the loans are fulfilling their objectives.

The report will be presented in appropriate form, to the president of the bank. Address: 625 WBA Building, Washington, D.C. 20005.

**4.** *Determining the profile of luggage and leather goods dealers.* Assume the role of a research specialist for *Leather and Luggage Goods*, the trade publication for the industry. At the oral request of Mike M. Henning, managing editor, you conducted a survey of dealer-subscribers to your publication. Now you are ready to write up your findings.

The objective of your research, as Mr. Henning worded it, is to "get a profile of leather and luggage goods dealers." A description of their operation, Mr. Henning reasoned, would be most helpful for organizations engaged in selling to the retailers as well as for the retailers themselves. The manufacturers, and in some instances their wholesale representatives, would be able to use such information in planning and assessing their sales efforts. Retailers would find such information helpful in comparing the various phases of their operations with others.

So it was with this general objective in mind that you designed the survey that would get you the information you feel is needed. From the publication's list of dealer-subscribers, you mailed 700 questionnaires.

You got a return of 116—a percentage of over 16, which you feel is good, considering the work involved in supplying the answers. Of this total, however, 15 turned out to be not usable for one reason or another. Counting branches of the 101 companies in the sample, 196 stores are represented.

As questionnaires are somewhat useless in their initial form, you tabulated them and you worked up some summary statistics from your tabulation. There may be still more to do, but at the moment your tabulations and statistical treatment of the data for the questions are as they appear at the end of this problem description.

You are now faced with the task of preparing a comprehensive writeup of your findings. You will use formal report form, and you will prepare the report for Mr. Henning. This report will form the permanent record of your investigation, and it will serve as the source of an article that will summarize the research for readers of your publication. With perhaps only minor change, the report probably will be duplicated and made available at cost to subscribers who want more details than the article will provide.

*Question:*    How many stores are you operating at present?

| Number | Number of stores operated |
|--------|---------------------------|
| 56 | 1 |
| 22 | 2 |
| 10 | 3 |
| 6 | 4 |
| 3 | 5 |
| 2 | 6 |
| 1 | 7 |
| 1 | 8 |

*Question:*    What is the size of your main store in square feet?

| Number of stores | Square feet of space |
|------------------|----------------------|
| 7 | Under 2,000 |
| 14 | 2,001–4,000 |
| 36 | 4,001–6,000 |
| 22 | 6,001–8,000 |
| 9 | 8,001–10,000 |
| 7 | 10,001–12,000 |
| 5 | Over 12,000 |
| Average size: | 6,160 square feet |
| High: | 20,000 |
| Low: | 1,200 |

*Question:*   How many square feet of space in your main store are devoted to selling, warehousing, and administration functions?

| | 1,000 and under | 1,001– 2,000 | 2,001– 3,000 | 3,001– 4,000 | 4,001– 5,000 | 5,001– 6,000 | Over 6,000 |
|---|---|---|---|---|---|---|---|
| Number of stores: | | | | | | | |
| Selling . . . . . . . | 6 | 12 | 31 | 28 | 15 | 5 | 4 |
| Warehousing. . . . | 7 | 13 | 35 | 24 | 12 | 6 | 5 |

| | 200 and under | 201– 400 | 401– 600 | 601– 800 | Over 800 |
|---|---|---|---|---|---|
| Number of stores: | | | | | |
| Administration . . . . | 5 | 15 | 48 | 30 | 3 |
| Average: | | | | | |
| Selling space. . . . . . . . . . . . . . . . | | | 3,009 | | |
| Warehouse space . . . . . . . . . . . . . | | | 2,688 | | |
| Administration space. . . . . . . . . . . | | | 613 | | |

*Question:*   What is (are) the size(s) of your branch store(s) in square feet?

| 1,000 and under | 1,001– 2,000 | 2,001– 3,000 | 3,001– 4,000 |
|---|---|---|---|
| 16 | 29 | 38 | 12 |

Average: 2,144 square feet.

*Question:*   How many employees (full-time equivalent) do you have (other than stock voting officers of the firm) in your main store?

Number of stores reporting, by area of employment

| Number employees | Selling | Adminis- tration | Warehouse* and other |
|---|---|---|---|
| 0 . . . . . . . . . . | 4 | 17 | 17 |
| 1 . . . . . . . . . . | 14 | 38 | 31 |
| 2 . . . . . . . . . . | 27 | 33 | 37 |
| 3 . . . . . . . . . . | 27 | 11 | 7 |
| 4 . . . . . . . . . . | 13 | 1 | 4 |
| 5 . . . . . . . . . . | 7 | 1 | 2 |
| 6 . . . . . . . . . . | 4 | — | 1 |
| 7 . . . . . . . . . . | 2 | — | 2 |
| 8 . . . . . . . . . . | | — | — |
| 9 . . . . . . . . . . | 2 | — | — |
| 10 . . . . . . . . . . | 1 | — | — |

* Large number of warehouse workers reported in stores supporting branch stores.

*Question:*  How many employees (full-time equivalent) are employed at each branch store?

| Number employees | Selling | Adminis- tration | Warehouse* and other |
|---|---|---|---|
| 0. . . . . . . . . . | 0 | 81 | 62 |
| 1. . . . . . . . . . | 37 | 14 | 33 |
| 2. . . . . . . . . . | 45 | — | — |
| 3. . . . . . . . . . | 10 | — | — |
| 4. . . . . . . . . . | 2 | — | — |

\* In some cases, administration and warehouse functions performed at main stores.

*Question:*  What was your total payroll to employees last year?

| Payroll | Number of stores |
|---|---|
| Under $10,000 . . . . . . . . . . . . . . . . . . . | 5 |
| $10,001–$20,000. . . . . . . . . . . . . . . . . . | 9 |
| $20,001–$30,000. . . . . . . . . . . . . . . . . . | 17 |
| $30,001–$40,000. . . . . . . . . . . . . . . . . . | 31 |
| $40,001–$50,000. . . . . . . . . . . . . . . . . . | 24 |
| $50,001–$60,000. . . . . . . . . . . . . . . . . . | 7 |
| $60,001–$70,000. . . . . . . . . . . . . . . . . . | 3 |
| $70,001–$80,000. . . . . . . . . . . . . . . . . . | 2 |
| Over $80,000 . . . . . . . . . . . . . . . . . . . | 3 |

Average: $ 38,431
High:    $112,400
Low:     $  3,600

*Question:*  What was your gross sales volume?

Sales, all stores including branches

| Gross volume | Number of stores |
|---|---|
| $200,000 and under . . . . . . . . . | 17 |
| $200,001–$400,000 . . . . . . . . . | 42 |
| $400,001–$600,000 . . . . . . . . . | 29 |
| $600,001–$800,000 . . . . . . . . . | 8 |
| $800,001–$1,000,000 . . . . . . . . | 3 |
| Over $1,000,000 . . . . . . . . . . | 2 |

Average: $  394,450
High:    $1,700,000
Low:     $   60,000

Sales of branch stores

| Gross volume | Number of stores |
|---|---|
| Under $100,000. . . . . . . . . . . . | 53 |
| $100,001–$200,000 . . . . . . . . . | 24 |
| $200,001–$300,000 . . . . . . . . . | 9 |

Average: $108,500
Low:     $ 40,000
High:    $284,000

*Question:* What percentage of gross sales volume was done in luggage, briefcases, personal leather goods, and gifts.

|  | Main store | Branches |
|---|---|---|
| Luggage . . . . . . . . . . . . . . . | 33.14% | 31.00% |
| Personal leather goods . . . . . . . . | 19.19 | 14.33 |
| Gift items . . . . . . . . . . . . . . | 17.13 | 26.20 |
| Handbags. . . . . . . . . . . . . . | 16.02 | 7.41 |
| Briefcases . . . . . . . . . . . . . | 14.52 | 21.16 |

*Question:* What percentage of your total sales volume was done in each of the 12 months last year?

| Monthly average for all reporting stores | |
|---|---|
| January. . . . . . . . . . . . . . . . . . . | 5.44% |
| February. . . . . . . . . . . . . . . . . . | 4.73% |
| March. . . . . . . . . . . . . . . . . . . | 6.17% |
| April . . . . . . . . . . . . . . . . . . . | 5.72% |
| May. . . . . . . . . . . . . . . . . . . | 7.54% |
| June . . . . . . . . . . . . . . . . . . | 9.12% |
| July. . . . . . . . . . . . . . . . . . . | 6.46% |
| August . . . . . . . . . . . . . . . . . | 7.37% |
| September . . . . . . . . . . . . . . . . | 10.11% |
| October . . . . . . . . . . . . . . . . | 6.15% |
| November . . . . . . . . . . . . . . . . | 10.09% |
| December . . . . . . . . . . . . . . . . | 21.10% |
| | 100.00% |

*Question:* What percent of sales do you spend on promotion?

| Percent of sales | Number of stores |
|---|---|
| Under 2. . . . . . . . . . . . . . . | 7 |
| 2–4 . . . . . . . . . . . . . . . . . | 49 |
| 4–6 . . . . . . . . . . . . . . . . . | 35 |
| 6–8 . . . . . . . . . . . . . . . . . | 5 |
| 8–10. . . . . . . . . . . . . . . . . | 3 |
| Over 10 . . . . . . . . . . . . . . . | 2 |

Average: 4.4%
High: 11.0%
Low: 0.5%

*Question:* What is your average gross margin, including all discounts, in luggage, briefcases, personal leather goods, and gift items?

|  | Luggage | Briefcases | Personal leather goods | Gifts |
|---|---|---|---|---|
| Number of stores |  |  |  |  |
| Under 35%. . . . . . . . . . | 5 | 5 | 2 | 3 |
| 35%–40% . . . . . . . . . . | 18 | 16 | 12 | 14 |
| 40%–45% . . . . . . . . . . | 42 | 43 | 31 | 39 |
| 45%–50% . . . . . . . . . . | 27 | 29 | 41 | 36 |
| 50%–55% . . . . . . . . . . | 9 | 7 | 12 | 7 |
| Over 55% . . . . . . . . . . |  | 1 | 3 | 2 |
| Average gross margin (%). . . . | 42.56 | 43.94 | 49.07 | 47.07 |
| High (%) . . . . . . . . . . . . | 54 | 55 | 58 | 58 |
| Low (%) . . . . . . . . . . . . | 32 | 35 | 37 | 37 |

*Question:*  How many manufacturers are represented in your luggage, briefcase, personal leather goods, and gift lines?

|  | Number of stores | | | | |
|---|---|---|---|---|---|
|  | Under 5 | 6–10 | 11–15 | 16–20 | 21–25 |
| Luggage . . . . . . . . . . . . | 8 | 39 | 47 | 7 |  |
| Briefcases . . . . . . . . . . . | 44 | 48 | 9 | — |  |
| Personal leather goods . . . . | 3 | 17 | 49 | 17 | 15 |

|  | Number of stores | | | | | |
|---|---|---|---|---|---|---|
|  | Under 20 | 21–40 | 41–60 | 61–80 | 81–100 | Over 100 |
| Gifts . . . . . . . . . . . . . . | 8 | 13 | 28 | 37 | 11 | 4 |

Average:
Luggage . . . . . . . . . . . . . . . . . . . . . . 11.15
Briefcases . . . . . . . . . . . . . . . . . . . . . 5.10
Personal leather goods . . . . . . . . . . . . . 13.00
Gifts . . . . . . . . . . . . . . . . . . . . . . . . 79.00

*Question:*  What percentage of your merchandise is imported?

| Percentage | Number of stores |
|---|---|
| Under 5. . . . . . . . . . . . . . . . | 65 |
| 6–10 . . . . . . . . . . . . . . . . . . | 27 |
| 11–15 . . . . . . . . . . . . . . . . . | 5 |
| 16–25 . . . . . . . . . . . . . . . . . | 3 |
| Over 20 . . . . . . . . . . . . . . . . | 1 |

Average:  5.7%
High:   28 %
Low:    1 %

**5.** *Determining the profile of a corporate executive.* Write a report for the American Association of Manufacturers, presenting a profile on its top executives. Such a study, the Association directors reason, should be most interesting, and it should also serve as a guide to executive manpower planning for the years ahead. It is with this planning point in mind that you will develop your report.

As a research specialist for the Association, you have been working on this assignment for the past eight weeks. First, from 183 cooperating companies you obtained the personnel records of 220 recently promoted executives at the presidential or vice presidential levels. Of the 220, 68 had been promoted to president, 30 to executive vice president, and 122 to various vice presidential positions. Then, from these records you extracted the information you feel will be needed in your report (see summary table at end). Now, you are ready to begin the task of organizing and analyzing the data for the final task of presenting them in report form.

Because your report will be published and made available to Association members who request it, you will take care to present it in appropriate form. Its formality and moderate length suggest some prefatory parts —perhaps a title page and preface (or an impersonal letter of transmittal addressed to all members). Whether you will need a table of contents and a synopsis will depend on the length of the finished report. If you find that a synopsis is not justified, you will be wise to begin your report in the direct order with a quick review of highlights.

| Company size of promoted executives* | Number of executives (all types) |
|---|---|
| Under 10 | 9 |
| 10–24 | 8 |
| 25–49 | 15 |
| 50–74 | 15 |
| 75–99 | 12 |
| 100–199 | 26 |
| 200–499 | 53 |
| 500–749 | 13 |
| 750–999 | 14 |
| 1000 and over | 18 |

\* Annual sales in dollars; 000,000 omitted.

Functional and corporate experience

| Principle work area | Presidents | Number of vice presidents | Total |
|---|---|---|---|
| Marketing | 18 | 30 | 48 |
| Administration | 18 | 26 | 44 |

| Principle work area | Presidents | Number of vice presidents | Total |
|---|---|---|---|
| Finance. . . . . . . . . . . . . . . . . | 6 | 28 | 34 |
| Operations. . . . . . . . . . . . . . . | 15 | 13 | 28 |
| Manufacturing. . . . . . . . . . . | 3 | 11 | 14 |
| Engineering . . . . . . . . . . . . . | 3 | 10 | 13 |
| Corporation planning. . . . . . . . | 3 | 7 | 10 |
| Personnel . . . . . . . . . . . . . . | 0 | 5 | 5 |
| Research and development. . . . . . . | 0 | 3 | 3 |
| Legal . . . . . . . . . . . . . . . . . | 1 | 5 | 6 |
| International . . . . . . . . . . . . . | 0 | 4 | 4 |
| Public relations . . . . . . . . . . . . | 0 | 3 | 3 |
| Other . . . . . . . . . . . . . . . . | 1 | 7 | 8 |
| Total . . . . . . . . . . . . . . . | 68 | 152 | 220 |

| Years with present employers* | Percent |
|---|---|
| Hired from outside . . . . . . . . . | 4.2 |
| Less than 1 year. . . . . . . . . . . | 13.7 |
| 1–5 years . . . . . . . . . . . . . . | 13.1 |
| 6–10 years . . . . . . . . . . . . . | 9.2 |
| 11–15 years . . . . . . . . . . . . . | 14.6 |
| 16–20. . . . . . . . . . . . . . . . | 15.3 |
| 21–25 years . . . . . . . . . . . . . | 11.0 |
| Over 25 years . . . . . . . . . . . . | 18.9 |

| Years in immediate past position | Percent |
|---|---|
| 1 years or less . . . . . . . . . . . . | 21.1 |
| 2 years . . . . . . . . . . . . . . . | 14.6 |
| 3 years . . . . . . . . . . . . . . . | 15.6 |
| 4 years . . . . . . . . . . . . . . . | 8.2 |
| 5 years . . . . . . . . . . . . . . . | 9.2 |
| 6 years . . . . . . . . . . . . . . . | 7.3 |
| 7 years . . . . . . . . . . . . . . . | 4.1 |
| 8 years . . . . . . . . . . . . . . . | 2.7 |
| More than 8 years. . . . . . . . . . | 17.0 |

* All executives.

| Education (highest level completed) | Presidents | Vice presidents | Total |
|---|---|---|---|
| H. S. graduates . . . . . . . . . . . . . . . . . | | 9 | 9 |
| Attended college . . . . . . . . . . . . . . . | 3 | 17 | 20 |
| Bachelor degree . . . . . . . . . . . . . . . . | 43 | 86 | 129 |
| Attended graduate school . . . . . . . . . . . | 6 | 17 | 23 |
| Advanced degree . . . . . . . . . . . . . . . | 16 | 23 | 39 |

| Undergraduate major | Presidents | Vice presidents | Advanced degree | Presidents | Vice presidents |
|---|---|---|---|---|---|
| Business administration . . . . . . . | 32 | 61 | M.B.A. . . . . . . | 7 | 11 |
| Engineering . . . . . . . | 17 | 45 | M.A. . . . . . . . | 2 | 2 |
| Liberal arts. . . . . . . . | 7 | 15 | LL.B. . . . . . . | 2 | 4 |
| Others . . . . . . . . . | 12 | 31 | M.S. . . . . . . . | 4 | 6 |
| | | | Others | 1 | — |

Summary tabulations of survey statistics

| Ages | Presidents | Executive vice presidents | Vice presidents |
|---|---|---|---|
| Under 35. . . . . . . . | 1 | 0 | 3 |
| 35–39. . . . . . . . . . | 5 | 0 | 9 |
| 40–44. . . . . . . . . . | 12 | 5 | 17 |
| 45–49. . . . . . . . . . | 25 | 7 | 44 |
| 50–54. . . . . . . . . . | 14 | 13 | 26 |
| 55–59. . . . . . . . . . | 8 | 2 | 18 |
| 60–65. . . . . . . . . . | 3 | 1 | 5 |

| Compensation* | Presidents | Executive vice presidents | Vice presidents |
|---|---|---|---|
| Under 30. . . . . . . . | 2 | 2 | 39 |
| 30–49 . . . . . . . . . | 16 | 6 | 62 |
| 50–69 . . . . . . . . . | 22 | 9 | 17 |
| 70–89 . . . . . . . . . | 17 | 8 | 3 |
| 90–109 . . . . . . . . | 6 | 3 | 1 |
| 110–129 . . . . . . . . | 3 | 2 | 0 |
| Over 130 . . . . . . . . | 2 | 0 | 0 |

* Base annual salaries in thousands of dollars.

**6.** *Determining competition's advertising for a local retailer* (requires research). You have been hired by a local retailer (a department, grocery, drug, or other store to be selected by your instructor) to construct a summary of the advertising done by the store's competition and to compare this advertising with the store's own efforts. Your goal, in general, is to inform the store management of its relative position with its competition and to inform it of any conditions that may be of value to it in its competitive effort. More specifically, your study will cover what the competition advertises, how much they advertise, and when and how often they advertise.

To get this information, you will collect the local newspapers for one full week. Then, you will go through them, page by page, recording the advertising information on forms you will design for the purpose. You will record the volume of the advertising, probably in columns (eight to the page) and inches. You will record the information on the merchandise advertised, prices, appeals, and such. Just how you will classify this information you will have to think out, but you know you will need such information for your report. The time (morning, evening) and position placement of the ad may also be of importance. In the end, you have sufficient information to give the company a good profile of the advertising of its competition in relation to its own.

After you have collected the data, you will tabulate it. Then you will analyze it and prepare it for presentation in a meaningful report for the store's management. The report will be dressed in formal style with all the prefatory elements.

**7.** *A study of the import and export toy market.* The American Association of Toy Manufacturers has employed you, a business analyst with the management consulting firm of H. Y. Larry and Associates, to conduct a study of the import-export market for toys.

Understandably, AATM is concerned with the continuing threat of toy imports. From time to time in the past, they have conducted studies to determine the extent of the import-export toy trade. The last study was made only two years ago, but according to talk in the trade it is now obsolete. Things are changing fast, they say.

So it was that AATM hired you to study the import and export toy business over the past two years. In general, they want a summary picture of what has happened in toy imports and exports over this period, with an emphasis on any changes that may have come about. More specifically, they want this summary to show from what countries we import what toys. And they want to know the same thing for our exports. As a general conclusion, they want to know the severity of our changes in import-export balance.

From the U.S. Department of Commerce, you quickly find the data that will form the basis of your study (see tables pages 446–49). You will need to study them for their meanings and to organize them for the most effective order of presentation. Then, you will write them up in the form of a formal report, using all the conventional prefatory pages. Address the report to the Association's board of directors, which authorized the study.

United States foreign trade in toys with major countries of origin and destination (value in U.S. $1,000)

| Countries | Last year | | This year | | Percentage change | |
|---|---|---|---|---|---|---|
| | U.S. imports | U.S. exports | U.S. imports | U.S. exports | U.S. imports | U.S. exports |
| Japan . . . . . . . . . | 44,195 | 6,183 | 50,028 | 3,784 | +13.2% | −38.8% |
| Hong Kong. . . . . . | 19,926 | 302 | 23,068 | 562 | +15.8 | +86.1 |
| United Kingdom . . | 5,845 | 2,224 | 8,977 | 2,235 | +53.6 | + 0.5 |
| Italy . . . . . . . . . | 2,802 | 783 | 4,823 | 1,056 | +72.1 | +34.9 |
| West Germany. . . . | 3,938 | 1,480 | 4,233 | 1,888 | + 7.5 | −27.6 |
| Canada . . . . . . . . | 1,178 | 8,084 | 1,302 | 8,756 | +10.5 | + 8.3 |
| Venezuela . . . . . . | — | 4,218 | — | 3,277 | — | −22.3 |
| Australia . . . . . . . | 63 | 880 | 72 | 1,404 | +14.3 | +59.5 |
| France . . . . . . . . | 594 | 745 | 748 | 1,122 | +25.9 | +50.6 |
| Other countries . . . | 2,900 | 9,304 | 3,423 | 11,234 | +18.0 | +20.7 |
| Total. . . . . . | 81,441 | 34,203 | 96,674 | 35,318 | +18.7 | + 3.3 |

United States toy imports for consumption by major countries, last two years (foreign value in U.S. dollars)

| Country of origin | Dolls and doll clothing | | Toys and games | | Wheeled goods | | Total | |
|---|---|---|---|---|---|---|---|---|
| | Last year | This year | Last year | This year | Last year | This year | Last year | This year |
| Canada | 7,060 | 5,010 | 980,914 | 928,876 | 190,081 | 367,897 | 1,178,055 | 1,301,783 |
| Mexico | 8,164 | 21,848 | 135,268 | 205,206 | — | — | 143,432 | 227,054 |
| Panama, Rep. of | — | 802 | 1,803 | 76,866 | — | — | 1,803 | 77,668 |
| Haiti | — | — | 5,173 | 6,738 | — | — | 5,173 | 6,738 |
| Peru | — | — | 6,221 | 2,464 | — | — | 6,221 | 2,464 |
| Sweden | 1,791 | 1,896 | 305,938 | 363,975 | 4,705 | 1,472 | 312,434 | 367,343 |
| Norway | 1,841 | 2,293 | 23,715 | 6,935 | 36,729 | 28,868 | 62,285 | 38,096 |
| Finland | 2,307 | 2,849 | 89,858 | 79,185 | — | — | 92,165 | 82,034 |
| Denmark | 2,699 | 1,195 | 164,654 | 138,957 | 16,512 | 14,741 | 183,865 | 154,893 |
| United Kingdom | 247,156 | 255,651 | 5,166,345 | 8,324,674 | 431,486 | 396,975 | 5,844,987 | 8,977,300 |
| Ireland | 5,374 | 440 | 5,561 | 1,599 | — | — | 10,935 | 2,039 |
| Netherlands | 4,202 | 2,058 | 51,323 | 94,080 | 16,614 | 59,912 | 72,139 | 156,050 |
| Belgium and Luxembourg | 2,218 | 373 | 9,844 | 13,553 | 12,402 | 11,625 | 24,464 | 25,551 |
| France | 87,715 | 75,143 | 503,050 | 671,563 | 2,777 | 1,585 | 593,542 | 748,291 |
| West Germany | 186,121 | 158,128 | 3,729,686 | 4,039,421 | 22,524 | 35,437 | 3,938,331 | 4,232,986 |
| East Germany | 5,760 | 4,249 | 9,087 | 8,513 | — | — | 14,847 | 12,762 |
| Austria | 3,844 | 3,762 | 139,071 | 156,296 | — | 406 | 142,915 | 160,464 |
| Czechoslovakia | 3,293 | 2,807 | 16,105 | 23,670 | 378 | 6,552 | 19,776 | 33,029 |
| Hungary | 11,949 | — | 7,117 | 13,844 | — | — | 19,066 | 13,844 |
| Switzerland | 23,900 | 2,370 | 94,207 | 94,353 | 1,390 | 1,322 | 119,497 | 98,045 |
| Poland | 102,161 | 144,376 | 28,023 | 34,569 | — | — | 130,184 | 178,945 |
| U.S.S.R. | 410 | 1,260 | 877 | 2,666 | — | — | 1,287 | 3,926 |
| Spain | 100,954 | 66,878 | 190,259 | 317,853 | 25,836 | 9,745 | 317,149 | 394,476 |
| Portugal | 32,919 | 61,361 | 467,781 | 299,041 | — | 273 | 500,700 | 360,675 |
| Italy | 470,850 | 456,115 | 2,020,164 | 3,595,081 | 311,003 | 772,060 | 2,802,017 | 4,823,256 |
| Yugoslavia | 2,285 | 284 | 120,190 | 251,219 | — | — | 122,475 | 251,503 |
| Greece | 12,210 | 2,955 | 5,099 | 10,239 | — | — | 17,309 | 13,194 |
| Israel | 4,740 | 2,001 | 3,354 | 9,984 | — | — | 8,094 | 11,985 |
| India | 9,786 | 2,029 | 15,864 | 8,314 | — | — | 25,650 | 10,343 |
| Indonesia, Rep. of | 150 | — | 6,038 | — | — | — | 6,188 | — |
| Korea, Rep. of | 1,825 | 13,256 | 61,811 | 66,063 | — | 4,027 | 63,636 | 79,319 |
| Hong Kong | 6,054,644 | 7,104,406 | 13,867,337 | 15,959,433 | 3,595 | — | 19,925,576 | 23,067,866 |
| Taiwan | 19,959 | 84,800 | 419,438 | 538,989 | — | — | 439,397 | 623,789 |
| Japan | 14,471,366 | 14,962,524 | 29,685,514 | 35,054,027 | 37,734 | 11,094 | 44,194,614 | 50,027,645 |
| Nansei + Nanpo Island | 5,783 | — | 666 | 280 | — | — | 6,449 | 280 |
| Australia | 337 | 547 | 62,973 | 71,281 | — | — | 63,310 | 71,828 |
| Other countries | 9,058 | 6,444 | 22,097 | 30,265 | — | — | 31,155 | 36,709 |
| Total | 21,904,831 | 23,450,110 | 58,422,525 | 71,500,072 | 1,113,766 | 1,723,991 | 81,441,122 | 96,674,173 |

United States toy exports by kind and by major countries, last two years (value in U.S. dollars)

| Country of destination | Dolls | | Indoor games | | Toys | | Wheeled goods | | Total | |
|---|---|---|---|---|---|---|---|---|---|---|
| | Last year | This year | Last year | This year | Last year | This year | Last year | This year | Last year | This year |
| Canada | 551,472 | 438,045 | 1,063,509 | 1,103,267 | 5,950,117 | 6,491,000 | 519,095 | 723,421 | 8,084,193 | 8,755,733 |
| Mexico | 80,113 | 109,456 | 205,019 | 32,273 | 523,648 | 619,227 | 107,166 | 105,750 | 915,946 | 866,706 |
| Guatemala | 42,325 | 31,224 | 26,479 | 7,161 | 205,175 | 220,615 | 86,860 | 45,204 | 360,839 | 304,204 |
| El Salvador | 25,568 | 18,217 | 10,047 | 10,344 | 151,733 | 121,275 | 32,039 | 40,781 | 219,387 | 190,617 |
| Honduras | 8,433 | 5,648 | 8,486 | 5,435 | 98,870 | 85,331 | 29,224 | 32,990 | 145,013 | 129,404 |
| Nicaragua | 7,305 | 8,653 | 10,620 | 4,743 | 119,591 | 100,485 | 81,737 | 59,595 | 219,253 | 173,476 |
| Costa Rica | 29,850 | 13,122 | 3,528 | 6,049 | 124,573 | 124,565 | 39,216 | 47,108 | 197,167 | 190,844 |
| Panama | 49,011 | 73,249 | 68,992 | 52,980 | 410,444 | 314,587 | 55,683 | 63,396 | 584,130 | 504,212 |
| Bermuda | 18,216 | 12,366 | 12,129 | 8,642 | 102,277 | 128,415 | 12,059 | 13,700 | 144,681 | 163,123 |
| Bahamas | 15,841 | 30,033 | 121,785 | 46,911 | 116,485 | 152,275 | 19,229 | 19,709 | 273,340 | 148,928 |
| Jamaica | 4,100 | 10,918 | 2,087 | 5,124 | 119,612 | 87,009 | 7,766 | 4,382 | 133,565 | 107,433 |
| Dominican Republic | 8,612 | 17,345 | 3,894 | 16,425 | 92,683 | 137,798 | 18,871 | 31,262 | 124,060 | 202,830 |
| Trinidad | 5,952 | 2,710 | 2,452 | 22,218 | 28,133 | 21,501 | 1,770 | 3,765 | 38,307 | 50,194 |
| Netherlands Antilles | 12,767 | 7,436 | 24,586 | 18,779 | 45,526 | 112,505 | 16,959 | 7,117 | 99,838 | 145,837 |
| Colombia | 3,520 | 18,802 | 2,243 | 558 | 8,350 | 32,722 | 600 | 4,626 | 14,713 | 56,708 |
| Venezuela | 277,691 | 277,218 | 863,409 | 515,711 | 2,600,760 | 2,113,605 | 476,167 | 370,843 | 4,218,027 | 3,287,377 |
| Ecuador | 3,233 | 1,474 | 4,616 | 3,164 | 93,669 | 109,258 | 18,054 | 13,093 | 119,572 | 126,989 |
| Peru | 90,453 | 130,310 | 59,057 | 18,592 | 292,608 | 433,641 | 101,045 | 150,718 | 543,163 | 733,361 |
| Bolivia | 13,600 | 6,487 | 3,853 | 57,732 | 30,513 | 23,848 | 730 | 1,758 | 48,696 | 89,825 |
| Chile | 7,234 | 9,765 | 2,400 | 45,597 | 22,512 | 32,354 | 1,156 | 915 | 33,302 | 88,631 |
| Brazil | 404 | 2,848 | 200 | — | 2,678 | 21,219 | 350 | 1,191 | 3,632 | 25,258 |
| Argentina | 116,378 | 159,296 | 1,830 | 684 | 90,200 | 102,948 | — | — | 208,408 | 262,928 |
| Iceland | 2,569 | 1,517 | — | 3,604 | 23,421 | 76,257 | 3,105 | 1,382 | 29,095 | 82,760 |
| Sweden | 35,203 | 10,494 | 61,706 | 182,730 | 442,200 | 395,963 | 1,158 | 2,750 | 540,267 | 591,938 |
| Norway | 10,350 | 6,402 | 5,341 | 6,784 | 58,913 | 104,687 | 850 | — | 75,454 | 117,873 |
| Finland | 2,450 | 1,006 | 6,076 | 3,442 | 82,424 | 79,375 | — | — | 90,950 | 83,822 |
| Denmark | 6,347 | — | 9,968 | 1,959 | 95,937 | 114,111 | — | — | 112,252 | 116,070 |
| United Kingdom | 105,074 | 193,882 | 871,972 | 588,388 | 1,215,066 | 1,402,499 | 31,420 | 49,960 | 2,223,532 | 2,234,729 |
| Ireland | — | — | 56,402 | 125,517 | 11,992 | 288,056 | — | 332 | 68,394 | 413,905 |
| Netherlands | 20,852 | 17,752 | 31,070 | 37,360 | 524,523 | 789,265 | 4,692 | 4,628 | 581,137 | 849,005 |

| | | | | | | | | | | |
|---|---|---|---|---|---|---|---|---|---|---|
| Belgium | 13,390 | 7,214 | 95,909 | 72,435 | 370,198 | 267,661 | 2,461 | — | 481,958 | 347,310 |
| France | 62,078 | 136,947 | 50,451 | 140,495 | 631,402 | 843,915 | 1,224 | 505 | 745,155 | 1,121,892 |
| West Germany | 143,402 | 271,068 | 389,369 | 254,541 | 901,802 | 1,358,166 | 45,845 | 3,849 | 1,480,418 | 1,887,624 |
| Austria | 657 | 6,869 | 1,080 | 1,686 | 35,728 | 145,662 | — | — | 37,465 | 154,217 |
| Switzerland | 31,315 | 22,439 | 28,372 | 113,784 | 348,671 | 502,895 | 2,291 | 592 | 410,649 | 639,118 |
| Spain | 51,571 | 109,705 | 244 | 4,258 | 76,699 | 125,680 | 212 | 1,052 | 128,726 | 240,235 |
| Portugal | 646 | 5,655 | 15,891 | 554 | 53,414 | 164,179 | — | 5,078 | 69,951 | 171,440 |
| Italy | 77,508 | 44,191 | 59,342 | 105,213 | 640,200 | 901,423 | 5,459 | 1,770 | 782,509 | 1,055,905 |
| Greece | 2,703 | 4,270 | — | — | — | 22,479 | — | 16,334 | 2,703 | 28,519 |
| Lebanon | 2,076 | 2,169 | 6,116 | 6,307 | 57,318 | 41,536 | 14,460 | 5,611 | 79,970 | 66,346 |
| Saudi Arabia | — | — | 7,419 | 22,016 | 11,584 | 15,357 | 3,235 | 10,244 | 22,238 | 42,984 |
| Thailand | — | — | 77,480 | 107,772 | 10,323 | 24,777 | 4,727 | 458 | 92,530 | 142,793 |
| Malaysia | 2,596 | 1,630 | 64,288 | 3,908 | 105,031 | 26,699 | 4,110 | 2,314 | 176,025 | 167,067 |
| Singapore | — | 3,409 | — | 23,524 | — | 137,820 | — | — | — | 290,049 |
| Philippines, Rep. of | 4,211 | 852 | 47,443 | 99,693 | 182,810 | 171,928 | 6,525 | 17,576 | 240,989 | 290,049 |
| Korea, Rep. of | — | — | — | 43,678 | 623 | 600 | — | — | 623 | 44,278 |
| Hong Kong | 13,102 | 94,636 | 36,776 | 153,210 | 221,230 | 296,929 | 31,109 | 17,715 | 302,217 | 562,490 |
| Taiwan | — | — | 3,450 | 93,696 | 218 | 2,065 | — | 3,668 | 3,668 | 95,761 |
| Japan | 180,486 | 391,808 | 5,086,226 | 2,962,374 | 882,685 | 388,606 | 33,214 | 40,840 | 6,182,611 | 3,783,628 |
| Nansei + Nanpo Island | 458 | — | 345,739 | 348,631 | 6,768 | 7,431 | 912 | 581 | 353,877 | 356,643 |
| Australia | 37,248 | 26,456 | 52,763 | 94,900 | 773,870 | 1,273,133 | 15,996 | 9,802 | 879,877 | 1,404,291 |
| New Zealand | 5,293 | 4,416 | — | 1,198 | 120,655 | 98,450 | 648 | 238 | 126,596 | 104,302 |
| French Pacific Islands | 1,255 | 1,726 | 384 | 532 | 36,775 | 43,162 | 3,787 | 3,942 | 42,201 | 49,362 |
| Libya | 764 | — | 15,614 | 49,694 | 3,716 | 8,691 | 494 | 364 | 20,588 | 58,749 |
| Spanish Africa | 894 | 628 | — | 376 | 6,176 | 26,858 | — | — | 7,070 | 27,862 |
| Liberia | 911 | 368 | 1,041 | 2,949 | 20,311 | 39,206 | 5,817 | 4,635 | 28,080 | 47,158 |
| Rep. of South Africa | 110,825 | 57,509 | 23,877 | 12,790 | 581,736 | 700,261 | 2,935 | 1,028 | 719,373 | 771,588 |
| Other countries | 17,556 | 17,497 | 70,223 | 88,696 | 218,159 | 313,464 | 29,141 | 19,245 | 335,079 | 438,902 |
| Total | 2,315,868 | 2,827,137 | 10,023,253 | 7,741,083 | 19,982,735 | 22,785,458 | 1,881,603 | 1,964,149 | 34,203,459 | 35,317,827 |

8. *What will business be like during the months ahead?*  As assistant to the president, De Berry Stores, Inc., you have drawn the assignment of writing a concensus forecast to be presented at the meeting of the board next Wednesday. President George De Berry of this chain of 24 major department stores in the East and Midwest gave you the assignment personally. The company does not employ an economist. De Berry does not believe in such "frills." "Why should we pay for them," he says, "when we can get free forecasts of all the top economists merely by reading through current periodicals."

De Berry's instructions, as usual, were quite vague; so much of what you will do is left to your good judgment. All the man said was that he wants you to survey the predictions of the nation's leading economic forecasters for the months ahead and to present your findings in a clear and meaningful report to the board. He wants the forecasts consolidated as much as it is practical—that is, he does not want merely a succession of individual forecasts. Your coverage will, of course, be largely of a general nature, covering all of the country's economy. But you will give special emphasis to whatever information you can find pertaining especially to department stores and to the eastern and midwestern regions.

In good short-report form your report will begin with a title page. Because the board will want the facts quickly, you will include a fast-moving synopsis. Whether you will need additional prefactory parts will depend on how voluminous your presentation turns out to be.

9. *Evaluating effectiveness of Ace distributors' salesmen.*  For the past three years, Ace Manufacturing has failed to keep pace with its competition in the home appliance industry. Quite naturally, Ace executives have become alarmed; and they have been searching hard for remedies to the situation. In their efforts to find the information they need in solving their problem, they have engaged the marketing consulting services of Central Research Institute. You work for Central, and you have been given the assignment.

You began your task about a month ago. Your first efforts consisted of gathering background facts about Ace's operations. Among other things, you learned that Ace is one of the five leading television manufacturers in the United States, the other four being Todd Manufacturing Company; Apco, Inc.; Davis Manufacturing Company; and Barr Industries, Inc. Until recently, Ace ranked first in volume of sales. Now it is down to third. As to its competitors, Ace sells to exclusive distributors; and the distributors sell to dealers in their territories. Obviously, Ace is highly dependent on its distributors, for its sales can be no better or worse than the sales efforts of the distributors' sales personnel.

Because Ace is so dependent on its distributors, Ace executives suspect that much of the blame for the sales decline should be placed on these distributors. But they can't be certain without proof. So they want you to check out their hypothesis. In addition, they want you to find any additional information which will give them an overall picture of the operations of appliance dealers at the retail level.

After collecting the necessary background data, you designed and conducted a personal interview survey among appliance dealers. You conducted the interview in three major retail areas (Dallas, Chicago, and New York). In each area you interviewed a proportionate number of randomly selected dealers of all five leading brands.

Now you have the survey findings, all neatly tabulated in two tables. In one (Table 1), you have tabulated the answers you asked concerning the dealers' experiences with distributors' salesmen. In the other (Table 2), you have assembled the summary percentages of the factors which tell about the overall operations of dealers.

**TABLE 1**

Tabulation of replies to TV dealer-distributor questionnaire

|  | Ace | | Todd | | Apco | | Davis | | Barr | |
|---|---|---|---|---|---|---|---|---|---|---|
|  | No. | % | No. | % | No. | % | No. | % | No. | % |
| Total dealers . . . | 199 | 100.0 | 120 | 100.0 | 125 | 100.0 | 110 | 100.0 | 133 | 100.0 |
| *1. Salesmen called* | | | | | | | | | | |
| Weekly . . . . . . . . | 76 | 38.2 | 40 | 33.3 | 44 | 35.2 | 31 | 28.2 | 44 | 33.1 |
| Every two weeks . . | 67 | 33.7 | 41 | 36.7 | 38 | 30.4 | 37 | 33.6 | 41 | 30.8 |
| Every three weeks . | 25 | 12.6 | 15 | 12.5 | 18 | 14.4 | 27 | 24.5 | 15 | 11.3 |
| Every four weeks . . | 10 | 5.0 | 9 | 7.5 | 11 | 8.8 | 5 | 4.6 | 13 | 9.8 |
| Over a month ago . . | 15 | 7.5 | 8 | 6.7 | 11 | 8.8 | 3 | 2.7 | 14 | 10.5 |
| Don't know . . . . . | 3 | 1.5 | 3 | 2.5 | 1 | 0.8 | 1 | 0.9 | 2 | 1.5 |
| Never . . . . . . . . | 3 | 1.5 | 1 | 0.8 | 2 | 1.6 | 5 | 4.6 | 4 | 3.0 |
| No answer . . . . . . | — | — | — | — | — | — | 1 | 0.9 | — | — |
| *2. Asked for window* | | | | | | | | | | |
| Yes . . . . . . . . . . | 39 | 19.6 | 25 | 20.8 | 31 | 21.8 | 19 | 17.3 | 28 | 21.0 |
| No . . . . . . . . . . | 155 | 77.9 | 95 | 79.2 | 88 | 70.4 | 88 | 80.0 | 102 | 76.7 |
| D.K. and N.A. . . . . | 5 | 2.5 | — | — | 6 | 4.8 | 3 | 2.7 | 3 | 2.3 |
| *3. Installed window* | | | | | | | | | | |
| Yes . . . . . . . . . . | 10 | 5.0 | 5 | 4.2 | 4 | 3.2 | 1 | 0.9 | — | — |
| No . . . . . . . . . . | 185 | 93.0 | 115 | 95.8 | 119 | 95.2 | 105 | 95.5 | 130 | 97.7 |
| D.K. and N.A. . . . . | 4 | 2.0 | — | — | 2 | 1.6 | 4 | 3.6 | 3 | 2.3 |
| *4. Brought displays* | | | | | | | | | | |
| Yes . . . . . . . . . . | 40 | 20.1 | 35 | 29.2 | 23 | 18.4 | 8 | 7.3 | 17 | 12.8 |
| No . . . . . . . . . . | 138 | 69.3 | 73 | 60.8 | 86 | 68.8 | 84 | 76.4 | 97 | 72.9 |
| D.K. and N.A. . . . . | 21 | 10.6 | 12 | 10.0 | 16 | 12.8 | 18 | 16.3 | 19 | 14.3 |
| *5. Explained line's features* | | | | | | | | | | |
| Yes . . . . . . . . . . | 67 | 33.7 | 65 | 54.2 | 45 | 36.0 | 22 | 20.0 | 48 | 36.0 |
| No . . . . . . . . . . | 131 | 65.8 | 55 | 45.8 | 78 | 62.4 | 85 | 77.3 | 83 | 62.5 |
| D.K. and N.A. . . . . | 1 | 0.5 | — | — | 2 | 1.6 | 3 | 2.7 | 2 | 1.5 |

**TABLE 1**   (*continued*)

| | Ace | | Todd | | Apco | | Davis | | Barr | |
|---|---|---|---|---|---|---|---|---|---|---|
| | No. | % | No. | % | No. | % | No. | % | No. | % |
| 6. *Dealer has folders* | | | | | | | | | | |
| Yes . . . . . . . . . . | 134 | 67.3 | 87 | 72.5 | 89 | 71.2 | 66 | 60.0 | 91 | 68.3 |
| No . . . . . . . . . . | 65 | 32.7 | 33 | 27.5 | 36 | 28.8 | 43 | 39.1 | 42 | 31.5 |
| D.K. and N.A. . . . . | – | – | – | – | – | – | 1 | 0.9 | – | – |
| 7. *Salesman sold on floor* | | | | | | | | | | |
| Yes . . . . . . . . . . | 8 | 4.0 | 10 | 8.3 | 4 | 3.2 | 2 | 1.8 | 6 | 4.5 |
| No . . . . . . . . . . | 190 | 95.5 | 110 | 91.7 | 120 | 96.0 | 106 | 96.4 | 126 | 94.7 |
| D.K. and N.A. . . . . | 1 | 0.5 | – | – | 1 | 0.8 | 2 | 1.8 | 1 | 0.8 |
| 8. *Helped plan advertising* | | | | | | | | | | |
| Yes . . . . . . . . . . | 29 | 14.6 | 17 | 14.2 | 18 | 14.4 | 6 | 5.5 | 19 | 14.3 |
| No . . . . . . . . . . | 169 | 84.9 | 103 | 85.8 | 106 | 84.8 | 102 | 92.7 | 113 | 84.9 |
| D.K. and N.A. . . . . | 1 | 0.5 | – | – | 1 | 0.8 | 2 | 1.8 | 1 | 0.8 |
| 9. *Understands problems* | | | | | | | | | | |
| Thoroughly . . . . . | 37 | 18.6 | 28 | 23.3 | 19 | 15.2 | 11 | 10.0 | 20 | 15.0 |
| To some extent . . . | 85 | 42.8 | 54 | 45.0 | 53 | 42.4 | 43 | 39.1 | 55 | 41.4 |
| Not at all . . . . . . . | 55 | 27.6 | 32 | 26.7 | 40 | 32.0 | 41 | 37.3 | 46 | 34.6 |
| D.K. and NA. . . . . | 22 | 11.0 | 6 | 5.0 | 13 | 10.4 | 15 | 13.6 | 12 | 9.0 |
| 10. *Helped with financial arrangements* | | | | | | | | | | |
| Yes . . . . . . . . . . | 6 | 3.0 | 2 | 1.7 | 2 | 1.6 | – | – | 7 | 5.3 |
| No—no need . . . . . | 181 | 91.0 | 116 | 96.7 | 118 | 94.4 | 103 | 93.7 | 117 | 87.9 |
| No—needed help . . | 5 | 2.5 | 1 | 0.8 | 2 | 1.6 | 3 | 2.7 | 5 | 3.8 |
| D.K. and N.A. . . . . | 7 | 3.5 | 1 | 0.8 | 3 | 2.4 | 4 | 3.6 | 4 | 3.0 |
| 11. *Interested in window service* | | | | | | | | | | |
| Yes . . . . . . . . . . | 87 | 43.7 | 36 | 30.0 | 45 | 36.0 | 39 | 35.5 | 62 | 46.6 |
| No . . . . . . . . . . | 108 | 54.3 | 82 | 68.3 | 78 | 62.4 | 70 | 63.6 | 69 | 51.9 |
| D.K. and N.A. . . . . | 4 | 2.0 | 2 | 1.7 | 2 | 1.6 | 1 | 0.9 | 2 | 1.5 |
| 12. *Prominence of display* | | | | | | | | | | |
| Best . . . . . . . . . . | 30 | 15.1 | 54 | 45.0 | 44 | 35.2 | 11 | 10.0 | 23 | 17.3 |
| Second best . . . . . | 46 | 23.1 | 34 | 28.3 | 39 | 31.2 | 22 | 20.0 | 41 | 30.8 |
| Third best . . . . . . | 43 | 21.6 | 13 | 10.8 | 27 | 21.6 | 42 | 38.2 | 34 | 25.6 |
| Fourth best . . . . . | 42 | 21.1 | 7 | 5.8 | 6 | 4.8 | 16 | 14.5 | 24 | 18.0 |
| No answer . . . . . . | 8 | 4.0 | 8 | 6.7 | 8 | 6.4 | 8 | 7.3 | 8 | 6.0 |
| 13. *Attractiveness of displays* | | | | | | | | | | |
| Excellent . . . . . . . | 53 | 26.6 | 54 | 45.0 | 48 | 38.4 | 9 | 8.2 | 21 | 15.8 |
| Good . . . . . . . . . | 43 | 21.6 | 34 | 28.3 | 26 | 20.8 | 41 | 37.3 | 39 | 29.4 |
| Fair . . . . . . . . . . | 44 | 22.1 | 16 | 13.3 | 27 | 21.6 | 28 | 25.4 | 36 | 27.0 |
| Poor . . . . . . . . . | 51 | 25.7 | 11 | 9.2 | 19 | 15.2 | 25 | 22.7 | 29 | 21.8 |
| No answer . . . . . . | 8 | 4.0 | 5 | 4.2 | 5 | 4.0 | 7 | 6.4 | 8 | 6.0 |

*Key to questions asked on Table 1:*
No.                              *Question*
  1.   Which of the following comments best explains how often the distributor's salesman calls on you?
  2.   On the last call, did he ask to set up a window display?
  3.   On the last call, did he set up a window display?

4. On the last call, did the salesman bring displays with him?
5. On the last call, did the salesman present his line's selling points to your personnel?
6. Do you now have a supply of booklets, brochures, envelope stuffers, etc., left by distributor's salesman?
7. Did the salesman actually work with your salesman selling his product on your floor within the last 30 days?
8. Has the salesman helped you plan any advertising, promotions, etc., in the past six months?
9. How well do you think this salesman understands your problems in handling his products.
10. Has the salesman given you any assistance in working out financial arrangements within the past year?
11. Would you be interested in window trimming services provided by the distributor?
12. How would you rank the quality of the displays you have seen for each of the five brands?
13. How would you rank the attractiveness of the displays of the five brands?

## TABLE 2

Comparative data regarding inventories and dealer attitudes

1. Number of leading brands stocked by Ace dealers (in percent)

| | |
|---|---|
| Only Ace | 14.1% |
| Ace and one other brand | 12.6 |
| Ace and two other brands | 30.1 |
| Ace and three other brands | 17.3 |
| Ace and all four leaders | 24.7 |

2. Percent of Ace dealers who also handle:

| | |
|---|---|
| Todd | 60.3% |
| Apco | 62.8 |
| Davis | 55.3 |
| Barr | 66.8 |

3. Average number of sets of each make per store

| | |
|---|---|
| Ace | 7.5% |
| Todd | 14.2 |
| Apco | 11.1 |
| Davis | 6.6 |
| Barr | 8.4 |
| All other makes | 25.2 |

4. Percent of Ace dealers with each type of Ace set in stock

| | |
|---|---|
| Portable (miniature) | 90.2% |
| Portable (regular) | 55.6 |
| Table model | 58.2 |
| Console | 28.1 |

5. Percent of dealers with Ace sets in windows, by type of set

| | |
|---|---|
| Portable (miniature) | 22.2% |
| Portable (regular) | 51.0 |
| Table model | 20.1 |
| Console | 10.8 |

**TABLE 2  (continued)**

6. Percent of dealers who suggested that:
   a. Manufacturers stop tie-in sales and
      overloading. . . . . . . . . . . . . . . . . . . . . . . . . 36.5%
   b. Provide better salesmen. . . . . . . . . . . . . . . . . 27.4
   c. Restrain price-cutters . . . . . . . . . . . . . . . . . . . 23.6
   d. Provide better margins . . . . . . . . . . . . . . . . . . 18.9
   e. Improve service . . . . . . . . . . . . . . . . . . . . . . . 13.8

Your next step is to interpret your findings as they apply to Ace's problem. Then you will organize the material for the best possible communication effect; and you will write the report. Hopefully, you will be able to draw a clear conclusion on the major hypothesis; and in the process you will be able to give Ace an overall picture of the current market. Should you need additional background information, problem facts, etc., use your imagination logically to supply it. And take care to consider using graphic aids wherever they can be used effectively in telling the report story. Use the formal report structure that this situation demands. Address the report to Mr. Eugene E. Orsag, vice president of marketing.

## SUBJECTS FOR LIBRARY RESEARCH REPORTS

The following topic suggestions may be used for library research reports. With most of the topics the specific facts of the case must be created through the student's (or perhaps the instructor's) imagination before a business-type problem exists.

### Accounting

1. Design a proposal for the inventory control system of X Company, a large manufacturer of electronic equipment and parts.
2. As the head accountant for X Company, justify your treatment of goodwill acquired by the takeover of Y Company.
3. Advise X Company on the question of whether it should change to a system of interperiod allocations of corporate income tax.
4. Recommend a treatment of lease transactions in the books of a certain lessee company.
5. Evaluate the alternative accounting methods available to X Company, which is committed to a policy of tax allocation.
6. As accountant for X Company, justify your treatment of the assets acquired by the takeover of Y Company.
7. Advise X Company management on the question of uniformity of accounting procedures between X Company and its nearest competitor.

8. Recommend to X Company a policy on the translation of foreign currencies in the consolidation of overseas subsidiaries.
9. Advise the chief accountant of X Company on the maintenance of capital in company accounts.
10. Advise X Company management on the accounting problems that will come about if it begins overseas operations.
11. Advise X Company management on the problems of departmentalization of factory overhead.
12. Develop a policy for X Company on the costing of joint products and by-products.
13. Advise the management of X Manufacturing Company on the question of whether to use process costing or job costing procedures.
14. Analyze break-even analysis as a decision-making tool for X Company.
15. Evaluate for X Company management the validity of the traditional matching process in determining corporate net income.
16. Analyze the relative effects upon income of the Fifo and Lifo methods of inventory valuation during a prolonged period of inflation.
17. Write a report for the American Accounting Association on the effects of computers on the demand for accountants.
18. Evaluate the utility of traditional variance analysis as a means of cost control.
19. Develop a proposal for the accounting treatment of the costs of a research program in X Oil Company.
20. Justify your progressive accounting treatment of revenues received under a four-year construction contract.
21. Establish a bad-debts policy and design a collection systems for X Company.
22. Determine the feasibility of a consolidated delivery service for City Y.
23. How should X Company handle the state sales tax on its books?
24. Design an inventory control plan for X Company.
25. Advise X Company management on the validity of return on investment as a measure of performance.
26. What are the methods X Company can use in handling errors which affected net income in prior years?
27. How should X Company handle its patents and copyrights on its books?
28. Report on the status of the use of operations research as a decision-making tool for accountants and managers.
29. How should X Company use cast-flow analysis as a guide in and for profit planning?
30. Evaluate alternative methods of measuring return on investments for X Company.
31. Report to X Company management on the trends in content and design of corporate annual reports.
32. Report to the American Accounting Association on the status of professional ethics in public accounting.
33. Summarize for the accounting department of X Company the most recent trends and developments in accounting theory.

34. Advise partners X and Y of the XY Company how priorities should be determined for cash distribution in the liquidation of their partnership.
35. Advise X Company management on income tax considerations in the selection of a form of business organization.
36. Report to X Company management on the advantages and disadvantages of the uniform cost accounting system.
37. Should X Company use an accelerated method of depreciation?
38. Recommend to X Company the proper disclosure of long-term leases in its financial statements.
39. Recommend to X Company management how it can make better use of the accounting department and accounting information.
40. How should X Company account for pension costs?

## Business education

1. Evaluate the effectiveness of closed-circuit television instruction.
2. How effective is programmed instruction in business education?
3. What should be the content of the business communication (or other subject) course?
4. How should teaching ability be measured?
5. What should be the role of the student in course and curriculum planning?
6. What should be the role of the business executive in developing courses and curricula for business education?
7. Should business teachers be unionized?
8. Examine the present status of business education teaching as a true profession.
9. Outline historical developments in business education.
10. What are the advantages and disadvantages of national business teacher organizations?
11. Make a comparison of business teacher training to the B.B.A. degree.
12. Describe the ideal certification program for business teachers.
13. Assess placement responsibilities of business education in secondary schools.
14. Describe how distributive education programs are coordinated.
15. Assess the function of career guidance in business education.
16. Describe the ideal education for careers in business.
17. Discuss the financing of business education programs at the secondary level.
18. Evaluate job training as a supplement of creating better consumers.
19. Examine the supervision of business education programs in secondary schools.
20. Outline the ideal training program for business education teachers.
21. Detail coordinating research efforts in business education.
22. Should a program for exceptional youths be developed in business education?
23. What are the effects of automation and data processing on teaching business subjects in secondary schools?
24. Describe the emerging role of the junior college in business education.

25. How are standards of achievement in the business education curriculum set?
26. What is the role of economics education at the secondary level?
27. Evaluate student achievement in course X.
28. Evaluate audio-visual aids as a supplement to teaching business subjects.
29. Outline various theories of learning applied to the teaching of business subjects.
30. Describe management techniques in the office.
31. Discuss the place of student opinions and evaluations in curriculum revisions.
32. Explore work measurements in the office.
33. Set up ideal testing procedures in business education.
34. Should business education be offered in the public secondary school or in a technical vocational school?
35. Should the business curriculum be specialized or should it provide a generalized, well-rounded education?
36. Trace the development of federal aid to business education.

## Finance

1. Advise overcapitalized X Company on the possibility of repurchasing shares.
2. Justify the use of ratio analysis to a major client of your brokerage firm.
3. Evaluate the advantages and disadvantages of issuing "no par" stock for X Company.
4. Advise the medical doctors at X Clinic as to whether they should incorporate their operation.
5. Should X Company lease or buy capital equipment?
6. Advise rapidly growing X Manufacturing Company on the form of organization it should take.
7. Advise faltering X Company as to whether it would be more valuable as a going concern than it would be in liquidation.
8. Should X Company establish a holding company in its corporate organizational structure?
9. Should X Company amend its policy of paying dividends at a constant proportion of earnings to one of paying on a constant per-share basis?
10. Examine the possibilities of factoring accounts receivable for X Company, which is experiencing a liquidity crisis.
11. Advise X Company as to whether it should seek to get its stock listed on a major stock exchange.
12. Develop a fundamental inventory control model for X Company.
13. Advise X Company on the policy it should follow in determining dividend payments.
14. Evaluate the utility of the payback method of investment analysis.
15. Recommend and justify a plan for financing expansion of X Company.
16. How will the present state of the market affect the success of the proposed rights offering of X Company?

17. Advise X Company as to whether it should select a capital structure that will serve to minimize the cost of capital and so promote maximum share prices.

18. Advise X Company management on how the prevailing condition of capital rationing in the company should affect its investment decision analysis.

19. What should be the role of the controllership function in cost control at X Company?

20. What is the most feasible way to finance newly formed X Company?


## Labor

1. For X Union investigate the impact technological evolution has had on unionism in the past decade.

2. Develop a new compensation for X Company that will best motivate employees.

3. Design a plan of employee discipline for X Company.

4. Evaluate the potential labor problems of X Company in _____ (country), where it is planning a new factory.

5. Advise X Company management on the use of the lockout as a means of dealing with its union.

6. For a specific national union make an objective report on union leadership in the United States during the past decade.

7. Evaluate the effects of a particular strike (your choice) on the union, the company, the stockholder, and the public. Write the report for a federal investigating committee.

8. Advise management of X Company on how to deal with Y Union, which is attempting to organize X's employees.

9. For a national union write a report on the trend of corruption in unions over the past 25 years.

10. How have union contracts limited the area of decision making?

11. Explore the relationships of the union and the white-collar worker.

12. Show trends and implications of teacher organizing.

13. Examine recent trends relative to the older worker and the stand taken by unions in this area.

14. Analyze the problem of automation and the unions' reactions to it.

15. Study the status and effects of the "right-to-work" laws.

16. Take a look at unions in business for themselves.

17. Set up plans for unionizing Company X.

18. Recommend a grievance system for Company X.

19. Should antitrust laws apply to unions?

20. Examine discrimination in unions.

21. What special problems arise in unionizing government employees?

22. Outline the power structure of unions and its implications.

23. Evaluate the future of process unionism.

24. Discuss unionism in retail stores and its effect on prices.

25. Describe labor regulation in state S.

26. Are unions monopolistic?

27. Now that the workers at X Company have been organized, what official attitude should management assume toward the union?
28. How should company X prepare for upcoming contract negotiations with the union?
29. What are the causes of industrial war and peace.
30. Should Company X join an employers' association?
31. Recommend a formal salary scale for X Company.

## Management

1. Advise Company X management on what it should do to overcome resistance to some basic change, such as a change in compensation plan.
2. Design an employee-selection procedure for X Company.
3. Recommend and justify to the board of directors of X Company a plan for exercising the firm's social responsibility.
4. Design a control system for preventing individual espionage at X Company.
5. Evaluate for X Oil Company the application of statistical decision theory in overcoming the problems of uncertainty in oil exploration.
6. Evaluate for X Company the possibility of using brainstorming sessions in strategic policy making.
7. Evaluate for X Manufacturing Company the use of the informal grapevine as a means of improving communication within the organization.
8. Using the best authoritative ideas available, design a management information system for X Company.
9. Design a public relations campaign for X Company.
10. Recommend an executive evaluation plan for X Company.
11. Develop for X Company a guide to ethics in its highly competitive business situation.
12. Analyze break-even analysis as a decision-making tool for X Company.
13. Evaluate the various methods of determining corporate performance and select the one most appropriate for Company X.
14. Design a program for evaluating a business, taking account of nonprofit measures of performance as well as profitability.
15. Determine the business outlook for the _____ industry.
16. Determine the effects of recent labor-management court rulings on X Company.
17. Recommend a suggestion system for X Company.
18. Recommend to X Company the feasibility of using a community computer center.
19. Report on the civil and criminal liabilities of corporate executives.
20. Advise X Company on the procedures for incorporating in _____ (state).
21. Recommend a profit-sharing plan for X Company personnel.
22. Can X Company profitably use a computer?
23. Would hiring handicapped workers be charity or good business for X Company?

24. Can creativity be taught to X Company executives?
25. Design a program for achieving optimum discipline in X Company.
26. Determine for X Company its policy toward aid to education.
27. Assess the extent of pollution control in _____ industry for an association of firms in the industry.
28. Should _____ Soap Company cease using phosphates in its detergents?
29. Determine the extent of minority recruiting, hiring, and training in the _____ industry for a legislative committee.
30. Determine the extent of discrimination against women in business for an asociation of businessmen.

## Personnel administration

1. Interpret for X Company the effects of court decisions on testing and hiring employees.
2. Develop and justify a program of fringe benefits for a large industrial company.
3. Recommend an equitable compensation program for the salesmen for X Company.
4. Design a program for breaking down line-staff barriers in X Company.
5. Analyze for X Company the problems of hiring under- and overqualified staff.
6. Recommend a retirement plan for X Company.
7. Devise an operational safety program for X Company.
8. Design a workable program for controlling activities of scientific and professional employees of X Company.
9. Survey the literature to find meaningful guides for selecting executives for foreign service for X Company.
10. Design a safety training program for X Company.
11. Develop a method to test morale in X Company.
12. Should X Company use the lie detector test to screen prospective employees?
13. Set up a secretary (or other position) selection plan for X Company.
14. Report to a major labor union the progress of women in the job market.
15. Evaluate the use of teaching machines (or some other innovative teaching technique) for the training programs of X Company.
16. Report to the management of X Company what information the employees need to know about the company and its operation.
17. Report to the safety director of X Company on the validity of the accident-proneness concept.
18. Report to the safety director of X Company on the effect of age and experience on accidents.
19. Develop a personnel testing program for X Company.
20. Report to X Company management on recent trends and developments in employee remuneration.
21. Advise X Company management on the merits and demerits of the guaranteed annual wage.

# Marketing

1. Determine the major opportunities in the environment for the marketing strategy of X National Bank.
2. Develop a plan for measuring the effectiveness of Company X advertising.
3. Design a PERT/CPM network for the marketing aspect of product management in Company X.
4. Develop a compensation plan for the salesmen of X Company.
5. Assuming a budget of $_____, develop an advertising plan for X Company.
6. For a major shopping center in your area, construct a plan for setting the advertising budget.
7. Develop a global advertising policy for the X Company, a multinational retail organization.
8. Determine the future for trading stamps for X Company, a major chain of department stores.
9. What problems will Company X encounter in trading with countries behind the iron curtain?
10. Set up and defend a multistage approach to pricing decisions for X Company.
11. Determine the problems X Company will encounter in introducing a new product to its line.
12. What is the importance of fixed ratios in setting pricing strategy for X Company?
13. Select the optimal channel of distribution for new product Y in your area and justify your choice.
14. Design a marketing strategy for your professional cleaning service.
15. Develop a segmented profile of the target market for product Y and analyze the utility of this information in the Company X's marketing management.
16. Explore the possibilities of trade with _____ (a foreign country) for X Company.
17. Determine changes in successful sales techniques for X Sales Company.
18. Report on the future of drive-in grocery stores for X Investment Company.
19. Determine the value of a college education in marketing work.
20. Should X Department Stores use credit cards?
21. Will pallet warehousing reduce costs for X Company?
22. Determine for Company X the social and ethical aspects of pricing for the market.
23. Determine for the American Consumer League whether advertising should be regulated.
24. Design a promotion campaign for the opening of Bank X.
25. Explore the possibilities of door-to-door selling for X Company.
26. Determine the best method to sell a new issue of common stock for well-established Company X.
27. Should X Company use contests to increase efforts of its salesmen?
28. Determine for a national department store chain the changing trends in service offered in the field.

29. Answer for the X Manufacturing Company the question of whether it should engage in "lease" sales.
30. Should Company X, a regional automotive supply chain, use centralized or decentralized warehousing?
31. Should Company X rent or lease trucks for distribution of its products?
32. How should X Company determine the amount to allocate to advertising.
33. Should X Company use its own advertising department or an agency?
34. Design a promotional program for introducing new product Y.
35. Where should X Company locate its next supermarket (or drugstore, service station, etc.) in your area?
36. Determine the influences on fashion in the _____ industry.
37. How can downtown merchants in _____ (city) cope with the trend toward suburban shopping centers?
38. Determine the trends in packaging in the _____ industry.
39. Make a market study of _____ (a city) to determine whether it is a suitable location for _____ (a type of business).
40. Should X Company establish its own sales force, use manufacturers' agents (manufacturers' representatives), or use selling agents?
41. Should X Petroleum Company attempt to increase its share of the market by engaging in active price competition?
42. Determine for X Company the best channel of distribution for _____ product line.
43. How should X Company evaluate the performance of its salespeople?
44. Should X Company enter the _____ market?
45. What price policy should X Company use on entering the _____ market?

# 16

# Oral communication

**P**ERHAPS LETTERS and reports are the business communication areas most in need of our improvement efforts. But they represent only a part of the communication that occurs in business. Oral communication is by far the most important communication area in business, at least on the basis of time consumed. Thus, our attention appropriately turns to this vital subject.

As we all know from experience, much of our oral communication is informal. Primarily it is of the person-to-person variety that occurs whenever people get together. Obviously, this is an activity in which all of us have considerable experience. And most of us do a reasonably good job of the communication that occurs in business. Oral communication is just too complex and involved for us to do otherwise. In fact, so complex and involved is this activity that a thorough review of it is beyond the scope of this book. In a sense, however, already we have covered the essentials of the subject, for much of the first six chapters of this book pertains to it. Especially is this true of the miscommunication patterns reviewed in Chapter 6.

In addition to the informal, personal communicating that goes on in business, there is some more formal, oral communicating. Specifically, we may refer to these communications as oral reports. Oral reports are not made frequently; but when they are made, usually they are extremely important. Frequently they determine the course of a business or the life plans of the people involved. Oral reporting is a subject in which most of us have had little experience and even less instruction. Thus, it is likely to be an area in which we genuinely need help. For this reason, it is the center of much of the following discussion.

Although not oral communication in the literal sense of the word, the techniques of listening also deserve our attention. Elementary and routine as this subject may appear to be, it is a communication area that most of us perform poorly. It is a major cause of the miscommunication that occurs in business. Thus, justifiably it is our second major subject for review in the pages which follow.

## THE NATURE OF ORAL REPORTS

A logical first step in the study of oral reporting is to define the term. Certainly it makes sense to understand clearly just what is being studied. And because the preceding chapters have covered written reports extensively, a logical second step is to distinguish between written and oral reports. Thus, in following paragraphs these two topics serve as a logical introduction to this review of oral reporting.

### A definition of oral reports

In its broadest sense, an oral report is any presentation of factual information using the spoken word. A business oral report logically would limit coverage to "factual business information." By this definition, an oral business report covers much of the information exchanged daily in the conduct of business. It varies widely in degree of formality involved. At one extreme it covers the most routine and informal reporting situations. At the other, it includes the highly formal and proper presentations that take place in business. As the more informal exchanges are little more than routine conversations, the emphasis in following pages is on the more formal ones. Clearly, these are the reports which require the most care and skill in preparation and presentation. They are the ones most deserving of formal study.

### Differences between oral and written reports

As written reports have been covered thoroughly in preceding chapters, a logical next step in studying oral reports is to note differences between them and oral reports. Differences do exist; and they are significant. Three in particular stand out.

*Visual advantages of the written word.* The first major difference between oral and written reports concerns the differences between the written and spoken word. It is that the written word permits greater use of visual aids to communication than do spoken words. With the written word, you can use paragraphing to show the reader the structure of the message and to make the thought units stand out. In addition, by writing your message, you can use punctuation to show relationships, subordination, and qualification of the information. The result of these techniques is to improve the communication effect of the entire message.

On the other hand, when you make an oral presentation, you can use none of these techniques. Of course, you can use others—techniques peculiar to oral communication. For example, you can use inflection, pauses, volume emphasis, and changes in rate of delivery. Depending on the situation, both oral and written techniques are effective in aiding communication. But the point is, they are different.

*Reader control of written presentation.* A second difference in oral and written reporting is that in a written report your reader controls the pace of the communication. He can pause, reread, change his rate of reading, or stop as he chooses. Since the reader sets the pace, you can develop your communication stylistically and with some complexity and still communicate. When receiving an oral report, one cannot control the pace of the presentation. One must grasp the meaning intended as the speaker chooses to present the words. Because of this limiting factor, good oral reporting must be relatively simple and gauged for quick, easy understanding.

*Emphasis on correctness in writing.* A third difference in oral reporting is in the degree of correctness permitted in each. Because your written work is likely to receive considerable scrutiny and study, you are likely to work for a high degree of correctness. That is, you are likely to follow carefully the recognized rules of grammar, punctuation, sentence structure, and so on. When you present an oral report, on the other hand, you may be much more lax in following these recognized rules. For one reason, your work is not indelibly recorded for others to scrutinize at their leisure. For another, established oral communication standards permit a less rigid application of established rules.

Other differences exist, of course, but these are the ones which are most significant. Hopefully, they serve as foundations from which to explain the techniques of oral reporting. At least, they give you some basic understanding of the relative nature of these two forms of reporting. In addition, they point to some of the topics of concern in studying oral reporting. As will become obvious in the pages ahead, much of the coverage of the subject deals with these basic differences.

## GENERAL ASPECTS OF ORAL REPORTING

In beginning to work on an oral report, you should consider carefully all the factors which combine to determine the effectiveness with which you perform your task. Such factors are many. They are complex. And they may be considered in many arrangements. The arrangement selected for this review begins with the logical first step in all endeavor—the planning of the effort. Next, it takes up the personal aspects which bear upon the effectiveness of the oral presentation. Then it reviews the aspects of audience analysis which can influence the report.

## Planning the oral report

As in written reports, planning is a logical first step in the work of oral reports. For the short, informal report, of course, planning may be minimal. But for the more formal presentations, particularly those involving audiences of more than one, proper planning is likely to be as involved as that for a comparable written report.

*Determination of report objective.* Logically, your first step in planning an oral report is to determine your objective. Just as it was described for the written report in Chapter 12, in this step you should clearly state the report goal in clear, concise language. And then you should clearly state the factors involved in achieving this goal. These steps give you a clear guide to the information you must gather and to the framework around which you will build your presentation.

In the process of determining your specific goal, you must be aware of your general objective. That is, you must decide on your general purpose in making the presentation. Is it to persuade? To inform? To recommend? Your conclusion here will have a major influence on your development of the material for presentation and perhaps even on the presentation itself.

*Gathering the report information.* With the report purpose clearly in mind, you next turn to the task of gathering the information you need to achieve this purpose. Your task may involve any of the formal research methods. Your task may also involve informal research—that is, personal inspection and study of a problem, perhaps with suggested solutions. A production engineer, for example, might carefully study a certain production problem, applying his specialized knowledge. He would work out a proposed solution. Then he would try to explain and justify.

*Organizing the content.* After you have all the information you need for your report, your next step is to give it order. Again, the procedure is quite the same as that used in written reports. You may follow either of the organization plans used in written reports (direct, indirect), but the organization requirements for the same report information presented both orally and in writing are not necessarily the same. Time pressure, for example, may justify direct presentation for an oral report. The same report problem presented in writing might be best arranged in indirect order. Obviously, a reader can always skip to the conclusion or ending of the report. The listener does not have this choice.

Although oral reports may use either direct or indirect order, the indirect is by far the most widely used order as well as the most logical. Because your audience typically is not likely to be intimately acquainted with the problem, some introductory comments are needed to prepare the audience to receive the message. In addition, you may need introductory words to arouse interest, stimulate curiosity, or to impress the audience with the importance of the subject. The main goal of the introductory remarks, of course, is to state the purpose, define unfamiliar terms, explain limitations, describe scope, and generally cover all the necessary introductory subjects (see discussion of introduction, Chapter 12).

In the body of the oral report, you should develop the goals you have set. Here, also, there is much similarity with the written report. Division of subject matter into comparable parts, logical order, introductory paragraphs, concluding paragraphs, and such are equally important to both forms.

The major difference in organization of the written and oral report is in the ending. Both forms may end with a conclusion, a recommendation, a summary, or a combination of the three. But the oral report is likely to have a final summary tacked on, regardless of whether it has a conclusion or a recommendation. In a sense, this final summary serves the purpose of a synopsis by bringing together all the really important information, analyses, conclusions, and recommendations in the report. It serves also to assist the memory by placing added emphasis on the points that should stand out.

## Consideration of personal aspects

After you have organized the contents of your report, you may next turn to the matter of how best to present the information. And in this process, you would do well to consider yourself as a speaker. In a well-written report, the reporter is behind the scenes. But in an oral report, you, the speaker, are in a very real sense a part of the message. Your audience takes in not only the words you communicate, but also what they see in you. And what they see in you can have a most significant effect on the meaning that develops in their mental filters. Thus, you should carefully evaluate your personal effect on the message you present, and you should do whatever you can to detect and overcome shortcomings and to sharpen any strengths you might have.

Although the following summary of such characteristics may prove to be useful, probably you know them from experience. The chances are you can easily recognize the good qualities and the bad. The problem is to some extent recognizing these characteristics, or the lack of them, in yourself. To a greater extent, it is doing something about improving your bad characteristics when you recognize them. The following review should help you to pinpoint these problem areas and should give you some practical suggestions of how to overcome them.

*Confidence.* A primary characteristic of effective oral reporting is confidence. Included are your confidence in yourself as well as confidence of the audience in you, the speaker. Actually, the two are complementary, for your confidence in yourself tends to produce an image that gives your audience confidence in you. Similarly, your audience's confidence in you can give you a sense of security, thereby making you more confident in your ability.

Confidence of your audience in you typically is earned over periods of association. But there are things you can do to project an image which invites confidence. For example, you can prepare your presentation diligently, and you can practice it thoroughly. Such careful preliminary work produces confidence in yourself. Having confidence leads to more effective communication, which in turn builds confidence in your listener's mind. Another thing you can do to gain confidence is to check carefully your physical appearance. Unfair and illogical as it may be, certain manners of dress and certain hair styles create strong images in people's minds ranging from one extreme to the other. Thus, if you want to communicate effectively, you should analyze the audience you seek to reach. And you should work to develop the physical appearance which projects an image in which your audience can have confidence. Yet another suggestion for being confident is simply to talk in strong, clear tones. Such tones do much to project an image of confidence. Although most people can do little to change their natural voices, they can try to add sufficient volume.

**Sincerity.** Your listeners are quick to detect insincerity in you. And when they detect it, they are likely to give little credence to what you say. On the other hand, sincerity is a valuable aid to conviction, especially if the audience has confidence in your ability. As to what you can do to project an image of sincerity, the answer is clear and simple. You must *be* sincere. Rarely is pretense of sincerity successful.

**Thoroughness.** When you are thorough in your presentation, generally your message is better received than when your coverage is scant or hurried. Thorough coverage gives the impression that time and care have been taken, and such an impression tends to make the message believable. But you can overdo thoroughness. If you present the information in too much detail, your listeners may become lost in a sea of information. The secret is to select the significant information and to leave out the cluttering trivia. To do this, of course, requires that you exercise good judgment. You must place yourself in your listeners' shoes and ask yourself just what do the listeners need to know and what they do not need to know.

**Friendliness.** A speaker who projects an image of friendliness has a significant advantage in communicating. People simply like people who are friendly, and they are more receptive to what friendly people say. Like sincerity, friendliness is difficult to feign. It must be honest if it is to be effective. But with most people, friendliness is honest, for most people want to be friendly. Some just are not able to project the friendly image they would like to project. With a little self-analysis, a little mirror watching as you speak, you can find ways of improving the friendliness of your image.

These are but some of the characteristics that should aid you as an oral reporter. There are others such as interest, enthusiasm, originality, and flexibility. But the ones mentioned are the most significant and the ones most speakers need to work on. Through self-analysis and dedicated effort to improve the personal aspects of oral reporting, you can make marked improvement in your communication ability.

## Audience analysis

Equally as important as considering your own communication characteristics is your need to be alert to the unique aspects of your audience. The end goal of the report, of course, is a specific audience response. Thus, what goes on inside your listeners as the communication takes place is a key part of oral reporting. Unfortunately, all too often you are likely to be so preoccupied with your problem (your nervousness, importance of your task, selection of graphic aids, etc.) that you give little thought to the uniqueness of your audience.

*Preliminary audience analysis.* For best communication results you should learn the pertinent characteristics of your audience in advance. What is pertinent will vary by situation. It is your task to learn the pertinent characteristics in your one case and to adapt your presentation to them.

Determining the pertinent characteristics is a thought problem requiring the use of good logic. You merely analyze your audience, searching for any characteristics which would have any effect on the best manner of presenting your report. For example, size of the audience may be a significant characteristic, for the manner of presentation, use of graphic aids, detail of explanation, and formality of the communication is influenced by the number of listeners involved. Similarly, the personal characteristics of the audience can be vital to the communication effectiveness—characteristics such as age, experience, extent of knowledge, and interests. With such information in mind, you can aim your words for the one audience. The importance to the speaker of being informed about the audience has been stressed for centuries. It was Aristotle, in fact, who advised speakers to consider carefully the characteristics of their audiences. He recorded the major audience characteristics of people in youth, in the prime of life, and in old age. And he admonished speakers to remember the differences in interest and experience in planning their messages.[1] His advice remains good.

---

[1] Lane Cooper, *The Rhetoric of Aristotle,* Appleton-Century Crofts Co., New York, 1932, pp. xx–xxi.

*Audience analysis during presentation.*    You can benefit further by continuing your audience analysis into the presentation. Called feedback, this phase of audience analysis gives you information which allows you to adjust your report as you present it to your audience.

Your eyes and ears will give you feedback information as you talk to your audience. You can gain from facial expressions some indication of how your listeners receive your information. You can detect from sounds coming from your audience whether you have their attention, whether they understand you, whether they are listening, and the like. If questions are in order, you can learn directly how your message is received and how you must alter it. In general, by being intensely alert to your audience as you communicate with them, you can make adjustments in your presentation to improve the communication of your message.

## PRESENTATION OF THE ORAL REPORT

Report planning and consideration of personal and audience aspects give you some general guides to the presentation of your message. But the most significant part of the oral reporting procedure is the presentation itself. It is, so to speak, the final product—the end result of all the work that preceded it. Good technique in this effort is vital to your success.

Probably you have a good idea of what is good technique. Certainly, you can recognize good speaking when you hear it. And you are likely to nod your head in agreement when you hear the following techniques of good oral presentation reviewed. Even so, probably you do not follow these techniques as well as you could. Thus, it is worthwhile for you to put them in mind any time you face an audience.

There are many such techniques, and they may be classified in many ways. In the following review of them, they are arranged in four groups: (1) use of language style and conversational mode; (2) bodily action; (3) voice quality; and (4) characteristics of good and bad delivery.

### Language style and the conversational mode

It is an elementary point to note that language is the principal medium used in oral communication. And whether a report is confused or clear, weak or forceful depends heavily on the words selected and on their arrangement. Without question, the language used in oral reporting is most vital to the success of the communication. It deserves most careful consideration.

Just as in written communication, you should adapt oral report language to your audience. That is, you should use words that are easily understood by your listeners—preferably words that are in their speaking vocabularies. And you should arrange these words clearly in sentences no more involved than your readers' abilities to comprehend. In fact, these techniques of adaptation apply even more to oral reporting, for the spoken message cannot be reviewed as can a written message. Communication must occur as the words are spoken or it does not occur.

In addition to selecting words and structures your readers easily comprehend, you should also work for a variety in sentence forms. Variety adds interest to the presentation. And as we noted in our review of theory, interest is an aid to communication. In acquiring variety, you should develop an interesting mixture of sentence types. Or, more specifically, you should develop an interesting rhythm of alternating loose and periodic sentences. What is an interesting pattern is difficult to describe. It is a matter of what is pleasing to the mind and to the ear. Good speakers and good writers recognize it. They have a feel for it. But they are not able to explain precisely what it is. The novice writer or speaker has no choice but to try to acquire an understanding of it.

In giving the spoken sentence the variety that produces interest, you should mix the two basic forms of sentence—the *loose* and the *periodic*. The periodic sentence is one in which meaning is not clear until the very end. In contrast, the loose sentence gives the essentials at the beginning and has the supporting and modifying parts at the end. Illustrating these two forms are these two sentences:

| *Periodic* | *Loose* |
|---|---|
| During the business convention, right in the middle of Robert's presentation about the new advertising proposal, Harry fainted. | Harry fainted during the business conference, right in the middle of Robert's presentation about the new advertising proposal. |
| In a case like this, without giving further consideration, our company should sue. | Our company should sue, in a case like this, without giving further consideration. |

Each of these forms of sentence arrangement has advantages. The periodic sentence structure is best for holding attention, for marshaling thought, and for giving added emphasis. The loose arrangement is best for bringing out essential ideas sooner. But it is not a question of using one arrangement or the other. The well-presented oral report will have a pleasing mixture of both, as well as of other contrasting techniques. More specifically, it will have loose sentences mixed with periodic sentences, comparisons mixed with contrasts, negations mixed with positives, and simple thoughts interspersed with complex ideas.

In selecting the proper words and arrangements to communicate your message, you should use a technique previously discussed—feedback. As you deliver your message, you should continuously be alert to any sign of miscommunication that comes from the audience. When you detect signs of misunderstanding, you must adjust to them on the spot. Perhaps you will need to repeat a point; you may say it in a different way; you may illustrate by example; or you may need to elaborate. Whatever you sense that must be done, you do.

Because oral reporting is similar to conversation, usually you should do it in a conversational manner. The ways of conversation are familiar to all of us, and they communicate best. But this is not to say that informality is always desired. In conversation, informality is not always the rule. Some conversation is highly formal. And so it is with oral reporting. You should follow the degree of formality appropriate for the situation. It would be inappropriate to be too formal; and it would be inappropriate to be too informal. Thus, you should work to develop a conversational style appropriate for the one situation.

## Bodily actions

In face-to-face oral communication some degree of visual communication takes place. In everyday conversation, bodily actions are a significant part of the communication. So significant are they, in fact, that some people would be sorely limited if the use of their hands, shoulders, facial muscles, and so on, were denied them. As oral reporting is a form of face-to-face oral communication, bodily actions are an important communication technique. You should know them. You should be aware of how you use them; and you should use them to your best advantage.

*General impressions.*   In reviewing bodily actions, the general impression you make while speaking deserves mention. Although not bodily action in a literal sense, the general impression you make on a listener has much the same communication effect. Clearly, it is a part of the visual message your listeners receive. The general impressions you create are a synthesis of all the elements that you communicate to your audience. Included are momentary things over which you have no control, such as the lighting, the stage fixtures, the sound equipment, and so on. But there are some relatively simple things over which you have some control and which may contribute importantly to the general impression created. One of these is the problem of dress. The watchword here is "appropriate." Certainly, you should not appear conspicuous, and you should live up to the standards of dress the audience expects of you.

Another contributor to the general impression you form is the speaking position you take. You have two choices. You may sit; or you may stand. Small, informal audiences may prefer that you sit while speaking. In fact, you might feel awkward standing on a platform with only a few people in the audience. On the other hand, some small groups may be affronted if you sit. Such a group may get the impression that you think that they are not important enough for a stand-up presentation. Generally, there is less risk in standing, even before a small group.[2] You have no choice but to appraise the situation carefully and to take the position that appears to be most appropriate.

*Posture.* Posture is another part of the image you communicate to your audience. Not only does it influence meaning in your listeners' minds, but also it has an effect on your reactions to yourself as you speak. Such reactions can have a negative effect on your communication effectiveness. Most of us recognize good posture. But all too often we do not recognize bad posture in ourselves. Self-analysis is the answer along with a conscious effort to improve.

In your effort to improve your posture, you should keep in mind what must go on within your body to form a good posture. Your body weight must be distributed in a comfortable and poised way consistent with the impression you want to make. You should keep the body erect without appearing stiff, and comfortable without appearing limp. Your bearing should be self-poised, alert, and communicative. And you should do all this naturally. The great danger with posture, as with all studied bodily action, is that of appearing artificial, conspicuous, or out of phase.

*Walking.* The way you walk before your audience can create meanings in the listeners' minds both before and during the presentation. A strong, sure walk to the speaker's stand can project an image of confidence. Hesitant, awkward steps can convey the opposite impression. During the presentation, you may employ walking as a form of physical punctuation. You may reinforce transitions and pauses with a few steps to the side, and you may emphasize a point with a step forward. Additionally, walking has emphatic qualities for the audience, as the movement may break the monotony of the presentation. Too much walking, however, calls attention to the walking and detracts from the message. In determining the amount and kind of walking desired, a good rule to follow is this: the more formal the situation, the less pronounced the walking should be; the larger the audience, the more definite the steps may be.[3]

*Facial expression.* Probably the most apparent and communicative bodily movements are facial expressions. The problem is, however, that you may unconsciously use facial expressions which convey meanings not intended. For example, a frightened speaker may tighten his jaw unconsciously and begin to grin. The effect may be an out-of-taste image that detracts from the entire communication effort. A smile, a grimace, a puzzled frown all convey clear messages. Without question, they are effective communication devices, and you should use them.

---

[2] Raymond S. Ross, *Speech Communication: Fundamentals and Practice,* Prentice-Hall, Inc., Englewood Cliffs, N.J., 1965, p. 64.

[3] *Ibid.,* p. 65.

Equally important in considering facial expressions is the matter of eye contact. The eyes have long been considered "mirrors of the soul" and provide most observers with information about your sincerity, good will, and flexibility. Some listeners tend to shun speakers who refuse to look at them, perhaps in the belief that the communicator should not be trusted or that he does not really care for his listeners. On the other hand, discriminate eye contact tends to show that you have a genuine interest in your audience.

*Gestures.* As does posture, gestures add to the message you communicate. Just what they add, however, is hard to say, for they have no definite or clear-cut meanings. A clinched fist, for example, certainly adds emphasis to a strong point. But it also can be used dramatically to convey defiance, to make a threat, or to signify respect for a cause. And so it is with other gestures. They register vague meanings.

Even though the meanings of gestures are vague, they are strong; and they appear to be natural adjuncts to communication. It appears quite natural, for example, for you to emphasize a plea by gesturing with palms up. And it is quite natural for you to support verbal rejection or disagreement with a palms-down movement. You may reinforce a division of points by using first one hand and then the other. Or you may use only one hand and with vertical palm suggest several divisions as you slice the air, moving your hand on a level plane from left to right. The general stereotype in using such gestures usually is recognizable, although no two people will use all gestures exactly alike.

In summary, it should be clear that you can use body movements effectively to aid in communicating. Just which movements you should use in a given situation, however, is difficult to say, for they are clearly related to personality, physical makeup, and to the size and nature of the audience. A very formal speaker appearing before a formal group would wisely use poised but relatively restricted bodily action. Grandiose movements, grand sweeps of the arms, and such would be inappropriate. An informal speaker appearing before an informal audience could use effectively a much wider range of action. In general, the larger the audience, the more gross and unrestricted the bodily action may become. Just what you should do on a given occasion cannot be predetermined, but is a matter for you to work out through your own logical interpretation of the situation.

## Use of voice

Good vocal quality is an obvious requirement of good oral reporting. Like bodily movements, the voice should not hinder the listener's concentration on the message presented. More specifically, it should not call attention away from the message to itself. Voices that cause such difficulties fall generally into four areas of fault: (1) lack of pitch, (2) lack of variety in speaking speed, (3) lack of emphasis by variation in volume, and (4) unpleasantness in voice quality.

*Lack of pitch variation.* A speaker who talks in a monotone is not likely to hold the interest of his listeners for long. Most voices are capable of wide variations in pitch; so the problem rarely is a physiological one. Most often it is primarily a matter of habit—of voice patterns developed over long years of talking without being aware of effect.

*Lack of variation in speaking speed.* Determining how fast to talk is a major problem in oral reporting. As a general rule, that part of the message that can be understood easily is presented best at a fairly rapid rate. If such information is presented at a deliberately slow pace, the effect is likely to be irritating and distracting. Some information, however, by its very nature is complex and requires a slower pace. Thus you would do well to vary your pace with the difficulty of the material.

A common problem related to the pace of speaking is the incorrect uses of pauses. Of course, pauses used at the appropriate time and place are effective. When properly used they add emphasis to the upcoming subject matter, and they are an effective means of gaining attention. But frequent pauses at points where they add little or nothing to the presentation are irritating, and they break the listener's flow of comprehension. The error compounds when the speaker fills in the pauses with "uh's" or other meaningless sounds.

*Lack of vocal emphasis.* A secret of good oral reporting is to give the words the emphasis due them by variations in the manner of speaking. You can achieve this desired effect by employing three techniques: (1) varying the pitch of the voice, (2) varying the pace of your presentation, and (3) varying the volume of your voice. As the first two have been discussed, only the use of voice volume requires comment.

Obviously, you must talk loudly enough for all of your audience to hear. Thus, the loudness (voice force) for a large group is different from that used for a small group. Regardless of group size, however, variety in force is essential for interest and emphasis. It produces contrast, which is one means of giving emphasis to the subject matter. Some speakers incorrectly believe that the only way to gain emphasis is to get louder and louder. But just as much emphasis may be had by going from loud to soft. It is a contrast with what has gone on before that provides the emphasis. Again, variety is the watchword in making the voice more effective.

*Unpleasant voice quality.* It is a hard fact of communication that some voices are more pleasing than others. Fortunately, most voices are reasonably pleasant. But there are some that are raspy, nasal, or in some other way unpleasant. Although therapy often is effective in improving such voices, some speakers are destined to live with what they have.

Even so, most of us do not do as well as we can with what we have. By concentrating on variations in pitch, speed of delivery, and volume, even the most unpleasant voices can be effective.

*Improvement through self-analysis.*  You can overcome any of the foregoing voice problems through hard work and concentration. The technique is through simple self-analysis. In this day of tape recorders, it is easy to hear yourself talk. And since you know good speaking when you hear it, it should be easy for you to improve your presentation. Certainly, some people have vocal limitations; but few speakers learn to do the best that is possible with the abilities they have.

## USE OF VISUAL AIDS

As was noted earlier, the spoken word is severely limited in communication effectiveness. Sound is here a brief moment and it is gone. If the message is missed, there may be no chance to hear it again. Because of this severe limitation, oral reporting often needs strong visual support— charts, tables, blackboards, film, and so on. Using them may be as vital to the success of your presentation as the words themselves.

### Proper use of design

Effective visual aids are those drawn from the message. They fit the one report and the one audience. To be shunned are any picked up from similar reports. Rarely do they fit.

In selecting visual aids, you should follow generally the procedure a report writer should follow. That is, you should search through your presentation for topics that appear vague or confusing. Whenever a picture or other form of visual aid will help to clear up this vagueness, you should use one. Visual aids are truly a part of your message, and you should look upon them as such.

After you have decided that a topic deserves visual support, you determine the form the support should take. That is, should it be a chart, a slide, a picture, or what? You should base your decision primarily on the question of which form best communicates the message. As simple and obvious as this point may appear, all too often reports violate it. All too often they select visual aids more for their appearance and dramatic effect than for their communication effect.

### Forms of visual aids to consider

Because no one form of visual aid is best for all occasions, you should have a flexible attitude toward these aids. You should know the good and bad qualities of each; and you should know how to use each most effectively.

In considering selection of a visual aid, you should keep in mind the types available. First, there are the various forms of photographed or drawn illustrations—charts, graphs, tables, diagrams, pictures, and so on. Each of these forms has its own special strengths and weaknesses, as is described in Chapter 15. Each may be displayed in various ways—by slide, overhead, or opaque projector; by flip chart; by easel display; on a blackboard; on a felt board; or in other ways. And each of these display forms has its own strengths and weaknesses. In addition, visual aids may take the form of motion pictures, models, samples, demonstrations, and the like. There is no shortage of possibilities.

Because so many forms of visuals and means of displaying them exist, a review of the subject would be somewhat voluminous and perhaps trivial. It is more logical to suggest that you plan your visual displays by first determining the possibilities available to you. In doing so, you would need to take into account factors of time, cost, availability, practicality, and such. Then you should consider the strengths and weaknesses of each possibility available to you. Especially should you consider the strengths and weaknesses relative to your own unique abilities to use the techniques. Such a logical thought process should lead you to select the most appropriate visuals for the one case.

## Techniques in using visuals

As properly designed visuals carry key parts of the report message, they are properly points of emphasis in your oral presentation. You use them to illustrate your key points. You point out key parts of them. Generally you blend them in with your words to communicate your findings. How you do all of this is to some extent an individual matter, for techniques vary. They vary so much, in fact, that it would be illogical to study the techniques used. It is more practical to review some general procedures—some do's and don't's—which you can apply to most individual techniques. Such a list is the following:

1. Make certain the visual aids are clearly visible to all in the audience. Too many or too light lines on a chart, for example, can be difficult to comprehend. Too small an illustration can be meaningless to people far from the speaker.
2. Explain the visual aid if there is any likelihood that it will be misunderstood.
3. Organize the visuals as a part of the presentation. Fit them into the plan of the presentation.

4. Emphasize the visual aids. Point to them with bodily action and with words.
5. Talk to the audience—not to the visual aids. Look at the visuals only when the audience should look at them.
6. Avoid blocking the listener's view of the visual aids. Make certain that lecterns, pillars, chairs, etc., do not block anyone's view. And take care not to stand in anyone's line of vision.

## A SUMMARY CHECKLIST

The foregoing review of oral reporting is scant at best. The subject is a broad one. In fact, entire textbooks are devoted to it. But hopefully this review has covered the high points—especially those that are easily transferred into practice. Certainly more concise and perhaps even more practical is a summary checklist of good and bad reporting practices. Such a checklist is the following:

1. Organize the report so that it leads the hearer's thoughts logically to the conclusion.
2. Move surely and quickly to the conclusion. Do not leave a conclusion dangling, repeat unnecessarily, or appear unable to close.
3. Use language specifically adapted to the audience.
4. Articulate clearly, pleasantly, and with proper emphasis. Avoid mumbling and the overuse of "ah," "er," "uh," etc.
5. Speak correctly, using accepted grammar and pronunciation.
6. Maintain an attitude of alertness, displaying appropriate enthusiasm and confidence.
7. Employ bodily language to best advantage. Use it to emphasize points and to assist in communicating concepts and ideas.
8. Avoid stiffness or rigidity of bodily action.
9. Look the audience in the eye and talk directly to them.
10. Avoid excessive movements, fidgeting, and signs of nervousness.
11. Punctuate the presentation with reference to visual aids. Make them a part of the report story.
12. Keep your temper even, even when faced with unfair opposition. To lose your temper is to lose control of the presentation.

## LISTENING

To this point our review primarily has concerned the sending (talking) side of oral communication. Certainly, this is a subject in which business people need help. And it is a subject about which an abundance of information has been developed. But evidence indicates that it is the receiving (listening) side of oral communication that causes the bulk of oral miscommunication.

## The inefficiency of listening

Just how inefficient we human beings are as listeners is difficult to say. Estimates range widely, but most evidence indicates that only a small portion of spoken words are actually received and that much of that which is received is not retained over time. According to one authority on the subject, only about 25 percent of what is heard will be remembered as long as two months.[4] Generally, the authorities agree that listening is the weakest link in the chain of communication activities.

## An explanation of our listening inefficiency

Why we do not retain spoken messages very well is easily explained by our review of the communication process. As you will recall, our sensory receptors continually pick up stimuli from the world about us. The perceptions picked up then flow through the nervous system to the brain. The resulting flow of stimuli to the brain, however, varies from moment to moment. At times the flow is fast, and at times it practically comes to a stop. Or, in other words, there are times when we are extremely alert to the stimuli around us. There are times when we are virtually in a stupor and have little input. And there are times when we are somewhere between these two extremes. Thus, how well we pick up the stimuli (including words) from our environment varies significantly. All too often, the rate of input is on the low side.

## Improving listening ability

Improving your input of stimuli is what our subject of listening is all about. Doing it primarily is a matter of mental conditioning. That is, you will have to want to do it first. Listening is a willful act. If you are like most of us, frequently you are tempted not to listen, for it is easier this way. As we all know, we human beings tend to be lazy. We tend to avoid that which requires work; and listening requires work.

Once you have decided that you want to listen better, you must make conscious effort to pay attention. You must work at it. What you do specifically in this regard will depend on your individual mental makeup, for the effort is primarily one of disciplining the mind to be alert to the

---

[4] J. Vernon Jensen, *Perspectives on Oral Communications,* Holbrook Press, Boston, 1970, p. 118.

words spoken. The following Ten Commandments of Listening should serve you as a general guide.[5]

1. *Stop talking.* Unfortunately, most of us prefer talking to listening. Even when we are not talking, we are inclined to concentrate on what to say next rather than on listening to others. So you must stop talking before you can listen.

2. *Put the talker at ease.* If you make the talker feel at ease, he will do a better job of talking. Then you will have a better input to work with.

3. *Show the talker you want to listen.* If you can convince the talker that you are listening to understand rather than oppose, you will help to create a climate for information exchange. Specifically, you should look and act interested. Doing things like reading, looking at your watch, and looking away distracts the talker.

4. *Remove distractions.* Things you do can also distract the talker. So don't doodle, tap with your pencil, shuffle papers, or the like.

5. *Empathize with the talker.* If you will place yourself in the talker's position and look at things from his point of view, you will help to create a climate of understanding. With such a climate established, a true exchange of information can result.

6. *Be patient.* You will need to allow the talker plenty of time. Remember that not everyone can get to the point as quickly and clearly as you. And do not interrupt him. Interruptions merely serve as barriers to information exchange.

7. *Hold your temper.* From our review of the workings of our mental filters, we know that angry minds do not contribute to communication. Angry people build walls between themselves. They harden their positions and block their minds to the words of others.

8. *Go easy on argument and criticism.* Argument and criticism tend to put the talker on the defensive. Thus, he tends to "clam up" or get angry. Even if you win the argument, you lose. Rarely does either party benefit from such controversy.

9. *Ask questions.* By frequently asking questions you display an open mind. You show that you are listening. And you assist in developing the message and in improving correctness of meaning.

10. *Stop talking!* The last commandment is to stop talking. It was also the first. All other commandments depend on it.

In summary, it should be clear that to improve your listening ability you have to set your mind to the task. Poor listening habits are ingrained in our living patterns. We can alter these habits only through conscious efforts.

---

[5] To some anonymous author goes a debt of gratitude for these often quoted and classic comments about listening.

## QUESTIONS AND PROBLEMS

1.  Explain the principal differences between written and oral reports.
2.  Compare the typical organization plans of oral and written reports. Note the major difference between the two plans.
3.  Explain how one's personal aspects influence the meanings of his spoken words.
4.  A reporter presented an oral report to an audience of 27 middle- and upper-level administrators. Then he presented the same information to an audience consisting of the three top executives in the company. Note some of the differences that probably took place in these two presentations.
5.  What is meant by the language style of an oral report? What advice would you give to one trying to achieve good style?
6.  Explain the role of feedback in oral reporting.
7.  Discuss how the general impression one receives of a reporter has an effect on the message received.
8.  By description (or perhaps by example) identify good and bad postures and walking practices for speaking.
9.  Explain how facial expressions can miscommunicate.
10.  Give some illustrations of gestures that can be used for multiple meanings. Demonstrate them.
11.  "We are born with voices—some good, some bad, and some in between. We have no choice but to accept what we have been given." Comment.
12.  What should be the determining factor in the use of a visual aid?
13.  Discuss (or demonstrate) some good and bad techniques of using visual aids.
14.  In presenting an oral report to a group made up of his peers as well as a few of his superiors, a speaker is harassed by the questions of one of his peers. Apparently, this person is just trying to embarrass the reporter. What advice would you give this reporter? Would your advice be different if the critic were one of his superiors? What if it were one under him in position?
15.  Discuss why we have difficulty listening. Use communication theory as a basis for your discussion.
16.  What can you do to improve your listening?

## ORAL REPORT PROBLEMS

1.  Assume that you have visited a certain business organization for your company (your choice). Your objective was to inspect a new procedure, machine, facility, equipment, or such (your choice). Make an oral report of your visit to the top administrators of your company. (Some suggested topics for your report: a safety program; pollution control; hiring of

minority groups; a training program; inventory control system; executive compensation plan; retirement program; bonus plan; a new computer; use of budgets.)

2. As a financial analyst, present a report to an investment club recommending how they should invest $100,000. Make any logical assumptions about the club's objective, other investments, and so on.

3. A national chain of food stores has hired you to evaluate two locations in your city as sites for a new store. Select two likely sites, do the research necessary, and present your report orally to the chain's executives.

4. Using the most current information available from published sources, present a report on the state of the economy to a company's board of directors.

5. Present a report analyzing a campus problem of your choice and recommending a solution. (Some problem suggestions: the library, registration, parking, cheating, dormitory regulations, admission policy, attendance requirements, athletic events, ticket policy, etc.)

6. Select a corporate annual report for a company of your choice. Present the information orally to a hypothetical group of the company's stockholders.

7. As vice president in charge of sales for _____ (a company of your choice) present to your sales manager a report on your company's progress by sales district for the past year. You may use your imagination logically to supply the facts.

8. As chairman of the site selection committee for a national association, prepare an oral report recommending one city over another for the association's next meeting (choose cities with which you are acquainted). The convention typically attracts about 400 delegates and their families. Adequate hotel accommodations and recreation facilities are important. Make any other assumptions which you think are necessary.

# Appendixes

# appendix A

## Physical presentation
## of reports

**W**HEN YOUR READERS look at your report, they see not only the message you have formed; they see also the overall appearance of your work. As with the words and illustrations, the appearance of your report becomes a part of the communication they receive and has an effect on the messages formed in their minds.

If, for example, they look at your work and see a neat, well-arranged document, a favorable impression is likely to form in their minds. Such favorable impressions probably will make them more receptive to the information in your message. At the other extreme, if they see an untidy, poorly arranged paper, they are likely to form a negative impression. And this impression will negatively affect their receptiveness to the information you seek to communicate. In other words, the impression of appearance of your work formed in your readers' minds becomes a part of their filter content. Thus, it serves to affect the meanings they give to the information communicated.

You can do much to insure the communication effect of your report by giving it the typing care and arrangement which will help in your communication effort. Hence, you should make good use of the following guide to the physical arrangement of reports.

### General information on physical preparation

Because your reports are most likely to be typed, you should have a general knowledge of the mechanics involved in manuscript typing. Even if you do not have to type your own reports, you should know enough about report form to make certain that justice is done to your work. You cannot be certain that your report is presented in good form unless you know good form.

*Conventional page layout.*   For the typical text page in the report, a conventional layout is that which appears to fit the page like a picture in a frame (see Figure A–1). This eye-pleasing layout, however, is arranged to fit the page space not covered by the binding of the report. Thus, you must allow an extra half of an inch or so on the left margins of the pages of a left-bound report and at the top of the pages of a top-bound report.

As a general rule, top, left, and right margins should be equal and uniform. For double-spaced manuscripts, about 1 inch is recommended. From 1¼ to 1½ inches is considered ideal for single-spaced work (see Figure A–2). Bottom margins are customarily made slightly larger than those at the top—about half again as much. The left margin, of course, is easily marked by the characters which begin the line. The right margin is formed by the average lengths of the full lines. As nearly as possible, this right margin should be kept straight—that is, without dips or bulges.

You may find it advisable to mark off in black ink a rectangle of the size of the layout you are using. Then you may place the rectangle beneath each page as you type, so that you can see the dimensions you are using and can end your typed lines appropriately.

*Special page layouts.*   Certain pages in the text may have individual layouts. Pages displaying major titles (first pages of chapters, tables of contents, synopses, and the like) conventionally have an extra half inch or so of space at the top (see Figure A–3). This technique has long been followed by publishers and is illustrated in almost all published books.

Letters of transmittal and authorization also may have individual layouts. They are typed in any conventional letter form. In more formal reports they may be carefully arranged to have the same general outline or shape as the space upon which they appear (see Figure A–7).

*Choice of typing form.*   It is conventional to double-space the typed report. This procedure stems from the old practice of double spacing to make typed manuscripts more easily read by the proofreader and printer. The practice has been carried over into typed work that is not to be further reproduced. Advocates of double spacing claim that it is easy to read, as the reader is not likely to lose her line place.

In recent years the use of single spacing has gained in popularity. The general practice is to single-space the paragraphs, double-space between paragraphs, and triple-space above all centered heads. Supporters of this form of presentation contend that it saves space and facilitates fast reading, as it approximates the printing most people are accustomed to reading.

*Patterns of indentation.*   You should indent double-spaced typing to

**FIGURE A–1**

Recommended layout for normal double-spaced page

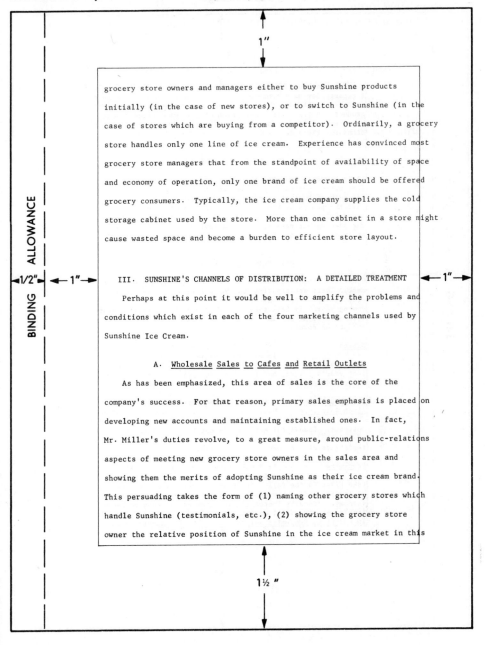

grocery store owners and managers either to buy Sunshine products initially (in the case of new stores), or to switch to Sunshine (in the case of stores which are buying from a competitor). Ordinarily, a grocery store handles only one line of ice cream. Experience has convinced most grocery store managers that from the standpoint of availability of space and economy of operation, only one brand of ice cream should be offered grocery consumers. Typically, the ice cream company supplies the cold storage cabinet used by the store. More than one cabinet in a store might cause wasted space and become a burden to efficient store layout.

III. SUNSHINE'S CHANNELS OF DISTRIBUTION: A DETAILED TREATMENT

Perhaps at this point it would be well to amplify the problems and conditions which exist in each of the four marketing channels used by Sunshine Ice Cream.

A. Wholesale Sales to Cafes and Retail Outlets

As has been emphasized, this area of sales is the core of the company's success. For that reason, primary sales emphasis is placed on developing new accounts and maintaining established ones. In fact, Mr. Miller's duties revolve, to a great measure, around public-relations aspects of meeting new grocery store owners in the sales area and showing them the merits of adopting Sunshine as their ice cream brand. This persuading takes the form of (1) naming other grocery stores which handle Sunshine (testimonials, etc.), (2) showing the grocery store owner the relative position of Sunshine in the ice cream market in this

**FIGURE A–2**

Recommended layout for a normal single-spaced page

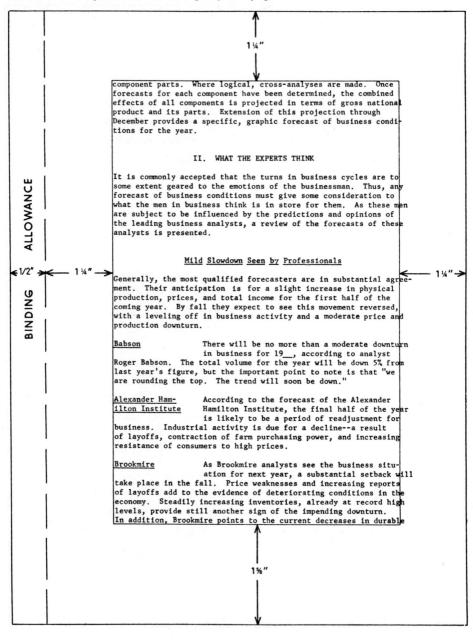

**FIGURE A–3**

Recommended layout for double-spaced page with title displayed

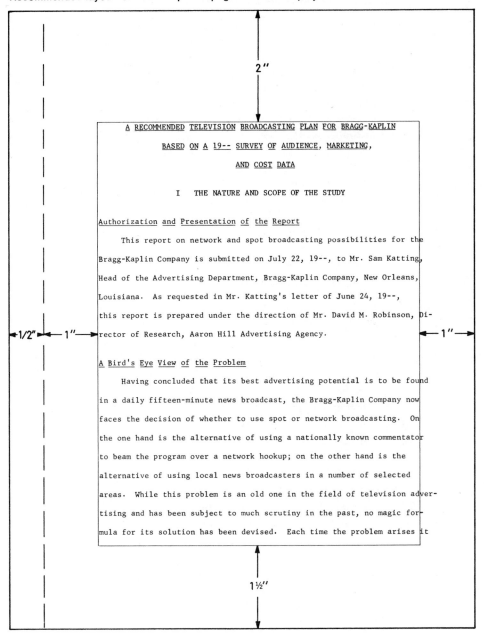

show the paragraph beginnings. On the other hand, because its paragraphs are clearly marked by extra line spacing, you should block single-spaced typing.

There is no generally accepted pattern of indentation. Some sources advocate a distance of four spaces; some prefer five; some like eight; and others like ten and more. Any decision as to the best distance to use is purely arbitrary and left up to you, although you would do well to follow the practice established in the office, group, or school for which you write the report. Whatever the selection, the important rule to follow is that of consistency.

*Neatness in typed work.* Even with the best typewriter available, the finished work is no better than the efforts of the typist. But this statement does not imply that only the most skilled typist can turn out good work. Even the inexperienced typist can produce acceptable manuscripts simply by exercising care.

You should take care in correcting your typing mistakes, for obvious corrections (strikeovers, erasure holes in the page, and the like) stand out in the manuscript like a sore thumb. With a little bit of care, this operation can be done so well that the casual reader doesn't detect the error.

Possibly nothing detracts more from a report than type which the eye must strain to read. So you should take care to see that your typewriter is equipped with a good, black ribbon—one that will make legible letters. A medium-inked ribbon is recommended for most typing work. Because the ink is likely to smear a bit on the first few pages typed with a new ribbon, it may be wise to type really important work only after a ribbon has had the excess ink worn off. Because of the sharp contrast in type it would cause, you should avoid changing ribbons in the middle of a manuscript.

For neat and clearly legible typing, you should clean the typefaces regularly. Ink from the ribbon tends to collect and dry in the typefaces. If allowed to remain, it will fill the enclosed portions of the type characters. Smudged or fuzzy typing is the result. Any small, stiff brush may be used for this purpose.

*Numbering of pages.* Two systems of numbers are used in numbering the pages of the written report. Arabic numerals are conventional for the text portion, normally beginning with the first page of the introduction and continuing through the appendix. Small roman numerals are standard for the pages preceding the text. Although all of these prefatory pages are counted in the numbering sequence, the numbers generally do not appear on the pages preceding the table of contents.

Placement of the numbers on the page varies with the binding used for the report. In reports which are bound at the top of the page, you should center all page numbers at the bottom of the page, a double or triple space below the layout used in the typing.

For the more widely used left-side binding, you should place the numbers in the upper right corner of the page, a double space above the top line of the layout and in line with the right margin. Exception to this placement is customarily made for special-layout pages which have major titles and an additional amount of space displayed at the top. Included in this group may be the first page of the report text; the synopsis; the table of contents; and, in very long and formal works, the first page of each major division or chapter. Numbers for such pages as these are centered a double or triple space below the imaginary line marking the bottom of the layout.

*Display of captions.* Captions—or headings, as they are sometimes called—are titles to the various divisions of the report. They represent the organization steps worked out previously and are designed to help the reader find his way through this organization plan. Thus, it is important that the captions show the reader at a glance the importance of their part in the report.

You may emphasize this importance of captions in two ways—by type and by position. You may use any logical combination of type and position to show differences in the importance of captions. In actual practice, however, a few standard orders of captions have become widely used.

There are four major positions of captions, as shown in Figure A–4. Highest of these four in order of rank is the centered caption. This caption is on a line by itself and is centered between left and right margins. Next in order is the marginal caption. Beginning on the left margin, this caption is also on a line by itself. The box caption is third in this ranking, but it normally is used only in single-spaced copy. It begins on the left margin and is surrounded by a box of space formed by indenting the first few lines of the text. The box indentations are kept of equal width throughout the report, although the heights of the boxes will vary with the number of words in the captions enclosed. Fourth in importance is the run-in caption. This caption simply runs into the first line of the text it covers and is distinguished from the text only by underscoring.

Were your report to be printed, there would be a wide variety of typefaces and sizes that you could use to show different degrees of importance in the captions. But most reports are typed and thereby limited by what type variations can be made with an ordinary typewriter. Except when unusual typefaces are available, you can show type distinctions in only two ways—by the use of capitals and the underscore. Spacing between letters is sometimes used, although the space requirements of this technique normally eliminate it from consideration.

**FIGURE A–4**

Caption positions in order of importance

But even though you are limited to two means of showing importance by type selection, you are able to construct four distinct ranks of type:

<u>SOLID CAPITALS UNDERSCORED</u>

SOLID CAPITALS

<u>Capitals and Lowercase Underscored</u>

Capitals and Lowercase

In theory, any combination of type and position which shows the relative importance of the captions at a glance is acceptable. The one governing rule to follow in considering types and positions of captions is that no caption may have a higher ranking type or position than any of the captions of a higher level. It is permissible, however, that two successive steps of captions appear in the same type, if their difference is shown by position, or in the same position, if their difference is shown by type selection. Also, there is no objection to skipping over any of the steps in the progression of type or position.

Although the possibilities of variation are great, some practices have become almost conventional, possibly because they excel in showing each caption's importance at a glance. Also, these practices are no doubt widely accepted because of their simplicity of construction. One such scheme of captioning is the following, which is recommended for use in reports with three orders of division.

The first order of captions in this scheme appears on a separate line, centered, and typed in solid capital letters. Although solid capitals underscored may be used, this high type normally is reserved for the report title, which is the highest caption in the report. Second-order captions are also on separate lines, beginning with the left margin and typed with capitals and lowercase underscored. Third-degree captions are run into the paragraph they cover. To distinguish the line from the text, underscoring is used, and the caption ends with a strong mark of punctuation, usually the period.

Other acceptable schemes include the following:

1. Centered, solid capitals
2. Centered, capitals and lowercase underscored
3. Marginal, capitals and lowercase underscored
4. Run-in, capitals and lowercase underscored

1. Centered, solid capitals
2. Marginal, capitals and lowercase underscored
3. Box cut-in, capitals and lowercase underscored
4. Run-in, capitals and lowercase underscored

1. Centered, solid capitals
2. Centered, capitals and lowercase underscored
3. Box cut-in, capitals and lowercase

1. Centered, solid capitals
2. Marginal, capitals and lowercase underscored
3. Box cut-in, capitals and lowercase underscored

## Mechanics and format of the report parts

The foregoing notes on physical appearance apply generally to all parts of the report. But for the individual construction of the specific report pages, additional special notes are needed. So that you may be able to get and follow these special notes, a part-by-part review of the physical construction of the formal report follows. Much of this presentation is left to illustration, for volumes could be written about the minute details of construction. Major points, however, are indicated.

***Title fly.***  Primarily used in the most formal reports, the title fly contains only the report title. In constructing the page, place the title slightly above the vertical center of the page in an eye-pleasing arrangement. Center all lines with regard to left and right margins. And type it in the highest ranking type used in the report (usually solid capitals underscored); and double-space it if you need more than one line.

***Title page.***  The title page normally contains three main areas of identification (Figure A–5), although some forms present the same information in four or five spots on the page (Figure A–6). In the typical three-spot title page, the first item covered is the report title. Preferably type it in the highest ranking type used in the report, usually solid capitals underscored. Center it; and if more than one line is required, break the lines between thought units and center both lines. Double-space the lines.

The second area of identification names the individual or group for whom the report is prepared. Precede it with an identifying phrase such as "Prepared for" or "Submitted to"—words which indicate the individual's role in the report. In addition to the name, include identification by title or role, company, and address, particularly if you and your recipient are from different companies. If the information below the identifying phrase requires three or more lines of type, single-space it. If you have fewer than three lines, double-space them. But regardless of how you space this information, the identifying phrase appears best set off from the facts below it by a double-space.

The third area of information identifies you, the writer of the report. It, also, is preceded by an identifying phrase. You may use "Prepared by," "Written by," or any such wording which describe your role in the report. You, also, may give your title or role, company, and address. As a final part of this group of information, you may include the date of publication. You should single-space this identification information if four lines are required. Double-space it if three lines or less are required. Likewise, set off the identifying phrase with a double space. Preferably double-space the date line from the information preceding it, regardless of previous spacing. Placement of the three spots of information on the page should conform to an eye-pleasing arrangement.

One such arrangement begins the title about 1¼ inches from the top of the page. The final spot of information ends about 2 inches from the page bottom. The center spot of information appears so as to split the space between the top and bottom units in a 2-to-3 ratio, the bottom space being the larger. Line lengths of the information units, of course, are largely governed by the data contained; yet you will have some opportunity to combine or split units. Preferably, the lines will have sufficient length to keep the units from having an overall "skinny" appearance.

***Letters of transmittal and authorization.***  As their names imply, the letters of transmittal and authorization are actual letters. Therefore, they

**FIGURE A–5**

Good layout for the three-spot title page

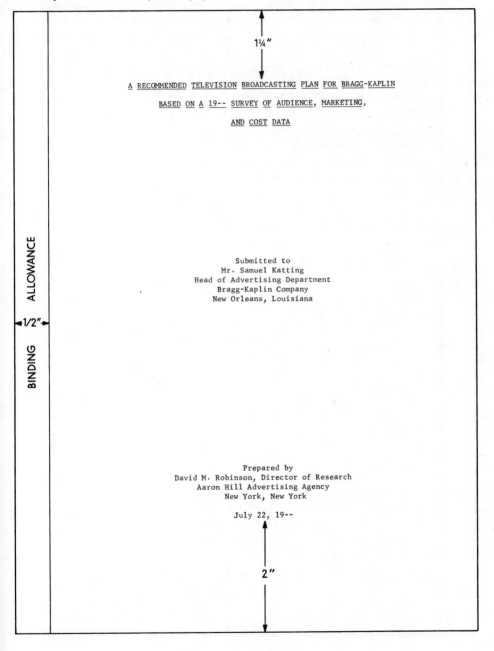

**FIGURE A–6**

Good layout for the four-spot title page

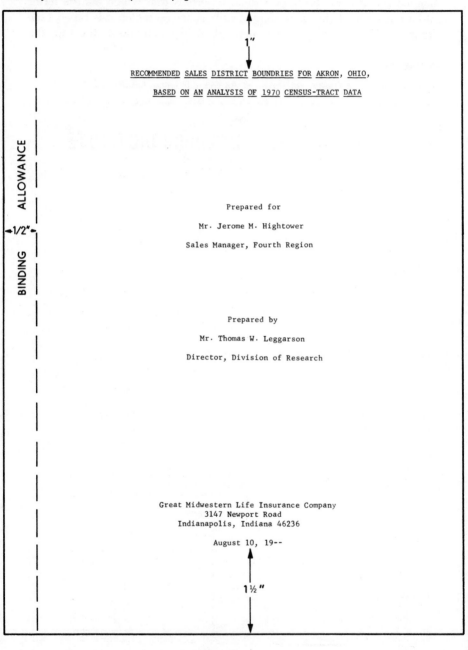

should appear as letters. You should type them in any acceptable letter form—pure block, modified block, or indented. A layout plan recommended for at least the more formal reports is that which fits the letter into a rectangle of the same shape as the space on which it is typed (see Figure A–7). This rectangle is marked by the dateline at the top, the

**FIGURE A–7**

Letter of transmittal fitted to the shape of the space in which typed

**MIDWESTERN RESEARCH INSTITUTE**
**3241 MONROE STREET**
**CHICAGO, ILLINOIS**

July 22, 19--

Mr. Joel D. Karp, President
The Munson Company
2121 Oldham Road
Cleveland, Ohio 44103

Dear Mr. Karp:

Here is the recommendation report on Munson's radio advertising policy that you requested in your May 9th letter.

As you read the report, undoubtedly you will be (as I was) surprised to see the facts point so clearly to one decision. The simple explanation is that this is one of those instances in which all pertinent data lead down the same path to one conclusion.

Perhaps you will want to question the matter of cost analysis. It's true that the recommended plan is going to cost a bit more initially. But the long-run outlook is much more positive. If you would like more information on the cost question, let me know and I'll rush it to you.

I am grateful to you for this assignment. And I'll be looking forward to helping you again with other problems that you might have.

Sincerely yours,

James W. Worthington
Director of Research

JWW:ek

BINDING ALLOWANCE

initial characters of type at the left, the average of the line lengths at the right, and the last line in the signature at the bottom. For the best optical effect, the rectangle should ride a little high on the page, with a ratio of top margin to bottom margin of about two to three.

*Acknowledgments.* When you are indebted to the assistance of others, it is fitting that you acknowledge the indebtedness somewhere in the report. If the number of individuals is small, you may acknowledge them in the introduction of the report or in the letter of transmittal. In the rare event that you need to make numerous acknowledgments, you may construct a special section for this purpose. This section is headed with the simple title "Acknowledgments" and is typed with the same layout as any other text page which has a title displayed.

*Table of contents.* The table of contents is the report outline in its polished, finished form. It lists the major report captions with the page numbers on which these captions appear. Although not all reports require a table of contents, one should be a part of any report long enough for a guide to be helpful to the readers.

The page is appropriately headed by the caption "Contents" or "Table of Contents," as shown in Figure A–8. The page layout is that used for any report page with a title display. Below the title you should set up two columns. One contains the caption, generally beginning with the first report part following the table of contents. You have the option of including or leaving out the outline letters and numbers. If you use numbers, arrange them so that their last digits are aligned. In the other column, which is brought over to the right margin and headed by the caption "Page," place the page numbers on which the captions may be found. Align these numbers on their right digits. Connect the two columns by leader lines of periods, preferably with spaces intervening.

As a rule, you should type all captions of the highest level of division with line spaces above and below them. Captions below this level you should uniformly single-space or double-space, depending on the overall lengths of the captions. If the captions are long, covering most of the line or extending to a second line, uniform double spacing between captions is recommended. Short captions appear bulky in consistent single-spaced form. Some authorities, however, prefer double spacing all of the content entries when double spacing is used in the text.

In the table of contents, as in the body of the report, you may vary the type to distinguish different levels of captions. But the type variations of the table of contents need not be the same as those used in the text of the report. Usually, the highest level of captions is distinguished from the other levels, and sometimes second-level captions are distinguished from lower captions by type differences. It is not wrong to show no distinction at all by using plain capitals and lowercase throughout.

*Table of illustrations.* The table of illustrations may be either a continuation of the table of contents or a separate table. This table, as shown in Figure A–9, lists the graphic aids presented in the report in much the same way as the report parts are listed in the table of contents.

In constructing this table, head it with an appropriately descriptive title such as "Table of Charts and Illustrations," or "List of Tables and Charts," or "Table of Figures." If you place the table on a separate page, this page layout is the same as that for any other text page with title displayed. And if you place it as a continued part of the table of contents, you should begin the table of illustrations after spacing four or more lines from the last contents entry.

The table is made up of two columns—one for the graphic-aid title and the second for the page on which the aid appears. Head the second column with the caption "Page." And connect the two columns by leader lines of spaced periods. Line spacing in the table is optional, again depending on the line length of the entries. Preceding each entry title, place that entry's number; and should these numbers be roman or otherwise require more than one digit, align the digits appropriately on their right members. If your report contains two or more illustration types (tables, charts, maps, etc.) and you have given each its own numbering sequence, you may list the entries successively by types.

## Variations in forms of reports

Much of the discussion to this point has been about the long, formal report form—the form containing numerous prefatory and appended parts in addition to a complete text. But not all reports need be of this type. In fact, most reports are not of this arrangement. Yet they do employ much the same writing, organization, and layout principles—so much so, in fact, that a knowledge of how to prepare the longer report forms is usually adequate for the preparation of shorter types. That is, there is a close relationship in all reports, and an understanding of this relationship will allow the writer to apply the same layout, writing, and organization principles to all reports.

*Format of letter and memorandum reports.* All the stages discussed in the preceding progression of report types, with the exception of the last two named, involve similar problems and instructions of physical presentation. But there is little similarity in the physical structure of the various letter-type reports.

The physical layout requirements of the letter report are the same as those for any other letter. Any conventional letter form may be used; and as was explained in the discussion of layout of the transmittal and authorization letters, the letter report might well approximate the shape of the space in which it is typed.

**FIGURE  A–8**

Good layout and mechanics in the first page of the table of contents

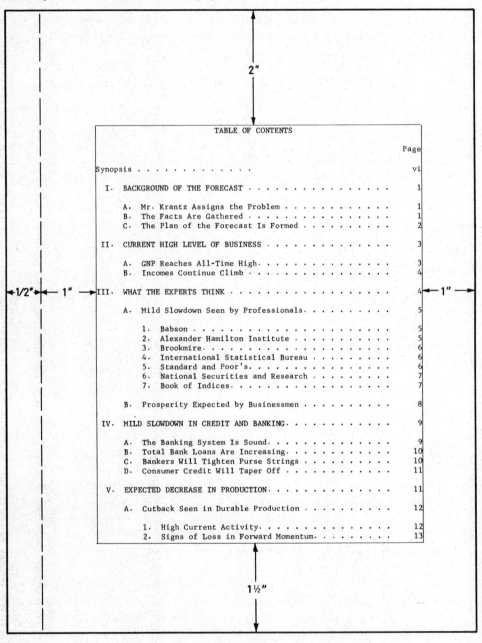

**FIGURE A–9**

Good layout and mechanics in the last page of the table of contents showing the table of illustrations attached

1"

1/2"  1"

1"

1½"

**FIGURE A-10**

Good form for a memorandum report

## Campus Correspondence

LOUISIANA STATE UNIVERSITY

FROM:    Committee on Courses and Curricula
        J. William Hughes, Chairman

TO:      Faculty, College of            DATE:  December 15, 19--
        Business Administration

SUBJECT:  Report of progress and plans on the study of the business
         administration curricula

Progress for the Period October 1 to December 15

On October 10 the Committee mailed questionnaires (copy attached) to the
deans of 24 selected colleges of business administration.  To date, 21 of
the deans have returned questionnaires.

Professors Byrd, Calhoun, and Creznik have tabulated the replies received
and are now analyzing the findings.

Future Plans

Professors Byrd, Calhoun, and Creznik will present their analyses to the
Committee at its February 4th meeting.  At this time, the Committee expects
to study these analyses and to make final recommendations.

Professor Byrd will record the Committee's recommendations in a written
report.  The Committee will distribute copies of this report to all voting
members of the faculty at least one week before the faculty meeting scheduled
for May 9.

Memorandum reports, although they are a type of informal letter, do not necessarily follow conventional letter format. The most popular form (see Figure A–10) uses the military arrangement of introductory information: *To, From, Subject*. Generally, this information is followed by informal presentation of facts in organized fashion. Other forms of the memorandum vary widely. Some resemble questionnaires, in that they are comprised of lists of topics or questions with spaces provided for the written answers. Others are simply handwritten notes on standard inter-office communication forms.

# appendix B

## Form of the business letter

**W**HEN WE APPLY communication theory to the business letter situation, it becomes apparent that the appearance of the letter is a part of the message. The reader judges the writer by what she sees as she looks at the typed page. And her judgment of the writer becomes a part of her filtering process through which she gives meaning to the message. Thus, for the very best communication result, you should make certain that your letter looks good—that it gives a good impression of you. For your guidance in this effort, the following brief review of letter form is presented.

### The ideal layout

Ideally, the best letter layout is one which has the same shape as the space in which it is typed. It fits the space much like a picture in a frame. That is, a rectangle drawn around the typing that makes up the letter would have the same shape and be in proportion to the space under the letterhead of the page. This layout would be marked at the top by the dateline, on the left by the line beginnings, on the right by the average line length, and at the bottom by the last line of the typed signature. Because it looks better to the eye, the layout is best placed a little high on the page (see Figure B–1). Side margins should be equal and no less than an inch.

Such layouts take time and generally are used in business for really important letters or those on which the extra time required can be justi-

**FIGURE B–1**

Modified block, blocked paragraphs, margins adjusted to make ideal layout

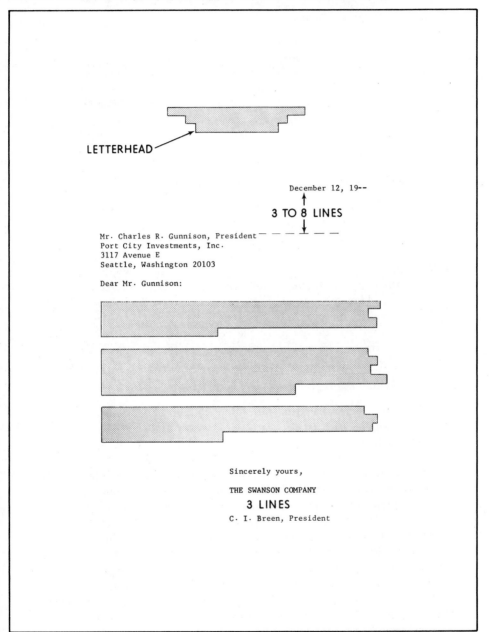

fied. Sales letters are almost always arranged this way, for after one good design has been worked out, the other thousands of letters can benefit from the effort. Most offices, however, do not find it practical to make individual layouts for letters.

## Fixed margins

Offices which use a fixed margin for all letters (usually about 6-inch lines are used) vary the heights of the letters by using more or less space, as needed, between date and inside address. The arrangements in Figure B–2 and B–3 are typical of this practice.

## Style preferences

A variety of styles is available, and any generally recognized one is acceptable. The two most popular ones are the block and the modified block. They are the ones illustrated.

The exact practices to follow in setting up the parts of the letter are not all agreed upon. The suggestions which appear below, however, follow the bulk of authoritative opinion—at least, in most instances.

*Dateline.* The conventional form (December 9, 1968) should be used, with day, month, and year. Abbreviated forms such as 12–9–68 or Dec. 9, '68, are informal and do not leave the best impression on some people.

*Inside address.* The mailing address, complete with title of the person addressed, makes up the inside address. Preferably, it is typed without abbreviations, except for those words commonly abbreviated (Dr., Mr., Mrs., etc.)

*Salutation.* The choice of salutation should be determined by the degree of familiarity between reader and writer and the formality of the situation. If they know each other well, the address may be by first name (Dear Joan). An address by last name (Dear Mr. Baskin) is appropriate in most cases, but especially is it appropriate when the people involved are to some extent acquainted. In situations that are formal or impersonal, the forms (Dear Sir, Gentlemen, Madam, etc.) are in order.

There is some movement nowadays to eliminate the salutation and the complimentary close. The style advocated by the Administrative Management Association and other groups favors such omission. Although these groups should be encouraged for promoting a logical change, their letter styles have not yet gained the support of a major section of business.

In recent years, advocates of women's rights have criticized strongly the use of Mrs. and Miss in addressing women. Why distinguish between married and single women, they argue, when we make no such distinction between married and single men? Their solution is to use Ms. for all women, just as we use Mr. for all men.

Although this term is gaining widespread acceptance, some people oppose it. So you may want to use the form with some precaution. Probably you would be wise to check the correspondence you are answering, your knowledge of the reader, or any other source of information for any hint of how your reader prefers to be addressed. When you have no such information to guide you, you will have to follow your own best judgment.

The impersonal salutations "Gentlemen" and "Dear Sirs" are in a similar status. Clearly, they greet the readers as males when in fact they might include females. At this point in time, however, no suitable substitutes have been proposed. Thus, we must continue to use these salutations until something more appropriate comes along.

*Subject block.* So that sender and receiver may quickly identify the subject of the correspondence, many offices use the subject block on their letters. As illustrated in Figure B–2, it tells what the correspondence is about. In addition, it contains any specific identifying material that may be helpful—date of previous correspondence, invoice number, order number, and the like. Usually it is placed on a line below the salutation, although some companies prefer to place it higher—often in the upper right corner of the letter layout. The block may be headed in a number of ways, of which the following forms are representative:

Subject: Your July 2nd inquiry about . . .

In reply please refer to File H-320

Reference your October 17th order for . . .

About your order No. 712-A dated . . . .

*Attention line.* Some companies prefer to emphasize the company address rather than the individual offices. Thus, they address the correspondence to the company in the inside address. Then they use an attention line (Figure B–3) to direct the letter to a specific officer or department. Typical forms of this reference are as follows:

Attention of Mr. Clayton E. Haney, Office Manager

For Mr. Charles E. Blake, Director

Attention: William O'Brien, Vice President

Attention Abraham E. Rubbicon, Sales Manager

*Second page heading.* When a letter must go beyond one page, the following pages should be set up for quick identification. Following pages always are typed on plain paper (no letterhead). Of the various

**FIGURE B–2**

Block style, fixed margins, using subject line

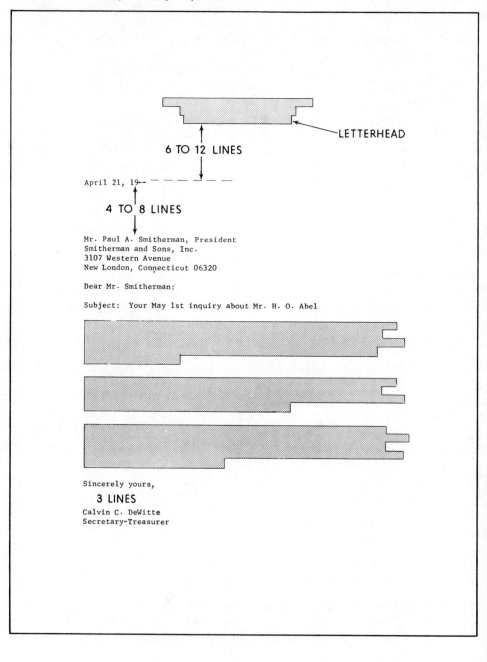

**FIGURE B–3**

Modified block, indented paragraphs, fixed margins

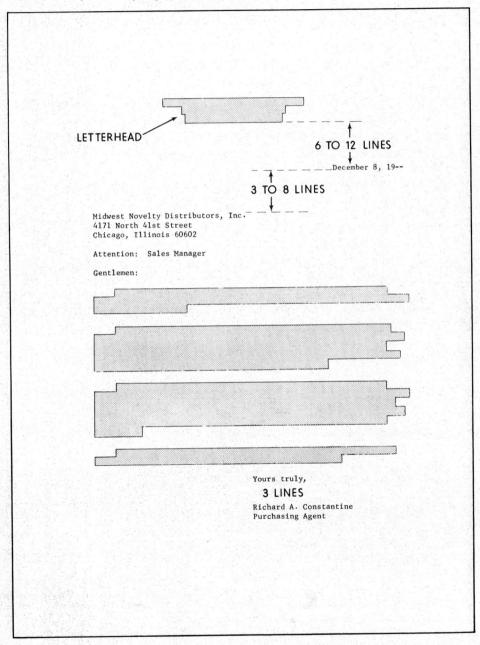

forms used to identify these pages, the following three are the most common:

Ms. Helen E. Mann                -2-                    May 7, 1976

Ms. Helen E. Mann
May 7, 1976
Page 2

Ms. Helen E. Mann, May 7, 1976, page 2

After each the letter continues following a triple or quadruple space.

*Complimentary close.* A form of "truly" is best used with impersonal salutations (Dear Sir, Yours truly), and a form of "sincerely" is generally used with salutations in which names appear (Dear Mr. Brown, Sincerely yours). Forms of "cordially" and other less used salutations are appropriately used on occasion.

*Signature block.* The typed signature conventionally appears on the fourth line below the complimentary close, beginning directly under the first letter for the block form. A short name and title may be typed on the same line and separated by the comma. If either is long, the title is typed on the following line and blocked under it. Of course, the writer's signature appears in the space between complimentary close and typed signature.

Some firms prefer that their name appear in the signature for strict legal responsibility. The conventional form for this arrangement places the firm name in solid capitals and blocked on the second line below the closing phrase. The typed name of the person signing the letter is on the fourth line below the firm name.

*Information notations.* In the lower left corner of the letter may appear abbreviated notations of enclosures (Enc., Enc.—3, etc.) and initials of dictator and stenographer (WEH:ga). Indications of carbon prepared for other readers also may be included (cc: William E. Sutton, Copy to William E. Sutton, etc.). Originally, initials of the person who dictated the letter were useful in helping readers decipher illegible signatures. Now with typed signatures, these initials are not so useful. But many firms use them. Stenographers' initials are useful for office checking.

*Folding.* The carelessly folded letter is off to a bad start with the reader. Neat folding will complete the planned effect by (1) making the letter fit snugly in its cover, (2) making it easy and handy for the recipient to remove, and (3) making it appear neat when opened out.

The two-fold pattern is easiest. It fits the standard sheet for the No. 10 envelope, the monarch sheet for its special envelope, and the note sheet (or "hotel" size) for the No. 6¾ envelope.

First fold of the two-fold pattern is from the bottom up, taking 1/12 inch less than a third of the sheet. Second fold goes from the top down, taking exactly the same panel as the bottom segment. (This measurement will leave the recipient a quarter-inch thumbhold for easy unfolding of the letter.) Folded thus, the letter should be slipped into its envelope with the second crease toward the bottom and the center panel at the front of the envelope.

The three-fold pattern is necessary to fit the standard sheet into the commonly used No. 6¾ envelope. Its first fold is from the bottom up, with the bottom edge of the sheet riding about a quarter inch under the top edge—to allow the thumbhold. (If the edges are exactly even, they are harder to separate.) The second fold is from the right-hand side of the sheet toward the left, taking 1/12 inch less than a third of the width. The third fold matches the second: from the left-hand side toward the right, with a panel of exactly the same width. (This fold will leave a quarter-inch thumbhold at the right, for user's convenience.) So that the letter will appear neat when unfolded, the creases should be neatly parallel with top and sides—not at angles that produce "dog ears" and irregular shapes. In the three-fold form it is especially important for the side panels (produced by second and third folds) to be exactly the same width; otherwise the vertical creases are off-centered and tend to throw the whole carefully planned layout off center.

The three-fold letter is inserted into its cover with the third crease toward the bottom of the envelope and the loose edges toward the stamp end of the envelope. (From habit, most recipients of business letters slit envelopes at their top and turn them face down to extract the letter. The three-fold letter inserted as described thus gives its reader an easy thumbhold at the top of the envelope to pull it out by, and a second one at the top of the sheet for easy unfolding of the whole.)

*Envelope address.* So that the optical character reader may be used in sorting mail, the Post Office requests that all envelopes be typed as follows (see illustration below):

1. Use the new two-letter abbreviations for states.

| | | | |
|---|---|---|---|
| AL | (Alabama) | IN | (Indiana) |
| AK | (Alaska) | IA | (Iowa) |
| AZ | (Arizona) | KS | (Kansas) |
| AR | (Arkansas) | KY | (Kentucky) |
| CA | (California) | LA | (Louisiana) |
| CO | (Colorado) | ME | (Maine) |
| CT | (Connecticut) | MD | (Maryland) |
| DE | (Delaware) | MA | (Massachusetts) |
| DC | (D.C.) | MI | (Michigan) |
| FL | (Florida) | MN | (Minnesota) |
| GA | (Georgia) | MS | (Mississippi) |
| HI | (Hawaii) | MO | (Missouri) |
| ID | (Idaho) | MT | (Montana) |
| IL | (Illinois) | NB | (Nebraska) |

| | | | |
|---|---|---|---|
| NV | (Nevada) | RI | (Rhode Island) |
| NH | (New Hampshire) | SC | (South Carolina) |
| NJ | (New Jersey) | SD | (South Dakota) |
| NM | (New Mexico) | TN | (Tennessee) |
| NY | (New York) | TX | (Texas) |
| NC | (North Carolina) | UT | (Utah) |
| ND | (North Dakota) | VT | (Vermont) |
| OH | (Ohio) | VA | (Virginia) |
| OK | (Oklahoma) | WA | (Washington) |
| OR | (Oregon) | WV | (West Virginia) |
| PA | (Pennsylvania) | WI | (Wisconsin) |
| PR | (Puerto Rico) | WY | (Wyoming) |

2.  Leave three spaces before the ZIP number.
3.  Type any on-arrival instructions ("Confidential," "Personal," etc.) four lines below the return address.
4.  Block the address lines.

Illustration of proper envelope address using number 6¾ envelope

5.  Single space the address, regardless of how many lines are needed.
6.  On the Number 10 envelope, start four inches from the left edge of the envelope; on the Number 6¾ envelope, start two inches from the left margin.

Although the Post Office does not mention placement with regard to vertical dimensions, a good eye-pleasing arrangement is to begin with the first line just under the center of the envelope.

# appendix C

## Documentation, footnotes, and the bibliography

$I$N WRITING REPORTS, you will frequently use information from other sources. As this material is not your own, you may need to acknowledge it. Whether and how you should acknowledge such data is the subject of this brief review.

### When to footnote

Your decision to use or not to use a source footnote should be determined mainly on the basis of giving credit where credit is due. If you are quoting the words of another, you must give credit. If you are paraphrasing (using someone else's ideas but your own words), you should give credit unless the material covered is general knowledge.

### Mechanics of footnotes

Footnotes usually are best placed at the bottom of the page, separated from the text by a line 1½ to 2 inches long (which begins at the left margin). Footnotes go inside the page layout, are single-spaced, and are indented or blocked just as the text is typed. They are keyed with the text references by means of superscripts (raised arabic numbers). The numbering sequence used may be consecutive by page, by chapter, or by the whole work.

### Form of the footnote

Although footnote form varies from one source to another, one generally accepted procedure is presented here. It permits two structures: an abbreviated one which may be used when a bibliography is present in the report, and one for use when no bibliography is present.

In the abbreviated form (not universally accepted in principle) the footnote reference needs to contain only these parts: (1) author's surname; (2) title of the article, bulletin, or book; and (3) page number.

> [3] Wilson, *The Report Writer's Guide,* p. 44 (book reference).
> [4] Allison, "Making Routine Reports Talk," p. 71 (periodical reference).

For the complete reference (usually preferred) the descriptive points are listed in the order mentioned below. The points are separated by commas, and the entry ends with a period. Capitals need to be used only with proper nouns, and abbreviations are acceptable if consistently used.

In these lists, all of the items that could possibly be placed in each type of entry are named in the order of arrangement. Those items not available or not pertinent in a given source should be passed over. In other words, the following lists are intended only to give the maximum contents in the order of arrangement of the footnote parts. Only as much of the list should be used as fits the source involved.

Book entry:

1. *Superscript.* Arabic numeral keyed with the text reference and placed before the first part of the entry without spacing.
2. *Name of the author, in normal order.* If two or more authors are involved, all may be presented. If the number of authors is too great to list, the first author followed by the Latin *et al.* or its English equivalent "and others" may be used.
3. *Capacity of the author.* Needed only when contribution to the publication is not truly that of the author, such as *editor* or *compiler.*
4. *Chapter name.* Necessary only in rare instances when the chapter name helps the reader to find the souce, as in references to encyclopedias.
5. *Book name.* Book names are placed in italics. In typewritten work, italics are indicated by underscoring or by solid caps.
7. *Publishing company.*
8. *Location of publisher.* If more than one office, the one nearest the writer should be used. United States cities alone are sufficient if population exceeds half a million; city and state are best given for smaller places.
9. *Date.* Year of publication. If revised, year of latest revision.
10. *Page or pages.* Specific page or inclusive pages on which the cited material is found.

The following are examples of book entries.

A typical book:

[1] J. H. Menning and C. W. Wilkinson, *Writing Business Letters,* 5th ed., Richard D. Irwin, Inc., Homewood, Ill., 1971, pp. 17–18.

A book written by a staff of writers under the direction of an editor (chapter title is considered helpful):

[2] W. C. Butte and Ann Buchannan, editors, "Direct Mail Advertising," *An Encyclopedia of Advertising,* Binton Publishing Company, New York, 1974, p. 99.

A book written by a number of coauthors:

[3] E. Butler Cannais and others, *Anthology of Public Relations,* Warner-Bragg, Inc., New York, 1960, p. 137.

Periodical entry:

1. *Superscript.*
2. *Author's name.* Frequently, no author is given. In such cases the entry may be skipped, or if it is definitely known to be anonymous, the word *anonymous* may be placed in the entry.
3. *Article name.* Typed in quotation marks.
4. *Periodical name.* Placed in italics, which are indicated by underscoring in typed work.
5. *Publication identification.* Volume number in roman numerals followed by specific date of publication in parentheses.
6. *Page or pages.*

Examples of periodical entries are shown below:

[1] Mildred C. Kinnig, "A New Look at Retirement," *Modern Business,* Vol. XXXVII (July 31, 1971), pp. 31–32.

[2] William O. Schultz, "How One Company Improved Morale," *Business Leader,* Vol. XVII (August 31, 1975), p. 17.

[3] Mary Mitchell, "Report Writing Aids," *ABWA Bulletin,* October, 1971, p. 13.

Newspaper article:

1. *Superscript.*
2. *Source description.* If article is signed, give author's name. Otherwise, give description of article such as "United Press dispatch" or "editorial."
3. *Main head of article.* Subheads not needed.
4. *Newspaper name.* City and state names inserted in brackets if place names do not appear in newspaper title. State names not needed in case of very large cities, such as New York, Chicago, and Los Angeles.
5. *Date of publication.*
6. Page. May even include column number.

The following are typical newspaper article entries:

[1] United Press dispatch, "Rival Unions Sign Pact," *Morning Advocate* [Baton Rouge, Louisiana], September 3, 1970, p. 1–A.

[2] Editorial, "The North Moves South," *Austin* [Texas] *American,* October 3, 1971, p. 2–A.

Letters or documents:

1. *Nature of communication.*
2. *Name of writer.*  ⎡With identification by title and
3. *Name of recipient.*  ⎣organization where helpful.
4. *Date of writing.*
5. *Where filed.*

An example of an entry citing a letter is given below:

[1] Letter from J. W. Wells, president, Wells Equipment Co., to James Mattoch, secretary-treasurer, Southern Industrialists, Inc., June 10, 1971, filed among Mr. Mattoch's personal records.

The types of entries discussed in the preceding paragraphs are those most likely to be used. Yet, many unusual types of publications (not clearly books or periodicals) are likely to come up. When they do, you should classify the source by the form it most nearly resembles—a book or a periodical. Then you should attempt to construct the entry which most correctly describes the one source. Frequently, you will need to improvise—to use your best judgment in determining the source description.

## Standard reference forms

Certain forms are conventionally used in handling repeated references. The more common of these are the following:

*Ibid.*   Literally, *ibid.* means "in the same place." It is used to refer the reader to the preceding footnote, but to a different page. The entry consists of the superscript, *ibid.*, and the page number.

*Op. cit.*   Meaning "in the work cited," this form is used to refer to a previously cited footnote but not the one directly preceding. That is, the two similar citations are separated by at least one intervening footnote to another source. The entry consists of the superscript, last name of the author, *op. cit.*, and page number.

*Loc. cit.*   This form means "in the place cited," and its use follows its literal meaning. The form refers to a preceding entry, either the one directly preceding or one further back in the footnote series. It is used only when the page numbers of the two references to the same source are identical. If the entry refers to the footnote directly preceding, *loc. cit.*

alone is adequate. If the form is used to refer to an entry further back in the series, the author's last name and *loc. cit.* make up the entry.

The following series of entries illustrates these possibilities:

[1] Janice Smith, *How to Write the Annual Report,* Small-Boch, Inc., Chicago, 1965, p. 173.

[2] *Ibid.,* p. 143 (refers to Smith's book but to a different page).

[3] William Curtis, "An Experiment with Records," *Business Leader,* Vol. XIX (December 5, 1970), p. 28.

[4] Smith, *op. cit.,* p. 103 (refers to Smith's book but to a different page than in footnote 2).

[5] Curtis, *loc. cit.* (refers to Curtis' article and to same page as in footnote 3).

[6] *Loc. cit.* (refers to Curtis' article and to same page as in footnote 3 and 5).

Other abbreviations used in footnote entries are as follows:

| *Abbreviation* | *Meaning* |
|---|---|
| cf. | Compare (directs reader's attention to another passage) |
| cf. ante | Compare above |
| cf. post | Compare below |
| ed. | Edition |
| e.g. | For example |
| et al. | And others |
| et passim | And at intervals throughout the work |
| et seq. | And the following |
| i.e. | That is |
| infra | Below |
| l., ll. | Line, lines |
| MS, MSS | Manuscript, manuscripts |
| n.d. | No date |
| n.n. | No name |
| n.p. | No place |
| p., pp. | Page, pages |
| f., ff. | Following page, following pages |
| supra | Above |
| vol., vols. | Volume, volumes |

## Discussion footnotes

In sharp contrast with source footnotes are the discussion footnotes. Through the use of discussion footnotes the writer strives to explain a part of his text, to amplify discussion on a phase of his presentation, to make cross-references to other parts of the paper, and the like. The following examples illustrate some possibilities of this footnote type.
Cross-reference:

[1] See the principle of focal points on page 72.

Amplification of discussion and cross-reference:

> [2] Lyman Bryson says the same thing: "Every communication is differ-
> ent for every receiver even in the same context. No one can estimate the
> variation of understanding that there may be among receivers of the
> same message conveyed in the same vehicle when the receivers are sepa-
> rated in either space or time." See *Communication of Ideas*, p. 5.

Comparison:

> [3] Compare with the principle of the objective: Before starting any
> activity, one should make a clear, complete statement of the objective in
> view.

## Placement of quoted and paraphrased information

You may use data obtained from secondary sources in two ways. You
may paraphrase the information (cast it in your own words), or you may
use it verbatim (exactly as the original author worded it). In typing
paraphrased material, you need not distinguish it from the remainder of
the report text. Information which you use verbatim, however, must be
distinguished clearly from the other material.

The conventional rule for marking this difference is simple. If the
quoted passage is four lines or less in length, it is typed with the report
text and is distinguished from the normal text by quotation marks. But if
a longer quotation (five lines or more) is used, the conventional practice
is to set it in from both left and right margins (about five spaces) but
without quotation marks. If the text is typed with double spacing, the
quoted passage is further distinguished from the report writer's work by
single spacing, as illustrated in Figure C–1.

Frequently, you will find it best to break up or use only fragments of
the quoted author's work. Because omissions may distort the meaning of
a passage, you must clearly show them. You make these omissions clear
by use of the ellipsis (a series of three periods typed with intervening
spaces) at the points where material is left out. If it appears at the end of
a sentence, you must use four periods—one for final punctuation plus the
ellipsis. A passage with such omissions is the following:

> . . . many companies have undertaken to centralize in the hands of
> specially trained correspondents the handling of the outgoing mail. Usu-
> ally, centralization has been accomplished by the firm's employment of a
> correspondence supervisor. . . . The supervisor may guide the work of
> correspondents . . . , or the company may employ a second technique. . . .

In long quotations it is conventional to show omissions of a paragraph
or more by a full line of periods, usually typed with intervening spaces.

**FIGURE C-1**

Segment of a report showing mechanics of typing a quoted pasage

```
of those opposing the issue, Logan Wilson makes this penetrating ob-

servation:

                  It is a curious paradox that academicians display a
                  scientific attitude toward every universe of inquiry
                  except that which comprises their own profession. . . .
                  Lacking precise qualitative criteria, administrators
                  are prone to fall back upon rather crude quantitative
                  measures as a partial substitute.5

         These logical, straight-forward, and simple arguments of the pro-

ponents of teacher evaluation appear to be irrefutable.
```

## The bibliography

A bibliography is an orderly list of published material on a particular subject. In a formal paper the list covers references on the subject of the paper. The entries in this list very closely resemble source footnotes, but the two must not be confused.

The bibliography normally appears as an appended part of a formal paper and is placed after the appendix. It may be preceded by a fly page containing the one word *Bibliography*. The page which begins the list is headed by the main caption *Bibliography*, usually typed in solid capital letters. Below this title the publications are presented by broad categories and in alphabetical order within the categories. Such groupings as "Books," "Periodicals," and "Bulletins" may be used. But the determination of groups should be based solely on the types of publications collected in each bibliography. If, for example, a bibliography includes a large number of periodicals and government publications plus a wide assortment of diverse publication types, the bibliography could be divided into three parts: "Periodicals," "Government Publications," and "Miscellaneous Publications."

As with footnotes, variations in bibliographical style are numerous. A simplified form recommended for business use follows the same procedure as the described above for source footnotes, with four major exceptions:

1. The author's name is listed in reverse order—surname first—for the purpose of alphabetizing. If coauthors are involved, however, only the first name is reversed.
2. The entry is generally typed in hanging-indention form. That is, the second and all following lines of an entry begin some uniform

distance (usually about five spaces) to the right of the beginning point of the first line. The purpose of this indented pattern is to make the alphabetized first line stand out.

3. The bibliography entry gives the inclusive pages of the publication and does not refer to any one page or passage.

4. Second and subsequent references to publications of the same author are indicated by a uniform line (see bibliography illustration). In typed manuscripts this line might be formed by the underscore struck ten consecutive times. But this line may be used only if the entire authorship is the same in the consecutive publications. For example, the line could not be used in a situation in which consecutive entries have one common author but different coauthors.

## BIBLIOGRAPHY

### Books

Burton, Helen, *The City Fights Back,* Citadel Press, New York, 1970, 318 pp.

Converse, Paul D., Harvey W. Huegy, and Robert V. Mitchell, *The Elements of Marketing,* 5th ed., Prentice-Hall, Inc., New York, 1952, 968 pp.

Kiernan, Gladys M., *Retailers Manual of Taxes and Regulation,* 12th ed., Institute of Distribution, Inc., New York, 1971, 340 pp.

Koontz, Harold D., *Government Control of Business,* Hougton Mifflin Company, Boston, 1941, 937 pp.

Surrey, N. M. M., *The Commerce of Louisiana during the French Regime, 1699–1763,* Columbia University Press, New York, 1916, 476 pp.

### Government Publications

United States Bureau of the Census, "Characteristics of the Population," *Nineteenth Census of the United States: Census of Population,* Vol. II, Part 18, United States Government Printing Office, Washington, D.C., 1971, 248 pp.

————, *Statistical Abstract of the United States,* United States Government Printing Office, Washington, D.C., 1970, 1056 pp.

United States Department of Commerce, *Business Statistics: 1971,* United States Government Printing Office, Washington, D.C., 1971, 309 pp.

————, *Survey of Current Business: 1970 Supplement,* United States Government Printing Office, Washington, D.C., 1970, 271 pp.

## Periodicals

Montgomery, Donald E., "Consumer Standards and Marketing," *The Annals of the American Academy of Political and Social Science,* Vol. VII (May, 1973), pp. 141–49.

Phillips, Emily F., "Some Studies Needed in Marketing," *The Journal of Marketing,* Vol. V (July, 1940), pp. 16–25.

————, "Major Areas of Marketing Research," *The Journal of Marketing,* Vol. XI (July, 1972), pp. 21–26.

## Miscellaneous Publications

Bradford, Ernest S., *Survey and Directory, Marketing Research Agencies in the United States,* Bureau of Business Research, College of the City of New York, 1975, 137 pp.

*Reference Sources on Chain Stores,* Institute of Distribution, Inc., New York, 1974, 116 pp.

Smith, T. Lynn, *Farm Trade Centers in Louisiana, 1901 to 1975,* Louisiana Bulletin No. 234, Louisiana State University, Baton Rouge, 1976, 56 pp.

## The annotated bibliography

Frequently, in scholarly writing each bibliography entry is followed by a brief comment on the value and content of the entry. That is, the bibliography is annotated. Form and content of annotated bibliographies are shown in these entries:

Donald, W. T., editor, *Handbook of Business Administration,* McGraw-Hill Book Co., Inc., New York, 1974, 731 pp.

Contains a summary of the activities in each major area of business. Written by foremost authorities in each field. Particularly useful to the business specialist who wants a quick review of the whole of business.

Brown, Stanley M., and Lillian Doris, editors, *Business Executive's Handbook,* 3d ed., Macmillan Co., New York, 1973, 644 pp.

Provides answers to most routine executive problems in explicit manner and with good examples. Contains good material on correspondence and sales letters.

# appendix D

# A guide to correctness
# in writing

I N THE FOLLOWING pages you will find a review of the punctuation and grammar standards that should be most helpful to you in your efforts to communicate clearly. This review is not complete, so you should not look at it as a thorough English handbook. For the finer points you may need to consult any of a number of current handbooks on the subject. For your convenience in finding them and for use as grading marks on your papers, the standards are coded with letters and numbers.

**Apos 1** *The apostrophe.* The possessive case of nouns and indefinite pronouns is shown by the use of the apostrophe. If the nominative form of the word concerned does not end in *s*, an apostrophe and an *s* are added. But if the word does end in *s*, only an apostrophe is added.

| *Nominative form* | *Possessive form* |
|---|---|
| company | company's |
| employee | employee's |
| companies | companies' |
| employees | employees' |

Proper names and singular nouns which end in *s* sounds, however, are exceptions to this practice. Such words add the apostrophe and the *s* to the nominative singular; to the nominative plural only an apostrophe is added.

| *Nominative form* | *Possessive form* |
|---|---|
| Texas (singular) | Texas's |

| | |
|---|---|
| Joneses (plural) | Joneses' |
| Jones (singular) | Jones's |
| countess (singular) | countess's |

Adding only the apostrophe to the nominative singular also is gaining acceptance. (Jones', Texas')

**Apos 2** The place in a contraction where letters are omitted is marked with the apostrophe.

$$has\ not = hasn't$$
$$cannot = can't$$
$$it\ is = it's$$

**Apos 3** The apostrophe is used in the plural of letters, numbers, and words considered merely as words.

*Examples*

There were three *17's* recorded in the final tabulation.

The first list ended with the *k's.*

If you are to achieve the conversational tone, you must use more *I's* and *you's* in your writing.

**Bkts** *Brackets.* Brackets are used to set off words which the author wishes to insert in a quotation. (With the typewriter the left bracket is made by striking the diagonal, backspacing once, striking the underscore, rolling the platen up a line space, and striking the underscore again.)

*Examples*

"Possibly the use of this type of supervisor [the trained correspondence expert] is still on the increase."

"At least direct supervision has gained in importance in the past decade [the report was written in 1961], during which time 43 percent of the reporting business firms that started programs have used this technique."

**Cln 1** *The colon.* The colon is used to introduce a statement of explanation, an enumeration, or a formal quotation.

*Examples*

*Statement of explanation:* At this time the company was pioneering a new marketing idea: It was attempting to sell its products direct to consumers by means of vending machines.

*Enumeration:* There are four classes of machinists working in this department: apprentice machinist, journeyman machinist, machinist, and first-class machinist.

*Formal quotation:*   President Hartung had this to say about the proposal: "Any such movement which fails to have the support of the rank-and-file worker in this plant fails to get my support."

**Cln 2**   The colon should not be used when the thought of the sentence should continue without interruption. If it is a list that is being introduced by a colon, the list should be in apposition to a preceding word.

### Examples

*Below standard:*   Cities in which new sales offices are in operation are: Fort Smith, Texarkana, Lake Charles, Jackson, and Biloxi.

*Acceptable:*   Cities in which new sales offices are in operation are Fort Smith, Texarkana, Lake Charles, Jackson, and Biloxi.

*Acceptable:*   Cities in which new sales offices are in operation are as follows: Fort Smith, Texarkana, Lake Charles, Jackson, and Biloxi.

**Cln 3**   Words or phrases that introduce lists, such as *namely, that is, for example,* or *i.e.,* are preceded by the colon and followed by the comma if the lists are clauses or long phrases. But a lighter mark—a dash or a comma—may precede the listing word introducing a single item.

### Example

There is a man among us, namely Mark, who can fill the bill.

**Cma 1**   *The comma.* Principal clauses connected by a coordinating conjunction are separated by a comma. The coordinating conjunctions are *and, but, or, nor,* and *for.*

### Examples

Only two of the components of the index declined, and these two account for only 12 percent of the total weight of the index.

New automobiles are moving at record volumes, but used-car sales are lagging well behind the record pace set two years ago.

Exceptions may be made to this rule, however, in the case of compound sentences consisting of short and closely connected clauses.

### Examples

We sold and the price dropped.
Sometimes we profit and sometimes we lose.

**Cma 2.1**  Elements listed in series should be set apart by commas. In order to avoid misinterpretation in rare instances when some of the elements listed have compound constructions, it is best to place the comma between the last two items (before the final conjunction).

### Examples

Good copy must cover facts with accuracy, sincerity, honesty, and conviction.

Direct advertising can be used to introduce salesmen, fill in between salesmen's calls, cover territory where salesmen cannot be maintained, and keep pertinent reference material in the hands of prospects.

A survey conducted at the 1975 automobile show indicated that black and cream, blue and grey, dark maroon, and black cars were favored by the public. (Note how this example illustrates the need for a comma before the final conjunction.)

**Cma 2.2**  Coordinate adjectives in series are separated by commas when they modify the same noun and if there is no *and* connecting them. A good test to determine whether adjectives are coordinate is to insert an *and* between the words. If the *and* does not change the meaning of the expression, the words are coordinate.

### Examples

Miss Pratt has been a reliable, faithful, efficient employee for 20 years.

We guarantee that this is a good, clean car.

Light green office furniture is Mr. Orr's recommendation for the stenographic pool. [If *and* were placed between *light* and *green,* the word meaning would be changed.]

A big Dawson wrench proved to be best for the task. [The *and* won't fit between *big* and *Dawson.*]

**Cma 3.1**  A nonrestrictive modifier is set off from the sentence by commas. By a nonrestrictive modifier is meant a modifier which could be omitted from the sentence without changing the meaning of the sentence. Restrictive modifiers (those which restrict the words they modify to one particular object) are not set off by commas. A restrictive modifier cannot be left out of the sentence without changing the sentence meaning.

*Examples*

*Restrictive:*    The salesperson who sells the most will get a bonus. [*Who sells the most* restricts the meaning to one particular salesperson.]

*Nonrestrictive:*    James Smithers, who was the company's top salesperson for the year, was awarded a bonus. [If the clause *who was the company's top salesperson for the year* is omitted, the statement is not changed.]

*Restrictive:*    J. Ward & Company is the firm which employs most of the physically handicapped in this area.

*Nonrestrictive:*    J. Ward & Company, the firm which employs most of the physically handicapped in this area, has gained the admiration of the community.

Notice how some sentences could be either restrictive or non-restrictive, depending on the meaning intended by the writer.

*Examples*

*Restrictive:*    All of the suits which were damaged in the fire were sold at a discount. [Implies that a part of the stock was not damaged.]

*Nonrestrictive:*    All of the suits, which were damaged by the fire, were sold at a discount. [Implies that all the stock was damaged.]

**Cma 3.2**    Note that *as* and *since* in their original use as time words introduce restrictive clauses and take no punctuation, but in their derived use as cause words they introduce added or nonrestrictive clauses, which require comma punctuation.

*Examples*

*Restrictive—time:*    I have not seen him since he returned.

*Nonrestrictive—cause or reason:*    I shall see him Tuesday, as we shall meet at Rotary.

**Cma 4.1**    Parenthetic expressions are set off by commas. A parenthetic expression consists of words which interrupt the normal flow of the sentence. In a sense, they appear to be "stuck in." In many instances they are simply words out of normal order. For example, the sentence "A full-page, black and-white advertisement was run in the *Daily Bulletin*" contains a parenthetic expression when the word order is altered: "An advertisement, full-page and in black and white, was run in the *Daily Bulletin*."

*Examples*

This practice, it is believed, will lead to ruin.

The Johnston Oil Company, so the rumor goes, has cut back sharply its exploration activity.

Although the dash and the parentheses may also be used for similar reasons, the three marks differ as to the degree to which they separate the enclosed words from the rest of the sentence. The comma is the weakest of the three, and it is best used when the material set off is closely related to the surrounding words. Dashes are stronger marks than commas and are used when the words set off tend to be long or contain internal punctuation marks. Parentheses, the strongest of the three, are primarily used to enclose material which helps to explain or supplement the main words of the sentence.

**Cma 4.2** A comma is used to set off an appositive (a noun or a noun and its modifiers inserted to explain another noun) from the rest of the sentence. In a sense, appositives are forms of parenthetic expressions, for they do interrupt the normal flow of the sentence.

*Examples*

The Baron Corporation, our machine-parts supplier, is negotiating a new contract.

St. Louis, home office of our midwest district, will be the permanent site of our annual sales meeting.

President Carthwright, a self-educated man, is the leading advocate of our night school for employees.

But appositives which identify very closely are not set off by commas.

*Examples*

The word *liabilities* is not understood by most laboring men.

Our next shipment will come on the steamship *Alberta*.

**Cma 4.3** Commas are used to set off parenthetic words such as *therefore, however, in fact, of course, for example,* and *consequently.*

*Examples*

It is apparent, therefore, that the buyers' resistance has been brought about by an overvigorous sales campaign.

After the first experiment, for example, the traffic flow increased 10 percent.

The company will, however, be forced to abandon the old pricing system.

Included in this group of introductory words may be interjections (*oh, alas*) and responsive expressions (*yes, no, surely, indeed, well,* etc.). But if the words are strongly exclamatory or are not closely connected with the rest of the sentence, they may be punctuated as a sentence. (*No. Yes. Indeed.*)

*Examples*

Yes, the decision to increase production has been made.

Oh, contribute whatever you think is adequate.

**Cma 4.4** When more than one unit appears in a date or an address, the units are set off by commas.

*Examples*

*One unit:* December 30 is the date of our annual inventory.

*One unit:* The company has one outlet in Ohio.

*More than one unit:* December 30, 1906, is the date the Johnston Company first opened its doors.

*More than one unit:* Richmond, Virginia, is the headquarters of the new sales district.

**Cma 5.1** Subordinate clauses which precede main clauses are usually set off by commas.

*Examples*

Although it is durable, this package does not have eye appeal.

Since there was little store traffic on aisle 13, the area was converted into office space.

**Cma 5.2** Introductory verbal phrases usually are followed by a comma. A verbal phrase is one which contains some verb derivative—a gerund, a participle, or an infinitive.

*Example*

*Participle phrase:* Realizing his mistake, the foreman instructed his workers to keep a record of all salvaged equipment.

*Gerund phrase:* After gaining the advantage, we failed to press on to victory.

*Infinitive phrase:* To increase our turnover of automobile accessories, we must first improve our display area.

**Cma 6.1** The comma is used only for good reason. It is not a mark to be inserted indiscriminately at the whims of the writer. As a rule, use of commas should always be justified by one of the standard practices previously noted.

**Cma 6.1.1**　Do not be tripped into putting a comma between subject and verb.

*Example*

The thought that he could not afford to fail spurred him on. [No comma after *fail*.]

**Cma 6.1.2**　Ordinarily, do not set off the second element of a compound predicate with a comma. (The compound predicate is usually a weak and unemphatic structure and needs recasting instead of bolstering with an apologetic comma.)

**Cma 6.2**　The only exception to the preceding notes should be in instances where clarity of expression may be helped by the insertion of a comma.

*Examples*

*Not clear:* From the beginning inventory methods of Hill Company have been haphazard.

*Clear:* From the beginning, inventory methods of Hill Company have been haphazard.

**Dsh**　*The dash.*　The dash may be used to set off an element for emphasis or to show interrupted thought. Particularly it is used with long parenthetic expressions or those containing internal punctuation. With the typewriter, the dash is made by striking the hyphen twice, without spacing before or after.

*Examples*

Budgets for some past years—1974, for example—were prepared without consulting the department heads.

The test proved that the new process is simple, effective, accurate—and more expensive.

Only one person—the foreman in charge—has authority to issue such an order.

If you want a voice in the government—vote.

**Ex**　*The exclamation mark.*　The exclamation point is used at the end of a sentence or an exclamatory fragment to show strong emotion. This mark should be used sparingly; never should it be used with trivial ideas.

*Examples*
We've done it again!

No! It can't be!

**Hpn 1**  *The hyphen.*  Division of a word at the end of a line is indicated by the hyphen. The division must be made between syllables. It is generally impractical to leave a one-letter syllable at the end of a line (*a-bove*) or to carry over a two-letter syllable to the next line (*expens-es*).

**Hpn 2**  Hyphens are placed between the parts of some compound words. Generally, the hyphen is used whenever its absence would confuse the meaning of the words.

*Examples*
Compound nouns: *brother-in-law, cure-all, city-state*

Compound numbers under 100 and above 20: *thirty-one, fifty-five, seventy-seven*

Compound adjectives (two or more words used before a noun as a single adjective): *long-term* contract, *50-gallon* drum, *door-to-door* selling, *end-of-month* clearance.

Prefixes (most have been absorbed into the word): *de-emphasize, ex-chairman, vice-chairman, antilabor*

**Hpn 2.1**  A proper name used as a compound adjective needs no hyphen or hyphens to hold it together as a visual unit for the reader: The capitals perform that function.

*Examples*
*Correct:*   A Lamar High School student
*Correct:*   A United Airlines pilot

**Hpn 2.2**  Two or more modifiers in normal grammatical form and order need no hyphens. Particularly, a phrase consisting of an unmistakable adverb (one ending in *ly*) modifying an adjective or participle which in turn modifies a noun shows normal grammatical order and is readily grasped by the reader without the aid of the hyphen. But an adverb not ending in *ly* had better be joined to its adjectives or participle by the hyphen.

*Examples*
*No hyphen needed:*   A poorly drawn chart
*Use the hyphen:*   A well-prepared chart

**Ital 1**  For the use of italics to set out book titles, see **QM 4**. Note that this device is also used to set out names of periodicals, of works of art or music, and of naval vessels and aircraft.

**Ital 2**  Foreign words and abbreviations thereof should be italicized—if you must use them. Italicize standard foreign (usually Latin) words and abbreviations used in footnotes and book references. This list includes, *circa, c.* ("about"); *et al.* ("and others"); *ibidem, ibid.* ("in the same place"); *idem* ("the same"); *infra* ("below"); *supra* ("above"); *loco citato, loc. cit.* ("in the place cited"); *opere citato, op. cit.* ("in the work cited"); *passim* ("here and there"); *sic* ("so," "thus"); *quod vide, q.v.* ("which see"). But the commonly used "versus," or "vs.," or "v." has become anglicized and needs no underscoring.

**Ital 3**  Italicizing a word, letter, or figure used as its own name, or as a physical unit instead of a symbol of an idea, is a prime requisite for clearness. Without this device, we could not write this set of rules. Note the use of italics all through to label name words.

*Examples*

The little word *sell* is still in the dictionary.

The pronoun *which* should always have a noun as a clear antecedent. [Try reading that one without the italics: It becomes a fragment ending in mid air!]

**Ital 4**  If your entire passage is already italicized or underlined (as in the case of a caption underlined for emphasis), how should you distinguish a title, a foreign word, or a word normally italicized? Your best resort is to shift back to the roman type, or in typing to *omit* the underline.

**Paren**  *Parentheses.*  Parentheses may be used to set off words which are parenthetic or which are inserted to explain or to supplement the principal message (see **Cma 4.1**).

*Examples*

Dr. Samuel Goppard's phenomenal prediction (*Business Week,* June 20, 1971) has made some business forecasters revise their techniques.

Smith was elected chairman (the vote was almost 2 to 1), and immediately he introduced his plan for reorganization.

**Pd**  *Use of the period.*  The period is primarily used to indicate the end of a declarative sentence. But it does have some other vital uses.

**Pd 1**    After abbreviations or initials, the period is used.

*Example*

Ph.D., Co., Inc., A.M., A.D., etc.

**Pd 2**    The ellipsis (a series of periods) may be used to indicate the omission of words from a quoted passage. If the omitted part consists of something less than a paragraph, three periods are customarily placed at the point of omission (a fourth period is added if the omission comes at the sentence end). If the omitted part is a paragraph or more, however, a full line of periods is used. In either case the periods are appropriately typed with intervening spaces.

*Example*

Logical explanations, however, have been given by authorities in the field. Some attribute the decline . . . to the changing economy in the state during recent years. . . .

. . . . . . . . . . . . . . . . . . . . . . . . . . . . . . . . . . . . . . .

Added to the labor factor is the high cost of raw material, which has tended to eliminate many marginal producers. Too, the rising cost of electric power in recent years may have shifted many of the industry leader's attention to other forms of production.

**Q**    *The question mark.*    Sentences which are direct questions are ended with the question mark.

*Examples*

What are the latest quotations on Ewing-Bell common stock?

Will this campaign help to sell Dunnco products?

Note, however, that the question mark is not used with indirect questions.

*Examples*

The president was asked whether this campaign will help to sell Dunnco products.

He asked me what the latest quotations on Ewing-Bell common stock were.

**QM 1**    *The quotation mark.*    Quotation marks are used to enclose the exact words of a speaker or, if the quotation is short, the exact words of a writer.

By short written quotations is meant something four lines or less. Longer quoted passages are best displayed with additional right and left margins (see Appendix C), in single spacing (where double spacing has been used in the text), and without quotation marks.

### Examples

*Short written passage:*   H. G. McVoy sums up his presentation with this statement: "All signs indicate that automation will be evolutionary, not revolutionary."

*Verbal quotation:*   "This really should bring on a production slowdown," said Ms. Kuntz.

If the quoted words are broken by explanation or reference words, each quoted part is enclosed in question marks.

### Example

"Will you be specific," he asked, "in recommending a course of action?"

**QM 2**   A quotation within a quotation is indicated by single quotation marks.

### Example

President Carver said, "It has been a long time since I have heard an employee say, 'Boss, I'm going to beat my quota today.'"

**QM 3**   Periods and commas are always placed inside quotation marks. Semicolons and colons always go outside the marks. Question marks and exclamation points go inside if they apply to the quoted passage and outside if they apply to the whole sentence.

### Examples

"If we are patient," he said, "prosperity will some day arrive." [The comma is within the quotes; the period is also within the quotes.]

"Is there a quorum?" he asked. [The question mark belongs to the quoted passage.]

Which of you said, "I know where the error lies"? [The question mark applies to the entire sentence.]

I conclude only this from the union's promise to "force the hand of management": Violence will be their trump card. [Here the colon is not a part of the quotation.]

**QM 4**   Titles of the parts of a publication (articles in a magazine, chapters in a book, etc.) are enclosed in quotation marks. Titles of a whole publication, however, are placed in italics. Italics in typewritten material are indicated by underscoring.

*Examples*

The third chapter of the book *Elementary Statistical Procedure* is entitled "Concepts of Sampling."

Joan Glasgow's most recent article, "A Union Boss Views Automation," appears in the current issue of *Fortune*.

**SC 1**  *The semicolon.*  Clauses of a compound sentence that are not joined by a conjunction are separated by a semicolon.

*Examples*

Cork or asbestos sheeting must be hand-cut; polyurethane may be poured into a mold.

The new contract provides substantial wage increases; the original contract emphasized shorter hours.

Covered by this standard are main clauses connected by conjunctive adverbs. Conjunctive adverbs are really not conjunctions but are such words as *however, nevertheless, therefore, then, moreover, besides,* etc.

*Examples*

The survey findings indicated a need to revise the policy; nevertheless the president vetoed the amendment.

Small-town buyers favor the old models; therefore the board concluded that both models should be manufactured.

**SC 1.1**  Standard lists of "weak" connectives of independent clauses include the little words *also, hence, yet,* and *still* and such introductory phrases as *that is, in fact, in other words,* and the like. The test of their weakness as connectives is that, to perform a complete conjunctive function, these words or phrases each need the support of a coordinating conjunction (**and** *therefore,* **and** *yet,* **and** *still,* **but** *nevertheless,* **or** *in other words*). With the coordinating conjunctions these forms would take comma punctuation, naturally; but standing alone, they need the semicolon support.

**SC 1.2**  Note that *so that* introducing a dependent clause of purpose ("They incorporated so that they might limit liability") needs no punctuation mark because its clause is always restrictive.

**SC 2**  Independent clauses connected by a coordinating conjunction (*and, but, or, for, nor*) may be separated by a semicolon if the clauses are long or have internal punctuation. Sometimes short compound sentences with coordinating conjunction are separated in order to achieve special emphasis. The purpose of this practice is to help the reader see the break between clauses by not allowing him to be misled by the other punctuation marks.

### Examples

The FTU and the IFL, rivals from the beginning of the new industry, have shared almost equally in the growth of membership; but the FTU predominates among workers in the petroleum-products crafts, including pipeline construction and operation, and the IFL leads in memberships of chemical workers.

The market price was $4; but we paid $7.

**SC 3** Elements in a series which contains internal commas are separated by semicolons.

### Examples

The following gains were made in the February year-to-year comparison: Fort Worth, 7,300; Dallas, 4,705; Lubbock, 2,610; San Antonio, 2,350; Waco, 2,240; Port Arthur, 2,170; and Corpus Christi, 1,420.

Elected for the new term were Anna T. Zelnak, attorney from Cincinnati; Wilbur T. Hoffmeister, stockbroker and president of Hoffmeister Asociates of Baltimore; and William P. Peabody, a member of the faculty of the University of Georgia.

**SC 4** Use the semicolon between coordinate units only. Do not use it to attach a dependent clause or phrase to an independent clause.

**SC 5** Use punctuation marks in consistent echelons of descent—major marks for major units, smaller marks for smaller ones. Do not mix them or reverse them. To use a semicolon, colon, or dash as internal punctuation within a clause or unit already set off by commas is illogical and confusing.

### Examples

*Not this:* His itinerary, which included New York; Portland, Maine; Springfield, Ohio; and Chicago, was revised by the sales manager.

*But this:* [You'd better recast the whole thing, but this would do.] His itinerary, which included New York, Portland (Maine), Springfield (Ohio), and Chicago, was revised. . . .

Be careful also not to start a parenthetical expression with one mark and end it with another.

## Standard for correctness in grammar

Maintaining high standards of grammar is vital to the business writer who desires to excel at his work. Although it is not always necessary that high standards of grammar be followed in order to communicate, little can be said in favor of abandoning these standards. To illustrate, the statement "He ain't never done nothing to nobody" has little chance of not communicating its message. But doesn't it communicate more than the message intended? Doesn't it also communicate some idea as to the intellectual level of the writer? Certainly, such impressions would not help the communication of a typical report or letter.

As with the review of punctuation standards, the following summary of grammar standards is not intended to be a complete handbook on the subject. Rather, it is a summary of the major trouble spots encountered by most business writers. Mastery of these grammar principles would almost assure the business writer of achieving the high standards which are vital to the communication of his report or letter.

**AA** *Adjective-adverb confusion.* Adjectives should not be used for adverbs, nor should adverbs be used for adjectives. Adjectives modify only nouns and pronouns; and adverbs modify verbs, adjectives, or other adverbs.

Possibly the chief source of this confusion is in statements where the modifier follows the verb. If the modifier refers to the subject, an adjective should be used. If it limits the verb, an adverb is needed.

> *Below standard:*   She filed the records *quick.*
> *Acceptable:*   She filed the records *quickly.* [Refers to the verb.]

> *Below standard:*   John doesn't feel *badly.*
> *Acceptable:*   John doesn't feel *bad.* [Refers to the noun.]

> *Below standard:*   The new cars look *beautifully.*
> *Acceptable:*   The new cars look *beautiful.* [Refers to the noun.]

It should be noted that many words are both adjective and adverb (*little, well, fast, much*). And some adverbs have two forms: One form is the same as the adjective, and the other adds the *ly* (*slow* and *slowly, cheap* and *cheaply, quick* and *quickly*).

> *Acceptable:*   All of our drivers are instructed to drive *slow.*
> *Acceptable:*   All of our drivers are instructed to drive *slowly.*

**Agmt SV** *Subject-verb agreement.* Nouns and their verbs must agree in number. A plural noun must have a plural verb form; a singular noun must have a singular verb.

> *Below standard:   Expenditures* for miscellaneous equipment *was* expected to decline. [*Expenditures* is plural, so its verb must be plural.]

*Acceptable:*   *Expenditures* for miscellaneous equipment *were* expected to decline.

*Below standard:*   The *president,* as well as his staff, *were* not able to attend. [*President* is the subject, and the number is not changed by the modifying phrase.]
*Acceptable:*   The *president,* as well as his staff, *was* not able to attend.

Compound subjects (two or more nouns joined by *and*) require plural verbs.

*Below standard:*   The *welders* and their *foreman* is in favor of the proposal. [*Welders* and *foreman* are compound subjects of the verb, but *is* is singular.]
*Acceptable:*   The *welders and* their *foreman are* in favor of the proposal.

*Below standard:*   *Received* in the morning delivery *was a typewriter and* two *reams* of letterhead paper. [*Reams* and *type-writer* are the subjects; the verb must be plural.]
*Acceptable:*   *Received* in the morning delivery *were a typewriter and* two *reams* of letterhead paper.

Collective nouns may be either singular or plural, depending on the meaning intended.

*Acceptable:*   The *committee have* carefully *studied* the proposal. [*Committee* is thought of as separate individuals.]
*Acceptable:*   The *committee has* carefully *studied* the proposal. [The *committee* is considered as a unit.]

As a rule, the pronouns *anybody, anyone, each, either, everyone, everybody, neither, nobody, somebody,* and *someone* take a singular verb. The word *none* may be either singular or plural, depending on whether it is used to refer to a unit or to more than a unit.

*Acceptable:*   *Either* of the advertising campaigns *is* costly.
*Acceptable:*   *Nobody* who watches the clock *is successful.*

**AN**   Do not use an adverbial clause as a noun clause. Clauses beginning with *because, when, where, if,* and similar adverbial connectives are not properly used as subjects, objects, or complements of verbs.

*Not this:*   He did not know *if* he could go or not.
*But this:*   He did not know *whether* he could go or not.

*Not this:*   The reason was *because* he did not submit a report.
*But this:*   The reason was *that* he did not submit a report.

*Not this:*   A time-series graph is *where* [or *when*] changes in an index such as wholesale prices are indicated.

*But this:*   A time-series graph is the picturing of. . . .

**Awk**   *Awkward.*   Awkward writing attracts attention to its structure and should be avoided. Writing is awkward when its word arrangement is unconventional or uneconomical, or simply not the best for quick understanding.

**Dng**   *Dangling modifiers.*   Avoid the use of modifiers which do not logically modify a word in the sentence. Such modifiers are said to dangle. They are both illogical and confusing. Usually, sentences containing dangling constructions can be corrected in either of two ways: The noun or pronoun which the modifier describes may be inserted, or the dangling element may be changed to a complete clause.

*Below standard:*   Believing that credit customers should have advance notice of the sale, special letters were mailed to them.

*Acceptable:*   Believing that credit customers should have advance notice of the sale, we mailed special letters to them. [Improvement is made by inserting the noun modified.]

*Acceptable:*   Because we believed that credit customers should have advance notice of the sale, we mailed special letters to them. [Improvement is made by changing the dangling element to a complete clause.]

Dangling modifiers are of four principal types: participial phrases, elliptical clauses, gerund phrases, and infinitive phrases.

*Below standard:*   Believing that District 7 was not being thoroughly covered, an additional salesman was assigned to the area. [Dangling participial phrase.]

*Acceptable:*   Believing that District 7 was not being thoroughly covered, the sales manager assigned an additional salesperson to the area.

*Below standard:*   By working hard, your goal can be reached. [Dangling gerund phrase.]

*Acceptable:*   By working hard, you can reach your goal.

*Below standard:*   To succeed at this job, long hours and hard work must not be shunned. [Dangling infinitive phrase.]

*Acceptable:*   To succeed at this job, one must not shun long hours and hard work.

*Below standard:*   While waiting on a customer, the radio was stolen. [Dangling elliptical clause—a clause without noun or verb.]

*Acceptable:* While the salesperson was waiting on a customer, the radio was stolen.

There are, however, a few generally accepted introductory phrases which are permitted to dangle. Included in this group are *generally speaking, confidentially speaking, taking all things into consideration,* and such expressions as *in boxing, in welding,* and *in farming.*

*Acceptable:* Generally speaking, business activity is at an all-time high.
*Acceptable:* In farming, the land must be prepared long before planting time.
*Acceptable:* Taking all things into consideration, this applicant is the best for the job.

**Frag**  *The sentence fragment.* The sentence fragment should be avoided. Although it may sometimes be used for effect, as in sales writing, it is best omitted by all but the most skilled writers. The sentence fragment consists of any group of words which cannot stand up alone as a complete and independent statement. Probably the most frequent violation of this rule results from the use of a subordinate clause as a sentence.

*Below standard:* Believing that you will want an analysis of sales for November. We have sent you the figures.
*Acceptable:* Believing that you will want an analysis of sales for November, we have sent you the figures.

*Below standard:* He declared that such a procedure would not be practical. And that it would be too expensive in the long run.
*Acceptable:* He declared that such a procedure would not be practical and that it would be too expensive in the long run.

**Pn 1**  *Pronouns.* The antecedents of all pronouns should be unmistakably clear. Failure to conform to this standard causes confusion. Particularly is confusion likely to come about in sentences where two or more nouns are possible antecedents of the pronoun or where the antecedent is far removed from the pronoun.

*Below standard:* When the president objected to Mr. Carter, he told him to mind his own business. [Who told whom?]
*Acceptable:* When the president objected to Mr. Carter, Mr. Carter told him to mind his own business.

*Below standard:* The mixture should not be allowed to boil; so when you do it, watch the temperature gauge. [*It* doesn't have an antecedent.]

*Acceptable:*   The mixture should not be allowed to boil; so when conducting the experiment, watch the temperature gauge.

*Below standard:*   The model V is being introduced this year. Ads in *Time, The Saturday Evening Post,* and big-city newspapers over the country are designed to get sales off to a good start. It is especially designed for the novice boatman who is not willing to pay a big price.

*Acceptable:*   The model V is being introduced this year. Ads in *Time, The Saturday Evening Post,* and big-city newspapers over the country are designed to get sales off to a good start. The new model is especially designed for the novice boatman who is not willing to pay a big price.

Confusion may sometimes result from using a pronoun with an implied antecedent.

*Below standard:*   Because of the disastrous freeze in the citrus belt, it is necessary that most of them be replanted.

*Acceptable:*   Because of the disastrous freeze in the citrus belt, it is necessary that most of the citrus orchards be replanted.

Except when their reference is perfectly clear, it is best to avoid using the pronouns *which, that,* and *this* to refer to a whole idea of a preceding clause. Many times the sentence can be made clear by the use of a clarifying noun following the pronoun.

*Below standard* (following a detailed presentation of the writer's suggestion for improving the company suggestion-box plan):   This should be put into effect without delay.

*Acceptable:*   This suggestion-box plan should be put into effect right away.

**Pn 2**   The number of the pronoun should agree with the number of its antecedent. If the antecedent is singular, its pronoun must be singular. If the antecedent is plural, its pronoun must be plural.

*Below standard:*   Taxes and insurance are necessary evils in any business, and it must be considered carefully in anticipating profits.

*Acceptable:*   Taxes and insurance are necessary evils in any business, and they must be considered carefully in anticipating profits.

*Below standard:*   Everybody should make plans for their retirement. [Words like *everyone, everybody, anybody* are singular.]

*Acceptable:*   Everybody should make plans for his retirement.

**Pn 3**   Care should be taken to use the correct case of the pronoun. If the pronoun serves as the subject of the verb, or if it follows a form of the infinitive *to be,* a nominative case pronoun should be used. (Nominative case of the personal pronouns is *I, you, he, she, it, we, they.*)

> *Acceptable:*   He will record the minutes of the meeting.
> *Acceptable:*   I think it will be he.

If the pronoun is the object of a preposition or a verb, or if it is the subject of an infinitive, the objective case should be used. (Objective case for the personal pronouns is *me, you, him, her, us, them.*)

> *Below standard:*   This transaction is between you and *he.* [*He* is nominative and cannot be the object of the preposition *between.*]
> *Acceptable:*   This transaction is between you and *him.*

> *Below standard:*   Because the investigator praised Ms. Smith and *I,* we were promoted.
> *Acceptable:*   Because the investigator praised Ms. Smith and *me,* we were promoted.

The case of relative pronouns (*who, whom*) is determined by the pronoun's use in the clause it introduces. One good way of determining which case should be used is to substitute the personal pronoun for the relative pronoun. If the case of the personal pronoun which fits is nominative, *who* should be used. If it is objective, *whom* should be used.

> *Acceptable:*   George Cutler is the salesperson who won the award. [*He* (nominative) could be substituted for the relative pronoun; therefore, nominative *who* should be used.]
> *Acceptable:*   George Cutler is the salesperson *whom* you recommended. [Objective-case *him* would substitute. Thus, objective-case *whom* is used.]

Usually the possessive case is used with substantives which immediately precede a gerund (verbal noun ending in *ing*).

> *Acceptable:*   *Our* selling of the stock frightened some of the conservative members of the board.
> *Acceptable:*   *Her* accepting the money ended her legal claim to the property.

**Prl**   *Parallelism.*   Parts of a sentence that are used to express parallel thoughts should be parallel in grammatical form. Parallel constructions are logically connected by the coordinating conjunctions *and, but,* and *or.* Care should be taken to see that the sentence elements connected by these conjunctions are of the same grammatical type. That is, if one of the parts is a noun, so should the other parts be nouns. If one of the parts is an infinitive phrase, so should the other parts be infinitive phrases.

> *Below standard:*    The company objectives for the coming year are to match last year's production, higher sales, and improving consumer relations.
> *Acceptable:*    The company objectives for the coming year are to match last year's production, to increase sales, and to improve consumer relations.

> *Below standard:*    Writing copy may be more valuable experience than to make layouts.
> *Acceptable:*    Writing copy may be more valuable experience than making layouts.

> *Below standard:*    The questionnaire asks for this information: number of employees, what is our union status, and how much do we pay.
> *Acceptable:*    The questionnaire asks for this information: number of employees, union affiliation, and pay scale.

**Prl 1**    After each member of a correlating pair of conjunctions (*either, or; both, and; not only, but also*), use exactly the same grammatical form.

**Prl 2**    Comparisons in particular need to be kept on consistent bases. Do not fall into the ditch of jargonese shortcuts.

**Prl 3**    Avoid the faulty parallelism of the illogical *and which* construction. Do not tie a lone relative clause to the main clause with *and*, as if it were parallel with a minor adjective, participial modifier, or implied quality.

> He warned of the high and frightening cost-of-living index, and which is still rising.

> *Better:*    He warned of the cost-of-living index, which is frighteningly high and which is still rising.
> *Or:*    He warned that the frightening, high cost-of-living index is still rising.

**Tns**    *Tense of the verb, infinitive, and participle.*    The tense of each verb, infinitive, and participle used should reflect the logical time of happening of the statement: Every statement has its place in time. If this place in time is to be exactly communicated, the writer must take care of his selection of tense. Even though tense usually is determined by the subject of the statement being reported, a few trouble spots may be mentioned.

**Tns 1**  *Statements of fact that are true at the time of writing should be worded in the present tense.*

> *Below standard:*  Boston was not selected as a site for the aircraft plant because it *was* too near the coast. [Boston still is near the coast, isn't it?]
>
> *Acceptable:*  Boston was not selected as a site for the aircraft plant because it *is* too near the coast.

**Tns 2**  Past tense is used in statements covering a definite past event or action.

> *Acceptable:*  Mr. Burns *said* to me, "Bill, you'll never make an auditor."
>
> *Below standard:*  Mr. Burns *says* to me, "Bill, you'll never make an auditor."

**Tns 3**  The time period reflected by the past participle (*having been . . .*) is earlier than that of its governing verb. For the present participle (*being . . .*), the time period reflected is the same as that of the governing verb.

> *Below standard:*  These debentures are among the oldest on record, *being* issued in early 1937.
>
> *Acceptable:*  These debentures are among the oldest on record, *having been* issued in early 1937.

> *Below standard:*  Ms. Sloan, *having been* the top salesperson on the force, was made sales manager. [Possible but illogical.]
>
> *Acceptable:*  Ms. Sloan, *being* the top salesperson on the force, was made sales manager.

**Tns 4**  Verbs in subordinate clauses are governed by the verb in the principal clause. When the main verb is in the past tense, usually the subordinate verb must also be in a past tense (past, present perfect, or past perfect). Thus, if the time of the subordinate clause is the same as that of the main verb, past tense is used.

> *Acceptable:*  I *noticed* [past tense] the discrepancy, and then I *remembered* [same time as main verb] the incidents which caused it.

If the time of the subordinate clause is previous to that of the main verb in past tense, past perfect tense is used for the subordinate verb.

> *Below standard:*  In early July we *noticed* [past] that he *exceeded* [logically should be previous to main verb] his quota three times.
>
> *Acceptable:*  In early July we *noticed* that he *had exceeded* his quota three times.

The present perfect tense is used for the subordinate clause when the time of this clause is subsequent to the time of the main verb.

> *Below standard:* Before the war we *contributed* [past] generously, but lately we *forget* [should be time subsequent to the time of main verb] our duties.
>
> *Acceptable:* Before the war we *contributed* generously, but lately we *have forgotten* our duties.

**Tns 5** The present perfect tense does not logically refer to a definite time in the past. Instead, it indicates time somewhere in the indefinite past.

> *Below standard:* We *have audited* your records on July 31 of 1970 and 1971.
>
> *Acceptable:* We *audited* your records on July 31 of 1970 and 1971.
>
> *Acceptable:* We *have audited* your records twice in the past.

**WU** *Word use.* Misused words call attention to themselves and detract from the writing. Although the possibilities of error in word use are infinite, the following list contains a few of the most common ones.

| *Don't use* | *Use* |
|---|---|
| a long ways | a long way |
| and etc. | etc. |
| anywheres | anywhere |
| different than | different from |
| have got to | must |
| in back of | behind |
| in hopes of | in hope of |
| in regards to | in regard to |
| inside of | within |
| kind of satisfied | somewhat satisfied |
| nowhere near | not nearly |
| nowheres | nowhere |
| off of | off |
| over with | over |
| seldom ever | seldom |
| try and come | try to come |

## Standard for the use of numbers

Quantities may be spelled out or they may be expressed in numeral form. Whether to use one form or the other is often a perplexing question. Especially is it perplexing to the business writer, for much of his work is with quantitative subjects. Because the means of expressing quantities is so vital to the business writer, the following notes on the use of numbers are presented.

**No** *Numbers.* Although authorities do not agree on number usage, the business writer would do well to follow the rule of ten. By this rule, one spells out number ten and below. He uses figures for numbers above ten.

> *Correct:* The auditor found 13 discrepancies in the stock records.
> *Correct:* The auditor found nine discrepancies in the stock records.

**No 1** An exception to the rule of ten is made when a number begins a sentence. In this position the number is spelled out regardless of size.

> *Correct:* Seventy-three bonds were destroyed.
> *Correct:* Eighty-nine men picketed the north entrance.

**No 2** In comparisons it is best to keep all numbers in the same form. The form used should be the one that according to the rule of ten, would be used most often in the series.

> *Correct:* We managed to salvage three lathes, one drill, and thirteen welding machines.
> *Correct:* Sales increases over last year were 9 percent on automotive parts, 14 percent on hardware, and 23 percent on appliances.

**No 3** When two series of numbers appear in one sentence, one should be spelled out, and the other should be in numeral form.

> *Correct:* Three salesperson exceeded $1,500, fourteen exceeded $1,000, and thirty-one exceeded $500.

**No 4** Days of the month are typed in figure form when they are preceded by the month.

> *Correct:* July 3, 1971

When they appear alone, or when they precede the month, the days of the month may be either spelled out or in numeral form according to the rule of ten.

> *Correct:* I shall be there on the 13th.
> *Correct:* The union scheduled the strike vote for the eighth.
> *Correct:* Ms. Millican signed the contract on the seventh of July.
> *Correct:* Sales have declined since the 14th of August.

# appendix E

## A report checklist

THE FOLLOWING LIST of the most common violations in report construction may serve two purposes. First, it may be useful as a guide to one preparing a report. Second, it may serve as a convenient grading aid. As a grading aid, it permits the grader to point out violations by merely writing symbols rather than writing out longhand comments. Although the checklist covers the longer, more formal types of reports, it can easily be adapted to other forms.

1. *The report title*
    a. Is this title complete? The title should tell the reader what he may expect to find in the contents, and it should rule out what he may not expect to find. Although requirements differ with the case, these aspects of the problem should be considered in constructing the title:
        (1) Who
        (2) What
        (3) Where
        (4) When
        (5) Why
        (6) How
    b. This title is too long. Try to be more economical with words.
    c. This title is too short. A scant title is broad and usually covers too much ground.
    d. In typing the title, break it at convenient breaking points—that is, at the ends of thought units.

2. *Title page*
   a. For best optical effect, center the parts between left and right margins. Here the lines are off center.
   b. Too much or too little space between the parts detracts from the appearance of the page. Check the text illustrations for better placement of the parts.
   c. For better balance, use (1) fewer and longer lines (by combining some of the items) or (2) more and shorter lines.
   d. Check this part for completeness. Usually, the recipient and the writer should be identified by name, title, company or organization, and address.
   e. Date the report specifically—by month, day, and year, if possible, but at least by year.
   f. Preferably single-space units of three lines or less. Double-space longer units.

3. *General layout and mechanics*
   a. Fit the layout of the page to the space available (see instructions in Appendix A). This page is
      (1) Too fat
      (2) Too low, high, or off center (as marked)
      (3) Too tall and thin
   b. Neat typing? Strikeovers, smudges, and erasures detract from the report's message.
   c. Keep the right margins relatively straight. Successive lines falling under or over the right-margin boundary offend the eye.
   d. The spacing could be improved here.
      (1) Too much space used here.
      (2) Not enough space here.
   e. Follow the conventional system of page numbering:
      (1) Use small roman figures (i, ii, etc.) for the prefatory pages.
      (2) Use arabic figures (1, 2, etc.) for all other pages.
      (3) No numbers are needed on the pages preceding the table of contents. But these pages are counted in the numbering sequence.
   f. This page is choppy. Consider lengthening or combining the paragraphs for more logical organization and better appearance.
   g. This page is too heavy. Consider breaking down these paragraphs into shorter ones.
   h. Your system of captioning could be improved. The captions should tell the reader at a glance the relative importance of each part. Better check the instructions in Appendix A.

      *i.*  Don't let a caption appear at the bottom of the page without at least two lines of text. Captions placed this way appear to be headings to nothing.

4. *Letter of transmittal*

    *a.*  Begin the letter with a direct presentation of the report. The primary objective of the letter is to transmit the report, and there is no reason for delaying the message with slow explanation or other material.

    *b.*  Refer incidentally to the authorization by date and nature (oral, written) somewhere early in the letter.

    *c.*  For combination transmittal-synopsis letters: Move smoothly into a review of the highlight facts and conclusions of the report. (For additional checklist points on this type of letter, use the appropriate notes under "5. Synopsis.")

    *d.*  For letters which do not serve also as a synopsis: A digest of the report findings is better left for the synopsis.

    *e.*  Your choice of subject matter for the letter could be improved. Perhaps the best choice is some appropriate talk about the report—comments which will help the reader to understand or appreciate the report.

    *f.*  A statement of your personal attitude toward the assignment is appropriate. It may well come at the close of the letter.

    *g.*  Make this part sound more sincere. It is easy to overdo words of appreciation, and it is easy to make them sound like "rubber stamps." You are most likely to avoid these pitfalls by making your words fit this one case and by writing in good conversational language.

    *h.*  A friendlier, livelier style would improve this letter. Except in the more formal situations, the transmittal letter is best written in good personal language (with personal pronouns *I, we, you,* and the like). This is your one chance to address the recipient personally.

5. *Synopsis*

    *a.*  If direct order assigned: Begin with a statement of your main finding, conclusion, or recommendation.

    *b.*  If indirect order assigned: Begin with a brief orientation to the study.

    *c.*  Briefly summarize the essential introductory facts. Consider these for completeness: for, by whom, when, what about, and how solved.

  *e.* Coverage of this part is out of proportion.
    (1) This coverage is scant. Highlight more of the supporting facts. The synopsis is not just a review of conclusions. It includes all of the foundation facts, their analyses, and the conclusions—in summary form.
    (2) This coverage is too much in detail. The task of the synopsis is to summarize.
  *f.* Your writing is not so concise as it should be. The objective of a synopsis is to cover the ingredients of the report in a minimum of space. Economy in the use of words is a main requirement.
  *g.* This writing tends to be dull. Try not to let your efforts to write concisely deaden your writing style. Your objective is to summarize concisely without sacrificing good writing style.

6. *Table of contents*
  *a.* Be consistent in the use of type and capitals. Although you may choose from a number of type forms (capitals, capitals and lowercase underscored, and the like), consistency is a logical requirement.
  *b.* This spacing is not the best for eye-pleasing effect.
    (1) These parts are crowded. Better double-space here.
    (2) Here the parts are strung out too much. Single spacing would be better.
  *c.* Use leader lines (preferably periods with spaces intervening) to relate the part to the page number.
  *d.* Keep the parts in line. Captions on the same level should begin at the same spot. Roman numerals in the outline and page numbers should be aligned on their right digits. Periods in the leader lines should be lined up.
  *e.* Elements which precede the contents table need not be listed. Thus, the only prefatory part listed in the contents table of the conventional long, formal report is the synopsis.
  *f.* Do not give the appendix and the epitome roman number status in the outline. They are appended parts of the report and are not part of the report message.
  *g.* These parts are not arranged in the best order of coherence. Review the logic of your plan for a better sequence.
  *h.* These topics overlap. In general, each section of the report should be mutually independent. Although some repetition and relating of points may be in order, too much of this is a sign of illogical organization.
  *i.* Do not let one major section account for the entire body of the report. Except in the very minor problems, it is a rare case in

which more than one aspect of the problem does not need to be discussed.

   *j.*  One-item subdivisions are illogical. You cannot divide an area without coming up with at least two parts.

   *k.*  More control captions are needed here. Subcaptions to this caption would show better organization.

   *l.*  The subcaptions, in good order, should cover all of the territory fenced in by the major captions—no more or less.

   *m.*  This organization plan is not the best. Restudy the problem for a more logical plan of presenting this report.

   *n.*  These parts are not equal in importance. So do not treat them as being equal in the development of the problem.

   *o.*  If talking captions assigned: These captions do not talk so well as they might. Talking captions not only give the subject covered, but they also tell what is said about the subject.

   *p.*  Coordinate headings should be parallel in grammatical structure. That is, if caption A is a noun phrase, so should captions B and C be noun phrases. If 1 under A is a sentence, so should 2 and 3 be sentences.

   *q.*  These captions tend to be too long. Good captions use the minimum wording which will convey the meanings intended.

   *r.*  Avoid monotonous repetition in the captions. Vary the wording or the construction patterns.

7.  *The introduction*

   *a.*  Although the reader's needs for orientation will change with the problem, these areas generally should be covered in the report introduction:

     (1)  How the report came about: time and nature of the origin of the problem, identification of the participants, and the like.

     (2)  What the problem is: objective, scope, definitions, background information, etc.

     (3)  How the problem is solved: description of the sources of information or research procedure employed in solving the problem.

     (4)  How the information is presented in the report: a preview to the organization of the report.

   *b.*  Work for a smooth, natural writing style in this part.

8.  *Coherence and tight connection*

   *a.*  For the long, formal reports, short summary previews are needed at important stages of the progress. These parts complement the preview section which typically ends the introduc-

tion of a formal report. Summary-preview parts are useful to let the reader know periodically where he is in the report plan.
b.   Your transition is weak here. Avoid abrupt changes of thought.
c.   Here you could improve your paragraph construction by selecting a topic sentence and leading from it.
d.   Don't lean heavily on the captions. A well-written report should read clearly even if all captions are taken out.
e.   This section ends abruptly. A summary or concluding statement would help.

9.   *The writing of the report*
a.   Is this writing adapted to the audience? It appears to be (1) too heavy or (2) too light for your reader. In general, this criticism concerns the length of your sentences and your choice of words. Better test your writing for readability.
b.   Avoid the overuse of passive voice.
c.   This writing style is dull. Work for a fast-moving and interesting writing style—one that is alive with concrete and action words.
d.   Your writing should be more concise. Be economical. Try to cut down on words without sacrificing meaning.
e.   If conventional formality is required: Write in the third person. Avoid these slips from impersonal to personal writing.
f.   Be consistent in time viewpoint. Illogical shifts from past to present and from present to past confuse the report message. Preferably, write in the present-time viewpoint, treating all things as they relate to the time of writing.

10.   *Miscellaneous*
a.   The text must tell the story, so don't just refer the reader to a chart or table and let it go at that.
b.   Supporting facts are necessary for any conclusions. Your presentation is (1) lacking in supporting fact or (2) cluttered with too much detailed fact. (Minute detail might well be presented in summary tables.)
c.   Don't lose sight of your objective. You must do more than present information. Adapt this information to the problem.
d.   Beware of unsupported, unqualified statements. Back up these parts with fact.
e.   Opinions and facts should be clearly differentiated. Label opinions as such.

11.   *Graphic display*
a.   The layout arrangement appears to be crowded or awkward at the points indicated. Particularly, don't crowd the illustration or

table with the text. It would be well to triple-space (at least) before and after it.

*b.*   Here the layout appears to be needlessly spaced out.

*c.*   If you have three or more of one type of illustration (charts, tables, maps, etc.), group them together for the numbering sequence within the report. For example, a report with three charts, four maps, and three illustrations would have these graphic aids numbered like this: Charts 1, 2, and 3; Maps 1, 2, 3, and 4; and Illustrations 1, 2, and 3. If you have a mixture of types, with only one or two of each, refer to them as "Figures" and number them all in the same series. For example, a report with one chart, two maps, and three illustrations would be numbered like this: Figures 1, 2, 3, 4, 5, and 6.

*d.*   Titles for all tables are appropriately placed above the table. Titles for all other graphic devices conventionally appear below the illustration.

*e.*   The table or graphic display number may appear either on the line with the caption or on a line by itself, centered above the caption.

*f.*   It is conventional to number tables with roman numerals and all other displays with arabic numerals. There is convention, too, for placing the caption of tables in a higher type than the titles of other forms of graphic display.

*g.*   You have too much here for one clear picture. Consider (1) breaking it into logical parts for regular display or (2) placing it in the appendix section.

*h.*   If the table or chart cannot be considered essential to a clear understanding of the context, it should be placed in the appendix section.

*i.*   Tables are useful, but tables alone are not enough. They are not in the true sense graphic—they don't tell the story instantly.

*j.*   Place each graphic aid as near as is practical to the spot where you talk about it. Placing all your graphic aids in the appendix is easy for the writer but hard on the reader, who must flip pages back and forth for reference.

*k.*   The type of illustration chosen here is not the most appropriate one to display this set of factors.

*l.*   Possibly this is your best work, but it falls down in overall appearance and quality. Clear, straight-inked lines neatly drawn, possibly with the use of cross-hatching or color, are necessary for the best graphic display.

*m.*   Overlarge illustrations break the continuity of the reading.

Couldn't you have reduced the size here without hurting the effectiveness?

*n.* Tie together the illustration and text by referring the reader to the illustration, and do it when you want him to look at it.

*o.* Make incidental your references to illustration material. Instead of using a separate sentence, use statements such as "as shown in Figure 2," "(see Chart 5)," and the like.

# appendix F

## A general checklist
## for letter grading

### The opening

**Buf N**  *Buffer needed.* This situation requires an indirect opening. Your opening is too direct.

**Buf Q**  *Buffer quality.* The quality of your opening buffer leaves something to be desired. It should be more on-subject, logical, and/or interesting.

**Buf S**  *Buffer strategy.* Your buffer does not do the best job of setting up the strategy of your letter.

**Dir**  *Directness.* This opening is slow in getting to your objective. It wastes words. In this letter situation, opening directness is required.

### Coverage

**Comp**  *Completeness.* You have not covered all the points essential to this problem.

**Ex M**  *Excess material.* You include more information than is necessary to achieve your objective.

**Exp**  *Explanation.* You need more explanation here. The reader needs to know more before he can do what you want him to do.

**ID**  *Identification of the situation.* If you are answering a letter, writing about a specific purchase, and the like, you need to make clear identification of these facts in your letter. Your identification is inadequate.

**ID Sub**   *Identification, subject line.*   A subject line would help in this case to identify the situation.

## The close

**Ac S**   *Action, strong.*   This drive for action is too strong for this problem.

**Ac W**   *Action, weak.*   When action is the desired result of your letter, make it direct and clear, not as a hint. This one is weak.

**Cl IT**   *Close, individually tailored.*   Make your closing remarks fit the one case as well as you can. This one could fit other situations.

**Cl OS**   *Close, off subject.*   An off-subject close is desired in this case. Yours brings back to the reader's mind things you want him to forget.

## Technique

**Adp**   *Adaptation.*   Your words should be adapted to the one reader. Here yours are (1) above or (2) below him.

**Awk**   *Awkward word arrangement.*

**Bky**   *Bulky arrangement.*   Make your paragraphs more inviting by breaking them into shorter units of thought.

**Chop**   *Choppy writing.*   A succession of short sentences produces an irritating effect.

**Dl**   *Dull writing.*   Bring your writing to life with vivid, concrete words.

**Emp +**   *Emphasis, too much.*
**Emp −**   *Emphasis, to little.*
Here you have given too much or too little (as marked) emphasis by (1) placement, (2) volume, or (3) words or mechanical means.

**Intp**   *Interpretation.*   Do more than just present facts. In this situation something more is needed. Make the data meaningful in terms of the reader's situation.

**Los**   *Loose writing.*   Take more care to use words economically. Write concisely.

**Ord**   *Order of presentation.*   This information does not fall in a logical order. The information is mixed up and confusing.

**RS**   *"Rubber-stamp" expression.*   Timeworn words from the past have no place in modern business writing.

**Trans**   *Transition.*   Abrupt shift of thought here.

## Effect

**Conv**  *Conviction.*  This is not so convincing as it should be. More fact or a more skillful use of words is needed.

**GW**  *Goodwill.*  The letter needs more goodwill. Try to make your words convey friendliness. Here you tend to be too dull and matter-of-fact.

**Hur**  *Hurried treatment.*  Your coverage of the problem appears to be hurried. Thus, it tends to leave an effect of routine or brusque treatment. Conciseness is wanted, of course, but you must not sacrifice your letter's objectives for it.

**Log**  *Logic.*  Is this really logical? Would you do it this way in business?

**Neg**  *Negative effect.*  By word or implication, this part tends to be more negative than it should be.

**Pers +**  *Too persuasive.*  Your words are too high-pressure for this situation.

**Pers −**  *Not persuasive enough.*  More persuasion, by either words or facts, would help your letter.

**Ton**  *Tone of the words.*  Your words create a bad impression on the reader. Words that talk down, lecture, argue, accuse, and the like work against the success of your letter.

**YVP**  *You-viewpoint.*  More you-viewpoint wording and adaptation would help the overall effect of your letter.

# Index

# Index

*This book has been set in 10 and 9 point Caledonia, leaded 2 points. Part numbers are 24 point (large) Helvetica Medium and part titles are 24 point (small) Helvetica. Chapter numbers are 42 point Helvetica Medium and chapter titles are 18 point Helvetica. The size of the type page is 27 x 45½ picas.*